WRESTLING WITH WORDS
AND MEANINGS

WRESTLING WITH WORDS AND MEANINGS

Essays in Honour of Keith Allan

Edited by
Kate Burridge & Réka Benczes

© Copyright 2014
Copyright of the collection is held by the editors.
Copryright of the chapters is held by the chapter authors.
All rights reserved. Apart from any uses permitted by Australia's Copyright Act 1968,
no part of this book may be reproduced by any process without prior written permission
from the copyright owners. Inquiries should be directed to the publisher.

Monash University Publishing
Building 4, Monash University
Clayton, Victoria 3800, Australia
www.publishing.monash.edu

Monash University Publishing brings to the world publications which advance the best
traditions of humane and enlightened thought.

This title has been peer reviewed. Monash University Publishing titles pass through a
rigorous process of independent peer review.

www.publishing.monash.edu/books/wwm-9781922235312.html

Series: Linguistics

Design: Les Thomas

Cover image: Csontvary, Tivadar. *The Solitary Cedar*. 1907. Oil on convas. Csontváry Múzeum.

National Library of Australia Cataloguing-in-Publication entry:

Author:	Burridge, Kate, editor; Benczes, Réka, editor.
Title:	Wrestling with words and meanings : essays in honour of Keith Allan / Kate Burridge and Réka Benczes (editors).
Series:	Linguistics
ISBN:	9781922235312 (paperback)
Notes:	Includes index
Subjects:	Allan, Keith, 1943-; Linguistics; English language--Etymology; English language--Usage.
Dewey Number:	410

Printed in Australia by Griffin Press an Accredited ISO AS/NZS 14001:2004
Environmental Management System printer.

The paper this book is printed on is certified against the Forest
Stewardship Council ® Standards. Griffin Press holds FSC chain
of custody certification SGS-COC-005088. FSC promotes
environmentally responsible, socially beneficial and economically viable
management of the world's forests.

CONTENTS

Introduction vii

PART 1: WORDS AND MEANINGS

1. Bastards and buggers 3
   Historical snapshots of Australian English swearing patterns
   Simon Musgrave and Kate Burridge

2. Diachronic properties of the lexicon 33
   Semantics, stability and diversity
   Olav Kuhn

3. The non-redundant nature of English tautological compounds 55
   Réka Benczes

4. French gender 73
   It's not (all) about sex
   Margaret H. à Beckett

5. Trendy new trends in wine terminology 103
   Adrienne Lehrer

6. Semantic prosody of hyperbolic adverbial collocations 124
   An empirical, corpus-based study
   József Andor

PART 2: DISCOURSE AND PRAGMATICS

7. The metaphorical conceptual system in context 143
   Zoltán Kövecses

8. Frightful names 161
   Barry J. Blake

9. On politic behaviour 176
   The personal pronoun as an address term in the Ndebele language of Zimbabwe
   Finex Ndhlovu

10. Response words are anaphors 198
    Thorstein Fretheim

11. Cultural schemas as 'common ground' 219
    Farzad Sharifian

12. Elaborativeness in academic writing 236
    A study of three research papers
    Zofia Golebiowski

13. Communication disorders and mental health 262
    The link we can't ignore
    Deborah Perrott

PART 3: SEMANTIC THEORY AND PHILOSOPHY OF LANGUAGE

14. *Nihil tam absurde dici potest quod non dicatur ab aliquo traductorum philosophorum* 283
    What some philosophers and scientists have said according to their translators
    Pedro José Chamizo Domínguez

15. Radical lexicalism in modelling grammar and language 303
    Mike Balint

16. Articles revisited 335
    A view from Extended Vantage Theory
    Adam Głaz

17. Delimiting lexical semantics 359
    A radical contextualist view
    Kasia M. Jaszczolt

18. Where did Proto Nuclear Micronesians come from? 381
    A linguistic-typological perspective
    Jae Jung Song

Notes on contributors 419

Index 425

INTRODUCTION

Wrestling with Words and Meanings is a celebration publication that honours the life and career of Professor Keith Allan, commemorating at the same time the occasion of his 70th birthday. The eighteen papers that make up the volume come from colleagues, collaborators and former students. They form an eclectic assemblage, to be sure, but all are connected in some way to Keith's linguistic interests.

Any good Festschrift must begin with some sort of review of the honorand's life; so before we outline the three broad themes that characterize this volume, we need to say something about Keith. It goes without saying that a person worthy of a Festschrift will be distinguished – and clearly, as one among the world's most notable scholars in the fields of semantics and linguistic pragmatics, as well as the history of linguistics, Keith is no exception. But let us begin at the beginning with a brief account of Keith's life. Born in the UK on 27th March 1943, Keith was schooled in London, after which he went to the University of Leeds. It was there that he discovered the joy of studying language. Abandoning his original idea of doing drama, Keith started out on his long journey with linguistics, and in 1964 gained his BA (Hons). After then spending some time in Ghana, he went back to studies and in 1970 completed an MLitt in Linguistics at the University of Edinburgh (his thesis topic *Aspect in English*). After three years of lecturing in the English language in Nigeria at the Ahmadu Bello University, Keith took up a lecturing position back in the UK, this time at the University of Essex. This was followed by another three-year stint in Africa, this time in Kenya at the University of Nairobi, after which he began his doctoral studies at Edinburgh, receiving his PhD in 1977 (*Singularity and Plurality in English Noun Phrases: A Study in Grammar and Pragmatics*). In the following year, he took up a position at Monash University and, with the exception of various visiting fellowships elsewhere, it was there he stayed until retirement in 2011. Currently, Keith is Emeritus Professor of Linguistics at Monash University's School of Languages, Cultures and Linguistics, and also Honorary Associate Professor at the University of Queensland.

Now we turn to some of the highlights of Keith's distinguished academic career. Since 1994 he has been a fellow of the Australian Academy of Humanities, and was for several years chair of its Linguistics panel. In 2003, he was a recipient of the Centenary Medal for Service to Australian Society and the Humanities in Linguistics. Keith has published extensively on different facets of language, with a focus on aspects of meaning, and the history and philosophy of linguistics. As he describes it, 'I see language as a form of social interactive behaviour believing this to be an important consideration in any thorough account of meaning in natural language'. This view of language clearly also drives his other research interests – these include topics to do with censorship, discourse analysis, dysphemism, euphemism, grammaticalization, jargon, language policy, linguistic metatheory, morphology, politeness, pragmatics, prosody, psycholinguistics, semantics, sociolinguistics, speech act theory, syntax and taboo.

His most significant books are *Linguistic Meaning* (Routledge, 1986); *Euphemism and Dysphemism: Language Used as Shield and Weapon* (with Kate Burridge, OUP, 1991); *Natural Language Semantics* (Blackwell, 2001); *Forbidden Words: Taboo and the Censoring of Language* (with Kate Burridge, CUP, 2006); *Concise Encyclopaedia of Semantics* (Elsevier, 2009); *The Western Classical Tradition in Linguistics Second Expanded Edition* (Equinox, 2010, first edition 2007); *The English Language and Linguistics Companion* (with Julie Bradshaw et al., Palgrave, 2010); *The Cambridge Handbook of Pragmatics* (with Kasia Jaszczolt, CUP, 2012); *Salient Meanings, Default Meanings, and Automatic Processing* (with Kasia Jaszczolt, Mouton de Gruyter, 2012); *The Oxford Handbook of the History of Linguistics* (OUP, 2013). Keith has also published more than 20 book chapters, 35 articles in encyclopaedias, more than 45 articles in journals and about the same number of book reviews – figures that are more than likely out-of-date by the time this volume appears, given that retirement to Queensland doesn't seem to have slowed Keith down in any way. He continues to be Editor of *The Australian Journal of Linguistics* (which he has done since 2006), and remains on the editorial boards of several other journals including *Language Sciences, Journal of Pragmatics, Journal of Philosophical Pragmatics, Odisea: Journal of English Studies, International Journal of Language Studies* and the series *Empirical Foundations of Theoretical Pragmatics*.

Keith's contribution to postgraduate supervision has been impressive. Since 1981 he has had nearly thirty successful PhD completions (for which he was the main supervisor), and several of these former students now have university teaching positions. It came as no surprise when in 2007 he received the Faculty of Arts Award for Excellence in Higher Degree by Research Supervision. (As an aside, this award came with substantial prize money, which Keith generously shared with colleagues and students on a celebratory lunch.) Keith has continued supervision even into his retirement – he once remarked that he regards the nurturing and mentoring of research students as the most rewarding aspect of his university work. And on his homepage he writes: 'I prefer students who have the urge to discover what there is to know and who question the current paradigms in linguistics – even those I hold dear'. Contributors to this volume, Margaret à Beckett, Olav Kuhn, Zofia Golebiowski, Finex Ndhlovu, Deborah Perrott, Mike Balint and Jae Jung Song, were exactly such students.

Keith's commitment to academic collegiality and the enrichment of higher education in Australia has been impressive over many years. He has chaired numerous conference organizations, most notably chairing the local organizing committee for the 11th International Pragmatics Conference held at Monash University in July 12–17, 2009. Keith has also been responsible for bringing many scholars to Australia to share and trade ideas about language. He himself has had brief forays into a number of exotic locations around the world to study, to teach and to interact, and not surprisingly contributions to this volume have come from around the globe – they attest to the internationality of current-day academia, and they show the extent of Keith Allan's influence. These papers cover a lot of the ground that characterizes Keith's linguistics work, though of course no slim volume such as this one could ever hope to capture his extraordinarily diverse research interests – everything from quantity implicatures, clause-type and illocutionary force to English terms of insult invoking sex organs and furry animal nicknames for bawdy parts. There is indeed something for everyone in Keith Allan's research!

We have divided the appropriately eclectic contributions into three themes of Keith's multifaceted and multifarious (perhaps even nefarious?) research: word meaning; pragmatics and discourse; semantic theory and philosophy of language.

Part 1: Word meaning

The opening paper in the first part of the volume by Simon Musgrave and Kate Burridge ('Bastards and buggers – Historical snapshots of Australian English swearing patterns') investigates the development of usage, meanings and cultural significance of two key expressions in Australian English vernacular: *bastard* and *bugger*. By drawing on extensive corpus linguistic data, Musgrave and Burridge demonstrate that there are significant differences with regard to their usage: while *bastard* appears more often in singular phrases, *bugger* tends to occur with a restricted range of adjectival modifiers. This difference in usage is an indication of their differences in meaning: as the authors elaborate, *bastard* codes a more negative attitude to the person referred to, and as a *bastard* is a 'bastard' for some particular reason, a wide range of adjectives co-occur with this noun. *Bugger*, however, is more generic, and we rarely have a proper reason why someone is considered a 'bugger' – which explains the restricted range of generic adjectives that appear with this word.

Still within the field of historical linguistics, Olav Kuhn ('Diachronic properties of the lexicon: Semantics, stability and diversity') explores the applicability of lexicostatistics, more precisely glottochronology, in estimating the lexical stability rates for a number of Indo-European and neighbouring languages based on the observed lexical diversity in groups and subgroups that are known to be related. Kuhn uses these rates to assess different hypotheses of historical relationship by analysing the distribution of shared vocabulary with the patterns of stability actually observed in known relationships. The performance of this approach is employed for two word lists used in the literature (one containing 100 lexical items, the other 40 items). Kuhn concludes that although the results of the two lists are indeed compatible, the method should nevertheless be considered more as a complementary approach that can enhance the level of predictability so that productive separation of lexical strata becomes feasible.

The third paper in the section, 'The non-redundant nature of English tautological compounds' by Réka Benczes, looks at the role of compounds that have been loosely referred to as 'tautological' in academic discourse. Benczes specifies this group of compounds in question as being comprised of two major subtypes: 1) the hyponym-superordinate type (such as *tuna fish* and *oak tree*); and 2) the synonymous type (such as *subject matter* or *courtyard*). By drawing on etymological data among others, Benczes argues that the meaning of such compounds is by no means redundant. Hyponym-superordinate compounds are remnants of our early acquisition of taxonomical relations by making the link between the hierarchical levels explicit. At the same time, such compounds are also used to dignify and upgrade concepts via the conceptual metaphor MORE OF FORM IS MORE OF CONTENT. Synonymous compounds have been shown to possess an emphatic feature, which has been exploited mainly in poetic language. However, according to Benczes, synonymous compounds are still alive in everyday language, though in a slightly different form – as blends.

Margaret H. à Beckett's contribution, 'French gender: It's not (all) about sex', looks at one of the most perplexing questions of French: namely, on what basis are the genders of nouns assigned. While previous approaches have failed to provide an adequately watertight explanation, à Beckett claims that French gender assignment and word-final pronunciation can be accounted for more comprehensively by treating French gender as a semantic system similar to the morpho-syntactically complex noun class and classifier systems that exist in a large number of languages in the world, including Africa, Asia, Australia and South America. Such an approach takes a more subtle look at attributes, as opposed to previous attempts that focused on global and absolute semantic properties. Accordingly, à Beckett proposes that French involves two separate and independent, semantically determined noun classification systems: the first one is related to gender, which is semantically determined in terms of a limited number of oppositional features (such as dead vs. alive, hard vs. soft, closed vs. open, etc.), which is indicated in masculine/feminine agreements outside the noun. The second system reflects other oppositions (such as part vs. whole, textured vs. smooth, slow vs. speedy, etc.), which are made manifest on nouns via word final contrasting vowel/consonant pronunciations.

Adrienne Lehrer's study on 'Trendy new trends in wine terminology' investigates the changes that have undergone in the past decades in writing (and talking) about wine, as well as the possible causes of this phenomenon. As pointed out by Lehrer, there is a plethora of new wine descriptors, based on the new uses of old words that have not typically been employed as wine descriptors before, such as *muscular* and *aggressive*, which signal the appearance of novel sets of metaphors. According to Lehrer, the major sources of these 'trendy' expressions happen to be the wine writers themselves. As the descriptions for the various categories of wines most probably converge with regard to their taste, smell and feel, wine writers need to employ increasingly imaginative and creative terms to grab the attention of their readers (who might eventually buy the product). Such attention-seeking naming processes can often be observed in the advertising and marketing of many other foods and beverages as well.

The last paper in the section by József Andor ('Semantic prosody of hyperbolic adverbial collocations: An empirical, corpus-based study') is an investigation of the hyperbolic function of four degree adverbs, *inconceivably*, *incredibly*, *unbelievably* and *unthinkably*, at the semantics–pragmatics interface (and as such, the paper can be considered as a precursor to the second section of the volume). Andor first examines the lexical entries of the adverbs in five corpus-based learner's dictionaries, and comes to the conclusion that the treatment of the adverbs in the dictionaries is very varied and unsystematic. In order to gain a more precise picture of the hyperbolic use of the adverbs under analysis, Andor provides an analysis of their collocational occurrence and frequency with adjectives using the British National Corpus; the data indicate that the adverbs do lean towards degrees of positive or negative polarity (dependant on encyclopaedically-based background knowledge). Native speaker judgments (representing three major regional varieties of English: British English, Irish English and American English) also point to the acceptance and recognition of the hyperbolic potential of the expressions.

Part 2: Pragmatics and discourse

The second part of the volume opens with Zoltán's Kövecses' contribution, 'The metaphorical conceptual system in context'. While plenty of work within cognitive linguistics has focused on the role of embodied experience in shaping our conceptual system, not much has been yet said about the significance of context. By drawing on an array of examples, Kövecses demonstrates that conceptualizers are very much aware and make use of the various factors that constitute both the immediate (local) and the nonimmediate (global) context in which metaphorical conceptualization takes place. The linguistic and discourse context, the social and cultural environment, as well as the larger physical world all affect and influence the way we conceptualize the world. Since these contextual factors change all the time, the abstract concepts in our conceptual system – as well as the system as such – are constantly in flux, and at the same time they also shape the way we metaphorically conceptualize the world.

The next contribution by Barry Blake, 'Frightful names', focuses on the beliefs and taboos associated with personal names. While the form of the personal name may be arbitrary and is assigned rather than being innate, once it is assigned, the name is thought to be an 'inalienable possession' of the bearer, i.e., there is a real link between the name and the referent in people's conceptualizations. There are numerous cultures where a name can be used in sorcery, with the effect that names become a source of taboo. By providing a wealth of intriguing examples, Blake also highlights how names are used in magic and for religious purposes. All in all, the paper highlights that an iconic relationship also exists between the performance of the name and the effect of that performance on the bearer of the name. Blake emphasizes that the power of names – and the superstitions that go along with them – is very much alive in every culture with varying degrees: after all, the naming customs in 'modern societies' also heavily rely on the associations that personal names evoke.

Leaving behind the immediate personal sphere, but remaining still within the close interpersonal context, Finex Ndhlovu ('On politic behaviour: The personal pronoun as an address term in the Ndebele language of Zimbabwe') looks at the use of the singular (*wena* – you SING) and plural (*lina* – you PL) forms of the personal pronoun as address terms in the Ndebele language. By tapping into previous studies on pragmatics and politeness strategies, the current chapter also underlines the significance of differences in cultural norms, expectations and practices in determining interlocutors' linguistic behaviours. Accordingly, in the Midlands Ndebele speech community the singular second person pronoun (*wena*) is used more rather as a pronoun of mutuality and powerlessness, while the plural second person pronoun (*lina*) is considered as the pronoun of power and deference. Nevertheless, Ndhlovu stresses that there is significant 'uneasiness' in the use of the personal pronouns, which is due to a lack of clarity about when it is deemed appropriate to be euphemistic, when to display social solidarity or endearment and when to express social distance.

Thorstein Fretheim's contribution ('Response words are anaphors') claims that response words such as *yes* and *no* are very similar to discourse-anaphoric items like personal pronouns. Fretheim analyses Norwegian in detail, which has three response words (with the effect that anaphor and antecedent can be matched in a greater variety of ways than what a response word system with just two values allows for). The chapter argues that the positive response word *jo*, which expresses a denial of a negative proposition (i.e., similar to German *doch*), can become a legitimate choice in discourse even if no negative proposition can be derived from the antecedent that *jo* responds to. When the producer of the antecedent expresses his/her personal opinion or asks for the addressee's personal opinion, the latter is allowed to choose between *ja* and *jo* in identical environments. In such situations *jo* can signal either a reduced degree of commitment to the proposition expressed or a playing down of the significance of that which the first speaker's utterance refers to.

Moving further out in the socio-cultural sphere, Farzad Sharifian ('Cultural schemas as "common ground"') examines the significance of 'common ground' – that is, knowledge that is assumed to be shared, and is required for the uptake of pragmatic meanings, between interlocutors – within a cultural linguistics framework. While Keith Allan made a distinction between two levels of common ground, the universal versus the very restricted, Sharifian claims that there is a further level of common ground situated between these two, that is, a culturally constructed common ground. By drawing on the Persian cultural schema of *târof*, the chapter reveals how this schema is associated with the communication of several speech acts among speakers of Persian, such as making requests and refusals, as well as offering and accepting invitations. As Sharifian underlines, unfamiliarity with this cultural schema (and thus a lack of common ground) results in a communicative challenge when Persian speakers come into contact with non-Persian speakers.

Zofia Golebiowski's chapter on 'Elaborativeness in academic writing: A study of three research papers' investigates the application of elaborative rhetorical strategies in three research papers written in English and published in international sociological journals. By applying a close textual analysis, Golebiowski explores how the authors elaborate their texts through various elaboration relations, such as amplification, extension, explanation, instantiation, reformulation and addition strategies. According to the analysis, elaboration is the most prominent feature of all three texts, which is due to the shared stylistic conventions and traditions of the discipline. Nevertheless, variations in the mode of employment of elaborative structures have also been uncovered, which can be explained by the writers' differing linguistic backgrounds and discourse community memberships.

The final contribution of the section by Deborah Perrott, titled 'Communication disorders and mental health: The link we can't ignore', calls attention to the increasing evidence that demonstrates a strong relationship between childhood communication disorders on the one hand and adolescent/adult psychiatric disorders on the other: phonological problems have been shown to be related to external problems (such as aggression), while semantic language problems have been linked with internalizing ones (depression, anxiety and emotional issues for example). Perrott underlines that the impact of a communication disorder affects both an individual and the community. Consequently, she examines some of the possibilities in which linguists (including researchers and clinical communication experts, such as speech pathologists) can assist in the alteration of the vertical transmission of communication and mental health problems at the individual, family and societal levels.

Part 3: Semantic theory and philosophy of language

The opening contribution of the third section, by Pedro José Chamizo Domínguez (*'Nihil tam absurde dici potest quod non dicatur ab aliquo traductorum philosophorum*: What some philosophers and scientists have said according to their translators'), raises a very fundamental problem in philosophy and general linguistic theory: the mistranslation of original philosophical (and scientific texts) and the consequences thereof. As Chamizo Domínguez asserts, when a given text is ambiguous in the source language, and such ambiguity cannot be reproduced in the target language, the translator has to opt for only one among the various possible options. Consequently, the different possible interpretations of the text in question cannot be taken into account in the translated text. The chapter reveals how problems originating in ambiguities, archaisms, false friends, gender, idioms, interpolations and polysemies can lead the translator to say something very different from what was actually said in the original text.

Entering into the field of semantic theory, in 'Delimiting lexical semantics: A radical contextualist view', Kasia M. Jaszczolt first assesses the minimalist–contextualist debate and provides new arguments in favour of the abolition of such a divide. Instead, Jaszczolt proposes that a radical form of contextualism is the way forward in the form of a pragmatics-rich account of word meaning, where meanings with different degrees of salience, cancellability (entrenchment), and proximity to what is standardly considered to be the abstract conceptual core are also included, in order to best reflect the speaker's intended content. Nevertheless, Jaszczolt also underlines the necessity of a principled account that would search for precise constraints and algorithms for the composition of meaning.

Still within the topic of the mental lexicon, Mike Balint ('Radical lexicalism in modelling grammar and language') proposes a Radical Lexicalism (RL) approach, which is viewed as a repository of both an internalised knowledge of grammar and the knowledge of how to use this information in producing and understanding the sentential components of utterances. RL, however, is firmly grounded in contemporary knowledge representation theory, and posited as the core conceptual driver of the cognitively plausible model of interlocutory language usage (CoP). Balint argues that it is the semantic and pragmatic compositional needs of the meaning-content to be conveyed that will drive the choice of syntactic structure rather than the other way around. In other words, the RL position is diametrically opposite to that of the Chomskyan and other syntactocentric positions that place the locus of what Chomsky terms 'lingusitic creativity' in a postulated syntactic module of internalised language knowledge.

In 'Articles revisited: A view from Extended Vantage Theory', Adam Głaz outlines a model for describing English articles, called Extended Vantage Theory (EVT), which is based on Robert E. MacLaury's Vantage Theory (VT). VT is a dynamic model of categorization and category construction, which has been applied in several analyses of language, such as the English number system (as put forth by Keith Allan). As Głaz argues, non-standard and surprising article uses also have a cognitively based motivation, since it is the speakers' cognitions that are responsible for the construction of points of view, and a proper linguistic theory needs to be able to accommodate both regular and irregular language uses. The chapter convincingly demonstrates that EVT can account for both the cognitive motivations behind the use of articles, grounded in fundamental processes of attention to similarity and difference, and the speakers' agency in constructing points of view on the situations being talked about. In sum, it is the language users' systematic cognitive operations, acting in parallel with their ability to override the apparently irresistible forces of context, that function as the main source of linguistic creativity.

With the final contribution of the third section by Jae Jung Song ('Where did Proto Nuclear Micronesians come from?: A linguistic-typological perspective') the volume goes full circle. While a number of hypotheses have been outlined in the literature, no conclusive linguistic evidence has been put yet forward on the Proto Nuclear Micronesians' migration route. Song draws on the so-called population-typology model, developed to investigate geographical distributions of structural properties with a view to making inferences about human migration, in an attempt to understand Proto Nuclear Micronesians' migration route better. By analysing the structural property of possessive classifiers, a defining characteristic of Micronesian languages, Song traces back the migration route of Proto Nuclear Micronesians back to their immediate homeland, which the author identifies as the Santa Cruz Islands.

It has been a joy to assemble and edit these insightful contributions – we trust you will enjoy them.

Kate Burridge and Réka Benczes

PART 1
WORDS AND MEANINGS

Chapter 1

BASTARDS AND BUGGERS

HISTORICAL SNAPSHOTS OF AUSTRALIAN ENGLISH SWEARING PATTERNS

Simon Musgrave and Kate Burridge
Monash University

The vernacular has always had a special place in Australian English history and remains an important feature today. But just how uniquely Antipodean are the swearing patterns that we can observe in Australian English? At first blush, there is much that is common to the Northern Hemisphere and Antipodean expressions used. We need more studies and more detailed accounts of individual expressions, and certainly more comparisons with the slang, swearing and terms of insult used in other varieties of English, especially British and American English. This paper is an attempt to describe two key expressions in the Australian English vernacular: *bastard* and *bugger*. It takes an historical perspective, examining corpus data from the Australian National Corpus to explore the developing usage, meanings and cultural significance of these expressions.

1. Introduction – Swearing in Australian English[1]

Which one of you bastards called this bastard a bastard?[2]

The Australian love affair with the vernacular goes back to the earliest English speaking settlements of the eighteenth and nineteenth centuries. During those crucial years of dialect formation, among the main ingredients in the linguistic melting pot were the slang and dialect vocabularies of London and the industrial Midlands, Ireland and Scotland – the cant (or

---

[1] We are grateful to Pam Peters and Réka Benczes for their helpful comments; these have assisted us greatly.

[2] Allegedly uttered by Australian cricket captain Bill Woodfull during the Bodyline series of 1932–3 in response to the English captain Douglas Jardine's complaint that one of the Australian players had called him a bastard.

'flash') of convicts, the slang of sailors, whalers and gold-diggers mingled with features of the emerging 'standard' language (cf. Ramson 1966: 49–50) to produce the new 'colonial parlance'. Fuelled by anti-authoritarian sentiment, the colloquial part of the language was expanded to become the feature that best distinguished the established citizen from the 'stranger' (or 'old chum' versus 'new chum'), and numerous eyewitness accounts point to the flourishing of 'bad' language during those early rough and macho years.

> Young Australia makes a specialty of swearing. High and low, rich and poor, indulge themselves in bad language luxuriantly; but it is amongst the rising generation that it reaches its acme. The lower-class colonial swears as naturally as he talks. He doesn't mean anything by it in particular; nor is it really an evil outward and visible sign of the spiritual grace within him. On the prevalence of larrikinism I wrote at length in a former epistle. (Twopenny 1883: 224–5)

> The base language of English thieves is becoming the established language of the colony. Terms of slang and flash are used, as a matter of course, everywhere, from the gaols to the Viceroy's palace, not excepting the Bar and the Bench. No doubt they will be reckoned quite parliamentary, as soon as we obtain a parliament. […] Hence, bearing in mind that our lowest class brought with it a peculiar language, and is constantly supplied with fresh corruption, you will understand why pure English is not, and is not likely to become, the language of the colony. (Wakefield 1829: 106–7)

> It is altogether frightful to what extent cursing and blaspheming are carried on and have increased among the people in the bush. People are apt to fancy that this is one of the chief and most striking vices of sailors, who are but too prone to give vent to their feelings in this manner. But sailors are surpassed by the 'old hands' in the bush: indeed, no comparison can be made between the two. Almost every word they speak, even the most indifferent, is accompanied by an oath, which is but a friendly and well meaning locution among them. (Gerstäcker 1857: 9–10)[3]

---

[3] Many thanks to Brian Taylor (1994–5) for pointing out the joys of Frederick Gerstäcker.

Notwithstanding their possibly over-keen noses for linguistic impurity, commentators such as these appeared in agreement that an informal culture and colloquial style of discourse were emerging as the 'mark of the Antipodean'.[4]

The current climate of growing informality has seen an increasing colloquialization of English usage worldwide; yet, as Peters and Burridge (2012) conclude, Australian (and New Zealand) English goes go well beyond the kinds of vernacular and informal grammar and lexis noted for varieties elsewhere. Moreover, in the modern world of global interconnection, the positioning of English as a worldwide *lingua franca* has seen non-standard and vernacular features become even more meaningful signals of cultural identity and the expression of the local. Many Australians see their colloquialisms, nicknames, diminutives, swearing and insults as important indicators of their Australianness, and linguistic expressions of cherished ideals such as friendliness, nonchalance, mateship, egalitarianism and anti-authoritarianism (Lalor and Rendle-Short 2007; Seal 1999; Stollznow 2004; Wierzbicka 1992).

This paper takes an historical perspective, using corpus data to examine the developing usage, meanings and cultural significance of two key expressions in the Australian English vernacular: *bastard* and *bugger*. Since the usual linguistic corpora (especially written) are not always fruitful when it comes to yielding illustrations of 'bad' language, examples in this paper draw largely on language from a range of sources (including creative writing, spontaneous public speech and private conversation) from various collections in the Australian National Corpus (AusNC). For the historical data, we use the Corpus of Oz Early English (COOEE, specifically texts written in Australia between 1788 and 1900) and also AustLit, a corpus which provides access to select samples of out of copyright poetry, fiction and criticism ranging from 1795 to the 1930s. For the modern data, we use the Australian Corpus of English (ACE, written texts collected from the 1980s); the Australian Radio Talkback Corpus (ART, collected 2004–6 from Australia-wide ABC and commercial radio stations); informal Australian speech from the International Corpus of English, (ICE-AUS Corpus, Australian spoken English collected 1991–5); the Monash Corpus of Australian English (MCE, conversations of Melbourne school children recorded in 1997); and the Griffith Corpus of Spoken English (GCSAusE, collected 1990 to 1998).

---

[4] This is a phrase Gordon and Deverson (1985: 19) use to describe the early Australian and New Zealand accent.

1.1. Changes in swearing patterns

Foul language changes across time and from place to place, and in order to understand the position of *bastard* and *bugger* in Australia's swearing history, we need to consider what makes something a swearword in the first place. There are still no laboratory or neuroimaging studies that have conclusively identified the exact neuroanatomical sites where 'dirty' words are stored, or that have evaluated specifically the neurological processing of obscenities, but the evidence seems overwhelming: 'bad' language is rooted deeply in human neural anatomy. What actually goes to clothe the expression is then the socio-cultural setting, in particular the taboos of the time – those things that go bump in the night (see Allan and Burridge 2006: Ch. 10; Pinker 2007: Ch. 7). These taboos will furnish the language with its swearwords and, because taboo is dynamic, there will always be shifts of idiom employing terms of opprobrium. As Hughes (1991) nicely outlines, the history of foul language in English has seen the sweeping transition from the religious to the secular in its patterns of swearing. When blasphemous and religiously profane language was no longer considered offensive (at least by a majority of speakers), what stepped in to fill the gap were the more physically and sexually based modes of expression. As we will later discuss, the terms *bastard* and *bugger* were the first of these to be pressed into maledictory service – risqué body parts and bodily functions were not generally used as swearwords until into the twentieth century.

This transition is evident in imprecatives such as *Bugger you!* This syntactically incongruous expression has its model in earlier phrases such as *God damn X* (where God is invoked as the agent of the malefaction). The abbreviated forms such as *Damn X* (euphemized in order to avoid explicit blasphemy) now provide the model for more sexually based modern imprecatives such as *Shit on X, Fuck X, Bugger X, Screw X* etc (see Dong 1992 [1971]). It is in these forms that religious profanity (blasphemy) remains a source for dysphemism (albeit indirect), despite the on-going secularization of English speaking communities.

Changes in social attitudes mean that sex and bodily functions no longer provide the powerful swearwords they once did. In most varieties of English, *bastard* and *bugger* have weakened considerably in strength and wounding capacity, and bans placed on this kind of profanity have eased. Far more potent expressions are now the racial and ethnic slurs, so that the swearwords today include expressions such as *faggot, dike, queer, dago, kike, kaffir, nigger, mick, wog, boong, abo* and so on. New taboos have meant that sexist, racist, ageist, religionist, etc. language (or –IST language, as Keith

Allan once dubbed it) has surpassed in significance irreligious profanity, blasphemy and sexual obscenity, against which laws have now well and truly been relaxed. As a simple illustration of the evolving sensitivities, take the various permutations of the expression *pot calling kettle black arse > pot calling kettle black > pot calling kettle* (the saying used to claim that someone is guilty of that which they accuse another). Societal queasiness around the Victorian era saw *arse* dropped from the end of the phrase, while more recent times have seen further euphemistic omission with the occasional dumping of *black*; indeed, the internet has much discussion on the racist nature of the idiom (see for example the piece by Jonah Goldberg, 'Racist Pot Calls Kettle a Bigot', in the *National Review Online* http://www.nationalreview.com).

1.2. Why do we swear?

Allan and Burridge (2011) have identified at least four functions for swearing: the expletive function, abuse and insult, expression of social solidarity, and stylistic choice – the marking of attitude to what is said. Though it is sometimes difficult for an outsider to pinpoint the role that swearing has in a conversation or in a written text (and frequently these roles will overlap), where possible we have given examples from the corpus data examined here.

1.2.1. The expletive function

Expletives are a kind of exclamatory interjection which, like other interjections, have a highly expressive function; cf. *Wow!, Ouch!, Omigosh!, Shit!* They are uttered in intense emotional situations, as when a speaker is angry and frustrated, under pressure, in sudden pain, or confronted by something unexpected and usually (though not necessarily) undesirable. In the case of swearwords, it is the taboo quality that provides the catharsis the speaker seeks in order to cope with the situation that provoked the expletive in the first place: the breaking of the taboo is what triggers the release of energy. Cusswords are uttered to let off steam, and they belong to the kind of 'automatic speech' that bubbles up from the limbic system of the brain when something has gone horribly wrong (e.g., that 'onosecond' when you realize you've just pressed the 'send' button and dispatched an e-mail message that really should not have been sent).

In the data, there are several examples of *bugger (it)* used as an expletive. Though it can can have a cathartic effect, *bastard* cannot fulfil this role, at least in Australian English (as we discuss in sections 2 and 3, its uses are contrained by its grammatical limitations).

(1) No, too late, it's too close. Well, it is going slow, I could make it. Bugger, too late now. (Hall 1986; B22a-plain.txt)

(2) Like I went for a drive trying to find where [Name] was playing soccer. I couldn't find it so I said Bugger it I'll go for a drive (ICE; conversation between friends S1A-062-plain.txt)

1.2.2. Swearing as abuse or insult

Malediction can also 'add insult to injury', and we do this by means of curses, name-calling, any sort of derogatory or contemptuous comments to intentionally slight, offend or wound a person in some way. Abusive language includes personal insults aimed at a second person (*You rotten bugger!*) or said of a third person (*The bastard stole my pen*); it also includes curses which may be imprecatives (*Bugger you!*) or (pseudo-)imperatives (*Be buggered! Bugger off!*). Speakers may also resort to swearwords to talk about the things that irritate and annoy them, things that they disapprove of and wish to disparage, humiliate and degrade (*Writing grant applications is a bugger*).

(3) 'e says. 'Well, take that, you fuckin' bastard' says Madeley, an' sloshes 'im one (Manning 1929; AustLit:manmidd-plain-1.txt)

Abusive swearing is also cathartic when it involves highly emotional language produced in anger or in frustration. However, while expletives are not generally addressed to any hearer (though they may be used with an audience of ratified participants or bystanders), in the case of abusive language (e.g., *Bastard!*) the release of extreme emotional energy can be directed at someone or something, typically the source of the misfortune or the annoyance (e.g., the lid that has just come off the food blender, spraying soup over the kitchen ceiling).

(4) Larry slunk out. In the darkness he stumbled over a bucket and kicked it across the yard. 'Bastard,' he muttered. (Penton 1936; AustLit: peninhe-raw.txt)

Offensive expressions may pick on a person's physical appearance and mental ability, name, character, behaviour, beliefs, family, and so on. Of course, they do not have to be 'bad' – *You dag!* can be an insult, but it is not a swearword. Abusive language that involves tabooed words, however, will always have that extra layer of emotional intensity and extra capacity to offend. When Aurelio Vidmar, the coach of soccer team *Adelaide United*, lashed out (in the wake of the Reds' 4–0 loss to Melbourne Victory in February 2009) and described Adelaide as a 'pissant town', he used an unusual insult that embraced both an insect and one of the tabooed bodily effluvia – an effective double-whammy to invoke something inconsequential, irrelevant and worthless.

1.2.3. The social function of swearing

Across a range of different studies, social swearing emerged by far as the most usual type (e.g., Ross 1960; Allan and Burridge 2011), and it appears to be a common function for the two expressions examined in the corpus data here. This is the use of swearwords to display in-group solidarity (especially when directed against outsiders), as a part of verbal cuddling or simply friendly banter:

> (5) The man squats down, blotting at beer-wet skin with his towel. 'Oh, bugger off,' Leigh says without malice. 'Hey, an accident, swear to God!' The man turns towards Cass and winks. (Hospital 1990; *Bondi* W2F-017-plain.txt)

This category includes expressions of mateship and endearment, as in the following:

> (6) Speaker 1: let me explain the night let me explain the night
> We we we went to the
> There was four of us went [Name] and myself and two of her friends
> Speaker 2: Oh right well you didn't invite me you bastard
> (ICE; conversation between male friends S1A-064-plain.txt)

This usage is routine in Australian English, as in other native varieties of English, and speakers often report that the more affectionate they feel towards someone, the more offensive the language can be towards that person.

1.2.4. Stylistic function of swearing

The function of swearing can also relate to the manner of expression. For example, speakers might choose a taboo word (over a more benign synonym) and use it descriptively to display a particular attitude to what is being said (e.g, describing someone as a *bastard* rather than *illegitimate, born out of wedlock*, etc.); or they might use swearwords simply to make an utterance more noteworthy than if orthophemism (= straight-talking) had been used (for example, Tourism Australia's TV advertisement and memorable

Australian invitation to the rest of the world: *So where the bloody hell are you?*; Feb. 2009[5]). Our corpus data had many examples where swearwords were used emphatically or to simply spice up the discourse:

(7) With sheep you've got two ways out – you can wear 'em or eat 'em. All you can do with cattle is eat the bastards. There's only a few molls, poofters 'n weirdos who wear leather pants. Wool will come back, when people realise synthetics aren't as good. (Thorne 1986; ACE: R09-plain.txt)

(8) This one I struck wasn't hungry. He just stood up on his hind legs and bellowed at me, like a bull. Frightened buggery out of me. (Cook 1986; ACE: R10-plain.txt)

Studies show that there are clear sociocultural and psychological benefits in using tabooed words and phrases – the thrill of transgression (it is liberating to defy prohibition by violating linguistic taboos) and the psychological gain in letting off steam and expressing extreme emotion through cascading expletives and forbidden words.[6] There is also the obvious link between hostility and the use of tabooed words in curses, name-calling and terms of insult. On the other hand, swearwords can act as in-group solidarity markers within a shared colloquial style. Like the 'incorrect' language of non-standard grammar, these words fall outside what is good and proper, and they help to define the gang; they can be a cultural indicator, a sign of endearment, a part of steamy pillow talk and are an important component of joke-telling. Swearing is a fact of linguistic life, not just a nasty habit to be broken, and attempts over the centuries to stamp it out have had little success. In fact, as Hughes (1991) shows, censorship and repression, whether they amount to full-blown sanctions or merely social niceties, seem only ever to coincide with more exuberant times of swearing. Clearly, it is a flourishing feature of Australian English, but it remains to be seen whether Australians really do live up to their popular image of having an unusually

---

[5] It can now be viewed at http://www.youtube.com/watch?v=TebeNC-_VjA.

[6] Studies over the years have shown that at times of extreme stress swearing will typically diminish. Writing of the use of *fuck* by British soldiers in World War I, Brophy and Partridge (1931: 16f) report that to omit the word was an effective way of indicating emergency and danger; Ross (1960) examined swearing among a group of five male and three female British zoologists in the Norwegian Arctic and reported that 'under conditions of serious stress, there was silence' (p. 480); in his analysis of swearing by psychiatric ward personnel at staff meetings over a six month period, Gallahorn (1971) reported expletive usage reduced when ward tension was intense.

rich and creative 'bad' language, as popular accounts so often portray them. At first blush, there is much that is common to the Northern Hemisphere and Antipodean expressions used; yet the censoring of the TV ad 'Where the bloody hell are you' in North America and its banning in the UK suggest there are significant differences.

2. *Buggers* and *bastards* – A brief history

> Swearing draws upon such powerful and incongruous resonators as religion, sex, madness, excretion and nationality, encompassing an extraordinary variety of attitudes. (Hughes 1991: 3)

All language groups have derogatory expressions available for other groups they come in contact with (especially where religious or military rivalry is involved), and in his historical accounts of English swearing, Hughes (1991 and 2006) shows how deeply embedded xenophobia ('antipathy to foreigners') is in the language. Over the years, however, there have been interesting changes to these racist dysphemisms. Earlier taunts displayed strong moral stereotyping, often with religious overtones (e.g., extended uses of *pagan*, *heathen*, *witch*). In contrast, modern expressions typically play more on superficial characteristics to do, for example, with appearance or dietary habits (e.g., Australian English *slants / slanties*, *slopes* and *RGBs*, 'Rice Gobbling Bastards', for people from east and south-east Asia).

Bugger is a prime example of early linguistic xenophobia with a strong moral and religious basis. The word derives from French *bougre*, ultimately Latin *bulgarus*, 'Bulgarian'. It carried the sense of 'heretic' from the fourteenth century and from the sixteenth century both 'sodomite' and 'practiser of bestiality'. The medieval religious sense derives from the fact that Bulgarians were members of the Eastern Orthodox Church, and therefore against accepted beliefs of the time (originally the name was given to a specific sect of heretics who came from Bulgaria; it then extended to other heretics). The second sexual sense arises from the common dysphemistic practice among human groups to attribute vice and immorality to outsiders; in this instance we see the prejudicial association of 'deviant' sexual behaviour with 'deviant' religious beliefs.[7]

---

[7] The bigotry that links purported decadence with 'other' thinking is evident elsewhere in the lexicon, such as the history of names for nasty diseases In the sixteenth century syphilis was known as *Spanish needle*, *Spanish pox*, *Spanish pip and Spanish gout*, reflecting Spain's status as number one enemy of the day. These labels were later replaced by *the disease of Naples* and *Naples canker* (Shakespeare referred to the disease

Bugger appears as a swearword as early as the first half of the eighteenth century; it was the first of the sexual terms to be extended in this way. As a general expression to insult or curse, it makes regular appearances in witness accounts in the transcripts of the eighteenth and nineteenth centuries from the Old Bailey (London's central criminal court), typically as a direct personal insult or curse, but more usually euphemistically rendered as *bougre*, *bouger* or *b–g–r*.

(9) 'D - n your eyes, you bloody bouger, stop; he drove on a little way, and he followed the chaise and called out, D - n your eyes, you bloody bouger, stop, and he put a pistol close up to him. (4 Dec 1776; t17761204)

(10) I said, don't shoot me before you rob me; he said, D - n you, you bougering soul, your money? (4 Dec 1776; t17761204)

(11) I spoke to one of the young gentlemen of the association, to present his piece at her, in order to intimidate her; he did; she was leaning out of the window, and seemed very much in liquor. She said he might fire and be buggered. (28 Jun 1780; t17800628)

(12) 'Tom, if you are going to settle with me I will play;' he said he be b - g - d if he would pay me if he had a pocket full of money. (15 July 1824; t18240715)

In transcripts of the eighteenth century, *bugger* appears as a strengthener in negative constructions, predating parallel examples cited in the *Oxford English Dictionary* by a good century:

(13) 'It cannot be helped now, I should not care a b - dy b - gg - r if I was going to be hung up for it.' I said the less he said of that sort the better. (12 Sep 1821; t18210912)

Given these Old Bailey examples, there is no reason either to think that epithets in reference to things undesirable or unpleasant (such as 'It's a bugger') would also not have been around at this time, though we have no records supporting this use. Of course dating swearwords is notoriously difficult on account of taboo; these expressions can have a life on the streets long

---

as 'Neapolitan bone-ache'), and finally in the eighteenth century, it was the French who featured in the xenophobic epithets for syphilis: *malady of France*, *French pox*, *French disease*, *French aches*, *French fever*, *French malady*, *French gout* and *French marbles* (French *morbilles*, 'small blisters'); cf. Allan and Burridge (1991: 174; 2006: 206–7).

before they happen to make an appearance in print. Documentary evidence of its use as an expletive (*Bugger!*) is so far missing before the nineteenth century; phrasal verbs such as *bugger up, bugger off, bugger about/around* and intensifying expressions such as *bugger all* also don't appear until late (well into the twentieth century).

Clearly there would have been no shortage of *bugger* users transported to Australia in those early years; however, as noted in section 3 we have only one example before 1900. It must be among the invisible words in Corbyn's reports of the Sydney Police Office (Corbyn, 1854; see also Burridge 2010).

(14) Mr Denton: She and another gal was on top of my house; I ordered her down, when she called me a possum stomached old —. (Corbyn 1854/1970: 101)

Corbyn was reporting the language of Sydney's criminal (or at least lower) class in the 1850s; however, the texts were not official court proceedings (like those of the Old Bailey), but were published in newspapers of the time for entertainment; hence Corbyn had to be more mindful of the sensitivities of his reading audience.

In recent years, *bugger* has weakened considerably both in sense and in wounding capacity. It is now considered a mild expression to insult or let off steam, and routinely shows up in the public arena in expressions of frustration, surprise or disbelief (*Bugger me! I'll be buggered!*), of mateship and endearment (*you lucky bugger*), and a range of other lighthearted expressions (*playing silly buggers*). Its loss of potency is evident in its regular media appearances; for example, the TV advertisement using *bugger* to sell the new Toyota Hilux utility truck became so successful that it gained something of a cult following, especially in New Zealand.[8]

Bastard also has a straightforward etymology, though it has ended up going down a slightly different dysphemistic track from *bugger*. Derived from Old French *bastard* (*bast* 'pack-saddle' + the pejorative suffix *–ard*, as in *drunkard, coward, sluggard*, etc.), the word first appears in English in the thirteenth century, used to denote an illegitimate child. It would originally have been a sneering reference to 'a child of the pack-saddle' (French *fils de bast*), the pack-saddle being the make-shift bed of itinerants. In this regard, it is interesting that *bastard* shares its pedigree with *batman*, the man in charge of the cavalry bat-horse and its load (< Modern French *bât* 'pack-saddle'). Figurative uses of *bastard* appear early on (fourteenth century),

---

[8] This can be viewed at http://www.youtube.com/watch?v=1Sn9L94YrNk.

often in reference to things of an inferior quality or grade (*bastard scarlet* and *bastard diamonds*); in scientific labels it denotes varieties that resemble a legitimate species of the same name (*bastard hellebore, bastard parsley* and *bastard rhubarb*), and is similar to the epithet *horse* in varietal names such as *horse chestnut, horse parsley, horseradish* and so on.

Bastard was another early recruit among the sexually based terms for use as a swearword – though clearly it was the stigma of illegitimacy that drove this development. In the early 1800s it can be found as a general (though strong) term of abuse for men or boys (considered vulgar). In his 1830 history of Morley (in Yorkshire), for example, Norrisson Cavendish Scatcherd writes 'nothing is more common also in this district than to hear a person abused by the word "Bastard"' (p. 96), and in his later glossary he defines it as 'a term of reproach for a mischievous or worthless boy' (p. 168).

As we go on to demonstrate, *bastard* has nothing like the grammatical flexibility of *bugger*. Though the *Oxford English Dictionary* has a handful of entries from the sixteenth and seventeenth centuries for transitive and intransitive verbal uses of *bastard*, these forms were short-lived. Being now limited to noun and nominal modifier, it has a more restricted cussing potential and inspires a smaller range of expressions. Curiously though, it can appear as an infix in some varieties of English (though not Australian English). Speakers may insert *bastard* inside words of three of more syllables, though, unlike other classic infixes (such as *bloody*), only words referring to objects able to be qualified with the epithet *bastard* (*telebastardvision* versus **fanbastardtastic*); cf. responses to infixing query Linguist List Sat, 13 Jul 1996; http://linguistlist.org/issues/7/7-1019.html; also Burridge (2004: 11) for a general discussion of infixing and 'the bloody insertion rule'.

As in the history of other swearwords, semantic bleaching, changing taboos and societal changes have rendered *bastard* a far milder swearword these days. Like *bugger*, it makes regular public appearances, sometimes to express anger or frustration at something or someone (*sneaky conniving bastard*), and under different circumstances to signal positive attitudes, such as compassion *(poor bastard)* or affection (*he's a good bastard*). Note that many Australian speakers distinguish these uses with different vowel sounds – a short vowel signals positive nuances (*good old bastard*), a long vowel negative nuances (*useless bludgin' baastard, right baastard*).

2.1. Bastards and buggers in the dictionary

The dynamic nature of taboo is always reflected in the dictionary-making conventions of different eras, in particular the pressures put on lexicographers to alter definitions or even omit entries entirely. In keeping with changing sensitivities, early dictionary makers (as arbiters of semantic goodness) cheerfully included religious and racial swearwords (the obscenities of more modern times), but were reluctant to admit the sexually obscene words. In contrast, the twentieth century saw mounting pressure on editors to change, or omit the racial and political definition of words; it is now religion, race and disability that create the linguistic minefield for lexicographers.[9]

The taboo quality of *bastards* and *buggers* has differed in strength over time (though as we'll see not consistently), and this has meant a different public life and official history for the two expressions. While dictionary entries for *bastard* abound in the earliest collections, *bugger* was banished to the 'Dark Continent of the World of Words' (to draw on J.S Farmer's description of the invisible obscenities of early Modern English).[10] Its absence from Samuel Johnson's dictionary is telling. Johnson didn't baulk at vulgar words for bodily functions and bawdy parts. Full entries appear for expressions like *turd, belly, bum, arse, piss, fart* and *bastard* (both in the literal sense 'a person born of a woman out of wedlock' and the extended sense 'any thing spurious or false') – and none of these words show any of the usual derogatory labels ('low', 'cant', 'barbarous', 'vulgar', 'bad', etc.) with which Johnson branded other expressions (cf. Hudson 1998; Burridge 2008). Moral code of the time might have prevented those in polite society from uttering these words; yet they were not slang, colloquial or cant and (important for Johnson) they had a well-documented pedigree, so he didn't mark them. There is, however, no mention of *bugger* (whose origin was established) in either the first edition (1755) or any of the subsequent revised editions (which introduced noted vulgarisms such as *bloody*). *Bugger* joined other invisible words such as *swive, cundum, twat* and the most potent of the so-called 'four letter words' (or 'monosyllables' as they were known in Johnson's day); hence, the now famous exchange between Johnson and the lady who had noted (and approved of) the omission of all the improper words from the dictionary – Johnson's alleged response was

---

[9] Robert Burchfield (1989) recounts the fierce debates in the early 1970s while he was editor of the *Oxford English Dictionary* over the inclusion in the dictionary of opprobrious senses of the word *Jew*. Lakoff (2000) details the 1990s dispute between the publishers of the *Merriam-Webster's Collegiate Dictionary* (10th edition) and members of the African-American community over the definition of *nigger*; see also Perrin (1992: Ch. 11) and Hughes (1991: Ch. 11) for accounts of various crusades over the years.

[10] J.F. Farmer, together with W.E. Henley, compiled the remarkable seven-volumed *Slang and its Analogues* 1890–1904.

'No, Madam, I hope I have not daubed my fingers. I find, however, that you have been looking for them'.[11]

Johnson's aim was to register the language and not to shape it, and he was clearly no Mrs Grundy – as Hudson put it, 'Johnson's Dictionary was not, in short, a "polite" book' (1998: 89). We also know that the real life Johnson didn't shirk from full-blown obscenity. Read (1934: 270), quoting Boswell described how he could 'talk the plainest bawdy', and of course many of his critics condemned his work precisely because it did include vulgar language (which he often justified on the authority of Shakespeare).[12] The question then is – why are these particular words missing?

Johnson tabooed words and word usage (polite and low) that he believed threatened the identity of the culture – what eighteenth-century grammarians referred to as the 'genius' of the language. He rejected ephemeral slang, so those words that he felt had no future. He also targeted words that he saw as having little or no etymological legitimacy (see Hudson 1998). But neither of these explanations condemn *bugger* as a lexical outlaw – it 'had legs' and a clear etymology. It was more likely the case that *bugger* was among the handful of words that couldn't appear – not because they were elusive cant, or because they were low or bad – but because they were too direct. The reality they conjured up was blunt, unlike their slangy counterparts that blurred the edges.

There were other early dictionaries (around Johnson's time or even before) that showed no such squeamishness. However, these were specialist dictionaries like Stephen Skinner's *Etymologicon Linguae Anglicanae* (1671). It offered scholarly accounts of many full-blown obscenities, though the collection was in Latin; so the text would have been uninterpretable to the young and innocent. Latin was often used as a euphemistic smokescreen in dictionary definitions, as in those of Nathan Bailey's *An Universal Etymological English Dictionary* (1724). John Ash's *New and Complete Dictionary of the English Language* (1775), however, used no coy abbreviations and no Latin for his risqué entries, which included the verb *bugger* and noun *buggery*,

---

[11] This version of the famous incident was noted by Sir Herbert Croft in the front of his *Dictionary* (1755); Allen Read (1934: 271) (who owned this book) cites this as the first appearance of the anecdote, predating by more than thirty years the now frequently quoted version published by H.D. Best in 1829.

[12] In a letter to David Ramsay, the puritanical Noah Webster roundly criticized Johnson for including 'vulgar words and offensive ribaldry' (*Letters*, pp. 286–7, edited by Warfel); despite Webster's view of dictionaries as an inventory of all words belonging to a language, his collections (of 1806, 1807, 1817, 1828, 1841) were well and truly sanitized (Webster was after all the man who cleaned up the Bible; cf. Perrin 1992).

as well as an historical entry for *buggers* glossed 'the Bulgarians'; there is no mention, however, of its extended use as a swearword. Notable in this regard is Captain Frances Grose's *Dictionary of the Vulgar Tongue* (first published in 1785, with fuller editions appearing in 1788, 1796 and 1811). Among the 4,000 colloquialisms and vulgarisms (reputedly collected at midnight in the slums of St. Giles) were the notable obscenities, though sometimes disguised with asterisks or dashes. The earliest editions contain entries for *bastard*, clearly showing its use in curses (though the *Oxford English Dictionary* cites this use only from the 1800s). However, *bugger* only appears in the new (and enlarged) release of the third edition in 1811 (the *Lexicon Balatronicum*), where *bugger* is defined as 'a blackguard, a rascal, a term of reproach. Mill the bloody bugger; beat the damned rascal'; we know it was well and truly in use in insults and curses from the early 1700s (as shown by the Old Bailey transcripts), so its omission from the earlier editions of the *Vulgar Tongue* is unexpected.

As lexicographer Jack Lynch points out, 'as dictionaries became authoritative reference ... some began to worry that the inclusion of bad words would harm impressionable readers. [...] Nearly every dictionary followed Johnson's practice until the 1960s' (2009: 239–40). When risqué words fell from grace in this way, they had no place to go but slang anthologies, even if they were standard (though colloquial) terms. The earliest edition of the *Oxford English Dictionary* (a century and a half after Johnson's dictionary), gave into Victorian sensitivities omitting the full-blown sexual obscenities of the 'Dark Continent' – even critics like John Hamilton in their passionate defense of why such words should appear in the dictionary never actually spelled out the words. Of course by then there was also a legal guardian, in the form of the Obscene Publications Act 1857, to ensure these words dropped from public record. However, there were some surprises that managed to sneak through the controls, including items of coarse slang such as *piss*, *shitsack*, *twat*, *windfucker* and even *bugger*.

Clearly, *bugger* was too potent a term to make public appearances until more modern times when its imagery was sufficiently buried; no such restrictions were ever placed on *bastard*. These days, however, it is *bastard* that packs more of a punch. In a joint study carried out by the Advertising Standard Authority, the British Broadcasting Corporation, the Broadcasting Standards Commission and the Independent Television Commission, 1,500 participants were asked to respond to the perceived 'strength' of 28 swearwords (Millwood-Hargrave 2000): *bastard* was ranked sixth most offensive (and fifth in the survey of 1997), while *bugger* was ranked twenty-first (as in

1997) – nearly 70% described it as either 'mild' or 'not swearing' (compared to the nearly 70% that rated *bastard* 'very' or 'fairly severe'). Unfortunately, a similar study carried out by the Australian Broadcasting Corporation (Urbis Pty. Ltd. 2011) didn't explicitly identify the coarse language items in its survey. Nonetheless, our findings presented in section 3 strongly suggest that *bastard* is a more loaded personal insult (even in friendly banter) than *bugger*.

3. The data on bastards and buggers

We now move on to the corpus data to explore the developing usage, meanings and cultural significance of *bastard* and *bugger*. All the four functions we outlined earlier were well attested (occasionally overlapping), though there were some significant differences between the two expressions. In the case of *bastard*, the abusive function dominated; in all but a handful of examples, it was used as a direct insult or as a dysphemistic epithet. It could also add intensity to what was being said or referred to (the stylistic function), and was occasionally used to express mateship or endearment (the social function); as earlier described, it lacks the ability to occur as an expletive. In the case of *bugger*, the social and stylistic functions dominated; it was occasionally used as an expletive, but only rarely to insult or curse.

In this section, we look at these functional aspects, but also focus on the structural characteristics of the swearing patterns. We start with the basic information. There are 98 instances of the forms *bastard* and *bastards* in the Australian National Corpus (AusNC). Of these, 84 are nominal uses, 11 are prenominal modifiers and 3 are oddities discussed later. There are 131 instances of forms based on the word *bugger* in the collections. Nominal uses account for 83 of these; there are also 6 instances of the noun *buggery*, 29 verbal instances, 4 exclamations, 2 instances of the phrase *bugger all* and 7 instances which are mentions rather than uses. These numbers suggest that, at least for their use as nouns, these two words occur at quite similar rates in Australian English.[13]

The collections which currently make up the AusNC are not designed to be balanced chronologically, with the partial exception of the Corpus of Oz Early English (COOEE). Therefore the comments which we can make about the distribution of forms across time are very limited, particularly as one text (Manning 1929) provides a disproportionate number of examples

---

[13] From this point, we use forms in small capitals (BASTARD) to indicate lemmas and forms in italics (*bugger*) to indicate actually occurring word forms.

for both words. However, it is worth noting that BASTARD appears in 8 texts originating before 1900, while BUGGER only appears once in that period:

(15) There was a general cry among the party coming down to me, of 'shoot the bugger'. (Court Report 1833, published in Ingleton 1988; COOEE 2-083)

It is also worth noting that of the 11 uses of BASTARD as a prenominal modifier, 8 are in texts from before 1900. Three of these instances occur in the diaries of Ludwig Leichardt and all refer to a plant species:

(16) I travelled west by north about eight miles, along the foot of Bastard-box and silver-leaved Ironbark ridges. (Journal of Ludwig Leichardt, published in Fitzapatrick 1956; COOEE 2-283)

Both words tend to appear in a wider range of texts from the more recent collections. This is an artefact of the corpus structure (in particular, the Australian Corpus of English [ACE] and the Australian component of the International Corpus of English [ICE] include material from 1983 and 1992 respectively); however, it is also what we would predict from the history of swearing patterns (in terms of changing taboos and the processes of semantic weakening).

3.1. Nominal uses

3.1.1. Singular and plural

There is a difference in the relative occurrence of singular and plural forms for the two nouns in this dataset. BASTARD occurs 64 times as a singular noun and 20 times as a plural, while BUGGER is singular in 47 instances and plural in 36. Table 1 shows these figures and also shows the relative proportions as percentages, as well as data for the pairs *man/men* and *woman/women*.

The numbers for the man and woman pairs suggest that we should not expect a strong preference for either singular or plural reference with words referring to humans. However, bastard appears to be an exception to this generalisation, and the tendency is apparent even in the case of the expression *you bastard*, which occurs with singular referent on 13 occasions as against 5 instances with plural reference.[14]

---

[14] There are only three instances of *you bugger*, all singular.

Table 1. Nominal uses: singular v. plural.

	Singular		Plural	
	Occurrences	%	Occurrences	%
BASTARD	64/84	76.0	20/84	24.0
BUGGER	47/83	57.0	36/83	43.0
MAN	2491	50.1	2479	49.9
WOMAN	1216	49.9	1219	50.1

3.1.2. Determiners and quantifiers

In the data from the AusNC, articles are the only determiners and quantifiers with which BASTARD co-occurs. There are 33 instances of this type, with 27 singulars and 6 plurals. Of the singulars, 14 instances are definite (with *the*) and 13 are indefinite (with *a*). BUGGER occurs with a wider range of determiners and quantifiers. There are 31 singular phrases of this type; 18 of them with definite *the*, 3 with indefinite *a*, 7 with *that*, 1 with *this* and 2 with *every*. The 18 plural phrases are made up as follows: 11 with *the*, 2 with *these*, 1 with *some* and 3 with *them*.

Two further facts about this group (BUGGER + determiner) are notable. Firstly all but 6 of the 31 examples come from a single text (Manning 1929). This work depicts the lives of ordinary soldiers during the First World War, and the author has depicted BUGGER as the more typical epithet used by this group.[15] In comparison, only 5 out of the 33 determiner + BASTARD examples come from this source. Secondly, the 3 examples of *a* + BUGGER are all predicative:

> (17) but that's nature for you What a bugger (ABC-TV script 1994; ICE:S2B-035-plain.txt)

> (18) 'It's a bugger, ain't it' exclaimed Martlow. (Manning 1929; AustLit:manmidd-plain.txt)

BASTARD only appears once in a construction of this type:

> (19) It's these sand greens that are a bastard to play. (*Australian Geographic*, January 1986; ACE:F39-plain.txt)

---

[15] Interestingly, in his annotated edition of Grose's *Dictionary of the Vulgar Tongue* (1931), Partridge makes the point under the entry for *bastard* that 'during the War [World War I] it was very frequent among British troops of all countries and most counties'.

3.1.3. Adjectives

The two words have very similar rates of occurrence with adjectives in the data (BASTARD – 33 instances and BUGGER – 30 instances), but the patterns of collocation are very different. Of the 30 examples for BUGGER, all but 6 include the adjective *poor* or the adjective *other* (see Table 2).

BASTARD, on the other hand, occurs with a wider range of adjectives (see Table 3).

Table 2. Occurrence with adjectives: bugger.

poor	*other*	misc.
18 (includes 2 x *poor old*)	6	*artful crafty little lucky miserable stubborn*

Table 3. Occurrence with adjectives: bastard.

colour	*fucking*	*old*	*poor*	*dodgy*	*little*	*total*	*not bad*	misc.
2 x black 2 x yellow	4	3 (1 x old black)	3	2	2 (1 x little Aussie)	2	2	*drunken hippie lying moral nasty looking rich Scotch smug worthless Yank*

All of the examples of *fucking* + BASTARD are in address terms (with the abusive function):

(20) 'e says. 'Well, take that, you fuckin' bastard' says Madeley, an' sloshes 'im one. (Manning 1929; AustLit:manmidd-plain-1.txt)

(21) a drunk … performing his pain-wracked aria Oh Ya F-ing Bastards Ya Bastards, Ya F-ing Bastards. (*Good Weekend*, December 1986; ACE:G72a-plain.txt)

The adjective *bad* only co-occurs with BASTARD in the phrase *not a bad bastard*:

> (22) Well, I reckon you're not a bad bastard, Cabell. I've seen plenty worse. (Penton 1936; AustLit: peninhe-raw.txt)

In respect of the miscellaneous adjectives which co-occur with the two words, the only noticeable pattern is that BASTARD occurs three times with adjectives indicating nationality: *Yank*, *Scotch* and *Aussie*:

> (23) I'll get you you little Aussie bastard. (TV show *Live and Sweaty*, 1992; ICE:S1B-023-plain.txt)

> (24) the men cried in righteous fury. 'Let the Yank bastard fix that bloody lot for you!' (Roberts 1986; ACE: P15-plain.txt)

The two instances of *black* + BASTARD indicate racial origin rather than nationality:

> (25) Seen a boss give a black bastard a lift when he'd passed me by. (Penton 1936; AustLit: peninhe-raw.txt)

The examples with *yellow* + BASTARD, on the other hand, refer to moral qualities of the referent rather than racial origin:

> (26) you'd curse yourself for a yellow bastard to the end of your days. (Penton 1936; AustLit: peninhe-raw.txt)

There is one adjective which is used in a similar fashion with both of the words; *old* is used typically as one of a sequence of adjectives, and our impression is that it is not generally used to specify the age of the referent but has either a softening effect as in the first example (note also the difference between the first occurrence of *poor*, which expresses empathy, and the second, which ascribes indigence), or an intensifying effect, as in the second:[16]

> (27) the time they walked from Wave Hill, the poor old buggers were always poor and tired. (Interview recorded 2000; BraidedChannels:01_BC_DV_JESSOP-plain.txt)

---

[16] In his account of vernacular Australian English, Pawley (2008: 364) describes the use of the adjective *old* before common nouns and personal names to indicate salient nouns in the discourse.

(28) He was a proper old bastard. He's got everybody dead scared.
(Penton 1936; AustLit: peninhe-raw.txt)

To reinforce the point made above about the language of Manning (1929), in these examples with adjectives, 17 of the 30 occurrences with BUGGER are from Manning, but only 1 of the 33 occurrences with BASTARD are from that source.

3.1.4. Address terms

We have already noted that *fucking* + BASTARD only occurs as an abusive term of address. Overall, there are many more occurrences of BASTARD in this context than of BUGGER: 18 against 3, all of which are from Manning (1929). Typical examples are:

(29) See? You miserable bugger, you! (Manning 1929; AustLit:manmidd-plain-1.txt)

(30) so it was just, you know, 'Okay you bastards, get out and have your fight outside' (Interview recorded 2000; BraidedChannels:16_BC_DV_JACKSON-plain.txt)

Of the BASTARD examples, 5 are plural. There is a single example of BASTARD in this way without *you* preceding:

(31) In the darkness he stumbled over a bucket and kicked it across the yard. 'Bastard,' he muttered. 'Could he ride a brumby or chuck a steer? Skite.' (Penton 1936; AustLit: peninhe-raw.txt)

3.2. Other uses

3.2.1. Bastard – Prenominal modifiers

As mentioned in section 2, there are 11 instances of BASTARD used prenominally. Of these, 5 occur with plants (*box* as a tree 3 times, *bloodwood* and *fig* once each) and an additional instance is with another natural product (*tortoiseshell*). One of the remaining 5 instances occurs with a human noun (*wowsers*), and the last 4 modify abstract nouns (*God, recession, Latin* and *commodity*). This last example clearly refers to an abstraction, although *commodity* can have concrete referents:

(32) there is a certain bastard commodity called law. (Savery 1829; COOEE:2-036.txt)

3.2.2. Bastard – Oddities

There are 3 instances of BASTARD that are hard to classify, although one has been mentioned above, the use of *Bastard* alone as an address term. The remaining 2 oddities are, firstly, the occurrence of BASTARD as part of a proper name, in this case a reference to William the Conqueror (it was well known as a surname and records of famous Bastards include Roger Bastard of Northampton, the Bastard family of Kitley House, Devon and the Oxford clergyman Reverend Thomas Bastard):

> (33) not that of William the Bastard, but of Jack the Strapper.
> (Deniehy, 1884, COOEE:3-091-plain.txt)

and secondly an instance where the word is apparently truncated for euphonic effect:

> (34) Harvey you nasty basty (Talkback radio recorded 2005, ART:COMNE4-raw.txt)

In this case, the transcriber noted this as representing BASTARD.

3.2.3. Bugger – Mentions

One of the texts in the AusNC is a passage on colloquialisms in Australian English by Arthur Delbridge (Delbridge 1986). This passage has mentions of the word BUGGER illustrating various colloquial uses of the word (these metalinguistic uses are clearly special and fall outside the four functions identified earlier). A typical sentence from this source is the following:

> (35) According to Collins it is slang to say bugger about, but taboo slang to say bugger off. (Delbridge 1986; ACE: J35-plain.txt)

There is a total of 12 such mentions in the text included in the ACE.

3.2.4. Bugger – Verbal uses

There are 29 instances of BUGGER as a verb or as a part of a phrasal verb. The most common coherent grouping of such uses is the phrasal verb *bugger off*. There are 7 such examples, of which the following are typical:

> (36) Then they just bugger off and leave 'em. (Cook 1986; ACE: R10-plain.txt)
>
> (37) 'Oh, bugger off,' Leigh says without malice. (Hospital 1990; ICE: W2F-017-plain.txt)

There are 5 examples of *bugger about*, but two of these are mentions by Delbridge (see above) and the remaining 3 are all from Manning (1929). Interestingly, Delbridge claims that this phrase is used 'with the sense of occupying oneself in a desultory fashion (bugger about)'. Manning uses it with a different sense, perhaps 'being ordered around without reason and to no good effect', certainly with a sense of external agency:

(38) and then we're buggered about, and taken over miles o' ground. (Manning 1929; AustLit: manmidd-plain.txt)

In one case, Manning uses this as a transitive phrasal verb:

(39) What's the cunt want to come down 'ere buggerin' us about for, 'aven't we done enough bloody work (Manning 1929; AustLit: manmidd-plain.txt)

Manning also uses the phrase *buggered-up* as an adjectival predicate (2 instances):

(40) some o' these bloody conscripts. Seen 'em yet? Buggered-up by a joy-ride in the train from Rouen (Manning 1929; AustLit: manmidd-plain.txt)

There are 3 instances of the phrase *buggered if*, all with first person singular subject:

(41) You might have drowned! I'm buggered if I'd give you mouth-to-mouth. (Thorne 1986; ACE: R09-plain.txt)

The remaining 7 verbal instances all use the bare verb, but none of them denote the sexual act, which is the original sense of the word. All use the verb in a more metonymical way to indicate some negative impact on the patient of the action:

(42) Let's go home I'm buggered (Conversation recorded 1993; ICE:S1A-023-plain.txt)

3.2.5. Buggery

The use of the bare verb BUGGER contrasts with the use of the noun *buggery*. There are 6 such instances in the corpus, and in this case, 2 of them are used to refer to the sexual act:

(43) criminal sanctions against the abominable crime of buggery (Connell et al. 1990; ICE:W2A-011-plain.txt)

The remaining 4 examples use the noun in a metonymical way where the word denotes a bad state of indeterminate nature:

(44) Frightened buggery out of me. (Cook 1986; ACE: R10-plain.txt)

In two of these instances, the word is used in the phrase *go to buggery* (both of these are from Manning 1929):

(45) 'He told me to go to buggery, sir' replied Bourne very quietly. (Manning 1929, AustLit: manmidd-plain.txt)

3.2.6. Remaining cases

Perhaps surprisingly, there is only one clear case of the phrase *bugger all* in the corpus:

(46) I've gotta start by saying that I really know bugger all about the media (Scripted speech 1993; ICE: S2B-047-plain.txt)

Finally, there are two instances where BUGGER is used as an exclamation:

(47) 'oh did you take those movies back' 'I did' ' bugger' 'I'm sorry darl but they were were due' (Conversation recorded 2009; GCSAusE: GCSAusE16-plain.txt)

(48) Well, it is going slow, I could make it. Bugger, too late now. (Newspaper article 1986; ACE:B22a-plain.txt)

3.3. Summary

Given that BASTARD does not have the possibility of being used as a verb, we concentrate here on the similarities and differences between the two words in nominal uses. Two points are clear from the data discussed above. First, we note a tendency for BASTARD to occur more often in singular phrases than might be expected. This tendency shows up overall, and also in sub-groups of the data such as the examples of *you* + BASTARD and with determiners and quantifiers. The second point is that BUGGER co-occurs with a restricted range of adjectival modifiers. Collocations of *poor* + BUGGER and *other* + BUGGER are almost stereotypes in this data. It is, however, hard to know how much weight to attribute to this observation given that so many of the examples come from a single source.

4. Discussion

> Whether they are referred to as swearing, cursing, cussing, profanity, obscenity, vulgarity, blasphemy, expletives, oaths, or epithets; as dirty, four-letter, or taboo words; or as bad, coarse, crude, foul, salty, earthy, raunchy, or off-color language, these expressions raise many puzzles for anyone interested in language as a window into human nature. (Pinker 2007: 267)

The nature of the data assembled here does not allow us to make precise statements about historical changes in the use of these two words in Australian English. However, the data which we do have is consistent with the historical backdrop discussed previously. The force of taboos against 'bad' language clearly decreases in Australian usage as it did in wider usage over the time period represented here. The clustering of pre-nominal uses of BASTARD in the nineteenth century is one example of this; such usages still reference the sexual element of meaning carried by the word, by invoking something that is not legitimate, but the word lacks the overt force of a swearword in this position. The later appearance of BUGGER is also consistent with the more general historical picture. The greater strength of the taboo against BUGGER which is evident in the odd treatment accorded the word in Johnson's dictionary (and other collections around that time) may be considered to have operated here in keeping the word out of sight.

We suggest that there are important differences between the two nouns we have examined here, and we will begin our attempt to analyse the differences by considering the collocation *other bugger*. As noted previously, there are no examples of *other bastard* in the data. To sharpen this contrast, we would like to consider an old joke which includes the words *other bugger*. Under the Imperial honours system previously used in Australia (and still used in the United Kingdom), there is an award called the Order of the British Empire abbreviated as OBE. The joke is that this abbreviation actually stands for *other buggers' efforts*, and the point that we would like to make is that the joke doesn't work at all if we say *other bastard's efforts*. The essence of the joke, we suggest, is that some person or people have been exploited; BUGGER allows the sense that the referent has been exploited but BASTARD does not. In fact, BASTARD tends to a reading where the referent is one who exploits. It is true that BASTARD can have a more sympathetic reading when modified by an adjective such as *poor*:

> (49) That's the least we can do for the poor bastards, I thought. (Botsjtsuh 1986; ACE: N03-plain.txt)

But such examples are much more common with BUGGER than with BASTARD, 18 instances against 3. To return to *other bugger*, we suggest that the examples in the data express either a neutral attitude to the referent:

> (50) I were busy keepin' some o' the other buggers off 'im, (Manning 1929; AustLit: manmidd-plain.txt)

or a sympathetic attitude:

> (51) they don't care a fuck about wastin' the other bugger's life, do they? (Manning 1929; AustLit: manmidd-plain.txt)

Very speculatively, we would suggest that the connotations of sympathy associated with BUGGER may be a secondary effect from the adjectival participle *buggered*. Someone who is *buggered* is someone for whom we might feel sympathy:

> (52) Let's go home I'm buggered (Conversation recorded 1993; ICE:S1A-023-plain.txt; also appears as example 25)

With no verbal uses, no such association can have developed for BASTARD. BUGGER can be used with negative connotations, but this seems to be restricted to phrases which include an adjective:

> (53) 'No, but those crafty buggers are out there all right. Probably having smoko,' (Botsjtsuh 1986; ACE: N03-plain.txt)

On the other hand, *bastard* has inherent negative connotations:

> (54) MacKenzie was elated, the bastard had backed down. (Bullock 1986; ACE:N04-plain.txt)

As noted above, BASTARD occurs with a wider range of adjectives which serve to make specific what are the usually negative characteristics of the referent:

> (55) yeah dodgy bastard should've given me a (yells) job. (Interview recorded 1996–8; MCE:MECG4MA_Sanitised-plain.txt)

(56) But that's a Vietnam issue. I bet that hippie bastard was never there. (Roberts 1986; ACE:P15-plain.txt)

We are suggesting that BASTARD has more inherent semantic content than BUGGER, and that this content codes a more negative attitude to the person referred to.[17] This seems to us to also be consistent with the two patterns in the corpus data which we have noted above. It is easier, we would suggest, to think of less strongly characterized people in terms of groups. A *bastard* is a BASTARD for some particular reason; while it is not impossible that several people might share that characteristic, this is not often the case and therefore it is more common for BASTARD to be used as a singular noun. But we very often do want to specify the characteristic which makes someone a BASTARD; hence the wider range of adjectives which co-occur with this noun. BUGGER, on the other hand, is more generic and we rarely have reason to be specific about why someone can be considered a BUGGER; hence the restricted range of generic adjectives which appear with this word.

If we are correct in our analysis of the difference between the two words, we will conclude by saying that Keith Allan might be an *old bugger*, but he is not an *old bastard*.

References

Allan, Keith and Kate Burridge. 1991. *Euphemism and Dysphemism: Language Used as Shield and Weapon.* New York: Oxford University Press.

Allan, Keith and Kate Burridge. 2006. *Forbidden Words: Taboo and the Censoring of Language.* Cambridge: Cambridge University Press.

Allan, Keith and Kate Burridge. 2010. Swearing and taboo language in Australian English. In Pam Peters, Peter Collins and Adam Smith (eds), *Comparative Grammatical Studies in Australian and New Zealand English.* Amsterdam: John Benjamins, 295–347.

Ash, John. 1775. *New and Complete Dictionary of the English Language: In Which All the Words Are Introduced [...] and the Different Constructions and Uses Illustrated by Examples* (in two volumes). London: Dilly & Baldwin.

Bailey, Nathan. 1724. *An Universal Etymological English Dictionary: Comprehending the Derivations of the Generality of Words [...].* London.

---

[17] The grammatical flexibility of *bugger* means that it appears in a greater range of idioms and structural types than *bastard*; it is conceivable that this wider use (beyond insult) has contributed to its weakened semantics. Pam Peters (p.c.) has suggested that the conversion of the noun *bugger* to the verb could also have contributed to the more generic semantics.

Brophy, John and Eric Partridge. 1931. *Songs and Slang of the British Soldier: 1914–1918*. 3rd ed. London: Routledge & Kegan Paul.

Burchfield, Robert. 1989. *Unlocking the English Language*. London: Faber & Faber.

Burridge, Kate. 2004. *Blooming English*. Cambridge: Cambridge University Press.

Burridge, Kate. 2008. 'Corruptions of Ignorance', 'Caprices of Innovation': Linguistic purism and the lexicographer. *The Johnson Society of Australia Papers* 10: 25–38.

Burridge, Kate. 2010. 'A peculiar language' – The linguistic evidence for early Australian English. In Raymond Hickey (ed.), *Varieties in Writing: The Written Word as Linguistic Evidence*. Amsterdam & Philadelphia: John Benjamins, 295–348.

Dong, Quang Phuc. 1992 (1971). English sentences without overt grammatical subject. In Arnold M. Zwicky, Peter H. Salus, Robert I. Binnick and Anthony L. Vanek (eds), *Studies out in Left Field: Defamatory Essays Presented to James D. McCawley on His 33rd or 34th Birthday*. Reprint of the original edition (1971). Amsterdam & Philadelphia: John Benjamins.

Farmer, John S. and W.E. Henley. 1890–1904/1970. *Slang and Its Analogues* (7 vols). London. Reprint by Arno Press, New York.

Gallahorn, George E. 1971. The use of taboo words by psychiatric ward personnel. *Psychiatry* 34 (3): 309–21.

Gerstäcker, Frederick. 1857. *The Two Convicts*. London: Routledge and Co.

Gordon, Elizabeth and Tony Deverson. 1985. *New Zealand English: An Introduction to New Zealand Speech and Usage*. Auckland: Heinemann.

Grose, Captain Frances Grose. 1811. *Lexicon Balatronicum. A Dictionary of Buckish Slang, University Wit, and Pickpocket Eloquence. Compiled Originally by Captain Grose. And Now Considerably Altered and Enlarged, with Modern Changes and Improvements, by a Member of the Whip Club*.

Hudson, Nicholas. 1998. Johnson's 'Dictionary' and the politics of 'Standard English'. *The Yearbook of English Studies* 28: 77–93.

Hughes, Geoffrey. 1991. *Swearing: A Social History of Foul Language, Oaths and Profanity in English*. Oxford: Blackwell.

Hughes, Geoffrey. 2006. *An Encyclopedia of Swearing: The Social History of Oaths, Profanity, Foul Language, and Ethnic Slurs in the English Speaking World*. New York: M.E. Sharpe.

Johnson, Samuel. 1755. *A Dictionary of the English Language: In Which the Words Are Deduced from Their Originals, and Illustrated by Examples from the Best Writers. To Which Are Prefixed, a History of the Language, and an English Grammar* (2 vols). London: W. Strahan.

Lakoff, Robin T. 2000. *The Language War*. Berkeley: University of California Press.

Lalor, Theressa and Johanna Rendle-Short. 2007. 'That's so gay': A contemporary use of *gay* in Australian English. *Australian Journal of Linguistics* 27: 147–73.

Lynch, Jack. 2009. *The Lexicographer's Dilemma*. New York: Walker and Company.
Merriam-Webster's Collegiate Dictionary. 2001. (19th ed.) Merriam-Webster's Incorporated.
Millwood-Hargrave, Andrea. 2000. *Delete expletives?* London: Advertising Standards Authority, British Broadcasting Corporation, Broadcasting Standards Commission, Independent Television Commission.
Oxford English Dictionary (OED). 1989. 2nd ed. Oxford Clarendon Press. Also available on compact disc.
Partridge, Eric (ed.). 1931/1962. *A Classical Dictionary of the Vulgar Tongue*. New York: Dorset Press.
Pawley, Andrew. 2008. Australian Vernacular English: Some grammatical characteristics. In Kate Burridge and Bernd Kortmann (eds), *Varieties of English: The Pacific and Australasia*. Berlin: Mouton de Gruyter, 362–97.
Perrin, Noel. 1992. *Dr. Bowdler's Legacy: A History of Expurgated Books in English and America*. Boston: David R. Godine.
Peters, Pam and Kate Burridge. 2012. Areal linguistics in the South Pacific. In Ray Hickey (ed.), *Areal Features of the Anglophone World*. Berlin: Mouton de Gruyter, 233–60.
Pinker, Stephen. 2007. *The Stuff of Thought: Language as a Window into Human Nature*. New York: Penguin.
Ramson, William S. 1966. *Australian English: An Historical Study of the Vocabulary, 1788–1898*. Australian National University Press: Canberra.
Read, Allen. 1934. The obscenity symbol. *American Speech* 9 (4): 264–78.
Ross, Helen E. 1960. Patterns of swearing. *Discovery* 21: 479–81.
Scatcherd, Norrisson Cavendish. 1874. *The History of Morley, in the West-riding of Yorkshire, and Especially of the Old Chapel: With Some Account of Places in the Vicinity*. n.p.: S. Stead.
Seal, Graham. 1999. *The Lingo: Listening to Australian English*. Sydney: University of New South Wales Press.
Skinner, Stephen. 1671. *Etymologicon linguae Anglicanae; seu, explicatio locum Anglicarum etymologica ex propriis fortibus [...]*. London: T. Roycroft.
Stollznow, Karen. 2004. Whinger! Wowser! Wanker! Aussie English: Deprecatory language and the Australian ethos. In Christo Moskovskey (ed.), *Proceedings of the 2003 Conference of the Australian Linguistic Society*. (http://au.geocities.com/austlingsoc/proceedings/als2003.html)
Taylor, Brian. 1994–5. Unseemly language and he law in New South Wales. *The Journal of the Sydney University Arts Association* 17: 23–45.
Twopenny, Richard K.N. 1883. *Town Life in Australia*. London: Elliot Stock.
Urbis Pty Ltd. 2011. *Community Attitudes Towards Swearing*. Ultimo, NSW: the Australian Broadcasting Corporation.

Wakefield, Edward Gibbon. 1829. *A Letter from Sydney: The Principal Town of Australasia*. n.p.: J Cross [Original from the New York Public Library; Digitized 25 Sep 2007].

Warfel, Harry R. 1953. *Letters of Noah Webster*. New York: Library Publications.

Wierzbicka, Anna. 1992. *Semantics, Culture, and Cognition: Universal Human Concepts in Culture-specific Configurations*. New York: Oxford University Press.

Text sources

Botsjtsuh, R. 1986. *Operation Sea Dragon*. Nerang QLD: Ryebuck Publications.

Bullock, Kenneth. 1986. Sydney. In *Pelandah 1986*. Sydney: Brolga Press.

Connell, R.W., J. Crawford, G.W. Dowsett, S. Kippax, V. Sinnott, P. Rodden and R. Berg. 1990. Danger and context: Unsafe anal sexual practice among homosexual and bisexual men in the AIDS crisis. *Journal of Sociology* 26 (2): 187–208.

Cook, Kenneth. 1986. A couple of interesting specimens. In *The Killer Koala: Humorous Bush Stories*. Ludlow: Tortoise-shell Press.

Corbyn, Charles Adam. 1854/1970. *Sydney Revels (the Eighteen-Fifties) of Bacchus, Cupid and Momus; Being Choice and Humorous Selections from Scenes at the Sydney Police Office and Other Public Places, During the Last Three Years* [Presented by Cyril Pearl]. Sydney: Ure Smith.

Delbridge, Arthur. 1986. Colloquialism. In P.H. Peters (ed.), *Style in Australia: Current Practices in Spelling, Punctuation, Hyphenation, Capitalisation, etc.: Proceedings of 'Style Council 86'* (edited for the Dictionary Research Centre, Macquarie University, NSW, Australia).

Deniehy, Daniel. 1884. *Life and Speeches of Daniel Henry Deniehy*. Sydney: McNeil and Coffee.

Hall, Jon. 1986. Road to ruin your nerve. *The Sun-Herald*, 9 November.

Hitchcock, Tim, Robert Shoemaker, Clive Emsley, Sharon Howard, Jamie McLaughlin, et al. *The Old Bailey Proceedings Online, 1674–1913* (www.oldbaileyonline.org; 24 March 2012).

Hospital, Janette Turner. 1990. Bondi. In *Isobars*. St Lucia: University of Queensland Press.

Manning, Frederic. 1929. *The Middle Parts of Fortune*. London: The Piazza Press.

Penton, Brian. 1936. *Inheritors*. Sydney: Angus & Robertson.

Roberts, Kevin. 1986. The junkman. In A. Taylor (ed.), *Unsettled areas: Recent Short Fiction – A South Australian Collection*. Netley, SA: Wakefield Press.

Savery, Henry. 1829/1964. *The Hermit in Van Diemen's Land* (edited by Cecil Hadgraft). St. Lucia: University of Queensland Press.

Thorne, Sandy. 1986. *Battler's Block*. Cammeray, NSW: Horwitz Grahame Books.

Chapter 2

DIACHRONIC PROPERTIES OF THE LEXICON

SEMANTICS, STABILITY AND DIVERSITY

Olav Kuhn

Monash University

Lexicostatistical methods have achieved a fair level of acceptance for quantifying the degree of relationships between languages and the construction of family trees. Attempts to use these methods for glottochronology, i.e., to estimate the time depth of these relationships, have not met wide acceptance, because the stability of lexemes with different meanings, even within basic vocabulary, is not uniform. However, variation in lexical stability is itself a possible source of evidence for historical inference, as long as that variation exhibits consistent behaviour. This paper estimates lexical stability rates for a number of Indo-European and neighbouring languages based on the observed lexical diversity in groups and subgroups known to be related. These rates are employed to evaluate different hypotheses of historical relationship, by comparing the distribution of shared vocabulary with the patterns of stability actually observed in known relationships. The performance of this approach is compared for the 100-word Swadesh list and the shorter 40-word list proposed by Holman et al. (2008).

1. Introduction

Lexicostatistics is a method of quantitative analysis of language relationships developed by Morris Swadesh, based on evaluating the proportion of cognates shared by related languages on a standard test list of basic vocabulary. The first general and systematic presentation of the method was Swadesh (1952), using a 200-word list and a mathematical model based on radioactive decay; comparisons between older and more recent stages of languages with written histories suggested that the retention rate of the items on the test list was approximately 81% per 1,000 years (Swadesh 1952: 458; Lees 1953: 119).

Using lexical analysis to estimate the time-depth of language relationships (especially ancestral proto-languages) is glottochronology, effectively an extension of lexicostatistics with specific assumptions: that every word on the test list has the same retention rate, that all languages have the same overall retention rate, now and at all times in the past, and that borrowing has no impact on either of these rates. All three assumptions were seen by many as implausible, and they were readily disproven (see Hymes 1960; Bergsland and Vogt 1962; Embleton 1986).

Swadesh (1955) provided a massive revision of the standard word list, now reduced to 100 words, including 93 from the older version together with seven new items. Old items were removed for various reasons, including high susceptibility to borrowing, as well as practical reasons of obtaining suitable synonyms in all languages. The shorter list was reported to have an overall retention rate of 86% per millennium, which in itself confirms that lexical retention rates are not uniform. Swadesh himself calculated individual retention rates for 215 items he had worked with originally, including almost all of the items on the 200-word list, and found them to vary significantly. He also evaluated a rough correction factor for the 200-word list to approximate the results of the more homogeneous 100-word list (Swadesh 1955: 128).

In the absence of a uniform retention rate, glottochronology could not be accepted as a reliable method for dating languages, although lexicostatistics does continue to be employed for subgrouping purposes. However, this absence also raises the question of whether variation in retention rates can be explained by other factors which could themselves be identified. The variability reported in Swadesh (1955) would be consistent with individual lexical items having their own characteristic retention rates, as if basic vocabulary consisted of a mixture of different isotopes with distinct half-lives, rather than a uniform object as in carbon-dating.

Thomas (1960) compared the lexical retention rates from Swadesh (1955), based mainly on Indo-European languages, with the relative persistence observed in eight Mon-Khmer languages. In the absence of historical written records, Thomas estimated lexical persistence based on the diversity of non-cognate forms for the same concept in the modern languages. He found that while individual items varied greatly, semantic groups (e.g., numerals, body parts) tended to behave similarly as sets across both samples. The behaviour of individual items was not, however, completely random; the Pearson correlation coefficient between the two reported sets is $r = 0.27$, although a major contributor to this is the very high stability of the numerals from 'one' to 'ten' in both.

A much larger study of lexical stability was undertaken by Dyen (1964), examining 89 Austronesian languages. He found that the variation in retention rates for Austronesian was strongly correlated with that in other languages, including a set of 39 Indo-European languages, suggesting that such variation is consistent, at the aggregate level, between unrelated and geographically distant languages. The observed identity of stable and unstable words within a group of languages may be called a distribution; thus Indo-European and Austronesian exhibit similar distributions of stable vocabulary, which are variations of an underlying common stability distribution shared by both families, and Mon-Khmer may also possess a version of this. Is there a global distribution, shared by all languages and thus perhaps intrinsic to the human capacity for language?

Oswalt (1971) suggested that a standard lexicostatistical list should consist of items that exhibited comparable behaviour in different languages families, i.e., that they should be equally stable (within expected statistical variation) and resistant to borrowing; and that a universal test list be compiled from empirical evidence. Since most language families lack long-term written records, he proposed a metric for evaluating the relative stability of individual items from the number of unrelated terms used for each item in the different members of a family; his *relative stability indices* were also based on the internal complexity of the family in which the words occurred. Oswalt examined five language groups: Athapaskan (24 languages), Pomo (7 languages), Eastern Austronesian (6 languages), Japanese (5 dialects) and Coast Salish (4 speech forms).

Oswalt also calculated a set of values that combined the observed RSIs for these five families as a provisional approximation to a universal set. He scaled the values before adding them together, mainly to prevent the Athapascan set from completely overshadowing the other language groups, using weights of 4 for Athapaskan, 2 for Pomo and Eastern Austronesian, and 1 for Japanese and Coast Salish.

However, Oswalt did not verify whether the five groups were consistent in their distribution of stable and unstable lexemes. Table 1 gives the Pearson correlation coefficient r between the sets of RSIs for each pair of language groups, as well as with the combined set; shading indicates values that are not independent of each other. For these comparisons, the RSI of the combined set was recalculated from the values of the individual families to avoid the effect of rounding applied in the published list; this also led to a minor correction in the combined RSI for BLOOD, which is 47.33 instead of the 43.3 listed in Oswalt (1971:428).

Table 1. Correlation for RSI values from Oswalt (1971).

	Ath	Pom	EAu	Jap	CSa	Com
Ath	1.00	0.29	0.10	-0.11	0.21	0.75
Pom	0.29	1.00	0.46	-0.04	0.26	0.73
EAu	0.10	0.46	1.00	0.18	0.23	0.65
Jap	-0.11	-0.04	0.18	1.00	-0.09	0.19
CSa	0.21	0.26	0.23	-0.09	1.00	0.44
Com	0.75	0.73	0.65	0.19	0.44	1.00

Even when different groups do represent the same underlying distribution, if the actual diversity is low, then the observable impact of this may not result in convincing correlation (either because there are too few languages, or the languages are too closely related). It may be that the Japanese set does not show any positive correlation with three of the other four groups because of these limitations, or it may be that the underlying distribution is simply different. Correlation between the other groups also varies greatly, and based on this data it is not possible to be certain that there is a fully universal lexical stability distribution, or to what extent there may be local variation.

Holman et al. (2008) evaluated a much larger sample of 245 languages in 69 families and found strong and consistent correlation in lexical stability for the 100-word Swadesh list across families regardless of location; the lack of geographic variation supports a truly global distribution. Their values for the distribution S were derived by the automatic comparison of word lists (an algorithm called 'automated similarity judgment program' or ASJP). Although recognition of cognates by inspection is less accurate than applying the comparative method, the large number of relatively closely related families in their sample means that errors will tend to cancel each other out and the overall values for S should accurately reflect the historical retention rates of the sampled vocabulary.

Localised deviations from the universal distribution may be small even when significant, and may require detailed analysis to identify. This paper examines the lexical stability exhibited in 100-word Swadesh lists for European families and subfamilies. The groups examined are: Germanic (8 languages), Romance (6 languages), Balto-Slavic (13 languages, including Latvian and Lithuanian), Celtic (5 languages), Indo-European (all of the previous, and also Modern Greek and Albanian), and Finno-Ugrian (7 languages). The diversity distribution D of each group is calculated by the simple addition of non-cognate forms for each item on the word lists, which serves as an approximation to the number of replacements that must have taken place to produce the modern lexical diversity. The base used here is that D = 0 where there is no diversity, i.e. all languages have reflexes of the same word; this simplifies the mathematics involved in manipulating distributions. Cognacy decisions inevitably need to be made for borderline cases; the definition of cognacy employed here is fairly liberal: words are accepted as cognate if they are derived from the same root, regardless of derivational changes, and borrowings within the same low-level subgroup are treated as if fully cognate (e.g., English *round* and German *rund*), on the grounds that they would be difficult to identify in the absence of historical records or outgroup comparison, which is the situation of most language families. Table 2 shows the correlation between the diversity distributions of each language group. D_{Eu} indicates the sum of D_{IE} and D_{FU}, representing an overall European stability distribution. As before, shading indicates non-independent pairings.

Table 2. Correlation for D for European groups.

	Ger	Rom	BS	Cel	FU	IE	D_{Eu}
Ger	1.00	0.21	0.32	0.35	0.29	0.56	0.54
Rom	0.21	1.00	0.25	0.29	0.34	0.52	0.52
BS	0.32	0.25	1.00	0.45	0.31	0.77	0.71
Cel	0.35	0.29	0.45	1.00	0.35	0.70	0.67
FU	0.29	0.34	0.31	0.35	1.00	0.50	0.72
IE	0.56	0.52	0.77	0.70	0.50	1.00	0.96
D_{Eu}	0.54	0.52	0.71	0.67	0.72	0.96	1.00

All of the groups exhibit a convincing level of correlation with each other, demonstrating that there is a shared stability distribution underlying these European language families, and Finno-Ugrian is as close to it as the Indo-European groups. But is this merely a random manifestation of the global distribution, or are there meaningful and predictive variations in a locally calibrated version? Table 3 shows the correlation between the combined distributions S, RSI and D_{Eu} with each other and with the different language groups, including those from Oswalt (1971). As the distributions based on D are more stable for lower values, whereas the others increase with higher stability, the signs for comparisons involving D and a different measure of stability are inverted.

Overall the stability distribution S has the highest correlation with individual groups, including the Japanese set. However, the Eurocentric distribution D_{Eu} is more similar to the European families. In part this is because it is derived from them; but some of the values in table 2 show that a more similar underlying distribution is also a component. For example, the stability of items in Celtic is better predicted by any of the other European distributions (lowest value for $r = 0.29$) than by either S or RSI ($r = 0.15$ and 0.13 respectively).

Table 3. Correlation between combined distributions and individual language groups.

	S	RSI	D_{Eu}	Ger	Rom	BS	Cel	FU	IE	Ath	Pom	EAu	Jap	CSa
S	1.00	0.58	0.46	0.29	0.36	0.23	0.15	0.57	0.34	0.27	0.39	0.57	0.24	0.30
RSI	0.58	1.00	0.31	0.14	0.18	0.10	0.13	0.43	0.22	0.75	0.73	0.65	0.19	0.44
D_{Eu}	0.46	0.31	1.00	0.54	0.52	0.71	0.67	0.72	0.96	0.22	0.21	0.35	-0.05	0.25

The very notion of 'basic vocabulary' assumes that lexical stability is dependent on semantics, but the exact factors involved may be complex. Pagel et al. (2007) found that the frequency of use of words for the meanings in the Swadesh-200 list in corpora of four modern Indo-European languages correlates strongly with their long-term stability in that language family. Since these words, or at least most of them, share the 'basic' quality, it does not automatically follow that the same correlation applies to other parts of the lexicon; see Beckwith (2004: 198–208) for a discussion of data not restricted to the Swadesh lists. It has also long been known that more frequently used words tend to be shorter (Zipf 1935; see also Sigurd et al. 2004), and thus it is not surprising that longer words are more likely to be replaced, not only relative to shorter words, but also in absolute terms (Wichmann and Holman, in press).

If the variation in stability of basic vocabulary items is sufficiently consistent around the world, and at different times, then several applications to the comparative method would derive from this. The most obvious is that a narrower selection of the lexicon could be searched for cognates, and the increased proportion of putatively inherited material might be enough to make a distant relationship convincing (a prominent example is Dolgopolsky 1986); and establishing different lexical strata would help with subgrouping related languages, and help with identifying borrowings.

2. Cognate finding

Since the European groups examined here have diversified in patterns which are statistically similar over timespans of perhaps three millennia (a reasonable estimate for Proto-Celtic and Proto-Balto-Slavic), it is not unreasonable to suspect consistent patterns to have existed here even earlier, perhaps all the way back to Proto-Indo-European. If that is indeed the case, then it should be possible to predict the words likely to be cognate *between* these groups based on which concepts are most stable *within* the same groups.

Table 4 shows the number of cognates found on the 100-word list between English, hardly the most lexically conservative language in the sample, and Spanish, Russian and Welsh. These languages were chosen, somewhat arbitrarily, as having the largest number of speakers in the Germanic, Romance, Balto-Slavic and Celtic groups. The items on the list are separated into groups defined by $D_{IE4} = D_G + D_R + D_{BS} + D_C$; this being an estimate of the stability distribution shared by these four Indo-European groups. For three items that are often interpreted differently in the literature, two variants were included: CLAW vs NAIL, BREAST(S) vs CHEST, and WARM vs HOT. Thus a total of 103 concepts were compared.

The most stable set for the languages sampled is $D_{IE4} = 0$, with ten items showing no diversity *within* the four language groups: {I, WHO, WHAT, ALL, ONE, TWO, NAIL, SIT, ASHES, FULL}. Most of the English words are cognate with their equivalents in Spanish, Russian and Welsh, except *all* and *ash(es)*, which are not found in Romance, Balto-Slavic or Celtic, and *I*, where Celtic has generalised the cognates of *me* instead.

The other sets $D_{IE4} = 1 \ldots 13$ include lower proportions of cognates, except where the sets are too small to be statistically significant, and the cumulative proportions show an almost monotonic decline, until finally they become equal to that of the list as a whole. It is therefore clear that the diversity that has accumulated since the times of Proto-Germanic, Proto-Romance, Proto-Balto-Slavic and Proto-Celtic, is an effective predictor of the stability of words even before those proto-languages and going back several more millennia to their common ancestor of Proto-Indo-European.

Table 4. English cognates divided into diversity sets.

set	size		cognates			cum. cognates			cum. % of cognates		
D_{IE4}	n	cum	Spa	Rus	Wel	Spa	Rus	Wel	Spa	Rus	Wel
0	10	10	8	8	7	8	8	7	80	80	70
1	16	26	8	7	8	16	15	15	61.5	57.7	57.7
2	16	42	7	5	4	23	20	19	54.8	47.6	45.2
3	13	55	4	2	2	27	22	21	49.1	40	38.2
4	10	65	1	4	1	28	26	22	43.1	40	33.8
5	13	78	1	3	0	29	29	22	37.2	37.2	28.2
6	6	84	1	1	1	30	30	23	35.7	35.7	27.4
7	5	89	1	0	0	31	30	23	34.8	33.7	25.8
8	6	95	0	1	0	31	31	23	32.6	32.6	24.2
9	3	98	0	0	0	31	31	23	31.6	31.6	23.5
10	2	100	0	1	0	31	32	23	31	32	23
11	1	101	0	0	1	31	32	24	30.7	31.7	23.8
13	2	103	0	0	0	31	32	24	30.1	31.1	23.3

The diversity values of the three variant items is shown in Table 5. The semantic definitions used by Holman et al. (2008: 351) are listed on the left, together with the stability values calculated there; an alternative definition commonly used for each is given on the right. The definitions or labels originally published by Swadesh for the 100-word list are 'claw', 'breast' and 'warm (hot)' (1955: 124, 137).

Table 5. Relative stability of variant items.

stability	item	D_{IE4}	item	D_{IE4}
20.5	CLAW	13	NAIL	0
30.7	BREASTS	6	CHEST	6
11.6	HOT	4	WARM	3

The difference between these alternatives in the four Indo-European groups is enormous for CLAW vs NAIL, but only of low significance for the other two.

It should also be noted that many languages employ the same word for both concepts, for example Latin *unguis*.

If the purpose for which the word list is being utilised is to discover and identify cognates rather than comparing measurements of language similarity, then it is clearly preferable for compilers to focus on the items which are known to be more stable in the local context. Comparison is a different matter, of course. As was demonstrated in the data from Oswalt, it cannot be assumed that the stability distribution found in any given language family will be probative in every other family, let alone equally so.

The global stability rankings from Holman et al. (2008) do correlate statistically with the lexical diversity of the Indo-European groups, and thus should also have predictive value for locating cognates even without local calibration. Table 6 shows the number of cognates found in the 40 items most highly ranked for stability (left), and in the reduced 40-item list that skips three higher-ranked items to reduce the risk of morphological duplication (Holman et al. 2008: 337). On the right are the cognates in the top 40 items sorted by D_{IE4}; the highly stable NAIL has been removed to make the word lists more directly comparable.

Table 6. English cognates in 40-word lists.

	top 40 stability rankings			reduced 40-item list			top 40 diversity rankings		
	Spa	Rus	Wel	Spa	Rus	Wel	Spa	Rus	Wel
cogs	15	11	11	17	13	13	22	19	18
%	37.5	27.5	27.5	42.5	32.5	32.5	55	47.5	45

The proportion of cognates in reduced lists based on global stability rankings is not necessarily notably higher than in the Swadesh 100-word list, and is actually lower in the case of English/Russian. For the relationships examined here the reduced 40-item list with less expected morphological duplication performs better, but this is not necessarily replicable, since the skipped items had after all been ranked as intrinsically more stable than their replacements.

The behaviour of sorted word lists of different sizes will vary, and there is no reason for assuming that 40 is the optimal list length for concentrating cognates. For diversity rankings, the optimal subset is presumably D = 0, although for some language groups that set will be too small to be useful, or disappear altogether. Figure 1 shows the proportion of cognates in word lists of increasing size containing the highest ranking items from Holman et al. (2008). Figure 2 does the same for word lists based on the diversity D_{IE4}.

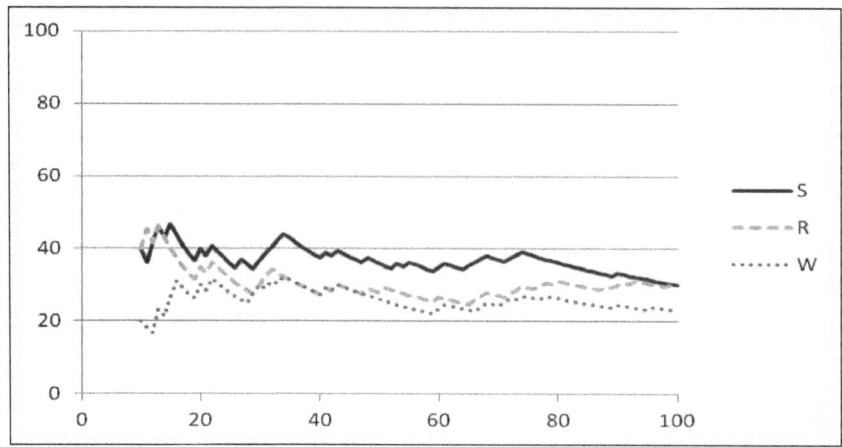

Figure 1. Word lists based on global stability (rankings in Holman et al. 2008).

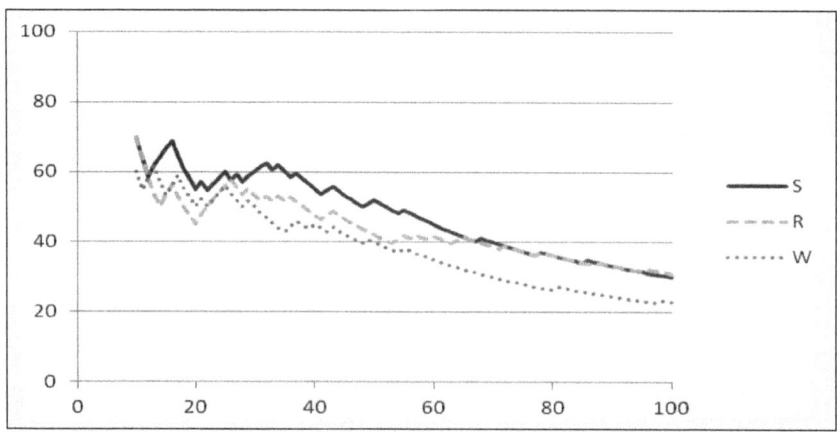

Figure 2. Word lists based on Indo-European diversity D_{IE4}.

Although there is a slight downward slope in Figure 1, the distribution of cognates is largely homogenous across the stability rankings. While this limits the value of evaluating different stability values, it is consistent with the purpose for which the reduced 40-item list was designed – serving as a proxy for the behaviour of the larger 100-item list.

The behaviour of word lists based on diversity in subgroups of the same family is quite different. It is highly predictive of words inherited from the more remote common ancestor, which is valuable for demonstrating a high proportion of cognates to make a genetic relationship appear plausible, or for concentrating the cognates to make it easier to sound correspondences by inspection. However, subgrouping is a different matter that may not benefit from the skewing observed, since the effect is not uniform. As shown in Figure 2, a subset of the word lists made up of low-diversity lexicon is likely to make it appear that Germanic (English) is more closely related to Romance (Spanish) than to Balto-Slavic (Russian), whereas the full 100-word list suggests that they are roughly equidistant. One possible explanation for this effect might be undetected borrowing between Proto-Germanic and Proto-Romance that is unevenly distributed across the diversity sets.

3. Subgrouping

The very oldest vocabulary is not always what is most useful in comparative historical linguistics. Subgrouping and the identification of intermediate branches will more often depend on lexical innovations after the breakup of the common ancestor. Any stability distribution that reliably predicts the contents of the oldest layer should also be able to make similar predictions for intermediate layers, and given an intermediate layer, estimate its relative age.

Within the Germanic family there is a division between the West Germanic group, possibly a dialect continuum for all periods after the breakup of proto-Germanic, and the more recent North Germanic group, which goes back to a unitary proto-Norse. The modern languages descended from these can vary in ways difficult to represent by a straightforward family tree. The lexicon of English has been greatly transformed under French and Old Norse influence, but the Continental Scandinavian languages have also borrowed significantly, with loans from Low German being particularly notable in the basic vocabulary.

Such factors can affect the reliability of lexicostatistics when attempting to draw up a family tree based on lexical data. Table 7 shows the number of cognates between pairs of Germanic languages in a simple phonetic comparison, without attempting to isolate intra-Germanic loanwords. Since the Continental Germanic languages are quite similar, other than for the West/North divide, the table has been simplified by only including the largest language from Continental West Germanic (i.e., German) and from Continental Scandinavian (i.e., Swedish).

Table 7. Intra-Germanic cognates.

	Eng	Ger	Swe	Ice
Eng	-	73	75	70
Ger	73	-	83	75
Swe	75	83	-	89
Ice	70	75	89	-

The highest percentage is 89, linking Swedish and Icelandic into a North Germanic node, which represents an Old Norse language still more or less unified centuries after the West Germanic languages had already been diverging. Other nodes, however, cannot be assigned unambiguously.

The next-highest value is 83 between German and Swedish, but before German should be linked to North Germanic, the lower score of 75 when compared with Icelandic needs to be explained. Since the difference between the latter and the German-English score of 73 is not significant, the discrepancy needs to be explained – and the fact that German is historically more closely related to English leaves lexicostatistics looking somewhat unconvincing.

The skewing of cognate counts between the different North Germanic languages has two possible explanations, other than mere chance variation: either Icelandic has undergone a higher rate of lexical replacement, or some of the cognates shared by German and Swedish in the data used here are actually cases of undetected borrowing.

The latter is historically true (mainly loans from Low German into the Continental Scandinavian languages), and the lexicostatistical data could thus be improved by identifying the loans; but this is not always possible with languages for which the history is less well known, and when the history is indeed known in that much detail, then lexicostatistics becomes almost redundant as a methodology. Making use of observed skewing between languages presumed to be equidistant for positing the existence of undetected borrowing was proposed by Dyen (1963), and this is utilised in analyses of relationship trees (for example, Black 2007, which examines Australian languages), but the problem remains: large differences in retention rates can cause similar skewing. An increased rate of lexical replacement is, of course, the reason for the lower cognate scores of English which obscure the existence of a West Germanic grouping in the example here.

However, if the relative stability of individual words is as predictable as seemed to be the case before, then this may result in a measurable difference between the skewing caused by borrowing and that which is the outcome of accelerated or retarded lexical replacement. If vocabulary of low cross-language diversity is more likely to consist of old inherited cognates, then this implies that old cognates will on average exhibit low diversity values, and more recent borrowings higher ones.

Obviously the observed diversity values will be unrepresentative of the actual history if there has been undetected borrowing. To test whether there is a difference in the distribution of loan words, the diversity of the Germanic lexicon should be ignored. Instead, and to ensure that the sample behind the distribution remains of a reasonable size, the Finno-Ugric family is included as representing a non-Indo-European neighbour of Germanic during much of its history. The distribution used here is therefore $D_{IE3+FU} = D_R + D_{BS} + D_C + D_{FU}$.

The average value of this distribution is $\bar{D} = 5.42$. If an item is chosen at random from the 100 on the list, then its expected diversity will, on average, be close to this value, and the same will be true for a set of items drawn randomly from the list. A set of unrelated words that only look similar by chance will normally be distributed randomly in the lexicon, and thus also have an average value of $\bar{D} = 5.42$. A set of inherited cognates, on the other hand, will be older and thus more stable on average, with a lower value of $\bar{D}$; and the fewer there are, the older they should be, and their average value of D should be lower as well.

Words that are being replaced would not be expected to be distributed randomly in the lexicon. If the language continues to have the same underlying stability distribution, then an item with $D = 10$ is ten times as likely to be replaced as one with $D = 1$. The average D of a random lexical replacement is therefore the sum of the squares of the individual values of D divided by their sum. For the distribution D_{IE3+FU} the average value of a random replacement is $D = 7.69$. There may be differences between borrowings and replacements from native material, but these have not been examined in this study.

Out of the 100 items, 64 are cognate across all four Germanic languages. Their average value of $\bar{D} = 4.53$, consistent with them being older, on average, than words selected at random. Smaller sets combine pairs of languages, which may thus provide clues to phylogenetic subgrouping. (There are also sets combining three languages, but these actually identify words common in Germanic, but missing in the fourth language, which only really tells us that the last is a distinct language, a point which is not disputed.) The largest exclusive subset is *North Germanic*, consisting of eight words found in Swedish and Icelandic, with $\bar{D}$ = 6.38. The next set is *West Germanic*, consisting of five words exclusive to English and German, with $\bar{D}$ = 4.20. It will be noted that West Germanic is indistinguishable from Common Germanic, whereas North Germanic appears distinctly younger – an observation consistent with known historical facts. It should also be noted that the two sets overlap, and have four items in common (FIRE, SLEEP, DRY, SEED), such that one pair of cognates is found in West Germanic, and the other pair in North Germanic.

Another four items are exclusively shared by German and Swedish; these could be designated *Continental Germanic*. As a phylogenetic node it is inconsistent with both of the previous, and its high $\bar{D}$ = 11.50 suggests that the set is significantly younger. If this lesser age is accepted, than the set must either be spurious and/or borrowed, whereas it would be consistent with the data if the West and North Germanic sets were genetic (although this is not a logical necessity).

Table 8. Distributional subsets of Germanic.

Set	Components	n	$\bar{D}$	$\bar{S}$
Common Germanic	all of Eng + Ger + Swe + Ice	64	4.53	23.66
West Germanic	only in English + German	5	4.20	23.84
North Germanic	only in Swedish + Icelandic	8	6.38	21.48
Continental Germanic	only in Swedish + German	4	11.50	23.73

Of the four words shared exclusively between Swedish and German in these lists (TAIL, BELLY, KILL, MOUNTAIN), only *svans* 'tail' is actually borrowed, but the use of the other three words as primary synonyms in modern Swedish may be the result of strong Low German influence. Other pairwise combinations of languages only share a single exclusive cognate (English/Swedish), or none at all (English/Icelandic, German/Icelandic), and thus cannot be analysed as sets.

Regardless of the details of individual word histories, as sets they exhibit distinct behaviour in terms of the metric $\bar{D}$ which was defined by observing the lexical diversity of equivalent items in neighbouring language families. While the differences in $\bar{D}$, and the sets themselves, are fairly small, they are consistent with each other and with the known history of the Germanic family tree. In the absence of a known history, comparable analyses based on local stability distributions can provide additional clues for determining prehistoric language events.

The behaviour of the global ASJP distribution does not allow for a comparable level of predictability; its gradient of lexical stability as exemplified in figure 1 is too level to discriminate amongst the Germanic strata. A randomly chosen word has the expected stability $\bar{S}$ = 23.37, and the lexical subsets in table 8 do not vary significantly from this mean.

4. Distant relationships

One approach to the lexical determination of distant language relationships has been to narrow the word list to a shorter set of presumably the most stable items, and this appears to be more productive when the search list is calibrated based on the local distribution of stable items, rather than a universal or global set of rankings.

The same observations suggest that since inherited cognates are more likely to be found in the more stable subsets of the vocabulary, then instead of using a reduced search list which could easily miss important data from what would be a small set of cognates to begin with, all putative cognates could be examined to see where they appear in the local stability distribution. The cognates from a genetic relationship should appear skewed towards the more stable end of the distribution, and this skewing should be more extreme the older the language family and the fewer the actual number of cognates.

Several studies have attempted to determine whether the lexical similarities between languages are more likely to be the outcome of borrowing or common descent by dividing the word lists into subsets based on criteria of basicness and stability; e.g., Black (1997) on Australian languages, where historical records are very limited, and there are suggestions of borrowing on a much larger scale than in Indo-European, or McMahon et al. (2005) who examined the distribution of related words between Quechua and Aymara. The latter languages were more similar in the less stable subset, suggesting convergence through borrowing, whereas Black identified Australian examples where lexical similarities were greatest in the more stable and basic subsets, supporting a genetic relationship with relatively superficial borrowing. The 'distillation method' of Wang (2004, 2006) also incorporates division into subsets, based on a model by Chen, that compares the proportion of putative cognates in the more stable (on average) Swadesh-100 list with that of words found only in the less stable (on average) Swadesh-200 list.

However, just as 'every word has its own history', so every item on a comparative checklist has its own stability, intrinsic to the human psyche in part, but also affected by cultural variation. A calibrated stability distribution may therefore be effective as a test on proposed long-distance language relationships.

The Indo-European and Finno-Ugric families examined here correlate strongly in their distributions of stable vocabulary, and have been proposed as likely candidates for a distant genetic relationship – and certainly as more plausible candidates than, say, a broader Nostratic. Since the two families have similar stability distributions, it is reasonable to project these further back in time beyond their respective proto-languages, to see whether the proposed lexical resemblances are also consistent.

The specific distribution used for this comparison is $D_{Eu} = D_{IE} + D_{FU}$, where IE refers to the assemblage of Indo-European groups (Germanic, Romance, Celtic, Balto-Slavic, Greek and Albanian), and this time including diversity counts across the individual subgroups, thus taking into account the diversification between Proto-Indo-European and the individual proto-languages, such as Proto-Germanic, etc. The average of this pan-European distribution is $\bar{D} = 8.79$, and a lexical subset inherited from a putative Indo-Uralic should have notably lower value of $\bar{D}$ than this.

There are 14 good candidates for an Indo-Uralic relationship on the Swadesh-100 list: {I ~ ME, THOU, THIS, THAT, WHO, NOT, MANY, KNEE ~ ELBOW, DRINK, HEAR, WATER, COLD, ROUND, NAME}. There is some morphological duplication here, as well as some semantic variation, but overall the case is fairly strong, and there seem to be too many lookalikes for coincidence. Only one more word (YEAR) is found in the longer 200-word list, which is itself a positive indicator; other items have a very restricted distribution, or are obvious loans, such as Finnish *sarvi* 'horn' and its relatives, which originate from Iranian. The average lexical diversity of the 14 items is $\bar{D} = 5.71$, much lower than chance, and therefore this set is more consistent with ancient inheritance than with borrowing.

It is of course possible for stable words to be borrowed, which would then naturally remain for a long period. However, it seems fairly unlikely for a large number of items to be stable in both language families, all the way back in time to their respective proto-languages, only to have been borrowed en masse in a brief period of great instability. It would certainly violate the principle of uniformity, which acts as a boundary on likely hypotheses in historical linguistics.

A similar situation is seen in a comparison of Uralic with Yukaghir, a relationship more generally considered more likely and more provable than Indo-Uralic (Abondolo 1998: 8). There are 14 strong candidates in the Swadesh-100 list amongst the suggestions made by Collinder (1977), with several more only found in the longer list, or having limited distributions: {I, THOU, WE, THIS, THAT, WHO, NOT, MANY, TWO, BIRD, BREAST, SAY, MOON, NAME}. The limited diversity within Yukaghir makes it difficult to derive a statistically meaningful diversity distribution for it; however, applying the distribution as for Indo-Uralic results in a plausible skewing of the similar vocabulary, with $\bar{D} = 6.29$. Assuming a general consistency in prehistoric lexical stability, this suggests that Uralic has a closer (or more convincingly genetic) relationship with Yukaghir than with Indo-European, although the two macro-families are not mutually exclusive, and the lexical sets provided in support overlap to a large extent.

There is no reason for assuming that a European stability distribution will have significant predictive power elsewhere in the world, and it may well be less useful than a more global approximation. Table 9 lists the values for the putative cognate subsets of Indo-Uralic and Uralic-Yukaghir, together with more accepted subsets from Tibeto-Burman and Sino-Tibetan, and some proposals for distant genetic relations that are morely likely to consist of chance lookalikes.

The Sino-Tibetan cognates are taken from the list by Peiros (1998: 184–5). There are 10 words in the Swadesh lists shared by all three of Burmese, Tibetan and Chinese; of these, nine are on the shorter 100-word list. Another 23 items are shared by Burmese and Tibetan, of which 18 are on the shorter list (including NAIL). Finally there are 14 words shared by Chinese with either Burmese or Tibetan, of which 13 are on the shorter list. The distributions of these sets are therefore generally consistent with inheritance, although skewing within the Swadesh-100 list would also be of interest.

The distant relationship proposals are (1) Indo-European and Northwest Caucasian, from Colarusso (1997); out of 20 putative cognates listed, seven are on the Swadesh lists in both proto-languages, and six are on the shorter Swadesh-100 list; (2) Indo-European and Dravidian, from Levitt (1998); out of 26 proposed cognates, ten are on the Swadesh lists, and seven are on the shorter list; (3) Uralic and Dravidian, from Tyler (1968), with 153 items, of which 38 are on the Swadesh lists, with 23 on the shorter list. The ratios of putative cognates in the generally more stable shorter list versus the longer list thus range from small but intriguing to large but unconvincing.

Table 9. Lexical comparisons.

Set	n	$\bar{D}$	$\bar{S}$
Indo-Uralic	14	5.71	24.43
Uralic-Yukaghir	14	6.29	24.31
Tibetan-Burmese	27	8.04	27.56
Sino-Tibetan	22	7.00	28.06
IE-NWC	6	9.67	19.92
IE-Dravidian	7	10.00	20.46
Uralic-Dravidian	23	8.00	24.37
All words	100	8.79	23.37

Although the distribution D used here is very much Eurocentric, the Sino-Tibetan set still appears convincingly skewed toward the more stable portions of the Swadesh-100 list. Tibetan-Burmese, however, seems no further removed from chance than the three long distance proposals that lack widespread support. Here the global ASJP distribution identifies the accepted relationships as having a higher proportion of stable words amongst its shared basic vocabulary, with average values of $\bar{S}$ higher than the list average. By contrast, proposals like Indo-Uralic and Uralic-Yukaghir are no more convincing than chance.

What does this mean in practice? Since there are regional and genetic variations from a truly global distribution, those variations are meaningful when they can be identified. A distribution like D_{Eu} quantifies the behaviour of the European lexicon as it existed several millennia ago. It is not only not unreasonable to project this further back in time for the same region, but it would be downright surprising for it to produce more spurious matches than a global distribution; after all, why should it? Such a scenario would involve massive borrowing of the same vocabulary between the proto-languages that would subsequently remain particularly stable and resistant to future replacement. Even if this were to be suggested, it would still be a highly significant historical event identifiable by a locally calibrated stability distribution but invisible to a global one.

5. Conclusions

The concept of a global or culture-free ranking of basic vocabulary holds great appeal, and would provide for multiple useful applications in historical and comparative linguistics. The ASJP-based stability ranking by Holman et al. (2008) is a comprehensive attempt at approximating such a universal scheme, and is convincingly homogeneous on the global scale (2008: 335). Its limited predictability for cognates in Indo-European suggests that a global distribution simply cannot provide some of the evaluations that historical linguists would hope for.

The reduced 40-word list provides a reasonable approximation to the lexicostatistical values of the Swadesh-100 list for the major IE languages compared here, and is thus a valuable shortcut, fulfilling its intended purpose; but it should not be seen as a short list of 'superstable' vocabulary as envisioned by researchers like Dolgopolsky (1986). Instead, calibrating vocabulary rankings based on local behaviour may be able to increase the level of predictability so that productive separation of lexical strata becomes feasible.

Appendix

Diversity values of the Eurocentric distribution D_{Eu} (= D_{IE} + D_{FU}) for items on the Swadesh-100 list, including alternatives for three items (marked by *).

Item	D_{Eu}	Item	D_{Eu}	Item	D_{Eu}	Item	D_{Eu}
who	0	stand	5	earth	9	hair	13
what	0	give	5	fire	9	mouth	13
two	0	sun	5	long	10	cloud	13
I	1	this	6	man	10	red	13
thou	1	louse	6	bone	10	woman	14
one	1	hand	6	liver	10	fat	14
name	1	hear	6	see	10	bite	14
we	2	die	6	burn	10	lie	14
night	2	star	6	green	10	rain	14
ear	3	smoke	6	white	10	sand	14
eye	3	that	7	bird	11	round	14
tongue	3	blood	7	dog	11	big	16
heart	3	stone	7	skin	11	neck	16
drink	3	human	8	meat	11	kill	16
water	3	seed	8	eat	11	road	16
full	3	leaf	8	sleep	11	mountain	16
new	3	feather	8	fly	11	many	17
horn	4	head	8	yellow	11	say	17
tooth	4	moon	8	good	11	*claw	17
knee	4	ashes	8	*hot	11	belly	18
sit	4	dry	8	tree	12	walk	18
not	5	all	9	bark	12	tail	21
fish	5	nose	9	black	12		
root	5	foot	9	cold	12	*nail	2
egg	5	know	9	*breasts	12	*warm	6
swim	5	come	9	small	13	*chest	12

References

Abondolo, Daniel (ed.). 1998. *The Uralic Languages*. London: Routledge.

Beckwith, Christoper I. 2004. *Koguryo: The Language of Japan's Continental Relatives*. Leiden: Brill.

Bergsland, Knut and Hans Vogt. 1962. On the validity of glottochronology. *Current Anthropology* 3: 115–53.

Black, Paul. 1997. Lexicostatistics and Australian languages: Problems and prospects. In Darrell Tryon and Michael Walsh (eds), *Boundary Rider: Essays in Honour of Geoffrey O'Grady*. Pacific Linguistics, Series C-136. Canberra: Australian National University, 51–69.

Black, Paul. 2007. Lexicostatistics with massive borrowing: The case of Jingulu and Mudburra. *Australian Journal of Linguistics* 27 (1): 63–71.

Colarusso, John. 1997. Proto-Pontic: Phyletic links between Proto-Indo-European and Proto-Northwest Caucasian. *Journal of Indo-European Studies* 25: 119–51.

Collinder, Björn. 1977. *Fenno-Ugric Vocabulary*. 2nd edition. Hamburg: Buske.

Dolgopolsky, Aaron B. 1986. A probabilistic hypothesis concerning the oldest relationships among the language families in Northern Eurasia. In Vitalij V. Shevoroshkin and Thomas L. Markey (eds), *Typology, Relationship and Time*. Ann Arbor: Karoma Publishers, 27–50.

Dyen, Isidore. 1963. Lexicostatistically determined borrowing and taboo. *Language* 39 (1): 60–6.

Dyen, Isidore. 1964. On the validity of comparative lexicostatistics. In Horace G. Lunt (ed.), *Proceedings of the Ninth International Congress of Linguists*. The Hague: Mouton, 238–52.

Embleton, Sheila M. 1986. *Statistics in Historical Linguistics*. Bochum: Brockmeyer.

Holman, Eric W., Søren Wichmann, Cecil H. Brown, Viveka Velupillai, André Müller and Dik Bakker. 2008. Explorations in automated language classification. *Folia Linguistica* 42 (2): 331–54.

Hymes, D.H. 1960. Lexicostatistics so far. *Current Anthropology* 1: 3–44.

Lees, Robert B. 1953. The basis of glottochronology. *Language* 29: 113–27.

Levitt, Stephan Hillyer. 1998. Is there a genetic relationship between Indo-European and Dravidian? *Journal of Indo-European Studies* 26: 131–59.

McMahon, April, Paul Heggarty, Robert McMahon and Natalia Slaska. 2005. Swadesh sublists and the benefits of borrowing: An Andean case study. *Transactions of the Philological Society* 103 (2): 147–70.

Oswalt, Robert L. 1971. Towards the construction of a standard lexicostatistic list. *Anthropological Linguistics* 13: 421–34.

Pagel, Mark, Quentin D. Atkinson and Andrew Meade. 2007. Frequency of word-use predicts rates of lexical evolution throughout Indo-European history. *Nature* 449: 717–20.

Peiros, Ilia. 1998. *Comparative Linguistics in Southeast Asia*. Pacific Linguistics, Series C-142. Canberra: Australian National University.

Tyler, Stephen A. 1968. Dravidian and Uralian: The lexical evidence. *Language* 44: 798–812.

Sigurd, Bengt, Mats Eeg-Olofsson and Joost van de Weijer. 2004. Word length, sentence length and frequency – Zipf revisited. *Studia Linguistica* 58 (1): 37–52.

Swadesh, Morris. 1952. Lexico-statistic dating of prehistoric ethnic contacts. *Proceedings of the American Philosophical Society* 96: 452–63.

Swadesh, Morris. 1955. Towards greater accuracy in lexicostatistic dating. *International Journal of American Linguistics* 21: 121–37.

Thomas, David D. 1960. Basic vocabulary in some Mon-Khmer languages. *Anthropological Linguistics* 2 (3): 7–11.

Wang, Feng. 2004. *Language Contact and Language Comparison: The Case of Bai*. PhD dissertation, City University of Hong Kong.

Wang, Feng. 2006. *Comparison of Languages in Contact: The Distillation Method and the Case of Bai*. Language and Linguistics Monograph Series B: Frontiers in Linguistics III. Taipei: Institute of Linguistics, Academia Sinica.

Wichmann, Søren and Eric W. Holman. In press. Languages with longer words have more lexical change. In Lars Borin and Anju Saxena (eds), *Approaches to Measuring Linguistic Differences*. Berlin: Mouton De Gruyter.

Zipf, George K. 1935. *The Psycho-Biology of Language*. Boston: Houghton Mifflin.

Chapter 3

THE NON-REDUNDANT NATURE OF ENGLISH TAUTOLOGICAL COMPOUNDS

Réka Benczes

Eötvös Loránd University & Indiana University

Tautological compounds, which are composed of a hyponym and a superordinate term (such as *oak tree*) or two synonyms (such as *subject matter*), are one of the quirkiest – and least researched – phenomena of English compounding. Their quirkiness can be attributed to two main reasons. First, at face value such combinations can be considered as prime examples for the redundancy of language. Second, such combinations do not follow normal compound-forming rules in the sense that both constituents can function as the semantic head (as opposed to 'normal' English compounds, which follow the Right-Hand Head Rule).

Perhaps it is the quirkiness of tautological compounds that can be accounted for the fact that not much has been said about them in traditional accounts of compounding, which typically relegate them to a marginal area of the English language. However, there is more to tautological compounds than meets the eye. The study aims to give an account of the various roles that tautological compounds play in language, thereby demonstrating their non-redundant nature – in order to relegate this much-neglected category to its proper, well-deserved place within English word formation.

1. Introduction[1]

The term 'tautological compound'[2] has often been used in academic discourse to describe two distinct – but closely related – phenomena: 1) compounds whose constituents are synonymous with one another (such as *subject matter*); and 2) compounds where the meaning of the second member is

---

[1] I am indebted to Kate Burridge for her valuable comments and to Amanda Young for her careful editing. The paper has also greatly benefited from the inspirational discussions I had with Jonathan Lum and Jonathan Schlossberg on the topic.

[2] Note that some works use the term 'pleonastic compound' instead of 'tautological compound' – see, e.g., Carr (1939) or Cooper (1904).

already included in the meaning of the first member (such as *oak tree*). Often, researchers meshed the two categories into one and have not paid particular attention to differentiating between them (e.g., Fay 1913: 113; Woods 1957: 50). In his analysis of tautological compounds in Coleridge's works, Cooper (1904) also applies the term to both types indiscriminately.[3] Others, however, have used the term 'tautological compound' for either one of the processes mentioned above. Accordingly, Bloomfield (1920: 343) and Reppert (1954: 8), and more recently Harbus (2003: 99) and Renner (2008: 610), use the expression to refer to a compound that has two synonymous constituents. At the same time, Emerson (1919: 505) and Willetts (1960: 73) refer to 'tautological compound' as an expression where the meaning of the first element is included in that of the second.

Perhaps the reason why there is such inconsistency as to what lexical item a tautological compound denotes is that not much has been said about them in traditional accounts of compounding (e.g., Bauer 1983; Fabb 1998; Jespersen 1954; Katamba 2005), which typically relegate them to a marginal area of the English language. Furthermore, such coinages are deviant in two senses of the word. First, at face value such combinations can be considered as prime examples for the redundancy of language; after all, what is the point of denoting an entity as *tuna fish*, if *tuna* would suffice?[4] Second, they do not follow normal compound-forming rules in the sense that both constituents can function as the semantic head – as opposed to 'normal' English compounds, which follow the Right-Hand Head Rule (Williams 1981), meaning that the right-hand member denotes the larger semantic category to which the compound as a whole belongs (i.e., *apple tree* is a subcategory of *tree*).[5] Marginality and deviancy, however, are no proper reasons to discard tautological compounds from a linguistic analysis. As underlined by Bauer and Renouf (2001: 120), there are plenty of 'unexpected trends' (Bauer and Renouf

---

[3] Thus, *fog-smoke* and *living-life* (which are compounds based on synonymous constituents) are treated eseentially the same as *skiff-boat* and *harbour-bay* (where the meaning of the left-hand constituent is already included in the meaning of the right-hand member). All examples are from *The Ancient Mariner*.

[4] Note that redundancy is in fact a basic feature of language and communication. According to Darian (1979: 57) the 'redundancy factor' of the world's languages is between 35 to 50%, with isolating languages like Samoan at the lower end of the scale and case-governed, highly inflected types such as German at the other end.

[5] Although *tuna fish* is a type of fish, and *oak tree* is a type of tree, the right-hand member spells out the larger semantic category to which the *left-hand member* belongs to (and not the compound as a whole, as in the case of the majority of English compounds). In pairings of synonyms, such as *subject matter*, the Right-Hand Head Rule does not work either, as both constituents, in principle, can function as semantic heads.

2001: 120) in English word formation, and a full analysis or description of the English language needs to fit these exceptional types in and provide an explanation for them. Bauer and Renouf's observation is highly relevant for the present study as well, since they question one of the most basic questions in word formation: if a pattern is atypical, does it also mean that it is exceptional? Their paper suggests that the answer to this question is negative.

Therefore, the aim of the present chapter is alleviate this gap in English morphology by examining the various functions that tautological compounds play in language. As it will be argued below, such coinages are by no means redundant, as they serve a number of purposes – such as categorization, upgrading of concepts, emphasis and clarification. The structure of the chapter is as follows: section 2 offers an overview of how (and under what name) tautological compounds have been treated (if at all) in morphological literature and clarifies the concept by establishing two subcategories. Section 3 and section 4 are devoted to the analysis of the functions that the two subtypes of tautological compounds have in English, while section 5 concludes.

2. What is a tautological compound?

In morphological literature, tautological compounds have rarely solicited a separate section or subcategory; instead, they have been typically relegated to and discussed under 'coordinate compounds', which, very loosely speaking, are units where both constituents are of equivalent status and can be considered, therefore, as heads (see Spencer 1991: 311). Note, however, that there is no agreement on the label 'coordinate' in the literature for that matter: Spencer (ibid.), on the one hand, treats 'coordinate' as an interchangeable term with 'appositional' or 'dvandva'. Jespersen (1954: 147–8), on the other, uses the term 'appositional' for the same phenomenon,[6] and in his discussion of appositional compounds, he also lists a couple of examples that are tautological (namely *subject matter*, *pathway* and *courtyard*). Unfortunately,

---

[6] Jespersen (ibid.) defines an 'appositional compound' as a combination of two words where the members are of equal status, but points out that this equality of the constituents is misleading, as one of the members in the compound enjoys a more 'superior status' than the other. Therefore, *boy-king* is not a boy and a king at the same time, but a 'boy who is also a king', or 'a king who is still a boy'. Jespersen also remarks that the order of the constituents in an appositional compound is difficult to predict (i.e., whether the compound will be *boy-king* or *king-boy*), although he immediately contradicts this observation by asserting that the first constituent typically determines the sex or the age of the entity that the compound denotes (see, e.g., *maid servant*, *hen pheasant* or *doe rabbit* – all examples are taken from Jespersen). Here, compounds where the first element is a sex/age-marker will not be considered as tautological, and thus will not be discussed in detail.

Jespersen makes absolutely no allusion to the tautological nature of these expressions.[7]

Clarification of the topic is offered by Bauer (2008: 2), who makes note of the fact that the term 'dvandva' has been applied in the morphological literature (imprecisely) to various different phenomena – others than that originally defined in Sanskrit grammar, according to which a dvandva compound is a combination of two elements linked by *and*.[8] From this it follows that a dvandva has two semantic heads. Appositional compounds (where the compound refers to two aspects of a single individual, and not to two separate individuals, such as *girlfriend*) are not considered by Bauer as a type of dvandva. Instead, it is proposed that both dvandvas *and* appositional compounds (among others) form subtypes under the general category of 'coordinated compounds' (compounds whose constituents are of equal status). In a later article, Bauer (2010: 203) relegates tautological compounds under 'co-compounds',[9] but as his use of 'co-compound' is more-or-less equivalent to that of 'coordinated compound' (see above), following Bauer (2008) I will also use the term 'coordinated compound' and will consider tautological compounds as constituting one of its subclasses.

However, as already alluded to in section 1, 'tautological compound' is an umbrella term that includes two distinct, but related subtypes: compounds where the left-hand member is a hyponym of the right-hand member, and those which are based on the pairing of two synonymous words. Therefore, I will differentiate between two different types of tautological compounds: 1) hyponym-superordinate compounds (such as *oak tree*, *smoking habit*, etc.);[10] and 2) synonymous compounds (such as *pathway* and *subject matter*). The following sections will analyse both types in detail and propose various functions for them.

3. Hyponym-superordinate compounds

Hyponym-superordinate compounds are only 'semitautological' (Hatcher 1952: 15), as in such cases we have a species–genus relationship between

---

[7] Fabb (1998) also does draw attention to the fact that appositional compounds can be a combination of synonyms – as an example he cites the Haitian word *toro-bèf*, literally 'bull-cow', which denotes the male species.

[8] Dvandva actually means 'two-by-two' or 'pair' (Bauer 2008: 2).

[9] Wälchli (2005: 1) also uses the term 'co-compound' for the phenomenon in question and defines a co-compound as a coinage whose constituents denote 'semantically closely associated concepts'.

[10] I.e., there is a species–genus relationship between the two entities. I have borrowed the term 'hyponym-superordinate compound' from Bauer (2008: 14–5).

the two referents of the compound. Yet it seems plausible to include them as referent tautologies; they can be paraphrased as '*A* is by definition [a member of the class] *B*' (ibid., emphasis as in original). That is, the question necessarily arises why we need an explicit *B* element in the compound expression if *A* is already included within the set of *B*. Explanations are few and far between in the morphological literature. In Bauer's (1983: 94–5) definition, for instance, the left-hand member of an endocentric nominal compound carries the 'primary defining characteristic of the subgroup denoted by the compound as a whole' – accordingly, the primary defining characteristic of *policedog* is that it is used in connection with the police. One of the consequences of this observation is that hyponym-superordinate type formations should not in principle exist. The fact that they are part of everyday language is explained by Bauer on the basis of the following: 1) the compound has either a non-redundant meaning, as in the case of *vegetable marrow*, where the modifier serves to contrast the entity from *bone marrow*; 2) or the modifier is indeed redundant, but 'fits with the primary defining features', as exemplified by *puppy dog* or *palm tree*. The reasoning in the second point is somewhat contradictory, since the main feature of a primary defining characteristic (as put forth by Bauer) is that it is, in essence, non-redundant.

Further perspectives on the topic are offered by Marchand (1969: 40), who lays down two important points in his brief discussion of hyponym-superordinate compounds (and to which I will turn to later in detail).[11] First of all, he makes a distinction between *oak tree* and *teaching profession*: while an oak 'can only be a tree' (p. 41), *profession* is an *ad hoc*, assumed 'genus' of teaching (as teaching can be a number of things: 'a vocation, a pastime, a bore' – ibid.). Second, he calls attention to a significant restriction with regard to hyponym-superordinate compounds: the order of the entities is fixed in the sense that the species must precede the genus. There is no **tree oak* or **profession teaching* for that matter.

The most in-depth and noteworthy analysis of hyponym-superordinate compounds has been offered by Hatcher (1952), who discusses them under the category of appositional compounds.[12] When an appositional compound [X Y] provides two names for the same entity (as in *pumice stone*), then the first constituent [X] 'assigns' (p. 4) the second constituent [Y] to a subdivision of the species, that is, we have a species–genus relationship

---

[11] Marchand (ibid.) refers to hyponym-superordinate compounds as 'subsumptive' or 'subordinative' compounds within the larger group of 'copula compounds'.

[12] Hatcher (1952: 4) defines an appositional compound as a unit that is composed of 'two names for the same object'.

between the two elements (also referred to by Hatcher as a relationship between specific and general). Compounds of such type abound in the English language: *elm tree, oak tree, daytime, winter season, tennis game, teaching profession, growing-up process, smoking habit, marriage relationship* – just to name a few (all examples are taken from Hatcher). Why do such compounds exist, however? In Hatcher's view, two main reasons can be cited. First, the general terms of *process* in *growing-up process* or *profession* in *teaching profession* provide a 'framework' (p. 13) for the specific term (i.e., *growing-up* and *teaching* respectively), thereby focusing the attention on one particular aspect of the specific term and assigning the entity denoted by the specific term in the more general 'scheme' of things (ibid.).[13] Second, by adding *profession* to *teaching*, or *process* to *growing-up*, we 'add at least a note of dignity with a suggestion of the official' (ibid.). In the following discussion of the functions of hyponym-superordinate compounds, it will transpire that Hatcher's observations have been remarkably acute.

3.1. Categorization

Hyponym-superordinate compounds (such as *oak tree, chess game, hound dog, tuna fish, jaybird*, etc. – to name but a few) are characterized by a lower-order category label in the modifier position and a higher-order category label in the head position. They have been around in the English language for a rather long time: one of the oldest hyponym-superordinate compounds is *greyhound*, whose first citation is from 1000.[14] The compound is derived from Old English *gríghund*, whose first constituent is etymologically related to Old Norse *grøy*, meaning 'bitch', while its second constituent is derived from *hund*, meaning 'dog'. As the meaning of *bitch* ('the female of the dog', first citation also from 1000, as in the case of *greyhound*) already includes the information that the entity is a dog, the compound can be considered as an example of the hyponym-superordinate type.[15]

The tautological or redundant nature of hyponym-superordinate compounds stems from the fact that any category within a taxonomy is always included in the category immediately above it (Rosch et al. 1976: 383).

---

[13] This function has also been highlighted by Marchand (1969) – see above for details.
[14] All definitions and etymologies come from the *Oxford English Dictionary* (*OED*), unless otherwise stated.
[15] C.f. Reppert's (1954: 8) analysis, who argues that *grey* was used in the sense of 'dog' in Chaucer, and, consequently, *greyhound* is a pure tautology.

In sum, hyponym-superordinate compounds can be depicted by a simple diagram, as exemplified by *oak tree* (see *Figure 1*).

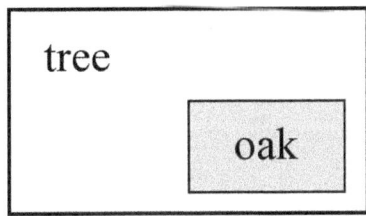

Figure 1. Oak tree as a series of inclusive sets (after Bauer 2008: 15).

Why do hyponym-superordinate compounds exist, however, if the entity denoted by the first constituent is already included conceptually by the entity denoted by the second one? One possible answer lies in the acquisition of categories. One of the most important characteristics of categorization is that children categorize differently from adults. While adults group things on the basis of taxonomies, children often put things together on the basis of associations, subjective preferences, etc. (Rosch et al. 1976: 414). Moreover, the taxonomic hierarchies used by adults are often difficult to grasp for children, who 1) have more difficulty in learning the terms for the subordinate and superordinate levels than that of the basic level; and 2) are often unwilling to acknowledge that the same thing can be called by both a basic-level term (such as *cat*) and a superordinate one (such as *animal*; Gelman et al. 1989: 310). These difficulties in acquiring taxonomies can be traced back to the fact that children do not understand the inclusive nature of categories (ibid.). However, as pointed out by Clark (2009: 274), children start producing root compounds that denote subcategories from the age of two. In such expressions, children consistently put the term denoting the higher-order category in the right-hand position, and use these coinages especially for contrastive purposes, as in the case of *car smoke* ('exhaust') versus *house smoke* (which comes from a chimney). Consequently, hyponym-superordinate compounds might be remnants of this early process of acquiring taxonomies; they quite simply 'make the relation between [taxonomical] levels explicit … [s]o it may be easier to understand that an *oak-tree* is a tree than that an *oak* is a tree' (Gelman et al. 1989: 310).[16]

---

[16] A somewhat similar explanation is provided by Hatcher (1952: 10) as well, who claims that such coinages typically denote animate entities and exemplify our 'naïve, cautious approach to the problem of species and genus'. Note that there are plenty of examples of

Nevertheless, the problem with this reasoning is that it does not explain why this process does not extend over *all* of our subordinate categories, and why it is limited to a group of compounds only. Therefore, a further explanation needs to be sought here to adequately justify the existence of *oak tree* and similar coinages. A hint is provided in Clark (2009: 268), who states that children 'rely on the paradigms they know, particularly when trying to contrast two objects, actions, or properties that are near neighbours'. These 'paradigms' are already existing forms and compounding patterns. Consequently, *oak tree* fits in with the compound-forming pattern of X+*tree*, such as *apple tree* and *plum tree* – where the head element is not redundant in the sense that we do not say *apple or *plum to denote an 'apple tree' or 'plum tree', respectively. In these cases, *apple* and *plum* are used exclusively as basic-level terms for the fruit that such trees bear, and the X+*tree* pattern denotes 'a tree that bears X'. The entrenchment of this pattern might have led to its extension to those cases as well where X denotes the tree itself, and not exclusively the fruit.

Evidence for the hypothesis that hyponym-superordinate compounds serve important categorization purposes can also be based on the fact that the order of the constituents within this compound type is not random (Marchand 1969: 42). It is always the superordinate term that features in the right-hand slot, while the hyponym occupies the left-hand position (i.e., we do not get examples such as *tree oak, *game chess, *dog hound or *fish tuna).[17] Therefore, in all of these compounds the right-hand constituent serves a rather similar categorizing function as the right-hand constituent of the vast majority of English compounds that adhere to the so-called Right-Hand Head Rule (whereby the right-hand member of a compound is the expression's semantic head, specifying the category to which the compound as a whole belongs – e.g., a *dog house* is a type of house, an *apple tree* is a type of tree, etc.). This ordering of the constituents is in line with the familiarity hierarchy, which spells out that the more familiar (i.e., the hyponym in the case of hyponym-superordinate compounds) always precedes the less familiar in noun phrase sequences (Allan 1987: 52).

---

the hyponym-superordinate compound type which can be linked to children's language and CDS ('child-directed speech'): *billy goat, pussy cat, puppy dog, teddy bear,* etc. These examples might also bear witness to the significance of hyponym-superordinate compounds in acquiring taxonomies.

[17] This ordering of the constituents is in direct opposition to scientific taxonomies, where the genus is followed by the species name, as in *Canis familiaris* ('domestic dog') and *Canis lupus* ('wolf'). For a discussion, see Allan (1986: 253).

3.2. Upgrading concepts

Apart from categorizational purposes, a further function hyponym-superordinate compounds can be linked to bureaucratic language or officialese, where it is rather common to use coinages such as *marriage relationship*, *smoking habit*, *growing-up process*, *teaching profession* or *panic reaction* (to name but a few; examples from Hatcher 1952). This feature can be explained by three motivational factors. One, bureaucratic language – influenced by legalese – is especially abundant in nominalizations[18] (Allan and Burridge 1991: 205), which are typically more difficult to process by hearers/readers than their longer, non-nominalized equivalents and do not require an explicit subject (which means that the speaker/writer does not have to assume responsibility for what is being said).[19] Second, as both Allan and Burridge (1991: 206) and Hatcher (1952: 13) argue, the role of assigning a somewhat redundant superordinate category to any concept is to elevate or dignify it by the process. In Allan and Burridge's (ibid.) words, the matters that bureaucrats manage are often 'so mundane' and 'trivial' that they use this special word formation process to 'obfuscate the mundane ... and endow it with gravity'. Similar opinion is formed by Hatcher (1952: 13), who claims that hyponym-superordinate compounds add 'a note of dignity with a suggestion of the official'. The reason why hyponym-superordinate compounds feel more 'dignified' than their single-unit counterparts can be accounted for by the conceptual metaphor MORE OF FORM IS MORE OF CONTENT (Lakoff and Johnson 1980: 127), whereby a linguistic unit that is longer (i.e., has a larger form, such as a compound unit) is perceived to carry more information (more content) than a single-word unit. Last, but not least, hyponym-superordinate compounds also have a categorizational role in bureaucratic language. In this role, the head element serves as a handy means to 'isolate and label' (Hatcher 1952: 14) various aspects of our personal, social and professional lives. At the same time, the head element – by virtue of its 'categorizational' role – helps us to zoom in on one particular aspect of the entity in question (that is specified by the first constituent of the compound).

---

[18] See also Hatcher (1952: 14), who argues that it is a general trend of official language to 'streamline' the 'Y of X' genitive phrase into a more condensed (compound) form, which lends it a more 'technical' sense – e.g., 'profession of teaching' becomes *teaching profession*.

[19] Consider the following example, cited in Allan and Burridge (1991: 205): 'a number of years ago the governor of California, when asked why he had allowed a man to die in the gas chamber (a highly unpopular act at the time) replied: "There was insufficient evidence on which to base a change of decision." He could have said *I couldn't find enough evidence to make me change my mind and decide to save a man's life*.' (Emphasis as in original.)

Accordingly, *marriage relationship* focuses on the reciprocal partnership of the individuals in marriage, while *marriage*, as a single unit and without the superordinate element, is a more collective and general term that can be applied to a number of things that are elements of the category of marriage: the length of the marriage, the individuals who are married, the legal aspects of marriage, the benefits of marriage, the hardships of marriage, etc. Such compounds are a reflection of a trend; according to Hatcher (p. 15), there is a growing tendency nowadays to relate the specific to a more general scheme 'in the midst of a never-ending attempt to "make order" within the complex relationships and categories of our civilization' (ibid.). This trend is especially noticeable nowadays with the adding of *event* and *incident* to nouns that denote events and incidents, respectively, as in the case of *birthday event*, *launch event* or *fire incident*.[20]

4. Synonymous compounds

In general, not much has been said in the morphological literature on compounds, which are based on two synonymous terms.[21] Where, however, they have been mentioned, reference is typically made to their tautological nature. Renner (2008: 610), for instance, alludes to synonymous compounds as 'tautological compounds',[22] and notes that they can function as nouns (e.g., *pathway*), verbs (e.g., *hustle-bustle*) or even adjectives (e.g., *squiggly-wiggly*). In his comparative analysis of co-compounds, Wälchli (2005: 143–4) terms synonymous compounds as 'synonymic co-compounds', and argues that in various languages of the world, they serve two main functions. On the one hand, they are used to express more abstract entities, as in the case of Khalkha, where *üzel bodol* ("view-thought") denotes 'opinion'. Second, synonymic compounds can also refer to the collective: the meaning of Chuvash *jurǎ-kĕvĕ* ("song-motif/melody") is 'songs'. These two functions, however, do not seem

---

[20] *birthday event*: 'Stephen Hawking misses 70th birthday event' (http://news.smh.com.au; 30 March 2012); *launch event*: 'Apple's next-gen iPad launch event is tomorrow, get your liveblog right here!' (http://www.engadget.com; 30 March 2012); *fire incident*: 'Chevron Confirms Fire Incident on Rig Offshore Nigeria' (http://www.chevron.com; 30 March 2012)

[21] Synonymy will be interpreted here loosely, as the relationship between two words that are similar in meaning. I agree with Palmer (1981: 89–91), who has emphasized that there are no real synonyms in language, since there are no two words with identical meanings. 'Synonyms' differ with respect to dialectal, stylistic, evaluative or collocational properties.

[22] Renner (2008: 607) considers tautological compounds as a subtype of coordinate compounds (which are 'composed of two elements which belong to the same lexical category and are co-hyponyms').

to hold for English synonymous compounds, whose motivations, therefore, must be searched for elsewhere. In what follows, I will present two possible motivational forces for the coinage of synonymous compounds in English.

4.1. Emphasis

It has already been noted that the collocation of synonyms can be used as an emphatic device in order to express strong emotions (Ullmann 1977: 153). See, for instance the following examples from the starting lines of Hamlet's first soliloquy (cited by Ullmann ibid.): 'O, that this too too solid flesh would melt, / Thaw, and resolve itself into a dew!' (Act I, scene 2). In the quoted lines the collocation of the synonymous verbs intensifies the emotions felt by Hamlet (and note also the reduplicated *too*, which has a similar function). Collocation is relatively common on the phrasal level as well – as exemplified by binomials, which are often formed by the conjoining of two synonyms, as in the case of *null and void, rules and regulations* or *ways and means* (Gustafsson 1975; Malkiel 1959; Norrick 1988). The main function of synonymous binomials is to emphasize 'the mutual semantic ground of the two members' (Gustaffson 1975: 12), although at the same time the two synonyms side-by-side might also evoke a sense of contrast, as they can 'arouse different connotations from one another and their combination may suggest an inclusiveness neither member can alone' (Norrick 1988: 79).[23]

It is questionable whether synonymous compounds in English are productive at all.[24] The question of productivity is indeed an intriguing one, especially in light of the fact that the collocation of synonyms in units larger than compounds, such as binomial expressions, is rather common in present-day American English (Gustaffson 1975; Malkiel 1959). Works on the subject of synonymous compounds (such as Renner 2008) typically mention *pathway* as a prime example of the phenomenon, which is in no accounts a recent coinage, as its first citation dates back 1450. Interestingly,

---

[23] See the following examples (from Norrick 1988: 80): in the case of both *bought and paid for* and *over and done with*, the second constituent (*paid for* and *done with*) adds a note of 'finality' to the expression that the first constituent would not have been able to achieve independently.

[24] There are some instances of the use of synonymous compounds in English poetry. See, for instance, Coleridge, who often paired synonyms with one another to increase the poetic or epic effect, as in the case of the already cited (fn. 2) *fog-smoke* or *living-life* (Cooper 1904: 224). The Old English epic verse *Solomon and Saturn II* has also exploited this word-formation process: the two elements of the compound *mōdsefa* ("mind","disposition") individually denote 'mind'. According to Harbus (2003: 99), the pairing of the two words simply adds emphasis.

pathway cannot be considered as a synonymous compound; it is in actual fact a hyponym-superordinate coinage. The first constituent, *path*, is derived from Old English *pæth*, meaning 'narrow path' or 'one-by-one path', while *way* is also of Old English origin and denotes a 'track prepared or available for travelling along'. Therefore, a *pathway* is a type of *way* (similar to *highway*, *carriageway*, etc.). In a similar vein, *yardstick*, mentioned by Reppert (1954: 8) as a tautological compound since the constituents have more-or-less identical meaning, can also be classified as a hyponym-superordinate type. Although both *yard* and *stick* are of Old English origin and originally denoted very generally 'stick', the meaning of the former was more specific, as it referred to 'a straight slender shoot or branch of a tree, a twig, a stick'. *Stick*, however, meant 'a rod or staff of wood' used for a special purpose; this purpose was indicated by the first constituent.[25]

Nevertheless, Renner's (2008) other examples, *teeny-tiny* or *hustle-bustle*, can be considered as synonymous compounds that have been conjoined for most likely an emphatic effect. According to the *OED*, *teeny* was originally a playful, 'childish' variation of *tiny* (the first citation of *teeny* is from 1825). *Hustle-bustle* ('a bustle in which there is much hustling or jostling'), a rhyming compound,[26] points to a very interesting phenomenon of English: namely, quite a few rhyming compounds, especially those denoting sound, are constituted of two meaningful and synonymous units, which at the same time are semantically related to the overall meaning of the compound as well. Examples include *crack-rack* ('an echoic word representing or describing a succession of cracks'), where the second constituent, *rack* ('a rush; a rapid advance, esp. towards or into collision with something; a hard blow or push'), is very close in meaning to both *crack* and the overall meaning of the expression. A similar process can be observed in *huff-puff* ('moved with every puff of wind'), which is yet again a concatenation of two meaningful – and synonymous – words. As elucidated by Benczes (2012), the rhyming feature of such expressions serves two aims: 1) it intensifies the meaning (i.e., it is used for an emphatic purpose); and 2) the partial reduplication (via rhyme) reflects the repetitive and/or rhythmical character of the sounds that these expressions denote.

---

[25] Examples include *potstick* ('a stick for stirring the contents of a pot or tub') or *setting stick* ('a stick used for making holes for "setting" or planting').

[26] Rhyming compounds are based on the partial reduplication of the base word, with a change in the initial consonant, as in *namby-pamby* or *nitty-gritty*. For a full account of the semantics of rhyming compounds, see Benczes (2012).

The examples cited above are all lexicalized, and the question necessarily arises whether contemporary English uses synonymous compounding at all. I believe that the answer to this question is a tentative 'yes', although synonymous compounds are now appearing in a new, blended form, as the following examples illustrate: *chilax* ('to calm down or relax'; from *chill+relax*),[27] *chivers* ('chills or shivers'; from *chill+shivers*), *confuzzled* ('a heightened state of bewilderment and puzzlement, usually caused by the individual in question not understanding the situation or conversation'; *confused+puzzled*).[28] Blends are not very distinct from compounds – Lehrer (2003: 371) alludes to them as 'underlying compounds'. Although blends were rather peripheral in English word-formation in the past (Bauer 1983), they are now on the increase, as they are considered as 'clever, trendy, eye-and-ear-catching words' (Lehrer 2003: 371) that people enjoy to create. Therefore, this shift from synonymous compounds to 'synonym-based blends' is a simple reflection of the current trends in English word-formation.

4.2. Clarification

The collocation of synonyms can also be used to 'make one's meaning clearer' (Ullmann 1977: 153). Many of the collocations of the English language, such as *liberty and freedom*, stem from the desire to clarify one's message as best as possible. As Ullmann argues, in the Middle Ages it was common to explain the meaning of a French word in a text by adding its native synonym. This trend also showed up in compounds, motivating the creation of synonymous coinages such as *courtyard* and *subject matter*.[29]

As regards to the former compound, the second constituent, *yard* ('a comparatively small uncultivated area attached to a house or other building

---

[27] Source: Merriam-Webster online dictionary; http://www.merriam-webster.com (01 May 2012).

[28] The definition of *chivers* and *confuzzled* are from the Urban Dictionary; http://www.urbandictionary.com (01 May 2012).

[29] According to Kate Burridge (p.c.), it is reasonable to assume that the practice of adding a native synonym to a French word quickly became a stylistic feature of prose. Legal doublets (and triplets) might have started off with a clear function, but the original motivation became obscured and such expressions turned into self-perpetuating idiosyncrasies of the jargon. With time the process has become a matter of stylistic choice, a conventionalised earmark of the variety. This phenomenon has its counterpart in art history as well – skeuomorphs are features that were once necessary (on a building for example) but are now applied for purely decorative purposes. Skeuomorphs also abound on artefacts – such as the note-taking application of Apple computers, which resembles a physical binder. Gessler (1998: 229) refers to skeuomorphs as 'material metaphors' that serve an important function: they help to familiarize us with the new and unfamiliar by drawing on conventionalized and widely accepted patterns.

or enclosed by it') is the Old English equivalent of the first constituent. *Court* derives from French *court*, denoting 'enclosure' (*Barnhart Dictionary of Etymology*; henceforth *BDE*). In fact, the *BDE* gives 'courtyard' as one of the definitions of the French *court*, which in itself points to the tautological nature of the compound. Nevertheless, it should be noted that the compound *courtyard* is not fully tautological, as it refers to an enclosure 'within the precincts of a large house, castle, homestead, etc.', that is, the compound's meaning specifies the nature of the building a courtyard can belong to. While any home could have a *yard* or a *court* for that matter, only larger and more prominent buildings could come with a *courtyard*. Accordingly, a courtyard must be larger in size than a yard or a court.[30] In this respect, *courtyard* can be considered as being motivated by the MORE OF FORM IS MORE OF CONTENT metaphor (as in the case of the examples in section 3.2), whereby the effect of the two synonyms 'add up' to an increase in the overall size of their referents.

Subject matter is a quite straightforward case as well. *Matter*, which is of Anglo-Norman origin, predates the Latinate *subject* (< Old French *suget*) by at least one hundred years (the first citation of *matter* is from 1230; ibid.). Therefore, it seems plausible to assume that *subject matter* (first citation from 1380) was also an instantiation of the trend to clarify non-native words with their native (or more conventionalized) synonyms.

The use of collocations based on synonyms in order to clarify what is being meant is especially prevalent in legal language (e.g., *goods and chattels* or *last will and testament*; Ullmann 1977: 154). Iglesias-Rábade's (2011) study has shown that the use of synonyms has already appeared in Late Middle English legal texts (as observable in the use of collocations such as *trewly and feithfully* or *mekely and devoutely*. This phenomenon can be explained by the fact that court proceedings were mostly in French during the early years of the English judicial system (Tiersma 1999: 31). Nevertheless, as Twardzisz (2011: 240) has pointed out, such seemingly tautological phenomena do have an important function in legal texts, as they serve 'to remove any possibility of ambiguity'. (See also Tiersma 1999: Chapter 5, for an overview on the tradition of precision in legal language.)[31]

---

[30] See also the definition of *yard*: 'a comparatively *small* uncultivated area...' (my emphasis – RB).

[31] In a similar vein, Gustaffson (1984, cited in Norrick 1988) claims that the synonyms of binomials in legal texts complement one another. Note that in all four examples cited in the above lines, one of the pairs is a native word (*goods*, *will*, *trewly* and *mekely* respectively), while the other pair is of non-native origin: *chattel* is derived from Old

5. Conclusions

The chapter set out to examine the role of compounds that have been loosely referred to as 'tautological' in academic discourse. As it has been shown above, there has been much confusion with regard to 1) what lexical items the term 'tautological compound' denotes; and 2) under what larger class of compounding (appositional, co-ordinate, dvanda, etc.) tautological compounds actually belong to. With regard to the first issue, the chapter has differentiated between two distinct, but related subtypes of tautological compounds: the hyponym-superordinate type (such as *tuna fish* and *oak tree*), and the synonymous type (such as *subject matter* or *courtyard*). As to the second point raised above, it has been argued that tautological compounds should be treated as a subclass of coordinated compounds.

It has also been demonstrated that the two subtypes of tautological compounds are by no means redundant: they, in fact, serve a number of diverse and important roles. Accordingly, hyponym-superordinate compounds are remnants of our early acquisition of taxonomical relations by making the link between the hierarchical levels explicit. At the same time, hyponym-superordinate compounds are also used to dignify and upgrade concepts via the conceptual metaphor MORE OF FORM IS MORE OF CONTENT, whereby a linguistic unit that has a larger form is perceived to carry more information (that is, more content) than a single-word unit.

Synonymous compounds have been shown to possess an emphatic feature, which has been exploited mainly in poetic language (as in the works of Coleridge). However, it has been maintained that synonymous compounds are still alive in everyday language, though in a slightly different form – as blends. Synonymous coinages have also been motivated by the need to clarify a non-native word with its native counterpart.

While tautological compounds have been around for a rather long time in the English language, they have received only very little attention (if at all) from linguists. Yet they provide fascinating insights into the motivational processes behind compounding. It is hoped, therefore, that the chapter has managed to relegate this much neglected category to its proper, well-deserved place within English word formation.

French *chatel* ("property, goods", from Latin *capitāle*), *testament* is from Latin *testāmen-um* ("will"), *faith* comes from Old French *feid* or *feit*, derived from Latin *fidem* ("trust"), while *devout* is of Old French origin and comes from *devote* (originally from the Latin *dēvōt-us*, "devoted"). Therefore, all of these collocations are based on the principal of combining a native word with a non-native synonym. In Tiersma's (1999: 32) view, the native and non-native pairing ensured that anybody would understand at least one of the terms.

References

Allan, Keith. 1986. *Linguistic Meaning: Volume 1*. London: Routledge and Kegan Paul.

Allan, Keith. 1987. Hierarchies and the choice of left conjuncts (with particular attention to English). *Journal of Linguistics* 23 (1): 51–77.

Allan, Keith and Kate Burridge. 1991. *Euphemism and Dysphemism: Language Used as Shield and Weapon*. Oxford: Oxford University Press.

Barnhart Dictionary of Etymology, The. 1988. Bronx, NY: H.W. Wilson Co.

Bauer, Laurie. 1983. *English Word-formation*. Cambridge: Cambridge University Press.

Bauer, Laurie. 2008. Dvanda. *Word Structure* 1: 1–20.

Bauer, Laurie. 2010. Co-compounds in Germanic. *Journal of Germanic Linguistics* 22 (3): 201–19.

Bauer, Laurie and Antoinette Renouf. 2001. A corpus-based study of compounding in English. *Journal of English Linguistics* 29 (2): 101–23.

Benczes, Réka. 2012. Just a load of *hibber-gibber*? Making sense of English rhyming compounds. *Australian Journal of Linguistics* 32 (3): 299–326.

Bloomfield, Maurice. 1920. Notes on the Divyāvadāna. *Journal of the American Oriental Society* 40: 336–52.

Carr, Charles T. 1939. *Nominal Compounds in Germanic*. Oxford: St Andrews University Publications.

Clark, Eve V. 2009. *First Language Acquisition*. 2nd edition. Cambridge & New York: Cambridge University Press.

Cooper, Lane. 1904. Pleonastic compounds in Coleridge. *Modern Language Notes* 19 (7): 223–4.

Darian, Steven. 1979. The role of redundancy in language and language teaching. *System* 7 (1): 47–59.

Emerson, Oliver Farrar. 1919. Middle English clannesse. *PMLA* 34 (3): 494–522.

Fabb, Nigel. 1998. Compounding. In Andrew Spencer and Arnold M. Zwicky (eds), *The Handbook of Morphology*. Oxford: Blackwell, 66–84.

Fay, Edwin W. 1913. Composition or suffixation? *Zeitschrift für vergleichende Sprachforschung auf dem Gebiete der Indogermanischen Sprachen* 45 (2): 111–31.

Gelman, Susan A., Sharon A. Wilcox and Eve V. Clark. 1989. Conceptual and lexical hierarchies in young children. *Cognitive Development* 4: 309–26.

Gessler, Nicholas. 1998. Skeuomorphs and cultural algorithms. In V.W. Porto, N. Saravanan, D. Waagen and A.E. Eiben (eds), *Evolutionary Programming VII: 7th International Conference, EP98 San Diego, California, USA, March 25–27, 1998 Proceedings*. Berlin & Heidelberg: Springer, 229–38.

Gustaffson, Marita, 1975. *Binomial Expressions in Present-Day English*. Turku: Turun Yliopisto.

Gustaffson, Marita. 1984. The syntactic features of binomial expressions in legal English. *Text* 4: 123–41.
Harbus, Antonina. 2003. The situation of wisdom in *Solomon and Saturn II*. *Studia Neophilologica* 75 (2): 97–103.
Hatcher, Anna Granville. 1952. Modern appositional compounds of inanimate reference. *American Speech* 27 (1): 3–15.
Iglesias-Rábade, Luis. 2011. Collocations in law texts in Late Middle English: Some evidence concerning adverbs ending in –lī. *Studia Neophilologica* 83 (1): 54–66.
Jespersen, Otto. 1954. *A Modern English Grammar on Historical Principles, Part VI: Morphology*. London: Bradford and Dickens.
Katamba, Francis. 2005. *English Words: Structure, History, Usage*. 2nd ed. London & New York: Routledge.
Lakoff, George and Mark Johnson. 1980. *Metaphors We Live By*. Chicago, IL: The University of Chicago Press.
Lehrer, Adrienne. 2003. Understanding trendy neologisms. *Rivista di Linguistica* 15 (2): 371–84.
Malkiel, Yakov. 1959. Studies in irreversible binomials. *Lingua* 8: 113–60.
Marchand, Hans. 1969. *The Categories and Types of Present-Day English Word-Formation: A Synchronic-Diachronic Approach*. 2nd, revised edition. Wiesbaden: Otto Harrassowitz.
Norrick, Neal R. 1988. Binomial meaning in texts. *Journal of English Linguistics* 21 (1): 72–87.
Oxford English Dictionary, The. 1989. Second edition; online version. Oxford: Oxford University Press.
Palmer, Frank R. 1981. *Semantics*. 2nd ed. Cambridge & New York: Cambridge University Press.
Renner, Vincent. 2008. On the semantics of English coordinate compounds. *English Studies* 89 (5): 606–13.
Reppert, J. D. 1954. Tautological compounds. *Word Study* 30 (1): 8.
Rosch, Eleanor, Carolyn B. Mervis, Wayne D. Gray, David M. Johnson and Penny Boyes-Braem. 1976. Basic objects in natural categories. *Cognitive Psychology* 8: 382–439.
Spencer, Andrew. 1991. *Morphological Theory*. Oxford & Cambridge, MA: Blackwell.
Tiersma, Peter M. 1999. *Legal Language*. Chicago and London: The University of Chicago Press.
Twardzisz, Piotr. 2011. Metaphors in commercial contracts. In Christina Alm-Arvius, Nils-Lennart Johannesson and David C. Minugh (eds), *Selected Papers from the 2008 Stockholm Metaphor Festival*. Stockholm: University of Stockholm, 237–53.
Ullmann, Stephen. 1977. *Semantics: An Introduction to the Science of Meaning*. Oxford: Basil Blackwell.
Wälchli, Bernhard. 2005. *Co-Compounds and Natural Coordination*. Oxford: Oxford University Press.

Willetts, R. F. 1960. Χρυσώνητος. *Glotta* 39 (1–2): 71–3.

Williams, Edwin. 1981. On the notions 'lexically related' and 'head of a word'. *Linguistic Inquiry* 12: 245–74.

Woods, Frank L. 1957. Nominal Compounds of the Old High German 'Benedictine Rule'. *The Journal of English and Germanic Philology* 56 (1): 42–51.

Chapter 4

FRENCH GENDER

IT'S NOT (ALL) ABOUT SEX[1]

Margaret H. à Beckett

Monash University

Why are some French nouns masculine and others feminine? The French gender system seems to have defied all efforts to describe it comprehensively. Biological distinctions account for only a small percentage of nouns in the language, even humans. Word-final phonology does not prove, of itself, to be sufficient explanation of gender. In à Beckett (2010) it is argued that French gender assignment and word-final pronunciation can be explained more adequately with reference to semantic principles similar to those of the morpho-syntactically complex classifier systems found in many languages of the world, including Africa, Asia, Australia and South America.

The present contribution suggests that French involves two separate, independent noun classification systems. The primary system relates to gender, which is semantically determined in terms of a limited number of oppositional features (dead:alive, hard:soft, closed:open, harmful:protective, fixed:changeable, etc.) expressed in masculine/feminine agreements outside the noun. An equally important secondary nominal classification system, also semantically determined, reflects other oppositions (part:whole, textured:smooth, slow:speedy, dull:shiny, spotted:striped, etc.) that are expressed directly on nouns via word-final contrasting vowel/consonant pronunciations (not orthography).

This contribution to the festschrift for Keith Allan illustrates these semantic principles at work among the animal and plant kingdoms and the world beyond.

1. Introduction

Grammatical gender is one of several noun classification systems in the world's languages, although its place alongside the semantic noun class and classifier languages has never been precisely determined (Aikhenvald 2000: 53; Grinevald 2002: 161). Of the many gender languages, French is

---

[1] An abridged version of this article appeared in *Inside Story* (15 April 2012).

generally considered to be the least transparent (Corbett 1991: 57). The sun and moon rise and set in much the same way, yet one is masculine, and the other feminine. But which one? And why?

Current explanations for French and other closely-related gender languages (Latin, Italian, Spanish) rest on semantic principles for some nouns, while 'formal' rules (related to their phonological/morphological forms) account for remaining nouns (Corbett: 1991, 33; Comrie 1999: 458). However, as Surridge (1993) points out for French, the precise nature of semantic, phonological and morphological interaction remains hidden by 'conflicting sets of rules' (pp. 87–8), 'exceptions' (p. 88), and 'limited applicability' (p. 89). The only certain way to identify the gender of any noun is through 'agreements' expressed in words (determiners, adjectives, etc.) syntactically related to the noun. The one area that offers ready explanation for these agreements is sex, where biological 'male'/'female' semantic distinctions correlate with contrasting masculine/feminine genders for various bird species, animal species, and certain human terms.[2]

Previous researchers (Tucker et al. 1977; Surridge 1993) have made reference to the regularity of gender assignments in other lexical sets (masculine for winds, seasons, months, days of the month, points of a compass, etc.; and feminine for females, academic disciplines, feast days, etc.). This regularity would suggest that semantic principles play a larger role than generally surmised, but lacking any obvious semantic explanation they have not previously warranted increased attention.

However, in her recent account of an extensive corpus of French noun classifications, à Beckett (2010) argues that gender distributions can be explained more adequately by semantic principles similar to those of other noun classification systems. She maintains that word-final sounds/segments relate to a secondary semantic system, a non-agreement system that reflects an independent set of semantic features such as rounded, striped, smooth, under, rough, toward, etc., and operates in tandem with the primary system that triggers agreements. Dual semantic systems are also found in other languages (Aikhenvald 2000: 185ff). While features associated with gender, the primary agreement system, are expressed *outside* the noun, those of the secondary system are expressed *on* the noun word-finally in terms of phonological contrasts between word-final vowels and word-final consonants, contrasts not always evident in the French orthography.

---

[2] 'Male'/'female' distinctions are not salient in certain European gender languages (Dutch, Danish, etc.).

À Beckett (2010) illustrates that the salient semantic features associated with French are not unlike those in other noun classification systems in the world's languages, including languages of Africa, Asia, Australia and South America. For example, 'vertical', or 'upright', is salient in French (most trees, seahorse and other fish), and also in Japanese, Palikur (Brazilian), and Akatek (Mayan) (Aikhenvald 2000: 193, 290, 187 resp.). Japanese classifiers also reflect features found in French, such as 'animate', 'inanimate', 'small', 'rounded', 'flat' (Downing 1986: 347), and Vietnamese contrasts between 'rigid' and 'flexible' (Adams 1986: 250, 252). Invisible:visible and dull:lustrous oppositions are salient in Anindilyakwa, an Australian Aboriginal language (Leeding 1989: 252ff) and also in French.[3] Illative:elative oppositions in motion and direction in Finnish case-marking (Branch 1987: 607) and Anindilyakwa locative clitics are salient in the French non-agreement system – as are certain shapes such as 'round' (observed in Minangkabau, Akatek, Palikur), 'irregular' (in Palikur). In Akatek, features associated with numeral classifiers include 'separate', 'curved', 'round', 'flat', 'extended', 'big' and 'small' (Aikhenvald 2000: 187, 290–1), which features are encoded in French. Chinese classifiers include a contrast between items that are 'flexible' (*tiáo*) and items that are 'rigid' (*gēn*), and while animals typically take the classifier *zhī*, for domestic animals we find *tóu* – semantic distinctions that are also encoded in French. In Arabic and Hebrew, duals of 'like' entities are feminine (Kaye 1990: 678; Heztron 1990: 699), as they are in French (dual nouns *couple* and *paire*) – except where they apply to 'unlike' or diverse items, when they are masculine (ATILF, à Beckett 2010: 311). A curious feature in French, 'harmful', is more closely associated with Australian Aboriginal languages, including Dyirbal (Dixon 1972; Harvey 1997).[4]

The discussion below reviews past accounts of French nouns, particularly irregular, unpredictable and unrelated changes in gender and final sounds and the challenge they pose for past explanations. It then explores the two semantic systems, and semantic features associated with each identified in à Beckett (2010) as they apply to living things and more generally across the French lexicon.

---

[3] Although these features are encoded somewhat differently in French.
[4] In Australian Aboriginal languages, 'harmful' is associated with a different gender from that found in French.

2. Past accounts

Past accounts of French gender by Mel'čuk (1974), Tucker et al. (1977) and Surridge (1993, 1995) recognise a semantic basis for some nouns (where contrasting masculine and feminine distributions relate to 'male' or 'female'), and offer a variety of explanations for remaining nouns. These accounts are examined extensively in à Beckett (2010) and are mentioned only briefly here. The most comprehensive of these studies is that of Tucker et al. (1977), which explores potential correlations between gender assignment and the (thirty) word-final phonemes for more than 30,000 French nouns. Results were expressed in terms of tabulations between gender and certain word-final sequences, and proved to have limited statistical viability. Commenting on these results, Surridge (1993: 83) notes: 'only one (sound) provides certainty as to gender, and in four cases the phonic ending would give the speaker no help at all. In between these extremes lie a range of different degrees of probability.'

Even so, other than the few semantically determined classifications related to male/female distinctions, it remains largely accepted that 'formal' principles (phonology, morphology) determine the gender of remaining nouns for gender languages, allowing French to be considered a rule-governed rather than 'irrational' system (Corbett 1991: 61). These generalisations fail to explain how competing semantic and 'formal' rules might interact. In their account of German gender, Zubin and Köpcke (1986) combine broad semantic principles (male/female distinctions, vague reference, contrasting superordinate/basic levels of meaning), with 'formal' morphological principles (masculine/feminine word-endings) and 'cognitive determinism' which incorporates various sets of parameters, including functional and perceptive notions. In their analysis, 'vague reference' and (most) superordinate level terms are neuter; (most) basic level terms for 'male' and 'female', as well as generic terms, are sex-related masculine or feminine according to various functional and behavioural domains – except where morphological masculine and feminine word-endings prevail. Superordinate exceptions, such as feminine terms for 'plant' and 'colour' are explained by 'the preconscious nature of grammatical classification', and 'preconscious cognitive determinism' accounts for irregular semantic shift and changes in noun class (Zubin et al. 1986: 176). However, as for French, determining when semantic rules prevail over formal rules in many cases can only be determined by reference to meanings.

3. Variations in gender and final phoneme

Of interest to an account of French gender is the way in which gender can vary over time. Gervais (1993) identifies such nouns 'doubt' *doute* and 'midnight' *minuit*, which were historically feminine and are now masculine, although final sounds for both remain unchanged.[5] Traditional accounts of French gender also overlook other variations in gender, such as different genders for singular/masculine and plural/feminine forms of 'organ' *orgue* and 'love affair' *amour*. À Beckett (2010: 77) identifies certain nouns that can be used with either masculine or feminine agreements, such as 'angora' *angora*, 'eagle' *aigle*, 'afternoon' *après-midi* and 'hymn' *hymne*. In these cases it seems unlikely that gender is determined by the final phoneme/final segment since they remain unchanged. Gender specifications of nouns can vary from one French dictionary to another, e.g., *pamplemousse* 'pomelo, shaddock, grapefruit', which is feminine in some sources (*Académie française* dictionaries, writers), masculine in others (*Larousse* dictionaries, botanists), while *Le Robert* offers alternative genders in *Petit Robert* (ATILF) but masculine-only in *Le Robert pour Tous* (LRPT 1994).[6] Even native speakers may not always agree on the gender of a noun, as the informative post from HeiDeas (http://HeiDeas:% 20February% 202008. webarchive, February 2008) notes:

> Fifty-six native French speakers, asked to assign the gender of ninety-three masculine words, uniformly agreed on only seventeen of them. Asked to assign the gender of fifty feminine words, they uniformly agreed (on) only *one* of them. Some of the words had been anecdotally identified as tricky… but others were plain old common nouns.

It is not that native speakers do not know the gender of nouns; as HeiDeas states, it is just that they disagree. These disagreements in gender are problematic for formal rules.

Another challenge comes from feminine nouns *personne* 'person' and *chose* 'thing' (à Beckett 2010: 77). In the case of *personne*, feminine agreements 'disappear' where its meaning expresses 'anyone'/'somebody/-one' (indefinite) or 'no-one' (negative), e.g.:

---

[5] In this article French terms and transcriptions are not generally provided, except for clarification.
[6] À Beckett (2010: 331) notes that 'bat' *chauve-souris* is masculine in the French/English section but feminine in the English/French section of the COFD (1986: 96, 16). The former is probably an error.

(1) *Il n'est pas question que personne est mort* (rather than *morte*, f.)
    'there is no question that someone has died'

(2) *Personne n'est parfait* (rather than *parfaite*, f.)
    'no-one is perfect'

For such examples, *personne* is described as an 'indefinite pronoun', with zero or masculine agreements (LRPT 1994: 836). These changes in gender are replicated for *chose* 'thing', which is feminine except where its meaning expresses 'another' (identity unknown), 'thingummy jig' (unnamed), or 'gadget' (unspecified) where it takes masculine agreements (LRPT 1994: 187). These 'indefinite', 'unspecified' and 'unnamed' notions are privative ('privative' meaning the absence, negation or loss of some property). Another 'privative' noun, *rien*, meaning 'nothing', is described as either an 'indefinite pronoun or masculine noun' (LRPT 1994: 989). A slightly different case is *légume* 'legume', which is masculine in its 'privative' sense as a vegetable (plant) of little value (and flavour), of use only in stockpots; however, *légume* is feminine in the phrase *grosse légume* 'big shot, top dog', 'outside of ordinary'. These changes in gender for *personne*, *chose* and *légume* cannot be related to changes in final sounds. Instead, à Beckett (2010: 77) argues, they appear to reflect semantic changes as meanings shift between polar opposites 'positive' and 'privative'.

Aigle 'eagle' is a vernacular term that applies to several large, dark, unrelated birds of prey. Its dictionary entry (LRPT 1994: 23–4) offers both masculine and feminine genders according to different usages. Masculine applies in the most general sense as the diurnal bird of prey. Feminine applies in the context of 'female' of the species (ATILF 2008), or at the nest (LRPT 1994: 23–4) which parents build in very high places for protection (they share parenting duties so we cannot know which is the male or female), and in expressions such as *l'aigle altière* 'eagle aloft', high above or *l'aigle déchaînée* 'eagle unchained', set loose (ATILF) – associated with height/protection and freedom.

Changes in classifications alongside changes in function are features of classifier languages (Löbel 2000: 23) and noun class languages. For example, in Murrinh-Patha, an Australian language of the Northern Territory, inanimate objects are in the *nanthi*-class, but as offensive weapons they are in the *thu*-class (Walsh 1993: 111). In French, the noun *orange* 'orange' is masculine as the colour term but feminine as the fruit (à Beckett 2010: 77). In Vietnamese and Murrinh-Patha, noun classifications are semantically determined.

3.1. Determining the final phoneme

If gender is determined by formal rules relating to word-final phone/segment, as Comrie (1999: 458) states, what principles determine the final sounds/segments? As à Beckett (2010: 66ff) points out, final phonemes of French nouns 1) can vary diachronically, e.g., *cou* 'neck' (orig. *col*); 2) may vary from dictionary to dictionary, e.g., 'navel' *nombril* ([–i] in COFD 1986: 374; [–i(l)] in LRPT 1994: 770); 3) have alternative phonemes for singular nouns, e.g., 'aniseed' *anis* [–i(s)] and 'tamarix' *tamaris/-ix* [–i(ks)]; and 4) have entirely different singular and plural forms, e.g., 'eye' sg. *œil* [–j] and pl. *yeux* [–ø] or 'canal' sg. *canal* [–l], and plural *canaux* [–o]. For loan words, the treatment of final sounds also varies as they enter the French lexicon. For example, the final [t] of 'wombat' is elided in French to *wombat* [–a], while 'cockatoo' adds an [s] to *cacatoès*, which is pronounced (ATILF 2005), although original forms present no obvious difficulty or structural impediment.

Orthography does not provide any certainty as to pronunciation. Some spellings preserve etymological connections over pronunciation, while others preserve pronunciation over etymological connections. Occasionally, alternative spellings may reflect both, e.g., 'spoon' *cuiller, cuillère* [–r], and 'key' *clé, clef* [–e]. But why is the final consonant pronounced for 'spoon' but not 'key', two feminine nouns, and for 'grapefruit' *grapefruit* [–t], but not 'fruit' *fruit* [–i], two masculine nouns? In many cases, non-pronunciation of the final letter(s) results in a final vowel sound, e.g., 'tobacconist's (shop)' *tabac* [–a], and 'respect' *respect* [–ɜ], but not for 'reverse' *revers* [–r], or 'crowbar' *anspect* [-k]. One might posit distinctive underlying representations where word-final orthographic consonants are pronounced, but even so, allocations would be arbitrary. As à Beckett points out (2010: 67), no principled system, historical or otherwise, has been offered to account for variations in what is pronounced and what is not pronounced word-finally. French dictionaries indicate that consonants at the ends of words are generally not pronounced, except where they are (LRPT 1994: 1236). This is a problem not only for learners but for native French speakers. LRPT (1994) attends to cases it considers problematic for native speakers by providing transcriptions (although it does not otherwise do so).[7] On first sighting of nouns such as *accroc* 'tear/rent', *étoc* (naut.) 'dangerous exposed rock', *dot* 'dowry', or *accul* 'blind alley', it is not possible to predict

---

[7] Unlike French/English dictionaries such as COFD (1986), which include transcriptions for every entry.

which final consonant will be pronounced and which will not (no, yes, yes, no, respectively), and both native and non-native speakers must call on authoritative sources such as dictionaries. More crucially, if final sounds are problematic for native speakers, 'formal' rules suggest that they would find it difficult to assign gender – yet gender seems less problematic than final phonemes, even with the variations noted above.

While Mel'čuk (1974: 11) suggests that infinitive forms used in extension as substantive nouns are masculine, this does not hold in the case of infinitive –*er* forms. Several nouns may be derived from the same infinitive, with different genders and different suffixes, sharing the same phonological form – as the infinitive verb *lever* 'to get up' illustrates (à Beckett 2010: 701): 1) *lever* [l(ə)ve] m. 'sunrise'; 2) *levé* [l(ə)ve] m. 'plan, survey'; 3) *levée* [l(ə)ve] f. 'embankment', 'gathering'. As à Beckett (2010: 701) points out, we can only distinguish the infinitive form from either of the other two terms through reference to orthography – but we cannot expect spellings to determine gender. Surely the different genders of these nouns must be related to their different meanings.

These issues are not raised by Mel'čuk (1974), Tucker et al. (1977) or Surridge (1993). In his monograph on gender, Corbett (1991) describes nouns that do not fit comfortably within a semantic, morphological or phonological framework as 'defective' (1991: 175), and treats such nouns as 'hybrids', particularly where they identify a 'male' referent but are feminine ('sentry', 'recruit', etc.) (p. 183ff). Härmä (2000) raises semantic inconsistencies in casual speech registers of young French speakers, where the gender of a noun is not reflected in pronouns/agreements, as in *Ma femme il est jaloux* 'My wife (he) is jealous' (cf. *ma femme elle est jalouse*). While this is described as a kind of 'gender neutralisation' related to *ça* 'this (/that)', Härmä (2000: 617) does not investigate further the precise motivation for gender neutralisations in the case of 'jealousy' and 'this/that' (item unspecified).

However, taking all of these factors into account, there is broad consensus on gender assignments in dictionaries and among native speakers (despite certain disagreements and irregularities). Conversely, final phones/segments of French nouns are not as closely tied to gender as would be expected were these two elements in some sort of causal relationship. The extent of unpredictable and unrelated variations in both elements suggest that gender assignments appear to be independent of the final phoneme and that final phonemes appear to be independent of gender. Evidence directs attention towards semantic features being independently relevant for both gender assignment and word-final syllable structure.

4. From sex to species

In one area, gender assignments appear relatively straightforward – sex, male or female. These biological distinctions are straightforward for various bird and animal species, and for certain terms. In such cases, 'male' correlates with masculine gender, and 'female' correlates with feminine gender, for example, in Table 1.

Table 1. French terms for 'male' and 'female' birds and corresponding (M/F) gender assignments.[8]

lexical item	gender	meaning
canard	M	'drake' (male)
cane	F	'duck' (female)
faisan	M	'pheasant' (male)
faisane	F	'pheasant' (female)
paon	M	'peacock' (male)
paonne	F	'peahen' (female)
coq	M	'rooster', 'cock' (male)
poule	F	'hen' (female)
dindon	M	'turkey' (male)
dinde	F	'turkey' (female)
jars	M	'gander' (male)
oie	F	'goose' (female)
merle	M	'blackbird' (male)
merlette	F	'blackbird' (female)
pigeon	M	'pigeon' (male)
pigeonne	F	'pigeon' (female)
sacret	M	'saker falcon' (male)
sacre	F	'saker falcon' (female)
laneret	M	'lanner falcon' (male)
lanier	F	'lanner falcon' (female)

---

[8] Taken from à Beckett (2010: Ch. 4, §4.3).

Among the more terrestrial fowl, the brilliant/flashy plumage of 'males' contrasts with the drab/dull colourations of 'females' – but one serves to camouflage, leaving the others exposed to danger. High visibility is precarious for daytime ground-dwellers. For the most part, speakers require only the generic or 'unmarked' term. More crucially, only one of each pair can serve. But which one? And why?

4.1. Which serves as the generic term, and why?

Among English pairs of terms for various bird species, it is typically the 'female' term that provides the generic or 'unmarked' sense for the species: *swan* (not *cob*), *goose* (not *gander*) – with a single exception, *peacock* (not *peahen*). In French, it is the other way round; it is the 'male' term that provides the generic or 'unmarked' sense for the species – with two exceptions, 'goose' *oie*, and 'saker' *sacre*, terms that would otherwise identify the 'female' of the species. *Sacre* is highly unusual. As its meaning changes from 'female saker' to the generic 'saker', its gender changes from feminine to masculine (ATILF 2005). This change in gender does not occur for 'goose' *oie* – it remains feminine in its generic sense (LRPT 1994: 786).

À Beckett (2010: 143–4) argues that the use of the feminine *oie* as the generic term for geese relates to its strikingly different responses to danger and threat from responses of other terrestrial and aquatic fowl in the above set. Whether feeding, flying or at rest, geese remain alert to potential threat or danger, and use constant and loud honking to communicate and keep members in touch; they collaborate to repel intruders in a way that avoids direct confrontation (www.wildfowling.co.uk, 2007; www.ducks.org/ Conservation/WaterfowlBiology/2112, 2004, Buffon, Tome 9.6, www.oiseau.net, 2006).

These responses are not shared by other terrestrial and aquatic fowl in Table 1. For example, the terrestrial fowl are strong flyers, yet they prefer to run/hop across the ground when danger threatens, and fly off only when it becomes immediate, and even then they do not fly far. Ducks and swans readily accept human intrusion, and with their head-under-water feeding, they cannot know what danger lurks below, nor can they sense or receive warning of any threat approaching from above.

For *sacre*, à Beckett (2010: 99) argues that the change to masculine gender in its generic sense as 'saker' (the species) relates to certain differences between 'diurnal' and 'nocturnal' birds of prey (the owls, the vernacular term for nocturnal birds of prey). Both share the same keen eyesight, but nocturnal birds of prey have other adaptations (extraordinary hearing, and wings 'rigged' for silent running that offer prey no advance warning to take cover) that offer more 'flexible' hunting when required, and enhance the chances of success in catching prey. In poor weather or times of scarcity, 'diurnal' birds lack the flexibility to extend their hunting when darkness comes, and may miss out entirely.[9]

These 'diurnal'/masculine and 'nocturnal'/feminine correlations are found in one other set – butterflies and moths. Butterflies face intense competition for nectar and increased danger from the immense numbers of other diurnal creatures that prey on insects; 'nocturnal' feeding provides cover of darkness and fewer predators for moths, a vastly safer environment. These 'harmful'/masculine and 'protective'/feminine associations account for all butterflies and moths – with the exception of Australia's masculine 'Bogong moth', which seeks relief from the heat of the day by hiding in caves and dark crevices in its native habitat and during its migratory flights (CSIRO 2011).[10] Seeking safety underground is argued to invite other dangers (see below).

The discussion above raises other properties associated with a specific gender in addition to 'male' and 'female':

Masculine: 'diurnal/inflexible', 'harmful', 'privative' (negation, absence, loss)

Feminine: 'nocturnal/flexible, 'collaborative', 'protective', 'positive'.

4.2. 'Harmful'

Taking just one of these properties identified above, 'harmful', à Beckett (2010) shows the correlation between masculine gender remaining regular and consistent not only for other birds but across an extensive corpus of living things and different lexical fields, including those in the set below:

- relying on speed to escape threat: hare, fox, roadrunner;
- ducking/diving for food: falcon, hawk, kite, gannet, guillemot, loon, diver, auk;
- hanging upside down: sloth;
- unwary of strangers: kookaburra, booby, gannet, puffin;

---

[9] Other diurnal birds of prey are also masculine (merlin, lanner, hobby and peregrine falcons, harrier, harrier hawk, goshawk, sparrow hawk, kite, lammergeyer, secretary bird, bald eagle, fish eagle, and 'snowy owl', the only diurnal owl) (à Beckett 2010: 117–8). Four feminine 'exceptions' are accounted for in à Beckett (2010: 125–7).

[10] The same correlations (masculine/*der Falter* 'butterfly' and feminine/*die Motte* 'moth') also occur in German (ELGD).

- inquisitive: cattle, emu, European robin, porpoise, dolphin;
- waiting for food to pass by: flounder, carpet shark, catfish, angelfish, stone fish; most snakes, crocodiles, alligators, lizards; most herons;
- preferring to run than fly: terrestrial fowl, whydahs, anis;
- seeking safety underground: wombat, hamster, sand eel, rabbit, cleaver wrasse, termite;
- individual night singing/calling: rail and crake, bittern, nightingale;
- inflexible diet: carnivores, herbivores;
- limited spread: Tasmanian devil; turbot; imperial pigeon (Solomon Is.), bird of paradise.

Living fast and dying too soon are notable features of this set, and roadrunners (real and cartoon) are iconic members. Waiting for prey to pass by may save energy in times of plenty but can lead to hunger when others get there first, or starvation in scarcity. Trees may be strong, but their vertical structures render them inherently unstable; like walls, lampposts and masts, they may be flattened in violent storms. Swifts are so exceedingly well adapted to their aerial existence that they cannot walk or take to the air if forced to land on the ground, and starve to death. Grebes respond to danger by diving rather than taking to the air. Also in this set are other aquatic species that feed head-under or dive below the surface, e.g., albatross, auk, dabbling duck, common guillemot, gannet, puffin, petrel, diver/loon, pelican, razorbill, shearwater, cormorant/shag, flamingo and kingfisher. This habit carries increased danger from injury through drowning and inability to call for help. However, several similar aquatic birds are feminine, e.g., avocet, (common) scoter, tern and coot, and these potential counter-examples are discussed below.

'Life-endangering' can also apply more generally to fire, inferno, storm, gale, black ice, fog, hazard, evil, danger, bridge, poison, gun, pistol, rifle, missile, boat and sword – but not 'flat-bottomed boats' with their increased stability, or 'side-arms' (*baïonette* and *épée*, the ceremonial dress sword, also used in the sport of fencing), which instruments are both light and portable, designed more for protection than offence and easily carried around on the body.

4.3. 'Protective'

In contrast, an adaptable nature and/or diet and 'protective' responses, particularly the ability to evade, avoid, or repel danger, are characteristic of the feminine set (à Beckett 2010), including those below:

- 'thorned' plants (hawthorn, honey locust tree, bramble, barberry, bougainvillea, blackthorn/sloe tree, coral tree) and 'spiny' fish (weever, stickleback, scorpionfish);
- wary: European smooth snake, grass snake, viper; trout; cockroach; mouse, otter, ostrich, quail, partridge;
- able to lure prey: death adder, certain herons, anglerfish;
- hard shell: tortoise/turtle; hazelnut, walnut, almond; crab, clam, oyster, mussel, scallop;
- additional prehensile grip: op/possum, lamprey, tick, some caterpillars, opknots, octopus;
- collaborative response to threat: tern, avocet, crane, guinea fowl, moorhen, wasp;
- emit a repellent odour: skunk, weasel, marmot, mole, mongoose; cantharis (beetle), grass snake;
- 'flexible' structure: Canadian/Eastern hemlock, fern, branch;
- able to veer/jump (suddenly change direction): shrew, dace, rainbow wrasse; frog, flea; mouse, gazelle, ant, tern, swallow, wagtail; frigate bird; prawn; grasshopper; locust;
- able to fly from harm: certain beetles (ladybird) and insects (fly, honey bee, cicada;
- 'adaptable' diet: hyena, goat, common buzzard/*buse*, Atlantic cod; carrion crow, seagull;
- 'adaptable' nature: carp, European perch, minnow; certain doves; goat; heath/heather, lavender, alder buckthorn, Canadian white spruce.

Fieldfares (large European migratory thrushes) collaborate to ram predatory birds or 'escort' them away from the colony. Swan-geese have a swan-like appearance but the manner of geese, and their loud and immediate collaborative response to strangers also makes them good 'watchdogs'. Wariness helps avoid threat, sudden changes in direction help evade threat, and nauseous smells, thorns or hard shells help repel threat. Such attributes are strongly associated with feminine gender.

More generally, 'life-protecting' can apply to warmth, food, lookout, sentry, sentinel, marina, barricade, portcullis, citadel, fortress, palisade, fence, bar, lock, police, customs, barn, cabin and house (protecting entities/items within). Marinas offer protection in all but the most violent weathers, where (masculine) harbours are 'fixed' in position and shelter depends on prevailing winds. Across the range of 'protective' properties in à Beckett (2010) and above, feminine gender is regular and consistent.

4.4. Potential counter-examples

Not included among the 'thorned' feminine set is the quintessential 'thorned', but masculine, rosebush – its thorns cannot protect against sap-sucking insects and fungal infections that kill. Most nuts and shellfish have rigid, thick walls that protect living matter within and are feminine, but an acorn shell protects its kernel only in part, and shells of other entities are brittle (egg, snail, peanut) and easily broken; for these entities, masculine gender reflects less 'harmful' than 'privative', lacking the protection offered similar feminine entities.

Scoters (sea ducks) dive for their food and might therefore fall into the masculine set, yet they are feminine. They have developed 'synchronous surfacing', which safeguards their catches from gulls waiting overhead. The aquatic avocets, terns and coots use co-operative responses to protect individuals and flocks against threat. The feminine osprey is an exception among masculine diurnal birds of prey, but it has waterproof feathers which other 'fish/sea eagles' lack. After submersion in water, ospreys can become airborne where other fish or sea eagles may drown, and if prey is too heavy for birds to lift, ospreys can swim to shore where other fish-eating eagles must release their catch. Certain members of 'nocturnal' owls are masculine. Many owls have rounded facial discs that amplify sound waves and locate prey, but in 'horned' owls they take the form of ear tufts that look much like horns, an attribute strongly associated with 'male' in the animal world.[11] These contrasting genders allow French speakers to distinguish 'diurnal' birds of prey from 'nocturnal' birds of prey, and separate the 'horned' (masculine) owls from the 'heart-shaped' and 'earless' faces of the larger set of feminine relatives (including Australia's barking owls, boobooks, mopokes and hawk-owls all of which are feminine) (à Beckett 2010: 124).

4.5. Competing properties

Entities can have more than one crucial property, and they may not necessarily be associated with the same gender; in such cases, they may

---

[11] 'Horned' is not salient for 'horned' ruminants since in it offers no indication of sex; in some species male and female are both 'horned'.

give rise to alternative genders, e.g. afternoon, eagle, or synonyms with different genders, e.g. 'tricoloured heron', which is known as both *aigrette tricolore* and *héron tricolore*. This heron species has both 'protective' and 'harmful' properties – it has an extensive and complex range of fishing strategies, but builds its nests on mud flats leaving its young with little protection from cold and predation, or drowning when water levels change abruptly. Speakers may use the feminine in the context of feeding and more generally, using the masculine term during the breeding season and abrupt changes in weather.

The inherent dangers of sheltering underground suggest that 'mole' *taupe*, the quintessential burrowing animal, would also be masculine, but it is feminine. 'Defined' by their molehills, moles can swiftly tunnel out of danger using scooped 'hands'; they can repel intruders by emitting a foul odour, and use their paralysing toxin to keep prey alive, stored for on-demand consumption for creatures that require constant food intake. This example suggests that a 'private' attribute is outweighed by 'positive' attributes that allow this creature to flourish, even in this dangerous environment.

The example for 'mole' is supported by bats and fruit bats which hang upside down at rest, a habit one might expect to be associated with masculine gender as it is for sloths, etc., but these creatures are winged and can fly to safety, an attribute that is not only 'protective' but 'exceptional' since bats are the only winged mammals – and both properties are associated with feminine gender in French. This association between 'standing out' or 'outstanding' and feminine gender applies not only to bats, and the meaning of the feminine *grosse légume*, above, but elsewhere in the lexicon:

- whale (the only fully aquatic mammal);
- bat/fruit bat (the only winged mammal);
- star anise tree (unique in its star-shaped fruits);
- 'holm/holly oak' (evergreen where other temperate climate oaks are deciduous);
- 'larch' (deciduous where all other cool climate conifers are evergreen);
- cream (the liquid that rises to the top when milk is left to stand);
- crest (the topmost piece of something);
- face (face, the outer/front-most surface of a head (person, animal) or building);
- thumb, the opposable digit (which all other digits lack);
- head and shoulders (the top and outermost parts of the body).

This set includes larch, the only deciduous cool climate conifer, which was officially reclassified from feminine to masculine in 1765[12] (to fit with other tall trees, most of which are masculine – but not holm oak). However, feminine gender remains in use among regional speakers in the Dauphiné where these trees grow. The precise date of its reclassification is in marked contrast to the more gradual change for 'hawthorn' from masculine to feminine, and for 'midnight' in its gradual change from feminine to masculine as clock towers and clocks became more commonplace to provide an ever-increasing awareness of 'midnight' not as a 'flexible' amount of time but as a 'fixed' point (as sundials had long indicated for the masculine 'midday').[13]

The notions 'exceptional', 'outstanding' and 'standing out' also apply to various terms for people, whether as 'exceptionally good' ('elite') or clearly noticeable ('dupe', the 'mark' picked out from other potential targets, as for 'victim'), 'sentry' (on the perimeter) and 'scout' (ahead of the rest) which are all feminine, including several considered by Corbett (1991) to be 'hybrid' (see above).

Despite our genderless modern English, we have little difficulty understanding the notion 'outstanding' in terms such as 'elite', 'cream of society', 'cream of the crop', 'mother lode' and 'mother of all storms' (one that 'stands out' from all others in living memory). What fascinates here is the association between 'female'/feminine and 'outstanding' in English and French. English expressions also attend to many of the same oppositions that are salient in French, such as 'furniture and fittings' (portable:fixed), 'tooth and nail' (living:dead), 'hand over fist' (open:closed, semantic features also distinguishing 'slap' and 'punch'), although such contrasts are perhaps less related to any gendered past than to the universality of oppositions ('everything is opposition') argued by Saussure (in Harvey 1997: 34) in his deliberations on the meaning of signs.[14]

5. Gender: Other semantic features

Other features are equally regular in their association with a specific gender. 'Dead' entities such as corpse, cadaver and wood (as lumber) are masculine,

---

[12] The only formal body authorised to undertake such reclassifications is the *Académie française*. Two centuries earlier, court-appointed authorities also regularised 'willow' as masculine (ATILF 2005), and today it remains feminine only in place names, being more resistant to change.

[13] Interestingly, the feminine Latin noun 'ides of March' identified a 'flexible' point in Roman calendar.

[14] Colons between semantic features indicate polar opposites (such as 'dead:alive').

as are all 'extinct' species (dinosaur, dodo, solitaire, tarpan, trilobite, aurochs, etc.). Support for this 'extinct'/masculine correlation comes from the American 'passenger pigeon', once one of the most numerous birds on earth, whose original French name was feminine (*tourtre*). Hunted to the point of extinction in the nineteenth century, the last passenger pigeon died early in the twentieth century, after which it has come to be known as *pigeon migrateur*, a masculine term. In contrast, 'alive/living' is associated with contrasting feminine gender, e.g., flora, fauna and other more unexpected examples such as 'recruit' (a living body to replace one lost through death or injury), and 'flatfish' (which lie on their sides, which position typically indicates 'dead' for fish' when they are not), and 'bleeding heart' pigeons (where colouration of feathers suggests 'dead' when they are 'alive').

Other oppositions identified above remain regular and consistent in their association with specific masculine or feminine gender elsewhere in the lexicon – see Table 2.

Table 2. Masculine and feminine oppositions.

Masculine	Feminine
'life-threatening' (hurricane, lightning, disaster)	'life-generating' (female, water, light, warmth, grain, seed, nut)
'inflexible' (chassis, bench, bone)	'flexible' (form, skin, season, moon)
'restricted' (bus, system, train, tram)	'free/open' (road, way, space, hand)
'indirect' route (*chemin* 'road' – follows the lie of the land), passage, voyage	'direct' (highway, route)
'indefinite' (salon, animal, game, instrument, object)	'definite' (bedroom, kitchen, bathroom, etc.)

Further 'privative' examples (beyond those for 'indefinite', 'indirect', 'inflexible', etc., above) include boudoir, secret, shipwreck, tool, device, equipment, price/prize, destiny, future, change, result, sport, even money (lacks the same intrinsic value), and are all masculine.

As for classifier and noun class languages, similar objects may be in different sets. Opposable thumbs (feminine) have a flexibility that fingers and toes (masculine) lack. Masculine trams, trains, buses and trucks are 'fixed' or 'restricted' to certain routes; feminine cars (*voiture, automobile*) are 'flexible', can go in any direction, and take to the open road. Pumpkins grown for competition are masculine (*potiron*), and those used for All Hallow's Eve are feminine (*citrouille*); the former are 'filled', the latter are 'hollow'. Time is a continuum from past to future, but our experience is 'fixed' firmly in the present while colour, another continuum is 'flexible', allowing us to move forwards and backwards, separating and combining different colours at 'fixed' points.

What other opposites are there? The answer is fewer than for many classifier languages (with up to six hundred or so distinctions), and more than those already identified (à Beckett 2010), since we can now add 'true:false', and 'perfumed:odourless' – feminine for the former in each pair, masculine for the latter. 'True:false' contrasts can account for feminine/masculine distributions for truth and lie; 'perfumed:odourless' can account for yellow citrus fruits, 'perfumed'/feminine for the bergamot (orange, although yellowish), and 'odourless'/masculine for lemon, citron, grapefruit[15] (see à Beckett 2010). A more extensive set of semantic features is presented in Appendix 1.

More importantly, how do we know which semantic features to look for, and what their correlating genders will be? The answer lies partly in entities themselves, partly in meanings expressed lexically, and partly the environment in which an object or entity sits. In the lexical field 'fruits', we use sight, smell, touch and taste, each sense called on to judge the moment when maturity is reached, against 'unripe' or past its prime. Each sense offers a limited set of semantic features – 'bright/light:dark', 'perfumed:odourless', 'soft:hard', 'thick-:thin-skinned', 'hollow:filled', 'sweet:sour' and so on, requiring closer and closer contact. Using our intuitions and stereotypical associations, it is not difficult to distribute opposites for each pair between the two genders. For 'hard:soft', we are more likely to associate 'hard' with masculine and 'soft' with feminine than vice versa – and so we find masculine for fruits that remain hard even when ripe, such as passionfruit, watermelon and quinces (where softness indicates rotting), and feminine for raspberries, red/white currants, figs and dates, where soft indicates ripe.

'Hard:soft' opposites can also vary slightly to provide other sets of semantic opposites such as 'fixed:changeable', or 'rigid:flexible'. 'Restricted:free' can vary into 'closed:open' contrasts to create distinctions between fist (masculine) and hand (feminine) although they indicate the same body part, while the masculine bud opens out into feminine leaf or flower. Closed

---

[15] Although these fruits are argued somewhat differently in à Beckett (2010: §7.10–1)

geometric figures (circle, square, rectangle and triangle) are masculine; open figures (line, parabola, helix, curve and spiral) are feminine.

6. Gender and terms for human beings

Semantic properties also account for the many terms for humans in the corpus and their masculine/feminine distributions (see à Beckett 2010: Ch.8). Many have 'fixed' genders related to the semantic features salient for other lexical fields, and typically identify an individual according to some quality or characteristic. Others identify referents according to an activity, particularly employment (virtuoso, chemist, lawyer[16]), occupation (musician), rank (royalty, nobility), or a personal relationship (ally, friend). In such cases, the gender typically correlates with the sex of the real-world referent. 'Exceptions' with fixed masculine gender relate to high office (Secretary of State) or high prestige (judge, writer, artist), wealth (rich person) and property (land-owner, heir),[17] terms that offer cachet and prestige that remain fossilised in older social norms. 'Fixed' feminine exceptions involve low prestige (secretary, *garde*, meaning 'nurse', one who looks after small children). Such classifications are subject to change as social and cultural norms change (Aikhenvald 2000: 311), and in French changes have occurred in domains that were once sex-specific but now correlate with the real-world referent (mayor, president, chemist). Equally interesting are those that once correlated but now do not, e.g., scientist, soldier (cf. warrior).[18]

One French term that has fixed masculine gender is *familier* 'family friend'. Its stem suggests 'blood' relation, but masculine gender negates this ('not blood'). Other 'privative'/masculine correlations can be found in 'flightless', 'extinct', 'unlike', (each lacking some quality). 'Absence' is associated with meanings such as void (absence of matter), silence (absence of sound), nothingness (absence of anything) and even oblivion/oversight/forgetfulness (absence/loss of memory) and lie (falsehood), all of which are masculine.[19]

---

[16] 'Lawyer' remains masculine in official documents; *avocate* (f.) is only found in the spoken language (ATILF).

[17] 'Fossilised' exceptions include chancellor, monarch, land-owner, rich person, teacher, artist, sculptor, etc.

[18] For treatment of 'male'/feminine, 'female'/masculine nouns, and nouns for humans derived from other nouns or adjectives, etc., see à Beckett (2010: Ch.8, §8.8, 8.9).

[19] It is noted that 'privative' terms are neuter in Latin (cadaver, lie, silence, void, etc.).

7. Final sounds/segments and associated semantic features

Final vowel and consonant sounds/segments are also found to correlate with semantic features. Some features are associated with a final vowel, and others with a final consonant, and together they form pairs of binary opposites. Those identified in à Beckett (2010: 670) are set out in Table 3, with certain examples.

Table 3. Vowel and consonant sounds/segments and their correlation with semantic features.

Vowel-final	Consonant-final
comparative size: kitten, baby; raven	superlative size: blue whale; mote
immobile: mineral; bine (hops); doll	mobile: animal; ivy, clematis, grapevine
spotted: ocelot, Atlantic cod	striped: zebra, tiger, Tasmanian tiger, bar
slow: snail, tortoise, sloth	speedy: hare, fox, gazelle, zebra, deer, coyote
lumbering: ox, camel, elephant, water buffalo	agile: diplomat, acrobat, leopard, panther
delicate: bird, chick	strong: ox, horse, donkey, ass, tiger; liana
dull: blueberry, grape	shiny: cassis; redcurrant, light, gold
part: tail, foot, finger/toe, season, end, day, daydream	whole: animal, tree, figure, painting, dream
slender: heron, swift, kite, cormorant	bulky, solid: swan, duck, booby
narrowing: spruce, fir, tail	broadening: swan, oak, elm, willow
abstract: idea, thought, echo	concrete: bust, sculpture
unpalatable: lemon, citron, lime	palatable: orange, mandarin, grapefruit, cucumber
irregular: year, month, cypress	regular: week, curve, line
textured (rough, wrinkled): pineapple, walnut, skin	smooth: eel, mango, aubergine, hazelnut
narrow, slender: roadrunner, heron, poplar	broad, wide: oak, elm, swan, duck
convex: abutilon, coral plant	concave: geranium, lavender

under: petticoat; foot, trunk	over: skirt; head, crown
into: entry, exit	out of: north/south/east/west wind
odd: month, year, season	even: day (*jour*), week
distant: enemy	close: family, aunt, uncle, sister, brother
outward: prow, invitation	backward: stern, reply
separate: colony, peloton	together: marriage
behind: *passé*/past time, retreat	ahead: *future*/future time, advance

'Slow:fast' opposites are reflected in contrasting vowel and consonant word-final pronunciation for 'tortoise' *tortue* and 'hare' *lièvre*, quintessential 'slow:fast' exemplars. 'Dull:shiny' opposites can account for contrasting final vowel and consonant pronunciations for closely-related berries, 'blueberry' (*bleuet* [–ɛ]) and 'cassis' (*cassis* [–s]). Contrasting vowel and consonant word-final pronunciations for 'prow' *proue* [–u] and 'stern' *arrière* [–r] can now be understood in the context of semantic opposites 'outward-facing' and 'backward-facing'. Semantic opposites 'to' and 'fro' can be observed in final vowel and consonant contrasts in the expression *aller et retour* 'return journey'. However, for reciprocal notions such as 'to-and-fro' (tide, stairs, oscillation, train), and 'over:under' ('clothing'), vowel-final pronunciation appears to be regular and consistent – suggesting, perhaps, that for this non-agreement system, competing features associated with contrasting classifications 'resolve' to final vowel pronunciation.

8. Dual semantic systems, different semantic domains

Semantic features associated with gender, the primary system, suggest very different domains from those of the secondary system. Where features of gender, the agreement system, relate to form ('male:female', 'filled:hollow'), structure ('upright:recumbent') and mode of existence ('endangering: protective'), semantic features of the non-agreement system express temporal/spatial degrees – shape ('slender:bulky', 'unrounded:rounded', 'narrowing: broadening'), movement ('clumsy:agile', 'slow:fast'), location ('front:behind', 'under:over', 'nearby:elsewhere'), direction ('outward:backward', 'from:towards'), time ('past:future'), texture ('rough:smooth'), measure ('part:whole', 'unpalatable:edible') or size ('comparative:superlative').

Interaction between semantic features associated with the two systems and salient attributes of entities is reflected in the diagram below (Figure 1).

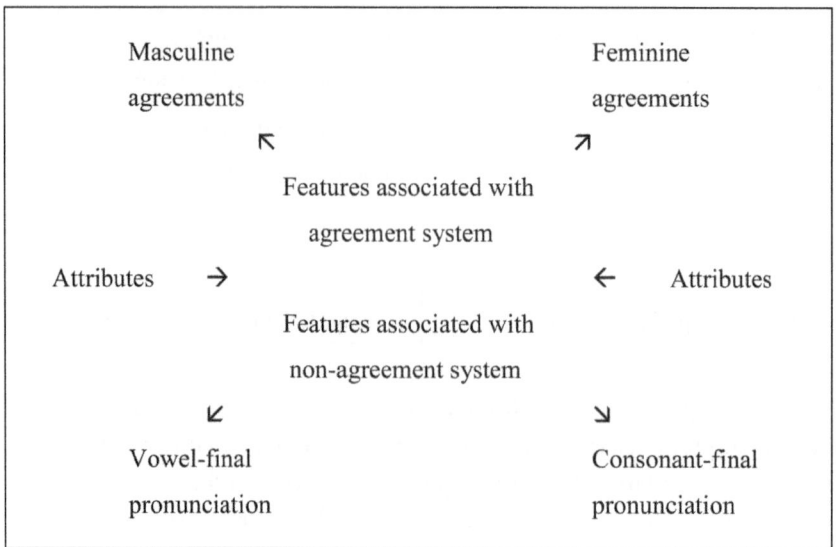

Figure 1. Dual agreement/non-agreement systems and operating principles.

Where other nominal classification systems have more extensive subsets, we should not be surprised to find such doubling up of semantic features in these two binary codes. Where we do not know these details about each entity, we cannot predict its gender, but knowing the gender narrows the field and tells us something about form, structure or mode of existence of an entity. And knowing even a small amount can provide a level of predictability as to both gender and/or the final sound not available through other accounts. 'Exceptions' prompt us to search among other crucial attributes of an entity for one associated with the contrasting gender. Once we become aware of the specific feature as something we know about an item, and recognise its relationship with the gender or word-final pronunciation of the designating term, it becomes a given. As such, it then requires little effort to memorise, and later recall.

As has been shown for both gender and word-final pronunciation systems, historical variations and changes (such as *cou/col* 'neck') can be shown to relate to changing saliencies of competing properties associated with different vowel and consonant word-final pronunciations. Aikhenvald (2000: 98) notes similar examples in classifier systems where '... nouns may have alternative choices of classifier depending on which property of the noun is in focus.' It is this change in focus that allows similar variations in the two French systems. Walsh (1993: 111) provides examples from Murrinh-Patha, an Australian Aboriginal language, where the classification of inanimate objects can change as perceptions change. We can observe similar examples in Latin, where 'box tree' is feminine as the living tree, and neuter as the dead wood (ELD 1966: 98). Adams (1986) refers to Vietnamese research (Huynh Sang Thong in Adams 1986: 244) where gardeners employ different classifiers when discussing plants from those in the general populace. In French, the highly-perfumed freesia is masculine for botanists and feminine for florists; the common European 'woodpecker', is masculine for ornithologists (*pic épeiche*) while the vernacular term is feminine (*épeiche*). In German, vernacular and specialist hunting terms for the same animals have different genders (Zubin et al. 1986: 155).

9. Comparison with other noun classification systems

It is interesting to compare semantic features of the French agreement and non-agreement systems with Minangkabau (a Western Austronesian language), a language that has both noun classifiers and numeral classifiers. In this language, Marnita (cited in Aikhenvald 2000: 189) shows that numeral classifiers for animate entities are associated with 'human:non-human' contrasts, and for inanimate entities distinctions relate to form and shape, such as 'flat', 'foldable', 'round and hollow', 'long', 'vertical', 'flat/long/thin', 'round', 'solid', 'thread-like'. These same features are also found in French and are split between the agreement and non-agreement systems (see à Beckett 2010, above vowel and consonant sets, and Appendix 1 and 2).

It can now be seen that many of the semantic features that are crucial in the French agreement and non-agreement systems are found in other languages. Indeed, many can be related to the schema of eight parameters developed by Allan (1977, 2001): material, shape, consistency, size, location, arrangement, quanta (1977), and function (2001). For example, 'material' covers a range of parameters such as 'hard:soft', 'textured:smooth', 'man-made:naturally occurring', 'abstract:concrete', while 'location' can incorporate contrasting notions 'under:over', 'to:from', 'here/there:elsewhere' – some located in the gender system, and some in word-final phonology. 'Quanta' is significant in distinctions observed among singular nouns, dual nouns, and collective nouns, but not in relation to each other.

It is of considerable significance that the same phonological forms relating to word-final pronunciation are also found in agreements relating to the gender system, particularly adjectival masculine/feminine agreements, and suffix alternations. The many phonological forms shared by these two French systems seem not unlike the 'alliterative concord' referred to by Corbett (1991) in his analysis of gender agreement for Swahili, where the form expressed in gender outside the noun may also be the same as the form expressed on the noun (1991: 117) – although Corbett considers both to be overt gender markers. Aikhenvald (2000: 35, 396) also refers to a similar 'alliterative concord' for !Xóõ, a Southern Khoisan language where noun class markers 'bear a strong phonological similarity to agreement markers' (p. 396) and to Ngan'gityemerri (Reid 1997, cited in Aikhenvald, 2000: 95) where 'overt noun class markers of Ngan'gityemerri, too, are (most often) the same as agreement noun class markers on adjectives' (p. 95). In other classifier/noun class languages such as Mayali, an Australian Aboriginal language, nouns denoting male or female animate referents trigger agreements 'that may be different from the noun class prefix that appears on the noun' (Aikhenvald, 2000: 396). In Latin, 'agreements' are alliterative in some cases, but not in others; nominative case markers ending in *–us*, *–a* and *–um*, and nominative agreement markers *–us*, *–a* and *–um* do not necessarily go together. It may be this 'alliterative concord' that has given rise to the premise of some connection between the two.

10. Concluding remarks

The analysis above and in à Beckett (2010, 2012) challenges previous explanations. It provides an innovative approach to understanding French gender and the principles underlying distributions between masculine and feminine genders. Previous studies restrict semantic motivation to various bird and animal species, and less successfully, to humans, with 'formal rules' determining remaining nouns according to final sounds/segments. À Beckett's approach dissociates formal rules from gender on the grounds that word-final sounds/segments offer only a limited statistical correlation with gender, and cannot account for unpredictable and unrelated changes in gender and word-finally, particularly determinations that depend on orthography (as for infinite *–er* verbs).

In this approach, French gender is treated as a semantic system on a par with the morpho-syntactically complex noun class and classifier systems found in many languages of the world, including Africa, Asia, Australia and South America, with similar semantic principles. This explanation allows a much more nuanced treatment of attributes rather than global and absolute semantic characteristics of previous attempts.

Word-final pronunciation is now treated as a secondary, non-agreement semantic system, expressed directly on nouns via vowel and consonant phonological distinctions. In that this second system is independent of other constituents inside or outside of the noun phrase, word-final pronunciation seems more like a device that occurs in classifier languages. Semantic features in the two French systems are fewer than for classifier systems (such as several hundred for Japanese) but more extensive than those offered for various noun class languages.

Each semantic system is limited not by hierarchy but by the salience of relevant features. For these binary systems, the extensive doubling-up of features in the same set would make any hierarchical organisation unwieldy. Instead, salience is determined by the entity itself, in comparison with others and the environment in which it sits, by semantic properties already encoded in the lexeme, and properties that can be taken as 'given' (such as 'alive' for living entities) – and by 'contrariety', which deals with the nature of opposition and inconsistency rather than 'variety', which concerns diversity and difference. For example, 'sun' and 'moon' have a limited set of crucial features relating to form and shape. Some may regard the 'sun' as having a 'fixed' form (and thus masculine) and the 'moon' as 'changeable' (and thus feminine) – as occurs in French, Latin, Italian, etc. Others may see the sun's form as 'constant/same' (and thus feminine) and the moon as 'different' (and thus masculine), and in German we find the feminine *die Sonne* and masculine *der Mond*. These constraints allow meanings to be codified in two ways – they separate 'some' from 'others, and separate 'one' from 'another/ some others/all others'.

The two French semantic systems are maintained through their binary frameworks and different spheres of operation – gender relating to structure and form, and word-final pronunciation relating to temporal/spatial degrees. There is some evidence to suggest that semantic features of word-final pronunciation apply also to other grammatical classes in the French language, i.e. adverbs ('inside:outside'), prepositions ('away:towards') and infinitive verb forms ('enter:exit') (à Beckett 2010: 698). For example, semantic opposites 'without' *sans* [–ã] and 'with' *avec* [–k] have contrasting final vowel and final consonant pronunciations, as do 'in(side)' *(de)dans* [–ã], and 'out(side)' *(de)hors* [–r] (see Appendix 2).

Understanding distributions between masculine and feminine is not difficult using our intuitions and/or stereotypical associations. For instance, we are more likely to associate 'hard' with masculine (if not 'male') and 'soft' with feminine (if not 'female') and likewise, 'fixed' and 'changeable'. Lakoff (1987: 1) suggests that, although the presence of entities in the same class has the potential to create a 'chain of inference – from conjunction to categorization' that might lead us to infer that they have something in common, this is not necessarily so. However, the semantic links between 'soft' and 'flexible/adaptable', a 'changeable' nature, and notions such as 'free', 'open', and 'continuous/flowing' associated with feminine are elements to ponder. Equally interesting are the semantic links between 'inflexible', 'endangering', 'domesticated', 'closed', 'fixed', 'hard', 'stop' and 'privative' associated with masculine. Sex is clearly salient in the French language in a number of ways, however, not to the extent argued by Grimm, and Zubin et al. (1986) since other features appear to be more fundamental 'life:death' distinctions bound in more ancient 'animate:inanimate' oppositions.

Ultimately, what is exciting about this research is the similarity between many of the semantic features that are salient in French to features already identified in other noun classification systems of the world's languages. With its dual agreement and non-agreement semantic systems, French calls into question the dichotomy generally drawn between noun class languages on the one hand, and classifier languages on the other, since this explanation of French reflects characteristics of both.

Appendix 1

French semantic features and correlating masculine/feminine gender.

Masculine	Feminine
dead	alive
inanimate	animate
indefinite	definite
indirect	direct
stop	continuous
life-taking	life-generating
harmful	protective
invisible	visible
unrelated	related
extinct	extant
closed	open
different/unlike	same/alike
bound	free
restricted	movable
dark	light
man-made	natural
sour	sweet
hard	soft
fixed	changeable
vertical	flat
upright	recumbent
inflexible	flexible
domestic	wild
uneven	even
constrained	spreading
filled	hollow
commonplace	outstanding/standing out/unique
bottom(most)	top(most)

Appendix 2

Word-final pronunciation and semantic oppositions (for prepositions, pronouns, adverbs, etc.).[20]

Vowel-final			Consonant-final		
under	*sous*	[–u]	over	*sur*	[–r]
from	*de*	[–ə]	towards	*vers*	[–r]
without	*sans*	[–ã]	with	*avec*	[–k]
here/there	*ici/la*	[–i] [–a]	elsewhere	*ailleurs*	[–r]
present/here	*je, tu, nous/vous*	[–ə], [–j], [–u]	elsewhere	*il/ils, elle/elles*	[–l]
inside	*(de)dans*	[–ã]	outside	*dehors*	[–r]
back	*(au) fond*	[–ɔ̃]	front	*(en) face*	[–s]
far	*loin*	[–ɛ̃]	close	*proche*	[–ʃ]
to enter	*entrer*	[–e]	to depart/exit	*sortir*	[–r]
outward	*inviter*	[–ɔ̃]	backward	*répondre*	[–s]

---

[20] For further examples, see à Beckett (2010: 698).

References

à Beckett, Margaret H. 2010. *Gender Assignment and Word-final Pronunciation in French: Two Semantic Systems*. München: Lincom Europa.

à Beckett, Margaret H. 2012. French Gender: It's not (all) about sex. *Inside Story*. Canberra: Swinburne University Canberra Times. 11 April 2012 (abridged version).

Adams, Keith. 1986. Numeral Classifiers in Austroasiatic. In C. Craig (ed.), *Noun Classes and Categorization: Proceedings of a Symposium on Categorization and Noun Classification, Eugene, Oregon, October 1983*. Amsterdam: Benjamins, 241–62.

Aikhenvald, Alexandra Y. 2000. *Classifiers: A Typology of Noun Categorization Devices*. Oxford: Oxford University Press.

Allan, Keith. 1977. Classifiers. *Language* 53 (2): 284–310.

Allan, Keith. 2001. *Natural Language Semantics*. Oxford: Blackwell.

ATILF. *Le trésor de la Langue Française informatisé*. <http://atilf.atilf.fr.>, accessed March 2005.

Branch, Michael. 1989. Finnish. In Bernard Comrie, *The World's Major Languages*. New York: Oxford University Press, 593–618.

Buffon, G.-L. L. 1770–83. *Histoire naturelle des Oiseaux*. Paris: Bibliothèque National de France (édition Gallica).

The Commonwealth Scientific and Industrial Research Organisation (CSIRO). <http:www.csiro.au/en/Outcomes/Environment/Biodiversity/BogongMoths.aspx>, accessed June 2008.

Comrie, Bernard. 1999. Grammatical gender systems: A linguist's assessment. *Journal of Psycholinguistic Research* 28 (5): 457–66.

Concise Oxford French Dictionary (COFD). 1985. Oxford: Clarendon Press.

Corbett, Greville G. 1991. *Gender*. Cambridge: Cambridge University Press.

Corbett, Greville G. 2005. Systems of gender assignment. In: Martin Haspelmath, Matthew S Dryer, David Gil and Bernard Comrie (eds), *The World Atlas of Language Structures*. Oxford: Oxford University Press, ch. 23.

Dixon, R. M. W. 1972. *The Dyirbal Language of North Queensland*. Cambridge: Cambridge University Press.

Downing, Pamela 1986. The anaphoric use of classifiers in Japanese. In: Colette Craig (ed.), *Noun Classes and Categorization: Proceedings of a Symposium on Categorization and Noun Classification, Eugene, Oregon, October 1983*. Amsterdam: Benjamins, 345–76.

Easy Learning German Dictionary (ELDG). 2001. 2nd ed. Glasgow: Harper Collins.

Gervais, Marie-Marthe. 1993. Gender and language in French. In: Carol Sanders (ed.), *French Today: Language and Its Social Context*. Cambridge: Cambridge University Press, 121–38.

Grinevald, Colette. 2002. Making sense of nominal classification systems. In: Ilse Wisher and Gabriel Diewald (eds), *New Reflections on Grammaticalization*. Amsterdam: Benjamins, 259–75.

Härmä, Juhani. 2000. Gender in French: A diachronic perspective. In: Barbara Unterbeck, Matti Rissanen, Tertu Navalainen and Mirja Saari (eds), *Gender in Grammar and Cognition*. Berlin: Mouton de Gruyter, 609–19.

Harvey, Mark. 1997. Nominal classification and gender in Aboriginal Australia. In: Mark Harvey and Nicholas Reid (eds), *Nominal Classification in Aboriginal Australia*. Amsterdam: Benjamins, 17–62.

HeiDeas. You say feminine, I say masculine, let's call the whole thing off. (Crosspost from LL) (<http://heideas.blogspot.com.au> webarchive, accessed February 2008).

Hetzron, Robert. 1990. Hebrew. In Bernard Comrie (ed.), *The World's Major Languages*. Oxford: Oxford University Press, 686–704.

Kaye, Alan S. 1990. Arabic. In Bernard Comrie (ed.), *The World's Major Languages*. Oxford: Oxford University Press, 664–85.

Lakoff, George. 1987. *Women, Fire and Dangerous Things: What Categories Reveal about the Mind*. Chicago: University of Chicago.

Leeding, Velma J. 1989. *Anindilyakwa Phonology and Morphology*. University of Sydney, PhD diss.

Le Robert Pour Tous. 1994. Paris: Dictionnaires Le Robert.

Löbel, Elizabeth. 2000. Classifiers in Vietnamese. In: Barbara Unterbeck, Matti Rissanen, Tertu Navalainen and Mirja Saari (eds), *Gender in Grammar and Cognition*. Berlin: Mouton de Gruyter, 259–76.

Mel'čuk, Igor A. 1974. Statistics and the relationship between gender of French nouns and their endings. In V. J. Rozencveigh (ed.), *Essays on Lexical Semantics: Volume I*. Stockholm: Skriptor: 11–42.

Surridge, Marie E. 1993. Gender assignment in French: the hierarchy of rules and the chronology of acquisition. *International Review of Applied Linguistics* 30 (1–2): 77–95.

Surridge, Marie E. 1995 *Le ou La? The Gender of French Nouns*. Clevedon: Multilingual Matters.

Tucker, G. Richard, Lambert, Wallace E. and Rigault, André (eds). 1977. *The French Speaker's Skill with Grammatical Gender: An Example of Rule-Governed Behavior*. The Hague: Mouton.

Walsh, Michael. 1993. Classifying the World in an Aboriginal Language. In: Michael Walsh and Collin Yallop (eds), *Language and Culture in Aboriginal Australia*. Canberra: Aboriginal Studies Press: 107–22.

Zubin, David A. and Köpcke, K.-M. 1986. Gender and folk taxonomy: The indexical relation between grammatical and lexical categorization. In: Colette Craig (ed.), *Noun Classes and Categorization: Proceedings of a Symposion on Categorization and Noun Classification, Eugene, Oregon, October 1983*. Amsterdam: John Benjamins: 139–80.

Chapter 5

TRENDY NEW TRENDS IN WINE TERMINOLOGY

Adrienne Lehrer

University of Arizona

New wine descriptors have been appearing in recent years, along with new wines, new wineries, new wine publications, and greater interest in wine and talking about wine. When I first began my research on wine descriptors in 1973, there were several hundred common descriptors including many metaphors, but the number and type of wine words has increased, and the nature of talking and writing about wine has become more colorful (for some people, more outrageous), and new sets of metaphors have emerged. Technically, these are not new words at all but rather new uses of old words that have not historically been employed as wine descriptors, such as *muscular* and *aggressive*.

My conjecture is that wine writers have been responsible for generating most new descriptors in the past several decades. Although there were many books about wine, a few of which included a glossary of terms, and food magazines typically have a wine columnist, the growth of specific monthly wine magazines such as *The Wine Spectator*, *The Wine Enthusiast*, *The Wine Advocate*, as well as many local and regional newsletters on the topic appeared later. These journals have articles on a large number of wines specific to a type (dry reds, sweet dessert wines), a varietal (Cabernet Sauvignon, Zinfandel), a region (Spain, Napa Valley), or a good wine to serve with paella. Since the descriptions for each category are likely to overlap in their taste, smell, and feel, the wine descriptions could be repetitious. However, wine writers are not just interested in wine but also in good writing. It is boring the read similar descriptions over and over and equally boring to write them. Therefore, writers use the resources of the language to find interesting ways of saying the same thing.

1. Semantic concepts

The semantic concepts that I will use the most are those of *semantic fields* and *frames* (Allan 1986, 2001; Cruse 1986, 1992; Lehrer 1983, 1992, 2009; Lyons 1963, 1977). The most important lexical relations in the field are *synonymy*, *antonymy*, *hyponymy*, and *class inclusion*. In addition, we need to use the vaguer notion of *association*. Fields and frames are necessary for understanding some of the new metaphors, since more often than not, new word senses come in semantically related groups. (Kittay and Lehrer 1981; Kittay 1987; Lehrer 1983, 2009). Although synonyms are words with the 'same' meaning, many writers on language show that they are rarely substitutable in all contexts. We will see this clearly in observing synonyms among the wine descriptors. Antonyms and other types of oppositions are similarly restricted in the wine field (Murphy 2003; Lehrer 2009; Lyons 1963, 1977). Among the conventional wine words there is a scalar opposition between *sweet* and *dry*, but this opposition is found mainly for describing wine and other alcoholic beverages. More commonly, the opposite of *dry* is *wet*.

2. Wine descriptors

2.1. A brief review of wine description categories

Wine descriptions often use explicit categories for describing and evaluating wines, especially in formal settings such as classes on wine or wine judging. Writers for wine magazines assume acquaintance with all these categories although their descriptions will contain other relevant and non-obvious observations. The task of tasting and describing is largely analytic, where appearance, smell (*nose*), taste, and mouthfeel are separated (Amerine et al. 1965). In addition, most categories have some words that are affectively positive or negative, but some are neutral.

The following categories are the most common, and I supply only a couple of examples. The lexical structure of many categories is that of gradable antonymy.

- appearance: *clarity, color*;
- sweetness: *sweet* vs. *dry*;
- acidity: *sour, tart, lively, zestful, flat, flabby*;
- astringency (from tannin): *hard, harsh, puckery, soft, smooth*;
- age: *old, young, ripe, green*;
- body: *heavy, full-bodied, light, thin, watery*;
- smell (aroma and bouquet – most descriptors are based on nouns): *fruity, flowery, cherry, apple, chocolate*;
- evaluation: *complex, elegant, clean, insipid*;[1]

---

[1] Many of the wine words contain both a descriptive and evaluative component. For example, a sour wine is undesirable, while a tart wine is not, although *tart* can be glossed as 'a little sour'.

- temporal (beginning, middle, and end of the sensation): *attack, lingering*;
- spatial (the part of the tongue most affected): *frontal*.

Some of the dimensions are more complex in that they involve several categories:

- balance (proportions of sweetness, acid, and astringency): *harmonious, unbalanced*;
- complexity ('a desirability of many flavors along with depth, intensity, and balance', Steiman 2000): *complex, simple*.

Several of these categories have acquired many new descriptors, and I will contrast the early ones (mostly before the 1970s) with later ones. The first is *body*. The word *body* is a dead metaphor, and in wine it relates to sugars, acids, tannins, esters, and other dissolved things. Heavy or full-bodied wines have a lot of these, and light wines have fewer. Table 1 shows the older words and Table 2 some of the newer ones (Lehrer 2009).[2]

Table 1. Old words for body (before 1970) (Lehrer 2009).

Too little					Too much
Negative		Positive			Negative
		heavy		light	
coarse	strong	fully-bodied		delicate	thin
	chewy	big	rich	fragile	watery
		fat	deep		weak
		thick	powerful		small
		solid	forceful		flabby
		round	sturdy		little
		hearty	meaty		meager

Big appears in the earlier list as a synonym for *heavy* and *full-bodied*, as do *meaty* and *fat*. This relationship is only an association since big things tend to

---

[2] Page numbers for material from *Wine and Conversation* (1983) and which has been repeated in the second edition are from the second edition (2009). The early version is no longer in print.

be heavy. However, this association is not a law of nature, and we can think of many counter-examples. The newer body words take the notion of body more seriously, using words from the 'literal' sense of body, particularly the human body. Since *meaty* was already in use, the jump to *beefy* seems simple. Other words for 'heavy' (*big-boned, broad-shouldered, muscular, chunky*, and *stout*) are used as synonyms for *heavy* and *big*. The words in the 'heavy' column are not synonyms in the field of anatomy, since a person can be muscular without being big-boned or broad shouldered, but in the wine field, the differences are neutralized. Wine writers may disagree and insist that there are differences, though subtle among the words. But my speculation is that if experiments were carried out, where speakers were given 4 or 5 different heavy wines, all distinguishable, experts would not agree on which one was the most muscular, the most big-boned, the most broad shouldered, or the chunkiest. Another possibility is that each taster might have some individual consistency in applying these words to wine, but that there would be no general consensus. This is an empirical matter and I would be delighted if someone carried out the research.

Table 2. Newer words for body (Lehrer 2009: 34).

heavy	light
fleshy	lean
muscular	sleek
big boned	svelte
broad shouldered	
stout	
chunky	
beefy	
sinewy	

There are fewer new words on the light side. The ones I found are *lean, svelte*, an*d sleek*. These three also appear to be synonyms, where differences in meaning for bodies are neutralized. All of the new words in both columns are positive or neutral.

One influence for using the new words may be the popularity of fitness and sports. In any case, we see the role of semantic fields in metaphor and semantic extension. If a word in a field (human body type) is transferred to another field (wine mouthfeel), other words from the *donor* field are likely to be transferred as well. (Kittay and Lehrer 1992).

Another category of wine descriptors that has acquired a new set of words is that for balance. The basic lexical items for balance include two sets of antonyms: *balanced, harmonious* vs. *unbalanced, unharmonious*. Hyponyms for the negative terms could specify the problem, such as *sour, acidic* for too much acid or *cloying* for too much sugar. Table 3 presents the new sets of antonyms.

Table 3. New words for balance (Lehrer 2009: 35).

Positive	Negative
integrated	disjointed
focused	unfocused
well-defined	diffuse
formed	muddled
assembled	uncoordinated

Wines that are integrated are 'bound together harmoniously' (Asher 1974: 52). 'Wines that are focused have flavors that integrate. Also the scents, aromas, and flavors are precise and clearly delineated' (Parker 1998: 1403). In Table 3, the reader should treat all the words in each column as synonymous and each column as antonymous. Although *focused* and *unfocused* are clearly antonyms by virtue of their morphology, the other items listed could easily be rearranged.

Another category in which there has been an influx of new meanings for old words is one that I call *accessibility*. It concerns how easy or difficult it is to decide on the quality of the wine. Table 4 provides this vocabulary.

Table 4. Accessibility of flavor (Lehrer 2009: 37).

Wines that give out their flavor readily		Wines that hold back
assertive	generous	shy
bold	up-front	sly
sassy	approachable	reticent
brash	(straight)forward	
in-your-face		

Some of the words in Table 4 were used fairly early, such as *forward*. In addition, words taken from the semantic field of human personality were also used, for example, *masculine* and *feminine*, although these last two items are seldom used now. The terms in the right-hand column describes wines where on the first sniff and taste one knows immediately what the wine is like. Words in the second column refer to wines that also present their characteristics, but less strongly. The items in the last (right-hand) column are for wines whose properties are subtle. One needs to taste and smell the wine over many sips (sometime to the end of the bottle) is determine its properties.

All of the terms in Table 4 are positive. The word *mean*, a negative expression, has a sense of *stingy*. Since many of the items in Table 4 are not defined in any glossary, some wine writers who use them may have alternative interpretations.

The category of age, *old* vs. *young* has two parameters: 1) absolute age – the number of years since the wine was made and/or bottled; and 2) how ready-to-drink the wine is. The latter depends on the type of wine, the method of vinification, the carefulness of storage, and the preference of the taster. Some people prefer wines with a lot of acid and tannin, others do not. Table 5 presents the old words for age and Table 6 gives the newer ones.

Table 5. Old words for age (Lehrer 1983).

Too young				Too old
Negative	Positive			Negative
	young	old		
green	fresh	mature	rich	withered, dead
unripe		ripe	deep	dying, decrepit
immature		mellow	powerful	senile
		developed	forceful	small
		aged		flabby

Young and *old* are generally neutral, although in certain contexts they could be negative. The leading metaphors deal with life cycles of people and plants.

The newer words may use these, too. *Open* and *closed* could refer to flowers, or maybe doors, with an open door welcoming the drinker and a closed one barring her. *Forward*, *backward*, and *precocious* suggest human development, especially *precocious*, which suggests a wine that is ready before expected. *Dumb* has the sense of 'mute', not 'stupid', which for Parker is a negative term. 'Closed wines may need time to reveal their richness; dumb wines may never be better' (1998: 1430). A new image is that of a coil, tightly wound and in need of becoming looser over time.

Table 6. New words for age (Lehrer 2009).

Ready-to-drink	Not yet ready
open	closed
backward	backward
precocious	dumb
	tight, tightly wound, coiled

2.2 Olfaction

Sean Shesgreen (2003) notes that when the famous wine writer Frank Schoolmaker died in 1976, the language of wine descriptions changed from that of class and gender (*breed, noble, character, masculine, feminine*) to the language of fruits and vegetables. He makes fun of a description in *Wines and Spirits* 1998 as 'a garden of southern Italian flavors, from sun-baked black plums and fresh fuzzy figs to almonds, fennel, and cherries; crisp, lemon-link acidity provides the freshness of a sea breeze.'

Another influence may have been Robert M. Parker's popularity, whose descriptions refer to smells rather than tastes (McCoy 2005). William Langewiesche (2000) describes Parker as having a 'million dollar nose' for his ability to notice, remember, and re-identify the aromas of wines. Technically, *aroma* applies to the smell of the grape and *bouquet* to the vinification. However, Steiman (2000: 224) in his wine glossary says that they are used interchangeably nowadays. Although there are only five basic tastes: *sweet, sour, bitter, salty* and *umami* (often translated from Japanese as 'savory'), humans can distinguish thousands of smells, and in fact our sensation of taste is highly influenced by smell. Therefore, it figures that those who describe wines will focus on those aromas. Almost all expressions in English and probably in other languages as well describe smells in terms of some object that produces that smell. These are either nouns or adjectives derived from nouns: *fruity, cherry, cherry-like, stony, skunky, grass, weedy*.

Noble and her colleagues (1990) have constructed wheels to classify terms used in wine descriptions, with a taxonomy of three levels. The most popular wheel is for still wines, and there is another wheel for sparkling wines, with considerable overlap.

English vocabulary that denotes smells in general are shown in Table 7.

Table 7. General words for smell.

Positive		Negative
scent	smell, odor	stink
fragrance		stench
aroma		

When *smell* and *odor* are unmodified, their connotations are negative, but adjectives with pleasant associations cancels this implicature; as *a lovely apple odor, that delightful sweet smell*.

Novices may wonder how they can learn to discern these smells. One way is to take classes where samples of wine with certain aromas and bouquets are present as samples to learn from. Another option is to try to learn some of these on one's own. Noble et al. (1987) explain that one can learn what a cherry smell (and taste) in wine is by taking 10 milliliters of brine from canned cherries in 25 milliliters of red wine. For mint, one crushed mint leaf or one drop of mint extract in 25 milliliters of red or white wine provides a good sample. The wines should have a neutral flavor so as not to overpower the cherry or mint or other smell to be noticed. Some of the smells are not of food at all, but yet they appear in wine descriptions, such as *cedar* or *rubbery*. For cedar, add one drop of cedar oil or a few shavings of cedar wood to 25 milliliters of red wine; for a rubbery smell, use a 1 x 10mm x 5 mm piece of rubber tubing or bike tire in 25 milliliters of red or white wine. Let it sit for several hours. There are also commercial sensory kits available.

Wine writers presumably expect their readers to have the sensory ability and the experience to discern and identify the properties of the wines being described. However, after a presentation of *Wine and Conversation* (2nd ed., 2009) at a bookstore shortly after the book appeared, a young man approached me afterwards who said that he wrote for a local wine newsletter. He told me that wine writers often just make up these descriptions. He once described a wine as having a quince aroma, knowing that few of his readers had ever eaten a quince. Moreover, neither had he! But describing wine with a quince smell sounded cool.

WineSpeak (2009) by Bernard Klem is 'vinous thesaurus of (gasp) 36,975 bizarre, erotic, funny, outrageous, poetic, silly, and ugly wine tasting descriptors'. All items are attested in the wine literature.[3] The category of smell (nose) has 14 categories, which include the expected: fruit, flower, vegetable, other food, and wood. Many of the words are purely evaluative, and many would be known to most people, like the smell of a wet dog. But others are expressions that nobody would experience, like *angry octopus*, *decayed wombat*, or *monkey riding a horse bareback* (pp. 112–5). Although the latter expressions evoke a vivid visual image, can it evoke an olfactory one? Moreover, who would have smelled a monkey riding on a horse? My interpretation is that these are negative evaluators and the writer is using a colorful image to express his view that the wine is bad.

2.3. More on evaluation

As we have seen much of the vocabulary deals with likes and dislikes, preferences, and judgments. In my earlier work I listed some of the words which expressed evaluations not connected to other specific properties of wines. Table 8 summarizes those words.

Table 8. Evaluation (Lehrer 2009: 14).

High praise	Low praise	Mildly derogatory	Strongly derogatory
complex	clean	insipid	off
breed	sound	bland	
character	simple	ordinary	
great	refreshing	common	(general terms of disapproval: awful, ghastly, etc.)
fine			
elegant			
finesse			
distinguished			

---

[3] There is duplication in these entries: *light, light as a feather, light as a soufflé, light as chiffon, light as foam, light medium, not light, rather light* and several others receive their own entry (Klem 2009: 124).

Many of the items in Klem's collection are strictly evaluative, especially some of the strongly derogatory ones: *all the subtlety of a chain saw, absolute nightmare, angel of death of hovering overhead* (pp. 1–2).

New words of evaluation appear in Table 9.

Table 9. New words of evaluation (Lehrer 2009: 39).

High praise	Mid praise	Low praise
blockbuster	charming	polite
decadent	intelligent	unpretentious
graceful	intellectual	
agile	polished	
pizzazz	refined	
sculpted	well crafted	
hedonistic		

Decadent is interesting in that it illustrates the use of irony and intended amusement in wine descriptions, as we will see later with the names of wines and wineries. Parker (1998: 1402) uses this word frequently:

> If you are an ice cream and chocolate lover, you know the feeling of eating a huge sundae lavished with hot fudge, real whipped cream, and rich vanilla ice cream. If you are a wine enthusiast, a wine loaded with opulent, even luxurious texture can be said to be decadent.

2.4. Verbs of motion

My initial interest had been in the nouns and adjectives used as wine descriptors. However, there is a temporal aspect as well, since the sensation of taste lasts for several seconds, depending partly on how long one holds the wine in one's mouth and also on the characteristics of the wine itself. The temporal dimension is generally divided into three phases: the foretaste or attack, the mid-palate, and the finish or aftertaste.

Rosario Caballero's detailed analysis of the verbs of motion used in wine descriptions (2007) adds an important aspect to wine vocabulary. Some of the wine descriptions she collected are presented below.

> A racy young wine, with lots of class *starts* slowly on the palate, then *kicks in* with tight and pronouncedly silky tannins. (2100)

Classy Chablis that stands as a monument to the 2000 vintage. So elegant and refined, *powering its way across* the palate with a fireball of intensely concentrated lime, kiwi, pineapple, dried herbs, freshly cut grass and spices. (2102)

[This wine] *bursts from* the glass with violets, lilies, blueberries, cherries, blackberries, and buttery oak. (2102)

Bright and focused, offering delicious blueberry plum and spice flavors that *glide* smoothly *through* the silky finish. (2102)

Wow. A smoky, nutty component *leaps from* the glass, backed by apricot and a beguiling spice and mineral element. (2103)

Distinctive, very monolithic, clean, pure, and crisp, with fresh fruit *zipping along* the palate. (2104)

Caballero analyzes these verbs and connected prepositional phrases in terms of two dimensions: intensity and persistence. Table 10 gives a selection of the verbs in her paper.[4]

Table 10. Verbs of motion in wine writing: Force and persistence.

+ Force	+ Force	+ Force	Neutral	+ Force	– Force
Abrupt	+ Speed			– Speed	– Speed
kick, punch	swirl, run	emerge	go, come	sneak, creep	glide, bob
explode, dip	race, spin	cascade	come along	swim, dance	sail, float
leap, gush	shoot, ride	move	come in	weave	unfurl

+Persistence	– Persistence
sail on, spin, stretch (out), expand, branch out	kick, burst, erupt, punch pop
unfold, unfurl, fan out, glide, go on	tumble, gush, cascade, shoot

---

[4] I have modified Caballero's chart slightly to fit the page.

2.5. Terroir

A loanword from the French has been added to wine descriptions: *terroir*. Many wine experts pronounce it with the strong 'r' of American English, I assume by choice so as not to appear pretentious. There is apparently no exact English equivalent (hence the borrowing). *Terroir* refers to a vineyard's complete growing environment – soil, drainage, altitude, climate, slope of the terrain, and exposure to the sun. For some wine writers there is also something exalted and mystical. For winemaker Randall Grahm, terroir is the soul of the wine, 'the sense of belongingness of coming from somewhere' (2008: 222). Kramer's treatment evokes a similar sense in ineffability. '*Terroir* is everything that contributes to the distinction of a vineyard plot ... but it is more than air, water, draining, sunlight, temperature, precipitation – it is another dimension that cannot be measured, but it is still located and savored' (2008: 225–6).

3. Names of wines and wineries

The names selected for wines and wineries provide another interesting use of language in addition to the wine descriptors. The winery names are proper nouns, but the wine names are not, in spite of the fact that both are capitalized. (See Allan 2001: 85–93.)

The names of wineries are rigid designators (Kripke 1972), which are 'baptized' by those individuals who start and/or finance the enterprise. The name may be trade-marked or otherwise legally protected, and the name may be registered with various agencies, like the government revenue department, the directory department of the telephone company, and probably marketing services. Nowadays, of course, there is an Internet site as well.

The names of wines, even though capitalized, are common nouns. They function grammatically as mass or count (Algeo 1973):

(1) I bought two bottles of Quail's Gate Pinot Noir. They were deliciously decadent.

(2) I bought two Quail's Gate Pinot Noirs. They were deliciously decadent.

One criterion for proper names is that they are not normally preceded by a determiner, nor do they take plurals, but they can be converted into common nouns (Algeo 1973; Allan 2001):

(3) I bought a couple of Quail's Gates yesterday. Boy, are they expensive!

Many wineries have normal kinds of names, such as the name of the original owner; e.g., *Martin Ray, Mondavi, Châteaux Rothschild*, or *Charles Shaw*. Others take the name of the place, such as *Eden Valley, Sonoita Vineyard, Bonny Doon*. Wine names, if they are primarily varietals, take the name of that grape: *Cabernet Sauvignon, Pinot Gris, Zinfandel, Grüner Veltinger*. Sometimes the name of the wine is simply the color: *Red, Rosé, White*.

The labels on bottles of wine contain the names of the winery and the type of wine, of course, but they contain other information as well. They frequently have information on the grape varietals and descriptions of the wines. (All descriptions are favorable.) In addition, they may have pictures, some of which are related to the name of the wine or winery (Tresaco Belío 2010).

The question is: Do these names have meaning? My own view is that 'technically' they do not have meaning, but, they take on the associations connected to the word or words selected (Lehrer 1992). However, many of the new wine and winery names employ words that are taken from the common noun vocabulary, and they typically have nothing to do with wine at all. Yet the names given follow certain patterns which Carroll (1985: 16) calls schemes:

> A rule-scheme differs from a linguistic rule in being less complete, less permanently part of the language, and more discretionary from a speaker's point of view. ... Violating linguistic rules makes speech ungrammatical. In contrast, rule-schemes are relatively flexible; they narrow down the space of possibilities instead of making a single prediction. ... Nevertheless, rule-schemes have structure. People don't mechanically grind out new names, but surely they don't start completely from scratch each time either.

One of the favorite schemes involves animal names. Animal names are not completely new. *Black Swan* from Australia and *Schwartze Katze* from Germany have a long history. Sometimes the labels on bottles of wine include pictures of the animal named, and frequently there is an accompanying adjective, often one that is not especially appropriate to that animal, like *funky* or *arrogant*. Often there is an intended pun, allusion, or joke as well.

3.1. Mammals

- Big Moose (California)
- Dancing Bull Rancho Zabaco Winery (California)

- Grizzly Flat (California)
- Bear Ridge (California)
- Leaping Horse (California)
- Wild Horse (California)
- Stag's Leap (California)[5]
- Three Blind Moose (California; cf. *Three blind mice*)
- White Elephant (California)
- Foxhorn (California; picture of a fox)
- Horse Heaven Vineyard, Chateau St. Michael (Washington State)
- Mad Dogs (Spain)
- Funky Llama (Argentina)
- Goats Do Roam (South Africa; cf. *Côte du Rhone*)
- Goats in the Village (Goats Do Roam Winery)
- Bored Doe (Goats Do Roam Winery; cf. *Bordeaux*)
- Herding Cats (South Africa)
- French Rabbit (France)
- Monkey Bay (New Zealand)
- Kanga Reserve (Australia; picture of a kangaroo)
- Southern Roo (Australia; picture of a kangaroo)

3.2. Birds

- Quail's Gate (British Columbia)
- Burrowing Owl (British Columbia)
- Smoking Loon (California)
- Heron (California)
- Screaming Eagle (California)
- Falcon Ridge (California)
- Night Owl, Delicado Vineyard (California)
- Duck Pond (Oregon)
- Black Swan (Australia)
- Four Emus (Australia)

---

[5] This Cabernet Sauvignon won the famous Paris blind tasting.

- Eagle Hawk (Australia)
- Piping Shrike (Australia)
- Little Penguin (Australia)

3.3. Fish

- King Fish Delicado Vineyard (California)
- Fisheye (California)
- Sockeye (Australia)
- Mad Fish (Australia)
- Blue Fish (Germany)

3.4. Reptiles and amphibians

- Painted Turtle (British Columbia)
- Leaping Lizard (California)
- Frog's Leap (California; the association here is that frogs actually leap, and there may be a reference to Stag's Leap Winery)
- Toad Hollow (California)
- Arrogant Frog (France)

Arrogant Frog has several layers of association. It follows the scheme of an animal name. It also plays on the homonymy of *frog* as a derogatory name for French people, and its modifier *arrogant* reflects a negative stereotype of the French as arrogant. Since the wine is made is France, its self-deprecation is acceptable, whereas if this name were used by a wine-makers in any other county, it would be considered outrageously rude. I have been told that wine with this name is not sold in France.

3.5. Animal names in other languages

- Abrazo del Toro (Spain)
- Gato Negro (Argentina)
- Zarafa 'giraffe' (South Africa)
- Schwarze Katze (Germany)
- Chien Lunatique (California!)
- Paloma (California)

3.6. Other names with pictures of animals

- Château La Paws, Côte de Bone (California; picture of a bone)
- Fat Bastard (France; picture of a sitting hippopotamus)
- Flourish (New York State; pictures of a butterfly, different one for each variety), Belhurst Winery
- Toasted Head, RH Philips Wine Co (California; picture of a standing bear breathing fire)
- Singleback Shiraz (Australia; picture of a platypus)
- Yellowtail (Australia; picture of a wallaby. Although the most salient association of *yellowtail* is the fish, it might refer to the yellow-footed rock-wallaby, which has a yellow striped tail – en.wikipedia.org).

3.7. Plants

Besides animals, there is a scheme using plants:

- Blossom (British Columbia)
- Twisted Tree (British Columbia)
- Arrowleaf (British Columbia)
- Turning Leaf Vineyards E & J Gallo (California)
- Timberwood Vineyards E & J Gallo (California)
- Acacia (California)
- Sageland (Washington State)
- Thistle Wine (North Carolina)
- Silver Birch (New Zealand)
- Tall Poppy (Australia)

3.8. Other funny or unusual names for wine or wineries

- See YU Later Ranch, Hawthorn Mountain (British Columbia)
- Laughing Stock Vineyards (British Columbia)
- Therapy Vineyards, British Columbia: Freudian Sip (Cabernet), Alter Ego (blend of 4 white varietals), Pink Freud (Rosé; cf. *Pink Floyd*)
- Red Car Boxcar (California)
- Mi Sueño, Au Bon Climat (California)

- Critique of Pure Riesling, Bonny Doon Vineyards (California; *Critique of Pure Reason* by Immanuel Kant)
- Stargalaxy (California)
- Cardinal Zin, Bonny Doon Vineyards (California)
- 7 Deadly Zins, Michael and David Vineyards (California)
- Black Opal (Australia)
- Devil's Marbles (Australia)
- Two Left Feet, Mollydooker (Australia)
- Bicyclette (France)
- Tempra Tantrum (Spain; from Tempranillo grapes)
- Xplorador (Chile)

3.9. Discussion

The winemaker of *Critique of Pure Riesling*, Randall Grahm, studied philosophy at the University of California at Santa Cruz. There are probably personal and cultural associations of other wine and winery names of which I am not aware. For example, *Tall Poppy* from Australia calls up a set of associations.[6]

Although certain naming schemas have been identified, how do we account for the relationship between the meaning, connotation, and associations of the word and its selection as the name of a wine or winery? My earlier work on names looked at names for pets, automobile makes and models, rock bands, beauty salons, and streets as well as personal names. Automobiles names can be taken from animals associated with speed, strength, and agility (*Impala, Lark, Gazelle, Mustang, Cougar*) or place names with elegant and exotic references (*Malibu, Biarritz, Riviera, Windsor, Monte Carlo, Versailles*), and astronomical objects (*Comet, Meteor, Mercury, Galaxy*), items which suggest distance and travel. As Allan (2001: 92) remarks, names like *pigeon* would not be likely. The Volkswagen *Rabbit* was popular in the US, but this name was not used in Australia because rabbits there are considered a nuisance and have a bad connotation. Beauty salons employ puns and other forms of wit (*Swirl and Curl, Scissor Wizards, Mane Street Hair Stylists, A Head of our Time, Hair it is,* and *Curl Up and Dye*). In general they all have something to do with hair.

---

[6] Check out 'tall poppy syndrome' on the internet for a number of articles.

In white water rafting, major rapids are sometimes named with a word associated with the phenomenon: *The Pourover, Toilet Bowl, Lost Paddle, Iron Rug* (on the Gauley River in West Virginia), *The Chutes, Maytag, Great Falls, Cascades* (on the various rivers), and others I have heard are *Egg-beater* and *Whirlpool*.

But why should wines and wineries by named after animals and plants? In some cases the name may reflect some striking animal or plant in the location of the winery and pictures on the label show the fauna and flora of the region. In some obvious cases the animal is native to the country, such as *Black Swan* and *Emu* in Australian or *Llama* in Argentina (although other South American countries have llamas, too).

Perhaps a better model is the that of rock bands, some of whose names are especially interesting because many of them are outrageous, boarding on poor taste, referring to topic like death (*Grateful Dead, The Stranglers, Megadeath, Suicidal Tendencies*), dangerous animals (*Great White, King Cobra, Scorpions*), and weapons (*Guns N' Roses, B-52s, Sex Pistols*). What these names do, especially the last category, is call attention to themselves. (Lehrer 1992).

I speculate that wine and winery names are selected to do precisely that – to call attention to themselves. In a globalized world where a large wine shop carries hundred of wines, with new ones arriving frequently, a catchy name with an attractive picture on the label, is intended to get the attention of wine shoppers with the hope they will try it. There are certainly other factors as well. When *Yellowtail* from Australia was introduced into the American wine market, because of its value, a good wine for a reasonable price, it soon became popular. This fact may have encouraged other wineries to select animal names, too. Since this is an empirical question, one would have to contact the individuals who chose the names and interview them.

4. What else is like wine descriptions?

Lots of things. As it turns out, we find similar phenomena in describing other beverages, such as beer, coffee, and tea. Some beer descriptions are taken from Asimov (2006):

(4)   Dry, refreshing and tangy; espresso and mineral flavors.

(5)   Well balanced and assertive; not at all smoky...

(6)   Light-bodied and fresh; subtle, lingering flavors of coffee and chocolate.

(7) Big and rich with a pleasing texture and potent aromas of coffee and licorice.

There are terms like *hoppy* and *malty*, not used for wine, but the examples above could describe wines. For coffee I have found the following from an internet distributor www.cofferevier.com:

(8) Heavy-bodied, with mild acidities, bold flavor with spice aromas
(9) Bright and winey with hints of wild berries
(10) Lively shine with spicy chocolate undertones
(11) Rich flavor and a buttery smooth aftertaste
(12) Soft, mild with strong blueberry tones... sweet floral fragrance

Even the term *terroir* is used.
For tea from the Republic of Tea website:

(13) Concentrated character reminiscent of the depth and clarity of a fine Bordeaux.
(14) Complex, yet invigorating with a clean slightly flowery finish.
(15) Earthy aroma and a nutty roasted flavor that is robust yet subtle.
(16) A full-bodied, brisk, malty, very typical Irish brew with a dark potent character.

The last description might very well be a beer description. So we see that wines can have the taste of coffee, coffee can be winey, and tea can be beer-like. In fact, some descriptions could be for any of the above beverages, wine, beer, coffee, or tea:

(17) A sip begins with an elegant floral aroma and lemony flourish and finishes with a satisfying dark cocoa flavor.

The most reasonable guess would be a chocolate drink with a squeeze of lemon. However, this description is for Starbuck's Casi Cielo Coffee from Guatemala.

One finds descriptions of many foods and beverages in advertising and marketing for everything from tomatoes and cheeses to chocolate. And similarly the language for describing music, art, and even people has its own descriptors, many of which are borrowed from other sensory domains. We talk of *sweet* music, and *sweet*, *bitter*, and *sour* people (Lehrer 2009: 247–50). Although there are apparently some individuals who have synaesthetic abilities, I believe that as least some of these metaphorical transfers can be analyzed in terms of transferred semantic fields that retain (perhaps loosely) their lexical-semantic relationship along with other even looser associations.

There is every reason to expect new metaphors for the description of wine and other sensory experiences to be produced. The extension of word meaning shows the creativity of speakers and writers. For the receiver it may provide new ways of experiencing the wine, and it probably tickles one's fancy to hear these new expressions. And finally it is a wonderful new stimulus for parodies, jokes and cartoons.

References

Algeo, John. 1973. *On Defining the Proper Name*. Gainesville, FL: University of Florida Press.
Allan, Keith. 1986. *Linguistic Meaning*. London: Routledge and Kegan Paul.
Allan, Keith. 2001. *Natural Language Semantics*. Oxford and Malden, MA: Blackwell Publishers.
Amerine, Maynard and V.I. Singleton. 1965. *Wine: An Introduction for Americans*. Berkeley: University of California.
Asher, Gerald. 1974. Wine journal. *Gourmet* 34–5; 12–4, 52.
Asimov, Eric. 2006. A journey to the dark side. *New York Times*, 18 October, p. 18.
Caballero, Rosario. 2007. Manner-of-motion verbs in wine description. *Journal of Pragmatics* 39 (12): 2095–114.
Carroll, John M. 1985. *What's in a Name?* New York: Freeman.
Cruse, D. Alan. 1986. *Lexical Semantics*. Cambridge: Cambridge University.
Cruse, D. Alan. 1992. Antonymy revisited: Some thoughts on the relationship between words and concepts. In Adrienne Lehrer and Eva F. Kittay (eds), *Frames, Fields, and Contrasts*. Hillsdale, NJ: Lawrence Erlbaum, 289–306.
Grahm, Randall 2008. The soul of wine: Digging for meaning. In Fritz Allhof (ed.), *Wine and Philosophy*. Malden, MA: Wiley-Blackwell, 219–24.
Kittay, Eva F. 1987. *Metaphor: Its Cognitive Force and Linguistic Structure*. Oxford: Clarendon.
Kittay, Eva F. and Adrienne Lehrer. 1981. Semantic fields and the structure of metaphor. *Studies in Language* 5: 31–63.
Kittay, Eva F. and Adrienne Lehrer. 1992. *Frames, Fields, and Contrasts*. Hillsdale, NJ: Lawrence Erlbaum.
Klem, Bernard. 2009. *WineSpeak*. Stamford, CT: Winespeak Press.
Kramer, Matt. 2008. The notion of *terroir*. In Fritz Allhof (ed.), *Wine and Philosophy*. Malden, MA: Wiley-Blackwell, 225–34.
Kripke, Sol. 1972. Naming and necessity. In Donald Davidson and Gil Harman (eds), *Semantics for Natural Language*. Dordrecht: Reidel.

Langewiesche, William. 2000. Million-dollar nose: Wine critic Robert Parker, Jr. *Atlantic Monthly* 283: 42046–8.

Lehrer, Adrienne. 1983. *Wine and Conversation*. Bloomington, IN: University of Indiana Press.

Lehrer, Adrienne. 1992. Names and naming. In Adrienne Lehrer and Eva F. Kittay (eds), *Frames, Fields, and Contrasts*. Hillsdale, NJ: Lawrence Erlbaum, 123–43.

Lehrer, Adrienne. 2009. *Wine and Conversation*. 2nd edition. Oxford and New York: Oxford University Press.

Lyons, John. 1963. *Structural Semantics*. Oxford: Blackwell.

Lyons, John. 1977. *Semantics*. Cambridge: Cambridge University Press.

McCoy, Elin. 2005. *The Emperor of Wine: The Rise of Robert M. Parker, Jr. and the Reign of American Taste*. New York: Harper-Collins

Murphy, M. Lynn. 2003. *Semantic Relations and the Lexicon.* Cambridge: Cambridge University Press.

Noble, Ann C. 1990. The Wine Aroma Wheel. Davis, CA.

Noble, Ann C. et al. 1987. Progress toward a standardized system of wine aroma terminology. *American Journal of Viticulture and Enology* 35 (2): 107–9.

Parker, Robert M. Jr. 1998. *Bordeaux: A Comprehensive Guide*. New York: Simon & Schuster.

Shesgreen, Sean. 2003. Wet dogs and gushing oranges: Winespeak for a new millennium. *Chronicle of Higher Education* March 7, 2003.

Steiman, Harvey. 2000. *The Wine Spectator's Essentials of Wine*. New York: M. Shanken Communication.

Tresaco Belio, Maria Pilar. 2010. El lenguaje de las contraetiquetas (Rioja y Somotano). In Margarita Goded Rambaud and Alfedo Poves Luelmo (eds), *Proceedings of the First International Workshop on Linguistic Approaches to Food and Wine Description*. Madrid: UNED.

Chapter 6

SEMANTIC PROSODY OF HYPERBOLIC ADVERBIAL COLLOCATIONS

AN EMPIRICAL, CORPUS-BASED STUDY

József Andor
University of Pécs

Traditionally defined as a trope or figure of thought, hyperbole was a term used in rhetorics, stylistics, or semantics to express some kind of exaggeration in discourse. This paper provides an investigation of hyperbolic function at the semantics–pragmatics interface via providing empirical evidence on the intensifier function and delexicalization, and the non-compositional nature of four hyperbolic degree adverbs: *inconceivably, incredibly, unbelievably* and *unthinkably*. Following the critical evaluation of the definition of their senses represented in various learner's dictionaries of English, the study provides empirically relevant insight into the expressed hyperbolic, degree function of these adverbs via observing the nature of their potential polarity and semantic prosody, based on corpus-based data and native speaker testing of intuitive judgment using subjects representing three major regional varieties of English: British English, Irish English and American English. Results of the corpus-based investigation and native speaker testing are used as a control to enhance the empirically viable validity of the observations.

1. Introduction

The history of the linguistic term 'hyperbole' dates back to the times of the classic rhetorics of ancient Greece and Rome. It originates from compounding two lexical items in their literal sense: *over* or *beyond*, and *throw* or *cast*. Traditionally in Greek rhetorics it was used as a cover term, classified as a trope or figure of thought related to expressions of exaggeration, overstatement or understatement used in discoursal acts. In the history of the theory of linguistic thought, the character and scope of the term has been discussed primarily on semantic grounds, but was also interpreted syntactically, morphosyntactically and pragmatically. Although of these major levels of linguistic representation the last one, namely pragmatics, is considered to be the youngest to be analysed on more or less theoretical grounds, principally since the first decades of the 20th century, it is exactly ancient rhetorics where the roots, origins of linguistic pragmatics can be traced (Allan 2010: 82). Semanticists were deeply interested in studying the nature of deviation from truth and linguistics, as well as conceptual credibility embodied in and formulated by lexical expressions of hyperbole. Theoreticians of the field, however, failed to measure or even to recognize their gradability in discourse. As pointed out by Nemesi (2010: 383) in his seminal study, already as early as the 1st century AD, the great Roman orator Quintilian identified two basic functions of hyperbolic expressions: verbalization of amplification and attenuation. Let me add that in discussing the rhetorical status of hyperbole in his monumental study titled *Institutio Oratoria*, Quintilian stressed the critically important functional role of the linguistic phenomenon aiming to express a high degree of load of emotional content and lacking any degree of intentionally expressed deception, misleading or lying. He also expressed the communicative importance of discursive overstatement rather than understatement in case the speaker was not in a position to verbalise his idea with adequate realistic precision, truthfulness (2008: 560–2). Aims of this type clearly formulate pragmatic rather than semantic requirements of discursive representation.

A further question, which still requires in-depth investigation, is the unconscious versus conscious and intentional usage of hyperbolic expressions in the misrepresentation of truth during communication, violating Grice's maxims of truthfulness (Gibbs 1994: 391–4). Nemesi (2010) correctly points to the scalar nature of hyperbolic expressions in usage and investigates productive as well as receptive aspects of its measurement. Accepting this standpoint, I would like to stress that the lexical representation of hyperbole usually manifests cases of delexicalization of original lexical meaning, development in the direction of the non-compositionality of morphological representation frequently with the emergence of the expression of intensification, degree and evaluative potential in lexical usage, and simultaneous manifestation of scalarity and gradability of the arising lexical formulae. As such, I believe, its occurrence in spoken discourse is spontaneous; its emotional load and gradience are high; and its intentionality and conscious usage principally depend on discursive perspectivization and contextual schematic factors. Measuring the role and degree of such factors, however, requires further investigation in researching interactive discourse. A novelty of Nemesi's study is his bias toward speaker-oriented investigations, wherein he outlines the framework of a highly relevant research programme concerning identifying the reasons of using hyperbolic expressions rather than other alternatives in discourse, investigation of aspects of frequency of occurrence, factors of consciousness in usage, and genre related dependence (p. 388). It was pointed out by Norrick (1982, 2004) that hyperbolic expression was extensively used in all the major word classes of lexical density and that its occurrence in textual representation was highly genre specific. In her dissertation Cano Mora (2012), analysing the genre relatedness of hyperbolic expression, offered a speech act related, corpus-based, functional investigation. Allan (2001: 127, 165) treats hyperbole as acts of overstatement, providing the grounds towards a speect act oriented analysis. Leech (1983: 146) highlights the pragmatic force of hyperbolic expression by pointing to its high rate of frequency of occurrence in everyday language. McCarthy and Carter (2004: 151) refer to the fossilization, the high degree of conventionalization of hyperbolic expressions preventing their strict recognition, discursive decomposition as a means of expression of purposeful exaggeration in the thread of discourse on the part of the hearer. For instance, the lexical item *really* has a high potential to express intensification, losing its strict literal meaning in utterance formulation and interpretation. Beyond amplifying the force of adjectival meaning shown by (1a), it can also amplify the degree of intensification expressed by other degree adverbs, such as that of *very*, and also that of the adjectival construction in which *very* occurs, as exemplified by (1b).

(1) (a) Oh, that is really interesting!

(b) Oh, that is really very/greatly/extremely interesting.

In her corpus-based analyses of various types of hyperbole presented in her recent monograph, Claudia Claridge (2011: 48–9) points to the predominance of single-word hyperbolic expressions concerning frequency of occurrence, and, within that type, to the high rate of occurrence of hyperbolic nouns and adjectives. Most of her examples are taken from the spoken section of the British National Corpus. She highlights the fact that hyperbolic expressions are gradable and that they express a magnifying or minimizing, intensifying role in their pragmatic force of usage and as such, she stresses the close connection between the notion of hyperbolic usage and vagueness (pp. 5, 9, 51). Presenting statistically relevant data of corpus-based analysis at the semantics/pragmatics interface, she points to the significantly dominant hyperbolic meaning of adjectives such as *incredible* in opposition to their original literal understanding. She stresses that pragmatically based scales in hyperbolic representation are strictly grounded in their linguistic structure, but these are expressed via speaker assumptions and expectations originating from world, i.e., encyclopaedic knowledge (p. 8). She notes, I believe correctly (referring to Allan 1992), that it is exactly during the interaction of lexical and encyclopaedic types of information available to the speaker/hearer that 'the boundary between semantics and pragmatics becomes blurred' (p. 27). In her view, hyperbole is both semantic and pragmatic in nature. On page 37 of her monograph she notes that

> [n]o matter how the transferred meaning is arrived at, it will carry an evaluative or, more generally, attitudinal/emotional component. This makes overstatement one of the means for subjectivity in language. The transmission of this subjective meaning is the ultimate reason why hyperbole is used in the first place – although the emotional factor need not be either fully intentional or even fully conscious on the part of the speaker nor perceptually very pronounced for the hearer. The more conventional a hyperbolic interpretation is, the weaker will be its emotional impact.

Let me stress, however, that none of the above-mentioned seminal studies investigated the degree of delexicalization or grammaticalization (in terms of Hopper and Trauggot 2003) of the lexical core of hyperbolic expressions, their polar nature, and the extent to which they are related to semantic prosody.[1] The principal aim of the present study is to offer empirical evidence about these issues via native speaker testing and corpus-based data used as a comparative control.

---

[1] As a recent but intensively developing topic in corpus-based lexical semantics, investigations are carried out on identifying, interpreting the nature and measuring the degree of potential polarity of lexical items in their collocative matching and co-occurrence. A comprehensive description of the research program of semantic prosody is presented in Stewart (2010). The term itself was coined and its scope was outlined by Sinclair (1996: 87–8) as the following: 'A semantic prosody is … attitudinal, and on the pragmatic side of the semantics/pragmatics continuum. It is thus capable of a wide range of realisation, because in pragmatic expressions the normal semantic values of the words are not necessarily relevant. But once noticed among the variety of expression, it is immediately clear that the semantic prosody has a leading role to play in the integration of an item with its surroundings. It expresses something close to the "function" of an item – it shows how the rest of the item is to be interpreted functionally.'

It was also clarified and described by Louw (2000: 60) as 'a form of meaning which is established through the proximity of a consistent series of collocates, often characterisable as positive or negative, and whose primary function is the expression of the attitude of its speaker or writer towards some pragmatic situation'.

2. The study

In this research the meaning and frequency of occurrence, the semantic-pragmatic potential and force, and the semantic prosody of four lexical items: *inconceivably, incredibly, unbelievably* and *unthinkably* have been studied. Concerning their morphological structure, all four items are negatively prefixed; thus compositionally, in their literal sense, they should carry a negative meaning. All four are adverbial expressions with a double potential of syntactic functions: they can occur both as non-sentential adverbs modifying adjectival expressions (2a), and they can also have a sentential status referring to the whole of a proposition as in (2b and 2c), the latter function justified by acceptable clausal paraphrases in the form of (2d) and (2e) with the occurrence of a predicative adjective having the same root.

(2)   (a) That was an incredibly important exercise.

        (b) Incredibly, Peter never read fairy tales.

        (c) Peter, incredibly, never read fairy tales.

        (d) Peter, and this was incredible, never read fairy tales.

        (e) It was incredible that Peter never read fairy tales.

In their sentential role and function their meaning is processed literally, whereas their occurrence non-sententially is usually interpreted hyperbolically, functionally representing a degree adverbial status expressing a high grade of pragmatic force based on distinctively subjective stance. This type of difference of function occurring in the syntactic representation of these adverbs clearly provides usage-based evidence in justification of Claridge's (2011: 196–8) observation noted above according to which in single-word representations of hyperbole, delexicalization and grammaticalization resulting in the expression of gradability can be observed not only synchronically but also diachronically, with randomly occurring lexical and morphological gaps. According to her observation, hyperbolic usage developed from the strictly literal, original meaning of the lexical core of the makeup of such expressions. Let me add, furthermore, that in the case of expressions with an original negative polarity of their meaning, a powerful recent tendency can be observed in present day English, a markedly expressed shift of polarity potential from negativity towards positivity, a process which can clearly be traced during corpus-based investigations and analysis of spoken discourse. Observing and documenting this process is one of the chief objectives of the present paper.

2.1. Representation of the meaning of the four hyperbolic expressions in corpus-based learner's dictionaries of English

In order to provide a balanced view, a realistic interpretation of the nature of the definition of the senses of our lexical items observed, recent editions of five standard, desk-size learner's dictionaries have been used (see Table 1). All of them were based on corpora of a very large size: the *Collins COBUILD Advanced Dictionary* (5th edition, 2009) is based on *The Bank of English* corpus of 645 million words (2009: xi), the *Cambridge Advanced Learner's Dictionary*'s (3rd edition, 2008) underlying corpus, the *Cambridge International Corpus (CIC)* is a collection of over 1 billion words, the *Longman Dictionary of Contemporary English* (*LDOCE*, 5th edition) was compiled on the basis of the *Longman Corpus Network* of 450 million words, the *Macmillan English Dictionary for Advanced Learners* (2nd edition) is based on the 200 million words of the *World English Corpus*, and the *Oxford Advanced Learner's Dictionary* (8th edition, 2010) is based on the *British National Corpus (BNC)* of 100 million words as well as the *Oxford English Corpus* of 850 million words.

Table 1. Definitions of the hyperbolic expressions *inconceivably, incredibly, unbelievably* and *unthinkably* as given in five monolingual learner's dictionaries.

inconceivably	*COBUILD*: –, *inconceivable*: If you describe something as *inconceivable*, you think it is very unlikely to happen or be true. Ex.: *It was inconceivable to me that Toby could have been my attacker*. (2009: 800)
	Cambridge: –, *inconceivable*: 1. impossible to imagine or think of. 2. extremely unlikely. *inconceivably*: adverb. (2008: 730)
	LDOCE: –, *inconceivable*: too strange or unusual to be thought real or possible. *inconceivably*: adverb. (2009: 891)
	Macmillan: –, *inconceivable*: 1. impossible to think about or imagine = unimaginable. 2. so unlikely as to be difficult to believe. *inconceivably*: adv. (2007: 766)
	OALD: –, *inconceivable*: impossible to imagine or believe. *inconceivably*: adv. (2010: 788)
incredibly	*COBUILD*: –, *incredible*: 1. If you describe something or someone as *incredible*, you like them very much or are impressed by them, because they are extremely or unusually good. *incredibly*: Ex.: *Their father was incredibly good-looking*. 2. If you say that something is *incredible*, you mean that it is very unusual or surprising, and you cannot believe it is really true, although it may be. *incredibly*: Ex.: *Incredibly, some people don't like the name*. 3. You use *incredible* to emphasize the degree, amount, or intensity of something. *incredibly*: Ex.: *It was incredibly hard work*. (2009: 802)

	Cambridge: 1. used for saying that something is very difficult to believe. Ex.: *Incredibly, no one was hurt in the accident.* 2. extremely. Ex.: *He was incredibly rich/angry/quick.., An inredibly loud bang followed the flash.* (2008: 731)
	LDOCE: *informal* extremely. Ex.: *Nicotine is incredibly addictive.* (2009: 893)
	Macmillan: 1. extremely. Ex.: *It was incredibly difficult to fit everyone in.* 2. used for saying that something is difficult to believe. Ex.: *Incredibly, his wife did not know the truth.* (2007: 767)
	OALD: 1. extremely. Ex.: *incredibly lucky/stupid/difficult/beautiful.* 2. in a way that is very difficult to believe. Ex.: *Incredibly, she had no idea what was going on.* (2010: 789)
unbelievably	*COBUILD*: –, *unbelievable*: 1. If you say that something is *unbelievable*, you are emphasizing that it is very good, impressive, intense, or extreme. *unbelievably*: Ex.: *Our car was still going unbelievably well.*, *He beamed: 'Unbelievably, we have now made it to the final twice.'* 2. You can use *unbelievable* to emphasize that you think something is very bad or shocking. *unbelievably*: Ex.: *What you did was unbelievably stupid.*, *Unbelievably, our Government are planning to close this magnificent institution.* 3. If an idea or statement is *unbelievable*, it seems so unlikely to be true that you cannot believe it. *unbelievably*: Ex.: *Lainey was, unbelievably, pregnant again.* (2009: 1696)
	Cambridge: in a way that is very surprising or difficult to believe. Ex.: *He works unbelievably hard.*, *It was still an unbelievably stupid thing to do.* (2008: 1579)
	LDOCE: –, *unbelievable*: 1. very good, successful, or impressive. 2. very bad or shocking. 3. so extreme that it hardly seems possible. 4. very difficult to believe and therefore probably untrue. *unbelievably*: adv. Ex.: *an unbelievably bad movie.* (2009: 1910)
	Macmillan: –, *unbelievable*: 1. *informal* used for emphasizing how good, bad, impressive etc something is. 2. too unlikely to be true or believed. *unbelievably* adv.: Ex.: *The food was unbelievably cheap.* (2007: 1622)
	OALD: –, *unbelievable*: 1. (*informal*) used to emphasize how good, bad or extreme sth is. 2. very difficult to believe and unlikely to be true. *unbelievably*: adv.: *unbelievably bad/good, Unbelievably it actually works.* (2010: 1674)
unthinkably	*COBUILD*: –, *unthinkable*: 1. If you say that something is *unthinkable*, you are emphasizing that it cannot possibly be accepted or imagined as a possibility. 2. You can use *unthinkable* to describe a situation, event, or action which is extremely unpleasant to imagine or remember. (2009: 1723)

Cambridge: –, *unthinkable*: too shocking or unlikely to be imagined as possible (2008: 1596)
LDOCE: –, *unthinkable*: impossible to accept or imagine. (2009: 1930)
Macmillan: –, *unthinkable*: 1. impossible to imagine. 2. extremely unpleasant or frightening. (2007: 1642)
OALD: –, *unthinkable*: impossible to imagine or to accept. (2010: 1697)

The above dictionary definitions, as we can see, show an extremely varied picture from the point of view of the systematic nature of the representation of the observed lexical items both from the morpho-syntactic and the semantic points of view. In most cases of the lexical items observed, the dictionaries failed to treat the adverbial forms as independent lexical items; they occurred as mere morphological derivatives of their morphologically underlying adjectives only – their meaning and function were left unexplained. However, treating them as such was far from being systematic. Whereas the observation holds for *inconceivably* in the case of all of the five learner's dictionaries studied, it does not hold for *incredibly*, senses of which were described by four of the dictionaries with the exception of *COBUILD*, which dictionary only gave a corpus-based example of the adverb, this way at least acknowledging its existence in the language. However, whereas the other four dictionaries at least noted the lexical status of the adverbial *inconceivably*, there is not even a mention of its existence in *COBUILD*. Concerning *unbelievably*, only *Cambridge* treated it as a separate lexical item to be defined, while the rest of the dictionaries merely listed the presence of the adverbial under the heading of the adjective and gave examples for illustration of its meaning on a random basis. The representation of *unthinkable* is even more interesting. There is simply no mention of the existence of the adverbial by any of the dictionaries observed.

Concerning the syntactic status of the adverbial, no mention is made about the potential double role of fulfilling a sentential or non-sentential function. This kind of syntactic functional difference can at best be traced by studying some of the examples given for illustration. But even there, in the case of *incredibly*, the dictionaries do not agree in the double syntactic potential, and for *unbelievably* only representation of the more conventional non-sentential function can be identified. Due to this random treatment, learners using the dictionaries might not gain the slightest idea about the systematically present double syntactic, sentential vs. non-sentential, status of the adverbs concerned.

The same varied and unsystematic treatment concerns representation of the nature of the senses even in the case of the morphologically dominant adjectives described and their adverbial derivatives where given. The literal versus neutralized, intensifier, degree-based meaning of the items is randomly represented, and in so far as expectably, the ordering of the senses listed is based on commonality of usage, there are radical differences in the ranking of the facets of meaning representation in the dictionaries. For *inconceivably* the five dictionaries agree in giving a quasi-literal facet as the primary meaning with a randomly expressed modal tone. Concerning *incredibly*, the representation of the senses is more varied: *Cambridge* lists the modal character of the literal meaning as primary, whereas the same meaning facet occurs as secondary in *Macmillan*, *COBUILD* and *OALD*. Reference to a degree status is lexicalized as primary in *Macmillan*, *LDOCE* and *OALD*; it occurs as secondary in *Cambridge*, whereas it is represented *expressis verbis* as the tertiary sense in *COBUILD*. Concerning occurrence in style based registers, only *LDOCE* commits itself to representation. For *unbelievably*, *COBUILD* merely offers a literal-based sense representation. The same meaning facet is given as secondary in *Macmillan* and *LDOCE*, and fourth by *Cambridge*. Concerning *unthinkably*, there is complete agreement in the dictionaries to describe the meaning of the item in modal terms. Representation of the polarity potential of the adverbs is also highly varied. It is given no account of by any of the dictionaries for *inconceivably*. Both the positive and negative nature of the items are described or phrased in the examples by *COBUILD*, *OALD* and *Cambridge*, whereas examples given in *Macmillan* and *LDOCE* clearly suggest a negativistic tone of the expression. For *unbelievably*, positive and negative polarity are represented with the exception of *Cambridge*, which gives no account of the polarity of the item. In the case of *unthinkably*, *Macmillan* phrases negative polarity in its description of the second sense of the item, whereas the other four dictionaries give no reference to the expression of polarity at all. All of the dictionaries fail to provide any representation of the nature of semantic prosody of the lexical items. This aspect of meaning and usage can only be inferred by the user by studying the randomly chosen examples. All of the five dictionaries used fail to give any account of the nature of the degree or intensifier status of the adjectives or adverbs where noted. There is not even a single reference to hyperbolicity or even the sense of vagueness expressed as a component of the meaning or a usage-based factor in any of the senses of the lexical items described.

2.2. Investigating the representation of the adjectival collocations of the adverbs and their polarity as well as potential semantic prosody in the British National Corpus

With the aim to provide a more realistic, empirically based investigation of the polarity and consequent semantic prosody of the four hyperbolic adverbs, I studied their collocational occurrence and frequency with adjectives using the British National Corpus of 100 million words. I aimed to trace signs of lexically based salience-related meaning[2] in the constructions observed. Results of the investigation are given in Table 2.

Table 2. The collocational occurrence and frequency with adjectives of the four analysed lexical items using the British National Corpus.

inconceivably	Frequency of occurrence in corpus: 14, adjectival collocates: 9 (64%): *devastating, distant, far, horrible, large, powerful, tiny, vast, wealthy*
incredibly	Frequency of occurrence in corpus: 780, adjectival collocates in a sample of 250 concordances: 190 (76%): *advanced* 2, *aggressive, apologetic, atmospheric, attractive, austere, beautiful* 3, *big, blue, bold* 3, *boring* 4, *brave* 3, *bright, broad, calm, challenging, chatty, clever, clumsy, cold, comfortable, complacent, complex, crowded, dangerous* 2, *daring, deafening, deep, detailed, difficult* 6, *easy, effective, efficient* 2, *emotional, entertaining, erotic, expensive* 2, *fast* 2, *feminine, fit, foolish, friendly, full, funny* 2, *furry, generous* 4, *gentle, good* 3, *good-looking, graceful, handsome, hard* 2, *hard-working, heartening, helpful, high* 3, *high-heeled, homesick, hot, hungry, idiosyncratic, impatient, important* 2, *impractical, incompetent, interesting* 5, *international, kinky, kind* 2, *laborious, large, lazy, light, loud, low* 2, *lucky* 2, *mean, modest, muscled, nice* 2, *pallid, patient, peaceful, polite, powerful* 3, *pretty, productive, quick* 2, *reactive* 2, *real, relieved* 2, *revealing, rich, sad, self-centred, selfish, sensitive, sensual, sexy* 2, *short* 2, *silly, simple* 2, *sloppy* 2, *slow* 2, *small, smooth, soft, sorry, sound, steep, strong* 3, *stupid* 3, *stylish* 2, *successful, superstitious, swift, tall, thick, tedious, tidy, tired* 2, *tough, traumatic, troubled, upset, useful, vicious, wealthy, well written*

---

[2] 'Salience' – as a term used in cognitive, lexical pragmatics and in lexicology – refers to the conceptually based potential matching of lexical items in utterances and discourse. It is a graded notion influenced by degrees of conventionality, standardization, and frequency of occurrence, as pointed out by Giora (2003) in her theoretical model of graded salience. Allan (2012: 168) stresses the role of individual factors, the intuitive bases of conceptually grounded matching relations, those providing relative salience in the structuring of the mental lexicon, emphasizing the role of encyclopedic knowledge from which lexically represented information is saturated via the operation of default filtering mechanisms.

unbelievably	Frequency of occurrence in corpus: 165, adjectival collocates: 105 (63%): *advanced* 4, *alike, arrogant, bald* 4, *beautiful* 2, *boring, brutal* 2, *callous, catchy, charismatic, cheap, chic, churlish, cold* 3, *complex, complicated, cool, desolate, difficult* 5, *disheartened, distant, empty* 2, *excited* 2, *exciting, exultant, fast* 2, *feeble, foolish* 2, *fresh, good* 3, *handsome, hard, hateful, hot* 2, *impressive, intricate* 2, *kind, lazy, light, long* 2, *loud, lucky* 2, *naive, over-exulted, overactive* 2, *painful* 4, *petty, precocious, prim, rough, revolting* 2, *savage, shocking, shoddy, short* 2, *similar* 2, *simple, strong, stupid* 3, *sure, terrible, tight, tough, ugly* 2, *unprofitable, well, well-supported, white*
unthinkably	Frequency of occurrence in corpus: 1, adjectival collocates: 0 (0%)

2.2.1. Observations on the basis of corpus data

It has to be noted, first of all, that the data of frequency of occurrence of adverbial–adjectival collocations show radical differences. The two extremes are the cases of *incredibly* taking the top position in the rank order with the amount of 780 occurrences, and *unthinkably*, taking the last, lacking even a single collocate of this type. The rate of multiple occurrences of lexical items is relatively low, and even in the cases observed the figures are not high. The lists show a great variety of adjectival meanings strikingly lacking a representative amount of directly instigated specific conceptual frame domains or even semantically ordered or lexico-syntactically circumscribable types of adjectival classes. It can be observed by studying the contextual representation of the adjectival collocations listed that – contrary to the representation of literal senses given in dictionary definitions observed and discussed above – the meaning of constructions with adjectival collocates without exception pose the manifestation of hyperbolic representation and inferentially based interpretation on the part of the decoder, which fact clearly refers to conspicuous grades of the delexicalization of the diachronically traceable original meaning of the adverbs studied and the powerful emergence of hyperbolic load of content. For illustration see (3a–c) taken from BNC:

(3) (a) FP1 1762: The man was an aristocrat, *inconceivably wealthy*, brother to an Earl, a Member of Parliament, a Colonel …

(b) CA7 1252: Here the vineyards are *incredibly steep*, and heath tree hedges protect the crops from the wind as well, …

(c) AD9 560: What a worn-out, haggard, rakish, *unbelievably handsome* beast, she thought.

Concerning the expression of polarity of the three lexical items showing quantitative significance, the results, however, are balanced: whereas there is an abundance of directly neutral collocations, a quantitatively significant rate of occurrence of both positive and negative collocations is easy to identify from the body of evidence even without contextual representation. Where non-contextual observations identified neutral polarity of the collocating items, in their contextual representation the polarity of the given construction could definitely be traced (ex. *inconceivably large, incredibly blue, unbelievably white*). Due to the balanced rate of polarity strictly expressed and the extreme role of the necessity of contextual (for instance, frame-based) factors of judgment, the corpus-based data do not reveal strictly manifesting commitment to expressed semantic prosody. However, the lexical potential for expressed conceptual salience of the collocations judged to be neutral by themselves certainly reveals leaning towards the expression of degrees of positive or negative polarity, manifesting under conceptually based restrictions, depending on reliance of encyclopaedically-based background knowledge (scenic, frame-based, or scriptal) on the part of the interpreter. It remains the task of scalar semantics, lexical and experimental pragmatics to provide in-depth interpretation of these factors, especially those of conceptual salience, relying on insight gained from fine-grained, genre and register-specific corpus data, and extending the scope of analyses further to contrasting the results of corpora representing regional varieties of the language.

2.3. Testing native speakers' intuitive judgment of the polarity and potential adjectival collocability of hyperbolic adverbs

With the aim to have a control study over the results of corpus-based data and the dictionary representation of the four adverbs expressing hyperbolic force, I tested native speakers' intuitive judgment as to whether they accepted these expressions as standard, regularly used lexical items, the rate of their force expressing intensification and the nature of their collocability with adjectives, with special attention to the possible semantic prosody and polarity of such constructions in elicitation of their usage. Sixty native speakers participated in the experiment – 20 of them speakers of British English, 20 speakers of Irish English, and 20 speakers of American English – to be able to gain data from major regional varieties of English. The testees were university students or intellectual individuals aged 20–65. Results of the survey are given in Table 3.

Table 3. Test results gained from speakers of three regional varieties of English.

Variety	Expression	Rate of acceptance, recognition of hyperbolic function	Rank order of degree of intensification	Adjectival collocates (occurrence: 5 or higher)
British English	unbelievably	20	1.83	beautiful, boring, great, stupid
	incredibly	20	2.17	bad, exciting, sexy
	inconceivably	20	2.66	boring, perfect, stupid
	unthinkably	20	3.33	honest, unfair
Irish English	incredibly	20	1.60	awful, beautiful, brilliant, cold
	inconceivably	16	2.00	cheap, difficult, perfect, stupid
	unbelievably	20	2.20	delicious, good, quiet, smart, warm
	unthinkably	12	4.00	difficult, foolish, stupid
American English	inconceivably	20	1.33	brilliant, far, possible, stupid
	incredibly	20	2.83	bad, beautiful, good, huge, important
	unbelievably	20	2.83	hard, stupid, tasty, ugly
	unthinkably	20	3.00	correct, irresponsible, large, terrible

Items in the table were listed according to the rank order of degree of intensification. The lower the index given, the higher the intensifying potential of the hyperbolic expressions. It can be observed that the lexical items have markedly different intensifying potential in the three regional varieties studied. Furthermore, their distances from one another were more balanced and gradual in British English than in the other two varieties. Data of Irish English in this respect show a relatively balanced picture for *incredibly, inconceivably* and *unbelievably*, whereas *unthinkably* had the lowest potential, distant from that of the other three items. The situation was different concerning American English, where *inconceivably* was the clear winner in the ratings, whereas the other three expressions had a balanced intensifying potential.

Data of the rate of acceptance and recognition of the hyperbolic potential of the expressions was almost maximal, counter to the representation of adverbial meaning and function given in dictionaries. Exceptions to this can only be observed referring to judgment by speakers of Irish English, who gave lower rates of acceptance for *inconceivably*, and a considerably low rate for *unthinkably*. The high rate of recognition of hyperbolic meaning and function contradicts the varied and vaguely expressed nature of representation given in dictionaries, but at the same time, it corresponds to and confirms the observation of corpus-based evidence.

Concerning the nature polarity manifested in intuitively associated adjectival collocability, the results gained from British subjects refer to a balanced distribution of expressed negativity and positivity in the case of the four lexical items. Polarity judgments were different in the case of speakers of Irish English. Whereas for them *incredibly* and *inconceivably* expressed a balanced distribution of positive and negative senses, *unbelievably* was definitely judged to occur with a markedly positive semantic prosody, whereas according to the judgment of those who accepted the usage of the item as a hyperbolic expression in the language, *unthinkably* was rated as highly negative. These results are significantly different from those of the corpus-based investigations. Similar to British English subjects, the American informants noted positive and negative polarity of all four expressions in their adjectival collocations. A very important factor definitely has to be observed, however, referring to the associatively evoked set of collocating adjectives: almost all of the adjectives invoked as salient constructional partners of the hyperbolic adverbs had highly expressed negative or positive content, which fact refers to a markedly active rate of semantic prosody underlying the collocations given by subjects of all of the regional variants of English represented in the survey. Interestingly, the polar opposites of such lexical items were not associated with the hyperbolic adverbs. Although a varied representation of conceptually based frames invoked by the adverbial – adjectival constructions could not be observed strictly, however, the manifesting frame instigating potential of the constructions is judged to be significantly high in all of the three regional varieties investigated. An outstandingly commonly associated adjectival partner in construction was *stupid*, which occurred as an adjectival collocate with a marked frequency. Occurrence of this negatively polar adjective as a collocate of three of the hyperbolic adverbs studied (*inconceivably, unbelievably, unthinkably*) definitely refers to the emergence of semantic prosody of the respective constructions.[3]

---

[3] Let me note that the adjective *stupid* has a marked rate of frequency of occurrence as a collocate of *incredibly* in BNC's corpus data.

None of the collocations revealed strictly formulated reliance on selectional restrictions, marked representation of appearance, behaviour-related features or categorization along the lines of positively and negative rated animacy, eventhood, or the expression of stativity, for instance.

3. Concluding remarks

The empirical evidence gained from corpus-based investigations and empirical testing of native speakers' intuitive judgement of the meaning potentials of hyperbolic adverbs has revealed the important status of loss of compositionality, marked delexicalization and grammaticalization, and the development of the intensifier function expressed by the adverbs studied in this paper. Although the degree adverb status of such adverbs is noted in the description of their senses in corpus-based dictionaries of English at least on a random basis, their polarity potential and emerging semantic prosody is left without notice in such sources. The present study has revealed the necessity of accounting for the extent and type of polarity expressed by these adverbs, and also for their conceptually based conditions of salience, gradational potentials, as well as the nature and conditions of their semantic prosody in discourse. Investigations of these aspects and features require simultaneously performed methods of control studies in terms of scale-based lexical semantics, lexical pragmatics, corpus linguistics, as well as psycholinguistic testing.

References

Allan, Keith. 1992. Something that rhymes with rich. In Adrienne Lehrer and Eva Kittay (eds), *Frames, Fields and Contrasts: New Essays in Semantic and Lexical Organization*. Hillsdale, NJ: Lawrence Erlbaum: 355–74.

Allan, Keith. 2001. *Natural Language Semantics*. Oxford: Blackwell.

Allan, Keith. 2010. *The Western Classical Tradition in Linguistics*. 2nd ed. London: Equinox.

Allan, Keith. 2012. Graded salience: Probabilistic meanings in the lexicon. In Kasia M. Jaszczolt and Keith Allan (eds), *Salience and Defaults in Utterance Processing*. Berlin and New York: Mouton De Gruyter: 165–87.

Cano Mora, Laura. 2012. *This Book Will Change Your Life! – Hyperbole in Spoken English*. Valencia: Servicio De Publicaciones, Universidad De Valencia.

Claridge, Claudia. 2011. *Hyperbole in English: A Corpus-based Study of Exaggeration*. Cambridge: Cambridge University Press.

Gibbs, Raymond W. Jr. 1994. *The Poetics of Mind*. Cambridge: Cambridge University Press.

Giora, Rachel. 2003. *On Our Mind: Salience, Context, and Figurative Language*. Oxford and New York: Oxford University Press.

Hopper, Paul J. and Elizabeth Closs Traugott. 2003. *Grammaticalization*. Cambridge: Cambridge University Press.

Leech, Geoffrey. 1983. *Principles of Pragmatics*. London and New York: Longman.

Louw, Bill. 2000. Contextual prosodic theory: Bringing semantic prosodies to life. In C. Heffer and Susan Hunston (eds), *Words in Context: In Honour of John Sinclair*. Birmingham: ELR: 48–94.

McCarthy, Michael and Ronald Carter. 2004. There's millions of them: Hyperbole in everyday conversation. *Journal of Pragmatics* 36: 149–84.

Nemesi, Attila L. 2010. Data-gathering methods in research on hyperbole production and interpretation. In Enikő Németh T. (ed.), *The Role of Data at the Semantics-Pragmatics Interface*. Berlin and New York: Mouton De Gruyter, 381–417.

Norrick, Neal R. 1982. On the semantics of overstatement. In Klaus Detering, Jürgen Schmidt-Radefeldt and Wolfgang Sucharowski, *Sprache erkennen und verstehen*. Tübingen: Niemeyer: 168–76.

Norrick, Neal R. 2004. Hyperbole, extreme case formulation. *Journal of Pragmatics* 36: 1727–39.

Quintilianus, Marcus Fabius. 2008. *Szónoklattan [Rhetorics]*. Pozsony: Kalligram.

Sinclair, John. 1996. The search for units of meaning. *Textus* 9: 75–106.

Stewart, Dominic. 2010. *Semantic Prosody: A Critical Evaluation*. New York: Routledge.

PART 2

DISCOURSE AND PRAGMATICS

Chapter 7

THE METAPHORICAL CONCEPTUAL SYSTEM IN CONTEXT

Zoltán Kövecses
Eötvös Loránd University

The issue of context has been largely neglected in cognitive linguistic and much other work on how conceptual systems change and vary. In recent work on conceptual systems, the issues of embodied cognition and the universal nature of cognitive operations have been emphasized. By contrast, my major goal in this paper is to attempt to characterize some of the contextual factors that are involved in shaping the conceptual system. My focus will be on metaphorical concepts and on the interaction between metaphorical aspects of the conceptual system and contextual factors. I propose that in many cases abstract concepts do not come from pre-stored mappings in the conventional conceptual system (as suggested, e.g., by Lakoff and Johnson 1999) but result from the priming effect of contextual factors in real situations of discourse.

1. Introduction

One of the most comprehensive and detailed statements on the nature of the human conceptual system is Barsalou's (1999) paper 'Perceptual symbol systems'. In his paper Barsalou notes many similarities between his approach and the work on conceptual structure in cognitive linguistics (Johnson 1987; Lakoff 1987; Langacker 1987; Fauconnier 1997; Fauconnier and Turner 2002).

In my view, the most salient idea that distinguishes cognitive linguistics from other kinds of linguistics is the attempt to describe and explain language use with reference to a number of cognitive operations – commonly called construal operations. Some of the cognitive, or construal, operations that cognitive linguists use in their accounts of language are common knowledge in cognitive psychology and cognitive science, while others are more hypothetical in nature (see Gibbs 2000). All of these cognitive operations serve human beings by helping them make sense of their experience, including language.

Cognitive, or construal, operations play an essentially dual role in our mental life. On the one hand, it is through such operations that we build or acquire a conventional conceptual system in terms of which we conceptualize experience. The second role of cognitive, or construal, operations is that, given that conceptual system, the operations help us further interpret or conceptualize (new) experience, an ever-changing world, as a result of which the conceptual system also changes.

The conceptual system can be regarded as the way in which the brain organizes knowledge about the world. Most of this knowledge is unconscious. The conceptual system is not something transcendental. It is based on the brain, and the brain supports all the cognitive, or construal, operations we utilize in the process of conceptualizing the world. It is the brain's neurons and the functioning of neurons that create such systems. However, for lack of expertise, I do not deal with the neuronal activities that underlie the construal operations; I simply assume them (but see, e.g., Coulson 2008; Gallese and Lakoff 2005; Feldman 2008; Lakoff 2008, and several others, from a cognitive linguistic perspective).

Below is a list of construal operations that cognitive linguists typically work with (based on Langacker 2008):

- Schematization/abstraction
- Image-schemas
- Attention/focusing
- Figure-ground
- Scope of attention
- Scalar adjustment (granularity; fine-grained – coarse-grained conceptualization)
- Dynamic and static attention (sequential and summary scanning (fictive motion))
- Prominence/salience
- Profile – base
- Trajector – landmark alignment
- Perspective
- Viewpoint
- Subjectivity – objectivity
- Metonymy
- Metaphor

- Mental spaces
- Conceptual integration

The cognitive operations at our disposal produce a particular conceptual system informed by and based on embodiment. But conceptual systems emerge as a result of contextual factors as well. Both the cognitive operations and the conceptual systems function under the pressure of a vast range of contextual factors. Simply put, the cognitive operations and the resulting conceptual systems function in context. The conceptual system and the context in which it emerges are in continuous interaction. As the conceptual system is influenced by the context, it changes, and as a result of this change, it is this modified conceptual system that is used in the next application of the system.

The cognitive operations we use are universal in the sense that all (normal) human beings are capable of performing them. Much of the embodiment on which conceptual systems are based is universal (but see Casasanto 2009). Despite the universality of the operations and that of embodiment, the conceptual systems vary considerably both cross-culturally and within cultures, with individual variation as a limiting case. This is possible because the contexts are variable and in different contexts people often use differential operations. In addition, the prominence of certain cognitive operations may be greater or smaller across groups of people. The changeability of contexts and that of cognitive operations as affected by differential contexts leads to differential conceptual systems.

While I fully recognize the importance of universal embodiment in our conceptual system and that of the universality of cognitive operations, it seems to me that much of the work cited above does not pay sufficient attention to the role of contextual factors in shaping what we know and how we think about the world. My major goal in this paper is to attempt to characterize some of the contextual factors that are involved in this process and to show one possible way in which it can happen. My focus will be on metaphorical concepts and on the interaction between metaphorical aspects of the conceptual system and contextual factors.

2. Universality in human knowledge

Many of our most elementary experiences are universal. Being in a container, walking along a path, resisting some physical force, being in the dark, and so forth, are universal experiences that lead to image schemas of various kinds (Johnson 1987; Lakoff 1987). The resulting image schemas ('container', 'source-path-goal', 'force', etc.) provide meaning for much of our experience either directly (for literal concepts) or indirectly (in the form of conceptual metaphors). Conceptual metaphors may also receive their bodily motivation from certain universal correlations in experience, when, for instance, people see a correlation between two events (such as adding to the content of a container and the level of the substance rising), leading to the metaphor MORE IS UP (see Lakoff and Johnson 1980; Lakoff 1987). When meaning making is based on such elementary human experiences, the result may be (near-) universal meaning (content) – though under a particular interpretation (construal), that is, conceived of 'in a certain manner', to use Hoyt Alverson's phrase (Alverson 1991: 97).

I suggest that universal embodied experiences of this kind constitute a major factor in shaping the conceptual system. This does not mean that all embodied experiences actually shape concepts, but that they can potentially do so. When universal embodied experiences affect the system in some way, they contribute to establishing the universal aspects of the conceptual system.

3. Context in human knowledge

In addition to embodied experience, another major factor in shaping the conceptual system is context. The significance of context in shaping the conceptual system is also noted by Barsalou (1999: 598), who states:

> Variable embodiment allows individuals to adapt the perceptual symbols in their conceptual system to specific environments. Imagine that different individuals consume somewhat different varieties of the same plants because they live in different locales. Through perceiving their respective foods, different individuals develop somewhat different perceptual symbols to represent them. As a result, somewhat different conceptual systems develop through the schematic symbol formation process, each tuned optimally to its typical referents.

Here Barsalou talks about 'different locales', a kind of context that, following Kövecses (2005, 2010b), I will call the 'physical environment'. As we will see below, in addition to the physical environment, I recognize the influence of several other contextual factors.

I use the term context very broadly, to include both the linguistic and the nonlinguistic context. By the context of linguistic and nonlinguistic communication, I mean the following:

- Surrounding discourse (what comes before and after a particular unit of discourse);
- Nature of discourse itself (genre, formality, etc.);
- Intertextuality (recycling of phrases from culturally dominant discourse, e.g., the Bible);
- Goal of discourse (purpose of discourse);
- Knowledge about the main elements of the discourse (speaker/conceptualizer$_1$, topic/theme of discourse, hearer/addressee/conceptualizer$_2$);
- Physical environment (the physical setting in which a communicative act takes place, including physical circumstances, viewing arrangement, etc.);
- Social situation (social aspects of the setting);
- Cultural situation (cultural aspects of the setting);
- History (social or personal; the history of the group or person that participates in the discourse);
- Interests, concerns (social or personal; the major interests, or concerns, of the group or person participating in the discourse).

I propose that both universal embodiment and non-universal context affect the way people conceptualize the world in real communicative/discourse situations. I call this influence, following Kövecses (2005), the 'pressure of coherence'. This is a principle that states, in effect, that conceptualizers are under two kinds of pressure when they conceptualize the world. Conceptualizers try to be coherent both with their bodies (their basic embodied experiences) and their contexts (the various contextual factors), where the body and context function as, sometimes conflicting, forms of constraint on conceptualization. The outcome of the two pressures depends on which influence, or pressure, turns out to be stronger in particular situations.

The cognitive operations I mentioned in the introduction create a particular conceptual system. Conceptualizers also use the same cognitive operations in understanding the world in particular communicative situations. The cognitive operations thus have a double role: they create a (up to a certain point in time) conventional conceptual system and they are used to conceptualize (changing) aspects of the world. With a conventional conceptual system in place and with the help of cognitive operations, we further conceptualize aspects of the world. In the course of this latter function of conceptual operations, the conceptual system is constantly modified and changed. There are two major forces that effect changes in the already existing conceptual system. One is alternative construal, that is, the alternative application of particular cognitive operations (e.g., metaphor vs. metonymy). The other is differential experience (see Kövecses 2005), which means that the various contextual factors constantly influence the way we conceptualize the world. Since the contextual factors change all the time, the conceptual system changes with them. Some of the work on non-metaphorical concepts in cognitive linguistics can be interpreted as recognizing the importance of this interplay. Work on the differential salience of conceptual categories along the lines of Rosch (1978) and Lakoff (1987), on culturally significant concepts, such as HARA in Japanese (Matsuki 1995) and QI in Chinese (Yu 1998), on the differential representation of categories in different contexts (Langacker 1987; Barsalou 1992), and on mental spaces (Fauconnier 1985/1994, 1997) can all be considered as instances of this type of work.

4. The contextual grounding of metaphorical concepts

In this section, I demonstrate the dynamics between the conceptual system, cognitive operations, and context in relation to metaphorical concepts. In particular, I discuss the notion of the pressure of coherence as regards metaphor, the phenomenon of what I call 'experiential focus' as the motivation for conceptual metaphors, and the effect of various kinds of context on the production of metaphors.

4.1. The pressure of coherence in metaphor

The principle of the 'pressure of coherence' makes the user of language adjust his or her metaphors to the surrounding context. The principle can explain a large amount of metaphor variation in naturally occurring discourse on the basis of the interplay between universal embodiment, differential experience, and the changing context of communication. In this view, even universal embodiment can be seen as a special case of the pressure of coherence. That is to say, if there are no overriding factors, people can use certain universal metaphors for particular target domains – to use the terminology of conceptual metaphor theory (Lakoff and Johnson 1980; Kövecses 2010a). However, in the majority of cases of metaphor use there seem to be overriding factors that lead groups of people and individuals to employ non-universal metaphors.

In general terms, we can have two research interests, one primarily concerned with universality and another primarily concerned with variation. The causes of universality (predominantly basic embodied experience) and the causes of variation (predominantly variation in contextual factors) yield two general lines of research:

Embodiment – Universality

Context – Variation

In *Metaphor in Culture* (2005), I made an attempt to reconcile the two programs by making the claim that when we comprehend something metaphorically in particular situations, we are under two kinds of pressure: the pressure of our embodiment and the pressure of context. I called these two forces affecting metaphorical conceptualization the 'pressure of coherence', that is, conceptualizers trying to be coherent both with their bodies (i.e., correlations in bodily experience) and their contexts (i.e., various contextual factors), where the body and context function as, sometimes conflicting, forms of constraint on conceptualization.

To see an initial example of how context can prime the selection of metaphors, let us now take the following portion of a newspaper article from a Hungarian newspaper and its rough English translation:

Levelet írt Sepp Blatter a Nemzetközi Labdarúgó Szövetség (FIFA) svájci elnöke az ázsiai szövetség (AFC) vezetőinek, melyben elfogadhatatlannak minősítette a kontinens küldötteinek három héttel ezelőtti kivonulását a FIFA-kongresszusáról, ugyanakkor megígérte, hogy megpróbál segíteni az AFC gondjainak megoldásában – jelentette kedden a dpa német hírügynökség.

Nagyon elkeserített az Önök viselkedése a Los Angeles-i kongresszusunkon. Önöknek, mint a labdarúgáshoz értő szakembereknek tudniuk kellett volna, hogy az a csapat soha nem nyeri meg a mérkőzést, amelyik a lefújás előtt levonul a pályáról – áll a levélben. (*Zalai Hirlap* [The Chronicle of Zala County], July 28, 1999)

Sepp Blatter, the Swiss president of the International Football Federation (FIFA), wrote a letter to the leaders of the Asian Football Association (AFC), in which he deemed unacceptable the behavior of the association's delegates three weeks ago when they left the FIFA Congress prematurely. On the other hand, he promised that he would try to help solve the problems with which AFC is struggling – the German news agency dpa reported.

I was bitterly disappointed by your behavior at our Congress held in Los Angeles. You, as experts on football, should have known that the team that leaves the field before the game is called off by the referee can never win the game – states the letter. (My translation, ZK)

Here, the target domain is the politics of international football that is conceptualized as the real game of football. The delegates leaving the FIFA meeting ahead of time correspond to the football players who leave the playing field before the referee calls the game off. The pressure of coherence causes or enables the president of FIFA, Sepp Blatter, to choose the football game metaphor because the topic of the meeting is the international politics of football. In addition, the speaker is a (political and administrative) representative of football, which also facilitates the use of the football metaphor for what happens at the FIFA meeting. This is how major elements of discourse, the topic and the conceptualizer/speaker, can influence the choice of metaphors in discourse.

A further factor that plays a role in producing differential experience, and hence novel metaphors, involves what I call differential concerns, or interests (Kövecses 2005). For example, intense professional interest may lead a person to habitually think about and express target domains in terms of a source domain that is based on one's professional interests. A good way of studying this form of metaphor variation is to look at letters in newspapers that are sent in to editors of newspapers by readers. In Hungarian newspapers the authors of the letters often mention their profession. Consider the following letter by a Hungarian electric engineer concerning the issue of Hungary's new relationship with Europe in the late 1990s. (The quote is followed by my more or less literal translation of the original.):

> *Otthon vagyunk*, otthon lehetünk Európában. Szent István óta bekapcsolódtunk ebbe a szellemi áramkörbe, és változó intenzitással, de azóta benne vagyunk – akkor is, ha különféle erők időnként, hosszabb-rövidebb ideig, megpróbáltak kirángatni belőle. (italics in the original; *Magyar Nemzet* [Hungarian Nation], June 12, 1999)

> We are, we can be at home in Europe. Since Saint Stephen we have been *integrated/ connected* to this intellectual/spiritual *electric circuit*, and *with varying degrees of intensity*, but we have been in it – even though various powers, for more or less periods of time, have tried to yank us out of it. (my translation, ZK)

The target domain is Hungary's new relationship to Europe in the wake of major political changes in the country in the early 1990s. The interesting question is what constitutes the source domain. As the passage makes it clear, many of the words used reflect the professional interest of the author of the letter: *be integrated/connected, electric circuit, with varying degrees of intensity* are expressions that reveal electricity and electric circuitry as a source domain in the passage. The electric engineer reasons on the basis of his knowledge of this domain. The concept of electricity and electric circuitry as a source domain is not obvious for this target and is certainly not the only one that could be used. My claim is that it is made available and its use is facilitated by the professional interest of the person who does the thinking about this particular target domain. Doctors, teachers, athletes, scientists, and so on, often take their source domains from their fields of activity to characterize and reason about the various target domains they encounter, talk, and think about.

In sum, what we find in all of the cases discussed in this section is that when people use metaphors they tend to adjust them to various aspects of the communicative situation; they try to be coherent with the contextual factors that characterize the situation. In other words, people's choice of metaphor seems to be facilitated and thus primed by what I have called the principle of 'the pressure of coherence'. Future research will determine which aspects of the communicative situation can have this effect on the choice and creation of particular metaphors.

4.2. Differential experiential focus

Embodiment is one of the key ideas of cognitive linguistics that clearly distinguishes the cognitive linguistic conception of meaning from that of other cognitively-oriented theories. On this view, in the emergence of meaning, that is, in the process of something becoming meaningful, the human body plays a distinguished role (Johnson 1987; Lakoff 1987; Lakoff and Johnson 1999; Gibbs 2006). It is especially what is known as image schemas that are crucial in this regard. Image schemas are based on our most basic physical experiences and are inevitable in making sense of the world around us.

However, several researchers have pointed out that aspects of the view of embodiment in cognitive linguistics may lead to contradictions within the theory (e.g., Alverson 1994; Rakova 2002). It can be problematic that the theory of embodiment tries to account simultaneously for universality and cultural specificity. Rakova (2002) emphasizes that a theory that builds on image schemas and, in general, on the universality of essential physical experiences cannot in the same breath be a theory of cultural variation—especially not if embodiment is conceived naturalistically. Here is a quote that indicates her position:

> Thus, my claim is that experientialism is often relativism in the strong sense, and that the supposed universality of directly meaningful concepts and kinesthetic image schemas is not consistent with the idea of culturally defined conceptualizations. (Rakova 2002: 228)

Undoubtedly, the examples that Lakoff and Johnson (Johnson 1987; Lakoff 1987) provide (like the CONTAINER schema) may sometimes give the impression that Lakoff and Johnson regard image schemas and embodiment as universal experiences that make things (including language) meaningful 'in a natural way', that is, in a way that suggests that the universality of embodiment mechanically produces universal meanings.

In my view, we can refine and improve on this conception of the embodiment of meaning in cognitive linguistics, and, thus, we can meet the challenge of the criticism above. In order to do that, we need to change the way we think about embodiment; we should not see it as a homogeneous, monolithic factor that is conceived mechanically. This is made possible by the idea that embodiment consists of several components and that any of these can be singled out and emphasized by different cultures (or, as a matter of fact, even by individuals within cultures). I termed this idea 'differential experiential focus' in previous work (Kövecses 2005).

Let us take as an example the kind of embodiment that makes our concepts and words relating to anger meaningful in different cultures. According to physiological studies, anger is accompanied by several physiological reactions, such as increase in skin temperature, in respiration rate, blood pressure, and heart rate (Ekman et al. 1983). These are universal physiological reactions that derive from the human body and explain why we find the same generic-level conceptual metaphor in languages and cultures that are independent from each other (Kövecses 2010a).

At the same time, we can observe that the different languages and cultures do not attend to the same physiological reactions associated with anger. While in English and Hungarian a rise in body temperature and increase in blood pressure receive equal attention, in Chinese the presence of PRESSURE seems to be much more focal (Yu 1998). Moreover, as Rosaldo's (1980) work tells us, the main physiological characteristic of anger among the Ilongot of

New Guinea is an undifferentiated and generalized state of physiological arousal. In other words, it seems that different languages and cultures base their anger-concepts on different components and levels of embodiment, thereby creating partly universal, partly culture-specific concepts (Kövecses 2000). This account is made possible by evoking the process of differential experiential focus.

The phenomenon of differential experiential focus can also be observed historically. Gevaert (2001, 2005) suggests that in historical corpora of the English language the conceptualization of anger as HEAT was prominent between 850 and 950. (This can be established on the basis of the number of heat related anger metaphors in the various historical periods.) Later, however, anger was conceptualized mostly as PRESSURE, and, beginning with the 14th century, HEAT and PRESSURE jointly characterized the conceptualization of anger in English. The well-known metaphor ANGER IS A HOT FLUID IN A CONTAINER (Kövecses 1986; Lakoff and Kövecses 1987) is the end product of the process. Gevaert justifiably asks in this connection whether the Lakoff–Johnson view of embodiment can be maintained in light of such findings. After all, it would be unreasonable to propose that the physiological responses associated with anger change from one century to the next.

The idea of differential experiential focus can serve us again in responding to this criticism (Kövecses 2005). The embodiment of anger, as we saw above, is complex and consists of several components. Of these, as a result of certain cultural influences over the ages, different components may occupy central position in the metaphorical conceptualization of anger. In other words, the criticism formulated by Gevaert would only be valid if we thought about embodiment as a homogeneous and unchanging factor in how humans conceptualize various abstract concepts. But if we think of embodiment as a complex set of factors to which speakers can apply differential experiential foci in different historical periods, we can resolve the dilemma raised by Gevaert and others.

4.3. The effect of additional contextual factors on metaphor use

I distinguish between two kinds of context: global and local (Kövecses 2010b). By global context I mean the contextual factors that affect all members of a language community in a given period when they conceptualize something metaphorically. By local context I mean the immediate contextual factors that apply to particular conceptualizers in specific communicative situations. The global and local contexts are obviously intertwined and form a continuum.

4.3.1. Linguistic context

The linguistic-conceptual context is constituted by the various conceptual frames (including temporary mental spaces) and symbolic units (form-meaning pairs, or, simply, words) representing and activating the frames. Let us provisionally think of discourse as being composed of a series of concepts organized in a particular way. The concepts that participate in discourse may give rise to either conventional or unconventional and novel linguistic metaphors. Suppose, for example, that we talk about the progress of a particular process and want to say that the progress has become more intense. There are many ways in which this can be done. We can say that the progress *accelerates, speeds up, gains momentum, moves faster, picks up* or *gathers speed*, and many others. These are all relatively *conventional* ways of talking about an increase in the intensity of a process. They are all based on the conventional generic-level mapping INTENSITY IS SPEED, as it applies to the concept of progress (in relation to a process). The larger metaphors within which the mapping INTENSITY IS SPEED works are also well established ones: PROGRESS IS MOTION FORWARD and, even more generally, EVENTS ARE MOVEMENTS.

However, the particular concepts that denote the specific process we are talking about may influence the selection of the linguistic metaphorical expression in talking about the intensity of the progress at hand. The linguistic metaphors we actually use may be much *less conventional* than the ones mentioned above. As an example, let me take a headline from *The Wall Street Journal Europe* (January 6, 2003) from my book *Metaphor in Culture* (2005) and reanalyze it here. It reads: 'The Americanization of Japan's car industry shifts into higher gear.'

Here, the process is the Americanization of Japan's car industry and the suggestion is that it has become, or is becoming, more intense. Instead of describing the property of 'increase in intensity' by any of the conventional linguistic metaphors above, or, as a matter of fact, by a large number of additional ones that could be used (such as *galloping ahead*), the author uses the relatively *un*conventional linguistic metaphor *shifts into higher gear* (where shifting into higher gear results in, or enables, higher speed, that is, we rely on the specific metonymy SHIFTING GEAR FOR GOING FASTER).

I propose that this particular expression is selected because of the influence of the immediate linguistic context, that is, the concepts that surround the conceptual slot where we need an expression to talk about 'an increase in intensity' (of the progress of a process). Since the process is that of the Americanization of Japan's *car* industry, we find it natural and highly motivated that the author of the utterance uses the expression *shifts into higher* gear in that conceptual slot in the discourse. Since the surrounding context includes the 'car industry', it makes sense to use the motion of a car, and not the motion of some other entity capable of motion, in the metaphor. I believe that it is the pressure of coherence (i.e., trying to be coherent with the linguistic context) that is at work here.

Metaphorically-used expressions (i.e., metaphoric symbolic units) are placed into this flow of frames and words at appropriate points in the manner explained in the discussion of the example. Thus the most immediate context in which metaphorical expressions are used is the linguistic context; more specifically and precisely, the frames that immediately precede and provide the slot into which linguistic metaphors can be inserted. This flow of discourse can be imagined as a line of successive (though not necessarily temporally arranged) frames (with the frames commonly nested in more general frames).

4.3.2. Major entities that participate in the discourse

Sometimes it seems to be our knowledge about the entities participating in the discourse that plays a role in the selection of metaphors in real discourse. Major entities participating in discourse include the speaker (conceptualizer), the hearer (addressee/conceptualizer), and the entity or process we talk about (topic). I'll discuss two such examples, involving the topic and the speaker/conceptualizer.

To begin, I will reanalyze an example first discussed in Kövecses (2005). The Hungarian daily *Magyar Nemzet* (Hungarian Nation) carried an article some years ago about some of the political leaders of neighboring countries who were at the time antagonistic to Hungary. One of them, the then Slovak president, Meciar, used to be a boxer. This gave a Hungarian journalist a chance to use the following metaphor that is based on this particular property of the former Slovak president:

> A pozsonyi exbokszolóra akkor viszünk be atlanti pontot érő ütést, ha az ilyen helyzetekben megszokott nyugati módra 'öklözünk': megvető távolságot tartva. (*Hungarian Nation*, September 13, 1997)
>
> We *deal a blow* worth an Atlantic *point* to the ex-*boxer* of Bratislava if we *box* in a western style as customary in these circumstances: *keeping an aloof distance*. (My translation and italics, ZK)

Confrontational international politics is commonly conceptualized as war, sports, games, etc. There are many different kinds of war, sports, and games, all of which could potentially be used to talk about confrontational international politics. In all probability, the journalist chose boxing because of his knowledge (shared by many of his readers) about one of the entities that constitute the topic of the discourse (the prime minister).

In using the metaphor CONFRONTATIONAL INTERNATIONAL POLITICS IS BOXING, the author is relying both on some conventional and unconventional mappings. What is common to the war, sports, and games metaphors is, of course, that they all focus on and highlight the notion of winning in relation to the activity to which they apply. This is their shared 'meaning focus' (Kövecses 2000, 2002/2010a) and this is what makes up the conventional part of the metaphor. The boxer corresponding to the politician and the blows exchanged corresponding to the political statements made are explicitly present in the discourse in question. In addition, we also assume that both boxers want to win and that the participating politicians want the same (whatever winning means in politics). However, the manner in which the boxers box and politicians argue is not a part of the conventional framework of the metaphor. *Keeping an aloof distance* probably comes into the discourse as a result of the author thinking about the target domain of politics. In the author's view, politics regarding Meciar should be conducted in a cool, detached manner. What corresponds to this way of doing politics in boxing is that you box in a way that you keep an aloof distance from your opponent.

4.3.3. Physical environment

The physical setting may also influence the selection and use of particular metaphors in discourse. The physical setting comprises, among possibly other things, the physical *events and their consequences* that make up or are part of the setting, the various aspects of the physical *environment*, and the *perceptual qualities* that characterize the setting. I'll briefly discuss the case of environmental conditions.

We can conceive of *environmental conditions* as a part of the physical setting, as discussed by Kövecses (2010b). The physical setting as a potential cause of, or factor in, which metaphors we select was first studied by Boers (1999). He assumed that people will make more extensive use of a source domain when that particular source domain becomes more salient for them under certain circumstances. The specific hypothesis was that the source domain of HEALTH will be especially productive of linguistic expressions in the winter because this is the time when, at least in countries of the northern hemisphere, people are more aware of their bodies through the more frequent occurrence of illnesses (such as colds, influenza, pneumonia, bronchitis). The particular target domain that was selected for the study was ECONOMY. Given the ECONOMY IS HEALTH metaphor, the salience of the HEALTH domain was assessed in terms of the frequency of health-related metaphorical expressions for economy. Boers counted all the metaphorical expressions ('*healthy* companies', '*sickly* firms', 'economic *remedy*', '*symptoms* of a corporate *disease*') that have to do with economy and that are based on the HEALTH source domain in the editorials of all issues of the English weekly magazine *The Economist* over a period of ten years. Boers found that the frequency of the metaphor was highest between the months of December and March. The same result was found systematically for the ten years under investigation. This finding shows that when the HEALTH domain becomes more salient for people, they make more extensive use of it than when it is less salient. Since the physical setting is part of the communicative situation, it may play a role in selecting particular metaphorical source domains. In the present example, wintertime is more likely to lead to the selection of health-related metaphors than to other metaphors, simply because such metaphors may be higher up in awareness than others due to the adverse impact of the physical environment on conceptualizers.

4.4. Types of context: A summary

Discourses do not occur in a vacuum. The types of situations and their major elements discussed above additionally involve the *social setting* and the *cultural context*. This means that the speaker and the hearer are communicating about a topic (i.e., producing and reproducing a discourse) in a specific and immediate physical, social, and cultural context (see Kövecses 2010a, b). The use of metaphors is affected by less specific and less immediate contexts as well, such as the 'broader cultural context' (see Kövecses 2005). Moreover, as was noted above, each of these contextual factors comes in a variety of distinct forms, and they can shade into each other. Finally, all the factors can affect the use of metaphors in discourse simultaneously, and they can do so in various combinations.

We can imagine the three factors as frames that are nested in one another, such that the physical setting as the outermost frame includes the social frame that includes the cultural frame, where we find the speaker/conceptualizer, the hearer/conceptualizer, and the topic, as well as the diagram for the flow of discourse. These contextual factors can trigger, or prime, singly or in combination, the use of conventional or unconventional and novel metaphorical expressions in the discourse. We can represent the joint workings of these factors in Figure 1 (taken from Kövecses 2010a, b).

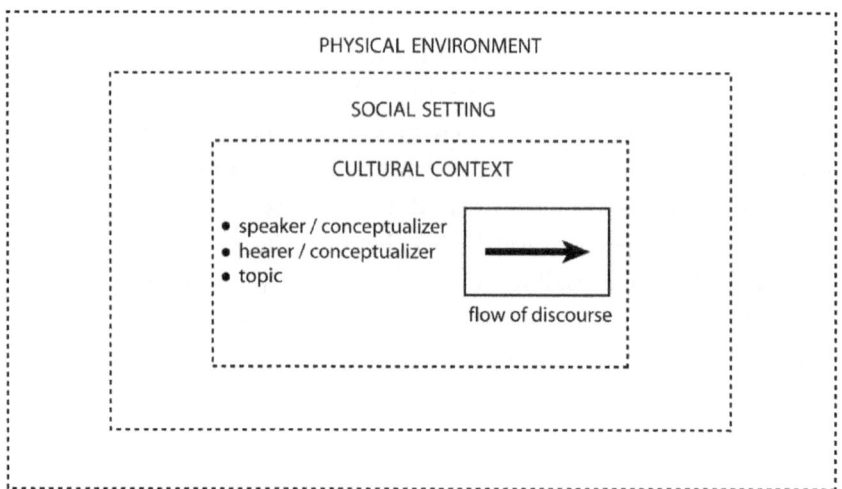

Figure 1. Contextual factors.

All the factors can trigger, or prime, the use of metaphors in discourse. Some of the metaphors so triggered will be conventional ones, but others will be genuinely novel. This is result of the 'pressure of coherence'. The pressure of coherence includes all the mechanisms that lead to the use of particular metaphors in discourse.

5. Conclusions

A number of contextual factors have been identified in the paper, but possibly there are more. The workings of these factors suggest that conceptualizers are very much aware and take advantage of the various factors that make up the immediate (local) and nonimmediate (global) context in which metaphorical conceptualization takes place. We can think of this contextual influence on conceptualization as large-scale priming by context that is occurring simultaneously (and competitively) with the influence of entrenched embodiment. As a result of this interaction (this 'in vivo' priming), the abstract concepts in the conceptual system and the system as such are constantly shaped and at the same time they shape the way we metaphorically conceptualize the world.

References

Alverson, Hoyt. 1991. Metaphor and experience: Looking over the notion of image schema. In J. Fernandez (ed.), *Beyond Metaphor: The Theory of Tropes in Anthropology*. Stanford: Stanford University Press, 94–117.

Alverson, Hoyt. 1994. *Semantics and Experience: Universal Metaphors of Time in English, Mandarin, Hindi, and Sesotho*. Baltimore: Johns Hopkins University Press.

Barsalou, Lawrence. 1992. Frames, concepts, and conceptual fields. In Adrienne Lehrer and Eva Feder Kittay (eds), *Frames, Fields, and Contrasts*. Hillsdale, NJ: Lawrence Erlbaum, 21–74.

Barsalou, Lawrence. 1999. Perceptual symbol systems. *Behavioral and Brain Sciences* 22: 577–609.

Boers, Frank. 1999. When a bodily source domain becomes prominent. In Raymond Gibbs and Gerard Steen (eds), *Metaphor in Cognitive Linguistics*. Amsterdam: John Benjamins, 47–56.

Casasanto, Daniel. 2009. Embodiment of Abstract Concepts: Good and bad in right and left handers. *Journal of Experimental Psychology: General* 138 (3): 351–67.

Coulson, Seana. 2008. Metaphor comprehension and the brain. In Raymond Gibbs (ed.), *The Cambridge Handbook of Metaphor and Thought*. New York: Cambridge University Press, 177–94.

Ekman, Paul, Wallace V. Friesen and R.W. Levenson. 1983. Autonomic nervous system activity distinguishes among emotions. *Science* 221: 1208–10.

Fauconnier, Gilles. 1985/1994. *Mental Spaces*. Cambridge: Cambridge University Press. (Originally published in 1985 by MIT Press.)

Fauconnier, Gilles. 1997. *Mappings in Language and Thought*. Cambridge and New York: Cambridge University Press.

Fauconnier, Gilles and Mark Turner. 2002. *The Way We Think*. New York: Basic Books.

Feldman, Jerome. 2008. *From Molecule to Metaphor*. Cambridge, MA: Bradford MIT Press.

Gallese, Vittorio and George Lakoff. 2005. The brain's concepts: The role of the sensory-motor system in conceptual knowledge. *Cognitive Neuropsychology* 22 (3–4): 455–79.

Gevaert, Caroline. 2001. Anger in Old and Middle English: A 'hot' topic? *BELL Belgian Essays on Language and Literature* 89–101.

Gevaert, Caroline. 2005. The ANGER IS HEAT question: Detecting cultural influence on the conceptualization of anger through diachronic corpus analysis. In Nicole Delbecque, Johan Van der Auwera and Dirk Geeraerts (eds), *Perspectives on Variation: Sociolinguistic, Historical, Comparative*. Berlin: Mouton de Gruyter, 195–208.

Gibbs, Raymond W. 2000. Making good psychology out of blending theory. *Cognitive Linguistics* 11: 347–58.

Gibbs, Raymond W. 2006. *Embodiment and Cognitive Science.* New York: Cambridge University Press.
Johnson, Mark. 1987. *The Body in the Mind.* Chicago: The University of Chicago Press.
Kövecses, Zoltán. 1986. *Metaphors of Anger, Pride, and Love.* Amsterdam: John Benjamins.
Kövecses, Zoltán. 2000. *Metaphor and Emotion.* New York and Cambridge: Cambridge University Press.
Kövecses, Zoltán. 2005. *Metaphor in Culture: Universality and Variation.* Cambridge and New York: Cambridge University Press.
Kövecses, Zoltán. 2006. *Language, Mind, and Culture: A Practical Introduction.* New York: Oxford University Press.
Kövecses, Zoltán. 2010a. *Metaphor: A Practical Introduction.* Second edition. New York: Oxford University Press. (Originally published in 2002.)
Kövecses, Zoltán. 2010b. A new look at metaphorical creativity in cognitive linguistics. *Cognitive Linguistics* 21 (4): 663–97.
Lakoff, George. 1987. *Women, Fire, and Dangerous Things. What Categories Reveal About the Mind.* Chicago: The University of Chicago Press.
Lakoff, George. 2008. The neural theory of metaphor. In Raymond Gibbs (ed.), *The Cambridge Handbook of Metaphor and Thought.* New York: Cambridge University Press, 17–38.
Lakoff, George and Mark Johnson. 1980. *Metaphors We Live By.* Chicago: The University of Chicago Press.
Lakoff, George and Zoltán Kövecses. 1987. The cognitive model of anger inherent in American English. In Dorothy Holland and Naomi Quinn (eds), *Cultural Models in Language and Thought.* New York: Cambridge University Press, 195–221.
Lakoff, George and Mark Johnson. 1999. *Philosophy in the Flesh.* New York: Basic Books.
Langacker, Ronald. 1987. *Foundations of Cognitive Grammar. Vol. 1: Theoretical Prerequisites.* Stanford: Stanford University Press.
Langacker, Ronald. 2008. *Cognitive Grammar: An Introduction.* New York: Oxford University Press.
Matsuki, Keiko. 1995. Metaphors of anger in Japanese. In John R. Taylor and Robert E. MacLaury (eds), *Language and the Cognitive Construal of the World.* Berlin: Gruyter.
Rakova, Maria. 2002. The philosophy of embodied realism: A high price to pay? *Cognitive Linguistics* 13 (3): 215–44.
Rosaldo, Michelle Z. 1980. *Knowledge and Passion: Ilongot Notions of Self and Social Life.* Cambridge: Cambridge University Press.
Rosch, Eleanor. 1978. Principles of categorization. In Eleanor Rosch and Barbara B. Lloyd (eds), *Cognition and Categorization.* Hillsdale, NJ: Lawrence Erlbaum, 27–48.
Yu, Ning. 1998. *The Contemporary Theory of Metaphor in Chinese: A Perspective from Chinese.* Amsterdam: John Benjamins.

Chapter 8

FRIGHTFUL NAMES

Barry J. Blake

La Trobe University

Though language is overwhelmingly arbitrary, at least in the lack of any motivated connection between forms and their referents, performance is iconic in that there is an analogue relationship between mode of delivery and factors such as respect or solemnity on the one hand, or enthusiasm or urgency on the other. However, many people appear to believe that there is considerable motivation in the form of words. If we look at the treatment of proper names in various cultures we find evidence of a belief in a real connection between a name and its referent and a belief in an iconic relationship between the performance of the name and the effect of that performance on the bearer of the name. Similar evidence can be found in the treatment of magic or religious texts.

1. Introductory remarks

One subject that attracted Keith Allan and his sometime collaborator, Kate Burridge, was the power of names, and the attendant taboo on using names (Allan and Burridge 1991, 2006). As a colleague of Keith Allan at Monash and later of Kate Burridge at La Trobe I became interested in name avoidance and other secretive linguistic practices, an interest developed in my book *Secret Language* (2010). In this paper I review a variety of practices involving names and texts aimed at evoking the supernatural.

It is a principle of language that there is an arbitrary relationship between the form of a word and its referent, though performance is iconic in the sense that the choice of syllables or words for emphasis is motivated, as is rate of delivery, choice of register and the like. In a few instances this motivation becomes part of the system. In English the adjectives *bad*, *glad*, *mad* and *sad* have acquired a longer vowel than that found in words such as *fad*, *lad*, *pad*, and *tad*, presumably from the fact that these adjectives are frequently emphasised (See references in Blake 1985).

Despite overwhelming evidence to the contrary, there is a widespread belief that there is a motivated or iconic relation between the form of a word and its referent. You occasionally hear people say something like, 'Slugs. That's a good name for them. That's what they are, dirty, slimy slugs.' Here the unpleasant properties of the referent are taken to be properties of the word, but people who say such things don't find any unpleasantness with words for slugs, excrement or whatever in an unfamiliar language.

It is recognised that there is a small proportion of the lexicon where the relationship between form and referent is at least partly motivated, and such cases perhaps help foster the belief in a more widespread motivation. In English we have a few onomatopoeic words such as *gong* and *thwack*, and some sets of words where there is a correlation between the rhyme and meaning as in *romp, stomp, chomp* and *clomp*, where *–omp* is associated with heavy, forceful or vigorous movement. There is a correlation in English between the form of given names and the sex of the referent. Traditional female names tend to be polysyllabic and end in a vowel, often the Indo-European feminine singular *–a* (*Angela, Barbara, Laura*), while traditional male names are more likely to be monosyllabic and end in a consonant (*John, Luke, Mark, Paul*). Perhaps this lies behind claims sometimes heard that names such as *Mark* are strong (Blake 2008: 138). I once heard someone remark of a young man whose surname was Quork, 'That's a good name for him. That's what he is, a real quork!' Here the shape of the word probably brought to mind other words such as *queer* and *dork*. While *queer* and *dork* may be arbitrary, the perceived resemblance between them and *quork* is motivated in the same way that a compound is motivated with respect to its components.

2. Names as inalienable possessions

Iconicity in performance and a belief in a non-arbitrary relationship between word and referent come together in the treatment of names and of words, phrases and longer texts directed to the supernatural. In this paper I would like to give examples of a belief that what is done to a word or text in performance can be reflected in an effect on a referent. Most of my examples are to do with proper names, mainly personal names. Here we encounter a widespread belief in a real link between name and referent. The form of the personal name may be arbitrary and is assigned rather than being innate, yet once assigned the name is thought to be bound to the person as if it were part of their make up.

Philip Peek, writing about African views of language, states, 'Deeply felt concern about names, their creation, use and avoidance, reflects this general point, in that to name something is to "know" its essence and possibly control it. Names do not simply describe; they are their referent' (Peek 1981: 27). It might seem an exaggeration to say that names are their referent, but there is evidence in some languages that they are part of their referent in the same way that body parts and effluvia are. It is widely believed that a body part such as a piece of hair or a substance excreted from the body can be used as a basis for sorcery, as can a footprint, and a personal name fits into the same category (Frazer 1911a: 52). In fact in some languages names are treated grammatically like body parts. This is widespread in Aboriginal Australia (Allan and Burridge 1991: 34, 2006: 125). For instance, in Kalkutungu one can use the dative *–ku* to mark a possessor as in *nyun-ku yuku* 'your spear' as in (1a), but not to mark the possessor of a body part or a name. With body parts and names the possessor and possessed bear whatever case is appropriate to their function in the clause (Blake 1979). There is no marking relating one to the other as can be seen in (1b) and (1c).

(1a) *Mani-ya*   *nyun-ku*   *yuku.*
     take-IMP   you-DAT   spear.
     'Take your spear.'

(1b) *Karri-ya*   *nyini*   *munthu.*
     clean-IMP   you   face
     'Wipe your face.'

(1c) *Panti-ya*   *nyini*   *ipal.*
     tell-IMP   you   name
     'Tell your name'

2.1. Names and word taboo

The idea that a name can be used in sorcery is reflected in the widespread taboo on revealing one's name. The Manambu of New Guinea are unwilling to have their name written down since these names could then be taken away and the life-force of their owners with them (Harrison 1990: 60). The same belief is reported from the Tolampoo of Sulawesi (Celebes) (Frazer 1911b: 319).

In the Bible there are a number of references to names being kept secret. In Genesis 32:29 when Jacob asks the angel who has wrestled with him during the night what his name is, the angel just replies, 'Wherefore is it that thou dost ask after my name?' In the Book of Judges an angel appears to Manoah and his wife to tell them they are to have a son (who is to be the hero Samson) and when Manoah asks the angel his name, the angel replies, 'Why asketh thou thus after my name, seeing it is secret?' (Judges 13:18). In Revelation 19:11–12 it is said of the rider of the white horse, 'His eyes were as a flame of fire, and on his head were many crowns; and he had a name written, that no man knew, but he himself.'

In European folklore, we have the story of Rumpelstiltskin who is prepared to give up his claim to the queen's baby if she can find out his name, and the knight of the swan who rescues a maiden in distress, but can remain with her only if she does not ask his name. Among the Persian stories of *The Thousand and One Days* there is the story of Prince Calaf who is prepared to give up his claim to the Princess Turandokht, and indeed his life, if the Princess can find out his name.[1]

While people may be concerned about revealing their name for fear they may be victims of sorcery, they also know their knowledge of names may give them power to curse an enemy or summon supernatural aid. There is, however, a widespread fear that uttering the name of certain creatures can antagonise the spirits of those creatures. There are often taboos on using the names of animals that are a threat to humans or their livestock, animals such as bears, foxes, weasels and wolves, or on using the names of prey, since idle use may frighten the prey. The taboo may apply to plants and even minerals. In Malaysia and Indonesia it is common for those who go into the forest to collect camphor to have to use special vocabulary in place of their everyday language, because camphor has a spirit which must not be disturbed.

A widespread taboo concerns the name of a dead person. This may be based on a fear of offending the spirit of the dead person or a fear that the spirit will remain in the locality and be malevolent, though respect may play a part too. Respect certainly plays a part in name taboo. In some religions, including Judaism, Brahmanism and Islam, the name of God is avoided (Ullmann 1957: 43; Blake 2010: 181–2). In many cultures there are taboos on using the name of certain kin or in-laws. In Arnhem Land in

---

[1] *Rumpelstiltskin* is a German fairy tale collected by the brothers Grimm in the early nineteenth century (See, for instance, Grimm 2002). The story of the knight of the swan serves as the basis for Wagner's opera *Lohengrin*, and the story of Turandokht provided the plot for Puccini's opera *Turandot*.

northern Australia a man cannot use the name of his sister. He refers to her as 'rubbish' or 'thing' (Berndt and Berndt 1964: 84). Among the Kambata of Ethiopia a woman was not allowed to use the name of her in-laws or any word beginning with the same syllable (Treis 2005). Among the Zulu and Xhosa a woman had to avoid her male in-laws' names and any word that contained a syllable of their names (Herbert 1990 a, b). It is not uncommon for there to be a taboo on using the name of a monarch or highly respected person. In China there was a taboo on pronouncing the name of the emperor or any word homophonous with the emperor's name. The taboo extended to the characters used to write the emperor's name. This was problematic where the emperor's name contained common characters and Emperor Xuan of the Han dynasty, whose given name *Bingyi* contained two very common characters, changed his named to *Xun*, which was written with a far less common character, to make it easier for his people to avoid using his name. One could avoid writing characters used in the emperor's name by substituting a synonymous character or omitting a stroke, usually the final stroke. In 1777, Wang Xihou wrote the name of the emperor Qianlong in his dictionary without leaving out any stroke. He and his family were executed and their property confiscated.[2]

3. Names and the power of language

Creation stories often deal with the origin of language. In cultures that accept the creation story in Genesis there has been in the past a widespread belief that Hebrew is the original language. Dante (*De Vulgari Eloquentia* 1: 4–7) believed that when the world was punished with a confusion of languages after building the Tower of Babel, the family of Shem, who had taken no part in the building, were able to preserve Hebrew and that this was the only reasonable language for Jesus Christ to speak as the Son of God. Ironically Jesus Christ, along with the Jews and many others of his time, spoke Aramaic.

Among Jewish scholars in the twelfth and thirteenth centuries in Provence and northern Spain a school of mystical speculation developed that came to be known as the *Kabbalah*. Within this philosophy there was not only the idea that Hebrew was the original language, but a belief that followed from that, namely that there was an inherent connection between Hebrew words

---

[2] See the Wikipedia entry on the naming taboo. During the time I was revising the manuscript of my book *Secret Language*, a report appeared in the press of a man being jailed for three years for including a derogatory reference to a member of the Thai royal family in a novel. He was subsequently granted a royal pardon.

and their referents. These notions became influential in Christian Europe in the Renaissance through the writings of scholars such as Giovanni Pico della Mirandola (1463–94), Johann Reuchlin (1455–1522) and Heinrich Cornelius Agrippa von Nettesheim (1486–1535). The following quotation from Manuel do Valle de Mouro, a sixteenth century Portuguese theologian, captures the essence of this belief (Maxwell-Stuart 1999: 137):

> The art of the Kabbalah is a Jewish tradition. The Jews believe that the predilections, conditions, powers and faculties of innumerable things are contained in Hebrew names in such a way that if anyone were to invoke properly the whole power of the Hebrew names, letters, accents and so forth, he could accomplish many extraordinary things. They claim that these same utterances create power over the whole universe, nature, evil spirits, angels and God himself, and that this happened because God himself or Adam, both of whom enjoyed the attributes of immortality and wisdom, gave things their substances, qualities, conditions, properties and descriptive names. Consequently, things are under the immediate control of the person who calls them by their names ...

The view that one can exercise control via words is widespread, but in the view expressed here the connection between words and their referents holds just for Hebrew, because the Hebrew names are considered to be the real, original names. The view was not confined to the Kabbalah and those influenced by it. It is an idea that has surfaced from time to time in Judaism and religions derived from that tradition. The third century Christian scholar Origen, for instance, believed Hebrew names had power in their original form, but lost it in transliteration or translation (Skemer 2006: 96). The mention of 'transliteration' reminds us that the written form was held to be significant and, of course, this was the only form available for languages like Hebrew when they were no longer spoken.

3.1. Language magic and cursing

In the culture of Ancient Greece and Rome it was common to inscribe curses on thin sheets of lead. These were buried near the home of a target or placed in a grave in the hope of enlisting the help of the spirit of the departed. The graves of those who had suffered untimely deaths or had not been given the proper burial rites were favoured, since it was thought their spirits were likely to remain in the vicinity of the grave. These *katadesmoi* (Greek) or *defixiones* (Latin) were directed against adversaries in business, the theatre and the courts. From the second century AD onwards they were directed against competitors in sport. A number of *defixiones* unearthed from the Roman Empire are directed against competitors in chariot races and their horses, and have been found buried near stadiums. Early curse tablets from as far back as the fourth century BC are aimed at getting rid of an unwanted partner or lover; from the second century AD onwards there are similar texts aimed at acquiring a lover (Ogden 1999: 4, 24). If the target of a curse is a woman, the curser may seek to have her made barren, to miscarry, or to produce deformed children. A belief in an iconic relationship between the direction of action and its intended effect is much in evidence in these tablets. Gager (1992: 5, 91), writing about the period of the Roman Empire, notes the practice of scrambling names in these curse tablets or writing them backwards with the intention of producing an analogous effect on the intended victim:

> Special forms of writing include either scrambling the names of the targets or writing them, and sometimes the full text of the spell, backwards … Such techniques clearly express a symbolic meaning … that the fate of the targets should turn backward or be scrambled, just like their written names. (Gager 1992: 5)

In some instances where the name is jumbled, it appears elsewhere in the text of the curse in normal form, so the purpose is not concealment. It seems distortion of the name is intended to have an analogous ill effect on the victim. This is confirmed by one tablet that asks that the target's words and deeds be jumbled as his name has been jumbled (Ogden 1999: 299–30).

The curse tablets also contain examples of alternate left-to-right and right-to-left (boustrophedon) writing long after this was the norm, upside-down writing, letters written backwards and individual words written backwards. One tablet contains the statement, 'Just as these words are cold and right-to-left [*eparistera*], so too may the words of Crates be cold and backwards' (Ogden 1999: 30). In some instances there are specific references to damaging the name in the hope of damaging the victim. One tablet that has been found with a nail hole through the name which suggests a nail pierced the name. It bears the words, 'I nail his name, that is, himself' (Cavendish 1967: 43).

The idea that the treatment of a word can be reflected in an effect on a referent can be seen also in the treatment of magic words and formulas. One magic word that is still known today is *abracadabra*. It appears in *De medicina praecepta* by Quintus Serenus Sammonicus, a learned writer of the late second century AD. He wrote that to recover from a tertian fever a sick person should wear an amulet around the neck containing a piece of parchment inscribed with a triangular formula derived from this word.

The triangular formula is derived by repeating the word with successive reductions. This is supposed to act like a funnel to drive the sickness out of the body. There is meant to be an analogy between the shrinking of the word and the reduction of the fever:

ABRACADABRA

ABRACADABR

ABRACADAB

ABRACADA

ABRACAD

ABRACA

ABRAC

ABRA

ABR

AB

A

This use of shrinking words was common from Hellenistic times and continued in the Roman Empire and later in Europe (Blake 2010; Budge 1978: 220).

Analogous to the shrinking word is the use of a formula containing a number, usually nine. This formula is repeated with the number being reduced by one with each repetition. As with the shrinking word, we have an example of mimetic magic (Frazer 1911a: 52). The disease or swelling or whatever is supposed to reduce as the series of numbers in the formula reduces, though it is not clear from the records what interval is allowed to elapse between repetitions (Jolly 2002: 39). Here is an example aimed at curing a skin disease (tetter) (Roper 2003: 20):

> Tetter, tetter; thou hast nine brothers,
> God bless the flesh and preserve the bone,
> Perish thou tetter, and be thou gone,
> In the name of the father, Son and Holy Ghost.
>
> Tetter, tetter; thou hast eight brothers, etc.
> Tetter, tetter; thou hast seven brothers, etc.

If it is accepted in a culture that humans can seek the aid of the supernatural to curse, cure, or divine, it is natural that there will be a belief in ways of countering a curse (and possibly a cure) or averting a prophesied disaster. There are counter-charms and rituals aimed at reversing spells including the possibility of destroying the image of a sorcerer, giving him back a bit of his own medicine, so to speak.

A name or a formula believed to have the power to summon supernatural forces can be read or written in reverse. In speech such reversals might be thwarted by phonotactic restrictions, but in writing no such limitation exists. One result of reversing a name or text is to undo the effect of the normal version. There is a kind of logic here. The Wayagga of Mount Kilmanjaro think that if someone has stepped over the body of another, they should at once turn back and leap over the body in the reverse direction, thus undoing the first action, but that if they fail to do so, the person stepped over will soon die (Frazer 1911b: 289).[3]

Reversals have sometimes been thought to turn good to evil. Over the centuries in Christian communities there have from time to time been those who conducted or attended Black Masses. These are basically versions of the mass directed to Satan and they involve a principle of opposites. The crucifix is inverted, the candles are black instead of white, and some 'sinful' actions are included. In some versions a naked woman serves as the altar and the ceremony ends with intercourse. Significantly as far as language is concerned, the text of the mass, or at least part of it, is said to be recited in reverse (Cavendish 1967: 335).

In Jewish folklore there are strong, dumb, human-like creatures known as *golem*. Some humans were thought to have the power to create a golem by shaping a figure out of clay and using the name of God to give it life, in particular by writing the name of God on a piece of paper and placing it in the mouth. To reverse the process, one removed the piece of paper. In another version of how to produce golem one had to shape the figure from clay and walk around it reciting a combination of letters from the alphabet and the secret name of God. Interestingly to kill the golem, one had to walk around the golem in the opposite direction and recite the words of creation backwards.

---

[3] When I was at school during World War II some boys were caught goose-stepping, giving the Nazi salute and shouting 'Heil Hitler!' When they were caught, they were sentenced to standing to attention and reciting 'God save the king' twenty times. Looking back I can see that this was an appropriate remedy. Standing to attention counteracted the goose-stepping and each 'God-save-the-king' was worth one 'Heil-Hitler'.

The 'opposite direction' is of course relative, but in Europe one particular direction was favourable and the other unfavourable. It was considered propitious to carry out various ceremonies, journeys and voyages in the same direction as the sun. In the Northern Hemisphere for a person looking south the sun appears to move from left to right or clockwise and this was a propitious direction in which to move around an altar, etc. The opposite direction, i.e., anticlockwise or counter-clockwise (*wythersŷnes* 'widdershins'), was considered unpropitious or having the power to bring about a reverse effect. In Chapter 79 of *Grettir's Saga* Thorbjorn Angle employs the services of his foster mother, Thurid, to help him overcome his enemy, Grettir. Thurid is well versed in sorcery and she curses Grettir by inscribing runes on the smooth surface of a large tree stump found by the sea. She fills the runes with her blood, recites a spell and walks backwards around the stump against the direction of the sun.[4]

One counter to reversal was the palindrome. Since a palindrome reads the same backwards as forwards, it cannot be reversed. The lead tablets of the classical world mentioned above contain lots of mysterious words and phrases, mostly gibberish as far as the users were concerned, but likely to be garbled words from Hebrew and possibly other languages such as Egyptian. Some of these *voces mysticae* or *voces magicae* 'mystic words or magic words' are palindromes. As Ogden (1999: 49) writes:

> One sort of *vox magica* well suited to the curse tablets was the palindrome: such words remained magically proof against the retrograde writing common on curse tablets. They appear in various lengths, but they are often very long indeed, and are the favourite bases for the formation of isosceles triangles, since they retain their symmetry and palindromic nature at each stage of reduction.

One palindromic *vox magica* in use among the Gnostics of the third and fourth centuries AD was the Greek palindrome ΑΒΛΑΝΑΘΑΝΑΛΒΑ (in Roman alphabet ABLANATHANALBA). It was popular in amulets, and is one of the long ones that Ogden alludes to that was used as the basis of an isosceles triangle or shrinking word. It is written out and then repeated below with the edge letters missing. These repetitions and reductions of the edges continue until only the middle letter is left (Gager 1992: 95).

---

[4] Runes were alphabet letters of Mediterranean origin found among Germanic peoples from the second century AD onwards. They were used mainly for inscriptions and when the Roman alphabet was introduced along with Christianity; they remained in use for occult and ornamental purposes.

ΑΒΛΑΝΑΘΑΝΑΛΒΑ

ΒΛΑΝΑΘΑΝΑΛΒ

ΛΑΝΑΘΑΝΑΛ

ΑΝΑΘΑΝΑ

ΝΑΘΑΝ

ΑΘΑ

Θ

Written material can be destroyed and destroying a written curse nullifies its effect. There is an example in *Egil's Saga*. Egil Skallagrimsson visits a farmer whose daughter has been ill for some time. The farmer tells Egil that in an attempt to help her overcome her illness he had the son of a neighbour carve runes and place them in her bed. Egil finds these runes in her bed scratched on a whalebone. Believing these are inappropriate runes inscribed by someone unskilled, he scrapes the runes from the bone and throws the bone in the fire. Egil then replaces them with his own runes and the young woman recovers (*Egil's Saga* 73). Behind this practice is the not unnatural belief that if writing is destroyed, then any effect that writing is supposed to bring about is thereby cancelled (Pálsson and Edwards trans. 1976).

As mentioned above, a name could be damaged with the intention of causing analogous damage to the bearer of the name. A name could also be destroyed in the belief that this would cause the death of the owner of the name, as in the ancient Egyptian practice of smashing pots inscribed with the names of enemies.

> An example of the coalescence of a symbol and the thing it stands for is the treating of a person's name as an essential part of him – as it were, in a way, identical with him. We have a number of pottery bowls which Egyptian kings of the Middle Kingdom had inscribed with the names of hostile tribes in Palestine, Libya and Nubia; the names of their rulers; and the names of certain rebellious Egyptians. These bowls were solemnly smashed at a ritual, possibly at the funeral of the king's predecessor; and the object of this ritual was explicitly stated. It was that all these enemies, obviously out of the pharaoh's reach, should die. But if we call the ritual act of the breaking of the bowls symbolical, we miss the point. The Egyptians felt that *real* harm was done to their enemies by the destruction of their names (Frankfort et al. 1949: 21–2).

3.2. Eating words

There is another kind of destruction of text and that involves a person or animal ingesting a text. It usually involves a text believed to have supernatural powers or the power to evoke a supernatural power and the purpose of ingesting the text is to unite the referent with the ingester. The text becomes part of the body and some assumed supernatural power is consequently linked to the body.

In the Bible there are a number of references to eating words, but most of these are metaphorical. However, there is a passage in Ezekiel 3:1–3 where the reference seems to be literal:

> Moreover he said unto me, Son of man, eat that thou findest; eat this roll [scroll], and go speak unto the house of Israel.
>
> So I opened my mouth, and he caused me to eat that roll.
>
> And he said unto me, Son of man, cause thy belly to eat, and fill thy bowels with this roll that I give thee. Then did I eat it; and it was in my mouth as honey for sweetness'

In Revelation 10:9–10 there is an even more explicit reference to eating text:

> And I went unto the angel and said unto him, Give me the little book. And he said unto me, Take it and eat it up; and it shall make thy belly bitter, but it shall be in thy mouth sweet as honey.
>
> And I took the little book out of the angel's hand, and ate it up; and it was in my mouth sweet as honey; and as soon as I had eaten it, my belly was bitter.

Over the last two millennia Christian texts have often been put in edible form and administered to patients (Clark 2002: 100). In Europe in the Middle Ages and later letters, whether runic or roman, were inscribed on dies (dice), which were used for stamping cakes given to rabid dogs in an attempt to cure them. Texts, including the Latin based gibberish *Pax Max D Inax* and *Pax, Max, Y, Vy* inscribed on apples or bread, were also used (Elliott 1957: 259f). A twelfth century manuscript from Germany recommends writing prayers on wafers and eating them barefoot, an interesting blend of the Christian and pagan (Kieckhefer 1989: 70). In the Anglo-Saxon Leechbok (lxii) a prescription for overcoming fever involves writing the opening words of the Vulgate version of John's gospel (*In principio erat verbum* 'In the beginning was the Word) on a paten and washing them into a drink. In a later manuscript they are to be written on parchment and scraped into a bowl and administered to a person thought to be possessed by a demon (Kieckhefer 1989: 74). The choice of words in this case is motivated by the part-for-whole principle, the first words of a text bringing to mind a larger text. The power of words can also be seen in a practice reported of Swedish peasants who would tear a page from the psalter, bake it in dough and feed it to cattle believed to be the victims of witchcraft (Ullmann 1957: 43). In China it has been the custom to ingest written words by writing them on rice paper and eating the paper or by burning the paper and putting the ashes in food.

Although there is a belief that a text absorbed by a creature can unite a supernatural power to the creature, it is worth noting that there is no evidence of a belief that eating a text gives one knowledge of the text. A distinction was made between the physical etic text and the emic text, as in riddles about bookworms who ate words but were none the wiser. The following example from Caelius Firmianus Symphonius, an otherwise unknown author from The Roman Empire, is typical, and theme was reworked in vernacular versions in the Middle Ages.

> XVI. Tinea
> Littera me pavit, nec quid sit littera novi;
> in libris vixi, nec sum studiosior inde;
> exedi Musas, nec adhuc tamen ipsa profeci.
>
> 16. Bookworm
> Letters fed me, but I did not know what a letter was.
> I lived in books, but I am no wiser am I for it.
> I consumed the Muses, but nevertheless I have not yet progressed

4. Concluding remarks

The examples given up to this point are all from cultures remote from our own in time and place. We probably feel we have advanced beyond the superstitions of our own past and we probably feel more advanced than other cultures despite the current fashion of showing respect for other cultures and being non-judgemental. Although we do not believe that names are an integral part of a person and need to be concealed from enemies for fear of sorcery, we naturally have feelings about names based on their associations. Surnames have ethnic associations and given names are often allusive as well, being chosen from Biblical characters, celebrities or our own ancestors.

The use of a name evokes the bearer of the name, and where enemies are concerned, there can be a strong taboo on the use of the enemy's name. The enemy may be a criminal, a bully, an abuser, or a former lover or partner after a bitter falling out. The aggrieved party can become seriously upset at the mention of the names of an opponent and will refrain from using it, and family, friends and acquaintances will be expected to observe the same taboo. This avoidance is the strongest echo in our culture of the widespread name taboo.

References

Allan, Keith and Kate Burridge. 1991. *Euphemism and Dysphemism: Language Used as Shield and Weapon*. New York: Oxford University Press.

Allan, Keith and Kate Burridge. 2006. *Forbidden Words: Taboo and the Censoring of Language*. Cambridge: Cambridge University Press.

Berndt, Ronald M. and Catherine H. Berndt. 1964. *The World of the First Australians*. Sydney: Ure Smith.

Blake, Barry. 1985. 'Short a' in Melbourne English. *Journal of the International Phonetic Association* 15: 6–20.

Blake, Barry. 1979. *A Kalkatungu Grammar*. Canberra: Pacific Linguistics.

Blake, Barry. 2008. *All About Language*. Oxford: Oxford University Press.

Blake, Barry. 2010. *Secret Language*. Oxford: Oxford University Press.

Budge, Ernest A.W. 1978. *Amulets and Superstitions*. New York: Dover (original edition: Oxford University Press, London, 1930).

Cavendish, Richard. 1967. *The Black Arts*. New York: Perigree.

Clark, Stuart. 2002. Witchcraft and magic in early modern culture. In Bengt Ankarloo and Stuart Clark (eds), *Witchcraft and Magic in Europe, Volume 4: The Period of the Witch Trials*. London: Athlone, 97–169.

Elliott, Ralph. 1957. Runes, yews, and magic. *Speculum* 32 (2): 250–61.

Frankfort, Henri, Henriette A. Frankfort, John A. Wilson and Thorkild Jacobsen. 1949. *Before Philosophy: The Intellectual Life of Ancient Man*. Harmondsworth: Penguin.

Frazer, James G. 1911a. *The Golden Bough: The Magic Art and the Evolution of Kings*. London: Macmillan

Frazer, James G. 1911b. *The Golden Bough: Taboo and the Perils of the Soul*. London: Macmillan.

Gager, John G. (ed.). 1992. *Curse Tablets and Binding Spells in the Ancient World*. New York: Oxford University Press.

Grimm, Jacob and Wilhelm. 2002. *The Complete Fairy Tales*. London: Routledge.

Harrison, Simon J. 1990. *Stealing People's Names: History and Politics in a Sepik River Cosmology*. Cambridge: Cambridge University Press.

Herbert, Robert K. 1990a. The relative markedness of click sounds: Evidence from language change, acquisition and avoidance. *Anthropological Linguistics* 32: 120–38.

Herbert, Robert K. 1990b. The sociohistory of clicks in Southern Bantu. *Anthropological Linguistics* 32: 295–315.

Jolly, Karen. 2002. Medieval magic: Definitions, beliefs, practices. In Karen Jolly, Catherina Raudvere and Edward Peters (eds), *Witchcraft and Magic in Europe, Volume 3: The Middle Ages*. London: Athlone, 1–71.

Kieckhefer, Richard. 1989. *Magic in the Middle Ages*. Cambridge: Cambridge University Press.

Maxwell-Stuart, P.G. (ed.). 1999. *The Occult in Early Modern Europe: A Documentary History*. New York: St Martin's Press.

Ogden, Daniel. 1999. Binding spells: Curse tablets and voodoo dolls in the Greek and Roman worlds. In Bengt Ankarloo and Stuart Clark (eds), *Witchcraft and Magic in Europe: Ancient Greece and Rome*. Philadelphia: University of Pennsylvania Press, 1–90.

Pálsson, Hermann and Paul Edwards (trans.). 1976. *Egil's Saga*. Harmondsworth: Penguin.

Peek, Philip M. 1981. The power of words in African verbal arts. *The Journal of American Folklore* 94 (371): 19–43.

Roper, Jonathon. 2003. Towards a poetics, rhetorics and proxemics of verbal charms. *Folklore* (Tartu) 24: 7–49 [www.folklore.ee/folklore/vol24/verbalcharm.pdf].

Skemer, Don C. 2006. *Binding Words: Textual Amulets in the Middle Ages*. Pennsylvania: Penn State University Press.

Treis, Yvonne. 2005. Avoiding their names, avoiding their eyes: How Kambaata women respect their in-laws. *Anthropological Linguistics* 47 (3): 292–320.

Ullmann, Stephen. 1957. *The Principles of Semantics*. Glasgow: Jackson and Oxford: Blackwell.

Chapter 9

ON POLITIC BEHAVIOUR

THE PERSONAL PRONOUN AS AN ADDRESS TERM IN THE NDEBELE LANGUAGE OF ZIMBABWE

Finex Ndhlovu

University of New England

The use of the personal pronoun as an address term in different speech communities around the world is widely documented. The pioneering work of Brown and Levinson (1987), Brown and Gilman (1968), Friedrich (1972), Gumperz (1982), and Gumperz and Hymes (1972) on politeness strategies long established that both singular and plural personal pronominal forms are often used to express respect, social distance, intimacy and solidarity. More recent studies (Watts 2003; Allan and Burridge 1991, 2006; Allan 2012) concur with the early studies on politeness strategies. Most of their conclusions are based on data mainly from French, Italian, Russian and English speech communities. This chapter presents the most recent empirical evidence from the Midlands Ndebele speech community of Zimbabwe to support the argument that the personal pronominal address system is more complex than is currently acknowledged in the literature. The data indicates that the use of both the singular (*wena* – you SING) and plural (*lina* – you PL) forms of the personal pronoun in the Ndebele language betrays an uneasy and unpredictable situation. This uneasiness and unpredictability revolves around a lack of clarity about when it is deemed appropriate to be euphemistic, when to display solidarity or endearment and when to express social distance.

1. Introduction and background

Geographically located roughly in the central part of Zimbabwe, the Midlands province is one of the most linguistically and culturally diverse regions of the country. It is home to people from diverse language backgrounds including the Karanga, Lemba, Ndebele, Nyanja, Shangwe, Tonga and Xhosa/Fengu. It is estimated that 16.5% of Zimbabweans speak Ndebele as their first language (Government of Zimbabwe 1982; Hachipola 1998; Ndhlovu 2009). While the Ndebele language is predominantly spoken in the country's south-western provinces of Matabeleland South and Matabeleland North, there are large pockets of Ndebele speech communities in many districts of the Midlands province including Gweru, Lower Gweru, Kwe Kwe, Zhombe, Gokwe, Zvishavane, Silobela and Mberengwa.

Among members of the Ndebele speech communities of Zimbabwe, particularly those from the Midlands province, the personal pronoun is frequently used as an address term in everyday speech. For instance, in commands – *Buya lapha wena* ('come here you-SING') and in interrogations as in *Lifunani lapha lina?* ('What do you want here you-PL?'). The personal pronoun is also used as an address term in association with other forms of address: with first names as in *Wena Jabulani* ('You-SING Jabulani'), with titles as in *Lina babalisi* ('you-PL teachers'); as a marker of respect to seniors or elders as in *Ngitsho lina baba* ('I am referring to you-PL father') and with endearments as in *Wena sithandwa* ('You-SING darling'). Personal pronominal usage is also evident in everyday speech where it conjugates verbs as a pluralising morpheme – *Libuye kusasa bomama* ('You-PL come tomorrow mothers'); or as a morpheme denoting power and respect – *Ngiyalibiza baba* ('I am calling you-PL father').

However, unlike other forms of address such as first names, titles, kinship names, nicknames and endearments, the Ndebele personal pronominal address system has so far received little attention in previous research. A few examples of such previous studies are worth mentioning here. More than half a century ago, Krige (1950) studied the relationship between language use and kinship relations among the Zulu people, a speech community whose linguistic practices and social systems are closely related to those of the Ndebele people by virtue of their shared histories and traditions. Both the Zulu and Ndebele languages (and their speakers) belong to the genetically related Nguni group that also includes Xhosa and Swati. The results of Krige's study project age as an important factor in determining the choice of an address term in the Zulu speech community. Krige suggested that all adults deserve to be respected in the way they are addressed and further examined the relationship between gender and the choice of an address term. Still focusing on the Zulu speech community, another scholar, Khumalo (1992: 346) presented evidence on how systems of address are changing with changes in socio-economic and political life of the Zulu people. Khumalo discussed a wide range of address forms including first names, titles, kinship names, nicknames and endearments.

Regarding the Ndebele forms of address, a general observation is made that women have to command a considerable vocabulary of archaic and euphemistic words compared to their male counterparts (Mhlabi 1978;

Sibanda 1987; Nzama 1989). For example, Sibanda observed the existence of what he termed sex varieties in the Bulawayo Ndebele speech community, noting that '[s]ex varieties are a result of different social attitudes towards the behaviour of men and women, and to the attitudes men and women themselves have towards language as a social symbol' (Sibanda 1987: 37).

This chapter builds on Sibanda's (1987) findings, extending them to the more specific issues on the pragmatic use of the personal pronoun as an address term in the Midlands Ndebele speech community. As can be seen from the few examples of previous studies cited here, most of what we know on Ndebele pragmatics is old and outdated. Therefore, one of the main goals of this chapter is to provide more recent analysis of how appropriate behaviour is socially indexed in the interactional parties' choices of personal pronominal address forms. Overall, this chapter is, in some aspects, a pioneer work as there is no known or published comprehensive work or recording of the Ndebele address system.

The diverse ways of using the personal pronoun as an address term are discussed in detail in this chapter, which is organised as follows. The next section deals with conceptual issues underpinning the entire chapter, namely Richard Watts' ideas on theories of politeness and politeness strategies (Watts 2003; Watts et al. 1992). This is followed by section three that presents the research methods and procedures of data collection. In the fourth section the chapter presents and analyses the research findings. The chapter concludes with a section that distils the overarching themes on personal pronominal usage within the Zimbabwean Ndebele speech communities and their implications for further understanding of the pragmatics of address terms across different speech communities.

2. Brief overview of theoretical framework

Fundamental to the arguments and discussion of this chapter is Richard Watts' concept of politic behaviour, which is defined as '[l]inguistic behaviour which is perceived to be appropriate to the social constraints of the ongoing interaction, i.e., as non-salient' (Watts 2003: 19). For Watts linguistic expressions are open to interpretation either as realisations of polite (politic behaviour) or as realisations of impoliteness. There are at least five key ideas that inform Watts' view on (im)politeness. First, he argues that it is necessary to make clear a distinction between the commonsense or lay notion of (im)politeness and the theoretical notion of the same. Second, and related to the first point, Watts considers politeness to be a binary notion that has a (i) socio-psychological dimension relating to the various ways in which members of sociocultural groups talk about polite language usage; and a (ii) theoretical linguistic dimension that is widely used in sociolinguistic theoretical research on politeness.

The third element in Watts' conceptualisation of politeness is that he considers the terms polite and politeness and their approximate lexical equivalents in other languages and cultures as being subject to variation in their meanings and connotations. Such variations are often registered in linguistic usages of different groups of speakers and even from one individual speaker to another. Fourth, for Watts, some examples of lay interpretations of polite language usage are 'the language a person uses to avoid being too direct, the language which displays respect towards or consideration for others, or language that displays certain polite formulaic utterances like *please*, *thank you*, *excuse me* or *sorry*' (Vilkki 2006: 327; emphasis as in original). Watts' fifth argument is that some people feel that polite behaviour is equivalent to socially correct or appropriate behaviour, while others may consider it to be the hallmark of a cultivated person.

Essentially, Watts' ideas on (im)polite linguistic behaviour do suggest that there are competing and contested meanings and understandings of what constitutes politic or politically correct/appropriate usage of language. His overall purpose in the theory of politic behaviour is to show that the nature of (im)politeness is inherently evaluative and constitutes another site for social struggles over discursive practices (Vilkki 2006). Therefore, because the notion of (im)politeness is a contested and disputed one, there are no linguistic structures that should be taken to be inherently polite or impolite.

Drawing on the above insights, this chapter seeks to unpack and tease out the underlying meanings of personal pronominal address terms within the Midlands Ndebele speech community of Zimbabwe. Like those of most southern African societies, the social systems of the Ndebele people are steeped in the use of *hlonipha* (respectful/euphemistic) register, which is often expressed in various linguistic, discursive, symbolic and metaphorical forms. All of these fall within the category of politic behaviour, which this chapter discusses and reflects on by specifically considering data on the use of personal pronouns *wena* (you-SING) and *lina* (you-PL) as address terms.

3. Research methods and procedures

The data presented and analysed in this section were collected through questionnaires, face-to-face structured interviews, and personal observations. With the questionnaire method, a pilot study was conducted using open questions the results of which were used to construct a closed questionnaire.

A total of 100 questionnaires were distributed as follows in rural and urban settings in the Midlands province. Sixty copies were sent to five secondary and two high schools where they were completed by students and teachers. Twenty copies were distributed to twenty residents of Mbizo high-density suburb in Kwekwe. Ten copies were sent to Zhombe Growth Point and the other ten were sent to Gokwe Growth Point. Out of the 100 copies distributed eighty were returned completed and useful. The other twenty were either not returned or were spoilt through misinterpretation of the questions. All the returned questionnaires were analysed following the conceptual framework of politeness strategies. The results were interpreted and tabulated (see Tables 1 and 2). Furthermore, the analysis considered the dynamics of pronominal usages by both the addressor and the addressee.

With regard to interviews, there were nine semi-structured guiding questions that formed the basis for discussions with participants, who were divided into five age groups: 4–12 years age group, 13–20 years age group, 20–40 years age group, 40–60 years and 60 years and above age group. The categorisation done after preliminary observations from the pilot study seemed to indicate that there were apparent similarities in linguistic usages by people in the respective age groups. Both male and female participants from different age groups were interviewed with the principle of theoretic saturation used to determine the total number of participants interviewed. It is important to note that the above age groups should not be seen as completely independent and water tight categories, since in reality they form a continuum. Each preceding age group overlaps into the next one and the age-ranges were simply designed for conveniences of analysis.

Personal observations were also made of how people of different ages and sexes spoke to each other in different social contexts, with a keen eye on their personal pronominal usages. People were observed as they addressed each other without any interference from the researcher in order to obtain what could approximate the most naturalistic data. The data on personal pronominal usages by pre-school children in particular were obtained solely through personal observations.

4. Results

4.1. Personal pronominal usage and the age variable

Results from observations and structured interviews conducted in the Midlands Ndebele speech community indicated that the youngest speakers in the 4–12 years age group and those in the 60 years and above age group use language in almost the same way. Pre-school children were often heard addressing all people as *wena* (you-SING) regardless of the individual's age. In a similar manner, those in the 60 years and above age group indicated that they would address any person as *wena* regardless of their age or sex. There is, however, a difference in the motivations for using the singular form of the personal pronoun by these two age groups. The old-aged use *wena* as a consequence of their knowledge and understanding that one person should be addressed thus. Furthermore, by virtue of their advanced age, people in the 60 years and above category are seniors in society and a majority of the people they address tend to be junior to them – hence their use of *wena* with an expectation to receive the more honorific *lina* (you-PL) in return. On the other hand, the default for pre-school children is to use *wena* because they are not yet in a position to tease out and separate politic from non-politic linguistic strategies. What they are certainly aware of is that they are addressing only one person. The politics of euphemistic and politeness associated with the use of *lina* when addressing an adult person is not apparent to these very young children.

Respondents in the 13–20 years and 20–40 years age groups indicated that they would address all adults with the second person plural pronoun *lina*, and young people with the singular pronoun *wena*. The primary school children, like their high school counterparts, opted to use *lina* to all adults and *wena* to their friends and acquaintances.

Eighty-seven percent of all questionnaire respondents across age-groups other than pre-school children and 60+ years indicated that they would address an adult stranger as *lina*. Nine respondents (11.25%) noted that they would use *wena* to an adult stranger. One respondent opted for the use of the term *baba* (father) to a male adult stranger, and *mama* (mother) to a female adult stranger. Interviewees in the 13–20 years age group reasoned that they would refer to an adult stranger as *lina* because the latter term shows respect. Those who opted for *wena* stated that their knowledge of Ndebele grammar indicates that it would be ungrammatical to address one individual using *lina*. Seventy-four respondents (92.5%) indicated that they would refer to a young stranger as *wena* while four respondents (5%) opted for *lina*. The remaining respondents (2.5%) chose to use other terms like the slang term *tshomi* (slang for friend) and *bhudi* (brother) when addressing male young people, and *sisi* (sister) for females.

Respondents in the 60 years and above age group, especially those from rural areas seemed to be sceptical about the changes that they claimed are taking place in the Ndebele address system. They condemned what they call *intsha* (the younger generation) as the cause of changes to the Ndebele language, particularly the use of slang and other colloquial forms of address. Nzama's (1989: 15) research in the Bulawayo Ndebele speech community had similar findings as she remarks that 'elderly people seem to be conservative in their use of linguistic forms. They associate new forms with the younger generation'.

Table 1. Questionnaire results: Personal pronominal usage and the gender and age variables.*

Persona addressed	Number of respondents who opted for:					
	wena		*lina*		Other terms	
		%		%		%
Father	8	10	68	85	4	5
Mother	8	10	68	85	4	5
Someone of father's age	8	10	68	85	4	5
Someone of mother's age	5	6.25	70	87.5	5	6.25
An adult stranger	9	11.25	70	87.5	1	1.25
Brother	44	55	27	33.75	9	11.25
Sister	45	56.25	27	33.75	8	10
Someone of brother's age	24	30	46	57.5	10	12.5
Someone of sister's age	26	32.5	44	55	10	12.5
Cousin	50	62.5	22	27.5	8	10
Aunt	12	15	62	77.5	6	7.5
Uncle	13	16.25	65	81.25	2	2.5
Grandmother	16	20	58	72.5	6	7.5
Grandfather	19	23.75	56	70	5	6.25

*Note: N=80.

The evidence adduced from the data (see Table 1) indicates that role-relationships are also a significant factor in determining choices of personal pronominal address terms within the Midlands Ndebele speech community. For instance, the common reason given for the use of *lina* to parents and all other adults is that they are breadwinners for their families. Examples of such reasons extracted from the data include the following: *Ngoba unginika engikuswelayo* ('Because he/she gives me what I need') and 'Because he/she is like my parent' [original response given in English].

While parents may address their children as *wena* or by using the children's first names, the system is always non-reciprocal. Children give the statusful and respectful *lina* to their parents, and receive the power-less *wena* in return. Most adults asserted that it is effrontery for a young person to address an adult person either by his/her first name or by using *wena* without being asked to do so. One adult participant (aged 55) from Mandombe area in Zhombe noted that "only a rude and disrespectful young person" would attempt to address an adult using *wena*. In other words, this is considered as impolite, dysphemistic and therefore, constitutes non-polit linguistic behaviour.

There is, however, evidence from this study that suggests that there are some adults who may be addressed as *wena*, for example elder brothers and elder sisters. Forty-four questionnaire respondents (55%) indicated that they would address their elder brother or elder sister as *wena*, while an almost similar number (56.25%) indicated they would address their elder sister using *wena*. The reasons that were given for this choice are: that they are children of the same parents with their brothers and sisters, that brothers and sisters do not deserve to be respected and that it is grammatical to say *wena* to any single (unmarried) person regardless of their sex or age. That children of the same parents may address each other using the second personal pronoun is not unique to the Midlands Ndebele speech community. Krige (1950: 24) noted the following about how siblings would address each other in Zulu society:

> Children of the same parents or siblings … are replicas of one another in social relationship, and come as near being socially identical as it is for human beings to be. The behaviour pattern between them is therefore on the whole, one of equality, friendliness and co-operation.

Again, what we see here is a clear case of politic behaviour that defies the generally accepted view that age is the key determinant of whether someone can be addressed using *lina* or *wena*. As Allan (2012: 4) observes:

> Speaking to others is a social activity, and like other social activities (such as dancing, playing in an orchestra, playing cards or football) the people involved mutually recognise – as part of the common ground –

that certain conventions govern their actions and their use of language, both when speaking and when interpreting the actions and utterances of their interlocutor.

The underlying meaning here is that in any communicative act, the participants or interlocutors are not passive recipients of pre-existing or laid down norms of social interaction. Rather they are active agents involved in the process of negotiating common ground to arrive at what constitutes appropriate linguistic behaviour relative to prevailing circumstances.

However, having said the above, the findings of this study as shown on Table 1 suggest that not all people would address their brother or sister as *wena*. For instance, twenty-seven respondents (33.75%) indicated that they would address their brother or sister using *lina*. Nine respondents (11.25%) opted for the use of other terms like *bhudi* (brother), *mnewethu* (my brother) and *mebra* (slang for my brother) to their brother while eight respondents (10%) indicated preference for the use of *sisi* (sister) or *dadewethu* (my sister). The brothers and sisters would in turn address their younger siblings as *wena* or use their first name. The respondents noted that all the above terms used to address brothers and sisters express both respect and intimacy.

The use of the personal pronoun as an address term can also be discussed with regards to how it is used within the extended family network. The extended family consists of one's grandparents, uncles, aunts, as well as children and grandchildren of these from both the maternal and paternal sides. Fifty of the questionnaire respondents (62.5%) indicated that they would address their cousins as *wena* regardless of their gender. Twenty-two respondents (27.5%) indicated a preference for *lina* when addressing their cousins. The remaining eight respondents (10%) opted for other address terms such as *mzala* (cousin), *mzawami* (my cousin), *khazi* (cousin) and *khazola* (slang for cousin).

Sixteen respondents (20%) noted that they would say *wena* to their grandmother while 72.5% of all participants indicated that they would use other address terms when they are in a conversation with their grandmother. Some of these terms are *gogo* (grandmother) or *gogas* (slang for grandmother).

With regard to how the grandfather would be addressed, nineteen respondents (23.75%) opted for *wena* while fifty-six respondents (70%) indicated that they would use *lina*. The other five respondents (6.25%) indicated a preference for other terms such as *khulu* or *babamkhulu* (grandfather).

On the question of how aunties would be addressed, twelve respondents (15%) indicated that they would use *wena* while sixty-two respondents noted that they would say *lina* to their aunt. The other six respondents (7.5%) opted for the use of alternative terms like *anti* (aunty) and *babakazi* (aunty). To their uncle thirteen respondents (16, 25) indicated that they would say *wena* while sixty-five respondents (81.25%) noted that they would address their uncle as *lina* (you-PL). The remaining two respondents (2.5%) opted for the use of kinship terms like *malume* (uncle), *lumes* (slang form of uncle) or *khule* (another slang version for uncle). (Refer to Table 1 for figures and percentages cited above).

4.2. Personal pronominal usage and the gender variable

Data gathered from respondents in the Midlands province's districts of Gokwe, Lower Gweru, Silobela and Zhombe show that there is no explicit gender differentiation in Ndebele when addressing people using the personal pronoun. For instance, eight respondents (20%) indicated they would address their father as *wena*. Sixty-eight respondents (85%) opted for *lina* to their father. Four respondents (5%) stated that they would say *baba* (father) or daddy to their father. A similar number of respondents appear for choices of personal pronominal address terms for mothers. The results in Table 1 show that the respondents would address their mother and father in similar ways when using personal pronouns.

Six respondents indicated that they would address someone of their mother's age as *wena* while sixty-nine respondents (86.75) opted for *lina* with five respondents indicating a preference for the use of the relationship term *mama* (mother). In a similar manner, five respondents (6.25%) indicated that they would address someone of their father's age as *lina* with a similar number indicating they would address someone of their father's age as *baba* (father).

With regards to how a sister or a brother would be addressed, the numbers of respondents who opted for particular personal pronominal forms is almost the same in both cases. The same goes for someone of brother's age. For instance, ten respondents (12.5%) indicated that they would address someone of their sister's age as *sisi* (sister) or *dadewethu* (my sister). A similar percentage (12.5%) also noted that they would address someone of their brother's age using the relationship terms *bhudi* (brother) and *mnewethu* (my brother).

An incident witnessed by the researcher in a bus from Bulawayo to Gokwe substantiates the views of the questionnaire respondents presented above. The bus conductor, a young man in his early twenties said to one adult female passenger:

Usubhadele yini *wena* mama?

('Have you paid [your bus fare] you-SING mother?')

In reply the woman expressed her disdain at being addressed as *wena* and retorted:

Ngilo mntwana ongangawe mina. Ungabongibiza ngokuthi '*wena*'!

('I have a child of your age. Do not refer to me as "you-SING"!')

The incident aroused commotion in the bus as most people argued that the conductor was wrong in addressing the woman as *wena*. Most passengers asserted that the conductor should have addressed the woman as *lina* because she was not only a grown up woman but was a mother too. The underlying meaning of all this is that personal pronominal choice is seen as tied to age and parenting.

Notwithstanding the implications of the above information, some witnessed cases indicate that people of different sexes use the personal pronoun differently. Some brides at Insukamini village (Lower Gweru), and Donsa area in Silobela were observed to be addressing any member of their husband's family as *lina* regardless of age and gender. The brides even addressed the young brothers and young sisters of their husband as *lina babomncane* (you-PL uncle) and *lina aunty* (you-PL aunty) respectively. On the contrary, the bridegrooms were heard referring to the young sisters of their wives as *wena* (you-SING).

Linguistic usages of male and female teachers at Manzamnyama, Donjani, St Judes, Nyaje, Rio Tinto, Loreto and St. Teresa Secondary Schools in the Midlands province were also observed. Young male teachers were seen to be comfortable with the use of such slang terms as *tshomi* (friend) and *majita* (gentlemen). On the other hand, their female counterparts were inclined to the use of *lina* when addressing their workmates, especially the elderly teachers. In speech events that took place among themselves, most lady teachers used the less formal mutual personal pronoun *wena*. That women are inclined to use the more formal linguistic forms while men are comfortable with the less formal one is not unique to teachers. This was found to be prevalent in most rural villages and urban locations that were visited during fieldwork trips in the Midlands Ndebele speech community.

4.3. Personal pronominal usage and social context

The social context of a speech event in this study has been taken to comprise the formality and informality of the situation, the nature of the topic of discussion and the physical circumstances under which a speech event is taking place. Language use is often context related; meaning that a style or way of speaking that is considered appropriate in certain situations might be deemed socially inappropriate in other situations. In other words, linguistic behaviour does not have to be appropriate to the individual only. It may also need to be suitable for particular occasions and situations. These situations could either be formal or informal.

4.3.1. Formal domains

The term formal as used here relates to a situation where certain socially or customarily prescribed norms of behaviour are to be observed. Examples of such situations that were included in this study include church services, African traditional ceremonies and business conversations. On the question on how they would address God when praying, thirty-one respondents (38.75%) indicated that they would use *wena*, while thirty-four respondents opted for *lina*. The other fifteen respondents (18.75%) noted that they would address God using alternative address terms such as *Thixo* (almighty), *Nkosi* (Lord), *Baba* (Father), *Nkulunkulu* (God), *Somandla* (all powerful), and *Mdali* (creator).

With regard to how they would address God when preaching, twenty-four respondents (34%) opted for the use of *wena*, with forty respondents (50%) indicating a preference for *lina*. The other sixteen people (20%) indicated that they would use tittles and relationship terms cited above. The common reason that was given for the use of *lina* and/or the relationship terms noted above is that God is considered to be all powerful. Some respondents also noted that because God is the creator of everything, he deserves to be addressed through formal and euphemistic terms. Those who opted for the use of *wena* on the other hand reasoned that there is only one God and that it would be inappropriate to address God using *lina* as if they were many. This would violate the Christian principle that there is only one God and those who believe in him should have no other gods. In addition to this another reason given for the use of *wena* is that God is believed to be loving and caring. The respondents who opted for *wena* noted that the singular form of the second person pronoun serves to express the intimacy that exists between God and those who worship and serve him.

Table 2. Questionnaire results: Personal pronominal usage and social context.*

Addressee & context	Number of respondents who opted for:					
	wena		*lina*		Other terms	
		%		%		%
God, when praying	31	38.75	34	42.5	15	18.75
God, when preaching	24	30	40	50	16	20
An adult in church	5	6.25	68	85	7	8.75
Young person in church	47	58.75	22	27.55	11	13.75
Ancestors in traditional ceremony	4	5	67	83.75	9	11.25
A friend when discussing business	66	82.5	6	7.5	8	10
A friend during informal conversations	69	86.25	–	–	11	13.75
A partner in public	58	72.5	9	11.25	13	16.25
A partner in private	58	72.5	3	3.75	19	23.75

*Note: N = 80.

However, from personal observations I discovered that in the Midlands Ndebele community, people rarely use *lina* when praying to God. The address terms that were found to be frequently used are *wena*, *wena baba* ('you-SING father'), *Mdali* ('Creator'), *wena Thixo* ('you Almighty'), *Nkosi* ('Lord'), and *Somandla* ('All powerful'). It seems that questionnaire respondents gave what they thought should be the correct way of addressing God rather than the exact way in which they address God. This points to some of the limitations of data collected through self-reporting, whereby respondents tend to misrepresent their linguistic practices by providing answers that they think are the most appropriate (though these answers in themselves are interesting and also revealing).

Regarding how they would address members of the congregation of different age groups, five questionnaire respondents (6.25%) indicated that they would say *wena* to an adult when in church while sixty-eight respondents (85%) opted for the use of *lina* (you-PL). The remaining seven respondents (8.75%) stated that they would address an adult member of their church using a range of kinship terms. To male adults they would use *baba* ('father') and to female adults they would use *mama* ('mother'). Concerning the preferred address term when speaking to a young member of their church forty-seven respondents (58.75%) indicated that they would use the second person singular pronoun *wena*. Twenty-two respondents (27.5%) opted for the use of *lina*, while eleven respondents (13.75%) noted that they would use other forms of address including first names and relationship terms such as *mngane* ('friend') and *mzalwane* ('brother or sister').

The reason that was given for the use of *wena* to both adults and young people in church is that all people are equal before God. Those who opted for the use of *lina* to an adult church member noted that although people are equal before God, respect for adults should always be maintained. One interviewee from Gwenzi Adventist church in Zhombe noted that:

Inhlonipho ivele ikhona ndawo zonke, sonke isikhathi.
('Respect is always there everywhere, all the time.')

The eleven respondents who indicated that they would refer to any member of their church as *mzalwane* (brother/sister) reasoned that the latter term carried both an element of respect and equality before God.

The data presented in Table 2 also shows that four respondents (5%) would address an ancestral spirit as *wena*, while sixty-seven people (83.75%) indicated that they would use *lina*. The other nine respondents, (11.25%) featured alternative forms of address: to female ancestral spirits they would say *gogo* ('grandmother') or *salukazi* ('elder woman'). When addressing a male ancestral spirit, they would say *babamkhulu* ('grandfather') or *khulu* (short form for 'grandfather').

The respondents who opted for the use of *lina* to an ancestral spirit noted that *ithongo* ('an ancestral spirit') represents all other *amathongo* ('ancestral spirits') in their family lineage. Thus, by addressing one ancestral spirit, the people would be indirectly talking to all their ancestors, hence the use of *lina*. One interviewee from Silobela stated that *lina* is used because ancestral spirits are never addressed individually. This is diametrically the opposite of how Christian respondents suggested they would address God using the personal pronoun. As already noted above the Christian view of the existence of only one God and the desire not to be seen as implying that there are several gods compels congregants to use the singular form of the personal pronoun during prayers. This is where non-linguistic religious belief systems are seen to be influencing the different ways in which respondents would use personal pronominal forms of address. All of this can be explained in terms of the contested nature of what constitutes polite and impolite linguistic usages in the sense that 'certain linguistic expressions might be open to interpretation either as realisations of politic behaviour or as realisations of impoliteness' (Watts 2003: 217).

Another major reason that was given for the use of *lina* to ancestors is that the dead are regarded as having extra-ordinary powers to protect and provide for the living. The importance of ancestral spirits in the everyday socio-economic and political lives of the Ndebele people is reiterated by Bozongwana (1983: 30), who states that '[t]he fertility of livestock, land, and also human beings is attributed to the cooperation and direction of the ancestral spirits and, as such all that man has is ordered by their governance.' However, data from oral interviews and personal observations suggest that, contrary to some of the questionnaire results noted above, personal pronouns are not frequently used when addressing ancestral spirits. The terms that are widely used in the *ukuthethela* ('appeasing of ancestral spirits') ceremony and *umbuyiso* ('calling home the dead') ceremony are relationship terms *babamkhulu* ('grandfather') and *gogo* ('grandmother') to a male and female ancestral spirit respectively.

Regarding personal pronominal usage in the work domain, some people addressed each other as either *lina* or *wena* depending on gender and role-relationships. The choice of the personal pronominal address term seemed to depend on the degree of intimacy between one worker and another. For instance, during a visit to Loreto High School in Silobela it was observed that teachers that were very close to each other exchanged the mutual *wena*. On the contrary, staff members not so close to each other were fond of exchanging the mutual *lina*. Both teachers and pupils addressed the headmaster as *lina hedimasta* ('you-PL headmaster') or simply *hedimasta* ('headmaster'). During lesson times, pupils referred to their teacher as *lina titsha* ('you-PL teacher') or simply *titsha/mbalisi* ('teacher'). In return, the teacher would address each pupil using *wena* or their first names. The system was asymmetrical although as will be shown in the next section of this chapter, the system of address changed to a reciprocal one between teachers and pupils as they shifted from the classroom situation to the less formal sports domain.

In marriage negotiations, it was observed that the *hlonipha* ('euphemistic') style is dominant. According to a sixty-five year old informant from chief Jahana's area in Gokwe, the go between should have a high command of isiNdebele *esilenhlonipho* ('respectful Ndebele language') when negotiating marriage proposals. While the go-between should address the would-be in-laws as *lina*, the system is not always reciprocal. The go-between may either receive the powerless *wena* or the statusful *lina* depending on the attitude of the host family. Nzama (1989: 13) made similar observations in her research with the Bulawayo Ndebele speech community:

In a marriage relationship and situations of marriage negotiations, address term selection entails the standard Ndebele and the *hlonipha* style. Of interest in recent years is the semantic pronoun of power and solidarity, the use of /li/...

This point substantiates the observations made by most interviewees that the plural form of the second person pronoun is dominant in marriage negotiation situations, which are largely considered as formal.

4.3.2. Informal domains

Informal situations as discussed in this chapter are those situations in which people interact in a relaxed mood with very limited or no constraints around choices of linguistic forms. The formality of a situation may be viewed in terms of general social behaviour or linguistic use or both. While the formal situations discussed above are classified as high domains, the informal situations are characterised as low domains, which Fasold (1984:183) defines as 'those [situations] in which the pronoun of solidarity and intimacy is commonly used...'

In this study, participants were observed and also asked to say how they would address people with whom they have different types of relationships both in public and in private. On the question on how they would address their partner in public, fifty-eight respondents (72.5%) said they would use *wena*. Nine respondents (11.25%) indicated that they would say *lina*, while fifteen respondents indicated that they would use a range of other address terms. Some of these alternative terms are *mngane* ('friend'), the slang term *tshomi* ('friend'), first names and endearments such as *s'thandwa* ('the one I love'), *dudu* ('darling'), *lovie* and *sweetie*.

Among the reasons given for the use of *wena* and endearments to partners were the following: 'We have something in common', *Ngoba ngimejwayele kakhulu* ('Because I am very much used to him/her'), *Ngumngane, ngakho ngisebenzisa loba luphi ulimi* ('He/she is a friend, so I can use any linguistic style'), 'We know each other well, so there is freedom to show love', *Siyabe siyintanga nye* ('We will be of the same age'), and *Akulanhlonipho enkulu edingakalayo njengoba silingana* ('There is no need to show respect since we are of the same age').

Of the questionnaire respondents, 86.25% noted that they would normally use *wena* when discussing informal matters with a friend of any gender or age. The other eleven (13.75%) opted for the use of slang and other relationship terms noted above. There were no respondents who would address a friend using *lina* when discussing informal matters. The absence of respondents who opted for the use of *lina* to a friend in any situation suggests that the relationship between friends is a mutual one, which does not warrant the use of the statusful *lina*. This is evident from some of the reasons that were given for the use of *wena* when addressing a friend in informal situations. For example: 'This is a sign of mutual understanding' and 'We will be sharing jokes and enjoying together'.

The personal observations made during field trips show that when pupils move out of class and go for sporting activities, they change the way they address their teachers. The observed students and teachers exchanged the reciprocal *wena...* (you-SING...) which expressed an atmosphere of free socialisation. Some students observed during a soccer training session at St Judes Secondary School were heard addressing the teachers they were playing with as follows:

Khabela ngapha titsha!

('Pass to this side teacher!')

While the personal pronominal marker is not apparent in the above statement the structure of the utterance allows for the insertion of *wena*, instead of *lina*. This would result in *Khabela ngapha wena titsha* ('Pass to this side you-SING teacher'). Inserting *lina* would render the utterance unacceptable – **Khabela ngapha lina titsha* ('Pass to this side you-PL teacher') is not a well-formed sentence in the Ndebele language. Thus, while the pupils would address their teacher as *lina titsha* ('you-PL teacher') in class, they shift to the less formal *wena titsha* ('you-SING teacher') as they go to places of socialisation with their teachers.

5. Discussion and analysis

The data presented above highlights some key factors that determine choices of personal pronoun as address terms in the Midlands Ndebele speech community. The data clearly indicates how personal pronominal usage is related to: the age and gender of addresser and addressee, role-relationships, level of intimacy between addresser and addressee, kinship relationships, as well as the formality and informality of the situation. Overall, the data indicates the need to show respect and the desire to express solidarity are both at the core of personal pronominal choices and usages.

The data presented in this chapter further confirms the findings of previous and current international research on pragmatics and politeness strategies (see for example, Watts 2003; Allan and Burridge 2006; Fukushima 2002; Eelen 2001). This body of literature has highlighted the significance of differences in cultural norms, expectations and practices in determining interlocutors' linguistic behaviours. The data for this study shows that in the Midlands Ndebele speech community, the singular second person pronoun (*wena*) is used as a pronoun of mutuality and powerlessness. On the other hand, the plural second person pronoun (*lina*) has been seen to be the pronoun of power and deference. The reasons that were given by respondents and interviewees for the use of either *lina* or *wena* to particular individuals were varied. But on the overall, most respondents noted that parents and any other adults deserve to be respected by virtue of their age and the role they play in the lives of those individuals and in society in general. Parents are the breadwinners for their families and hence they should be respected by being addressed as *lina*. On the contrary, people of the same age and those with a high degree of solidarity would exchange the mutual *wena*. The reason behind such symmetrical exchange of *wena* is that the individuals are close to each other and can talk freely on any subject matter. As Brown and Gilman (1968: 253) noted almost half a century ago, 'the personal pronouns are closely associated with two dimensions fundamental to the analysis of all social life – the dimensions of power and solidarity'.

On the relationship between personal pronominal usage and age within the Midlands Ndebele speech community, the study shows that the behaviour pattern towards the father seems to be the basis of behaviour towards all paternal relatives. In a similar manner, one's behaviour towards the mother seems to be the basis of behaviour towards maternal relatives. The data reveals that all adults on both the maternal and paternal side should be respected the same way that the father and mother are respected. Thus aunties, uncles and grandparents should be addressed as *lina* even if the individual is alone. It can be further deduced that grandparents, aunties and uncles are given a lot of respect because of the role they play in the life of an individual. Grandparents especially are regarded as beholders and custodians of social morality, customs and traditions. They guide and counsel the young on how to become morally upright citizens. In the final analysis it can be concluded that role-relationships play a significant role in determining appropriate personal pronominal usages by individuals and communities.

The study also shows that by virtue of there being no significant social distances between them siblings often address each other using *wena* regardless of age and gender. However, some exceptional cases were observed, which indicate that while children of the same parents may be friendly with each other, age sometimes determines the choice of an address term. These findings confirm studies on Zulu kinship terminology carried out in the 1950s. For example, Krige (1950: 24) found out that 'there are two factors, which create differences in the behaviour of one sibling to another. These are age and sex, which influence even the kinship terminology'.

This point supports personal observations made during the course of this study, which suggested that brothers, sisters and any other people of their age are sometimes addressed using *lina*. In view of the research findings of this study, it can be concluded that there is no one clear-cut way by which a brother or sister should be addressed. Whether they should be addressed using *lina* or *wena* solely remains at the addressor's discretion.

From the results presented in Table 1, it can also be noted that the sex of an addressee is not a very important determinant of how adults in particular are addressed using personal pronouns. The data show that regardless of their sex, all adults should be addressed as *lina*. Similarly both elder brothers and elder sisters are addressed as *wena* under similar circumstances.

On the question of personal pronominal usages and gender of the addressor, the study has shown that there is some degree of difference in the choices made by the two genders. Women are inclined to use the more formal form *lina* while men display an inclination towards the use of *wena* and an assortment of slang terms and other less formal forms of address. These results seem to confirm Trudgill's (1983: 87) findings in the English societies where he notes that 'men's and women's speech is not only different: women's speech is also socially "better" than men's speech. This is a reflection of the fact that generally speaking, more "correct" social behaviour is expected of women'.

This view came to light in personal observations at some schools in the Midlands province where lady teachers were seen to be very particular about their choice of proper address terms in particular situations. On the other hand their male counterparts predominantly used slang terms like *tshomi* ('friend') and *majita* ('gentlemen').

The study also found that the use of a personal pronoun as an address term in the Midlands Ndebele speech community is to a large degree related to some non-linguistic variables of the social context. Some of the social context variables investigated and analysed in this chapter include the classroom situation, church situation, work situation, the traditional ceremony (high domains) and the entertainment situation as well as discussions of informal matters (low domains). In all high domains, the plural form of the personal pronoun (*lina*) was found to be dominant while in all low domains, the singular form (*wena*) was more common. A clear conclusion of this study is that behaviour does not only have to be appropriate to the individual, it also needs to be suitable for particular occasions and situations.

The data also suggest that speakers in a social interaction are not kinds of sociolinguistic automata who should talk only within constraints laid down by the norms of their society (politic behaviour). Individuals living in urban areas tended to use modern address forms that transgress what is often considered to be politically correct ways of speaking. They do so because they are living in situations of rapid transition where traditional intergroup barriers are breaking down and norms of interaction are changing. The concept of 'politic behaviour' can, therefore, be seen as being multidimensional and, to some extent, something that is relative to the situation or context. What might be considered as appropriate linguistic behaviour in predominantly rural and countryside settings often turns out to be out of sync with linguistic norms that are generally expected in urban and peri-urban settings.

The study has also shown that people in the 60 years and above age group blame the youngsters and urbanisation for the changes that are taking place in the Ndebele system of address. The elderly perceive the incorporation of English linguistic forms in the Ndebele address system to be a negative thing. However, from the reasons that were given by various respondents and interviewees in the 13–20 years, 20–40 years and 40–60 years age groups, such changes should not be viewed negatively. In fact, the use of English forms of address facilitates and enriches communication. Furthermore, linguistic interference seems to be inevitable in cosmopolitan societies that continue to experience cross-linguistic and cross-cultural contact such as the Midlands Ndebele speech community.

6. Conclusion

In addition to demonstrating the dynamics of personal pronominal usages among people of different ages and different sexes in the Midlands Ndebele speech community, this chapter has also revealed that there are other forms of address that are widely used together with personal pronouns. The chapter has shown that the personal pronoun can be used in combination with first names, tittles, relationship terms, kinship terms, endearments, totems and nicknames. It can, therefore, be concluded that it is the availability of alternative choices than anything else that compels one to use a particular form of address in particular situations. The Midlands Ndebele speech community seems to be rich in diverse forms of address, which may be used in place of, or to complement, personal pronouns and still retain the intended communication purposes of showing respect or solidarity. It also came to light that everything else (topic, gender, situation) being equal, personal pronominal usage in the Midlands Ndebele speech community generally varies with age. People in different age groups use the personal pronoun differently and are addressed differently. This partly determines whether specific linguistic usages are considered as realisations of politic behaviour or realisations of impolite behaviour. Finally, the amount of interference from linguistic norms of other cultural groups varies from one age group to another and it is this variation that largely accounts for the dynamics of second person pronominal address in the Midlands Ndebele speech community.

References

Allan, Keith. 2012. The middle class politeness criterion. Seminar paper presented at the Linguistics Seminar Series, University of New England, 6 July 2012.

Allan, Keith and Kate Burridge. 1991. *Euphemism and Dysphemism: Language Used as Shield and Weapon*. New York: Oxford University Press.

Allan, Keith and Kate Burridge. 2006. *Forbidden Words: Taboo and the Censoring of Language*. Cambridge: Cambridge University Press.

Bozongwana, Wallace. 1983. *Ndebele Religion and Custom*. Gweru: Mambo Press.

Brown, Roger and Albert Gilman. 1968. The pronouns of power and solidarity. In Joshua Fishman (ed.), *Readings in the Sociology of Language*. Berlin: Mouton de Gruyter, 252–75.

Brown, Penelope and Stephen Levinson. 1987. *Politeness*. Cambridge: Cambridge University Press.

Eelen, Gino. 2001. *A Critique of Politeness Theories*. Manchester: St Jerome Publishing.

Fasold, Ralph. 1984. *The Sociolinguistics of Society*. New York: Basil Blackwell Publishers.

Friedrich, Paul. 1966. Structural implications of Russian pronominal usage. In William Bright (ed.), *Sociolinguistics: Proceedings of the UCLA Sociolinguistics Conference*. The Hague: Mouton, 214–59.

Friedrich, Paul. 1972. Social context and semantic feature: The Russian pronominal usage. In John Gumperz and Dell Hymes (eds), *Directions in Sociolinguistics: The Ethnography of Speaking*. New York: Holt, Rinehart and Winston, 407–34.

Fukushima, Saeko. 2002. *Requests and Culture: Politeness in British and Japanese*. Bern: Peter Lang.

Government of Zimbabwe. 1982. *August 1982 Population Census*. Harare: Government Printer.

Gumperz, John and Dell Hymes (ed.). 1972. *Directions in Sociolinguistics: The Ethnography of Speaking*. New York: Holt, Rinehart and Winston.

Hachipola, Simooya Jerome. 1998. *A Survey of the Minority Languages of Zimbabwe*. Harare: University of Zimbabwe Publications.

Khumalo, J. S. M. 1992. The morphology of the direct relative in Zulu. In Derek F. Gowlett (ed.), African Linguistic Contributions: Papers in Honour of Ernest Westphal. Pretoria: Via Afrika Limited, 210–226.

Krige, Eileen Jensen. 1950. *The Social System of the Zulus*. Pietermaritzburg: Shutter and Shooter.

Mhlabi, Stephen J. 1978 *Ndebele Register, Volume 1*. University of Zimbabwe: Department of African Languages and Literature.

Ndhlovu, Finex. 2009. *The Politics of Language and Nation Building in Zimbabwe*. Bern: Peter Lang.

Nzama, Sizanokuhle. 1989. Code selection, switching and social evaluation in the Bulawayo speech community. Unpublished MA thesis, University of Zimbabwe.

Sibanda, Galen. 1987. The interlanguage factor in the Ndebele community. Unpublished PhD dissertation, University of Zimbabwe.

Trudgill, Peter. 1983. *Sociolinguistics: An introduction to Language and Society*. Harmondsworth: Penguin Books Ltd.

Vilkki, Liisa. 2006. Politeness, face and facework: Current issues. *SKY Journal of Linguistics* 19: 322–32.

Watts, Richard J. 2003. *Politeness*. Cambridge: Cambridge University Press.

Watts, Richard J. Sachiko Ide and Konrad Ehlich (eds). 1992. *Politeness in Language: Studies in Its History, Theory and Practice*. Berlin: Mouton de Gruyter.

Chapter 10

RESPONSE WORDS ARE ANAPHORS

Thorstein Fretheim

Norwegian University of Science and Technology

There are some interesting similarities between response words like *yes* and *no* and discourse-anaphoric items like personal pronouns. Response words are discourse variables whose communicated truth-theoretic content is determined by a pragmatic process of saturation. It is argued that they encode a procedure, in the relevance-theoretic sense, as opposed to a concept. A hearer will locate a linguistic antecedent from which to extract conceptual information needed to determine the pragmatically derived content of the anaphoric response word. When the interlocutor's speech-act has the syntactic form of a complex sentence structure, the response word will not always direct the interlocutor to a unique coreferential antecedent, but this is a familiar situation in pragmatic processes of resolving the reference of anaphors. The most relevant antecedent-anaphor relation wins out. Special attention is given to certain data in Norwegian, a code with two response words that affirm a positive proposition and one that affirms a negative proposition. It is shown that the two positive ones, *ja* (cf. German 'ja') and *jo* (cf. German 'doch'), are not complementary. In certain contexts, *jo* conveys affirmation with a bit of reservation, which is consistent with the lexical constraint encoded by *jo*.

1. Anaphora relation[1]

I propose that the relation between a response word token and the truth-conditional content that it communicates in a context can profitably be described in terms of the concept of anaphora. Determination of the content communicated by the producer of a response word depends largely on a mental representation of information extracted from its linguistic antecedent.

In the introductory chapter of his book on anaphora, Huang (2000: 1) notes that in contemporary linguistics, the term 'anaphora' 'is commonly

---

[1] I am grateful to Kaja Borthen and Signe Rix Berthelin for comments on an early version of this paper.

used to refer to a relation between two linguistic elements, wherein the interpretation of one (called an anaphor) is in some way determined by the interpretation of the other (called an antecedent)'. With most kinds of anaphora it is only when the hearer has interpreted the two linguistic elements that the existence of an anaphora relation between them can be ascertained. Formal properties of antecedent and anaphor are normally not decisive. Ariel (1996: 16) notes that 'the process of antecedent selection cannot be performed without taking into consideration the nature of the potentially anaphoric expression itself', but even if anaphors are marked as such, antecedents are generally not marked by any distinguishing feature. There is nevertheless one recognized type of anaphora, between a reflexive and its antecedent, which may be defined in strictly morpho-syntactic terms, notably in grammars that keep reflexives and personal pronouns morphologically apart and demand by rule of grammar that the antecedent is the subject of the clause that contains the coreferential reflexive.

The relation between a response word and its antecedent is not like the relation between a reflexive and its antecedent. A response word is no bound variable. Its reference (i.e., its truth-conditional content) cannot be established on purely formal grounds. (Nor, for that matter, can the relation between a personal pronoun and its antecedent.) With response word anaphora, the presence or absence of the negation marker *not* in the first speaker's sentence constrains that person's search for the intended antecedent of the second speaker's *yes* or *no* to some degree but it does not fix the antecedent selection. Both a *yes* and a *no* may cause the hearer to identify a relatively larger or a relatively smaller syntactic chunk of the interlocutor's most recent utterance as the antecedent of the response word. The pitch profile of the monosyllabic response *yes* or *no* may reveal whether or not the speaker is in agreement with the addressee, which may in turn constrain the addressee's inference leading to resolution of the truth-conditional content of the response word. In the pragmatic process of interpreting tokenings of *yes* and *no*, a hearer must be sensitive to the presence of formal cues in the immediately preceding discourse both in order to determine the content of the response word and in order to determine whether the speaker agrees with the hearer in an act of confirmation or disagrees with him in an act of denial or refusal. For instance, if the interlocutor has first expressed a proposition with the help of a syntactic structure that includes an overt marker of negation like the English word *not* (or *nothing*, *no one*, the quantifying determiner *no*, etc.), the non-negative propositional anaphor *yes* is likely to be understood to oppose the hearer's most recently expressed proposition. Conversely, a given token of the negative propositional anaphor *no* is most likely to confirm the proposition that this anaphor addresses if there is a candidate antecedent that contains *not*, and to contradict it otherwise.

The antecedent of an anaphor offers important input to the inferential process of determining the reference or designatum of the anaphor, and often the speaker's choice of anaphor is itself the most important indicator of where in the preceding discourse to locate its antecedent (Gundel, Hedberg and Zacharski 1993). Occasionally there is no overt antecedent for a particular anaphor, in which case the reference of the anaphoric expression can only be resolved via a bridging implicature (e.g., Matsui 2000) inferred on the basis of information present in the preceding discourse.

The antecedent part of an anaphora relation has traditionally been viewed as a linguistic element, but this terminology is at odds with what Cornish (1999) calls an antecedent. For him the antecedent member of an anaphora relation is the semantic content that is the output of the saturation process. The linguistic element that I call an antecedent, he calls the 'antecedent trigger'. Although my inclusion of response words in the category of anaphoric expressions has, to the best of my knowledge, not been proposed before, my terminological practice deviates in a less dramatic way from established conventions than the distinction between 'antecedent trigger' and 'antecedent' proposed by Cornish. Still, the 'trigger' metaphor employed by Cornish is appropriate, because the job of the linguistic antecedent is to trigger contextually determined inference leading to saturation of the later anaphor.

The context-dependent resolution of the content of a token of *yes* or *no* is a pragmatic process that is triggered by a linguistic expression. A response word triggers the search for a contextual value, the contextual value that contributes the most to the relevance of the stimulus for the addressee. Such linguistically controlled inferential processes have come to be known as saturation processes. Recanati (2010: 4) says, 'Saturation is a pragmatic process of contextual value-assignment that is triggered (and made obligatory) by something in the sentence itself, namely the linguistic expression to which a value is contextually assigned.' He describes saturation as a 'bottom-up' process, because it is driven by the presence of a linguistic trigger, typically an indexical, including pronouns and demonstratives. This is the only kind of pre-semantic (pre-propositional) pragmatic process that is mandatory.

Some 'minimalist' philosophers (Cappelen and Lepore 2005; Borg 2004) hold that the only pragmatic processes which are pre-semantic in the sense that they affect truth-conditions are the mandatory saturation processes. For adherents of so-called truth-conditional pragmatics, or TCP (Recanati 2004, 2010; Bezuidenhout 2002; Sperber and Wilson 1995; Carston 2002), there are also optional, 'top-down' pragmatic processes. Recanati refers to these as 'modulations'. They cover metonymic transfer, sense-extension and what relevance theorists like Sperber, Wilson and Carston call free enrichment (see also Hall 2009), and they are characterized by the fact that they are 'not mandated by the linguistic material but respond to wholly pragmatic considerations' (Recanati 2010: 4). The truth-conditional pragmatics approach to the semantics-pragmatics interface sees information derived from such optional inferential processes as necessary for ascription of truth-conditions to utterances of sentences. Technically the relation between a response word and the antecedent material needed to identify its content is not of this optional top-down sort but of the bottom-up sort permitted even by minimalists who restrict pre-semantic pragmatic processes to cases of mandatory saturation. Still, philosophers and linguists who want to keep pragmatic intrusion to a minimum in their analyses of truth-conditional content have never been concerned with the special phenomenon of response word anaphora. For people of the opposite belief, those who argue for massive contextual input to mental representations of truth-conditional content and who therefore permit free enrichment processes and other kinds of modulation of the 'logical form' of a sentence (Recanati 2004, 2010), the analysis presented in this paper should not pose any serious problems, but response word anaphora has been largely ignored even by scholars of this 'contextualist' persuasion.

2. Identifying the content of occurrences of 'yes' and 'no'

Do response words like *yes* and *no* encode a concept? Some words that are commonly used as response words clearly do. One can respond to a statement or a question by saying *True!* or *Absolutely!*, which simultaneously signals agreement with the interlocutor, and one can respond to a statement, a question or an imperative by saying *Sure!*, or *No way!*, the latter signalling the contrary propositional attitude of disbelief or disapproval. However, it seems intuitively right to think that *yes* and *no* are not words that encode concepts in the same way as the four 'sentence substitutes' mentioned here. *Yes* and *no* can also convey information about the speaker's agreement or disagreement with the addressee, but only indirectly as a consequence of the mutually manifest context of the interlocutors, not as a lexically encoded part of their meanings.

I believe the primary lexical meaning of response words like *yes* and *no* to be what relevance theorists call a procedural meaning (Blakemore 1987; Wilson and Sperber 1993), because they instruct the addressee to pursue a specific inferential route in the endeavour to resolve the truth-conditional (semantic) content of an utterance consisting of one of these words and nothing else.[2] In this respect, a response word appears to be functionally rather similar to an indexical, like a personal pronoun, whose reference depends on information extracted from an accessible phrase or clause in the preceding discourse. In other words, *yes* and *no* behave like anaphors whose semantic value is fixed via conceptual 'transfer' from an antecedent.

In the following talk exchange between A and B, where B_1 and B_2 are to be read as alternative reactions to A's utterance, *yes* in B_1 and *no* in B_2 are seen to convey the same information. Intuitively, *yes* and *no* have contrary meanings, and it is natural to attribute this to the fact that the two response words encode opposite instructions for the hearer to follow in the inferential interpretation of the response word. How, then, can we account for the fact that *yes* and *no* seem to be interchangeable in (1)?

(1) A: It's clear that Isaac doesn't know what we decided to do.

   B_1: Yes. That's true.

   B_2: No. That's true.

The utterance of B_1 is a confirmation of the truth of A's preceding statement. The positive polarity of the main clause causes the hearer to infer that the answer *yes* affirms the hearer's proposition, but this proposition is actually the negative proposition that A claims to be true. Speaker A's sentence has two levels of embedding under the main clause but the negation marker in A's embedded complement did not affect B's choice of response word in B_1. In principle the demonstrative *that* in B_1 permits two interpretations. It can represent the belief that it is clear, or evident, that Isaac does not know what they decided to do, or it can represent the belief that Isaac does not know what was decided. Anyone who says that the truth of an arbitrary proposition *p* is clear to them is committed to the belief that *p* is true, but this communicated epistemic attitude is external to the proposition expressed. A's main clause *It's clear (that)…* and B's predicate *… is true* do not supply any semantic material to the negative proposition that A and B believe to be

---

[2] My approach to pragmatic analysis and the exploration of the semantics-pragmatics interface is basically that of Relevance Theory, as developed by Sperber and Wilson (1995), Carston (2002) and others.

true; these linguistic elements are non-truth-conditional indicators of A's and B's shared commitment to the negative proposition expressed, they are metalinguistic markers of propositional attitude.

The hearer's impression of the semantic status of the adjective *clear* in (1) depends to some extent on whether this word is accented or unaccented. An accent on *clear* combined with de-accentuation in the complement clause indicates that *clear* does contribute a truth-condition, while de-accentuation of the main clause of A's declarative indicates that *clear* is external to the proposition expressed (cf. van Dommelen and Fretheim 2012), just as in the syntactic alternatives of *Clearly, Isaac doesn't know what we decided to do*, *Isaac clearly doesn't know what we decided to do* and *Isaac doesn't know what we decided to do, clearly*, where the adverb *clearly* is unambiguously 'parenthetical'.

The positive response word *yes* in (1) B_1 expresses what relevance theorists call a higher-level (or higher-order) explicature, a communicated attitude to the proposition expressed (Blakemore 1992; Wilson and Sperber 1993). *Yes* matches the positive polarity of A's higher clause and therefore repeats the higher-level explicature first communicated by A, expressed in the lower clause *(that) Isaac doesn't know what we decided to do*.

In the alternative utterance of (1) B_2, the speaker's response is *no*. Here B's choice of response word is not dictated by what is found in A's higher clause. The antecedent selected by B is now A's negative embedded complement. B's utterance of *no* affirms the truth of the negative proposition associated with the complement. While *yes* instructs the hearer to locate a syntactic structure with an overtly expressed positive polarity, *no* in B_2 causes the hearer to look for the negation marker *not/n't* in the utterance responded to and to associate the negation there with whatever interpretation will make the utterance of *no* relevant to him. Consequently, *no* in B_2 signals B's agreement with A. This negative proposition is what relevance theorists call the (basic, or 'ground-floor') explicature of A's utterance (Sperber and Wilson 1995), the truth-conditional content explicitly communicated by A. Although the interpretation of *no* in B_2 described here may be more accessible than the alternative interpretation of *no* as an objection to A's statement, a token of *no* pronounced not on a rather flat, low-falling tone but on an energetic high fall or a rise-fall might cause the hearer to interpret the utterance as a sign of disagreement with A, as an act of objecting to A's higher-level explicature and therefore also to the basic explicature communicated by A. However, this disagreement interpretation is not supported by the continuation *That's true* in B_2.

In (2) below, the alternative responses of B_1 and B_2 are very likely to be given the same interpretation, just as in (1), but this is largely due to the meaning of the continuation *He does* with its positive polarity, which makes it manifest to the hearer that the inferred semantic value of *yes* and *no* in (2) B_1 and B_2 is the reverse of the inferred semantic value of the same response words in (1). *Yes* in B_3 and *no* in B_4 are not accompanied by a comment in the form of a declarative, so these two utterances will not be understood to express the same higher-level and basic explicatures. When the response word is not followed up by a comment that constrains the hearer's pragmatic interpretation of it, *yes* and *no* are likely to direct the hearer to contrary truth-conditional interpretations, both based on information extracted from A's statement. B_3 and B_4 illustrate this.

(2)   A: It's clear that Isaac doesn't know what we decided to do.

         B_1: Yes. He does.

         B_2: No. He does.

         B_3: Yes.

         B_4: No.

The utterance of *He does* in B_1 and B_2 expresses disagreement with A. As addressee A must backtrack and find an antecedent for the preceding response words *yes* and *no* which matches the interpretation of the follow-up declarative. *Yes* in B_1 is a denial of the negative proposition expressed in the lower clause: $\sim(\sim p) \equiv p$. *No* in B_2 is an example of external negation. It is literally a denial of the thought that it is clear that the lower-clause negative proposition is true. This does not entail a denial of that negative proposition but it implicates that B believes Isaac does know, and this implicature is corroborated by the next utterance *He does*.

The pragmatic interpretations of *yes* in (2) B_3 and *no* in (2) B_4 are not constrained by the meaning of a follow-up declarative, so *yes* in B_3 will normally be understood to confirm A's higher-level explicature and basic explicature, a sign of agreement with A, while *no* in B_4 will be interpreted as a sign of disagreement with A.

3. How to distribute positive and negative members of a tripartite response word system

A large number of the world's languages have a response word system with three rather than just two members. In German, for instance, *yes* in (2) B_1 above does not correspond to the German positive response word *ja* but to a different positive response word *doch*. An utterance of *doch* denies a negative proposition, and for this reason I call it a positive response word just like the word *yes* in (2) B$_1$. If the negative proposition negated by *doch* is one that the interlocutor believes to be true, then *doch* is a sign of disagreement with the interlocutor, but if the antecedent of *doch* is a negative interrogative, this word may be used to deny ~*p* in a context where both speaker and hearer believe *p*, as when *yes* is the answer to a biased English negative interrogative like *Didn't you forget your umbrella?*, or probably even more convincingly *Didn't you forget something?* where the positive-polarity item *something* indicates the speaker's bias.

3.1 Response words and concomitant head movements

I shall devote this subsection and the next one to an examination of the distribution of lexically contrastive response words in a language with a tripartite lexical distinction. I have chosen Norwegian as my source of data for two interrelated reasons: it is my native language and I was concerned with the interplay of response words and simultaneous head movements in Norwegian spoken discourse in a paper written thirty years ago (Fretheim and Vogt-Svendsen 1983). Video recordings were made of invented dialogues between a first (female) speaker who produced either an interrogative or a declarative Norwegian sentence and a second (male) speaker who responded to this by using either the response word *jo* ('yes'), corresponding to German *doch*, or the response word *nei* ('no') in conjunction with a simultaneous nodding or shaking of his head. The third response word, *ja* ('yes'), was of minor interest to us, because a head shake does not normally co-occur with *ja* – and if it does, what it conveys is something like 'This is really sad', which is not an indicator of the speaker's epistemic stance. *Ja* is never a sign of disagreement.

We were particularly concerned with denials with *nei* that would appear to be ambiguous because they could be associated either with an antecedent that was just one part of the first speaker's sentence and so with a narrow scope of negation, or with an antecedent that exhausted the first speaker's sentence and was therefore associated with a wide scope of negation. How might the extra-linguistic nod or shake contribute to native recipients' interpretations of the response *nei* in such cases? We found that, while the difference between a head nod and a head shake caused no significant difference with respect to which one of the two contrary interpretations available to the informants was selected when the first speaker's stimulus was an open yes/no-question, we observed systematic differences of a significant sort when the first speaker's stimulus was a declarative sentence used to perform a statement. (3) illustrates this difference between production of the vocal response *nei* and a contemporaneous head nod and production of the vocal response *nei* and a contemporaneous head shake.

(3)   A: Martin mente visst at de ikke ville komme.

'Martin apparently believed that they would not come.'

B_1: Nei ('No'-nod).

B_2: Nei ('No'-shake).

When the response word was accompanied by a nod, the utterance (B_1) was interpreted as an act of confirmation of A's belief by 50 out of a total number of 50 informants, but when the extra-linguistic indicator was a shaking gesture (B_2), the number of informant responses that signalled B's agreement with A was reduced to 29 (out of 50) and the number of informant responses that signalled B's disagreement with A was consequently increased from zero to 21. *Nei* was not an utterance produced with much amplitude in B_1 and B_2. A negative response word realized with more intensity is presumably easier to associate with an act of protest, and a contemporaneous head shake strengthens that interpretation.

The general conclusion expressed in Fretheim and Vogt-Svendsen (1983) was that a head shake will occasionally contribute to the hearer's overall comprehension of the stimulus when it accompanies *jo* and a head nod will contribute positively to the hearer's comprehension when it accompanies *nei*. These are the marked combinations of vocal response and head movement, as the two signs do not seem to be mutually supportive but to pull in opposite directions. The unmarked combinations of *nei*-cum-shake and *jo*-cum-nod often just strengthen the interpretation most likely to have been favoured anyway in the absence of a head movement, a disagreement interpretation in the former case and an agreement interpretation in the latter.

A head nod that accompanies *nei* supports the assumption that the speaker agrees with the interlocutor. As shaking of the head normally indicates disagreement with the opinion expressed by the interlocutor, an utterance of *nei*-cum-shake may constrain the interlocutor's pragmatic search for the truth-conditional content in a situation where more than one truth-conditional interpretation is possible. The fact that the shake in B_2 by no means caused a uniform acceptance of the disagreement interpretation may be due to the lack of energy with which the utterance *nei* was pronounced, as noted above.

While it appears that a variety of parameters may affect a native Norwegian addressee's interpretation of a given combination of response word and head movement, the results presented in Fretheim and Vogt-Svendsen (1983) did support the generalization that a head movement activates inference directed at non-truth-conditional aspects of what is communicated and the vocal response represents a truth-conditional content, by targeting either a proposition expressed by the hearer or a higher-level explicature in which the proposition expressed is a constituent.

With *jo*, the unmarked combination of a vocal response and a nodding gesture did nothing more than support whatever would be the unmarked interpretation of a given token of a 'bare' response word *jo*. While the head movement was generally judged to be meaningless when a head shake was produced simultaneously with *jo*, the test subjects' reactions to one such combination showed that the shake directed the majority to a disagreement interpretation, to the assumption that the speaker believes p ($\equiv$ ~(~p)) but attributes belief in ~p to the hearer.

Negative response words like English *no* or Norwegian *nei* encode the (procedural) information that the speaker believes a negative proposition, ~p, retrieved from the immediately preceding discourse to be true. They do not encode information about the speech act performed or the speaker's epistemic attitude to the proposition expressed. This has to be inferred on the basis of linguistic clues in the utterance that the response word addresses, the pitch profile imposed on the response word and the speaker's tone of voice, a possible extra-linguistic clue like an accompanying head gesture, and, obviously, the context at large. The speaker may employ a negative response word in order to confirm the truth of a negative proposition in an expression of agreement with the interlocutor, or in order to deny the truth of a positive proposition expressed by the interlocutor. Provided the response word is a reaction to a request, a third possibility would be that *no* and *nei* serve as refusals to act in a way desirable to the addressee. A head nod would be meaningless in an act of refusing to do something, so no act of refusal to comply with an imperative was included in the video test described in Fretheim and Vogt-Svendsen (1983).

3.2. *The Norwegian response words 'ja', 'jo' and 'nei' and their antecedents*

In this subsection I am going to examine the import of Norwegian response words in talk exchanges structured in much the same way as the English dialogues presented as (1) and (2) above, except for the fact that the stimulus produced by the first speaker Anders (m.) is not a declarative but an interrogative which the second speaker Birgit (f.) is requested to respond to. Unlike the main clause *It's clear (that)* in (1) and (2), the Norwegian higher clause *syns du (at)* ('do you think (that)') of the interrogative in (4) does belong to the propositional form of his question, because there is a difference between asking 'Do you think that *p*?' and saying 'I think that *p*'. Only the latter informs the hearer of the speaker's epistemic attitude to the proposition *p* and so contributes to a higher-level explicature. The present tense form *syns* of the verb *synes*, meaning 'think', 'be of the opinion', may be interpreted as a non-truth-conditional item when it occurs with a 1st person subject but otherwise this verb supplies a concept to the proposition expressed.

(4)   Anders: Syns du at pengene ikke skal fordeles likt mellom oss?
'Do you think that the money should not be distributed evenly between us?'

Birgit$_1$: Ja. Det syns jeg.
(literally: Yes. That think I.)
'Yes. That's what I think.'

Birgit$_2$: Jo. Det syns jeg.
'Oh yes! I think it should (be distributed evenly between us).'

Birgit$_3$: Nei. Det syns jeg ikke.
(literally: No. That think I not.)
'No. I don't think it should not be distributed evenly between us.'

The proposition that Anders in (4) wants Birgit to address and react to by either confirming or denying its truth is, in plain words, BIRGIT THINKS THAT THE MONEY SHOULD NOT BE DISTRIBUTED EVENLY BETWEEN ANDERS AND BIRGIT (I assume here that the 1st person pronominal form *oss*, 'us', is meant to be interpreted inclusively). This proposition is addressed directly by means of *ja* in Birgit$_1$, which affirms it, and *nei* in Birgit$_3$, which negates it. *Jo* in Birgit$_2$, however, disregards the conceptual material of the main clause. It instructs Anders to seek out a negative antecedent. There is one in Anders's lower clause, so Birgit's *jo* will be understood to deny the thought that the money should not be distributed evenly, that is, to affirm the contradictory counterpart of the proposition expressed in the lower clause.

Observe that the conceptual input that saturates the anaphoric demonstrative *det* in Birgit$_2$ is not Anders's interrogative but the interlocutor's semantic representation of Birgit's response word *jo*. If Birgit had answered *Det syns jeg* ('I think so') without first producing that response word, the only accessible interpretation of the following declarative would have been that Birgit endorses the negative proposition expressed in the direct object complement of the interrogative.

What I am saying here suggests that an anaphoric response word may in turn function as antecedent for an anaphoric demonstrative pronoun in the second speaker's next utterance. This would be an antecedent in the novel sense of Cornish (1999), not a linguistic element but the positive proposition explicated by the preceding response word *jo*. At the point in Birgit$_2$ where the speaker utters *Det syns jeg*, the saturated content of her response *jo* is activated in the minds of the interlocutors. This content is the positive proposition THE MONEY SHOULD BE DISTRIBUTED EVENLY BETWEEN ANDERS AND BIRGIT, and Anders will therefore identify the content of Birgit's anaphor *det* with this proposition. The declarative *Det syns jeg* in Birgit$_2$ expresses the higher-level explicature SPEAKER THINKS THAT THE MONEY SHOULD BE DISTRIBUTED EVENLY BETWEEN ANDERS AND BIRGIT.

The thought that a response word is the antecedent of another anaphor later in the discourse is, as was pointed out to me by Kaja Borthen, consistent with Huang's definition of anaphora quoted at the beginning of this paper but for me the relation of co-designation is not between an antecedent and an anaphor, nor between the meaning of an antecedent and the meaning of an anaphor, but between a content derived on the basis of an input that includes but is not exhausted by the interpretation of an antecedent and the content of the later anaphor. Thus the interrogative produced by Anders is the antecedent of both the anaphoric response word *jo* in B$_2$ and the indexical *det* in the following declarative, but just as the output of the process of saturating the response word produced by Birgit depends on an interpretation of the interlocutor's interrogative, the output of the process of saturating the demonstrative pronoun in turn depends on an interpretation of the response word. An antecedent of an anaphor is, for me, a descriptive segment or a proper name, a linguistic item whose interpretation triggers inferential processes necessary, but not always sufficient, for resolution of the reference of the anaphor. In (4) Birgit$_2$, the semantic value of *det* is determined by the semantic representation of the response word *jo*, whose semantic value is determined not just by the antecedent provided by Anders but also by the procedural meaning of *jo*. There are also cases where bridging contextual assumptions substitute for a non-existent linguistic antecedent (e.g., Gundel, Hedberg and Zacharski 2005).

Birgit₃ starts with a negative answer to Anders's question. The scope of negation is wide. While the use of *nei* in Birgit₃ might in principle be believed to indicate that Birgit embraces the judgement that the money should not be distributed evenly between them, this interpretation will not be accessible to the addressee – not unless the negation marker *ikke* is shifted to the main clause, as illustrated in (5).

(5) Anders: Syns du ikke at pengene skal fordeles likt mellom oss?

'Don't you think that the money should be distributed evenly between us?'

Birgit₁: #Ja. Det syns jeg.

Birgit₂: Jo. Det syns jeg.

'Oh yes! I think it should (be distributed evenly between us).'

Birgit₃: Nei. Det syns jeg ikke.

(a) 'No. I don't think it should be distributed evenly between us.' =

'No. I think it shouldn't be distributed evenly between us.'

or:

(b) 'No. I don't think it should not be distributed evenly between us.'

Comparing (4) and (5) we see that the surface-syntactic placement of the negator *ikke* in the first speaker's antecedent required for saturation of the second speaker's anaphoric response is a determinant of the distribution of the three response words *ja*, *jo* and *nei*. The speaker uttering *ja* is not allowed to ignore the negative polarity expressed in the higher clause and *ja* cannot affirm the complement clause proposition, because even though the negation marker is in the higher clause, Anders's question concerns a negative proposition, the same proposition as in (4).

Birgit₂ works in the same way in (5) as in (4). *Jo* requires a negative antecedent. In (4) the negator *ikke* was located in the first speaker's lower clause, but in (5) it is located in the higher clause. In both dialogues, *jo* in Birgit₂ is a denial of the negative proposition THE MONEY SHOULD NOT BE DISTRIBUTED EVENLY BETWEEN ANDERS AND BIRGIT.

English *think* and Norwegian *synes* are both so-called 'Neg-raising' verbs, which make available 'a lower-clause reading or understanding for a higher-clause negation' (Horn 1989: 308). The distribution of the response words *ja* and *nei* is sensitive to the polarity shown in the surface-syntactic form of the higher clause, which is positive in (4) and negative in (5). *Jo*, however, is insensitive to the syntactic placement of *ikke*, which may be either in the higher or in the lower clause. *Jo* denies the negative proposition that Anders wants Birgit to react to, regardless of the location of *ikke*.

One important difference between having *ikke* in the higher clause and having it in the lower clause is that only the former syntax permits an interpretation of the interrogative as a biased question, one that asks whether ~*p* and indicates that the speaker is inclined to believe *p* or to favour the truth of *p*. Unlike the situation in (4), Birgit's answers in (5) imply either agreement with Anders, as in Birgit$_2$, or disagreement, as in reading (a) of Birgit$_3$. Reading (b) of Birgit$_3$ is only consistent with Birgit's disregarding the possibility of a positive bias interpretation of Anders's interrogative.[3]

Based on the observations and comments made in the present section, I can now venture to offer what I believe to be the procedural meanings of the three Norwegian response words:

(i) The procedural meaning of JO:

Use contextual information to form in your mind an explicature that conforms to the logical formula ~(~*p*), a denial of a contextually activated negative proposition.

(ii) The procedural meaning of NEI:

Use contextual information to form in your mind an explicature that conforms to the logical formula ~*p*, a communicated negative proposition.

(iii) The procedural meaning of JA:

Use contextual information to form in your mind an explicature that conforms to the logical formula *p* and matches an antecedent with an expressed positive polarity.

---

[3] In spoken East Norwegian the choice between a low-pitched accent on the verb form *syns* in Anders's interrogative (accent 1) and a falling pitch movement on *syns* (accent 2) triggered by the unstressed negation marker *ikke* indicates the speaker's expected answer (Fretheim 2012). Accent 2 indicates that the speaker expects to receive an answer that affirms *p*, while accent 1 is indicative of an open question about ~*p*.

4. Norwegian 'jo' is insensitive to the polarity of its linguistic antecedent

While Norwegian *nei* instructs the hearer to identify an antecedent with a transparent negation marker (*ikke*) as opposed to the lexically incorporated negation of a Norwegian word like *misfornøyd* ('dissatisfied') where the negation is expressed in the prefix *mis-*, and while *ja* instructs the hearer to identify an antecedent with an overtly displayed positive polarity, the third Norwegian response word *jo* denies a negative proposition (ie affirms a positive proposition) but does not place any polarity constraint on its antecedent. *Jo* instructs the hearer to access a mental representation of a negative proposition $\sim p$ and communicates that the speaker denies this proposition, which may have been inferred via information expressed in the antecedent of *jo*.

Consider the dialogue between Anders and Birgit in (6), where Birgit$_1$, Birgit$_2$ and Birgit$_3$ are again alternative responses. Anders is asking for Birgit's evaluation.

(6) Anders: Er dette et spørsmål om estetikk?

'Is this a question of aesthetics?'

Birgit$_1$: Ja – og nei.

'Yes – and no.'

Birgit$_2$: Nei – og ja.

'No – and yes.'

Birgit$_3$: Nei – og jo.

'No – and yes.'

Birgit$_1$ is an answer that tells Anders that in one respect aesthetics is an issue but in another respect it is not. It is impossible to tell from the linguistic stimulus alone whether *nei* ('no') in Birgit$_1$ is to be understood as a speech act that addresses the polar question posed by Anders or as a mock contradiction of Birgit's own affirmation. I call it a mock contradiction, because the coordinating connective *og* ('and') precludes an interpretation of the negation in Birgit$_1$ as a repair operation, that is, a wholesale rejection of an affirmative answer found to have been produced too quickly. *Og* indicates that both propositions linked by this conjoining connective are to be construed as true, even though they appear to be contradictory (cf. the analysis of 'and'-conjunction in Blakemore and Carston 2004). The affirmative answer and the following negative answer in Birgit$_1$ may both be true, given certain qualifications of both answers. Anders's comprehension of the utterance of Birgit$_1$ does not require that Anders is able to activate a lucid idea of the two distinct yet putatively compatible concepts associated with the noun *aesthetics*, but he may expect her to follow up her utterance by explaining what it means that an affirmative and a negative answer may both be true when interpreted in the intended context. The utterance of Birgit$_1$ communicates that the answer is affirmative when the matter is regarded from one point of view but it is negative when viewed in a different perspective. The shift from 'yes' to 'no' means a change in the set of contextual assumptions brought to bear on the answer.

When the order of the positive and the negative response word is interchanged, as in (6) Birgit$_2$ and Birgit$_3$, *ja* in the former responds to the positive proposition expressed by Anders, while *jo* in the latter responds to the content of Birgit's own negative response *nei*. There is no difference in truth-conditional content between Birgit$_2$ and Birgit$_3$. These utterances differ only in that *jo* in Birgit$_3$ is presented as a self-addressed reaction to the earlier *nei*, while *ja* in Birgit$_2$ does nothing more than answer Anders's question in an act of qualifying the earlier *nei*. We know that *jo* is self-addressed because this item encodes the falsity of a negative proposition and the only negative proposition that would make the utterance of *jo* relevant is the result of a pragmatic process of saturating the earlier utterance of *nei* in Birgit$_3$ in light of information located in the antecedent provided by Anders.

The token of *jo* that appears in (7) Birgit$_1$ and the token of *ja* that appears in (7) Birgit$_2$ are both instances of acts of repair on the part of the speaker, but what is the difference?

(7)   Anders: Er dette et spørsmål om estetikk?

'Is this a question of aesthetics?'

Birgit$_1$: Nei. – Jo, forresten. / *Ja, forresten.

'No. – Yes, come to think of it.'

Birgit$_2$: Nei. – Ja, mener jeg. / *Jo, mener jeg.

'No. – I mean yes.'

It is hard to find an appropriate English gloss for the Norwegian adverb *forresten* (literally: for the rest) in Birgit$_1$. I have attempted to translate it as 'come to think of it'. What the utterance *Jo, forresten* implies is that the speaker found after a moment's reflection that she had to change her mind and negate her previous negative statement, hence the presence of the response word *jo* in Birgit$_1$, which may not be replaced by *ja*. Birgit$_2$, however, consists of a negative response followed by the speaker's eradication of it because she recognises that it was a slip of the tongue. She does not acknowledge that her prior negative answer was serious, and she makes it clear that *ja* was what she should have said and had intended to say the first time around.

Birgit expresses a single response word in the alternative answers of (8) Birgit$_1$, Birgit$_2$ and Birgit$_3$ below. Three out of ten native speakers who were consulted felt that, in order to make the answer *jo* in (8) Birgit$_2$ acceptable and coherent, Anders's interrogative should have had a negative syntactic form. The remaining seven informants said they found the response word *jo* acceptable even though there is no negation marker in the interrogative, but they felt that there is a slight difference in meaning between Birgit$_1$ and Birgit$_2$. While *ja* is an unqualified positive answer, they associated *jo* in Birgit$_2$ with an attitude of reservation or lack of full commitment on the part of the speaker.

(8)   Anders: Er du fornøyd med det nye kontoret ditt?

'Are you satisfied with your new office?'

Birgit$_1$: Ja.

'Yes.' = 'I am satisfied.'

Birgit$_2$: Jo.

'Yes.' = 'I am not dissatisfied.' / 'It's not that I'm not satisfied.'

Birgit$_3$: Nei.

'No.' = 'I am not satisfied.'

If Birgit intends to communicate that she is not a hundred percent satisfied with her new office, she is likely to let her verbal response be accompanied by what might be described as a disenchanted voice quality and possibly some other paralinguistic sign of reduced commitment to the proposition expressed by the response word. A special intonation contour or voice quality may also be imposed on *ja* in (8) Birgit$_1$, and probably with a similar pragmatic result, but while Birgit$_1$ may be produced with a prosody that reveals either enthusiasm or lack of enthusiasm, Birgit$_2$ would be misleading if produced by someone who has only positive things to say about her new office. Birgit$_1$ and Birgit$_2$ are both affirmative answers to Anders's question, unlike Birgit$_3$, but Birgit$_2$ sounds as if the speaker intends to say 'Yes but …', with an unexpressed second conjunct.

The use of *jo* in response to the statement in (9) appears to be less controversial among native hearers than its use in (8). Not a single one of my ten informants had a problem with *jo* in (9) Birgit$_2$.

(9)   Anders: Det kunne ha gått mye verre.
        'It could have been much worse.'
        Birgit₁: Ja.
        'Yes.'
        Birgit₂: Jo.
        'Well, yes, I guess so.'

Jo in (9) Birgit₂ causes the addressee Anders to activate a somewhat different context than *ja* in (9) Birgit₁, as *jo* is an act of denying a negative proposition. *Jo* in Birgit₂ therefore instructs Anders to activate the opposite thought that the outcome simply could not have been worse, a thought that is inconsistent with Anders's own statement, and it is this utterly negative thought that Birgit takes issue with in producing the answer *jo*: the situation could have been worse.

Speakers may use *jo* in response to an affirmative statement or to a question with a positive polarity if they do not fully endorse the proposition expressed, but they may also select *jo* if they agree with the positive proposition expressed but intend to communicate that they intentionally play down its importance or trivialise the fact that it represents a true state of affairs. In such cases the adversative connective *men* ('but') is a very frequent introducer of some added information that the speaker regards as more significant in the context at hand, as shown in Birgit's answers in the examples of (10)–(12).

(10)   Anders: Cecilie har lagt seg.
        'Cecily has gone to bed.'
        Birgit: Jo. Men hun leser på senga og hun burde virkelig sove.
        'Yes. But she's reading in bed and she really ought to sleep.'

(11)   Anders: Dette er det beste som kunne ha skjedd.
        'This is the best thing that could have happened.'
        Birgit: Jo. Men vi er ikke ved målet ennå.
        'Yes. But we have not reached our goal yet.'

(12)   Anders: Det ble sagt at de skal gi forskning et kraftig løft.
        'It was said that they are going to give research a tremendous boost.'
        Birgit: Jo. Men de har ikke fortalt oss hvordan de definerer forskning.
        'Yes. But they have not told us how they define research.'

By uttering *jo* in (10)–(12) instead of the equally acceptable response *ja*, the speaker conveys that she judges the fact represented by the positive proposition expressed to be relatively unimportant. This implied aspect of the overall meaning of *jo* in a discourse where no linguistic antecedent with a negative form can be found contributes significantly to the relevance of this response word. With *ja* the speaker's reservation will be manifest to the hearer only when the follow-up utterance introduced by the adversative connective *men* ('but') has been processed, and *jo* presumably makes the hearer more aware of what is ostensibly presented as a difference in importance between the explicature derived from the response word and the explicature derived from the follow-up declarative.

The discourse coherence and relevance of *jo* illustrated in the present section demonstrates that a negative linguistic antecedent cannot be a prerequisite for acceptable use of this response word in spoken Norwegian. Due to its procedural meaning, the lexical item *jo* makes the hearer realise that the speaker addresses a negative proposition (formed in her mind) and negates it. Identifying the antecedent of an utterance of *jo* is normally a fairly straightforward task when the response word is produced as a reaction to a linguistic stimulus that contains an overt negation marker but if no negative candidate antecedent occurs in the immediately preceding discourse, the speaker will be understood to convey that what the addressee has just said is not false but on the other hand not as pertinent as he apparently believes it to be.

5. Conclusion

I have argued that there are striking similarities between response words and indexical expressions like anaphoric pronouns whose reference is fixed by virtue of an inferred link between the anaphor and an identified antecedent needed to saturate the anaphor. Unlike the run-of-the-mill indexicals, response words are not expressions included in a sentence, but like indexicals they mandatorily trigger a bottom-up pragmatic process, receiving their semantic value through saturation in a context, in essentially the same way as the recognised standard indexicals that are typically integrated in a sentential form.

Special attention was given to Norwegian response words, their encoded meaning, their distribution, and the hearer's interpretation of the antecedent as input to the interpretation of the response word. There are three response words in the Norwegian lexicon, which means that anaphor and antecedent can be matched in a greater variety of ways than what a response word system with just two values permits. I have shown that the positive response word *jo*, which expresses a denial of a negative proposition, is sometimes a legitimate choice even if no negative proposition can be derived from the antecedent that *jo* responds to. In most contexts the two positive response words *ja* and *jo* are in complementary distribution. However, when the producer of the antecedent expresses his/her personal opinion or asks for the addressee's personal opinion, the latter is allowed to choose between *ja* and *jo* in identical environments. In such situations *jo* will be interpreted as if it denies the negative proposition which is the counterpart of the positive proposition associated with the antecedent, thus signalling either a reduced degree of commitment to the proposition expressed or a playing down of the significance of that which the first speaker's utterance refers to.

A response word communicates a proposition, and a communicated proposition is what relevance theorists call an explicature. Having adopted the relevance-theoretic framework myself, I have been using the term 'explicature' a number of times and I have said that a response word expresses an explicature. The relevance-theoretic explicature is defined as the result of an inferential development of an encoded logical form, but does a response word really encode a logical form? A logical form must contain at least a conceptual blueprint, even if it is a semantic representation that vastly underdetermines the proposition expressed, but the encoded meaning of a response word is not of a conceptual sort at all. This type of lexical item encodes a procedure, an instruction for hearers to follow so that they obtain an interpretation that makes the response word relevant to them. All concepts supplied to the fully developed explicature resulting from interpretation of a response word are contextually inferred, and the most important source of concepts supplied to the addressee's semantic composition resulting in an explicature is the antecedent structure located in that part of the discourse which triggers the speaker's use of the response word, most typically in the interlocutor's immediately preceding utterance. With response words there is no encoded conceptual schema that serves as input to context-driven inferential processes of enrichment, so technically an 'explicature' that is communicated by a response word does not come about in the way envisaged by proponents of Relevance Theory. This potential problem, however, is a topic for a different paper.

References

Ariel, Mira. 1996. Referring expressions and the +/− coreference distinction. In Thorstein Fretheim and Jeanette K. Gundel (eds), *Reference and Referent Accessibility*. Amsterdam: John Benjamins, 13–36.
Bezuidenhout, Anne. 2002. Truth-conditional pragmatics. *Philosophical Perspectives* 16: 105–34.
Borg, Emma. 2004. *Minimal Semantics*. Oxford: Clarendon Press.
Blakemore, Diane. 1987. *Semantic Constraints on Relevance*. Oxford: Blackwell.
Blakemore, Diane. 1992. *Understanding Utterances*. Oxford: Blackwell.
Blakemore, Diane and Robyn Carston. 2004. The pragmatics of sentential coordination with *and*. *Lingua* 115: 569–89.
Cappelen, Herman and Ernie Lepore. 2005. *Insensitive Semantics*. Oxford: Blackwell.
Carston, Robyn. 2002. *Thoughts and Utterances: The Pragmatics of Explicit Communication*. Oxford: Blackwell.
Cornish, Francis. 1999. *Anaphora, Discourse, and Understanding: Evidence from English and French*. Oxford: Clarendon Press.
Fretheim, Thorstein and Wim A. van Dommelen. 2012. A pragmatic perspective on the phonological values of utterance-final boundary tones in East Norwegian intonation. *The Linguistic Review* 29 (4): 663–77.
Fretheim, Thorstein and Marit Vogt-Svendsen. 1983. The semantics of head-nodding and head-shaking in Norwegian talk. In Fred Karlsson (ed.), *Papers from the Seventh Scandinavian Conference of Linguistics, vol. 2*. Helsinki: University of Helsinki Press, 445–69.
Gundel, Jeanette K., Nancy Hedberg and Ron Zacharski. 1993. Cognitive status and the form of referring expressions in discourse. *Language* 69: 274–307.
Gundel, Jeanette K., Nancy Hedberg and Ron Zacharski. 2005. Pronouns without NP antecedents: How do we know when a pronoun is referential? In Antonio Branco, Tony McEnery and Ruslan Mitkov (eds), *Anaphora Processing: Linguistic, Cognitive and Computational Modelling*. Amsterdam: John Benjamins, 351–64.
Hall, Alison. 2009. 'Free' enrichment and the nature of pragmatic constraints. *UCL Working Papers in Linguistics* 21: 93–123.
Horn, Laurence R. 1989. *A Natural History of Negation*. Chicago: The University of Chicago Press.
Huang, Yan. 2000. *Anaphora: A Cross-linguistic Study*. Oxford: Oxford University Press.
Matsui, Tomoko. 2000. *Bridging and Relevance*. Amsterdam: John Benjamins.
Recanati, François. 2004. *Literal Meaning*. Cambridge: Cambridge University Press.
Recanati, François. 2010. *Truth-conditional Pragmatics*. Oxford: Clarendon Press.
Sperber, Dan and Deirdre Wilson. 1995. *Relevance: Communication and Cognition*. Oxford: Blackwell (2nd edition with a Postface).
Wilson, Deirdre and Dan Sperber. 1993. Linguistic form and relevance. *Lingua* 90: 1–25.

Chapter 11

CULTURAL SCHEMAS AS 'COMMON GROUND'

Farzad Sharifian
Monash University

The notion of 'common ground', or its terminological variants, is of pivotal importance in studies of pragmatics. It refers to knowledge that is assumed to be shared, and is required for the uptake of pragmatic meanings, between interlocutors. Allan (2012) characterises the nature of common ground, and in doing so makes a distinction between two levels of common ground: the universal versus the very restricted. This chapter offers an account of a level of common ground that lies between these two, that is, culturally constructed common ground. The chapter argues that cultural schemas often serve as common ground between interlocutors, in particular for communicating pragmatic meanings. The chapter focuses on the case of the Persian cultural schema of *târof* and reveals how it is associated with the communication of several speech acts among speakers of Persian, including making requests and refusals, as well as offering and accepting invitations. The chapter also shows how unfamiliarity with this cultural schema (and thus lack of common ground) presents a communicative challenge when Persian speakers interact with non-Persian speakers.

1. Introduction

Keith Allan was always a source of inspiration, support and encouragement for me. In this paper I take the opportunity to engage with a topic of interest to Keith, that is, 'common ground', and explore it from the perspective of Cultural Linguistics (Palmer 1996; Sharifian 2011). The paper begins by a discussion of the notion of 'common ground' (CG) from Allan (2013), followed by a description of the sub-discipline of Cultural Linguistics.

In an attempt to characterise the notion of CG, Allan (2013, p. 286) maintains that '[o]ur understanding of linguistic utterances rests on an assumption of CG'. Allan notes that several terms have been used by different scholars to refer to CG in the relevant available literature. He offers a unified definition that captures the substance of all these terminological preferences as follows:

the terms *common knowledge, mutual knowledge, shared knowledge, assumed familiarity, presumed background information* and *common ground* are describing essentially the same thing, and it is what defines the pragmatic constituent of communicative competence: the knowledge and application of how and when to use utterances appropriately that combines with grammatical knowledge (of semantics, syntax, morphology, phonology) in the production of utterances to generate a coherent text comprehensible to its intended audience. (2013:291)

As for the extent to which CG is shared between speakers, Allan argues that:

Some CG is universal, e.g. knowledge of the sun as a heavenly body that is a source of light and warmth, rain as (among other things) a source of fresh water replenishing the earth, the physiological and socio-cultural differences between the sexes. Some CG is very restricted, e.g. between a couple who use the Hobgoblin to refer to the man's first wife. Usually S[peaker] can readily assess the probable CG with H[earer], and chooses his or her words accordingly. (2013:286)

In this paper, I offer a level of CG that may be placed between the two that Allan has identified (i.e., the universal and the restricted) and that is culturally constructed common ground established through *cultural schemas* serving as CG. The paper begins by a brief discussion of the theoretical framework of *cultural cognition* and its components *cultural conceptualisation* and language, as a preamble to the discussion of cultural schemas. This is followed by a discussion of the nature of cognitive schemas and cultural schemas. The later sections focus on the elaboration of the Persian cultural schema of *târof* and provide examples of how it serves as common ground and how it is verbally instantiated during the communication of pragmatic meaning among speakers of Persian.

2. Cultural cognition and cultural conceptualisations

I have used the term 'cultural cognition' (Sharifian 2008, 2009, 2011) to refer to a level of cognitive life that emerges from the interactions between the members of a cultural group across time and space. This view of cognition is parallel to the ones discussed by several cognitive scientists (e.g., Clark and Chalmers 1998; Sutton 2005, 2006; Wilson 2005). Two important and interrelated aspects of cultural cognition are language and cultural conceptualisations.

Cultural cognition is emergent in the technical sense of the term (e.g., Goldstein 1999). That is, it results from the interactions between parts of a system (here, the members of a group) which is more than the sum of its parts (in this case, more than the sum of the cognitions of the individual members). Like all emergent systems, cultural cognition is *dynamic* in that it is constantly being negotiated and renegotiated across the generations of the relevant cultural group, as well as modified through the contact that the members of that group have with other cultures.

As a central aspect of cultural cognition, language serves as (to use the term used by wa Thiong'o 1986), a 'collective memory bank' of the cultural cognition of a group. Many aspects of language are shaped by cultural cognition that was dominant at earlier stages in the history of a speech community. Historical cultural practices leave traces in current linguistic practice, some of which are in fossilized forms that may no longer be analysable. In this sense language can be viewed as storing and communicating cultural cognition. In other words language acts both as a memory bank and a fluid vehicle for the (re-)transmission of cultural cognition and its component parts or *cultural conceptualisations*, a term that I have used to collectively refer to conceptual structures such as 'cultural schemas', 'cultural categories' (including 'cultural prototypes'), and 'cultural metaphors' (Sharifian 2011). As mentioned above, cultural conceptualisations and their entrenchment in language are intrinsic to cultural cognition. In the following section I briefly discuss the notions of 'cultural category' and 'cultural metaphor' and will then elaborate on the notion of cultural schema, and how it can serve as CG.

Cultural categories are cognitive categories that have a cultural basis. Children usually begin by setting up their own categories, but as they grow up, they explore and discover, as part of their cognitive development, how their language and culture categorise events, objects, and experiences. As Glushko et al. (2008: 129) put it:

> Categorization research focuses on the acquisition and use of categories shared by a culture and associated with language – what we will call 'cultural categorization'. Cultural categories exist for objects, events, settings, mental states, properties, relations and other components of experience (e.g. birds, weddings, parks, serenity, blue and above). Typically, these categories are acquired through normal exposure to caregivers and culture with little explicit instruction.

I have used the term *cultural metaphors* to refer to conceptual metaphors (Lakoff and Johnson 1980) that are culturally constructed (e.g., Palmer 1996;

Sharifian 2011). Several studies have explored cultural schemas and models that give rise to conceptual metaphors, for example through ethnomedical or other cultural traditions (Sharifian et al. 2008; Yu 2009a and b; see also Idström and Piirainen 2012). One way this is manifest is by the differing way organs of the body are associated with emotions and mental life. For example, in Indonesian it is *hati* ('the liver') that is associated with love, rather than the heart (Siahaan 2008). Siahaan traces back such conceptualisations to the ritual of animal sacrifice, especially the interpretation of liver organ known as 'liver divination', which was practiced in ancient Indonesia. In some languages, such as Tok Pisin (Mühlhäusler, Dutton and Romaine 2003), the belly is the seat of emotions. Yu (2009b) observes that many linguistic expressions in Chinese reflect the conceptualisation of THE HEART IS THE RULER OF THE BODY. He maintains that the 'target-domain concept here is an important one because the heart organ is regarded as the central faculty of cognition and the site of both affective and cognitive activities in ancient Chinese philosophy' (Yu 2007: 27).

2.1. *(Cultural) schemas and language*

Cultural schemas are a culturally constructed sub-class of cognitive schemas. In cognitive psychology traditionally schemas (also known as schemata) are viewed as building blocks of cognition that help organize, interpret, and communicate information (e.g., Bartlett 1932; Bobrow and Norman 1975; D'Andrade 1995; Holland and Cole 1995; Minsky 1975; Rumelhart 1980; Sharifian 2001; Strauss and Quinn 1997). Schema theory has enjoyed considerable popularity under the dominant paradigms of cognitive psychology, in particular within classicism and connectionism (Rumelhart 1980; Rumelhart et al. 1986; Schank and Abelson 1977). Connectionists define schemas as patterns of activation among strongly interconnected units in human memory networks. Rumelhart et al. maintain that '[I]t is these coalitions of tightly interconnected units that correspond most closely to what have been called schemas' (p. 20).

Schemas serve different functions in the interaction between cognition and environment. Taylor and Crocker (1981) have identified seven functions of schemas as follows:

- Providing a structure against which experience is mapped;
- Directing information encoding and retrieval from memory;
- Affecting information processing efficiency and speed;
- Guiding the filling of gaps in the information available;

- Providing templates for problem solving;
- Facilitating the evaluation of experience;
- Facilitating anticipations of the future, goal setting, planning, and goal execution.

The concept of schema underlies terms such as script, frame, global concept, scenario, encyclopaedic entry, plan, etc. in cognitive studies. Several classifications of schemas have also been proposed. Cook (1994) makes a distinction between three types of schema: world schema, text schema and language schema. He uses 'world schema' to refer to the schematic organization of world knowledge and 'text schema' to refer to 'a typical ordering of facts in a real or fictional world' (p. 15); 'language schema' refers to generalized knowledge about the grammar of a language.

Derry (1996) identifies three classes of schemas in the literature: memory objects, mental models and cognitive fields. A memory object is 'a schema type that includes but is not limited to Piagetian logical-mathematical schemes' (p. 167). She states that mental models 'represent situational understandings that are context dependent and do not exist outside the situation being modelled' (p. 167). The definition of 'cognitive field' given by Derry matches a connectionist's interpretation of schemas, that is, they are distributed patterns of activation that occur in response to external stimuli. It seems that these different schema types are, in fact, no more than different interpretations of the same cognitive entity.

In an intercultural study, Nishida (1999) extracts eight primary types of schemas for social interactions as follows:

- Fact-and-concept schemas: these are schemas that include factual information such as 'The capital of Australia is Canberra' and conceptual information such as 'A room has walls'.
- Person schemas: these are schemas that include knowledge about types of people, including their personality traits, represented by sentences such as 'John is taciturn'.
- Self schemas: these are schemas that include knowledge about the social self and the individual self.
- Role schemas: these are schemas that include knowledge about achieved and ascribed social roles and the expected behaviour associated with these roles.
- Context schemas: these are schemas that include knowledge about situations and appropriate behaviour associated with them.

- Procedure schemas: these are schemas that contain knowledge about the appropriate sequences of events in common situations.
- Strategy schemas: these schemas include knowledge about problem-solving strategies.
- Emotion schemas: these schemas contain information about affect and evaluation. Emotion schemas are in fact activated through their association with other schemas.

Thus some of the schema types discussed in the literature are labelled by content. A major problem with this kind of labelling is its possibility of leading to further categories *ad infinitum* since human experience is unlimited in scope. Another potential problem is labelling the same content or experience differently and therefore coming up with taxonomies of schemas that may prove to be overlapping or redundant.

As mentioned earlier, cultural schemas are the sub-class of cognitive schemas abstracted from people's cultural, and therefore to some extent shared, experiences. They differ from schemas abstracted from an individual's idiosyncratic experiences. Cultural schemas enable individuals to communicate cultural meanings and serve as CG between interlocutors. In cognitive psychology, cultural schemas are located within individuals' cognition, albeit they are shared across a cultural group. However, within the framework of cultural cognition (Sharifian 2011), cultural schemas also have a collective life at the emergent level of the cognition that characterises a cultural group. I refer to this as the macro-level. Although speakers usually operate on the basis of shared cultural schemas, in reality (at the micro-level) they may share some but not all components of a cultural schema. This pattern of schema sharing may be diagrammatically presented as shown in Figure 1.

Figure 1 shows how a cultural schema may be represented in a *heterogeneously distributed* fashion across the minds of individuals. It schematically represents how members may have internalised some but not all components of a macro-level cultural schema that has been developed at the level of cultural cognition. It also shows how individuals may share some but not all elements of a cultural schema with each other. It is to be noted that the individuals who internalise aspects of a cultural schema may not be those who are viewed as insiders by the cultural group as a whole, but those 'outsiders' who have somehow had contact and interaction with others who have internalised aspects of these cultural schemas.

Cultural schemas are instantiated in many aspects of language. Palmer (1996) maintained that '[i]t is likely that all native knowledge of language

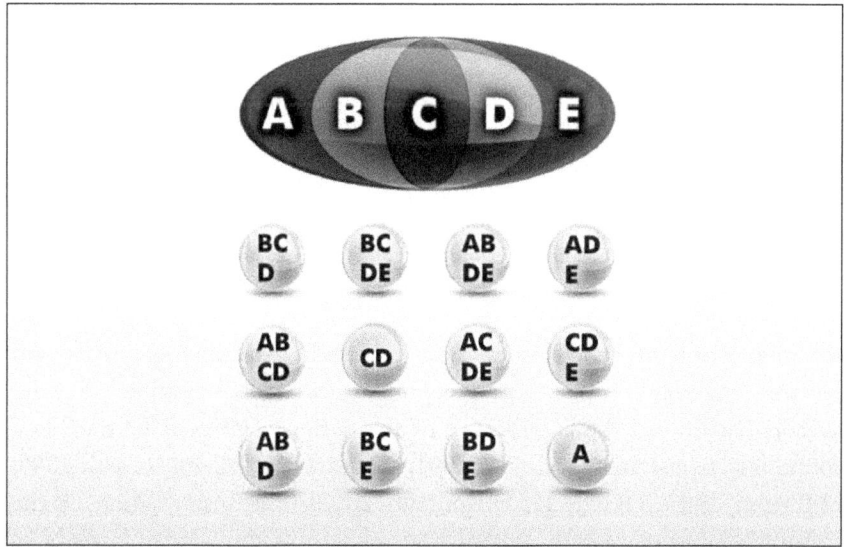

Figure 1. Diagrammatic representation of a cultural schema (from Sharifian 2011).

and culture belongs to cultural schemas and the living of culture and the speaking of language consist of schemas in action' (p. 63). Cultural schemas capture encyclopaedic meaning that is culturally constructed for many lexical items of human languages. Take an example of the word *privacy* in a variety of English such as American English. The pool of knowledge that forms a web of concepts that define *privacy* in relation to various contexts and factors is best described as the cultural schema of PRIVACY. The cultural relativity of this schema is reflected in complaints that some speakers from one cultural group make about members of some others, such as, 'They don't understand the meaning of privacy'.

Cultural schemas may also provide a basis for pragmatic meanings. Knowledge that is assumed by culturally constructed CG, and which underlies the enactment and uptake of speech acts is largely captured in cultural schemas. In some languages, for example, the speech act of 'greeting' is closely associated with cultural schemas of 'eating' and 'food', whereas in some other languages it is associated with cultural schemas that relate to the health of the interlocutors and their family members. Making inferences by interlocutors about the knowledge of how to appropriately greet the hearers is based on the general assumption of shared cultural schemas, and therefore CG. A mechanism of this sort is necessary for making sense of the enactment of speech acts. In short, cultural schemas represent pools of knowledge that provide the basis for a significant portion of semantic and pragmatic meaning in human languages, providing a substantial basis for the CG that exists between the members of a cultural group. The following section presents an example of a Persian cultural schema that serves as CG between speakers of Persian when communicating pragmatic meanings.

3. Persian cultural schema of *târof*

Târof is a cultural schema that underlies a significant part of everyday social interactions in Persian (Sharifian 2010) and serves as CG in the communication of several speech acts, including requesting goods and services, making refusals, and accepting offers and invitations. Several authors have noted the significance of the notion of *târof* in Persian, as a communicative strategy (Asdjodi 2001; Assadi 1980; Eslami Rasekh 2005; Hillmann 1981; Hodge 1957; Koutlaki 2002). The instantiation of the cultural schema of *târof* in conversations may be in the form of 'ostensible' offers and invitations, repeated rejection of offers, repeated instances of offers, hesitation in making requests, giving frequent compliments, etc. Often all the parties involved in a single conversation can make use of a combination of these realisations, in varying degrees. It is often not easy to tease out genuine offer and compliments from *târof*, and so speakers constantly ask each other not to engage in *târof*, in order to find out if the communicative act is a genuine one. The following excerpt, from the author's personal data, reveals the instantiation of this cultural schema in a conversation in Persian:

L: *Miveh*   *befarmâyin*
    Fruit   eat:polite.form
    'Please have some fruit'

S: *Merci*   *sarf*   *shodeh*
    thanks   I   have.had
    'Thanks, I have had some'

L: *Khâhesh*   *mikonam*   *befarmâyin,*   *ghâbel-e*
    shomâ   *ro*[1]*-*   *nadâreh*

---

[1] The morphemes *o* and *ro* in expressions like *khodesho* or *Cheshm-am ro* are the spoken form of *râ*, which is a DO-marker postposition in Persian. *râ* can be used in Persian as a definiteness marker, a specificity marker and a topicalisation marker. For more information see Dabirmoghadam (1992) and Shokouhi and Kipka (2003).

	beg	I do	eat:polite.form	worthy-of
	you	DO marker	it.is.not	

'Please have some, they are not worthy of you'

S: *Sâhâbesh nakoneh,*   *ghâbel-eh,*   *dast-e-toon*   *dard*

its.owner doesn't   worthy-is   hand-of-your   pain

'You are worthy, thanks'

L: *Torokhodâ*   *befarmâyin,*   *namak*   *adâreh*

for.God's.sake   eat:polite.form   salt   doesn't.have[2]

'For God's sake please have some, it has no salt'

S: *Târof khord-im*   *nemikon-am,*   *tâzeh*   *shâm*

târof had-we   don't-I   just   dinner

'I don't do târof, we just had dinner'

L: *Ye*   *doonehportaghâl*   *beoonjâhâ*   *nemikhoreh*

one   orange   is   not.too.much

'One orange wouldn't be that much'

S: *Chashm, nemikon-am*   *dast-e-toon*   *o*   *kootâh*

okay will.not-I   hand-of-your   DO marker   short

'Okay, I won't turn down your offer'

A Wikipedia page dedicated to the cultural schema of *târof* defines it as 'a Persian form of civility emphasizing both self-deference and social rank'[3] and observes that:

---

[2] This expression is associated with a traditional cultural belief that if you eat something that contains salt you will be indebted to the person who gave the food/fruit to you.

[3] http://en.wikipedia.org/wiki/Taarof (accessed 30/09/2012).

T'aarof also governs the rules of *hospitality*: a host is obliged to offer anything a guest might want, and a guest is equally obliged to refuse it. This ritual may repeat itself several times before the host and guest finally determine whether the host's offer and the guest's refusal are real or simply polite. It is possible to ask someone not to t'aarof ('t'aarof nakonid'), but that raises new difficulties, since the request itself might be a devious type of t'aarof. At times t'aarof can lead to one performing a task that one does not want to perform. For instance, if one friend offers a ride to another friend only because they are being polite, they may become stuck in the situation if the friend agrees to get the ride. Of course if one was going by the rules of t'aarof, one would refuse the offer many times before accepting.

The Urban Dictionary defines *târof* as follows:

> A Persian word for a custom that is ONLY applied in the Iranian culture. It is a way of denying your will to please your counterpart, however the will is only denied because of the custom and not to please the counterpart. But there are situations where tarof persist upon a request to make the counterpart genuinely satisfied. Tarof often causes misunderstandings between both parties and is a source for awkward situations in a social setting.[4]

The general aim of the cultural schema of *târof* is to create a form of social space for speakers to exercise face work and also to provide communicative tools to negotiate and lubricate social relationships. It also affords a chance for interlocutors to construct certain identities and images of themselves. For example, liberal use of *târof* can be used by hosts to portray themselves (either to themselves or to others) as very hospitable. Persian-speaking society traditionally revolves around social relations. Almost all forms of social institutions in Iran, from marriage to employment and business, hinge upon social relations. Usually a person's ability to exercise and respond to *târof* appropriately has a significant bearing on their social relationships. Beeman (1986) characterises personal relations in Iran as an art that requires sophisticated verbal skills. For many Iranians living outside Iran, the cultural schema of *târof* is closely associated with their identity as an Iranian. Maghbouleh (2012) reports of a US summer camp for Iranian-heritaged youth, called the '*ta'arof* Tournament', that makes a sport of *târof* rituals. She observes that by participating in this summer camp and engaging in

---

[4] http://www.urbandictionary.com/define.php?term=Tarof (accessed 30/09/2012).

the cultural performance of *târof* these second-generation young Iranians are provided with a chance to construct an Iranian ethno-national identity which serves as a 'powerful source material for group affinity and belonging in diaspora' (Maghbouleh 2012: 1).

Several authors have noted the absence of the Persian concept of *târof* in English. They have used various labels to describe it, including 'ritual courtesy' (Beeman 1986: 56), 'communicative routine' (Koutlaki 2002: 1741), 'ritual politeness' (Koutlaki 2002: 1740), and 'polite verbal wrestling' (Rafiee 1992: 96). Koutlaki observes that *târof* 'is a very complex concept, carrying different meanings in the minds of native speakers [of Persian] and baffling anyone endeavouring to describe it'. Beeman (1986: 196) maintains that '*tæ'arof* is the active, ritualised realisation of differential perceptions of superiority and inferiority in interaction. It underscores and preserves the integrity of culturally defined roles as they are carried out in the life of every Iranian, every day, in thousands of different ways'. Some non-Iranian writers have naively described *târof* as 'insincerity' or even 'hypocrisy'. For example, de Bellaigue (2004: 14) states that '[y]ou should know about *ta'aruf*. In Arabic *ta'aruf* means behaviour that is appropriate and customary; in Iran, it has been corrupted and denotes ceremonial insincerity. Not in a pejorative sense; Iran is the only country I know where hypocrisy is prized as a social and commercial skill'. Learners of the Persian language also often find it a challenge to learn this cultural schema and to apply it in an appropriate manner according to context. For example, an American learner of Persian observes that:

> Ta'arof has a built-in set of phrases and specific conditions in which these phrases are used. The challenge for a student of Persian, let alone a non-Iranian student of Persian who did not grown up ta'arof-ing (like me), is knowing when to ta'arof and when to not. For example, some months ago I invited an Iranian friend (who may or may not be an editor of this blog) to my home and offered him something to drink. He refused my offer and I figured that was that. Big mistake. I later learned that my friend was in fact rather thirsty, but he, being the polite Iranian that he is, did not ask me again for something to slake this thirst.[5]

Although the word itself is Arabic in origin, the root of the cultural schema of *târof* dates back to Pre-Islamic Persia, especially to the teachings of

---

[5] http://ajammc.wordpress.com/2011/12/06/the-treacherous-territory-of-taarof-3/ (accessed 30/09/2012).

Prophet Zartosht (Zarathushtra) (Asdjodi 2001; Beeman 1986). The core principles of Zoroastrian religion are 'good words', 'good thoughts' and 'good deeds', which are known in English as the three Gs. The use of 'good words' words in Zoroastrian religion is not merely a virtue but a kind of prayer.[6] It is also a pivotal part of one's identity as a Zoroastrian. At least part of the intention of using 'good words' is to break the human tendency to egotism by always elevating others *vis á vis* the self. It should also be emphasised that this use of 'good words' is not just a matter of verbal display but should be backed by 'good thoughts'. That is why I refer to the whole system as a cultural schema rather than just a set of linguistic strategies. In other words, *târof* is a conceptual system, which feeds not only into speech but also into behaviour, as 'good deeds'. O'Shea (2000: 122) observes that *târof* in Persian has both physical and verbal manifestations. She notes that 'the former consist of activities such as jostling to be the last through the door, seeking a humble seating location, or standing to attention on the arrival or departure of other guests'. Assadi (1980: 221) also observes that '*Ta'arof* is a generic term which denotes a myriad of verbal and *non-verbal* deferential behaviours in Persian' (emphasis added).

Two websites have discussed *târof* metaphorically in terms of 'war', 'dance' and 'game'. Taghavi[7] likens *târof* to war due to the repeated exchanges that take place between interlocutors, during which they constantly make offers, reject offers, make compliments, etc. The Persian Mirror webpage[8] views *târof* as 'a verbal dance between an offerer and an acceptor until one of them agrees'. On the same webpage *târof* is considered as an art that 'in the end becomes a ritual or a game that both participants are aware of playing'. The weblog of an Iranian residing in the US characterizes *târof* as 'A lie is no longer considered a sin when hospitality is the intention'[9] and remarks that 'Those of us who have lived in the West for decades may feel westernized, but when it comes to Ta'arof, we remain Persians'.[10] A Google search with the word 'taarof' yielded a large number of weblogs and webpages where speakers of Persian try to explain what *târof* is for non-Persian speakers. The following are examples of excerpts from such weblogs:

---

[6] http://www3.sympatico.ca/zoroastrian/Avesta.htm (accessed 30/09/2012).
[7] http://www.iranian.com/HamidTaghavi/Oct98/Tarof/index.html (accessed 30/09/2012).
[8] http://www.persianmirror.com/culture/distinct/distinct.cfm#art (accessed 30/09/2012).
[9] http://www.iranian.com/Ghahremani/2005/March/Taarof/index.html (accessed 30/09/2012).
[10] http://www.iranian.com/Ghahremani/2005/March/Taarof/index.html (accessed 30/09/2012).

ok, so the concept of taarof is something my friends and I discuss all the time, and how North Americans do not have this concept at all.[11]

It is a cultural phenomenon that consists of refusing something even though you might want it, out of politeness. On the giving end, it is offering something… to be polite… but not really wanting to give it away.[12]

Don't waste your time trying to find out what 'taarof' means in English. You HAVE to be an Iranian to understand that, it's not a 'word' to be translated, it's a whole dictionary on its own![13]

Since English does not have an identical cultural schema for *târof*, speakers of Persian English may use words such as 'compliment' or 'courtesy' to refer to it. They may also use the original Persian word in their English for intracultural communication with other speakers of Persian. Interestingly, the website of the Iranian Singles Network has a section under every person's profile with the title 'having etiquette/*tarof kardan*', where the members are asked to specify the extent to which they like or exercise *târof*.[14] As can be seen here, *târof* is translated as 'etiquette'. Other words that may be used in Persian English to capture the concept of *târof* are 'formal' and 'formality'. Consider the following example from a movie which was broadcast on Jam-e-Jam Satellite Channel:

(Speaker A is talking to speaker B at the door of B's house)

A: *Biâ too* (meaning 'Come in')

Subtitle: 'Come in'.

B: *Mozâhem nemisham* (meaning 'I won't bother you')

Subtitle: 'I won't trouble you'.

A: *Târof nakon* (meaning 'don't do târof")

Subtitle: 'Stop being formal'.

---

[11] http://persianculture.wordpress.com/2008/12/24/taarof/ (accessed 30/09/2012).
[12] http://www.plexusinstitute.org/blogpost/656763/120250/You-think-communication-is-complex-Try-Taarof (accessed 30/09/2012).
[13] http://www.iranian.com/main/cartoons/2007/mahmoud-taarof (accessed 30/09/2012).
[14] http://www.iraniansingles.com/ (accessed 30/09/2012).

B: *Na jooneh to, bâyad beram* (meaning 'no, really I have to go')

Subtitle: 'Thanks, I have to go'.

In light of the observations made so far in this chapter about *târof*, it is clear that it is not intrinsically a display of formality. In fact the above exchange does not reflect a formal conversation. Both speakers are using singular forms to address each other, which is one characteristic of a familiar style. If the conversation had been formal, they would have used plural forms: *biâyin* 'come:PL' instead of *biâ* 'come:SG', *nakonin* 'don't.do:PL' instead of *nakon* 'don't.do:SG, and *shomâ* 'you:PL' instead of *to* 'you:SG'. Overall, it should be clear from the examples presented in this section that unfamiliarity with the Persian cultural schema of *târof*, and therefore absence of common ground, on the part of non-Persian speakers could lead to significant miscommunication with speakers of Persian, when the parties speak either English or Persian.

4. Concluding remarks

In this paper I have made an attempt to show how cultural schemas can serve as common ground between interlocutors coming from the same cultural background, in particular when communicating pragmatic meanings. Often such cultural schemas are grounded in cultural traditions that are themselves grounded in fundamental worldviews such as religion. The paper elaborates on the case of the Persian cultural schema of *târof* and reveals how this cultural schema underlies the enactment of several speech acts among speakers of Persian and how unfamiliarity with this cultural schema presents a challenge for non-Persian speakers. As mentioned earlier, although the degree to which this schema is shared across the community of Persian speakers varies from one individual to another, speakers usually operate on the basis of the assumption of shared knowledge or 'common ground'.

References

Allan, Keith. 2013. What is common ground? In Alessandro Capone, Franco Lo Piparo and Marco Carapezza (eds), *Perspectives on Pragmatics and Philosophy*. Milan: Springer Verlag, 285–310.

Asdjodi, Minoo. 2001. A comparison between ta'arof in Persian and limao in Chinese. *International Journal of the Sociology of Language* 148 (1): 71–92.

Assadi, Reza. 1980. Deference: Persian style. *Anthropological Linguistics* 22: 221–4.

Bartlett, Frederick C. 1932. *Remembering*. Cambridge: Cambridge University Press.

Beeman, William O. 1986. *Language, Status, and Power in Iran*. Bloomington, IN: Indiana University Press.

Bobrow, Daniel G. and Donald A. Norman. 1975. Some principles of memory schemata. In Daniel G. Bobrow and Allan M. Collins (eds), *Representation and Understanding: Studies in Cognitive Science*. New York: Academic Press, 131–49.

Clark, Andy and David Chalmers. 1998. The extended mind. *Analysis* 58: 10–23.

Cook, Guy (1994). *Discourse and literature*. Oxford: Oxford University Press.

Dabir-Moghaddam, Mohammad. 1992. On the (in)dependence of syntax and pragmatics: Evidence from the postposition –*ra* in Persian. In Dieter Stein (ed.), *Cooperating with Written Texts: The Pragmatics and Comprehension of Written Texts*. Berlin: Mouton de Gruyter, 549–73.

D'Andrade. Roy G. 1995. *The Development of Cognitive Anthropology*. Cambridge: Cambridge University Press.

de Bellaigue, Christopher. 2004. *In the Rose Garden of the Martyrs: A Memoir of Iran*. London: HarperCollins.

Derry, Sharon J. 1996. Cognitive schema theory in the constructivist debate. *Educational Psychologist* 31:163–74.

Eslami Rasekh, Zohren. 2005. Invitations in Persian and English: Ostensible or genuine? *Intercultural Pragmatics* 2 (4): 453–80.

Glushko, Robert J., Paul P. Maglio, Teenie Matlock and Lawrence W. Barsalou. 2008. Categorization in the wild. *Trends in Cognitive Science* 12 (4): 129–35.

Goldstein, Jeffrey. 1999. Emergence as a construct: History and issues. *Emergence: Complexity and Organization* 1 (1): 49–72.

Hillmann, Michael C. 1981. Language and social distinctions. In Michael Bonine and Nikki R. Keddie (eds), *Modern Iran: The Dialectics of Continuity and Change*. Albany, NY: State University of New York Press, 327–40.

Hodge, Carleton. 1957. Some aspects of Persian style. *Language* 33: 355–69.

Holland, Dorothy and Michael Cole. 1995. Between discourse and schema: Reformulating a cultural-historical approach to culture and mind. *Anthropology & Education Quarterly* 26 (4): 475–89.

Idström, Anna and Elizabeth Piirainen. 2012. *Endangered Metaphors*. Amsterdam & Philadelphia: John Benjamins.

Koutlaki, Sofia A. 2002. Offers and expressions of thanks as face enhancing acts: *tae'arof* in Persian. *Journal of Pragmatics* 34 (12): 1733–56.

Lakoff, George and Mark Johnson. 1980. *Metaphors We Live By*. Chicago: University of Chicago Press.

Maghbouleh, Neda. 2012. The Ta'arof Tournament: Cultural performances of ethnonational identity at a diasporic summer camp. *Ethnic and Racial Studies* 35: 1–20.

Minsky, Marvin. 1975. A framework for representing knowledge. In Patrick H. Winston (ed.), *The Psychology of Computer Vision*. New York: McGraw-Hill, 211–77.

Mühlhäusler, Peter, Thomas E. Dutton and Suzanne Romaine. 2003. *Tok Pisin Texts:From the Beginning to the Present*. Amsterdam: John Benjamins.

Nishida, Hiroko. 1999. A cognitive approach to intercultural communication based on schema theory. *International Journal of Intercultural Relations* 23 (5): 753–77.

O'Shea, Maria. 2000. *Cultural Shock: Iran*. Portland, OR: Graphic Arts Publishing Company.

Palmer, Gary B. 1996. *Toward a Theory of Cultural Linguistics*. Austin, TX: University of Texas Press.

Rafiee, Abdorreza. 1992. Variables of communicative incompetence in the performance of Iranian learners of English and English learners of Persian. Unpublished PhD thesis, University of London.

Rumelhart, David E. 1980. Schemata: The building blocks of cognition. In Rand J. Spiro, Bertram C. Bruce and William F. Brewer (eds), *Theoretical Issues in Reading Comprehension*. Hillsdale, NJ: Lawrence Erlbaum, 33–58.

Rumelhart, David E., Paul Smolensky, James L. McClelland and Geoffrey E. Hinton. 1986. Schemata and sequential thought processes in PDP models. In James L. McClelland, David E. Rumelhart and the PDP Research Group (eds), *Parallel Distributed Processing: Explorations in the Microstructure of Cognition. Vol. 2: Psychological and Biological Models*. Cambridge, MA: MIT Press, 7–57.

Schank, Roger C. and Robert P. Abelson. 1977. *Scripts, Plans, Goals, and Understanding*. Hillsdale, NJ: Lawrence Erlbaum Associates, Inc.

Sharifian, Farzad. 2001. Schema-based processing in Australian speakers of Aboriginal English. *Language and Intercultural Communication* 1 (2): 120–34.

Sharifian, Farzad. 2008. Distributed, emergent cognition, conceptualisation, and language. In Roslyn M. Frank, René Dirven, Tom Ziemke and Enrique Bernárdez (eds), *Body, Language, and Mind. Vol. 2: Sociocultural Situatedness*. Berlin & New York: Mouton de Gruyter, 109–36.

Sharifian, Farzad. 2009. On collective cognition and language. In Hanna Pishwa (ed.), *Language and Social Cognition: Expression of the Social Mind*. Berlin & New York: Mouton de Gruyter, 163–82.

Sharifian, Farzad. 2010. Cultural conceptualisations in intercultural communication: A study of Aboriginal and non-Aboriginal Australians. *Journal of Pragmatics* 42: 3367–76.

Sharifian, Farzad. 2011. *Cultural Conceptualisations and Language: Theoretical Framework and Applications*. Amsterdam & Philadelphia: John Benjamins.

Sharifian, Farzad, René Dirven, Ning Yu and Susanne Neiemier (eds). 2008. *Culture, Body, and Language: Conceptualizations of Internal Body Organs across Cultures and Languages.* Berlin & New York: Mouton De Gruyter.

Siahaan, Poppy. 2008. Did he break your *heart* or your *liver*? A contrastive study on metaphorical concepts from the source domain organ in English and in Indonesian. In Farzad Sharifian, René Dirven, Ning Yu and Susanne Neiemier (eds), *Culture, Body, and Language: Conceptualizations of Internal Body Organs across Cultures and Languages.* Berlin & New York: Mouton de Gruyter, 45–74.

Shokouhi, Hussein and Peter F. Kipka. 2003. A discourse study of Persian *râ*. *Lingua* 113: 953–66.

Strauss, Claudia and Naomi Quinn. 1997. *A Cognitive Theory of Cultural Meaning.* New York: Cambridge University Press.

Sutton, John. 2005. Memory and the extended mind: Embodiment, cognition, and culture. *Cognitive Processing* 6 (4): 223–6.

Sutton, John. 2006. Memory, embodied cognition, and the extended mind. *Special Issue of Philosophical Psychology* 19 (3): 281–9.

Taylor, Shelley E. and Jennifer Crocker. 1981. Schematic bases of social information processing. In E. Tory Higgins, C. A. Herman and Mark P. Zanna (eds), *Social Cognition: The Ontario Symposium on Personality and Social Psychology.* Hillsdale, NJ: Erlbaum, 89–134.

wa Thiong'o, Ngugi. 1986. *Decolonising the Mind: The Politics of Language in African Literature.* London: Heinemann.

Wilson, Robert A. 2005. Collective memory, group minds, and the extended mind thesis. *Cognitive Processing* 6 (4): 227–36.

Yu, Ning. 2007. Heart and cognition in ancient Chinese philosophy. *Journal of Cognition and Culture* 7 (1–2): 27–47.

Yu, Ning. 2009a. *From Body to Meaning in Culture: Papers on Cognitive Semantic Studies of Chinese.* Amsterdam & Philadelphia: John Benjamins.

Yu, Ning. 2009b. *The Chinese HEART in a Cognitive Perspective: Culture, Body, and Language.* Berlin & New York: Mouton de Gruyter.

Chapter 12

ELABORATIVENESS IN ACADEMIC WRITING

A STUDY OF THREE RESEARCH PAPERS

Zofia Golebiowski

Deakin University

This paper investigates the employment of elaborative rhetorical strategies in three research papers written in English and published in international sociological journals: the first authored by native speakers of English, the second by a Polish writer working in an Anglophone discourse community, and the third by a Polish writer from the Polish discourse community. Elaboration relations are discussed with respect to their textual function, frequency of employment, hierarchical location and recursiveness, and discoursal prominence. I explore how the authors elaborate their texts through amplification, extension, explanation, instantiation, reformulation and addition strategies. The analysis reveals that Elaboration is a prominent feature of the examined texts. It is proposed that the similarities in the employment of Elaborations across the corpus result from the shared stylistic conventions and traditions of the disciplinary research community of sociology while variations in the mode of employment of elaborative structures may be caused by the writers' differing linguistic backgrounds and discourse community memberships.

1. Introduction

Academic texts are addressed to specific audiences with writers making assumptions about their readers' background knowledge and familiarity with similar texts. In the process of writing, authors monitor the unfolding text in respect to prospective readers' needs for clarifications of claims, explanations of concepts or reformulations of definitions. The identification of audience requirements regulates the appropriateness of reader engagement through the selection of appropriate rhetorical elaborative structures which aim at enhancement of text comprehension and facilitate its processing. Halliday (1994: 225) defined such rhetorical configurations as semantic relations of *Elaboration*, where 'one clause elaborates on the meaning of another by further specifying or describing it'. He distinguished Elaboration relations of Exposition, Exemplification and Clarification. Previously, Hobbs (1985) attempted to provide a definition of an Elaboration coherence relation and suggested that it fulfils two functions: to overcome misunderstanding or lack of understanding, and to enrich the understanding by 'expressing the same thought from a different perspective' (Hobbs 1985: 25). Grimes (1975) discussed a similar category of propositional structures calling them 'supporting predicates'. His 'supporting predicates' included Attributive, Equivalent, Specifically, Explanation, Evidence, Analogy and Manner categories. Elaboration relations were paid specific attention in the Rhetorical Structure Theory (RST) of Mann and Thompson (1988, 1987, 1986) and Mann, Matthiessen and Thompson (1989), and in Longacre's (1983) relational taxonomy. RST comprised Elaboration types of set–member, generalisation–instance, whole–part, process–step and object–attribute, while Longacre (1983) discussed 'paraphrase' and 'illustration' notional structures.

There are some emerging studies in academic discourse which address Elaborations as a key means by which writers engage with their readers. Although the RST discussion of Elaborations was largely focused on a persuasive discourse of short texts, a follow-up relational study by Kamyab (1997) made an attempt at examining Elaborations in scientific review articles. In 1997 Duszak investigated elaborative structures in cross-cultural academic settings. On the basis of her examination of Polish and English research papers, she defined Elaborations as 'thematic inserts that function as explication, precisioning, amplification or reformulation of author's view' (Duszak 1997: 1913). Elaborations were also the focus of Hyland's (2007) investigation of a large corpus of academic texts. Hyland focussed specifically on exemplifying and reformulating elaborative strategies, but restricted his investigation of the use of elaborative rhetoric to a clause, word, or numerical figure. Similarly, Biber and Gray's (2010) examination of elaborativeness in academic writing was limited to subordinate clauses and phrasal expressions.

This study extends the investigation of Elaboration in academic discourse to both macro and microstructural levels of text. It examines and compares the mode of employment of discoursal Elaboration across texts produced in Anglophone and Polish academic discourse communities by native and Polish speakers of English. Elaborations are discussed with respect to their textual functions, frequency of employment, hierarchical location and discoursal prominence. An attempt is made to examine the reflection of cultural conditioning in the choice of elaborative structures and to describe the interface of the variation in their utilisation and discoursal meaning.

2. The corpus

I will illustrate the occurrence of Elaborative relations in the following articles published in sociological journals: Text 1 (Clark and Seymour 1991) written by native speakers of English in the Anglophone (American) academic discourse community; Text 2 (Pakulski 1993) written by a native speaker of Polish in the Anglophone (Australian) academic discourse community; and Text 3 (Ziółkowski 1994) written by a native speaker of Polish in the Polish academic discourse community.

Studies which identified the greatest intercultural divergence in research writing concentrated on 'soft' science texts while those showing greater similarities tended to focus on 'hard' sciences (cf. Golebiowski and Liddicoat 2002, Kirkpatrick 1997, Liddicoat 1997). The selection of research papers for this study from sociology, representing a 'soft' science, was thus dictated by expectations that the ensuing analysis would yield rich cross-cultural stylistic evidence. According to Hyland (2002) 'soft knowledge fields represent heavier rhetorical investment in contextualisation, perhaps even a need to persuade the reader that the phenomenon actually exists'. Additional consideration for the selection of corpus was given to the fact that 'soft' science texts are more accessible for linguistic investigation than texts in 'hard' sciences, where the analysis of discourse may be hampered by lack of full comprehension of the subject matter (cf. Kaldor et al. 1997).

All three texts have been published in highly reputable journals: Texts 1 and 2 in *International Sociology*, the journal of the International Sociological Association, and Text 3 in *Polish Sociological Review* (PSR), a publication vehicle of the Polish Sociological Association. All texts address the theme of social changes. Texts 1 and 2 have a tight thematic connection: Text 2 is a direct response to the question of validity of the concept of class put forward by Text 1. An influential paper by Lipset and Clark (Text 1) provoked a number of responses, Pakulski's (Text 2) among them. This has provided a unique opportunity to examine and compare how writers influenced by Anglophone and Polish cultural traditions but working in Anglophone discourse communities organise their prose when discussing the same topic, according to the same organisational requirements. Text 3 addresses systemic changes effected by the post-communist transformation in Polish society. *PSR* is regarded as the most prestigious sociological journal publishing in

English in Poland. The majority of its contributions comprises state-of-the-art Polish-written papers judged by an editorial board to be of interest to international audiences and translated into English. However, the selected article was originally written in English. The selection of this journal as a source of the third text has allowed for the analysis and description of the style of presentation which is likely to be preferred and acceptable in journals published in English in Poland.

The authors of Text 1 are native English speakers, born, educated and working in an English speaking country. The author of Text 2 was born and completed his education up to tertiary level in Poland, followed by work in Polish academia. His doctoral study was undertaken in Australia and supervised by a Polish-born and Polish and British educated professor of sociology. When writing his paper the author had been a part of the Australian academy for three decades. The author of Text 3 was born and educated in Poland and, apart from research visits to universities in English-speaking countries, spent his working life in the Polish academy. All four writers are professors of sociology with significant publication records. Together they have authored and co-authored over 70 books and edited volumes and have written over 750 articles and book chapters. The most prolific is Martin Lipset, the co-author of Text 1. All publications of the authors of Text 1 are in English. Almost all publications of the author of Text 2 are in English, with 50% co-authored with native English speakers. About 25% of the publications of the author of Text 3 are in English, 65% are in Polish and 10% are in French. On the basis of examination of samples of the other overall written work of the four authors, I consider the selected texts to be representative of their usual writing style.

3. Methodology

In my investigation I utilise the Framework for the Analysis of the Rhetorical Structure of Texts (FARS), proposed and described by Golebiowski (2005, 2006, 2009, 2011). FARS provides a functional account of text organisation in terms of the strategies employed by writers to achieve their communicative purposes. FARS coherence relations obtain from the level of text as a whole to the level of a clause. The entire text represents a relational schema at the top hierarchical level. This top level schema entails a relation linking macropropositions at the global level of discourse. The top macropropositions include schemata entailing relations linking (mezzo) propositions at the mezzo level, which in turn include relational schemata linking propositions at the micro-level. FARS relational taxonomy includes the relational clusters of Elaboration, List, Causal, Adversative, Facilitation, Assessing and Digression (see Table 1). The Elaboration cluster is the largest and comprises six types of relations: Extension, Amplification, Explanation, Reformulation, Instantiation, Addition.

Table 1. FARS taxonomy of relations.

Relational cluster	Delicacy within cluster
Elaboration	Extension, Amplification, Explanation, Reformulation, Instantiation, Addition
List	Collection, Sequence, Disjunction
Causal	Cause, Circumstance, Condition, Evidence, Means
Adversative	Concessive, Contrast, Collateral, Comparison
Facilitation	Framing, Advance Organising, Introducing, Enumerating
Assessing	Conclusion, Evaluation, Interpretation
Digression	Explanation, Instantiation, Addition, Extended Reference

FARS identifies two types of relational functioning: paratactic, where all parts of a textual schema are equally prominent in terms of their discoursal functions, and hypotactic, where one part of a relational schema is more prominent than the other part(s). It is postulated that the majority of coherence relations can function both paratactically and hypotactically, depending on the world of texts in which they appear. In a way similar to Grimes' (1975) predicates, the adoption of paratactic or hypotactic forms depends on writer's communicative purposes. A relational textual schema is paratactic when both (or more) of its parts bear the same functional prominence, with writer taking no stance in advancing one argument over the other. A relational schema is hypotactic when one part of text is more prominent in terms of writer's functions than other part(s).

I treat clause, a basic information processing unit in human discourse (Givón 1983: 7) as a minimal analytical unit. In principle, following RST, I regard complements (subjects, objects, adverbials) and restrictive relative clauses as parts of their host clauses, and assign the status of separate, functionally significant units to non-restrictive clauses. However, I consider functional integrity a deciding factor in segmenting texts. For example, due the high sentential complexity of the examined texts, in particular Texts 2 and 3, expressions containing predications with ellipted subject groups, and functionally significant complements, especially those constituting large nominal and verbal groups, have been allocated a propositional status and treated as independent units of analysis.

The allocation of an independent status to ellipted expressions has been dictated by methodological considerations. Because Texts 2 and 3 exhibit a high level of syntactic and semantic congestion, the denial of a separate status to functionally significant elliptical units would have prevented the description of specific rhetorical characteristics of relational schemata of these texts. There has also been an effort exercised towards the factoring of texts into analytical units of comparable sizes. Table 2 shows a final number of analytical units and an average number of words per unit.

Table 2. Segmentation of texts.

	Text 1	Text 2	Text 3
Total number of units	362	439	635
Number of words per unit	12.8	12.9	13.6

3.1. Elaboration relations: Definitions and exemplifications

I will provide definitions of relations of the FARS Elaborative cluster, and will illustrate their presentation in the studied corpus. Elaboration relations occur in textual schemata where one member of the schema presents the thesis, and the other elaborates it or its part. There are different ways in which text may be developed through the use of Elaborations. A general tendency for an Elaboration is to facilitate text comprehension by elaborating concepts, assumptions, solutions, or part(s) thereof stated in the thesis through an in-depth development. Such development includes a clarifying, supporting, or instantiative material which assists and encourages the reader to become involved in the unfolding text. Elaborations may also expand the contents of the thesis sideways, developing related processes and discussing issues presented in the thesis from different points of view. They may rephrase and reinforce proposals, claims or suggestions made in the thesis. Elaborations can be signalled lexically by expressions such as *in particular, specifically, for example, for instance, let me illustrate, which* or by punctuation. A colon has often been found to indicate Amplification, Explanation, or Evidence, while a semicolon has a tendency to point to Extension or Addition. Signalling maybe helpful in identification of relations but it cannot be relied on as the same linking adverbials may indicate different relations and punctuation is frequently misleading.

The conceptual framework of an Elaboration relation and its categorisation in this study has been influenced by the RST theory and by treatment of elaborative structures by Halliday (1994), Longacre (1983) and Grimes (1975). The Elaboration relation joins two components: Antecedent A and Consequent B. Information presented in B elaborates information or part thereof presented in A. In a hypotactic Elaboration, A is functionally more prominent than B, and in a paratactic Elaboration, A is equal to B in terms of significance of their text functions. A canonical order of textual presentation is for A to precede B. While Elaboration relations of Extension, Amplification, Explanation and Reformulation are basically neutral and their paratactic or hypotactic realisations are contextually dictated, Elaborations Instantiation and Addition are deemed to appear in hypotactic variants only.

3.1.1. Elaboration Extension

In the Elaboration Extension schema the author seeks to convey particular meanings by extending the thesis. Segment B expands ideas from preceding segment A sideways, introducing related propositions which widen the sense in which the writer wants to be understood. Examples 1 and 2 illustrate paratactic and hypotactic varieties of this relation. In 1, text span B further extends the proposition expressed in segment A. The presentation of the features of the four systems in A is expanded and widened by the author's conceptualisation of these systems as analytical categories in B. Both members of the schema are functionally prominent and both propositions are developed in the ensuing text. In 2, the author's main focus is Weber's definition of class, which is based on economically determined classification. The elaborative proposition of segment B expands the author's understanding of such a concept of class in terms of the relationship between the emergence of class consciousness and general culture of a society. Although in segment B the author increases the accessibility of information provided in segment A, B has a lower degree of discoursal significance than segment A whose content is further explored in the unfolding text.

Example 1 (Text 3)

(A) I believe that these four systems of interests and values not only coexist and compete with each other in societies undergoing transformation, but also manifest themselves in different ways and reflect different phenomena

(B) I view these systems of normative order primarily as analytic categories, ones which only later give way to hypotheses concerning the different phases of transformation.

Example 2 (Text 1)

(A) Weber reserved the concept of class for economically determined stratification. He defined a class as composed of people who have life chances in common, as determined by their power to dispose of goods and skills for the sake of income. Property is a class asset, but not the only criterion of class. For Weber, the crucial aspect of a class situation is, ultimately, the market. His examination of past class struggles suggested that conflicts between creditors and debtors are perhaps the most visible economic cleavage. The conflict between employers and workers is highly visible under capitalism, but is just a special case of the more common struggle between buyers and sellers.

(B) Weber, like Marx, was concerned to identify conditions encouraging class consciousness. Yet for him there was no single set of classes or form of class consciousness. Rather, which groups develop a consciousness of common interest opposing other groups is a specific empirical question; Different groups join or conflict at different times and places. Variations depend heavily on the general culture of a society, including its religion and fundamental beliefs. These can foster or inhibit the emergence of class-conscious groups in ways that cannot be understood solely from a society's economic base.

3.1.2. Elaboration Amplification

Elaboration Amplification is a communication process through which meaning is clarified by a second segment that presents the statement made by the thesis in more detail or a more definite way, thus developing the thesis in depth. Amplification obtains between an object or value and its attribute, between a set and its members, or between a generalisation and its specific instances. It joins information presented in the elaborative member of schema that is semantically less inclusive, to the more inclusive and less precise information provided by the thesis. This Elaboration subtype bears similarity to Grimes' (1975) supporting predicate 'Specifically', Longacre's notional structure of 'Generic specific paraphrase' or 'Amplification paraphrase', and, to some degree, Halliday's 'Clarification'.

In Example 3, the Elaboration provided by segment B highlights specific seminal information about the 'second Left' introduced in A. The amplification of the thesis statement in B is mandatory for the understanding of the whole relational schema and enables the reader to follow the discussion of the unfolding text. Segment B is thus seen to be as functionally as prominent as the proposition in segment A.

Example 3 (Text 1)

(A) But a second Left is emerging in Western societies (sometimes termed New Politics, New Left, Post-Bourgeois, or Post-Materialist),

(B) which increasingly stresses social issues rather than traditional class political issues.

3.1.3. Elaboration Explanation

In an Elaboration Explanation schema, the discourse function of the elaborative segment is to elaborate the meaning of a preceding text segment or part(s) thereof by providing explication and/or definition in order to constrain the interpretation of the thesis and make the material more accessible. Elaboration Explanation is somewhat similar to Grimes' (1975) supporting predicate 'Explanation', which Grimes however applies to broader contexts including, for example, the cause–effect schemata.

In a paratactic Example 4, B explains which values are subsumed under the term 'all values' mentioned in segment A. Both members of this schema are of equal functional prominence and the content of the whole schema, including the types of 'values' is further discussed in the ensuing text. In contrast, in a hypotactic Example 5, a less prominent unit B explicates the notion of 'conceptual stretch' from unit A for readers who need this explanation.

Example 4 (Text 3)

(A) Polish society today seems to consider all other values secondary, subordinated and accepted only insofar as they are instrumental to the realization of economic and social-welfare related values.

(B) This refers to such values as individual freedom and rights, democracy, freedom of speech, law, order, self-government, and individual ownership.

Example 5 (Text 2)

(A) The concept of class suffers from what Sartori (1970) diagnosed as 'conceptual stretch'.

(B) Its denotation (coverage) has extended, mainly due to indiscriminate application, at the expense of its clarity and precision.

3.1.4. Elaboration Reformulation

In the Elaboration Reformulation schema, the elaborative segment expresses the idea of the thesis or a part of it in a different way. Reformulations include repetitions and paraphrases which restate previous utterances through alternative linguistic means, usually resulting in the reinforcement of statements already made, or aimed at a clearer presentation of the arguments advanced. Reformulations have generally been seen as repairs (cf. Blackmore 1993; Schegloff et al. 1977), but FARS Elaboration Reformulation resembles more Grimes' supporting predicate 'Equivalent or the RST "Restatement"'. However, contrary to RST, which proposes Restatement as a separate relational category, and following Duszak's (1997) categorisation, FARS Reformulation is included in the Elaboration cluster of relations.

In a paratactic variety of Reformulation in Example 6, unit B reformulates the propositions in segment A by summarizing them within the scope of the original formulation. The resulting clarifying reinforcement of the author's thesis is as functionally significant as the thesis itself. In Example 7, in segment B, the author declares that the 'traditional class–party alignment' has been 'crumbling' thus restating a part of the proposition in A about the 'class–party alignments weakening'. However, B is not viewed as mandatory for increasing the comprehension of A. This relation is therefore seen as hypotactic where unit A is more prominent than B.

Example 6 (Text 3)

(A) However, socialism was still accepted insofar as it played the role of a welfare state, offered protection, and safeguarded the system of distribution and social care.

(B) Society accepted the state as a guaranty of social security and satisfaction of basic individual needs.

Example 7 (Text 2)

(A) It is this tension [between the interests of people as consumers and the interest of people as producers] that may lead to the well documented weakening of the traditional class-party alignments.

(B) this alignment has been crumbling [and figures for union membership and voting patterns testify to that.]

3.1.5. Elaboration Instantiation

In the Elaboration Instantiation schema, the elaborative text segment clarifies proposition(s) of the thesis through an illustrative material. It develops the thesis in depth by contributing an example of the set which has been introduced in the principal member of the schema. Elaboration Instantiation reveals what the author predicts about his readers' knowledge of the topic and tends to make the abstract more concrete. It resembles the 'Exemplification' categories in Longacre (1983), Fahnestock (1983) and Halliday (1994). In Example 8, segments B and C exemplify propositions forwarded in A. Although text in B and C illustrates and clarifies the authors' claim made in A, examples of Wright's and Giddens' approaches are not seen to be mandatory for the understanding of the argument presented in segment A. The enfolding text in the paper further develops segment A.

Example 8 (Text 1)

(A) Many writers have, like Dahrendorf, retained terms from Marx, while substantially changing the meaning.

(B) Erik Wright (1985: 64–104) has sought to capture some of the same changes as Dahrendorf. He does so by developing a 12 category typology of class location in capitalist society that includes: 1. bourgeoisie, 2. small employers, 4. expert managers, 5. expert supervisors, 8. semi-credentialed supervisors, and continues up to 12. proletarians. It explicitly incorporates not just ownership, but skill level, and managerial responsibility. It is striking that Wright, a self-defined Marxist, incorporates so much of post-Weberian multi-dimensionality.

(C) Giddens (1980: 108–112) similarly emphasises the emergence of multiple cleavages within the workplace, the distinct importance of management, and the rise of an autonomous middle class, as undermining the Marxist approach.

3.1.6. Elaboration Addition

In Elaboration Addition, the elaborative segment includes material which is supplementary or auxiliary to what has already been presented in the thesis. Information presented in B is additional to the information or part thereof presented in A. For instance, in 9, the proposition in B provides superfluous information to the propositions forwarded by A. Although thematically relevant, it is not mandatory to the understanding of the text.

Example 9 (Text 3)

(A) The elements however seem to grow and do so in a double opposition: not only to materialism, [B] but also to some earlier, traditional values of preindustrial, mostly rural society.

(B) which is characteristic of capitalist-industrial culture

As can be seen in the examples cited, in spite of an effort made towards the achievement of the specificity of definitions, some degree of overlap inherently exists between the conceptual frameworks of the Elaboration subtypes. It is also possible for the writer to wish to communicate more than one kind of Elaboration relation. The elaborative segments may thus contain more than one elaborative element. For example, some Amplifications may simultaneously be illustrative, Extensions additive, or Reformulations explicatory.

4. Findings

Across the examined corpus the Elaborative systems have been found to be complex, not only in terms of textual pervasiveness but also in relation to the hierarchical location of Elaboration relations, the distribution of textual prominence within the relational schemata and the recursiveness of elaborative structures across the levels of text development.

4.1. Elaborative pervasiveness

Elaborations are the most frequent coherence relations identified in the studied texts, constituting almost 27% of all relations. Their pervasiveness is the highest in Text 3 where over 30% of relational schemata demonstrate elaborative configurations, with Text 1 closely following, and the author of Text 2 formulating one fifth of its relational structures as Elaborations. As seen in Table 3, the most pervasive elaborative category is Amplification, comprising almost half of all Elaborations. Its most frequent occurrence is in Text 3, followed by Text 1, with Text 2 at the low end of the frequency continuum. The greatest intertextual variation is observed in the distribution of Addition, the second most frequent Elaboration in the corpus, comprising about one fifth of all Elaborations, with Text 2 including over three times lower number of Additions than the remaining texts. Elaboration Extension, which occupies the third place in the elaborative pervasiveness, features similar frequency of occurrence in Texts 1 and 3, with slightly lower numbers of this relation employed in Text 2. Explanations and Reformulations show higher occurrence in Texts 2 and 3 than Text in 1: the frequency of Explanations is about double, and of Reformulations about triple in both texts in comparison with their occurrence in Text 1. On the other hand, Text 1, which tends to present numerous case studies, is much higher than Texts 2 and 3 in the number of Instantiations, with its frequency about double that in the remaining texts.

Table 3. The ratio of Elaboration relations to all relations (%).

Type	Text 1	Text 2	Text 3	Total
Amplification	12.8	10.5	14.3	12.7
Extension	3.6	2.8	3.6	3.3
Explanation	1,7	2.5	3.4	2.6
Reformulation	0.3	0.8	1.1	0.7
Instantiation	3.9	1.7	2.2	2.6
Addition	6.7	2	6.1	4.9
Total	29.0	20.6	30.6	26.9

4.2. Hierarchical location and relational taxis

The three articles differ in the level of hierarchical placement of Elaborations in the text and the distribution of taxis within the elaborative schemata. From Table 4 we can see that in Text 1 the majority (64%) of the Elaborative schemata are placed at bottom levels of text development, with almost all remaining Elaborations (35%) placed at mezzo hierarchical levels, leaving only one small-size (3 analytical units) Elaboration occupying a relatively low top macrostructural level. The picture of elaborative hierarchy of Texts 2 and 3 is considerably different. In Text 2 the heaviest concentration of Elaborative schemata (68%) is at mezzo levels, 21% of Elaborations appear at bottom levels and 11% are utilised in the text's top macrostructure. Text 3 also features a balanced elaborative density at mezzo and bottom hierarchical levels (40% and 46% respectively) but has the strongest top elaborative macrostructure of the three texts, with 14% of its Elaboration relations appearing at high hierarchical levels. Elaborative schemata employed in the top macrostructure of this paper occupy significant amounts of textual space. They include an Elaboration Explanation (comprising the paper's

Introduction), Elaboration Extension (including three sections of the paper), Elaboration Amplification (comprising a substantial part of the Conclusion section), and Elaboration Extension (comprising the penultimate section of this article).

Table 4. Hierarchical distribution of Elaboration relations.

Level	Text 1	Text 2	Text 3
1			
2			
3			1
4		2	3
5			6
6	1	2	6
7		6	10
8	1	8	16
9	2	7	9
10	3	8	13
11	2	9	12
12	8	8	6
13	9	11	5
14	11	10	16
15	16	8	18
16	13	5	15
17	12	5	14
18	10	1	14
19	5		6
20	4		10
21	6		7
22			3
23	1		1
Total	104	90	191

The overwhelming majority of Elaborations in all texts are hypotactic, but the paratactic–hypotactic ratio varies intertextually (see Table 5). Text 1 features the highest frequency of hypotactic Elaborations with hypotactic Amplifications constituting 85% of all Amplifications in this text. Text 2 features the most balanced distribution of elaborative taxis, largely attributed to an even balance of hypotactic and paratactic Amplifications and low frequencies of elaborative categories of Addition and Instantiation which have only hypotactic variants. Text 3 is closer to Text 2 in its distribution of elaborative taxis, with most of its Amplifications (81%) exhibiting hypotactic structures.

Importantly, there is a considerable intertextual variation in the distribution of the elaborative taxis across hierarchical levels of discoursal development. While the majority of paratactic relations in Text 1 appear at low hierarchical levels, 50% of Elaboration schemata included in the top structure of Text 3 and 59% of Elaboration schemata included in the top structure of Text 2 are paratactically structured, thus playing a critical role in the understanding of author's communicative messages.

Table 5. Paratactic and hypotactic ratio of Elaboration relations.

Elaborations	Text 1	Text 2	Text 3
Paratactic	15%	28%	30%
Hypotactic	85%	62%	70%

4.3. Recursiveness

All three texts are characterised by a complex system of elaborative recursiveness where Elaborative schema of lower hierarchical levels are embedded within elaborative configurations located at higher levels. Example 10 illustrates multi-stage elaborative recursiveness: segment A (in italics) is an Elaboration at the first stage of recursiveness, segment A includes a second stage Elaboration in segment B (italics), and segment B contains a third stage Elaboration in segment C.

Example 10

First stage Elaboration in segment A:

In the mainstream Marxist tradition, the concept of class is linked with property relations and is used to account for social conflicts and social change. *Such a concept and usage – let us call it 'generative/explanatory' – typically focuses on economic roles, stresses the polarity and conflict of classes, and ignores the issues of class boundaries. Classes mark objective positions in the societal production processes and what most Marxists see as 'objective and antagonistic' interests, which are attributed to these positions. It is these structurally imputed conflicting interests that are seen as the main propellant of historically important collective conduct, even if they are not always well articulated in the consciousness of social actors. If they do articulate – and many Marxists see the rise of 'class consciousness' of workers as inevitable – classes transform into historical actors capable of concerted action and, ultimately, revolutionary change. Thus, within the 'generative' concept-user camp one can find a division between structuralist objectivists, who see classes as principal internal conflict generator (labour vs. capital) accessible to theorists using proper abstractions (e.g., Althusser 1971) on the one hand, and actional subjectivists who identify classes with collective actors challenging the status quo in a radical way (e.g., Touraine 1985) on the other. For the former, classes are ubiquitous but typically hidden from an 'empiricist' gaze; class conflicts permeate social reality but reveal themselves only to those who use the right method of analysis (that is, presuppose their existence). For the latter, classes are also ubiquitous but more tangible: they appear whenever solidary groups form and challenge the dominant values, norms and institutions. [Note 1: 80–81] As Touraine (1985) suggests, this is regardless of the socio-economic positions of the challengers, forms of the challenge and identities of the actors.*

Second stage Elaboration in segment B:

Such a concept and usage – let us call it 'generative/explanatory' – typically focuses on economic roles, stresses the polarity and conflict of classes, and ignores the issues of class boundaries. Classes mark objective positions in the societal production processes and what most Marxists see as 'objective and antagonistic' interests, which are attributed to these positions. It is these structurally imputed conflicting interests that are seen as the main propellant of historically important collective conduct, even if they are not always well articulated in the consciousness of social actors. If they do articulate – and many Marxists see the rise of 'class consciousness' of workers as inevitable – classes transform into historical actors capable of concerted action and, ultimately, revolutionary change. *Thus, within the 'generative' concept-user camp one can find a division between structuralist objectivists, who see classes as principal internal conflict generator (labour vs. capital) accessible to theorists using proper abstractions (e.g., Althusser 1971) on the one hand, and actional subjectivists who identify classes with collective actors challenging the status quo in a radical way (e.g., Touraine 1985) on the other. For the former, classes are ubiquitous but typically hidden from an 'empiricist' gaze; class conflicts permeate social reality but reveal themselves only to those who use the right method of analysis (that is, presuppose their existence). For the latter, classes are also ubiquitous but more tangible: they appear whenever solidary groups form and challenge the dominant values, norms and institutions. [Note 1: 80–81] As Touraine (1985) suggests, this is regardless of the socio-economic positions of the challengers, forms of the challenge and identities of the actors.*

Third stage Elaboration in segment C:

Thus, within the 'generative' concept-user camp one can find a division between structuralist objectivists, who see classes as principal internal conflict generator (labour vs. capital) accessible to theorists using proper abstractions (e.g., Althusser 1971) on the one hand, and actional subjectivists who identify classes with collective actors challenging the status quo in a radical way (e.g., Touraine 1985) on the other. *For the former, classes are ubiquitous but typically hidden from an 'empiricist' gaze; class conflicts permeate social reality but reveal themselves only to those who use the right method of analysis (that is, presuppose their existence). For the latter, classes are also ubiquitous but more tangible: they appear whenever solidary groups form and challenge the dominant values, norms and institutions. [Note 1: 80–81] As Touraine (1985) suggests, this is regardless of the socio-economic positions of the challengers, forms of the challenge and identities of the actors.*

The volume and depth of elaborative recursiveness vary across the corpus. Because there is a greater presence of Elaborations at higher levels in Text 3, followed by Text 2, their recursiveness is also higher at these levels (see Table 6). Text 3 features the strongest recursiveness, exhibiting elaborative embedding up to seven stages. The longest first stage Elaboration, placed in the middle part of the article, comprises its three sections. The longest second stage Elaboration comprises almost an entire section, the longest third stage includes 29 analytical units, the longest fourth stage 23 units, the longest fifth stage 6 units, with sixth and seventh stages limited to 1–3 unit text spans. In a similar manner, in Text 2, massive first stage elaborative schemata comprising entire article sections or substantial parts of sections make room for heavy recursive second and third stage Elaborations, with the fourth stages limited to 1–3 unit text blocks. On the contrary, the longest first stage Elaboration in Text 1 constitutes 45 analytical units and its second to fifth stage Elaborations constitute relatively short text spans. The longest second stage Elaboration constitutes 13 units, the longest third stage Elaboration comprises 6 units, the longest fourth level Elaboration 3 units, and all fifth level Elaborations consist of 1-unit spans.

Table 6. Ratio of elaborative recursive stages.

Stage	Text 1	Text 2	Text 3
1	23%	38%	39%
2	36%	43%	14%
3	30%	15%	27%
4	7%	4%	11%
5	4%		6%
6			2%
7			1%

5. Discussion

The findings of the reported study demonstrate that Elaboration is a routine method by which the authors of the three research papers establish grounds for proposed claims and seek to make their research accessible and persuasive. Blocks of discourse textually formulated as various types of Elaborations cover extensive reviews of literature, including its assembling and interpretation, considerations and reconsiderations of the validity of previous claims as well as discussions and clarifications of related concepts and research methods. Golebiowski (2002), who investigated all relational structures in the same corpus, found Elaborative relations to be the most frequent of all coherence relations in Texts 1 and 3, and the second most frequent (after List) in Text 2. In the reported study we see that the most functionally significant elaborative category is Amplification whose pervasiveness significantly exceeds the frequency of all other Elaborations. The authors use it to detail features which are salient to their primary theses and to specify their statements more precisely. Amplification is assigned a primary role in all three texts – either through its abundant employment (in Texts 1 and 3) or by a tendency to appear in its paratactic variant (in Text 2).

The pervasiveness of the elaborative structures across the whole corpus suggests that elaborativeness may be a general characteristic of the style of writing sociology. The findings of the reported study support earlier descriptions of the prose of social sciences and of sociology in particular, as exhibiting tendencies to include broad elaborative bases for presented propositions. Hyland (2007) suggested that Elaboration is an important and recurrent feature of academic prose and Bazerman (1981: 370) claimed that sociological writers need to persuade their readers not only of the specific claims of their text, but of 'a larger framework of thought in which the claims are placed', and that construction of knowledge in this field usually requires 'a reconsideration of the validity of wide parts of the literature and not just of the specifically competing claims'.

Yet the analysis of the employment of Elaborative relations in the three papers shows intertextual variation across of all areas investigated. We saw that the Polish native speaker Text 3 demonstrates the highest elaborative strength. It features the greatest pervasiveness of Elaborations, the highest level of their recursiveness and the most frequent placement of Elaboration schemata in the textual macrostructure. It features the highest number of Amplifications, Explanations and Reformulation of the three texts. Elaborations occupy the largest amounts of this paper's textual space and demonstrate strong paratactic presence at top hierarchical levels of discourse development. Almost 50% of Elaboration relations located in the rhetorical top structure are paratactically developed, pointing to their critical role in the understanding of the communicative messages intended by the author.

It is likely that the writing style of Text 3 (and, to a lesser degree, Text 2) is influenced by the author's languaculture[1] and draws upon the socio-cultural beliefs and discourse conventions of his mother tongue. It has been claimed that Elaborations are the essence of Teutonic (including Polish) expository writing (Clyne 1987; Galtung 1985) and that a prolific use of elaborated meanings meets the requirement of an intellectualisation of the academic style (Duszak 1997). According to Duszak (1997), in Polish academic writing, the negotiation of the thematic base is often conducted through grounding in the form of auxiliary elaborative arguments. This phenomenon is clearly observable in Text 3 which is the highest in the

---

[1] I am using this term after Agar (1994) to refer to a linguistic-cultural discourse community.

frequencies of Amplifications, Explanations and Reformulations. Duszak (1998, 1994) claimed that the authors of Polish language studies papers she analysed attached special value to a detailed and early presentation of their 'research workshop'.[2] In a similar way, the author of Text 3 uses Explanation Elaboration to introduce and explicate the writers' 'tools', i.e., the concepts, terms and notions discussed. For example, the whole first section of the text is devoted to the explication of terms 'values' and 'interests', which constitute the core concepts of this article. The style of writing characterised by elaborative detours, needs strategies to bring the readers' focus back to the main line of argumentation. This is illustrated in this text's use of Reformulations which restate the author's theses after the elaborative inserts.

The comparatively lower frequency of Elaboration relations in Text 2 (written by a Polish native speaker and produced in an Anglophone academic environment) is compensated by considerable sizes of the elaborative segments and a high proportion of paratactic configurations. Although the visibility of Elaborations in the textual top structure is lower than in Text 3, a heavy presence of paratactic configurations across all hierarchical levels accords them a central position in the writer's argumentation. Coordinately organized elaborative structures of this paper reflect a significant focus on propositional content, at the same time resulting in a low degree of the presentational force. Highly placed paratactic relational schemata leave readers to their own resources in terms of the choice of information necessary for the understanding of the text. Such low level of reader guidance is seen as characteristic of Teutonic communication tradition in which academic writing is aimed at elitist audience (cf. Galtung 1985; Clyne 1994).

It is important to note here that the findings reported by Golebiowski (2002) show that the low percentage of Elaborations in Text 2 is offset by a high frequency of Digressions which are the most frequent relations in this text, with 16% of relational schemata classified as digressive. This finding suggests that Addition and Instantiation components of the relational schemata in Text 2 have been assessed as exhibiting very low functional levels and consequently classified as Digressions. A possible explanation of this phenomenon is a subtle distinction between hypotactic Elaborations (Additions and Instantiations) and Digressions. Digressive segments are

---

[2]   Interestingly, no other research concerned with academic prose produced in languacultures of the 'Teutonic' area of influence reported such findings. On the contrary, Clyne (1987) found more explanations of terms in papers written by English than by German scholars. The degree of discoursal elaboration presented in the form of Reformulations may be related to the level of linearity of textual argumentation.

seen to include additional, peripheral material perceived as superfluous to the understanding of text and deemed to convey peripheral information which disrupts the flow of discourse. On the other hand, although Elaborations tend to slow the flow of discourse, they are integrated in the main line of argumentation, facilitating the writer–reader communication.[3]

The frequency of Elaborative schemata in native English speaker Text 1 almost equals that of Text 3 but the majority of these schemata are placed at bottom hierarchical levels where they occupy limited discoursal spaces resulting in functional roles less prominent than those of Elaborations in the Polish native speaker texts 2 and 3. Elaborations are almost totally absent in the paper prominent top structure and are predominantly hypotactically structured, thus viewed as less relevant and more superfluous for text comprehension. To some degree, a high level of textual hypotaxis is caused by the pervasiveness of Additions which are always hypotactic and Instantiations which the authors use to describe numerous case studies. Through the employment of hypotactically structured relations the authors indicate the distribution of the functional weight of textual propositions to their readers, who are thus aided in the discovery of the text's coherence relations and consequently are able to view some information as more important than the other. By indicating their stance relating to the preferences in the line of argumentation, the authors place specific emphasis on functionally dominant propositions, pointing to their textual salience. Such high level of discoursal facilitation contrasts with the academic style of the Polish academic tradition (where Text 2 partially, and Text 3 clearly belong), where little recognition is assigned to the interactive properties of text (cf. Golebiowski 1998, 1999). The linear style of argumentation in Text 1 is also reflected in the practical non-existence of Elaboration Reformulations. While the styles of Texts 2 and 3 require reformulations of the authors' theses in order to bring their readers' attention back from the thematic detours to the main argument development, a more subordinate discoursal structure of Text 1 results in

---

[3] The Golebiowski (2002) study uses the degree of textual relevance and redundancy as a measure of digressiveness. A classificatory distinction between Digression and Elaboration is the detachability of a digressive textual segment without diminishing the degree of textual coherence. However, the assessment as to which relational structures are digressive and which are hypotactic elaborative can be subjective to a considerable degree and may differ between readers representing varied background knowledge and different discourse communities. The concept of digression also varies across cultures. Writers and readers, guided by their own cultural norms and rules of appropriateness, may differ in their perception relating to the relevance and value of textual material. For example, texts seen as digressive by members of Anglo-American academic community may be considered linear by representatives of Polish academic communities.

a linear organisation of text characterised by considerable value attached to the relevance of presented material.

Variations in the elaborative strength across the corpus may be also caused by the language–systemic determinants. For example, large numbers of Elaboration schemata in Texts 2 and 3 result from the occurrence of numerous intrasentential Elaborations. Their identification resulted from the subsegmentation of complex sentences which feature considerable elaborative expansion of their constituents. Such elaborate sentence structures mirror the syntactic complexity of a Polish sentence. The inflectional character of the Polish language, case marking in particular, increases the sentential capacity, allowing, for instance, for the use of genitive constructions to produce hierarchies of nominalised expressions (cf. Duszak 1997). In a style similar to Polish academic discourse, which exploits the flexibility of the Polish sentence, Texts 2 and 3 contain multiple embeddings and subsequent expansions of both leftmost and rightmost parts of a sentence. The elliptic constructions that result from these embeddings compact the discoursal structure of these texts. Duszak (1997) refers to 'expansionist' and 'reductionist' strategies in Polish academic writing, reflected in a high level of structural elaborative complexity. Such tendencies are clearly visible in texts 2 and 3, whose sentential constructions include heavy accumulations of meaning, resulting from a high compression of content and the accommodation of a closed reasoning structure within sentence boundaries.

As all of the writers are leading figures in their sociological research communities, it can be assumed that the writing styles they utilise are exemplary (in both senses of the word) of their socio-cultural academic communities. The representativeness of styles is reinforced by stylistic inputs from members of respective sociological discourse communities through the reviewing, revising, consulting and editorial processes. In case of Text 1, both authors needed to reach a consensus in terms of the final stylistic output of their text. The authors of Texts 2 and 3 used the assistance of native speakers of English in the process of their writing: the author of Text 2 consulted fellow members of his local academic discourse community on stylistic matters (Pakulski, p.c. 2001), and the author of Text 3 was assisted by an EFL teacher (Ziolkowski, p.c. 2001). There is evidence of editorial interference in both Text 2 and 3, reflected in differences between the manuscript and published text versions.[4]

---

[4] The authors of Texts 2 and 3 kindly made original manuscripts available for my examination. The manuscript of Text 1 has not been made available.

It has to be borne in mind that there are always external influences which shape the writer's style, and thus it is unlikely that there is any such thing as a pure English or pure Polish style. Influences of both Anglophone and Polish cultures and discourse communities seem indisputable in the case of the author of Text 2. Although the socialization of this author into a new academic discourse community has lead to the assimilation of this discourse community's practices and textual conventions, his writing style cannot escape being shaped by the characteristics and conventions of the first language and native culture. It is also likely that the discoursal styles of Texts 1 and 3 are influenced by stylistic norms other than Anglo in case of Text 1, and other than Polish in case of Text 3. For example, the second author of Text 1, although born in the U.S., has been a member of both American and Jewish communities (Lipset 1996), and the author of Text 3 has been exposed to norms and conventions of Anglo-American academy through contacts with native English speaking academics.

6. Conclusion

The description of elaborative relational structures of three selected papers from the field of sociology demonstrates that Elaboration is a prominent discourse feature of these texts. It is hoped that the approach to analysis of academic prose reported in this study will open a new line of enquiry into the investigation of discoursal organisation in the discipline of sociology as well as other fields of study. Further studies might shed more light in particular on writing conventions in soft sciences which, characterised by a less cohesive readership than hard sciences, might require a greater degree of elaboration for knowledge accomplishment (cf. Hyland 2002).

This paper argues that the variation in the mode of employment of elaborative structures by the writers of the three studied texts may be caused by their differing linguistic backgrounds and discourse community memberships. It proposes possible interpretations of the differences in elaborative styles which suggest that the rhetorical structure of a research article cannot escape being shaped by the characteristics and conventions of the first language as well as the cultural norms and traditions underlying the discourse community into which the author has been socialised. However, in view of evidence that the cultural conditioning of texts varies between disciplines (cf. Golebiowski and Liddicoat 2002), it is possible that cultural influences are particularly accentuated in the research writing of sociology, an ideology driven discipline. Other variables that may be causing the apparent variation in the elaborative rhetorical strategies across texts may include second language development, subdisciplinary differences and journal editorial policies. The reported findings should not thus be over-generalized as typical for the entire respective discourse communities. Although the four authors are academics of high reputation and their writing styles can be regarded as representative of their socio-cultural academic settings, some of the stylistic features observed and described may represent characteristics of the individual writing styles.

Finally, it has to be borne in mind that the observations and discussions carried out in this paper are based on a case study of three research papers that constitute only three points on the international map of transmission of sociological knowledge. The aim of the study has been to provide a close, detailed and specific description of one selected discursive strategy. It has not aimed to be prescriptive, or to provide a final conclusion.

References

Agar, Michael. 1994. *Language Shock: The Culture of Communication*. New York: Morrow.

Biber, Douglas and Bethany Gray. 2010. Challenging stereotypes about academic writing: Complexity, elaboration, explicitness. *Journal of English for Academic Purposes* 9: 2–20.

Bazerman, Charles. 1981. What written knowledge does: Three examples of academic discourse. *Philosophy of Social Sciences* 11: 361–87.

Blackmore, Diane. 1993. The relevance of reformulations. *Language and Literature* 2: 101–20.

Clyne, Michael. 1987. Discourse structures and discourse expectations: Implications for Anglo-German academic communication in English. In Larry Smith (ed.), *Discourse across Cultures: Strategies in World Englishes*. New York: Prentice Hall.

Clyne, Michael. 1994. *Intercultural Communication at Work*. Cambridge: CUP.

Duszak, Anna. 1994. Academic discourse and intellectual styles. *Journal of Pragmatics* 21: 291–313.

Duszak, Anna. 1997. Reduction and elaboration in Polish academic discourse. In Raymond Hickey and Stanislaw Puppel (eds), *Language History and Language Modelling*. Berlin: Mouton de Gruyter.

Duszak, Anna. 1998. *Tekst, dyskurs, komunikacja międzykulturowa*. Warszawa: Wydawnictwo Naukowe PWN.

Fahnestock, Jeanne. 1983. Semantic and lexical coherence. *College Composition and Communication* 34: 400–16.

Galtung, Johan. 1985. Struktur, Kultur and intellektueller Stil. In Alois Wierlacher (ed.), *Das Fremde und das Eigene*. München: Iudicum, 151–96.

Golebiowski, Zofia. 1998. Rhetorical approaches to scientific writing: An English–Polish comparative study. *Text* 18: 67–102.

Golebiowski, Zofia. 1999. Application of Swales' model in the analysis of research papers by Polish Authors. *International Review of Applied Linguistics* 37: 231–48.

Golebiowski, Zofia. 2002. *The Rhetorical Organisation of Academic Texts in English*. Unpublished PhD thesis. Monash University, Melbourne.

Golebiowski, Zofia. 2005. Globalisation of academic communities and the style of research reporting. *Transcultural Studies* 1: 57–72.

Golebiowski, Zofia. 2006. The distribution of discoursal salience in research papers: Relational hypotaxis and parataxis. *Discourse Studies* 8 (2): 259–78.

Golebiowski, Zofia. 2009. Prominent messages in Education and Applied Linguistic abstracts: How do authors appeal to their prospective readers? *Journal of Pragmatics* 41 (4): 753–69.

Golebiowski, Zofia. 2011. Scholarly criticism across discourse communities. In Salager-Meyer, Françoise and Beverly A. Lewin (eds), *Crossed Words: Criticism in Scholarly Writing*. Berlin: Peter Lang, 203–24.

Golebiowski, Zofia and A. Liddicoat. 2002. The interaction of discipline and culture in academic writing. *Australian Review of Applied Linguistics* 25 (2): 59–71.

Givón, Talmy (ed.). 1983. *Topic Continuity in Discourse. Vol. 3: Typological Studies in Language*. Amsterdam: John Benjamins.

Grimes, Joseph. 1975. *The Thread of Discourse*. The Hague: Mouton.

Halliday, M.A.K. 1994. The construction of knowledge and value in the grammar of scientific discourse, with reference to Charles Darwin's *The Origin of Species*. London: Routledge.

Hobbs, Jerry. 1985. On the coherence and structure of discourse. Technical Report CSLI-85-37. Center for the Study of Language and Information, Stanford University: Stanford, CA.

Hyland, Ken. 2002. Directives: Argument and Engagement in Academic Writing. *Applied Linguistics* 23 (2): 215–39.

Hyland, Ken. 2007. Applying a Gloss: Exemplifying and Reformulating in Academic Discourse. *ELT Journal* 28 (2): 266–85.

Kaldor, Susan, Michael Herriman and Judith Rochecouste. 1997. Cross-disciplinary and discipline-specific discourse features. In Zofia Golebiowski and Helen Borland (eds), *Academic Communication across Disciplines and Cultures*. Melbourne: Victoria University.

Kamyab, Ghodratollah. 1997. Rhetorical structure analysis of medical review articles. Unpublished PhD thesis. Monash University, Melbourne.

Kirkpatrick, Andy. 1997. Intercultural variation in academic communication. In Zofia Golebiowski and Helen Borland (eds), *Academic Communication across Disciplines and Cultures*. Melbourne: Victoria University, 140–56.

Liddicoat, Anthony. 1997. Texts of the culture and texts of the discourse community. In Zofia Golebiowski and Helen Borland (eds), *Academic Communication across Disciplines and Cultures*. Melbourne: Victoria University, 38–42.

Lipset, Seymour. 1996. Steady work: An academic memoir. *Annual Review of Sociology* 22: 1–27.

Longacre, Robert. 1983. *The Grammar of Discourse*. New York: Plenum Press.

Mann, William, Christian Matthiessen and Sandra Thompson. 1989. Rhetorical Structure Theory and text analysis. *ISI Research Report*. University of Southern California.

Mann, William and Sandra Thompson. 1986. Relational Propositions in Discourse. *Discourse Processes* 9 (1): 57–90.

Mann, William and Sandra Thompson. 1987. Rhetorical Structure Theory: A theory of text organisation. *ISI/RS Report* 87–190: 2–82.

Mann, William and Sandra Thompson. 1988. Rhetorical Structure Theory: Toward a functional theory of text organisation. *Text* 8 (3): 243–81.

Schegloff, Emanuel, Gail Jefferson and Harvey Sacks. 1977. The preference for self-correction in the organization of repair in conversation. *Language* 53: 361–82.

Texts used for the analysis

Clark, Terry Nichols and Seymour Martin Lipset. 1991. Are social classes dying? *International Sociology* 6 (4): 397–410.

Pakulski, Jan. 1993. The dying of class or of Marxist class theory? *International Sociology* 8 (3): 279–92.

Ziółkowski, Marek. 1994. The pragmatic shift in Polish social consciousness: With or against the tide of rising postmaterialism? *Polish Sociological Review* 4: 303–21.

Chapter 13

COMMUNICATION DISORDERS AND MENTAL HEALTH

THE LINK WE CAN'T IGNORE

Deborah Perrott

Lifespan Counselling and Rehab

Current evidence-based research and three decades of literature demonstrate a strong relationship between communication disorders and mental health disorders. Longitudinal studies now enable us to see the link between childhood communication disorders and adolescent/adult psychiatric disorders. Particular types of communication disorders in childhood co-exist with specific psychiatric disorders, and this paper will review the research that supports this link. More specifically, it will address what we know about the types of childhood communication disorders that relate to specific psychiatric disorders in adolescence and adulthood. The impact of a communication disorder affects an individual and community. At a broader level, life-long communication disorders are viewed as a significant strain on mental health budgets and service delivery, and policies that address this are paramount. Applied linguistics offers a wealth of knowledge to assist in the better understanding of mental health. This paper explores some of the possible ways linguistics can assist with psychiatric measures. Such linguistic knowledge, when applied, has the potential to positively impact by altering the vertical transmission of communication and mental health problems at the individual, family and societal levels.

1. Introduction

Applied linguistics, a sub-discipline in the field of linguistics, enables us to explore communication utilizing a variety of populations. A relatively new field in applied linguistics is the use of assessments and profiles that are communicatively focused in order to assess an individual's capacities. Broadly speaking, they aim to measure communication strengths and weaknesses. Such assessments vary in terms of their application. Assessments for infants may involve observations and parental interviews, whereas for youth or adults, they may be presented in a written or verbal form. Such assessment is implemented when a communication problem is highlighted by a parent or professional. Likewise, when an individual presents to a service with a mental health problem(s), they are assessed using medical and psychological measures. At this present time in Australia, mental health problems are addressed through providing community access to certain services (psychology, psychiatry, dietetics, social workers, speech pathology) for short-term, evidence-based treatments. Although assessment and treatment of mental illness are steps in the right direction, there is a need to emphasize that applied linguistic research links communication disorders to psychiatric disorders. This paper will argue that, based on our current understanding of the research, the impact of diagnosed (and undiagnosed) communication disorders over the lifespan is both detrimental to individuals and difficult for communities to manage. Suggested solutions target the need for: (1) Understanding the relationship between communication disorders and mental health; (2) Further developing communication assessments which support current models of assessment; (3) Utilizing experts in communication for assessment and educational and preventative measures; (4) Implementing routine, targeted assessment of communication in individuals from birth through to early adulthood; (5) Addressing the issue of prevention and education of communication disorders as the key to further reducing mental health presentations in society. This paper will propose that minimizing mental health budgets can be achieved through focusing on managing communication disorders. Such an approach is aimed at breaking the cycle of the transference of communication and mental health issues between families in the community.

Research allows us to view the relationship between communication disorders and psychiatric disorders. The Speech Pathology Association of Australia (2010a: 1) informs us that:

> As a pre-requisite to our understanding of the relationship we should note that some communication disorders form part of the diagnostic criteria along with several mental health disorders. Such disorders include; autism spectrum disorders, attention deficit disorders, behavioural disorders, developmental language and speech disorders, schizophrenia, psychosis and dementia.

Acknowledging the above diagnostic relationship, research now describes the link between particular communication capacities such as comprehension and expressive language and specific mental health presentations (see review by Sutherland, McNeill and Gillon 2009). This in itself is a step forward as it challenges prevailing models that have been our only way of measuring mental health problems. For example, the medical model used for assessing child, adolescent and adult depression acknowledges elements necessary for functional communication (short-term memory loss, reduced eye-contact) but does not *emphasize* the components of communication. Research now expands our boundaries of thinking to acknowledge that communicative factors are indeed another way of linking communication disorders to mental health problems.

So we ask ourselves, what have we learnt to bring us closer to an understanding of the link between communication disorders and mental health disorders? The Speech Pathology Association of Australia has developed both a Position Statement (2010a) and Clinical Guidelines (2010b) entitled *Speech Pathology in Mental Health Services*, which aim to assist in the understanding, treatment and education and prevention of infants, children, adolescents and adults presenting with communication and mental health issues. Both papers are founded on evidence-based research and are prime examples of how the relationship between communication and mental health can be addressed and cannot be ignored. Such papers are not only clinically relevant but arm organizations and governments with knowledge of how to support the need to address mental health problems. Similarly, *The Bercow Report* (2008) highlights the fact that there is a significant strain on mental health services due to life-long communication disorders. This extensive British review outlines research and recommendations for attacking the issue of communication disorders and their relationship to mental health at a national level. This prompts a need for serious consideration of what factors may contribute to mental health disorders in Australia – more importantly, what can be done to assist in the reduction of both communication and mental health disorders from the knowledge that we have available and that historically exists.

2. Brief literature review

The following literature review is based on international studies including both communicatively impaired populations that have been found to present with a psychiatric disorder, and psychiatric samples that have been found to present with communication disorders. This in itself demonstrates a commonality between the two disorders. The literature reviewed for this paper includes selected and recent research as opposed to an historic overview. Longitudinal studies provide us with the most compelling evidence to support the fact that communication disorders in early childhood show a correlation to psychiatric disorders in youth and adulthood (Beitchman et al. 1996, 2001; Clegg et al. 2005; Conti-Ramsden and Botting 2004; Law et al. 2009; Lindsay et al. 2007). In a comprehensive review, Sutherland et al. (2009) found that children with speech-language impairments and written language impairments correlate with behavioural and psychiatric disorders. Current research highlights the link between specific language and psychiatric disorder correlates. Van Daal et al. (2007), for example, noted that different types of communication disorders and specific behavioural problems correlate at a young age. Phonological problems relate to problem behaviour that can be defined as external (aggression). Semantic language problems relate to internalizing problems (depression, anxiety and emotional issues). Furthermore, problematic comprehension in children has also been found to be associated with emotional and social problems as contrasted with expressive problems (Beitchman et al. 1996; Lindsay and Dockrell 2000; Rutter and Mawhood 1991). Psycho-social, emotional and behavioural problems correlate with communication disorders, as demonstrated in child studies, with longitudinal studies showing similar patterns of results. Cantwell and Baker (1987) were innovators in this field, with work spanning many years. They observed that many children presenting to speech-language clinics also presented with numerous psychiatric diagnoses. Similarly, other research has shown correlations between psychopathology and psychosocial problems and poor language skills (Beitchman et al. 1996; Baltaxe and Simmons 1990).

The developmental period between childhood and adolescence is critical to the potential or likely genesis of mental health presentations in adolescence. Several longitudinal studies demonstrate that language problems in childhood can be a significant risk factor for antisocial behaviour in adolescence (Beitchman et al. 1996, 2001; Bor et al. 2004). Voci et al. (2006) report that poor psycho-social skills in children are likely to continue into adolescence. Poor social functioning, whether in childhood or adolescence, has an impact on many factors including individual and peer group interaction, the maintaining of play and the self-development of the child or adolescent. Poor social functioning has been found to have a negative affect on relationships (Fujuki et al. 2001), and studies that measure self-esteem have found that poorer self-esteem relates to reduced psycho-social functioning (Burgess and Younger, 2006; Jerome et al. 2002). There is a correlation between social competency functioning and psychopathology presentations (Burt et al. 2008) — and, specifically relating to youth, an association between poor interpersonal relationships and youth and adult crime and psychopathology (Brownlie et al. 2004; Sanger et al. 1999). An Australian study demonstrates that specific populations, such as juvenile young offenders, present with significant oral language problems (Snow and Powell 2004a, 2004b, 2005, 2008), and these problems have consequences in the juvenile justice system to do with issues such as police interviewing processes and fair representation for such youth within the justice system.

Pragmatic behaviours and depression in youth can be linked. An Australian community sample of depressed adolescents perceived that they used poor pragmatic skills in daily communication skills when compared to their non-depressed peers (Perrott 1998; 2011); these problems include difficulty with initiating, continuing and terminating conversations. They also report difficulty with managing topic change and extending topics and describe the use of stereotypic language as being easier than extending a topic of conversation, as it gives the impression that the speaker is being understood and it requires less energy than adding to a topic. Maintaining eye-contact is also a difficult task for depressed youth. Similar features have been reported for depressed youth in research utilising United States populations (Segrin and Flora 2000, Segrin et al. 2007; Segrin and Rynes 2009). Starling (2003) informs us that youth with a language learning disability are at risk and present with greater social and behavioural problems and reduced academic achievement. Clearly, such research leaves us to contemplate some of the issues that may arise for such youth regarding future employment and training opportunities.

The area of maltreatment of infants and children is specific and beyond the scope of this paper; however there is much to be gained from longitudinal studies that investigate this area. For example, language development, communication, social problems and academic performance can all be areas affected by childhood trauma, abuse and neglect (Klapper, Plummer and Harmon 2004). Snow (2009b) highlights how with Australian juvenile justice participants there is a transferal of children in child protection services to youth services.

Also supporting the link between communication profiles and mental health outcomes, a large-scale longitudinal British study has found that early language skills are a significant predictor of adult mental health (Schoon et al. 2010). This research also concludes that disadvantaged groups in society correlate with reduced receptive language in childhood. Likewise, this is supported by Snow's (2009a) Australian research which highlights the imbalance between social groups in Australia, concluding that socially disadvantaged groups in society are at a greater risk for both communication and mental health problems.

Do in patient psychiatric samples reflect similar results to community samples? Generally, in-patient samples would suggest more acute or complex mental illness(es). Such mental illnesses may also be accompanied by medical conditions; for example, anorexia nervosa. Therefore, complexity and severity of conditions are variables that may differ between community and out-patient samples. In an Australian study based in an adolescent long-stay unit, Clarke (2006) assessed the communication of in-patients and found a range of communication problems presented that were previously masked. Such problems included poor listening skills, reading and problem-solving; these varied between disorders, with psychosis scores representing the most negative scores overall. Such research allows consideration of more specific communication patterns correlated with psychiatric presentations. Additionally, a link between adolescent suicide attempts and social deficits has been addressed by Spirito et al. (1990), although research in this area is complex.

Equally worthy of note is the stress on families who have a child (or children) with language problems and associated psycho-social, emotional and behavioural problems. Such issues impact on family functioning and daily activity schedules (Long et al. 2008). Parent–child interaction is an example of the impact of a communication problem that may create stress on the caregiver(s) and on their ability to bond with the child. An example may be when a child is unable to communicate basic needs to a parent. Likewise, research informs us that siblings living with a communication disorder, such as an autism spectrum disorder, report managing and living with a sibling stressful at times (Perrott 1995). Chronic family stress (secondary to the diagnosed condition of a family member with a communication problem) may then become a mental health problem over time.

At an individual level, the consequences of a communication problem can impact at various times of a person's life and in different ways. For example, an infant with a language disorder may display aggressive behaviours in order to communicate their needs due to limited communication. An adolescent may fail to assimilate with a peer group due to reduced social competency or an adult may struggle with a job interview due to communication problems such as dysfluency. As Starling (2003) informs us, youth with a language learning disability have limited educational skills and reduced vocational skills. Similarly, communication problems do not stop and start with the individual but rather have an impact on the family, peer groups, colleagues and the wider community. Such consequences may interact and can include any of the following:[1]

a) Lifespan consequences

- Intergenerational transfer of problems for families not receiving early intervention, screening or education.
- Language and mental health problems for children exposed to maltreatment and trauma at an early age.
- Increased need for welfare and child protection services at early ages.
- Increased risk of criminal/justice involvement in adolescence/early adulthood.
- Illegal activity and substance abuse in young people/early adulthood.
- Early parenting/unplanned pregnancies creating further strain on families/communities.

b) Vocational consequences

- Difficulty securing and maintaining employment due to social communication and language challenges.
- Loss of employment opportunities and prospects.
- Reduced employment options for carers due to increased demands to care for an individual.

c) Familial consequences

- Family tension and conflict.
- Strained parent-child roles impacting attachment and emotional attunement with off-spring.
- Family violence and subsequent trauma impact.
- Reduced sibling and extended family contact.
- Secondary psychiatric problems of other family members.
- Difficulty in managing life transitions and a young person's move toward autonomy and independence.

---

[1] From *Speech Pathology in Mental Health Services, Clinical Guideline,* Speech Pathology Australia (2010b:10).

- Difficulty with developing and sustaining intimate (non-sexual) and romantic relationships.

d) Psychological consequences

- Social isolation and loneliness (costs of communication impairment and known precipitants of depression).
- Impact on personality development.
- Reduced tolerance for and avoidance of social communication.
- Specific psychological consequences-aggression, irritability, limited attention/concentration/ impulsivity, reduced responsiveness/lack of spontaneity, anxiety, depression and self-harm.
- Reduced sense of self-worth/self-identity, loss of hope and optimism and reduced self- advocacy.

e) Social consequences

- Problems coping with social situations, resulting in reduced social contacts, community involvement, recreational activities and social status.
- Difficulties with establishing peer relationships.

We must acknowledge that not all speech and language problems result in mental health issues and vice versa, particularly in adults. It may be that adulthood mental health clinical presentations may be associated with other variables; for example, work-place stress. And while mental health problems that do not present in childhood or adolescence may be associated with other factors, some adult presentations can be attributed to events in childhood; for example, trauma in childhood that displays itself in a form of anxiety in adulthood.

In both research and clinical practice, measuring and assessing communication disorders and mental health disorders is a complex task with many uncontrolled variables. When an individual is assessed, the process of assessment may involve a multidisciplinary team undertaking several assessments over a period of time. Individual differences and idiosyncrasies make measuring communication or one's perception of communication a complicated task. Likewise measuring mental health symptoms and an individual's clinical presentation is highly complex. Socio-economic factors impacting on individuals are also difficult to both measure and control.

Regardless of the ever-present complexities in controlling research, it is the awareness of communication disorders in childhood and youth that is the key factor to identifying those "at higher risk" for the development of potential mental health issues. But is an awareness simply enough to break the cycle between generations?

3. Where to from here? Suggested solutions for consideration

As a consequence of the above research, we are able to demonstrate a strong relationship between communication disorders and mental health disorders occurring across the lifespan of an individual. The National Research Council and Institute of Medicine (2009) state that more than half of all mental, emotional and behavioural disorders present in childhood. This leaves us to seriously contemplate what can be done at various levels of intervention. With the knowledge that we have available, we need to consider at a practical level the ways in which we can reduce the permeation of communication and mental health disorders between generations. The following five points are given as starting points for consideration and debate; they are presented in a broad sense and are aimed at suggestions that direct toward probable solutions. Though they are described systematically, all points can be applied simultaneously. For example, whilst we need more research in the area of communication disorders and mental health, we cannot sit back and ignore the pertinent issues of early intervention and prevention.

3.1. Acknowledge what we know

Our primary step is to acknowledge the research in the field. This research needs to be dispersed to those who are (a) training in the field of education and health; and (b) working in the field of education and health. It is a positive sign that there are several courses in Australia that now incorporate communication disorders and mental health training; these include medicine, psychiatry, speech pathology and specific courses in postgraduate applied linguistics. However, there are still so many courses that require inclusion of communication disorders and mental health training aimed at educating future practitioners and educationalists. Deliverers of tertiary course components in education and health subjects should consider providing such knowledge at either general or specific course levels. Both academic and clinical training would be a step in the right direction. Mental Health clinicians utilize communication as their primary medium and acknowledge the reciprocity of communication with their clients. Hence, mental health clinicians require knowledge of the communication disorders that may be part of the presenting psychopathology of their client (Perrott 2012).

3.2. Assessments as a step in the right direction

Although there are numerous communication screening assessments and profiles available for infants, toddlers and primary-aged children, there are fewer available for adolescents and young adults (see Andersen-Wood and Smith 1997). Such assessments provide us with valuable communication information and are constantly being updated for reliability and validity measures.

A low-cost form of assessment is to ensure that at secondary and tertiary institutions, adolescents and young adults are provided access to communication profiles that may identify communication and/or mental health disorders. The assessment of social skills as an adjunct to current depressive measures was initially presented by Kent et al. (1997). Their view is that an appraisal based on social skills and specific pragmatic skills may aid in the detection and ultimately the prevention of major depressive disorder in youth. Furthermore, traditional medical models of depression assessment rely on a multitude of factors including access to medical assessment, compliance to attend a session and costs. Only 40% of depressed individuals present for some form of care or treatment and only one in six receive evidence-based treatments (Andrews 2001). Disturbed adolescents are more likely to seek help from their peers (Offer et al. 1991). Surely the use of a communication screening assessment in a classroom setting for youth would warrant a cost effective and less complex process for both the young person and health services alike. In relation to adolescent depression:

> Traditionally, assessment and diagnosis of depression has focused on affective, cognitive and somatic symptoms. However, as evidence continues to amass, some are beginning to suggest that an analysis of interpersonal symptoms and problematic behaviors are a valuable addition to these traditional focal points. (Rehm 1988, cited in Segrin 2000: 389)

Evidence-based research is required to develop and test communication assessments that specifically assess the correlation with depression. There are however, sufficient communication screening tools and assessments currently available that can be implemented by experts.

3.3. Utilizing experts in communication as consultants

Assessments, whether screening or otherwise, require the targeting of populations by experts. Utilizing the professional expertise we currently have available is a starting point. A recent paper complied by Speech Pathology Australia highlights the critical roles that Speech Pathologists in Mental Health are able to undertake: (a) Screening, assessment and intervention for communication disorders in at risk populations, for example, in drug and alcohol services and trauma related youth programs; (b) Education and prevention programs, for example, in mother/parent-child and pediatric units; (c) Education of health professionals, teachers, parents and carers regarding the association between communication and swallowing disorders and mental health conditions (Speech Pathology Australia 2010a: 3).

A further role of the Speech Pathologist is to work in a consulting capacity with pre-school/crèche, kindergarten, primary and secondary educationalists with the view to the early detection of communication disorders. This is a collaborative approach and could include training educationalists regarding the collection of relevant data and communication assessment. Although this is the brief for many speech pathologists in practice today, it would seem that this service is limited to those infants, children and adolescents who are already identified as having a communication impairment. The role of the speech pathologist in the majority of educational setting is restricted to current case-loads and waiting lists. Therefore, infants through to young adults are not routinely screened for communication problems. Referral to date often depends on the judgement and opinion of the educationalist and/or parent. The collaboration of the educationalist, parent and speech pathologist assessments provide optimal data and forms a starting point for appropriate referral and intervention.

3.4. Early intervention from birth to young adulthood.

Educationalists and health professionals need to be systematically screening infants from birth through to early childhood and from early childhood to primary school level for communication disorders. Such screening and assessment of communication skills should also routinely include pragmatic and social skills assessments. Many nations of the world systematically monitor immunizations from birth throughout childhood. Screening assessments of communication from birth through to adolescence could also be undertaken utilizing a similar data base system. Maternal health practitioners make routine assessments for developmental anomalies from birth through to early childhood. This is a starting point, although access to service is voluntary and 'at risk' groups in the community may fail to attend. As the Bercow national recommendations state in relation to early identification and early intervention, 'If a child does not benefit from early intervention, there are multiple risks – of lower educational attainment, of behavioural problems, of emotional and psychological difficulties, of poorer employment prospects, challenges to mental health and, in some cases, of a descent into criminality' (2008: 14).

Adolescence is a critical period for the development of mental health problems. It is during this developmental period that problematic behaviours may be identified. So often such behaviours are simply masked communication problems. Drugs and alcohol (which are more accessible in youth) may further conceal difficulties with communication and social skills. Substance abuse in any form further perpetuates either communication or mental health symptomology, making it more difficult for a young person to seek help to break this cycle. As the research outlined above demonstrates, when adolescents have an unidentified communication disorder they are at greater risk for early school leaving. Such youth are often marginalized in society and are poorly monitored for communication, mental health, academic and workplace outcomes. Hence, adolescence becomes a critical time period for systematic screening and assessing.

Tertiary institutions could offer youth the opportunity to access communication assessments through the medical, health and/or counselling system of the tertiary institutions. Such institutions are the hub of youth activity and aim at employment outcomes in the long-term. It may be young adults graduating from tertiary institutions that find themselves (in the workplace or unemployed) with inadequate communication and social skills, which may then impact on their health and mental well-being. We need to consider ways to encourage and assess communication to support educational success and the follow-through of assimilation into employment in society. Communication assessment could include consideration of communication skills (oral skills) and strategies associated with employment. The result of successful employment is the reduction of mental health problems, again with their core link being communication competency.

3.5. Prevention and education

There is a need for general public education regarding communication disorders and their link to mental health. *The Bercow Report* (2008) states that approximately 50% of all children and youth in socio-economically disadvantaged populations have speech and language skills below their peers. Snow (2009a) highlights that individuals in low socio-economic contexts are at greater risk for both communication and mental health issues. Lower socio-economic groups need to be targeted in effective and positive ways. However, so often our 'at risk' groups in society are located in remote, rural or indigenous communities. They may not routinely be serviced by professionals or may 'fall through the gaps'. This so often occurs from birth throughout childhood. There is a critical need to screen and assess preschool and school-aged children. Again, 'at risk' families and communities require support and monitoring to achieve this. Speech Pathology Australia advocates the role of the Speech Pathologist in such contexts: 'Currently, speech pathology services are inadequate and underrepresented in mental health settings, particularly in the area of prevention for at risk populations' (The Speech Pathology Association of Australia 2010a: 1).

Isolated communities, rural communities and indigenous communities all need equal access to health and education assessments for communication disorders. Reaching such communities is often time consuming and complex to navigate, especially when translators are required. This issue of assessing communication should be tackled in ways that allow the development of trust and respect within each cultural context and viewed as an ongoing process. To put time, resources and costs into such a process is to invest in prevention and education, rather than managing issues at critical points of desperation with less chance of affecting change. Furthermore, every individual within each community requires different communication skills to meet their needs. To simply ignore a community is to perpetuate issues from one generation to the next. Lower socio-economic groups require access to services in order to avoid replicating problems between families.

In relation to prevention and education, The Speech Pathology Association is in strong support of 'speech pathologists providing education and consultancy services to professionals, university training courses and the broader community to improve the understanding of communication and swallowing disorders in mental health' (The Speech Pathology Association of Australia 2010a: 4).

In short, prevention and education strategies can be subdivided into areas focused on individual, peer group, family and community. Suggestions may be many and varied and are beyond the scope of this paper. However, all preventative and educational responses addressing the relationship between communication and mental health need to be strategically planned and founded on evidence-based research (see 3.1.).

4. Summary

Linguists, whether researchers or clinical communication experts, such as speech pathologists, are key players in the quest for supporting communication research and assessment tools that enable a greater understanding of mental health. Likewise, mental health experts are able to contribute to the field through research, and clinical expertise, including finely tuned observations and case examples that profile the communication attributes of those who are mentally ill. Our primary step is to acknowledge the link between communication disorders and mental health disorders and to build on this research. From such research we can further refine our application to assessments of communication that may highlight mental health issues. The key to implementing such assessments is undoubtedly early intervention. Assessments whether screening or more in-depth should be systematically undertaken and monitored on a National database. To screen all infants from the period of birth onwards provides a systematic approach aimed at targeting those 'at risk'. Tertiary assessments should also be made available for young adults to freely access, simply due to the fact that mental health problems may develop from adolescence through to early adulthood. Since the task of assessing infants through to young adults in communities is so immense, Speech Pathologists are well trained and equipped to take on the role of consulting and training other professionals. Finally, the ultimate solution to reduce mental health costs in society is to focus on the areas of prevention and education. Poorer socio-economic groups and 'at risk' groups in all communities need to be effectively reached and provided with relevant, accessible information and follow-up appropriate to the needs of that community. As our mental health systems around the globe become more financially top-heavy, we need to consider what we know and apply our knowledge to the reality that communication disorders and mental health are linked.

References

Andrews, Gavin. 2001. Should depression be managed as a chronic disease? *British Journal of Medicine* 322 (7283): 419–21.

Andersen-Wood, Lucie and Benita R. Smith (eds). 1997. *Working with Pragmatics: A Practical Guide to Promoting Communicative Confidence.* Milton Keynes: Speechmark.

Baltaxe, Christiane A.M. and James Q. Simmons, III. 1990. The differential diagnosis of communication disorders in child and adolescent psychopathology. *Topics in Language Disorders* 10 (4): 17–31.

Beitchman, Joseph H., E.B. Brownlie, Graham Inglis, Chris J. Wild, George B. Ferguson, Asher D. Schachter, W. Lancee, Beth Wilson and Sunu R. Matthews. 1996. Seven-year follow-up of speech/language-impaired and control children: Psychiatric outcomes. *Journal of Child Psychology and Psychiatry* 37 (8): 961–70.

Beitchman, Joseph H., Beth Wilson, Carla Johnson, Leslie Atkinson, Arlene Young, Edward Adlaf, Michael Escobar and Lorie Douglas. 2001. Fourteen-year follow-up of speech/language-impaired and control children: Psychiatric outcomes. *Journal of the American Academy of Child and Adolescent Psychiatry* 40 (1): 75–82.

Bercow, John. 2008. *The Bercow Report: A Review of Services for Young Children and Young People (0–19) with Speech, Language and Communication Needs*. Retrieved 20/11/12 from www.dcsf.gov.uk/bercow.

Bor, William, Tara R. McGee and Abigail A. Fagan. 2004. Early risk factors for adolescent antisocial behavior: Australian longitudinal study. *Australian and New Zealand Journal of Psychiatry* 38 (5): 365–72.

Brownlie, E.B., Joseph H. Beitchman, Michael Escobar, Arlene Young, Leslie Atkinson, Carla Johnson, Beth Wilson and Lori Douglas. 2004. Early language impairment and young adult delinquent and aggressive behavior. *Journal of Abnormal Child Psychiatry* 32 (4): 453–67.

Burgess, Keith B. and Alastair J. Younger. 2006. Self-schemas, anxiety, somatic and depressive symptoms in socially withdrawn children and adolescents. *Journal of Research in Childhood Education* 20 (3): 175–488.

Burt, Keith B., Jelena Obradovic, J.D. Long and Ann S. Maston. 2008. The interplay of social competence and psychopathology over 20 years: Testing transactional and cascade models. *Child Development* 79 (2): 359–74.

Cantwell, Dennis P. and Lorain Baker. 1985. Psychiatric and learning disorders in children with speech and language disorders: A descriptive analysis. *Advances in Learning and Behavioral Disabilities* 4: 29–47.

Clarke, Angela. 2006. Charting a life: Analysis of 50 adolescents in a long-stay mental health unit. *Conference Proceedings, 17th World Congress of the International Association for Child and Adolescent Psychiatry and Allied Professionals*. Melbourne, Australia.

Clegg, Judy, Chris Hollis, Lynn Mawhood and Michael Rutter. 2005. Developmental language disorders – A follow-up in later adult life: Cognitive, language and psychosocial outcomes. *Journal of Child Psychiatry* 46 (2): 128–49.

Conti-Ramsden, Gina, and Nicola Botting. 2004. Social difficulties and victimization in children with SLI at 11 years of age. *Journal of Speech, Language and Hearing Research* 47 (1): 145–61.

Fujuki, Martin, Bonnie Brinton, Ted T. Issacson and Connie Summers. 2001. Social behaviors of children with language impairment on a playground: A pilot study. *Language, Speech and Hearing Services in Schools* 32: 101–13.

Jerome, Annette, Martin Fujuki, Bonnie Brinton and James Shane. 2002. Self-esteem in children with specific language impairment. *Journal of Speech Language and Hearing Research* 45: 700–14.

Kent, Lindsey, Panos Vostanis and Catherine Feehan. 1997. Detection of major and minor depression in children and adolescents: Evaluation of the mood and feelings questionnaire. *Journal of Child Psychology and Psychiatry* 38 (5): 565–73.

Klapper, Stacy A., Nancy S. Plummer and Robert J. Harmon. 2004. Diagnostic and treatment issues in cases of childhood trauma. In Joy. D. Osofsky (ed.), *Young Children and Trauma: Intervention and Treatment*. New York: The Guilford Press, 139–54.

Law James, Robert Rush, Ingrid Schoon and Samantha Parsons. 2009. Modeling developmental language difficulties from school entry into adulthood: Literacy, mental health, and employment outcomes. *Journal of Speech, Language Hearing Research* 52 (6): 1401–16.

Lindsay, Geoff and Julie E. Dockrell. 2000. The behavior and self-esteem of children with specific speech and language difficulties. *British Journal of Educational Psychology* 70 (4): 583–601.

Lindsay, Geoff, Julie E. Dockrell and Steve Strand. 2007. Longitudinal patterns of behavior problems in children with specific speech and language difficulties: Child and contextual factors. *British Journal of Educational Psychology* 77 (4): 811–28.

Long, Carolyn E., Matthew J. Gurka and James A. Blackman. 2008. Family stress and children's language and behavior problems. Results from the national survey of children's health. *Topics in Early Childhood Special Education* 28 (3): 148–57.

National Research Council and Institute of Medicine. 2009. *Preventing Mental, Emotional, and Behavioral Disorders Among Young People: Progress and Possibilities*. Committee on the Prevention of Mental Disorders and Substance Abuse Among Children, Youth, and Young Adults: Research Advances and Promising Interventions. Mary Ellen O'Connell, Thomas Boat, and Kenneth E. Warner (eds). Board on Children, Youth, and Families, Division of Behavioral and Social Sciences and Education. Washington, DC: The National Academies Press.

Offer, Daniel, Kenneth Howard, Kimberley Schonert and Eric Ostrov. 1991. To whom do adolescents turn for help? Differences between disturbed and non-disturbed adolescents. *Journal of the American Academy of Child and Adolescent Psychiatry* 30 (4): 623–30.

Perrott, Deborah. 1995. Sibling support: An overview. *Autism Conference: Shaping the Future*. Victoria: Autism Victoria, 1–5.

Perrott, Deborah. 1998. Adolescent communication: Self-evaluation of the use and competency of pragmatic skills between depressed and non-depressed adolescents. Unpublished MA thesis, Macquarie University.

Perrott, Deborah. 2011. Adolescent communication: Pragmatic skills. Unpublished PhD thesis, Monash University.

Perrott, Deborah. 2012. Talk to me: The link between communication and psychiatric disorders. *Psychotherapy in Australia* 19 (1): 58–64.

Rutter, Michael and Lynn Mawhood. 1991. The long-term psychological sequelae of specific developmental disorders of speech and language. In Michael Rutter and Paul Casaer (eds), *Biological Risk Factors for Psychosocial Disorders*. Cambridge: Cambridge University Press, 233–57.

Sanger, Dixie D., Karen Hux and Mitzi Ritzman. 1999. Female juvenile delinquent's pragmatic awareness of conversational interactions. *Journal of Communication Disorders* 32 (5): 281–95.

Schoon, Ingrid, Samantha Parsons, Robert Rush and James Law. 2010. Children's language ability and psychosocial development: A 29-year follow-up study. *Pediatrics* 126 (1): 73–80.

Segrin, Chris. 2000. Social skills deficits associated with depression. *Clinical Psychology Review* 20 (3): 379–403.

Segrin, Chris and Natalie J. Flora. 2000. Poor social skills are a vulnerability factor in the development of psychosocial problems. *Human Communication Research* 26 (3): 489–514.

Segrin, Chris, Alesia Hanzal, Carolyn Donnerstein, Melissa Taylor and Tricia J. Domschke. 2007. Social skills, psychological well-being and the mediating role of perceived stress. *Anxiety, Stress, and Coping* 20 (3): 321–9.

Segrin, Chris and Kristina N. Rynes. 2009. The mediating role of positive relations with others in associations between depression, social skills, and perceived stress. *Journal of Research in Personality* 43 (6): 962–71.

Snow, Pamela C. 2009a. Oral language competence and equity of access to education and health. In Karen Bryan (ed.), *Communication in Healthcare: Interdisciplinary Communication Studies, Volume 1*. Bern: Peter Lang, 101–34.

Snow, Pamela C. 2009b. Child maltreatment, mental health and oral language competence: Inviting Speech Pathology to the prevention table. *International Journal of Speech Language Pathology* 11 (12): 95–103.

Snow, Pamela C. and Martine B. Powell. 2004a. Interviewing juvenile offenders: The importance of oral language competence. *Current Issues in Criminal Justice* 16 (2): 220–5.

Snow, Pamela C. and Martine B. Powell. 2004b. Developmental language disorders and adolescent risk: A public-health advocacy role for speech pathologists? *Advances in Speech-Language Pathology* 6 (4): 221–9.

Snow, Pamela C. and. Martine B. Powell. 2005. What's the story? An exploration of narrative language abilities in male juvenile offenders. *Psychology, Crime and Law* 11 (3): 239–53.

Snow, Pamela C. and Martine B. Powell. 2008. Oral language competence, social skills, and high risk boys: What are juvenile offenders trying to tell us? *Children and Society* 22 (1): 16–28.

Speech Pathology Association of Australia, The. 2010a. *Speech Pathology in Mental Health Services: Position Statement*. Retrieved 16/11/2012 from www.speechpathologyaustralia.org.au/.

Speech Pathology Association of Australia, The. 2010b. *Speech Pathology in Mental Health Services: Clinical Guideline*. Retrieved 16/11/2012 from www.speechpathologyaustralia.org.au/.

Spirito, Anthony, Kathleen Hart, James Overholser and Janya Halverson. 1990. Social skills and depression in adolescent suicide attempters. *Adolescence* 25 (99): 543–52.

Starling, Julia 2003. Getting the message across: Safeguarding the mental health of adolescents with communication disorders. *ACQuiring Knowledge in Speech, Language and Hearing* 5 (1): 37–9.

Sutherland, Dean, Brigid B. McNeill and Gail Gillon. 2009. Communication impairments and behaviour problems in children and adolescents: A review of the literature. *ACQuiring Knowledge in Speech, Language and Hearing* 11 (3): 132–5.

Van Daal, John, Ludo Verhoeven and Hans van Balkom. 2007. Behaviour problems in children with language impairment. *Journal of Child Psychology and Psychiatry* 48 (11): 1139–47.

Voci, Sabrina C., Joseph H. Beitchman, E.B. Brownlie and Beth Wilson. 2006. Social anxiety in late adolescence: The importance of early childhood language impairment. *Anxiety Disorders* 20 (7): 915–30.

PART 3

SEMANTIC THEORY AND PHILOSOPHY OF LANGUAGE

PART 2

Chapter 14

NIHIL TAM ABSURDE DICI POTEST QUOD NON DICATUR AB ALIQUO TRADUCTORUM PHILOSOPHORUM

WHAT SOME PHILOSOPHERS AND SCIENTISTS HAVE SAID ACCORDING TO THEIR TRANSLATORS

Pedro José Chamizo Domínguez

Universidad de Málaga

The aim of this paper is to show how some philosophers' thought can be misunderstood for the sake of their translator. Given that philosophy and science have been written in several and varied languages (from Greek and Latin to English, French, German or Spanish, to mention only a few Indo-European languages), and people, even scholars, are able to understand only a few, translation emerges as an unavoidable option when a given reader is interested in knowing a given thought which has been expounded in a language not known to him/her. And this happens not only when dealing with technical, philosophical terms, but also when dealing with ordinary language terms. In order to prove my thesis I am going to show how problems originating in ambiguities, archaisms, false friends, gender, idioms, interpolations and polysemies can lead the translator to say something very different from what was actually said in the original text.

1. Introduction

The Argentinean writer (and half-philosopher) J. L. Borges wrote that 'philosophy is nothing else than the imperfect argument (when not a lonely monologue) among some hundreds, or thousands, of perplexed men, *who are distant with regard to time and language:* Berkeley, Spinoza, William of Ockham, Schopenhauer, Parmenides, Renouvier...' (Borges 1986: 239; emphasis added; my translation). And given that 1) philosophers are distant not only with regard to time, but also with regard to language; 2) philosophy has been written in many different languages; and 3) a given person knows at best only a few languages in which philosophy has been written, translation emerges as an unavoidable option if we want to know what a given philosopher, whose language is unknown or imperfectly known by us, thought. In addition, we know or assume that there are readers who are interested in knowing the contents of the philosophy in question and who are not able to read the original version due to their lack of knowledge of the language in which a given philosophical thought has been expressed. Otherwise translation would make no sense.

Well then, many times problems occur that cannot be attributed to the lack of skill of the translator, but to the fact that the translator, consciously or unconsciously, sets his/her own theoretical convictions out – and these convictions differ from the theses or opinions of the original text's author. Sometimes a given translator seeks to 'set the author straight' and makes him/her say something similar to what the French architect and restorer, Eugène-Emmanuel Viollet-le-Duc (1814–79), theoretically held and put into practice with regard to the restoration of medieval buildings: 'Restoring a building is not to maintain, repair, or do it up, *it is to reestablish it to a complete state, which may never have existed at any given time*' (Viollet-le-Duc 1854–1868; emphasis added; my translation).[1]

In a short but substantial and witty article, A. Koyré (1973) refers to two cases where translators have projected in their translations their own convictions, although in all probability unconsciously. As a result of this, N. Copernicus and G. Galilei have been obliged to say what they never said, in German and English, respectively. The first case has to do with the title itself of *De Revolutionibus Orbium Coelestium* (1543), by Copernicus, whose translation into German turned out to be: *Über die Kreisbewegungen der Himmelskörper* (literally, *On the Revolutions of the Celestial/Heavenly Bodies*).[2]

---

[1] The original French text reads: 'Restaurer un édifice, ce n'est pas l'entretenir, le réparer ou le refaire, *c'est le rétablir dans un état complet qui peut n'avoir jamais existé à un moment donné*.'

[2] Translations of philosophical works' titles used to be very frequently deceitful. By way of example I will mention two further instances in addition to the one Koyré has referred to. The first one deals with the 1966 Italian translation of Quine's *From a Logical Point of View* (1953) that turned out to be *Il problema del significato* (literally, *The Problem of Meaning*). Indeed, Quine deals with the problem of meaning in this book, but I have to confess that, when I needed to consult the Italian translation of Quine's work and asked an Italian friend of mine for help in order to find the Italian translation of Quine's book, and after providing him with its original English title, he was not able to connect the Italian title with its original one. And the titles of Quine's

The second case has to do with a passage from Galileo's *Discorsi e dimostrazioni matematiche, intorno à due nuove scienze* (1638), where the Latin verb *comperio* has been translated into English as *I have discovered by experiment*. Koyré's ironic comment will exempt me from further remarks:

> I am not going to undertake to do here the critique of Mr Crew and Mr de Salvio's translation. It is enough for me to point out that not only does Galileo not say he discovered fall and throw's properties *by experiment*, but also that the term experiment (*experimentum*) has been not used by him. It has been used purely and simply by his translator, who, patently committed to empiricist epistemology, could not imagine that one could demonstrate or discover something other than by experiment. Therefore, where Galileo writes *comperio*, translator writes 'discovered *by experiment*', in this way annexing Galileo to empiricist tradition and thus irremediably distorting his thinking. *It is no wonder that the legend of an empiricist and experimenter Galileo is so firmly established in America. Since, alas! American historians, even the best, cite Galileo or the Discorsi at least, according to the English translation.* (Koyré 1973: 274; emphasis as in original except for last three sentences where emphasis has been added; my translation).[3]

If so, what we know (or think that we know) about what a given philosopher has said will arrive by means of the interpretation that his/her translator made of the original text. Sometimes, but very infrequently, it happens

---

books seem to be ill-fated when translated into other languages, as attested by the French translation of another book by Quine. I am referring here to the 1977 French translation of *Word and Object* (1960), whose French title reads *Le mot et la chose*. Again, this title reminds anyone who knows French philosophy the title of the well-known work *Les mots et les choses* (1966) by M. Foucault. It goes without saying that in philosophical jargon *thing* and *object* are not synonymous strictly speaking, since *object* is used in order to refer to any entity, even human beings, whereas *thing* cannot be used in order to refer to human beings, except if the speaker is derogatorily speaking.

[3] The original French text reads: 'Je ne vais pas entreprendre ici la critique de la traduction de MM. Crew et de Salvio. Il me suffit de faire remarquer que non seulement Galilée ne dit pas avoir découvert les propriétés de la chute et du jet *par expérience*, mais que le terme expérience (*experimentum*) n'est pas employé par lui. Il a été purement et simplement ajouté par le traducteur qui, visiblement acquis à l'épistémologie empiriciste, ne pouvait pas s'imaginer que l'on puisse démontrer ou découvrir quelque chose autrement que *par expérience*. Aussi, là où Galilée dit: *Comperio*, écrit-il: 'discovered *by experiment*', en annexant ainsi Galilée à la tradition empiriste et en faussant, par là même, irrémédiablement, sa pensée. *Il n'est pas étonnant que la légende de Galilée empiriste et expérimentateur soit si fermement établie en Amérique. Car, hélas ! les historiens américains, même les meilleurs, citent Galilée, ou du moins, les Discorsi, d'après la traduction anglaise.*'

that the translation of a philosophical text can be even clearer – and consequently more appreciated – than the original text itself is. This is the case of Jean Hyppolite's translation of Hegel's *Die Phänomenologie des Geistes*: 'Translation can illuminate, compelling the original, as it were, into reluctant clarity (witness Jean Hyppolite's translation of Hegel's *Phänomenologie*). It can, paradoxically, reveal the stature of a body of work which had been undervalued or ignored in its native guise' (Steiner 1975: 396).[4] But examples like this are worth mentioning precisely because they are extremely infrequent. The usual case is just the contrary – the case where, due to the translator's lack of skill, a translated text says something very different from the original or leads the reader into an interpretation which does not coincide with the most plausible interpretation of the original text. And this can happen, among other reasons, because the translator might not have noticed some of the most frequent linguistic problems that can lead a translation to be erroneous or, at least, capable of being misinterpreted and/ or that does not show all the nuances of the original text. In my opinion, the most relevant among these problems are the following: ambiguities, archaisms, gender, idioms and collocations, non-lexicalised metaphors and polysemies. I will try to show below how all these problems can be found in real translations of philosophical texts, by means of providing both actual translations and what such translations literally say for the speakers of the target language.

2. Ambiguities

A paradigmatic case of ambiguity can be found in a famous parenthesis from L. Wittgenstein's *Tractatus logico-philosophicus* that caused the well-known controversy about the Wittgensteinian solipsism. And whether Wittgenstein was a solipsist philosopher or was not will highly depend

---

[4] Steiner's opinion is endorsed by Alain Badiou as well: 'J'ai été extraordinairement frappé par une observation que m'a faite une fois un de mes traducteurs en allemand, Jürgen Brankel, un philosophe de Hambourg, qui m'a déclaré qu'il était passionné par la traduction française de la *Phénoménologie de l'esprit* par Jean Hyppolite, infiniment plus que par le livre de Hegel. Il considérait qu'en réalité, le livre de Hegel en Allemand était un livre passablement informe, brouillé, un typique livre de jeunesse, disait-il, et que Hyppolite en avait fait un véritable monument, tout à fait nouveau et que, en vérité, il fallait distinguer tout à fait la *Phénoménologie de l'esprit* de Hegel et la traduction de la *Phénoménologie de l'esprit* par Hyppolite, qui était un livre de plein exercice dans lequel selon lui la philosophie allemande devait immédiatement et impérativement puiser.' (Quoted in Anonymous 2012).

on how the original German sentence is understood and, consequently, translated:

(1) Dass die Welt *meine* Welt ist, dass zeigt sich darin, dass die Grenzen der Sprache (*der* Sprache die **allein** ich verstehe) die Grenzen *meiner* Welt bedeuten. (*Tractatus* 5.62; emphasis as in original; my bold type)

The sentence included inside this parenthesis is a paradigmatic case of structural ambiguity inasmuch as the German adverb *allein* could refer either to the pronoun *ich* or to the noun *Sprache* as well. And, given that the context does not provide any information for choosing between both options, the translator has to decide on whether this ambiguous sentence means either 'the language only I understand' or 'the only language I understand'. Now, if the translator opts for the first interpretation, the reader could infer that Wittgenstein was a solipsist philosopher;[5] while, if the translator opts for the second interpretation, the thesis about Wittgenstein's solipsism cannot be reasonably maintained, since he could understand many other languages in addition to this language which is understood only by him.

In any case, (1) was firstly translated into English as:

(1.1) That the world is *my* world, shows itself in the fact that the limits of the language (*the* language which I understand) mean the limits of *my* world. (Wittgenstein 1922; emphasis as in original)

Consequently, Wittgensteinian solipsism was allowed to be reasonably maintained until J. Hintikka (1958), in a seminal article on the topic, attracted readers attention on the problem. In fact, Hintikka stated in this article that 'the clause in the brackets is, beyond reasonable doubt, a mistranslation' (Hintikka 1958: 88), since the clause in question was understood as '*the* language, which I alone understand'. As far as the Spanish translations are concerned, the early one reads 'el lenguaje que yo sólo entiendo' [the language only I understand] (Wittgenstein 1957: 163) and, consequently, Wittgenstein would have defended solipsism; while a further translation opts for 'del solo lenguaje que yo entiendo' [the only language I understand] (Wittgenstein 2003: 235), and, accordingly, Wittgenstein had

---

5   In fact, this entailment would be properly speaking an implicature and not an implication, since the fact that only Wittgenstein was able to understand one language does not necessarily entail that he was not able to understand many other languages.

not been a solipsist at all. In any case, what the reader is allowed to think on whether Wittgenstein was a solipsist philosopher or not, depends on the translation s/he reads, but, if we assume that the ambiguity of (1) was deliberately introduced by Wittgenstein himself and is not a mere *lapsus calami*, such ambiguity will be irremediably lost for Spanish and English readers.[6]

And ambiguities emerge where one least expects them. Let us consider the instance of a short excerpt from Keith Allan's excellent *Natural Language Semantics*, where the ambiguity has been caused by the polysemous nature of the English noun *guerrilla*, in spite of the fact the English noun is a borrowing from the Spanish one *guerrilla*, which is not polysemous at all:

(2) Terror has become the mark of *guerrillas* and the petty dictator. (Allan 2001: 156; my emphasis)

In spite of the fact that the English noun *guerrilla* is a borrowing from the Spanish *guerrilla*, this noun means in English both 'a regular war carried on by small bodies of men acting independently' and 'one engaged in such warfare' (*Oxford English Dictionary*, OED hereinafter), while the Spanish noun only means *guerrilla band*: 'partida de paisanos, por lo común no muy numerosa, que al mando de un jefe particular y con poca o ninguna dependencia de los del Ejército, acosa y molesta al enemigo' (literally, band of civilians, generally few numerous, which in command of a particular chief and with few or none dependence on the chiefs of the Army, hounds and annoys enemy; *Diccionario de la Real Academia Española*, DRAE hereinafter).

If so, (2) can be understood as 'terror has become the mark of *guerrilla individuals* and the petty dictator' as well as 'terror has become the mark of *guerrilla groups* and the petty dictator'. But, given that the context does not provide any additional information which could allow the reader to opt for

---

[6] It is not clear whether or not Wittgenstein himself intended the ambiguity in (1). But there are many cases where a given ambiguity is consciously introduced, and, if there is a language where such ambiguity cannot be maintained, half of what the author tried to mean will be irremediably lost in the target language. Although, obviously, it does not deal with any philosophical text at all, I would like to mention the book entitled *La putain de la République* (1999), written by Christine Deviers-Joncour on the occasion of her love affair with the French socialist minister Roland Dumas. The title in question purposely means both *I am the whore of the (French) Republic* and *The (French) Republic is a whore*. Such double entendre can be maintained in Spanish, but I am afraid it cannot be maintained in English.

one of both alternative interpretations, the translator has to make his/her mind to translate (2) either as 'el terror se ha convertido en la marca de los *guerrilleros* y del dictador mezquino/insignificante', if s/he intends *guerrilla individuals*, or as 'el terror se ha convertido en la marca de las *guerrillas* y del dictador mezquino/insignificante', if s/he intends *guerrilla groups*.[7]

3. Archaisms

When a translator has to deal with an ancient text where, in the source language itself, some terms are used according to a meaning that is currently archaic, s/he has to opt between two mutually exclusive possibilities, namely, 1) s/he can bring up to date terminology, whose result will be that the archaic flavour of the text in the source language would be irremediably lost; or 2) s/he can maintain archaisms in the target language, whose result will be that the text runs the risk of being misunderstood.

This second option was chosen by Manuel García Morente in his classic translation of R. Descartes' *Discourse on Method*.[8] Accordingly, García Morente translated the original French text

(3) Ceux qui ont le raisonnement le plus fort, et qui *digèrent* le mieux leurs pensées, afin de les rendre claires et intelligibles, peuvent toujours le mieux persuader ce qu'ils proposent, *encore qu'ils ne parlassent que bas-breton*, et qu'ils n'eussent jamais appris de rhétorique. (Descartes 1973: 7; emphasis added; I have updated the original spelling)

as

(3.1) Los que tienen más robusto razonar y *digieren* mejor sus pensamientos para hacerlos claros e inteligibles son los más capaces de llevar a los ánimos la persuasión sobre lo que se proponen, *aunque hablen una pésima lengua* y no hayan aprendido nunca retórica. (Descartes 1968: 32; emphasis added)

In (3.1) there are two options which can create problems for understanding. The first problem has to do with the translation of the French verb *digérer*

---

[7] When I realised this ambiguity I asked Keith Allan for the exact meaning of (2) he had in mind when he wrote this sentence. Unfortunately, his answer was disheartening: 'I do not recall what I had in mind'.

[8] For other instances of archaisms in this translation by García Morente, see (Chamizo Domínguez 2008: 14–8).

as *digerir*. The French verb is being used by Descartes in this text according to the salient meanings of the Latin verb *digerere*, which are 'to arrange methodically' or 'to put in order',[9] and this would be the meaning of its Spanish cognate in this context. But this meaning is currently obsolete in French, just as in Spanish. As a result of this, neither a normal French speaker nor a normal Spanish speaker would correctly understand (3) or (3.1), respectively. In fact, the *Dictionnaire de la Langue Française* (*DAF*, hereinafter) reports 'Très vieilli. Ordonner méthodiquement un sujet' [literally, 'Very dated. To methodically arrange a subject'], while this old-fashioned meaning is neither included nor alluded in the *DRAE*. Currently the salient meanings of *digérer* and *digerir* are 'Transformer les aliments dans les voies digestives pour les rendre assimilables par l'organisme' [literally, 'to transform food at the digestive tract for rendering them easily absorbed by the organism'; *DAF*] and 'Convertir en el aparato digestivo los alimentos en sustancias asimilables por el organismo' [literally, 'to convert food into easily absorbed substances at the digestive tract'; *DRAE*] in French and Spanish, respectively. Consequently, the present-day reader of this Cartesian text, either in French or in Spanish, could understand that Descartes is using the verb in question metaphorically, since this verb is also used metaphorically according to the meaning 'Assimiler intellectuellement' [literally, 'to intellectually assimilate'] and 'Meditar cuidadosamente algo, para entenderlo o ejecutarlo' [literally, 'to carefully meditate something in order to understand or perform it'] in French and Spanish, respectively.

As far as the clause *encore qu'ils ne parlassent que bas-breton* [literally, 'though they should speak only in the language of Low Breton'] is concerned, we are dealing with a clear instance of a politically incorrect ethnic slur, which probably Descartes never would (and perhaps 'should' as well) write if he were writing in 20th or 21st centuries. Although I do not know whether García Morente translated the clause in question as *aunque hablen una pésima lengua* [literally, 'though they speak an awful language'] either in order to avoid the original ethnic slur or because the literal translation of *bas-breton* as *bajo bretón* would be not understood by Spaniards, or both,

---

[9] Surprisingly and in spite of the fact that the verb *digérer* was used by Descartes according to its Latin meaning, the Latin version of the *Discourse on Method* (*Specimina philosophiae, seu Dissertatio de methodo*) translates *digèrent* as *ordine disponunt* (Descartes 1973: 543). And this is particularly surprising if we take into account that this translation – made by Descartes' friend Étienne de Courcelles (Latin: Stephanus Curcellaeus) – was revised and approved by Descartes himself.

the result is that Descartes' ethnic slur has been concealed for Spanish speakers.

4. False friends

The subject of false friends is a fascinating topic for translators not only due to the many traps that false friends lay for translators, but also because they allow us to explain mental processes that speakers of different languages have carried out, whose result has been that a given shared signifier has, in fact, divergent meanings in two or more different languages. However, this topic has been scarcely studied from a theoretical point of view. Those I have called in another place 'semantic false friends' (Chamizo Domínguez 2008) are particularly relevant for translation, since they share a common etymologic origin, but differ with regard to their meanings. And semantic false friends are particularly deceitful inasmuch as translators, who believe in the meaning a given term has in their own mother language, often disregard the fact that the same signifier can have – fully or partially – different meanings in other languages. And this happens not only when dealing with translating novels or movies, but when translating philosophical texts as well. Translations of philosophical texts are riddled with errors which have been caused by this phenomenon of linguistic interference. As a result of these errors, the understanding of the text in question could become irremediably erroneous.

Let us illustrate this matter by resorting to the case of the following text excerpted from the translation into Spanish of a book by an American contemporary philosopher:

(4) Las doctrinas *comprehensivas* filosóficas y morales de este tipo no pueden ser aceptadas[10] por el común de los ciudadanos, y ya no pueden servir, si es que algunas vez sirvieron, como base *profesa* de la sociedad. (Rawls 1996: 40; emphasis added)

(4) is the translation of

(4.1) *Comprehensive* philosophical and moral doctrines likewise cannot be endorsed by citizens generally, and they also no longer can, if

---

[10] Given that the Spanish verb *aceptar* and the English verb *to endorse* are not false friends, I will avoid a fuller explanation of this translation, but I would point out that, in this context, a more plausible translation into Spanish of this English verb would be *aprobar*, *respaldar*, *suscribir* or *sancionar*.

they ever could, serve as the *professed* basis of society. (Rawls 2005: 10; emphasis added)

Now, there are two terms in (4) that are relevant for the topic of false friends. The first term is the case of a full semantic false friend, whereas the second term is the case of a partial semantic false friend. Indeed, the Spanish adjective *comprehensivo/comprehensiva* is a learned synonym of *comprensivo/comprensiva*, whose salient meanings are: 1) 'Que tiene facultad o capacidad de comprender (entender)' [literally, 'that has the faculty or ability to understand']; 2) 'Que comprende (contiene o incluye)' [literally, 'that comprises (covers or includes)']; and 3) 'Dicho de una persona, de una tendencia o de una actitud: tolerante' [literally, 'said of a person, tendency, or attitude: tolerant'; *DRAE*]. By contrast, the salient meaning of the English adjective *comprehensive* is 'Characterized by comprehension; having the attribute of comprising or including much; a large content or scope' (*OED*), and, consequently, synonymous with *all-inclusive, compendious, complete, encyclopedic, embracive, exhaustive,* or *universal*; but never synonymous with *understanding* or *tolerant*.[11]

As far as the adjective *profeso/profesa* is concerned, it has two meanings in Spanish: 1) 'Dicho de un religioso: Que ha profesado' [literally, 'said of a member of a religious order: someone who has professed (taken vows)']; and 2) 'Se dice del colegio o casa de los profesos' [literally, 'it is said of a school or house of professed people (who have taken vows)'; *DRAE*]. That is, the Spanish adjective only can be used when referring or alluding to nuns, friars, monks, or schools or houses managed by them. Conversely, the English adjective *professed* has two different salient meanings: 1) 'Self-acknowledge; openly declared or avowed by oneself; sometimes with an implication of 'not real', and so = Alleged, ostensible, pretended (Of persons or things)'; and 2) 'That has taken the vows of a religious order' (*OED*). Consequently, the Spanish adjective *profeso/profesa* is a hyponym with regard to its English cognate, while the English adjective is a superordinate term with regard to the Spanish one, since the Spanish adjective only can be used when referring to (Catholic) religious people.

As a result of all this, (4) would come across (to any normally constituted Spanish speaker) nonsensically as:

---

[11] Since it does not make sense in this context, I disregard the meaning 'Designating a secondary school or a system of education which provides for children of all levels of intellectual and other ability' (*OED*).

(4.2) *Understanding* (*indulgent* or *tolerant*) philosophical and moral doctrines likewise cannot be *accepted* by citizens generally, and they also no longer can, if they ever could, serve as the basis *which have taken the vows* of society.

5. Gender

Given that the English language is extremely sparing with gender markers, it is often unclear to the translator what gender the writer is meaning in reference to a human being or an animal. So, for instance, in order to illustrate the different meanings that the adjective *regular* has in American and in British English, the *OED* entry quotes a funny story about Gilbert Keith Chesterton on the occasion of his early visit to the United States. The *OED*'s text reads as follow:

(5) When G. K. Chesterton made his first visit to the United States he was much upset when *an admiring reporter* described him as a regular guy. (Emphasis added)

According to what (5) literally says one never would know whether *an admiring reporter* should be translated into Spanish as *un periodista admirador* or as *una periodista admiradora*. And, if we know that the alluded journalist was in fact a lady, we know it thanks to the Chesterton's text itself, where the matter of the gender of the journalist is clearly stated:

(5.1) An American friend congratulated me on the impression I produced on a lady interviewer, observing, 'She says you're a regular guy.' This puzzled me a little at the time. 'Her description is no doubt correct,' I said, 'but I confess that it would never have struck me as specially complimentary.' But it appears that it is one of the most graceful of compliments, in the original American. (Chesterton 1922: 43)

But what Chesterton himself says cannot be inferred from the *OED*'s text. And, if one assumes that someone is translating (5) into Spanish, Italian, French or German, s/he is obliged to attribute a particular gender to the journalist in question, in spite of the fact s/he runs the risk of being wrong. And this meanness of the English language with regard to gender markers can lead English readers to think that there is a text in which the Spanish philosopher Ortega y Gasset was politically incorrect, when he really was not. Let us consider the following text:

(6) Las versiones al alemán de mis libros son un buen ejemplo de esto. (…) Y es que *mi traductora* ha forzado hasta el límite la tolerancia gramatical del lenguaje alemán para transcribir precisamente lo que no es alemán en mi modo de decir. De esta manera el lector se encuentra sin esfuerzo haciendo gestos mentales que son españoles. Descansa así un poco de sí mismo y le divierte encontrarse un rato siendo otro. (Ortega y Gasset 1983a: 452; emphasis added)

It is patently clear that, in (6), Ortega y Gasset has been explicit with regard to the gender of his translator into German, since he makes clear that he is speaking about a lady and not about a gentleman. But this point, which is patently clear in the original text, has been covered up in its translation into English. The translation in question reads as follow:

(6.1) The German versions of my books are a good example of this. (…) And it is successful because *my translator* has forced the grammatical tolerance of the German language to its limits in order to carry over precisely what is not German in my way of speaking. In this way, the reader effortlessly makes mental gestures that are Spanish. He relaxes a bit and for a while is amused at being another. (Ortega y Gasset 2002: 63; emphasis added)

Well then, if we suppose that, by means of an unfortunate piece of bad luck, all the Spanish copies of (6) get lost and we only keep its translation into English, we will be not able to guess whether Ortega's translator into German was a male or a female. And if, in addition, we suppose that someone back-translates [6.1] into Spanish, it is highly probable that – in the absence of further information – s/he would opt for the masculine gender by default. If so, Ortega y Gasset could be found guilty of inexcusable male chauvinism by someone who positively knows that Ortega's books were translated into German by a lady and not by a gentleman.

6. Idioms and collocations

Both idioms and collations are typically syntagms that have a lexicalised meaning which differs from the literal meaning of the words that make up the idiom or collocation, although, if the speaker is not cooperative – on purpose and/or because of his/her lack of knowledge –, s/he can misunderstand the actual meaning of the idiom or collocation. Accordingly, if a given translator translates any idiom or collocation according to the literal meaning of the words, misunderstandings are unavoidable. And, given I illustrated the false friends subject by choosing to a text by Rawls, I will also illustrate the idiom subject by selecting another text by Rawls himself. So, when Rawls is treating the order of precedence when applying a principle, we find the following text:

(7) Esta prioridad significa que, al aplicar un principio (o al ponerlo a prueba en *casos difíciles*), asumimos que los principios están plenamente satisfechos. (Rawls 2002: 74; emphasis added)

According to what (7) literally says, it seems to be that Rawls is speaking of any (juridical) case which entails any kind of difficulty; and consequently one could guess that Rawls might have written in his original text something like *difficult/hard cases*. But what the original text says in fact is:

(7.1) This priority means that in applying a principle (or checking it against *test cases*) we assume that the prior principles are fully satisfied. (Rawls 2001: 43; emphasis added)

Instead of finding *difficult/hard cases* or something similar, we find the collocation *test cases*, which in the juridical English jargon means '(*Law*) a case, the decision of which is taken as determining that of a number of others in which the same question of law is involved' (*OED*; emphasis as in original), and this is said in Spanish *casos que crean/sientan jurisprudencia/precedente*. As it turns out, not necessarily any difficult case sets a precedent when ruled by a judge or a jury; and, conversely, a given case can set a precedent and, in spite of that, could be an easy case.

The famous English phrasal and prepositional verbs can be considered as a special case of collocations since the meaning of the single verb radically changes according to several different prepositions. And again, if the translator is not aware of this, the reader of his/her translation can misunderstand the text s/he is reading. Let us consider the following text:

(8) Una de las distinciones de mayor calado que pueden practicarse entre concepciones de la justicia es entre aquellas que *permiten* la coexistencia de una pluralidad de doctrinas comprehensivas, con diferentes y aun encontradas concepciones del bien, y aquellas que sostienen que no puede haber más que una concepción del bien que han de aceptar todos los ciudadanos que sean plenamente razonables y racionales. (Rawls 1996: 166; emphasis added)

The salient meanings of the Spanish verb *permitir* in this context are: 1) 'Dar su consentimiento para que otros hagan o dejen de hacer algo' [literally, 'let (someone) others do or cease doing something']; and 2) 'No impedir lo que se pudiera y debiera evitar' [literally, 'do not impede what could and should be avoided'; *DRAE*]. Accordingly, what is being stated in (8) is that there are conceptions of justice that admit, consent, allow, permit, or tolerate the coexistence of several doctrines of the good. If so, one could expect that Rawls would write one of the verbs aforementioned or any other of their synonyms. But what Rawls wrote in fact was:

> (8.1) One of the deepest distinctions between conceptions of justice is between those that *allow for* a plurality of reasonable though opposing comprehensive doctrines each with its own conception of the good, and those that hold that there is but one such conception to be recognized by all citizens who are fully reasonable and rational. (Rawls 2005: 134; emphasis added)[12]

Indeed, what one finds in (8.1) is not the verbs I previously guessed, but the prepositional verb *to allow for*, whose meaning is 'To allow what is right or fair, to make due allowance for; also *fig.* To bear in mind as a modifying or extenuating circumstance' (*OED*; emphasis as in original), which is synonymous with *to take into account* or *to take into consideration*. And, since the Spanish verb *permitir* can be glossed as *to give something one's approval*, it seems that, in (8) Rawls is stating that there are conceptions of justice that give their approval to the coexistence of different 'understanding/tolerant' doctrines as opposed to other doctrines that only would admit a unique conception of justice.

7. Non-lexicalised metaphors

Normally, when a metaphor is lexicalised in a given language, bilingual dictionaries include both the literal meaning (or meanings) of the term in question and its figurative meaning. But, when this is not the case and a given writer uses a term according to any new figurative meaning, then his/her translator can misunderstand it or, even when s/he correctly understands

---

[12] In order to apply Ockham's razor, I will avoid commenting on the following remarks: 1) the translator has missed the adversative conjunction *though* in 'though opposing'; 2) in spite of the fact that the English noun *distinction* can be translated in other contexts as *distinción*, I would prefer *diferencia*, since Rawls is speaking of opposite doctrines; and 3) the couple of false friends *comprehensive/comprehensivo*, which I previously mentioned.

this new meaning, can think that the metaphor in question might not work in the target language. Ortega y Gasset's philosophical writings are famous because of the many new metaphors routinely includes; and many of them are extremely striking even for native speakers of the Spanish language. For instance, he metaphorically describes the style as '*siempre unigénito*' (Ortega y Gasset 1983b: 263), whose plausible translation into English might be 'always unique'. But this translation does not do justice to the original Spanish metaphor, since, firstly, the Spanish metaphor emerges from theological jargon and alludes to The Only Begotten Son of God, and, secondly, this metaphor is striking even for native speakers of Spanish if they are not aware such metaphor originates from theological jargon. In any case, such metaphor is not usual among Spanish speakers.

This striking use of metaphors by Ortega led the translator into English of one of his works to provide a strange translation, which could then lead his English readers to misunderstand his original thinking. I am alluding to the following text:

(9) Escribir bien consiste en hacer continuamente pequeñas *erosiones* a la gramática, al uso establecido, a la norma vigente de la lengua. Es un acto de rebeldía permanente contra el contorno social, una subversión. Escribir bien implica cierto radical denuedo. (Ortega y Gasset 1983a: 434; emphasis added)

In principle, it seems that the Spanish noun *erosión* could have been translated into English by the English noun *erosion*, since both nouns share their literal meanings as 'Desgaste de la superficie terrestre por agentes externos, como el agua o el viento' (*DRAE*) and 'The action or process of eroding; the state or fact of being eroded' (*OED*) in Spanish and English, respectively. As well as they share their figurative meanings as 'Desgaste de prestigio o influencia que puede sufrir una persona, una institución, etc.' (*DRAE*) and 'the gradual destruction or diminution of something: *the erosion of support for the party*' (http://oxforddictionaries.com/),[13] in Spanish and English, respectively; especially if we take into account that such metaphor is odd and striking even in Spanish. Nevertheless, what in fact was translated into English was something very different:

---

[13] The printed version of the *OED* does not provide any definition with regard to its figurative meaning; it only states '*transf.* and *fig.*' (emphasis as in original). By contrast, the following example is quoted: 'About twenty per cent of the Government majority has disappeared by the natural erosion of by-elections.'

> (9.1) To write well is to make continual *incursions* into grammar, into established usage, and into accepted linguistic norms. It is an act of permanent rebellion against the social environs, a subversion. To write well is to employ a certain radical courage. (Ortega y Gasset 2002: 51; emphasis added)

As a result of this, Ortega y Gasset's intended meaning of *attrition, corrosion, undermining, waste, wearing away* or *wearing out*, turned out to be either 'The action of running in or of running against' or 'A hostile inroad or invasion; esp. One of sudden and hasty character; a sudden attack' (*OED*); that is, a *descent, foray, raid, inroad, invasion*, or *irruption*. And this, besides not being what Ortega y Gasset himself wrote, entails a premeditated act, which in principle is not entailed by the noun *erosión/erosion*.

8. Polysemies

I will finally deal with the subject of polysemy, which brings up very interesting problems as well when a translator opts for a given version of a term, if such term is particularly polysemous in its source language and has no unique, plausible synonym in the target language. In the interests of being brief, I will only refer to the problems of translating into English the title of W. F. Hegel's *Die Phänomenologie des Geistes*. Given that the German noun *Geist* is highly polysemous, it has to be translated, according to the context, by different English nouns. The main ones could be, among others less salient: *ghost, spirit*, and *mind*, since the 'word *Geist* is one of those German abstractions that can mean anything from spirit to mind to ghost to intellect to psyche' (Filkins 2012: B14).[14] But each of them brings with it a specific problem. Let us analyse such problems one by one.

Hegel's translator might have decided on translating *Geist* as *ghost*. And this option would have in its favour the fact that the English collocation *The Holy Ghost* has its exact equivalent in the German collocation *Der Heiliger Geist*. But the problem emerges since the salient current meaning of the noun *ghost* is 'The soul of a deceased person, spoken of as appearing in a visible form, or otherwise manifesting presence, to the living. Now the prevailing sense' (*OED*). If so, it seems reasonable for the English

---

[14] In order to be brief, I will disregard other possible terms such as *soul, nous, psyche* or the German noun *Geist* itself, which is also recorded at the *OED* as: 'Spirit; spirituality; intellectuality; intelligence.'

translator to reject this alternative inasmuch as the title of Hegel's work could be understood by English readers as:

(10) *The Phenomenology of Phantom, Spectre, Vision, or Apparition.

As far as the English noun *spirit* is concerned, one could think that it is a plausible choice for translating the German noun *Geist* in many contexts as well. So, in order to allude only to the previous case, *The Holy Ghost* is said in English *The Holy Spirit*. In addition, it means 'The soul or spirit, as a principle of life' (*OED*). But, in view of the fact that the English noun *spirit* also means either 'A liquid of the nature of an essence or extract from some substance, esp. one obtained by distillation; a solution in alcohol of some essential or volatile principle' or '*pl*. strong alcoholic liquor for drinking, obtained from various substances by distillation; *sing*. any kind of it' (*OED*; emphasis as in original), again the title of this Hegel's work could be misunderstood by any English unwary reader as

(10.1) *The Phenomenology of Alcohol.

Consequently, only the noun *mind* remained as a plausible option for the early translator into English of *Die Phänomenologie des Geistes*. And, indeed, the early translation into English of Hegel's work in question was:

(10.2) The Phenomenology of Mind. (Hegel 1910).

However, as time went by, this translation became problematic, since 'One of the main problems with Baillie was that he translated *Geist* as "mind", which may have been good enough in 1910, but after half a century of linguistic change, the word was too intellectual and too psychiatric, and by the 1970s Miller's "Spirit" was undoubtedly preferable.' (Rée 2001: 254; emphasis as in original). As a result of this, the new translation made in the 1970s was entitled:

(10.3) The Phenomenology of Spirit. (Hegel 1977)

And so because, as J. Rée has argued, the noun *mind* was contaminated by intellectual and psychiatric nuances in only 67 years, this made it unsuitable for translating the German noun *Geist*. And, although J. Rée does not allude to this point, I would add of my own creation that, currently, (10.2) could lead someone, who is not versed in Hegel's philosophy, to believe that the German idealist wrote about something similar to what nowadays is called *Philosophy of Mind*, if we allow for the fact that the German standard translation is precisely *Die Philosophie des Geistes*.

9. Conclusions

When we carry out the translation of any philosophical text, we do it because 1) we know or assume that there are readers who are interested in knowing a given thought, and 2) they cannot read the text in question because they lack of knowledge of the language in which the thought has been expressed. When a given text is ambiguous in the source language, and such ambiguity cannot be reproduced in the target language, its translator has to opt for only one among the various possible options, if all of them are reasonable. Consequently, the different possible interpretations of the text in question cannot be taken into account in the translated text. The translation problems of philosophical texts do not emerge only with regard to the technical, philosophical terms, but also, and perhaps more frequently, with regard to terms used in everyday language. If the translator has made a mistake and there is nothing incongruous or strange in the translated text, this mistake will go unnoticed by the reader. In such cases, the author's thought will become irremediably misunderstood.

References

Allan, Keith. 2001. *Natural Language Semantics*. Oxford & Malden: Blackwell.
Anonymous. 2012. http://fr.wikipedia.org/wiki/Jean_Hyppolite. Accessed 19 April 2012.
Borges, Jorge Luis. 1986. *Textos cautivos*. In *Obras completas: Vol. IV*. Barcelona: Emecé.
Chamizo Domínguez, Pedro José. 2008. *Semantics and Pragmatics of False Friends*.
    London & New York: Routledge.
Chesterton, Gilbert Keith. 1922. *What I Saw in America*. London: Hodder and Stoughton.
Dictionnaire de l'Académie Française (DAF). 1994. Paris: Julliard.
Descartes, René. 1968/1637. *Discurso de método. Meditaciones metafísicas*. Translated by
    Manuel García Morente. Madrid: Espasa-Calpe.
Descartes, René. 1973/1637. *Discours de la méthode*. In *Œuvres: Vol. VI*. Edition by
    Charles Adam and Paul Tannery. Paris: C.N.R.S.-J. Vrin.
Deviers-Joncour, Christine. 1999. *La putain de la République*. Paris: J'ai lu.
Diccionario de la Real Academia Española (DRAE). 2012. Madrid: Real Academia
    Española. Available from http://buscon.rae.es/draeI/
Filkins, Peter. 2012. The hidden lens: How translation shapes meaning. *The Chronicle of
    Higher Education*, March 16, 2012: B11–B14.
Foucault, Michel. 1966. *Les mots et les choses (Une archéologie des sciences humaines)*. Paris:
    Gallimard.
Hegel, Georg Wilhelm Friedrich. 1910. *The Phenomenology of Mind*. Translation by
    James Black Baillie. London: Dover Publications.

Hegel, Georg Wilhelm Friedrich. 1977. *The Phenomenology of Spirit*. Translation and introduction by de A. V. Miller. Analysis of the text and foreword by J. N. Findlay. Oxford: Clarendon Press.

Hintikka, Jaakko. 1958. On Wittgenstein's 'Solipsism'. *Mind* 67 (265): 88–91.

Koyré, Alexandre. 1973/1943. Traduttore-traditore. À propos de Copernic et de Galilée. In *Études d'histoire de la pensée scientifique*. Paris: Gallimard, 272–4.

Ortega Gasset, José. 1983a/1937. Miseria y esplendor de la traducción. In *Obras completas*. Madrid: Alianza-Revista de Occidente, V: 431–52.

Ortega Gasset, José. 1983b/1914. Ensayo de estética a manera de prólogo. In *Obras completas*. Madrid: Alianza-Revista de Occidente, VI: 256–63.

Ortega y Gasset, José. 2002/1937. The misery and the splendor of translation. Translated by Elisabeth Gamble Miller. In Lawrence Venuti (ed.), *The Translation Studies Reader*. London & New York: Routledge, 49–63.

The Oxford English Dictionary (OED). 1989. 2nd edition. Oxford: Clarendon Press.

Quine, Willard Van Orman. 1953. *From a Logical Point of View*. Cambridge, MA: Harvard University Press.

Quine, Willard Van Orman. 1960. *Word and Object*. Cambridge, MA: The MIT Press.

Quine, Willard Van Orman. 1966. *Il problema del significato*. Translated into Italian by Enrico Mistretta. Rome: Ubaldini.

Quine, Willard Van Orman. 1977. *Le mot et la chose*. French translation by J. Dopp & P. Gochet. Foreword by P. Gochet. Paris: Flammarion.

Rawls, John. 1996. *El liberalismo político*. Translated by Antoni Domènech. Barcelona: Crítica.

Rawls, John. 2001. *Justice as Fairness: A Restatement*. Edited by Erin Kelly. Cambridge, MA: The Belknap Press of Harvard University Press.

Rawls, John. 2002. *La justicia como equidad: una reformulación*. Translated by Andrés de Francisco. Barcelona: Paidós.

Rawls, John. 2005/1993. *Political Liberalism*. Expanded Edition. New York: Columbia University Press.

Rée, Jonathan. 2001. The translation of philosophy. *New Literary History* 32: 223–57.

Steiner, George. 1975. *After Babel: Aspects of Language and Translation*. Oxford: Oxford University Press.

Viollet-le-Duc, Eugène Emmanuel. 1854–1868. *Dictionnaire raisonné de l'architecture française du XIe au XVIe siècle*. 10 vols. Paris: Bance et Morel. Available from: http://fr.wikisource.org/wiki/Dictionnaire_raisonn%C3%A9_de_l%27architecture_fran%C3%A7aise_du_XIe_au_XVIe_si%C3%A8cle. Accessed 19 April 2012.

Wittgenstein, Ludwig. 1922. *Logische-Philosophische Abhandlung / Tractatus Logico-philosophicus*. Bilingual edition (German–English) by C. K. Ogden and F. P. Ramsey. London: Routledge and Kegan Paul.

Wittgenstein, Ludwig. 1957/1922. *Tractatus Logico-philosophicus*. Bilingual edition (German–Spanish) by Enrique Tierno Galván: Madrid: Revista de Occidente.
Wittgenstein, Ludwig. 2003/1922. *Tractatus logico-philosophicus*. Spanish translation by Luis M. Valdés Villanueva. Madrid: Tecnos.

Chapter 15

RADICAL LEXICALISM IN MODELLING GRAMMAR AND LANGUAGE

Mike Balint
Monash University

Radical Lexicalism (RL) as proposed here posits the mentally represented lexicon – or lexicons in the case of multilinguals – as the repository of both the internalised knowledge of grammar (or grammars) and of the knowledge of how to use that grammatical knowledge in producing and interpreting utterances in one or more languages. Grammarians of all schools will no doubt object to representing grammar as a mere subsidiary database within the mentally represented lexicon; Fregean philosophers of language will cry foul about the spectre of psychologism in theoretical explanation, and Chomskyans will be up in arms about the conjoint representation of competence and performance. RL however is firmly grounded in contemporary knowledge representation theory, and posited as the core conceptual driver of a cognitively plausible model of the architectural and operational Gestalt of interlocutory language usage (CoP), its thesis is solidly based in everyday observational evidence and common sense inference from interlocutory language usage in respect of the discourse context in which it occurs. The paper explores, within the CoP framework, the role of a cognitively plausible mental representation of the lexicon(s) in making available grammar(s) for purposes of licensing the encoding and parsing/decoding processes of the mental representations of the sentential components of utterances in interlocutory language usage.

1. Mental representations in language usage

The basic premise of the approach taken in this paper is that the function of language usage is to transfer information from the originator of an utterance (hereafter O) to its addressee (hereafter A).[1] Each utterance is

---

[1] Conventionally termed Speaker and Hearer, respectively, which however carry connotations of oral language usage. O and A are intended as neutral substitutes carrying no connotations in respect of the physical medium of utterance transmission.

taken as comprised of a sentential component[2] carrying a meaning-content explicitly encoded into its concatenation of grammatical constituents, and in most cases also triggering a nonencoded inferential meaning-content[3] which may be context-sensitive or context-dependent. The nonencoded inferential meaning-content may complement, supplement, support or even entirely supplant the explicitly encoded meaning-content. The information intended to be communicated as the total message-content (*intended* meaning-content) of an utterance is representable as a propositional merger of its encoded and nonencoded meaning-content (hereafter Merger Representation or MR; cf. Jaszczolt 2005: 53–73), where the nonencoded meaning-content is inferable from a propositional interaction between the explicitly encoded meaning-content of the sentential component of the utterance and a set of relevant common-ground presumptions mutually manifest to the interlocutors in the discourse context in which the utterance occurs.

The focus of radical lexicalism (RL), as put forward in this paper, is on modelling lexical licensing as the sole means of accounting for the grammatical structure of the sentential components of utterances, in other words of capturing *what can go with what* and *what can come after what or before what* in well-formed strings of listemes[4] that constitute the mental representations of the sentential components of utterances. Internalised language knowledge is thus posited as also driving the choice of context-dependent and/or context-sensitive inferential and referential[5] place-markers

---

[2] Definitions of the sentence in both traditional grammars and contemporary formal models of grammar – whether these be explicit or implicit, formal or working definitions – suffer from the same fundamental deficiency of offering functionally incoherent circular definitions of the definiendum in terms of the set of definiens forming its constituent parts and of the set of definiens in terms of their respective roles within the definiendum. The nature of the grammatical category of the sentence is discussed at length in Balint (2011: 66–9), where a functional, non-circular definition of the sentence is proposed in terms of the role(s) it plays in the pragmatic category of utterance.

[3] All communication through the medium of language presumes and indeed crucially relies on the ability of interlocutors to infer, whether in understanding the simplest reference, presupposition, conventional or conversational implicature carried by the sentential component of an utterance, or in being able to take a hint, recognise an understatement, get the message of dog whistle politics or understand and enjoy various forms of irony or comedy.

[4] Allan (2009: 249) defines listemes as 'language expressions whose meaning is not determinable from the meanings (if any) of their constituent forms and which, therefore, a language user must memorize as a combination of form and meaning.'

[5] Reference also presumes and relies on a mode of context-dependent inference for its interpretation, given that it is triggered by the meaning-content of explicitly encoded grammatical constituents operating as referential place-markers in the sentential

operating as grammatical constituents in the sentential components of utterances. These place-markers then trigger propositional interaction with common ground presumptions mutually manifest to O and A in the discourse context in which the utterance occurs, so as to yield inferences intended by O and thereby enable desired rhetorical effects with an economy of encoded grammatical form. RL thus postulates that the two principal structural enablers of the mentally represented encoding and decoding processes are (1) the knowledge of grammar immanent in a mentally represented lexical database and (2) the knowledge of context immanent in a mentally represented context database, and that it is the propositional interaction of these two dimensions that produce contextually interpretable mental representations of the sentential components of utterances, whether by O as their producer or A as their receiver.

Four kinds of meaning-content are potentially encodable into the physical manifestations of the sentential components of utterances transmitted from O to A: (1) intensional and grammatical meaning-content that is context-free in respect of the discourse context in which the utterance occurs; (2) context-dependent referential meaning-content; (3) compositional meaning-content; and (4) in most cases also an inferential meaning-content, which may be either context-sensitive or context-dependent. A variety of motor control functions is taken as converting mental representations of the sentential components of utterances into physical manifestations and vice versa, and facilitating the transmission of those physical manifestations from O to A. Encoding by O of the sentential component of an utterance is postulated as a non-linear cognitive process involving a multiplicity of language-specific dimensions and cognitive enabling capabilities. These include, among others, the conjoint and co-dependent operation of a multitude of phonological, morphological, syntactic, prosodic, semantic and pragmatic construction, construal, control, feedback and correction processes simultaneously scanning back and forth over some particular set of lexemes selected for producing the sentential component of a given utterance. The converse processes of parsing and decoding[6] on the part of A are taken as involving similar non-linear cognitive processing, though with opposite polarities.

---

components of utterances. In addition to deixis and denotation, inferentially enabled grammatical forms of reference also include long distance dependency relationships within and outside the sentence, such as discourse anaphora, gapping and other forms of ellipsis, all of which involve in effect dimensions of indexical reference; cf. Balint (2011: 11).

[6] As a simplifying assumption, parsing and decoding are posited as consecutive and distinctly different operations in the processing of incoming utterances by A. Parsing

The end result of encoding is posited as mentally represented linearisation in terms of the concatenation of the lemmas[7] of lexemes that form the grammatical constituents – morphemes, words, stock-standard phrases or whole clauses – of the sentential component of the utterance to be produced. Given that lemmas are in turn posited by RL as made up of sequences of *signemes*[8] and signemic segment boundaries, the linearisation of lemmas in effect produces a linearised sequence of signemic segments and signemic and other types of segment boundaries as the encoded mental representation of the form of the sentential component of the utterance. The mental representation of such linearised signemic sequences is in turn posited as instantly convertible into an intermediate level of mental representations which may take the form of phonemes or, in languages with written traditions, mental representations of graphemes,[9] Morse code, Braille signs, Auslan or other systems of hand signals or indeed those of ideograms or other kinds of phonologically unanalysable pictograms, hereafter collectively termed as *transemes* or mental representations of the strings of physical signals actually transmitted from O to A. One or another relevant motor control function

---

      is taken as involving the grammatical segmentation of the mental representation of an incoming stream of language signals into grammatical categories, functions and relations between identified morphosyntactic constituents. Decoding, on the other hand, is posited as involving the extraction and integration of meaning-content from the parsed strings, and the compositional merging of the intensional, grammatical, compositional, inferential, referential and propositional components of encoded and nonencoded utterance meaning-content, as interpreted and comprehended within and with reference to the relevant common ground presumptions mutually manifest to the interlocutors.

[7]   Lemmas are taken as the mentally represented lexical forms of listemes, which may or may not carry lexical meaning-content, whether intensional or propositional (Levelt 1989: 6).

[8]   Signemes or lexical prompts are posited as the smallest discrete non-meaning carrying units or building blocks into which mental representations of the lemmas of grammatical constituents of the sentential components of utterances may be segmented. The mental representations of signemes are commonly termed 'phonemes', taken as separated from one another by mentally represented phonemic segment boundaries, and with discrete sound segments in the form of phones or sets of allophones as their physical manifestations. However, as the grammatical constituents of the sentential components of utterances are transmissible from O to A not just in the form of strings of sound segments, a more general descriptor is needed for the mental representation of the smallest units of physically transmissible language signal segments, one that is not necessarily associated with sound, and it is in order to eliminate the inherent terminological bias of the term 'phoneme' toward sound as the physical medium for transmitting the sentential components of utterances from O to A that the term sigmeme is introduced.

[9]   All further references to graphemes are to be taken as applying only to languages with alphabetic writing systems.

operated by O is then posited as converting the mentally represented sequence of transemes, in consecutive order, into an incrementally realised stream of physically manifested *physemes*,[10] which may take the form of phones, graphemes, Morse code, Braille signs, Auslan or other systems of hand signals, ideograms or other kinds of pictograms, respectively.

The incremental stream of physemes received by A is then posited as re-converted in consecutive order into a sequence of mentally represented transemes by one or another relevant motor function operated by A. These intermediate mental representations are then postulated as in turn instantly re-converted into a mentally represented sequence of parsable and decodable signemes as preliminary to the construal of the mentally represented sentential component, and subsequently the interpretation and comprehension of the utterance by A within and with respect to the discourse context in which it occurred. It is of course the postulated linearised mental representation of the physical form of the sentential component of an utterance that makes possible its conversion and transmission in terms of an incremental stream of physically represented physemes (and in turn the reconversion of that physical sequence into a mental one) that is self-evidently the key enabler of the production and interpretation of the sentential components of utterances, and thus of the very possibility of using the medium of language for conveying information through time and space from an O to an A.

The correspondence between mental representations of spoken and written language may be close, as in Hungarian, distant, as in French, or entirely absent, as in Chinese. In many languages, furthermore, the spoken and written forms of language may involve significantly different encoding requirements, in that the switch from informal speech to formal writing may require an alternate choice of lemmas considered more appropriate to the medium of writing. On the whole, it seems that the longer a written tradition, the greater the divergence between the mental representations of the sequence of phonemic or non-phonemic representations inferable from the respective spoken and written or other non-spoken manifestations of lexemes. The greatest divergence is found in logographic systems of writing using ideograms or pictograms, such as Egyptian hieroglyphs, Sumerian cuneiform or Chinese characters, where the mentally represented lemma of the written form of a lexeme is a graphic symbol representing

---

[10] Physemes are posited as denoting the physical manifestations of the mentally represented signemes, as mediated by mentally represented transemes, irrespective of the medium of transmission.

an idea or concept in terms of what is essentially a diachronically evolved conventionalised picture of greater or lesser abstraction. In such languages, a mentally represented linearised sequence of signemes is evidently converted on a lemma-by-lemma, rather than signeme-by-signeme basis into the mental representation of a sequence of logographs, rather than the mental representation of a sequence of graphemes which would be the case in alphabetical systems of writing, where the encoded signemic sequences are converted into transemic mental representations of graphemic sequences on the basis of a more or less one-to-one correspondence.

Memory capacity does not appear to place any significant limitations on lexical storage or searchability, given that not only are the intensional content and potentially several parallel lemma forms available for each and every lexeme in the lexical database, but that this may easily be reduplicated for two or more languages in the case of multilinguals. Given this self-evidently vast capacity of the memory function, repetition, duplication and other forms of redundancy in the lexical database(s) or in the cognate encyclopedic and context database(s) do not appear to present any kind of issue (cf. Figure 1 below). This, in turn, has significant implications for cognitively plausible modelling of internalised language knowledge, since there is little reason to suppose that Occam's Razor or considerations of simplicity and elegance need or should play any role in cognitively plausible representations of the internalised knowledge databases of the language user.

2. Cognitive plausibility in representing language usage

The RL thesis as advanced in this paper is the core conceptual driver of a model of the architectural and operational Gestalt of interlocutory language usage first presented in Balint (2011). Interlocutory language usage is a quintessentially psychosocial phenomenon that functions in terms of the simultaneous, conjoint and co-dependent operation of language *system*, language *context* and the process flows of language *process* in interlocutory language usage. The result is a cognitively encodable, incrementally transmissible and decodable communication code (or codes in the case of code-switching and/or code-mixing multilinguals) capable of carrying and conveying message-content between interlocutors interacting with one another within a given mutually manifest discourse context that provides a propositionally relevant common ground for reference and inference in the production and interpretation of utterance and connected discourse. Cognitive plausibility is self-evidently a key requirement on this model, henceforth referred as the 'cognitive plausibility model' of interlocutory language usage, or CoP for short. That cognitive plausibility ought to be a fundamental requirement on modelling interlocutory language usage would seem to be a matter of plain common sense, at once uncontroversial and incontrovertible. After all, proposing a theory or model of language usage that does not aim at a cognitively plausible representation would make about as much sense as proposing a genetically implausible model of a life form. Self-evidently, therefore, a cognitively plausible representation of the Gestalt of interlocutory language usage – which functions in terms of the simultaneous, conjoint and co-dependent operation of language system and the context-sensitive or context-dependent process flows of language process – must perforce involve a conjoint and co-dependent representation of system and process within and with reference to the operating context.

This is in fact the position taken in contemporary knowledge representation theory – a branch of cognitive psychology – that specifically postulates that for a representation of either a cognitive system or a cognitive process to be valid, the two must be jointly accounted for:

> It makes no sense to talk about representations in the absence of processes. The combination of … [a represented world, a representing world, and a set of representing rules] … creates merely the potential for representation. Only when there is also a process that uses the representation does the system actually represent, and the capabilities of a system are defined only when there is both representation and process. … [Something] is a representation only if a process can be used to interpret that representation. (Markman 1999: 8)

> A central part of the definition of a representation is that some process must extract and use information from it. … One reason that specifying the processing assumptions for a given representation is important is that the implications of a representational formalism for psychological models are not clear until the processing assumptions have been laid out. … The specification of processes is also necessary because in an important sense, without specifying processing assumptions, there is no representation at all (there is at best only representation potential), so all further discussion begs many important questions. (Markman 1999: 289–90)

This makes nonsense of the Chomskyan insistence on considering 'competence' in isolation from 'performance', which Chomskyans regard as a kind of garbage bin of grammar into which all empirical data that the Chomskyan model *du jour* is unable to account for, may safely be dumped and forgotten about. Equally, it also makes nonsense of Fregean objections raising the spectre of psychologising in theoretical explanations as a consequence of a methodologically invalid mixing of the categories of theory and usage, as would seem to be the case in regard to CoP at a first glance.

Let us note at once, however, that Frege's stricture is aimed specifically against psychologising *the laws of logic*, although by extension it may also be taken as applying to any theory with propositions that are in the nature of eternal and unchangeable verities like the laws of logic, which of course linguistics theory certainly is not. In any case, there is a strict formal separation in the CoP model between the theory of internalised language knowledge and the theory of interlocutory language usage. For monolinguals, internalised language knowledge is posited as being immanent in four interacting structured relational databases:[11] (1) a lexical database, (2) a language system database embedded in the lexical database and functioning as the governance unit of both language system and language process, (3) a context database and (4) an encyclopedic database embedded in the context database and particularly closely interlinked with the lexical database. For multilinguals, internalised language knowledge will, of course, involve two or more lexical databases, and correspondingly two or more language system databases posited as embedded in the respective lexical databases (cf. Figure 1). Interlocutory language usage, on the other hand, is posited as *utilising* these databases in communicative action, where the language code is employed in combination with anchor points in the referential and inferential context to transfer explicit and/or implied information from O to A. Internalised language knowledge and interlocutory language usage are thus taken as forming a Gestalt, wherein the linkage between the two components is posited as formalisable in terms of sets of dynamic usage rules and constraints on language process, principally those pertaining to the processes of encoding, transmitting and decoding the sentential components of utterances. These cognitive processing rules and constraints are in turn postulated as being as much part of the language system as are the rules and constraints of grammar, and as such, are posited as listed in the language system database, or databases in the case of multilinguals, alongside and interacting with the static rules and constraints of grammar. The combined Gestalt effect of these static and dynamic rules and constraints are then

---

[11] A structured relational database is a hierarchical listing of data organised in terms of categories, where however each piece of data is a composite of distinctive properties or features that form referential networks and networks of networks across the database.

posited as governing the partly non-conscious and partly conscious choices in encoding, transmitting and decoding the sentential components of utterances transmitted from O to A.

CoP itself is a holistic procedural model of how internalised language knowledge is utilised in the various media and registers of interlocutory language usage. The holistic aproach is motivated by the author's experience in translating works of literature and works of literary scholarship across three unrelated languages – English, Hebrew, and Hungarian – and becoming aware that no existing linguistic theory properly illuminates the Gestalt or whole-of-language nature of language usage faced by the translator. For a translator, both source and target language usage are by definition Gestalts of (1) both system and process, (2) both form and content, (3) both text and context, and (4) both encoding and decoding, where the whole is greater than the sum of its parts. Language in fact presents itself to a translator as a complex open system of multilevel networks-within-networks that function conjointly, co-dependently and in seamless unison, to produce intended communicative and informative flows, impacts and effects within and with respect to the interlocutory cognitive context in which language usage occurs.

Unfortunately however, all current linguistic theories are fragmentary, in that none deals simultaneously with internalised language knowledge and interlocutory language usage in terms of a single coherent perspective on the gamut of phonology, morphosyntax, prosody, semantics, pragmatics, and discourse or text considerations that translators need simultaneous recourse to. Furthermore, significant segments of scholarship engaged in the development of some given model of internalised language knowledge are focused principally on proving model-internal theorems to internally validate one or another aspect of the particular model of their choice. Given however that many of these theories or models of internalised language knowledge are arbitrarily delimited in scope through simplifying and other exclusionary assumptions, it is unsurprising that model-internal analysis and argument will not necessarily get us closer to a deeper understanding of how the human faculty of language actually works. There is in fact no better teacher than translation – and in particular the translation of difficult-to-translate text containing complex ideas – to expose an aspiring language theorist to some humbling object lessons about the limitations of the reach, scope and relevance of the various reductionist theories of language competing for attention in the marketplace of scholarship. There is clearly a fundamental need for developing a big picture understanding of the nature of the architecture and operations of the entire faculty of language, rather than just a specialist view of one or another of its facets taken in isolation, which would in any case more than likely prove fundamentally inadequate precisely because it is in isolation of its big picture operating context. Hence the attempt in Balint (2011) to develop CoP as a unified, holistic procedural theory of interlocutory language usage.

CoP has no pretentions to 'prediction'[12]; it is a strictly descriptive model of mental representation and physical manifestation in interlocutory language usage, presenting an integrated perspective based in common sense inferences drawn from everyday empirical evidence. The model aims to fully account for the role of context[13] in producing and interpreting utterances and connected discourse, and to develop dynamic, process-oriented representations of goal-directed, inferential interlocution (cf. Balint 2011: 104–240 on the dimensions of inference in utterance production and interpretation). The message-content of an utterance is posited as self-generated by O within a postulated cognitive Conceptualiser function, in the form of thoughts, notions, ideas, cognitions or concepts which may then be chosen to be linguistically encoded, in one way or another, as the next step in producing an utterance.[14] In turn, a Reasonable Facsimile of the message-content intended by O is posited as being construed in the Conceptualiser of A upon having parsed and decoded, then contextually interpreted and comprehended a given utterance by O. All stages of the incremental processes of utterance production and interpretation are in turn seen as being under continuous online executive (cybernetic) process control by both O and A in their respective spheres of operation. CoP posits, furthermore, that interlocution – dialogue or Gricean 'conversation' – and multilingualism

---

[12] The position taken in particular by Chomskyan and many post-Chomskyan or quasi-Chomskyan grammarians is that the notational artefacts they postulate as outcomes that are by definition designed to be produced by the posited operations of their models (of what they regard as the supposedly *innate* knowledge of grammar or of 'language') are in fact 'predictions' similar in nature to predictions generated by mathematical models in hard science. This of course involves "a systematic distortion of such methodologically central terms as 'explanation' and 'prediction'" (Itkonen 1974: 221). In this connection, cf. also Harman (1980: 21–2), Botha 1989 (161–2, 224), Hawkings and Penrose (1996: 3–4, 134–5) and Allan (2001: 475).

[13] Context is taken as the applicable universe of discourse, including both the internal and the external contexts of a given discourse or text. An utterance may be context-free, context-sensitive or context-dependent in its interpretive requirements. cf. Balint (2011: 33–9) for the distinction between context-dependence and context-sensitivity.

[14] cf. Balint (2011: 17–20) for a discussion of the crucial ontological and phenomenological distinctions between thought and language.

are the canonical modes of language usage, where monolingualism is taken as a particular case of multilingualism and associated code-switching and/or code-mixing phenomena. Multilingualism is in turn postulated as an underlying capability immanent in all internalised language knowledge, thus potentially available in all interlocutory language usage.

CoP furthermore posits that the processes of linearised and therefore incrementalisable encoding and decoding of utterances are crucially dependent on a range of cognitive enabling and motor control functions that must be integrated into its structure and operations in order to guarantee the cognitive plausibility of representation. These include, among others, (1) conceptualisation – thought generation; (2) intention – executive, communicative and informative; (3) memory – lexical, encyclopedic and cognitive context database access, search and retrieval capacity; (4) executive decision on what to encode, how, why and when – the choice of lexical items, including constructional schemas (cf. footnote 17), and the lexical licensing or traffic control over the processes of concatenating the selected items into physically incrementalisable strings of mentally represented signemes; (5a) attention and awareness – attention to, awareness of, and utilisation of context, relevance[15] and coherence in linearised and therefore incrementalisable encoding and decoding; (5b) attention and awareness – attention to, awareness of, and catering by O, in the course of incrementally encoding an utterance, to the perceived interpretive needs of A; (6) cybernetic, goal-directed online executive control, including online hypothesis projection, online feedback loops, online corrective action and online inferential reasoning; (7) cognitive overlay processes linking language knowledge and usage, principally pertaining to the processes of encoding, transmitting and decoding the sentential components of utterances; and (8) motor control processes linking linearly encoded signemes (via transemes) with incrementally emerging physemes, and vice versa, in the production and interpretation of utterances and connected discourse (cf. Balint 2011: 17–49, 278–81, 302–33).

3. The mentally represented lexicon

CoP aims to integrate postulated representations of internalised language knowledge with representations of the way this knowledge is procedurally

---

[15] The cognitive function of relevance recognition and utilisation has nothing to do with Relevance Theory (Sperber and Wilson 1986/1995), which is readily demonstrable to be cognitively implausible; cf. Balint (2011: 44–8).

realised in interlocutory language usage in the form of utterance and connected discourse. Interlocutory language usage is thus posited as a Gestalt composite of (1) *language system*, or the largely static and tacit or non-conscious body of grammatical rules and constraints immanent in internalised language knowledge, which is independent of any particular timeline of delivery; and (2) *language process*, which comprises the dynamic procedural dimensions of interlocutory language usage, each instantiation of which operates along a distinct timeline. Language system and language process are in turn taken as operating conjointly and co-dependently across a range of 'levels of analysis'[16] of form, meaning-content, context and cognitive enablers that need to be simultaneously represented and accounted for as operating in seamless unison.

The language system is posited as stored in a subdivision of the lexical database, the operation of which is cognitively enabled in a manner similar to that of the rest of the lexicon, in that the key operational enablers are (1) the memory function; (2) the capacity to search for, select, retrieve and utilise listemes of grammatical, semantic or pragmatic rules, constraints or usage guidelines, such as cognitively entrenched schemas[17] for forming concatenations of grammatical constituents in the construction of the sentential components of utterances; and (3) the contextual comprehension of relevant common ground presumptions perceived as mutually manifest to the interlocutors. As is the rest of the mentally represented lexical database, the storage of the language system is posited as being in the form of a set of structured relational data entries which function as system and process operating instructions for the language processes involved in interlocutory language usage. These system and process operating instructions are essentially a range of declarative rules, constraints, schemas and usage guidelines that are inferable from interlocutory language usage as governing its operations, and in particular the processes of encoding grammatically

---

[16] 'Levels of analysis' refers to domains or fields of linguistic enquiry, such as phonology, morphology, prosody, syntax, semantics or pragmatics, inclusive of theoretical orientations that may be formal, functional, cognitive or various combinations and permutations of the three.

[17] Cognitively entrenched constructional templates of syntactic and/or morphosyntactic form. 'A schema can be defined as a cognitive representation comprising a generalisation over perceived similarities among instances of usage. Schemas arise via repeated activation of a set of co-occurring properties, and are used to produce and understand linguistic expressions. [...] schemas are used to categorize (or license) utterances. In syntax, schemas go by the name of constructional schemas or constructions.' (Barlow and Kemmer 2000: xxiii).

well-formed[18] and semantically, as well as pragmatically acceptable utterances by O, and the processes of recognising and construing the same by A in the converse processes of parsing and decoding. The declarative rules and constraints on grammatical well-formedness inferable from interlocutory language usage – the rules and constraints licensing grammaticality, as are of course also the rules licensing semantic and pragmatic acceptability and the constraints thereon – are essentially static categorising schematisations that grammarians and linguists abstract away from their instantiations in language usage. The licensing rules and constraints may in turn be posited, at the most general level of analysis, as:

1. Governing the encoding processes by O, in which the lemmas of lexemes selected from the lexical database are concatenated into linearised mental representations of the sentential components of utterances in terms of strings of signemes convertible first into likewise mentally represented transemes and then into physically manifested physemes incrementally transmissible to A in the selected medium of transmission by the agency of one or another relevant motor control function.

2. Governing the parsing and decoding processes by A, in which a linearised string of mentally represented signemes – converted from a likewise linearised string of mentally represented transemes recovered by the agency of one or another relevant motor control function from an incoming stream of physically manifested physemes – is segmented into lemmas of lexemes carrying decodable intensional, grammatical, referential and semantically compositional, as well as contextually interpretable inferential and propositional meaning-content.

3. Blocking cases of phonological, morphological, prosodic, syntactic, semantic and pragmatic error in utterance production and interpretation.

---

[18] Interestingly, not all representations of the syntactic dimension of internalised language knowledge aim to capture and account for grammatical well-formedness. Constraint-based grammars, for instance, such as Dynamic Syntax, Lexical-Functional Grammar or Head-driven Phrase Structure Grammar 'imply no commitment to determining all and only the well-formed strings of language… [Such systems] are thus able to be relatively liberal with the data, allowing other, e.g. pragmatic, constraints to be operative in determining judgements on acceptability.' (Cann et al. 2005: 223)

For any language, the full set of these declarative rules, constraints and usage guidelines on grammaticality and acceptability is then posited as operating in the form of a lexically listed rule component of the grammatical code, which is in turn complemented by the likewise lexically listed closed set of lexemes formed by grammatical function words and grammatical function morphemes. The rule component of the grammatical code is posited as governing the manner in which lexemes – lexically listed form-meaning pairs, including morphemes, words, stock-standard phrases and idiomatic expressions – encoded with intensional, grammatical, referential and semantically compositional, as well as contextually interpretable inferential and propositional meaning-contents, may be concatenated to form the sentential components of utterances. The grammatical code is in turn taken to operate in large measure simultaneously, conjointly and co-dependently with the correlated semantic and pragmatic codes governing the semantic and pragmatic acceptability of the sentential components of utterances. The mental representations of syllabic, word level, phrasal, clausal or sentential concatenations of listemic forms or lemmas of lexemes are in turn taken as analysable in terms of multi-level composites of phonological (P), morphological (M), prosodic (P) and syntactic (S) components, and will henceforth be referred as composite PMPS strings, or PMPS for short. For any given language, the term *grammar* is therefore taken as describing the lexically listed mental representations of the language code comprising the full set of rules, constraints and usage guidelines that drive and govern encoding by O (or parsing/decoding by A) of concatenations of mental representations of PMPS language forms in terms of a system of cognitively entrenched constructional schemas, grammatical constituencies, categories, functions and relations inferable from the physically manifested, empirically observable strings of PMPS constituents in the sentential components of utterances in interlocutory language usage.

The mentally represented knowledge base that makes interlocutory language usage possible is modelled by RL in terms of three structured reference and relational databases conceived as tightly integrated in both their architecture and operations. The first is a context database comprised of a list of propositions or images capable of being propositionalised that together represent the sum total of both the tacit and overt knowledge of a language user about the universe of discourse[19] within which an utterance

---

[19] RL posits the universe of discourse of an interlocutor – and within it any given specific discourse context or set of relevant common-ground presumptions – as interpretable

or connected discourse occurs. The second is a mentally represented encyclopedia comprising the full set of denotata within that universe of discourse, thus essentially a subsidiary database of the first. The third is a lexicon – or a parallel set of two or more lexicons, in the case of multilinguals – construed as the repository of all internalised language knowledge, both tacit and overt.

The lexical database is in turn conceived as comprising four distinctly different categories of internalised language knowledge, one an open set of lexemes, the other three closed sets. The open set of lexemes are the lexical representations of 'content words', in contradistinction to 'function words'. The open set of lexemes comprises a memorised list of mentally represented lexical form–meaning pairs, which are explicitly encodable and instantly searchable, recallable or recognisable in terms of their combination of lemma form and intensional, grammatical, referential and semantically compositional, as well as contextually interpretable inferential and propositional meaning-contents. The physical manifestations of this open set of lexemes are in the form of morphemes, words, stock-standard phrases or idiomatic expressions, each with its own unique one-to-one pairing of PMPS form and meaning-content in the sentential components of utterances,[20] whether conveyed in sound, writing, touch or hand signals. The vast bulk of lexically listed items belong to this open set of lexical form-meaning pairs, a set which is moreover capable of indefinite growth by integrating a potentially endless supply of additional words, phrases and other expressions memorised during the lifetime of a language user.

The closed sets are in turn posited as encompassing three distinct sets of data pertaining to grammatical coding and interlocutory language usage. The first of these is the closed set of lexemes comprised of the function words and function morphemes, which form part of the grammatical code of a given language, such as modal verbs or prepositions in English. The lexical representations of function words and mophemes will henceforth be termed *coder lexemes* or *coders* for short, with the term 'lexeme' reserved for members of the open set of non-coder lexemes only, which will thus be used in contradistinction to 'coder'. Lexemes and coders are similar in that (1) the mental representation of a coder possesses both lexical form and intensional

---

and representable in terms of a structured relational database of propositions constituting the entire body of the internalised knowledge of the universe of discourse as memorised and stored in the mind of the language user.

[20] Instances of homonymy form a small class of exceptions to the generally unique one-to-one correlation of lexical form and lexical meaning-content.

meaning-content, just like a lexeme; (2) that a coder is physically manifested as a stand-alone function word, a clitic or an inflectional affix, thus in the form of a PMPS constituent in the sentential component of an utterance, just like a lexeme; and (3) that lexemes and coders both carry a specification of their own grammatical category as part of their lexical meaning-content, as well as specifications of co-occurrence constraints in the form of subcategorisation frames and selectional restrictions.[21] But unlike lexemes, coders by definition carry grammatical meaning-content only, and as such are restricted in their meaning-content to the signification of grammatical relation, mood, aspect, tense, modality, case, thematic role, or of temporal or locational reference in the sentential component of the utterance.

The second category of closed lexical dataset includes the set of listemes that have a lemma form, but are empty of lexical meaning-content, such as the mental representation of cognitively entrenched constructional schemas or that of the individual members of the set of signemes utilised in a given language. The third category of closed lexical dataset is in turn posited as the set of listemes that carry lexical meaning-content, but are free of any specific lemma or lexical form, as for instance the propositional content of grammatical formation rules and constraints listed in the form of declarative statements, rather than as cognitively entrenched constructional schemas or templates. All memory-dependent items in the body of internalised language knowledge – whether lexical or grammatical, tacit or overt – are thus posited as listed in the lexicon in terms of listemes of one type or another. This mode of categorising and locating internalised language knowledge is at the conceptual core of RL, and does of course represent a departure involving a radical expansion of the conventional scope of what the notion of listeme denotes.

Two distinctly different kinds of representations may furthermore be distinguished in the lexical database, one structured like a dictionary, the other operating as an interactive instruction manual. The dictionary function is posited as operating the lexeme, coder and lemma-only sets of listemes, providing a searchable listing of lexical items memorised for active recall or passive recognition in encoding and parsing/decoding the

---

[21] A subcategorisation frame (or a strict subcategorisation feature) is a morphosyntactic co-occurrence constraint specified in terms of some mandatory morphosyntactic feature on the sentence constituent occurring before or after the sentence constituent to which the strict subcategorisation feature is attributed; a selectional restriction (or selectional feature) is a semantic co-location constraint specified in terms of a mandatory semantic feature on the sentence constituent occurring before or after the sentence constituent to which the selectional restriction is attributed (Chomsky 1965: 148ff.).

sentential components of utterances. The interactive instruction manual function, posited as operating the third of the closed set of listemes, is in turn construed as the repository of the internalised knowledge of the systems dimension of interlocutory language usage. In effect, the lexicon is seen as operating a tacitly known 'how to use' instruction manual for the user of language, interactive in the linkages it provides between the stasis of internalised language knowledge and the dynamic processes of utterance production and interpretation in interlocutory language usage. The interactive instruction manual function is in turn posited as incorporating three distinctly different sets of propositional representations pertaining to grammatical coding and the processes of utterance production and interpretation in interlocutory language usage. The first of these is postulated as comprising the grammatical formation rules and constraints governing the concatenation of PMPS constituents into sentential components of utterances; the second as including the interlocutory and in effect cybernetic *processing* rules and constraints governing grammatical encoding and parsing/decoding; the third as involving the conversational guidelines and conventions governing the manner in which the data drawn from the lexicon may be put to economic and efficient communicative use within and with respect to a given discourse context so as to achieve the rhetorical and stylistic parameters intended by O.

In essence, therefore, the 'how to use' function of the lexicon is postulated as an interactive set or list of propositionally expressed rules, constraints and conventions that must be mandatorily applied in interlocutory language usage by both O and A. The propositions, which form a closed set of listemes that is generally static and unchanging for mature language users past the language acquisition phase, will henceforth be termed *metalinguistic coder listemes*, or *metacoders* for short. Metacoders therefore include the following three categories: 1) declarative grammatical formation rules and constraints, generally in the form of mentally represented constructional schemata that 'license' the ways PMPS constituents may be concatenated into morphosyntactically, syntactically and semantically well-formed sentential strings carrying contextually interpretable meaning-contents; 2) cybernetic management-control principles, protocols and procedures that govern the actual case-by-case applications of 'licensing' by grammatical formation rules and constraints to the dynamic linarisation and incrementation processes of encoding and parsing/decoding of sentential components of utterances; and 3) conversational principles, conventions and guidelines enabling inference and reference utilising common ground presumptions and denotata perceived by O as mutually manifest with A in the discourse context in which interlocutory language usage occurs. It follows, therefore, that metacoders also include 1) segmentation boundaries inferable for signemes and for the mental representations of morpheme, word, phrase, clause and sentence; 2) cognitively entrenched lexical schemas serving as constructional templates inferable from the construction of the physical manifestations of the sentential components of utterances; and 3) language-relevant cognitive mediation protocols for utilising cognitive enablers in the simultaneous, conjoint and co-dependent operation of language system, language context and the language process flows of interlocutory language usage. Metacoders are thus taken as possessing lexical meaning-content, but unlike other listemes, no physically encodable lemmas of some specific lexical form. Physically, metacoders are expressible only in terms of metalinguistic propositions pertaining to the governance of interlocutory language usage, whether in the form of statements or equivalent structural specifications of one sort or another. The set of metacoders postulated as listed in the lexicon in effect constitute a cognitively entrenched body of tacit, habituated knowledge of how to use language, i.e. of how to utilise lexemes and coders in encoding the mental representations of the sentential components of intended utterances. It is a knowledge inferable as being applied automatically and instantaneously in interlocutory language usage, albeit mostly in non-conscious and non-aware ways, much like using a body part or driving a car.

All lexemes and coders are postulated, furthermore, as exhaustively analysable into bundles of basic lexical building blocks mentally representable in terms of sets of unary, binary or n-ary (scalar) distinctive features of lexical form or of intensional meaning-content. Each distinctive feature posited as being carried by a lexeme or coder is in turn seen as a node on an instantly accessible, structured and cross-referable lexical network that link lexemes and coders across the lexicon – or two or more lexicons in the case of multilinguals – on the basis of some shared property of lexical form or lexical meaning-content. The distinctive features of lexical form and intensional meaning-content are thus postulated as forming dense reference networks, and indeed networks of networks of sets of distinctive features that endow the lexicon with the relational structure of a structured relational database.

Thus, signemes are posited as comprised of bundles of signemic distinctive features separated from one another within signemic lemmas by signemic segmentation boundaries. When the medium of communication is to be sound, the mentally represented transemes derived from signemes are in turn posited as comprised of phonemic distinctive features separated from one another within the transemic lemmas by phonemic segmentation boundaries. Similar considerations are posited to apply when signemes are converted into mentally represented transemes appropriate to conversion into physemes in the mediums of alphabetic writing, Morse code, Braille signs, Auslan or other hand signals, ideograms or other kinds of pictograms. The lemmas of lexemes and coders are in turn analysable into morphological, syntactic and prosodic distinctive features of language form, and the applicable morphemic, word, phrasal and clausal segmentation boundaries. The intensional meaning-content carried by lemmas is itself posited as analysable in terms of networks of semantic and pragmatic distinctive features, and each such unary, binary or n-ary distinctive feature of intensional meaning-content, as inferred by analysis of the respective meaning-contents carried by the PMPS grammatical constituents of the sentential components of utterances, in effect operates as a stand-alone propositional predication pertaining to the meaning-content of the lemma under analysis.

The reference networks and networks of networks formed by the distinctive features of intensional meaning-content are posited as fully searchable for each such feature, and this of course is the underlying characteristic of lexical representation upon which categorisation and indexation depend in *thesauruses* of languages. In effect, lexical features enable the instant or virtually instant searchability, identification, selection and retrieval of groupings of lexemes or coders in terms of one or another distinctive feature of intensional meaning-content shared in common between them, just as the categories of indexation do in a thesaurus. Distinctive features of intensional meaning-content are thus conceived as readily utilisable lexical representations which enable the mentally operating encoding (or parsing/decoding) process to rapidly – in most cases instantly – track down a given lexical item with just the right shade of meaning, or, if there is a mental blockage for some reason or another, to track it down with the aid of a thesaurus, as also supported by monolingual or even bilingual dictionaries where the meaning of a previously unfamiliar word or expression needs to be tracked down.

4. Lexical licensing of grammatical form

But metacoders, too, are conceived under RL as in principle analysable in terms of propositional meaning-content properties representable as bundles of mentally represented metacoder lexical features pertaining to phonological, morphological, syntactic, prosodic, semantic or pragmatic rules, constraints or guidelines utilised on the one hand in encoding, and on the other hand in parsing and decoding the sentential components of utterances. In effect, the lexical listing of metacoders is posited in terms of (1) stand-alone propositions involving lexical meaning-content without specific lexical form, (2) 'off-the-shelf' cognitively entrenched constructional schemas involving lexical form without specific lexical meaning-content, or (3) 'off-the-shelf' cognitively entrenched constructional schemas with propositional meaning-content, involving both lexical form and lexical meaning-content. Furthermore, the mandatory co-occurrence constraints specified by grammatical features, such as subcategorisation frames and selectional restrictions are in effect lexeme- or coder-specific instantiations of metacoders pertaining to the permissible morphosyntactic and semantic compositional contexts within the phrasal, clausal or sentential concatenations into which given lexemes and coders may be inserted as PMPS constituents in the sentential components of utterances. The instant searchability, access, choice and utilisation of metacoders is thus postulated as in principle similar to that of lexemes and coders, although in the case of metacoders, the processes of lexical selection and utilisation are significantly more tacit than is the case for lexemes and coders. The lexical database is thus conceived as exhaustively enumerating the full corpus of tacitly known and internalised grammatical formation rules and constraints in terms of coder and metacoder listemes which are seen as further analysable into subsidiary networks of distinctive features. The metacoders are in turn posited as instantly available mandatory inputs[22] licensing the phonology, morphology, syntax, prosody, semantics and pragmatics of sentence formation, thus governing the mentally represented process dynamics of the linearised and therefore incrementalisable encoding and parsing/decoding of the sentential components of utterances.

It is metacoder listemes that are therefore postulated, under RL, as the lexical entities licensing or determining *what can go with what* and *what can go after or before what* in encoding the mentally represented meaning-carrying concatenations of lemmas of lexemes and coders that form the PMPS grammatical constituents of well-formed sentential components of utterances. RL therefore perceives syntax/morphosyntax as an epiphenomenon which is on the one hand self-evidently driven by the intended message-content of the utterance and on the other hand licensed

---

[22] Mostly, though not always; translation and the writing of complex text are cases where such inputs may not always be instantly available.

by mental representations of lexically listed declarative rules and constraints on grammatical well-formedness. These in turn are posited as operating conjointly and co-dependently with mental representations of lexically listed declarative rules, constraints and usage conventions licensing the semantic and pragmatic acceptability of intended intensional, intensional entailment, grammatical, referential and semantic compositional, as well as contextually interpretable inferential and propositional meaning-content. The rules, constraints and usage conventions licensing grammatical well-formedness conjointly and often co-dependently with those of semantic and pragmatic acceptability are in turn posited as governing the processes of encoding or decoding/parsing the sentential components of utterances. It is worth noting that although the contents and functional specifics of lexical licensing are patently language-specific or indeed dialect-, sociolect- or even idiolect-specific, at the same time the nature, structure and organising principles of the mental lexicon itself are clearly integral to the human cognitive function as a whole, and as such must be posited as being invariant from language to language.

In positing 'off-the-shelf' cognitively entrenched schemas or constructional templates abstracted by inductive generalisation from frequently used functional, relational or structural combinations of grammatical categories, RL is in agreement with a broad coalition of functionalist and cognitive approaches to language (cf. *inter alia* Givón 1995: 175–300; Goldberg 1995: 50; Hudson 2007: 157; Langacker 1990, 2000: 5; Taylor 2002: 38, Van Valin and La Polla 1997: 69). The lexicon is posited as listing this category of metacoders in the form of stand-alone symbolic constructions possessing both lexical form and high level propositional meaning-content. In principle, therefore, the lexical listing of these inductive generalisations is no different from that of 'off-the-shelf' stock-standard phrases used in what Alison Wray (2002, 2008) terms formulaic language. Hudson describes such symbolic constructions in the following terms:

> In short, I believe that the syntax of a language does in fact consist of a very large number of constructions, each with its own peculiar interactions with other constructions and with lexical items. This means that the syntax is basically a messy collection of inductive generalisations on which we impose some order by generalisation, rather than a small set of very simple, very abstract and very elegantly interacting patterns on which the imperfections of language have imposed some mess. (Hudson 2007: 153)

The position taken by RL follows from the usage-based principles of Cognitive Grammar which posit that the declarative rules, constraints and guidelines of 'grammar' – or the coding system of a given language – are self-evidently derived by grammarians abstracting generalisations from observed instantiations in actual language usage (cf. Langacker 1987, 1991). It would then appear to be a fairly minor further step in the same direction to posit the outcomes of these processes of abstraction as mentally representable in terms of lexically listed metacoders involving cognitively entrenched generalisations in the respective internalised language knowledge databases of participants in interlocutory language usage.

The purpose of usage-based and in general cognitive approaches to modelling internalised language knowledge is thus seen as identifying the most comprehensive possible empirically adequate taxonomy of rules, constraints and schemas abstracted from observed instantiations of language use. This contrasts very sharply with the *a priori* approach of Chomskyans and other generativists who set out to prove theorems internal to some abstract model of grammar supposedly capable of describing in a descriptively or even explanatorily adequate manner the internalised systemic knowledge of language that drives the processes of interlocutory language usage (cf. Chomsky 1965). All the same, a measure of lexicalism is not uncommon in some formal approaches to the theory of grammar, such as Lexical Functional Grammar, Head-Driven Phrase Structure Grammar, Word Grammar, or even the Government and Binding Theory of Chomsky, and in particular his Minimalist Program, which takes a radically lexicalist approach to sentence generation (cf. respectively, Bresnan 2001: 302; Sag et al. 2003: 303; Hudson 2006; Chomsky 1981, 1995, and Jackendoff 2002: 109). CoP, and within it RL, is in fact thoroughly eclectic in borrowing from and standing on the shoulders of giants: the idea of the CoP Conceptualiser borrows from Jackendoff's Conceptual Semantics, the ideas of lexically listed construals and cognitively entrenched schemas are borrowed from Langacker's Cognitive Grammar, the idea of grammatical network construal and representation is borrowed from Hudson's Word Grammar and in some respects also from Connectionism, and the idea of thought as the locus of linguistic creativity and the allied concept of mentally represented encoding of the sentential components of utterances are borrowed from Fodor's Language of Thought Hypothesis (LoTH); cf. Fodor (1975, 1995, 1998, 2008).[23]

---

[23] At the same time, looked at from an RL perspective, Fodor unfortunately creates more problems than he solves by in effect conflating the Conceptualiser function and the encoding function.

5. Representing the Gestalt and cybernetic decision processes of language usage

The CoP model and within it RL represent, however, a radical departure from all these approaches of modelling grammar, in that Balint (2011) sets out to capture the Gestalt simultaneity of the conjoint and co-dependent operations of the system, process, form, content, context and cognitive enabling dimensions in interlocutory language usage, and within it of the lexical licensing operations governing the nature and utilisation of the grammatical code in encoding and parsing/decoding the sentential components of utterances. The complexity of this Gestalt is enormous; consequently formulae of extreme complexity are required to anywhere near adequately represent it within the framework of a formal model. While it would be quite beyond the scope of this paper to enter into any kind of a presentation of the dimensions of formalisation developed in Balint (2011), it is worth mentioning that a large toolkit of terms, functions and operators new to language modelling had to be identified and formally defined in order to develop the formulae necessary to formally represent the architecture and operations of the CoP model and that of RL within the context of CoP. A crucially important new domain of representation developed for purposes of formalisation was that of *functors*, formalisms that work as functions from a system point of view, but as operators from a process point of view.[24] The principal functors fall into four major categories:

1. *Intentional Drivers* utilised as process governors:

    1.1   Executive Intention;

    1.2   Communicative Intention;

    1.3   Informative Intention;

    1.4   Illocutionary Force;

    1.5   Illocutionary Point.

2. *Online Cybernetic Facilitators* utilised for steering the encoding and parsing/decoding processes:

    2.1   Online Goal-Directed Executive Process Control;

---

[24] The term 'functor' is not intended to be used here in any Carnapian sense or the way it has come to be used in algebraic topology or mathematical category theory.

2.2 Online Hypothesis Projection – as to the expectable end result on reaching the goal of the sentence encoding process under way;

2.3 Online Self-Feedback and Self-Correction by O;

2.4 Online Interlocutor Feedback and Self-Correction by O.

3. *Online Sentence Shapers* utilised to perform the core RL functions:

   3.1 Online Executive Decision;

   3.2 Online Database Search and Reference;

   3.3 Online Lemma Choice and Retrieval;

   3.4 Online Grammatical Licensing/Traffic Control of proposed lemma concatenations;

   3.5 Online Linearisation into signemes convertible via transemes into physemes, and vice versa;

   3.6 Online Motor Control of body functions physically forming, transmitting and receiving physemes.

4. *Online Cognitive Enablers*:

   4.1 Conceptualiser;

   4.2 Memory – long and short term;

   4.3 Awareness – and awareness of awareness;

   4.4 Attention;

   4.5 Perception/Recognition;

   4.6 Relevance Recognition and Utilisation;

   4.7 Coherence Recognition and Utilisation.

In addition, two further functors are also posited, albeit purely as enablers for the construction of complex Gestalt formulae: (1) a *metalanguage functor* indicating that what follows is in the metalanguage of one or another level of analysis of language form or meaning-content, and (2) a *drill-down functor* indicating that what follows is at a high level of analysis of language form or meaning-content which may be drilled-down into, in order to access lower levels or micro levels of analysis.

Figure 1 provides a summary overview of the structural and operational relationships between the key internalised knowledge databases postulated for CoP and for RL within CoP, where L1, L2 … Ln represents parallel databases for multilinguals using two or more languages.

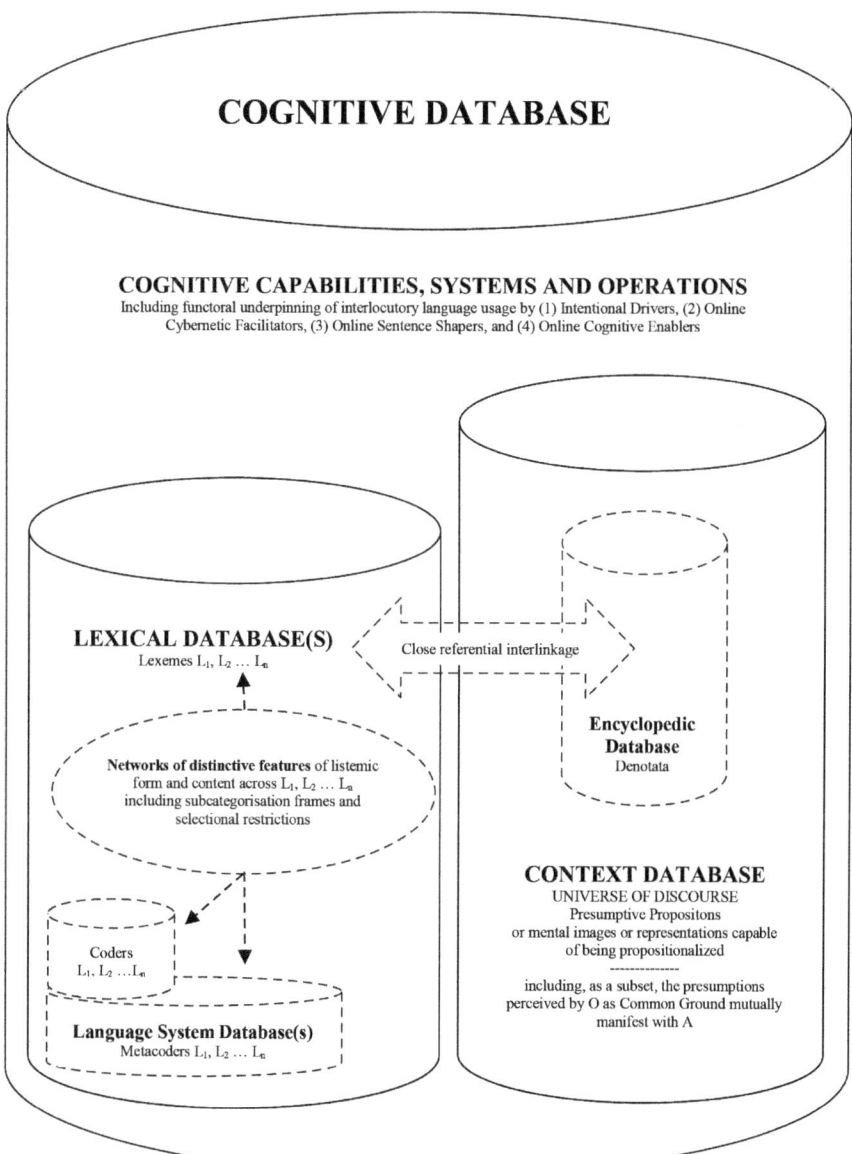

Figure 1. Summary overview.

From a procedural dynamics point of view, the lexical selection processes involved in utterance production and interpretation, and the goal-directed cybernetic/executive monitoring and steering process that control the decision processes involved in lexical and morphosyntactic selection, may be conceived as a *push* process in the case of utterance production and a *pull* process in the case of utterance interpretation. It is a *push* process in utterance production in the sense that a conceptualised message-content and its illocutionary point is being *pushed* by the communicative and informative intentions of O out towards A, whilst it is a *pull* process driven by the communicative and informative intentions of A, who is 'reeling in,' parsing, decoding and interpreting the utterance to construe a Reasonable Facsimile of the message-content intended by O. This push-pull dynamics is continuously monitored, steered and facilitated by the respective executive control (i.e., cybernetic) mechanisms and processes of O and A, both of which may be usefully viewed as operating in terms of the metaphor of a 'traffic control' process managing the choice, linearised concatenation and physical incrementalisation of mental representations of the PMPS constituents of the sentential components of utterances, with the traffic control process itself is in turn posited as being governed by the grammatical and semantic licensing properties of lexemes, coders and metacoders. The encoding process is thus conceived as progressively activating sequences of decision points along a decision tree, with binary accept/reject or 'go/no-go' gates operating where the choice is restricted to that between acceptable and unacceptable, and red-amber-green 'traffic lights' operating where the choice is between acceptable, borderline and unacceptable.

The traffic control points along the decision trees involved in lexical selection are posited as operating in terms of the lexical licensing system inferable from the grammatical and semantic analysis of the concatenations of physically manifested PMPS constituents in the sentential components of utterances. In other words, the decision trees involved in lexical selection are posited as operating in terms of the full set of metacoders and lexical co-occurrence features of listemic form and content inferable from the processes of interlocutory language usage. At each traffic control point in utterance encoding and parsing/decoding, the mental representation of the incrementally emerging utterance is therefore seen as being instantly checked – and if need be, appropriately adjusted – for simultaneous compliance with 1) the relevant grammatical metacoders, including cognitively entrenched schemas/templates or otherwise applying declarative rules and constraints on grammatical well-formedness; 2) the relevant semantic metacoders and lexical co-occurrence features governing semantic acceptability and co-location compatibility; 3) the skeleton meaning-content intended by the concatenation of explicitly encoded lexemes and coders selected to carry the semantically underdetermined logical form[25] of the sentential component of the utterance; 4) the intended full meaning-content of the explicitly encoded component of the utterance after the principal semantic completion and expansion processes[26] of referent assignment, indexical saturation, ellipsis unpacking, generality narrowing and contextual disambiguation (cf. Levinson 2000: 174–86); 5) the appropriateness and completeness of the inferential impacts and effects intended to be projected by the propositional interaction of the semantically fully determined logical form[27] of the sentential component with relevant common ground presumptions; and 6) the acceptability, appropriateness and felicity of the merger of the explicitly encoded and inferential meaning-content in terms of the norms and maxims of conversational dialogue[28] in interlocutory language usage.

6. Radical lexicalism in context

Ultimately, what the RL stance of CoP amounts to is a common-sense assertion to the effect that in encoding an intended message, the needs of

---

[25] The grammatically encoded meaning-content is taken as including all of the intensional, intensional entailment, grammatical, semantic compositional and propositional meaning-content components explicitly encoded into the PMPS constituents of the sentential component of the utterance, with some among the encoded PMPS constituents operating as referential and inferential place-markers or triggers intended to yield additional meaning-content through propositional interaction with contextual denotata or relevant common-ground presumptions mutually manifest to the interlocutors.

[26] cf. Bach (1994: 3ff.) for the processes of completion and expansion of the semantically underdetermined logical form of the sentential component of the utterance. The alternative terminology is enrichment and development, respectively, per Sperber and Wilson (1986/1995).

[27] In the literature, the term 'logical form' is used only in conjunction with the semantically underdetermined meaning-content of the sentential component of an utterance, as variously understood by competing schools of thought in syntax, semantics and pragmatics. It stands to reason however, that if the semantically underdetermined sentential meaning-content may be regarded as having a 'logical form', then so should the semantically fully determined sentential meaning-content, given that this latter is simply a referentially and inferentially completed and expanded variant of the former. As used here and hereinafter, the term 'semantically fully determined logical form' is thus shorthand for the merger representation (MR) of the full intensional, grammatical, referential and semantic compositional, as well as contextually interpretable inferential and propositional meaning-content components yielded after referential and inferential completion and expansion of the 'semantically underdetermined logical form' of the sentential component of an utterance.

[28] As formulated in Grice (1967a, 1967b, 1989) and in a sense complemented by the work of Searle (1965, 1969, 1975), and indeed that of Austin (1962), and elaborated on by subsequent post-Gricean schools of pragmatics.

how best to encapsulate the meaning-content of that message in language form will necessarily drive the choices of O in selecting a particular set of listemes and the mode of concatenating them into the sentential component of an intended utterance. The decision as to the particular grammatical form or morphosyntactic structure of the concatenation of mentally represented PMPS constituents forming the mental representation of the sentential component of an utterance is thus posited as *following* rather than preceding the decision on the message-content to be conveyed to A: in other words, RL posits that the 'what' of a message necessarily precedes, and is senior to, the 'how' of that message. Put simply, what is being asserted is that language form is merely a means to an end, and that it is the needs of the information content of an intended message that will necessarily drive the choice by O of the particular language form in which that information content is to be expressed. In other words, it is the semantic and pragmatic compositional needs of the meaning-content to be conveyed that will drive the choice of syntactic structure rather than the other way around, whether that syntactic structure is conceived and represented in hierarchical, networked or linear terms, or in some combination thereof. The RL stance is thus diametrically opposite to that of the Chomskyan and other syntactocentric positions that place the locus of what Chomsky terms 'lingusitic creativity' in a postulated syntactic module of internalised language knowledge, and in taking a position which is in some ways akin to Fodor's LoTH, which in effect locates the locus of linguistic creativity in what RL terms the Conceptualiser, it also goes some way beyond the position taken in Jackendoff (2002) which posits parallel domains of linguistic creativity in semantics and indeed in phonology as well:

> Traditional generative grammar assumes without argument that only syntax is 'generative', that is, that the combinatorial complexity of language arises entirely by virtue of its syntactic organization. This chapter presents a framework in which phonology, syntax, and semantics are equally generative. Syntax is thus only one of several parallel sources of grammatical organization. The generative components communicate with each other through 'interface' components; it is shown that these interfaces are of nontrivial complexity. It is also shown that many of the alternative frameworks for generative grammar share this sort of parallel organization. (Jackendoff 2002: 109)

At the same time, RL does appear to have aspects in common with the lexicalist dimension of Chomsky's Minimalist Program (MP), which Jackendoff (2002) describes in the following terms:

> The most recent variant, the Minimalist Program, responds to the attenuated roles of D-structure and S-structure in Government-Binding Theory by eliminating them altogether. Syntactic structures are built up by combining lexical items according to their intrinsic lexical constraints; the operation of combining lexical items into phrases and of combining phrases with each other is called Merge. (Jackendoff 2002: 111)

Interestingly, in Jackendoff's description of MP, Chomsky appears to conflate system and process, and does so, it would appear, seemingly unaware of the implication of this for the distinction between competence and performance. Where however RL and MP decisively part ways is in the following:

> Merge operations can be freely interspersed with derivational operations. However, at some point the derivation splits into two directions, one direction ('Spell-Out') yielding PF and the other LF. Despite all these changes, what is preserved is (a) that syntactic structure is the sole source of generativity in the grammar, and (b) that lexical items enter a derivation at the point where syntactic combination is taking place. (Jackendoff 2002: 111–2)

As a direct consequence of the Chomskyan revolution in the late fifties, the past six decades have seen a proliferation of a wide variety of formal, functional and cognitive approaches to the structure and operations of the grammatical component of internalised language knowledge. The only thing, however, that this plethora of approaches, models and paradigms of grammar prove is that there are many possible ways to slice, dice and formalise the rules, constraints and usage guidelines comprising the grammatical component of internalised language knowledge, as inferable from the empirical evidence adduced in interlocutory language usage. Recognition of the analysability and presentability of internalised grammar this way or that is, however, more a reflection of the ingenuity of the analyst than a necessarily valid indication of what is actually at work in the grammatical component of internalised language knowledge, and how that which is at work actually works, for it is hard to imagine that all explicit and implied approaches, models and paradigms of grammar are equally valid.

Logic tells us that given that the structure and operations of the cognitive faculty may safely be posited as being common to all humans, there can only be one grammatical paradigm at work, however Protean it might be in its manifestations in thousands of human languages, just as there is clearly one only paradigm at work in the natural sciences, however multi-faceted that paradigm may be.[29] After all, imagine the insanely chaotic nonsense of having as many explicitly and implicitly competing models and paradigms about the nature of the physical world in the natural sciences, as there are in linguistics about the nature of the grammatical component of internalised language knowledge! It is to be hoped that CoP, and within it RL, can go some way in providing evaluative criteria toward a cognitively plausible model or paradigm of the grammatical component of internalised language knowledge – however eclectically sourced and construed – that would validly represent the way the governance of the encoding/production and decoding/interpretation of utterances actually works.

References

Allan, Keith. 2001. *Natural Language Semantics*. Oxford: Blackwell.
Allan, Keith. 2009. *The Western Classical Tradition in Linguistics*. Second (expanded) edition. London: Equinox
Austin, J.L. 1962. *How to Do Things with Words*. Oxford: Clarendon Press.
Bach, Kent. 1994. Conversational Impliciture. *Mind and Language* 9: 124–62.
Balint, Mike. 2011. *Utterance and Discourse in Context: A Process Model of the Architectural and Operational Gestalt of Interlocutory Language Usage*. PhD thesis, Monash University.
Barlow, Michael and Suzanne Kemmer. 2000. *Usage-Based Models of Language*. Stanford, CA: CSLI Publications.
Botha, Rudolf P. 1989. *Challenging Chomsky: The Generative Garden Game*. Oxford: Basil Blackwell.
Bresnan, Joan. 2001. *Lexical-Functional Syntax*. Malden, MA: Blackwell.
Cann, Ronnie, Ruth Kempson and Lutz Marten. 2005. *The Dynamics of Language: An Introduction*. Amsterdam: Elsevier.
Chomsky, Noam. 1965. *Aspects of the Theory of Syntax*. Cambridge, MA: MIT Press.
Chomsky, Noam. 1981. *Lectures on Government and Binding*. Dordrecht: Foris.

---

[29] This was of course the main thrust of the reasoning that set Chomsky out on the trajectory he has been following for the past seven decades, though unfortunately the simplistic, essentially context-free and therefore cognitively implausible syntactic models of grammar that he has serially proposed in futile attempts to square the circle, have never really had a chance of surviving close empirical scrutiny.

Chomsky, Noam. 1995. *The Minimalist Program*. Cambridge, MA: The MIT Press.

Fodor, Jerry A. 1975. *The Language of Thought*. Cambridge, MA: Harvard University Press.

Fodor, Jerry A. 1995. *The Elm and the Expert: Mentalese and its Semantics*. Cambridge, MA: The MIT Press.

Fodor, Jerry A. 1998. *Concepts: Where Cognitive Science Went Wrong*. New York: Oxford University Press.

Fodor Jerry A. 2008. *LOT 2: The Language of Thought Revisited*. New York: Oxford University Press.

Frege, Gottlob. 1892. Über Sinn und Bedeutung. *Zeitschrift für Philosophie und philosophische Kritik* 100: 25–50.

Frege, Gottlob. 1897/1969. *Nachgelassene Schriften*. Hamburg: Felix Meiner.

Givón, Talmy. 1995. *Functionalism and Grammar*. Amsterdam: John Benjamins.

Goldberg, Adele, 1995. *Constructions: A Construction Grammar Approach to Argument Structure*. Chicago: The University of Chicago Press.

Grice, H. Paul. 1967a. Logic and conversation. In: Peter Cole and Jerry L. Morgan (eds), *Syntax and Semantics. Vol 3: Speech Acts*. New York: Academic, 41–58.

Grice, H. Paul. 1967b. Further notes on logic and conversation. In: Peter Cole (ed.), *Syntax and Semantics. Vol 9: Pragmatics*. New York: Academic, 113–27.

Grice, H. Paul. 1989. *Studies in the Way of Words*. Cambridge, MA: Harvard University Press.

Harman, G. 1980. Two quibbles about analyticity and psychological reality. *The Behaviour and Brain Sciences* 3: 21–2.

Hawkings, Steven and Roger Penrose. 1996. *The Nature of Space and Time*. Princeton, NJ: Princeton University Press.

Hudson, Richard. 2006. Word grammar. In: Keith Brown (ed.), *Encyclopedia of Language & Linguistics, Second Edition. Vol. 13*. Oxford: Elsevier, 633–42.

Hudson, Richard. 2007. *Language Networks: The New Word Grammar*. Oxford: Oxford University Press.

Itkonen, Esa. 1974. *Linguistics and Metascience*. Studia Philosophica Turkuensia Fasc II. Kokemäki: Societas Philosophica et Phaenomenologica Finlandae.

Jackendoff, Ray. 2002. *Foundations of Language: Brain, Meaning, Grammar, Evolution*. Oxford: Oxford University Press.

Jaszczolt, Kasia M. 2005. *Default Semantics: Foundations of a Compositional Theory of Acts of Communication*. Oxford: Oxford University Press.

Langacker, Ronald W. 1987. *Foundations of Cognitive Grammar. Vol. 1: Theoretical Prerequisites*. Stanford, CA: Stanford University Press.

Langacker, Ronald W. 1990. The rule controversy: A cognitive grammar approach. *CRL Newsletter* 4 (2). UCLA, San Diego.

Langacker, Ronald W. 1991. *Foundations of Cognitive Grammar. Vol. 2: Descriptive Application*. Stanford, CA: Stanford University Press.

Langacker, Ronald W. 2000. A dynamic usage-based model. In: Michael Barlow and Suzanne Kremmer (eds), *Usage-Based Models of Language*. Stanford, CA: CSLI Publications, 1–63.

Levelt, Willem J.M. 1989. *Speaking: From Intention to Articulation*. Cambridge, MA: The MIT Press.

Levinson, Stephen C. 2000. *Presumptive Meanings: The Theory of Generalised Conversational Implicature*. Cambridge, MA: The MIT Press.

Markman, Arthur B. 1999. *Knowledge Representation*. Mahwah, NJ: L. Erlbaum.

Sag, Ivan A., Thomas Wasow and Emily M. Bender. 2003. *Syntactic Theory: A Formal Introduction*. Stanford, CA: CSLI Publications.

Searle, John R. 1965. What is a speech act? In: Max Black (ed.), *Philosophy in America*. Cornell, NY: Cornell University Press, 615–28.

Searle, John R. 1969. *Speech Acts*. Cambridge: Cambridge University Press.

Searle, John R. 1975. Indirect speech acts. In: Peter Cole and Jerry L. Morgan (eds), *Syntax and Semantics. Vol 3: Speech Acts*. New York: Academic Press, 59–82.

Sperber, Dan and Deirdre Wilson. 1986/1995. *Relevance: Communication and Cognition*. Oxford: Blackwell.

Taylor, John R. 2003. *Cognitive Grammar*. Oxford: Oxford University Press.

Van Valin, Robert D. and Randy J. LaPolla. 1997. *Syntax: Structure, Meaning, Function*. Cambridge: Cambridge University Press.

Wray, Alison. 2002. *Formulaic Language and the Lexicon*. Cambridge: Cambridge University Press.

Wray, Alison. 2008. *Formulaic Language: Pushing the Boundaries*. Oxford: Oxford University Press.

Chapter 16

ARTICLES REVISITED

A VIEW FROM EXTENDED VANTAGE THEORY

Adam Głaz

Marie Curie-Skłodowska University

Off-mainstream cognitive linguistics includes Vantage Theory (esp. MacLaury 1997/2011), a model of categorization that, with adaptations and modifications, has been applied in several analyses of language. One major proposal is Allan's (2002) VT2, constructed to account for the English number, another is Głaz's (2012) Extended Vantage Theory (EVT), designed to model the use of the English articles. The latter is also the focus of the present paper.

Non-standard and surprising article uses are claimed to also have cognitive motivation, since it is speakers' cognitions that are responsible for the construction of points of view – cf. Allan's (2010) discussion of the issue in the light of linguistic relativity. The theoretical EVT framework is sketched and a classification of article uses in terms of EVT is offered. EVT thus continues MacLaury's line of reasoning about language and cognition but adds to it a 'toolbox' for analyzing a specific aspect of language, a hopeful incentive for further developments.

1. The problem

A viable account of English articles, their semantics, uses and systemic relationships, must reconcile two apparently contradictory requirements. On the one hand, a systemic perspective, focusing on oppositions and contrasts, cannot adequately deal with the more creative uses that apparently breach the system. On the other hand, in an idiosyncratic account of the creative uses, one does not want to lose what, after all, *is* systemic and contrastive.

The present account, a more condensed version of the proposal fully developed in Głaz (2012), attempts to meet the two requirements in a descriptive model that seeks cognitive motivation behind both systemic and innovative, and sometimes apparently illogical or inconsistent, uses of English articles. The scope of the study, however, only allows me to present a skeletal framework of the account, mainly concentrating on what is systemic, and the interested reader is referred to the above-mentioned monograph for a more comprehensive picture.

The model I am proposing is called Extended Vantage Theory (henceforth EVT), a modified version of Robert E. MacLaury's (e.g., 1995, 1997/2011, 2002) Vantage Theory (henceforth VT). After presenting the basics of VT, I will proceed to lay out its extended variant, and then to an analysis of selected aspects of article usage.

2. Vantage Theory in brief

2.1. Introductory comments

Between 1978 and 1981, Robert E. MacLaury and his associates, equipped with a set of Munsell colour chips (see Figure 1), interviewed around 900 speakers of 116 indigenous Mesoamerican languages.[1] When certain regularities were identified in the data, it proved impossible to explain them by means of the models available at the time, such as the classical account in terms of necessary and sufficient conditions, Zadeh's (1965) fuzzy sets or Rosch's (e.g., 1975, 1978) prototype approach. Thus arose Vantage Theory (VT): it postulates that categories are constructed as *vantages*, or points of view. These, however, are not mere locations for seeing but complex cognitive procedures constructed as arrangements of mental coordinates.

In the interviews, the informants were asked to apply three kinds of procedure: *naming, focus selection* and *mapping*. In *naming*, the informant is shown each of the Munsell chips in isolation and in random order, and asked to provide its name. The names are recorded and the chips are then arranged into the full array, which shows the ranges of colour categories. In *focus selection*, the informant is asked to choose the best example (focus) for each term he/she has used in the naming task. Finally, in *mapping*, the informant is shown the arranged set (without any of the categories marked on it) and asked to put a grain of rice on every chip he/she would name X, then Y etc. The boundaries of category ranges are delineated.

The results of the threefold procedure can be surprising. For example, the naming and mapping ranges of a category need not coincide, the focus of a particular term may fall on the area named with another term, or two terms can be used in reference to the same category by the same speaker

---

[1] The fieldwork was conducted as the Mesoamerican Color Survey, part of the more comprehensive World Color Survey, and its findings were later enriched with data from other language families.

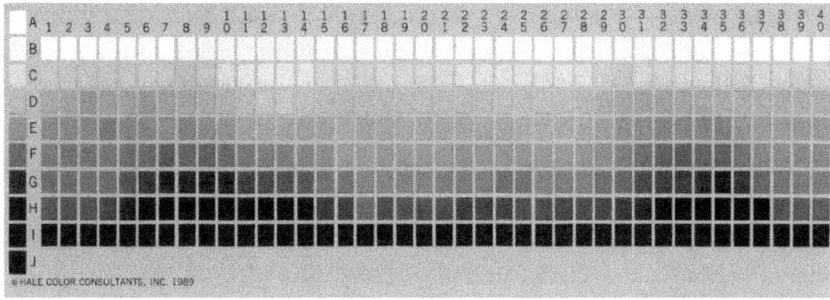

Figure 1. The Munsell chart or array

320 colourful chips arranged in rows according to hue (here cut in the red hue area) and in columns according to brightness, at maximum saturation. The additional column on the left contains ten achromatic colours from white at the top through shades of grey to black at the bottom.

© Hale Color Consultants, William N. Hale, Jr., reproduced with permission.

during a single interview. MacLaury concluded that conceptualisers look at a category from different points of view, which is performed by analogy to the way they orient themselves in space-time.

In space-time, a person locates him- or herself by plotting the spatial axes of up–down, front–back and left–right, unified into a single body of reference, with the temporal coordinate manifested as motion. The coordinates define the person's spatiotemporal location, or a series of locations through which the person progresses, as described by Einstein's (1920: ch. 3) example of a rock dropped from a moving train: for someone on the train, its trajectory is straight but for someone standing by the track it is parabolic (cf. MacLaury 1997/2011: 143). From the shape of the trajectory one can deduce the position of the viewer. Or consider locating an object in space through a series of figure-ground arrangements; eg in order to understand *The newspaper is on the living room table*, one *zooms in* by locating 'a living room in relation to the house design, the table in relation to the living room, and the newspaper in relation to the table' (MacLaury 1997/2011: 139). The reverse procedure is called *zooming out/ panning out*. Importantly, doing so need not involve physical movement: the conceptualiser may zoom in or pan out mentally. Thus, the processes of zooming in and out involve coordinates as mental constructs, and it is on this basis that one can postulate the existence of an analogy between space-time and categorisation. As a result of the subconsciously performed analogy, a conceptualiser establishes *inherently fixed coordinates*, characteristic of a given domain (in the domain of colour these are typically hue, less frequently brightness, and saturation as a theoretical possibility), and *inherently mobile coordinates* of reciprocally balanced emphases on *similarity* or *difference*. In the process of zooming in and out, a coordinate may change its status from fixed to mobile for immediate purposes, though retaining its inherent, 'default' value. A more precise formulation of the correspondences between space-time and categorisation (*equivalences* in MacLaury's terminology) is offered in MacLaury (2013a) and Głaz (2010).

2.2. Vantages

In the colour domain, when a person constructs a hue-based category called blue, the process starts with selecting the focus (a blue hue), after which other stimuli are incorporated into the category's range. As long as they are deemed similar to the focus, the range will expand; once they start being viewed as different from the focus, the range will be curtailed (see Figure 2).

Levels	Fixed Coordinates	Mobile Coordinates	Entailments
1	Bu	S	focus, range
2	S	D	breadth, margin

Figure 2. The modelling of the BLUE category in VT.

The inherently fixed Bu (for *blue*) is juxtaposed on Level 1 with the inherently mobile attention to similarity (S). Then, on Level 2, S is 'fixated': its status changes from new to old information, allowing for new information to be added. This is analogous to the zooming in process while locating the newspaper (where the table first functions as new information relative to the room, but once located, it is treated as known and capable of serving as a reference point for locating the paper). The new information on Level 2 is the attention to difference (D) at the expense of attention to similarity. These processes are hidden cognitions, whose existence is postulated on the basis of observable linguistic behaviours called *entailments* (see Figure 2). Crucially, the value of the whole arrangement derives from *all* of its levels as a coherent whole, even though only one level is focused on at any single moment.

The BLUE category thus modelled is characterised by only one arrangement of coordinates, one point of view or *vantage*. But there may be more than one, each being referred to by a separate term, as in COOL (usually blue-green) or WARM (usually yellow-red) categories in a number of world languages. Consider the COOL category in Zulu (the Bantu group, Niger-Congo family), in Figure 3.

Entailments	Dominant Vantage *hlaza*		Levels	Recessive Vantage *kosazana*		Entailments
	FC	MC		FC	MC	
focus, range	Bu	S	1	Gn	D	focus, margin
	↙			↙		
breadth	S	Gn	2	D	Bu	curtailment
	↙			↙		
margin	Gn	D	3	Bu	S	range

Figure 3. The modelling of the Zulu COOL category in VT.

The category is conceptualised as two vantages, called *dominant* and *recessive*. The dominant vantage starts with a blue focus and the stronger attention to similarity endows it with a wider range. At Level 2, S is fixated and the new mobile coordinate Gn (green) is introduced. This is in turn fixated at Level 3, when difference (D) enters the equation. In other words, as a result of the appearance of the green hue in the conceptualiser's field of attention, the role of similarity weakens to make way for difference: the vantage is endowed with a margin. The recessive vantage arises through a reversal of the coordinates: Gn is the primary fixed coordinate, while D is emphasised first and more than S. As a result, the margin of the vantage is established before its range: the range 'fills in' the portion of the colour spectrum between Gn and the margin thus instituted. The blue hue is introduced late as being weakly similar to the green starting point. The COOL category is an assembly of its coordinates plus their arrangement, or simply the sum of its vantages.

2.3. Cognitive distance and coordinate strength

In what follows, i.e., my elaboration of VT into a model for describing English articles, called Extended Vantage Theory (EVT), I will not be capitalising on several otherwise important constructs proposed in the theory as originally formulated, such as the variants of the dominant-recessive pattern, the universal width of purview, the spotlight effect, frames, stress, or detached vs. engaged viewpoints.[2] Instead, greater attention will be paid to two notions that figure in EVT in a more direct manner: (i) the contraction and protraction of cognitive distance and (ii) the strength of coordinates.

Attention to similarity causes contraction of the cognitive distance between the items being conceptualised: the items are brought closer together. With very strong attention to S, they become indistinguishable and may be treated as a homogeneous mass. Attention to difference, on the other hand, yields protraction of the distance, and the objects being conceptualised can be viewed as discrete entities.

But the degrees of attention to, or emphasis on, S or D produce different effects depending on their location in the vantage architecture. They result in what we will call, somewhat modifying MacLaury's terminology, *non-discriminatory*, *analytic* and *synthetic-systemic viewing modes*, or *modes of conceptualisation*. Figure 4 illustrates this (the double SS or DD symbols mark greater attention to a particular coordinate at the expense of the other).

	Dominant Vantage		Recessive Vantage	
non-discrimination	SS	1	DD	(autonomous) analysis
(grounded) analysis	D	2	S	systemic synthesis

Figure 4. Viewing modes/modes of conceptualisation arranged as two vantages.

Greater emphasis on similarity on Level 1 of the dominant vantage results in non-discrimination: the entities being observed are collapsed into a homogeneous mass. Against this background, attention to difference on Level 2 produces analysis, so that some of the entities can be viewed as distinct, though only in a coarse-grained fashion. The recessive vantage, in turn, starts with greater attention to difference, which results in significant protraction

---

[2] Note the confusing terminology: in VT, rather unfortunately, *viewpoints* are not the same as *points of view*. A *point of view* is a vantage (a 'take' on a category, in the sense specified), whereas a *viewpoint* rests on the degree of subjectivity (engagement)/objectivity (detachment) of viewing, from the most engaged (VP-1) to the most detached (VP-4). It is perhaps too late now to change this terminological awkwardness. Confusion sometimes arises even in MacLaury's own work. For a discussion of viewpoints, see MacLaury (1997/2011: 278ff., 2002: 528–9, 2013b; or Głaz 2012: 46–8).

of the cognitive distance between the objects within the conceptualiser's purview: this is analytic viewing. Then, on Level 2, attention to similarity takes over and contracts the distance again. But now the contraction is not so radical and, rather than being viewed as a homogeneous mass, the objects are synthesised or linked into 'an abstraction, a theory, or a systemic understanding' (MacLaury 1997/2011: 291). In other words, the dominant vantage is a progression from non-discriminatory to analytic viewing, while the recessive vantage progresses from analytic to synthetic-systemic viewing. Note that the two analytic viewing modes, on Level 1 of the dominant vantage and on Level 2 of the recessive vantage, are not the same. The former operates against the background of the Level 1 non-discriminatory mode, while the latter is the initial step in vantage construction. I will call them *grounded* and *autonomous analysis*, respectively. Figure 5a to 5d should help visualise the above.

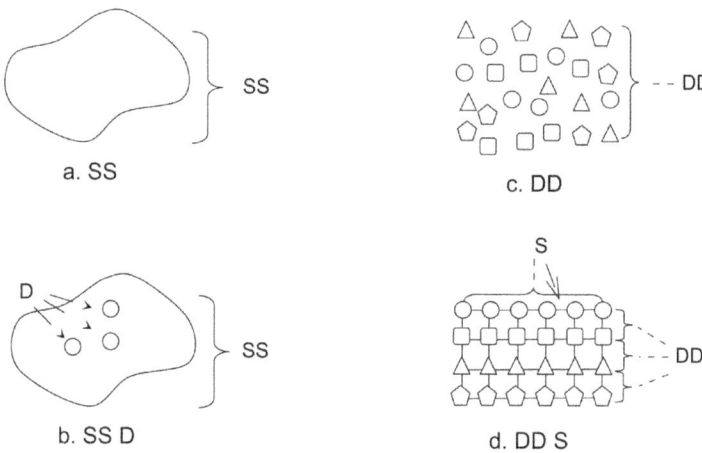

Figure 5. Viewing modes and vantages.

(a) Non-discrimination; (b) the dominant vantage, analysis grounded in non-discrimination; (c) autonomous analysis; (d) the recessive vantage, synthetic-systemic viewing against analytic viewing.

Moreover, apart from greater attention to, or emphasis on, either S or D, each coordinate can bear different *strengths* regardless of its position in the vantage architecture. That is, irrespective of which coordinate receives greater attention, each of the two can be of *neutral, augmented* or *reduced* strength. Attention to either S or D is thus tantamount to selecting it as the primary mobile coordinate for a vantage, whereas its strength is the amount of cognitive effort that the coordinate attracts, regardless of whether it has been selected or not.[3] I will mark coordinate strengths with nothing (regular strength), a '+' (for augmented strength or simply 'strong' S/D) and a '-' (for reduced strength or 'weak' S/D).

Four viewing modes in two vantages, coupled with three values of coordinate strength, yield twenty-four theoretically possible conceptualisations, a full list of which can be found in Głaz (2012: 164–7). Of these, eleven have been identified as underlying the conceptualisations behind the use of English articles (the remaining ones may be internally contradictory or, indeed, may emerge in the determiner systems of other languages, pending further research) – see Table 1.

Table 1. Conceptualisations underlying the use of English articles.

SS	regular-strength non-discrimination
SS+	strong non-discrimination
SS-	weak non-discrimination
SS D	the default dominant vantage: regular-strength non-discrimination followed by regular-strength grounded analysis
SS+ D-	strong non-discrimination followed by weak grounded analysis
SS+ D	strong non-discrimination followed by regular-strength grounded analysis
SS- D	weak non-discrimination followed by regular-strength grounded analysis
SS- D+	weak non-discrimination followed by strong grounded analysis
DD S	the default recessive vantage: regular-strength autonomous analysis followed by regular-strength synthesis
DD+ S-	strong autonomous analysis followed by weak synthesis
DD- S+	weak autonomous analysis followed by strong synthesis

Exemplification of how these are realised in the use of English articles will be provided in section 4 below. I will now summarise another modification of VT as originally formulated, one that has contributed substantially to the development of my EVT model, if not in specific solutions, then in its general approach. That modification is Allan's (2002) VT2.

---

[3] It is a pity that strength is not listed in the glossary to MacLaury (1997/2011), despite its crucial role in the internal differentiation of the dominant–recessive pattern (cf. for example MacLaury 1997/2011: 149–51, 2002: 504–5, 2013b; Głaz 2012: 36–7).

3. Inspiration from Keith Allan's VT2

There have been a few daring attempts to render VT more operational in linguistic analyses. Mention can be made of Preston's (1993) reformulation of internal vantage architecture and the process of constructing 'vantage chains', to a large extent followed by Fabiszak (2010), applied by these two authors to the analysis of conversational discourse. However interesting these attempts are, I have found more inspiration for my EVT framework in Allan's (2002) VT2, based on the distinction between aggregation and separation in conceptualising.

Allan's work is an account of some aspects of the category of number in English. The author considers pluralising expressions of the type *three giraffes* or *the herd are* vs. the collectivising ones of the type *three giraffe* or *the herd is*, or *coffee/wine* vs. *coffees/wines, four pieces of cake is* vs. *four pieces of cake are* and the like. These are different points of view (vantages), modelled as tables composed of frames, each of which includes a synthetic and an analytic subvantage. Synthesis results from attention to similarity or aggregation (a subvantage of the dominant type), analysis from attention to difference or separation (a subvantage of the recessive type). Or, more appropriately, the synthetic subvantage involves zooming in from attention to similarity (or aggregation) to analysis, while the analytic subvantage involves zooming out from attention to difference (or separation) to synthesis.

In contrast to standard VT, Allan's analytic subvantage is a successor to (not simultaneous with) the synthetic subvantage, and a reverse step from an analytic to a synthetic subvantage produces a new frame of conceptualisation, an element within a table. Thus, analytic and synthetic are subvantages and a vantage is 'the array of frames that would be represented within a table' (Allan 2002: 688) – cf. Figure 6. It takes the whole table, with all its conceptualising steps, to represent a complex conceptualisation like *three giraffe* or *three giraffes* (the formal-logic notation Allan uses need not concern us here).

But how is the difference between VT's dominant and recessive outlooks interpreted in VT2? Are the collectivised NPs (*three giraffe*) recessive because they are marked, or are they dominant because they express non-differentiation? Allan does not give a definitive answer but is more prone to treating the collectivised, unpluralised cases as recessive. This is at odds with the principle of constructing a simpler vantage with a simpler label for things more common. In the *giraffe/giraffes* case, it is the pluralised *giraffes* that calls for a longer and more complex table of frames, which suggests markedness (Allan 2002: 688–90).[4] Consider the form *fishes*, which, although morphologically perfectly regular, is a less frequent, contextually restricted and, therefore, marked option of the plural of *fish*. This lack of a consistent pattern in the arrays of conceptualisation for each of the two VT vantage types is a weakness of VT2 its author readily acknowledges.

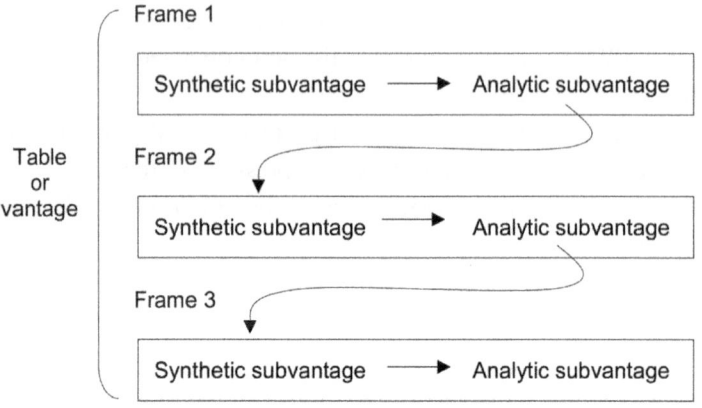

Figure 6. Architecture of a Table in Allan's (2002) VT2.

Regrettably, VT2 was not further elaborated into a theory of broader applicability. Although my Extended Vantage Theory does not follow VT2 directly, Allan's idea of capitalising on the notions of analytic vs. synthetic viewing proved seminal for its development.

4. EVT: A skeletal analysis

I will now proceed to exemplify the conceptualisations captured in the form of the EVT formulae with instances of article use. The reader is advised to bear in mind, however, that this is of necessity a skeletal framework and cannot make pretences to comprehensiveness – gaps, simplifications and inadequacies are inevitable. My aim here is predominantly to show that EVT is, hopefully, a promising model with descriptive and explanatory potential,

---

[4] The table for *three giraffe* consists of three frames, each being composed of a synthetic subvantage followed by an analytic subvantage. The table for *three giraffes* has one more conceptualisation frame. The difference results from the fact that the conceptualisation of the collectivised *giraffe* as opposed to the individualised *giraffes* does not involve analysis: the animals are viewed as constituting a homogeneous set. In the case of *giraffes*, in turn, the overt plural marker -*s* is an expression of analytic viewing (subvantage) in a distinct frame.

and a fuller account with a more in-depth justification can be found in Głaz (2012).

Also, for convenience and better logic, the formulae are discussed and exemplified below in a somewhat different order than that in their list in section 2.3 above.

SS   regular-strength non-discrimination

The regular-strength non-discriminatory mode (SS) is associated with article-less singular mass nouns. Typical examples are *bread*, *music* or *honesty*, which portray progressively more abstract entities conceptualised in a non-discriminatory fashion as undifferentiated, homogeneous masses. When the speaker maximally emphasises similarity, whatever is being conceptualised becomes conflated into an indistinguishable, homogenous substance (bread, water etc.). By extension, the process also pertains to less tangible entities (music, time) or to abstract ones (honesty, democracy etc.). Thus, 'mass' is used here in a technical sense: it is a way of conceptualising or *con*ceiving of, rather than merely *per*ceiving, an entity (where 'entity' need not be something accessible through the senses). This account follows Langacker's (1991: 18) notion of a mass noun profiling a region bounded in its domain of instantiation. The latter can be physical space, but also time or a social or abstract space.

SS+   strong non-discrimination

In some usages, however, a greater cognitive effort is necessary on the part of the conceptualiser to arrive at the homogeneous concept of mass. Such is the case in (1) and, for a different reason, in (2) below:

(1)   How to Run for *President* of the United States.
      (http://www.ehow.com/how_2165709_run-president-united-states.html; accessed 3 January 2011) SS+

(2)   After the accident, there was *cat* all over the road.
      (Taylor 1993: 218 and many other sources) SS+

The augmented value of SS+ is necessary because presidents are individuals not normally conceptualised as masses. The conceptualiser has thus to overcome the conventionalised conceptualisation of an individual and recategorise the image into a mass-like homogeneity (the role of president, i.e., an implication that all presidents have basically the same functions).⁵ In (2), in turn, extra cognitive effort is required to overcome the conventionalised meaning associated with the word *cat*. Although several parallel usages enjoy a conventionalised 'item' or 'mass' status (e.g., (*a*) *chicken*), *cat* does not. If *chicken* in the sense of 'meat' is SS, *cat* requires an extra cognitive effort, hence SS+.

Additional cognitive effort in attending to similarity also underlies collective nouns such as *audience*: the effort is necessary to override the real-life awareness of 'plurality' and portray it as a mass: SS+. Naturally, *audience* is usually used with the indefinite or definite article (*an/the audience*) and may also be used in the plural ((*the*) *audiences*). A full account of those in EVT terms is offered in Głaz (2012: 241–2); for *an audience* cf. below.

SS-   weak non-discrimination

Reduced strength of similarity (SS-) is typical of plural usages such as *lions, Italians, fractals, medieval mystery plays* or *boyfriends*. These are not fully homogeneous because they are conceptualisations of sets consisting of individual items. In other words, although *lions* reflects a conceptualisation of lions which are all 'the same' (hence SS), they are not conflated into an internally undifferentiated 'mass' (the *–s* suffix, hence the weaker SS-).

In all of the cases above (SS, SS+ or SS-) no specific item is isolated as a distinct entity, hence no role is attributed to D. Once D enters the scene, a 'loose', 'free-floating' mode becomes a fully-fledged vantage.

SS D   the default dominant vantage: regular-strength non-discrimination followed by regular-strength grounded analysis

When the initial non-discriminatory viewing mode (SS) is followed by a degree of emphasis on difference (D) a portion or an aspect of an otherwise homogeneous mass is being identified or isolated. Thus, instead of the homogeneous *bread, music* or *English* (language), there are usages as in examples (3) to (5):

(3)   Panforte, the traditional fruit cake of Sienna, is neither a conventional cake nor *a bread* but pressed dried fruits with cinnamon, coriander, cloves, nutmeg and white pepper.

---

⁵   Referring to German material, Porzig (1924) sees here a substantivising force of the article. In *er war König*, the last word has an adjectival nature (what *kind* of person was he?), whereas in *er war der König* it is a genuine substantive (the king of a specific country) (p. 148, quoted after Bühler 1990 [1934]: 345). But of course, Bühler notes (p. 353), substantivisation need not involve an article, as in *Envying is petty*.

(BNC simple search, http://bnc.bl.uk/, H06 2628: *BBC Good Food*, London: Redwood Publishing Company, 1991; accessed 4 November 2010) SS D

(4) The 1960s saw some hectic Australian searching for *a music* that was 'ours', not 'theirs'.

(BNC simple search, http://bnc.bl.uk/, ABE 627: *The Economist*, 1991; accessed 4 November 2010) SS D

(5) Sean's is *an English* full of the lilt of the Western Isles. (Allan 1980: 559, his example (73)) SS D

These are all cases of the default variant of the dominant vantage, SS D: a homogeneous mass (SS) constitutes the background for an isolation of a 'kind' of bread, music, English etc. as a result of analytic thinking (D).

SS+ D-   *strong non-discrimination followed by weak grounded analysis*

An augmented value of attention to S followed by a reduced value of attention to D is represented in example (6):

(6) I'd always been interested in ancient history and I'd always wanted to write *a historical novel*.

(Greenbaum 1996: 244) SS+ D-

The conceptualiser does not select any particular member of the set of novels but refers to the nature of the set (hence SS is augmented as SS+). Accordingly, the role of D- is not to isolate a specific member of the respective set, but merely to distinguish the set from other sets, i.e. to endow it with a boundary. I am following here Epstein's (2001: 357) idea that 'NPs that designate roles are used to refer to a fixed property, not to a particular individual.' Consider also example (7):

(7) *A 77-year-old Nebraskan* who lives in a house he bought in 1958 and reimburses his company for personal telephone calls might make an unlikely candidate to be the most revered capitalist of our day. Yet that's what Warren Buffett is.

(*Time* 171–20, 19 May 2008, p. 19) SS+ D-

Although a specific individual is mentioned, the description focuses on the person's characteristics, such as his age or habits. Alternatively, in a somewhat forced interpretation, one might claim that the use occasions an idiosyncratic category of '77-year-old Nebraskans who live...' etc, with Warren Buffett as its one and only member. In either case, the formula is SS+ D-, with the augmented strength of the properties of the person or the relevant set.

A similar conceptualisation takes place in this excerpt from an SF novel (reference is made to the mother of the main protagonist):

(8) But in the world not of an atevi lord's whimsy, one had to deal with *a mother* who didn't answer the phone, didn't answer telegrams, didn't answer messages on the island-wide system, and hadn't been in communication with Toby since his message.
(C. J. Cherryh, Invader, Legend Books, 1995: 245–6) SS+ D-

SS+ D   strong non-discrimination followed by regular-strength grounded analysis

It has been suggested above that the 'pure', 'articleless' conceptualisation *audience* requires an augmented value of emphasis on similarity to override the real-life awareness of 'plurality' and portray it as a mass: SS+. The indefinite article usage, *an audience*, results from conceptually selecting a portion or a kind of that mass (through analysis-entailing emphasis of difference), which is a variant of the dominant vantage: SS+ D.

SS- D   weak non-discrimination followed by regular-strength grounded analysis

Example (9) is another variant of the dominant vantage: SS- D:

(9) I'm looking for *a millionaire*, she says, but I don't see many around.
(Biber et al. 1999: 260) SS- D

Reference is made here to a random member (D) of the set of millionaires (SS-): no member is viewed as being more salient than any other. Alternatively, the noun preceded by *a/an* may be qualified by an attribute and/or a modifying clause (example (10)):

(10) Although I publish quite a lot I discovered a couple of years ago that no mainstream publisher wanted to publish *a negative analysis of the British monarchy that I've written*.
(Greenbaum 1996: 244) SS- D

The speaker adopts here the point of view of the hearer and/or the publishers. The status of the relative clause *that I've written* is interesting: even though it is a defining clause, a publisher is more likely to focus on the characteristics of the analysis as such, rather than on its being a specific work by a specific author. Note also the use of the Present Perfect (*I've written*) where one would have expected Past Perfect (*had written*, as prior to *I discovered a couple of years ago*). The Present Perfect suggests that the analysis referred to has the permanent characteristic of being 'negative' (i.e., of being that *kind* of work), and that the characteristic still obtains, as opposed to the temporally more limited Past Perfect reference. Hence, SS- D.

SS- D+ weak non-discrimination followed by strong grounded analysis

The next variant of the dominant vantage is the more analytic SS- D+, typical of those usages with the indefinite article in which the noun phrase has an indefinite but specific reference.[6] Consider example (11):

(11) She has just bought *a new car*.
       (Huddleston and Pullum 2002: 372) SS- D+

The conceptualiser 'zooms in' on a specific car and not any car: she owns this particular vehicle.[7] The process is induced by an augmented D+, which operates against the weakly homogeneous SS- background (a set of cars). But D+ is nevertheless too weak for the specific item to become unambiguously identified by means of the definite article – this is what happens in the examples to follow.

Before considering these examples, however, it is perhaps worth recalling that the role of S in the recessive vantage is different from its role in the dominant vantage. In the dominant vantage (level 1), attention to SS entails non-discrimination and homogeneity. In the recessive vantage, S is attended to on Level 2, i.e. against an already analytic background. Therefore, its strength is insufficient to produce non-discrimination; instead, it links the individual elements of the scene into a coherent class or system, but without conflating them into a mass. This is the synthetic-systemic viewing mode.

---

[6] Bill Sullivan proposes calling these unspecified but definite (p.c.), or unspecified but particular (Sullivan 2013). Sullivan agrees that it is somewhat counter-intuitive to refer to indefinite NPs as having definite reference, but that is because the terminology is flawed from the start: indefinites are, in fact, non-definites. Although there are undoubtedly good reasons to follow this proposal, I will continue to use 'indefinite but specific'.

[7] This is even more pronounced in *She's just had a baby*: it is hardly likely for the woman to want to trade the baby for another (Sullivan 2013).

DD+ S-   strong autonomous analysis followed by weak synthesis

The variant of the dominant vantage represented by the formula DD+ S- is typical of a number of usages in which the noun referent is unambiguously identified due to contextual or situational knowledge shared by the speaker and hearer. Consider examples (12) and (13):

(12)   Where did you park *the car*?
       (Huddleston and Pullum 2002: 368) DD+ S-

(13)   Could you do something about *the hum*? / Does *the draught* worry you?
       (Huddleston and Pullum 2002: 370) DD+ S-[8]

A particular car, hum or draught is referred to. Unambiguous reference can also be achieved through co-text, specifically a prepositional phrase (14) or a relative clause (15):

(14)   *The Door* to Your Heart [title of a song by Taylor Dayne] DD+ S-

(15)   He brought home *the picture* that he mentioned yesterday.
       (Low 2005: 190) DD+ S-[9]

DD- S+   weak autonomous analysis followed by strong synthesis

The other major non-default variant of the recessive vantage is the strongly synthetic-systemic DD- S+, typically associated with generic reference:

(16)   *The human brain* has fascinated me ever since I was a child.
       (Huddleston and Pullum 2002: 407) DD- S+

(17)   Wolfgang can play *the piano/the violin/the drums*.
       (Huddleston and Pullum 2002: 408) DD- S+

---

[8]   Similar usages are *Beware of the dog*, or the announcement *Mind the gap*, until recently used on the London underground. These are all specific and definite, although the dog/gap is either not known to the hearer (in fact, it is introduced as new information), or the hearer is reminded of its presence. Halliday and Hasan (1976: 71) refer to them as exophoric immediate situational instances. Löbner (2011: 285) interprets *dog* as a sortal noun shifted to a unique concept.

[9]   Interestingly, these two kinds of post-modification may also occur with the indefinite article (cf. *A house on the corner is for sale* and *A bicycle John bought has been stolen*, from Quirk et al. 1985: 272, 269, respectively). These are modelled as SS+ D- for reasons explained in Głaz (2012: 231–2).

The references in examples (16) and (17) are to the kind of organ/instrument, i.e. a certain type of entity within a larger context of entities of other kinds: the human brain vs animal brains and/or vs other human organs, the piano vs other kinds of instruments etc. Hence the formula involves a strongly synthetic-systemic S+. In other words, all the individual human brains are brought together as a category juxtaposed with other categories (the animal brain, the heart, the liver). Similarly, consider sentence (18):

(18)　I intended to write the definitive study of the present British monarchy.
(Greenbaum 1996: 245) DD- S+

DD is weak because the study is non-specific: it does not yet exist. However, it is definite in the sense of my expected, potential achievement; it occupies the uppermost position on the scale of 'studies of the present British monarchy' (S+). In other words, any product that would satisfy these criteria could be described in this way, but through systemic viewing focus is placed on the *type* of product, not on its concrete realisations. Similarly, Abbott's (2009: 187) example *She gave the wrong answer and had to be disqualified* may simply be described as 'idiomatic', as the author proposes, but with recourse to EVT it may be considered a strongly systemic generic statement: an unknown answer, but one that qualifies as *the* wrong one in a series or on a scale of answers.[10]

The hypothetical nature of a systemically portrayed referent is also found in negative contexts such as (19):

(19)　I don't have *the slightest idea*.
(Huddleston and Pullum 2002: 405) [DD- S+]–NEG

The idea cannot be definite specific because it does not exist. It can only be viewed as a systemic 'highest value' of 'slight ideas'. I propose to model it as [DD- S+]–NEG, where negation operates on the whole of the conceptualisation in square brackets.

DD S　the default recessive vantage: regular-strength autonomous analysis followed by regular-strength synthesis

Finally, the default variant of the dominant vantage (DD S) represents a kind of conceptualisation in which the conceptualiser makes a specific reference

---

[10] It seems, too, that we need not agree with Abbott's (2009: 188) treatment of *There was the nicest young man at the picnic* as a formally definite description with an indefinite meaning. Instead, *the nicest young man* can be viewed as a prime example of the category of 'nice young men', regardless of who the person actually is.

to an entity, but the reference also has a recognisable generic aspect. For example, in (20) the unique reference to the (this) sun is grounded in our folk view of the universe with one sun, entailed by the synthetic-systemic S:

(20) Today is Sunday 14th April, it's mid-afternoon and *the sun* is shining. (Greenbaum 1996: 244) DD S

Similarly, in (21) the reference to the forehead is specific (Mary's forehead), but also systemic (again, the 'kind of thing' that can be called *the forehead*, against the domain of the human body):

(21) Mary banged herself on *the forehead*. (Quirk et al. 1985: 270) DD S

It is perhaps also justified to analyse example (22) in the same way:

(22) 'What do you look for in a role?'
'I look for *the echo* inside me.'
('10 questions to Sir Ben Kingsley', *Time* 170–7, 20 August 2007: 4) DD S

This is a peculiar extension of the 'body context' illustrated in (21) above: there is a specific voice (echo) inside a specific person (me), but it is conceptualised in synthetic-systemic terms as the 'kind' of voice inside every person (on a par with the forehead, the heart, the liver, etc.).

5. Filling the gaps

At this point it is possible to deal with the use of the definite article with plural nouns and with pluralised mass nouns. These cases lie somewhat outside the dominant-vantage or the recessive-vantage paradigms, and require distinct notations.

5.1. Definite plurals [SS-] D

The formula [SS-] D means that D operates against the whole of SS- as a conceptual unit, rather than in tandem with SS- within a vantage. For example, let us recall that uses such as (9) *I'm looking for a millionaire* (any millionaire) are modelled as SS- D, i.e., a weakly homogeneous set of millionaires, from which the conceptualiser picks out a random member. In contrast, in [SS-] D the role of D relative to SS- is different: D endows the weakly homogeneous set with a boundary. In doing so, the conceptualiser distinguishes that set from everything outside it: such is the case with definite plurals, e.g., *the millionaires*. Importantly, the set of elements which is endowed with a boundary may be a subset or the total set. In other words, what lies beyond the set may be entities of the same type, but for some reason not included in it, or they may be entities of different kinds. In either instance, what lies beyond the boundary is less important than the boundary itself. Figure 7 represents it diagrammatically.

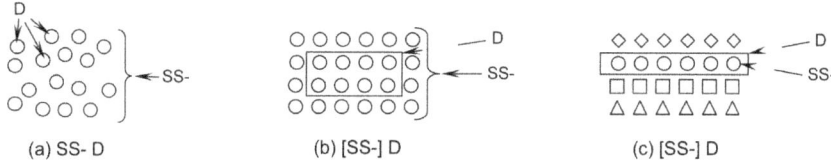

(a) SS- D   (b) [SS-] D   (c) [SS-] D

Figure 7. The different roles of D in relation to SS-:
(a) specific indefinite singular *I'm looking for a millionaire*; (b) definite plural *the millionaires* (a specific group); (c) *the millionaires* (all of them, as a 'category of people' opposed to other 'categories', eg *the nonaffluent*).

Example (23) represents a case in which the definite article marks a boundary of a portion of the set of performances (Figure 7b), whereas in (24), an appositive construction, the boundary embraces the complete set of the individuals being mentioned:

(23) Uhm < , > a couple of people can't make *the performances* but the majority of them yes.
(Greenbaum 1996: 165) [SS-] D

(24) You, *the students*, should form a society.
(Huddleston and Pullum 2002: 374) [SS-] D[11]

A rather typical context for a definite plural usage, [SS-] D, is postmodification, for example by means of a relative clause:

(25) *The few people who came to the meeting* all supported the proposal.
(Huddleston and Pullum 2002: 394) [SS-] D

---

[11] Consider also the ambiguous *The bathroom tiles are cracked* (Huddleston and Pullum 2002: 370). We can assume that only some tiles are actually cracked (cf. *The bathroom tiles are all cracked*) but, as Huddleston and Pullum observe, the impression is that of the whole of the wall/floor being cracked. On either interpretation, the formula is [SS-] D, with some variation in the role of the final D, which delimits (i) the set of cracked vs. good tiles, (ii) the set of tiles in this bathroom vs. other tiles, or (iii) the set of tiles in the bathroom vs. everything outside the set.

This is an internally homogeneous set of people, made definite through *the* and *who came to the meeting*, while *few* locates them on the scale of quantity below an expected standard.

A subcategory of the definite plural constructions are nominal uses of adjectives, as in (26):

> (26) the treatment of *the handicapped*, the fate of *the senile* and *the terminally ill*
> (Greenbaum 1996: 246) [SS-] D

These are elliptical structures (*the handicapped/senile/terminally ill people*) with the nominal element missing. Formally, then, even though there is no plural marker, a conceptual link is established with a set of individuals. Alternatively, the usages may be viewed as instances of ADJ > N recategorisation, which results in viewing the handicapped (people) as being distinct from the healthy ones. The formula [SS-] D symbolises a set, SS-, as well as the boundary imposed on that set, D.

A comparable formula can be proposed for modelling the use of *the* with mass nouns, such as *bread* or *music*. The non-discriminatory SS conceptualisation is endowed with a boundary, and hence *the bread* or *the music* (meaning 'this portion/kind of bread' and 'this kind of music', respectively) are entailed by [SS] D.

5.2. Pluralised mass nouns SS > SS-. Definite pluralised mass nouns [SS > SS-] D

Mass nouns can also be pluralised, e.g. *breads*, *teas* or even, surprisingly, *musics*.[12] These involve a conceptual recategorisation of a homogenous mass into a homogeneous set consisting of 'things of the same kind' (bread, tea, music, etc.). More precisely, the mass must be first conceptually segmented, and then the portions are grouped into a uniform assembly (rather than one of the portions being selected for individual attention, as in *the bread/the music*). Let us recall that plural count nouns (*lions*, *Italians*) are modelled as SS- (attention to similarity in the conceptualisation of a homogeneous set, but not mass – hence the similarity is weakened). By analogy, plural mass nouns are symbolised as SS- but recategorised from SS; we express this as SS > SS-. When these are made definite (*the breads, the teas, the musics*), the conceptualisation is endowed with a boundary: [SS > SS-] D.

---

[12] A Google search for *different musics* on 24 November 2011 yielded an amazing 151,000 hits.

6. More challenges

Because, regrettably, it is not possible to present here a broader range of the use of articles and their modelling in terms of EVT, I will only mention the major areas in which the model has been found useful.

First, EVT helps explain ambiguous and vague uses, such as *I intend to date a Norwegian* (Huddleston and Pullum 2002: 404) or *they wanted to see a film* (Greenbaum 1996: 245). These are analysed as either SS- D (any Norwegian or film is good enough) or SS- D+ (I know, though you probably don't, which Norwegian I want to date, and they had a specific film in mind).

Second, I propose to identify more complex cognitive processes, such as the use of reference points or the conceptual replication of a scene's fragment. The reference-point phenomenon obtains both at sentence level and at discourse level. An instance of the former is the relatively straightforward *the father of one of my students* (symbolised as STUDENT ▶ DD S), while the latter are cases of associative anaphora, such as *He found her blue Ford Escort in the car park*. The vehicle *was locked and* the lights *were off* (Biber et al. 1999: 264) (VEHICLE ▶ [SS-] D). Conceptual replication, in turn, can be recognised in *I usually have lunch with* a colleague (Huddleston and Pullum 2002: 406), i.e., repeatedly, as a recurrent motif. Interestingly, the latter example is also ambiguous: it can mean the same but unidentified colleague, or a random and a different colleague on each occasion.[13]

Finally, in a range of cases I (i) recognise the importance of the speaker's/hearer's encyclopedic knowledge and the hearer's expectations; (ii) propose to distinguish conceptual units of various lengths (equal to or larger than words); (iii) deal with uses traditionally classified as illogical or unmotivated (eg first-mention definites), as well as with special cases, such as nationality nouns (*French* vs *the French* vs *the Japanese*), (*the*) *sandflats* vs *a sandflat, the police are* vs *the police is, a British Isles* or *a Disunited Nations*. In each of them I seek cognitive motivation and oppose labelling them as arbitrary.

7. Conclusions

It is legitimate to ask at this juncture what makes the present EVT account of the use of English articles attractive? Or rather, what do both VT and EVT offer those engaged in cognitively-oriented linguistic inquiry?

---

[13] For details of the account cf. Głaz (2012: 234); suffice it to say here that the former meaning is symbolised by [SS- D+]xS, the latter by [SS- D]xD, where the x sign marks the process of mentally replicating 'the colleague' either through S or D.

Firstly, VT emphasises the dynamic nature of category construction: it addresses the emergence of different points of view (vantages) on a category in the conceptualisation of a single speaker, as well as across a language community. Secondly, it reconciles the systematic nature of categorisation with its plasticity and the diversity of categories constructed by speakers of diverse languages. Thirdly, it shows how the mechanism of categorisation is deeply rooted in the fundamental human experience of orienting oneself in space-time, familiar to all human beings, perhaps with the exception of the severely impaired. Fourthly, it ultimately reduces to the very basic cognitive processes of emphasising similarity or difference when dealing with reality.

This approach to categorisation entails a redefinition of two crucial concepts: that of a point of view and that of a category. Point of view is not treated here as a static physical or mental location of the conceptualiser, but as a dynamic cognitive procedure for viewing a category, a *vantage*. A category, then, may be viewed and termed in more than one way, with specific kinds of relationships obtaining between its vantages. A category is an assembly of its vantages. Crucially, the construction of various vantages on a category is not exceptional but rather a regularly occurring cognitive behaviour.

Naturally, the extent to which the analysis of English articles presented here is convincing is open to debate. This has as much to do with the theoretical model being employed as with the analyst's clarity of thinking and presentation. The latter issue I will leave for the reader to judge, but I hope that EVT goes some way to seriously responding to Michel Achard's challenge: 'It would be worth investigating whether Vantage Theory can be used successfully to describe linguistic data' (1999: 242). I believe EVT coherently deals with two major aspects of the data at hand: (i) the cognitive motivations behind the use of articles, grounded in fundamental processes of attention to similarity and difference, and (ii) the speakers' agency in constructing points of view on the situations being talked about. In other words, it is the language users' plastic, but systematic, cognitive operations, working in tandem with their ability to override the apparently irresistible forces of context, that function as the engine of linguistic creativity. For it must be appreciated that the recognition of the definiteness of a certain entity, an object or an event, involves two forces, which Karl Bühler (1990 [1934]: 347) refers to as 'what is definite and unmistakable in the coordinate system of the here and now... and what is *conceptually* unmistakably determinate' (emphasis in the original). Certainly, the same applies to indefiniteness; in short, what is at stake is both what is 'out there' in the world and what is 'in here' in the human mind when it categorises and conceptualises that world.

Ultimately, however, it is cognition that plays the decisive role, where the speakers impose their own interpretations on the objective situation, if such can ever be said to exist.

References

Abbott, Barbara. 2009. Definite and indefinite. In Keith Allan (ed.), *Concise Encyclopedia of Semantics*. Elsevier, 184–91.

Achard, Michel. 1999. Review of John R. Taylor and Robert E. MacLaury (eds), *Language and the Cognitive Construal of the World*. Berlin & New York: Mouton de Gruyter, 1995, 406 pp. *International Journal of American Linguistics* 65 (2): 240–2.

Allan, Keith. 1980. Nouns and countability. *Language* 56 (3): 541–67.

Allan, Keith. 2002. Vantage Theory, VT2, and number. *Language Sciences* 24 (5–6): 679–703.

Allan, Keith. 2010. Vantage theory and linguistic relativity. *Language Sciences* 32 (2): 158–69.

Biber, Douglas, Stig Johansson, Geoffrey Leech, Susan Conrad, Edward Finegan. 1999. *Longman Grammar of Spoken and Written English*. Harlow: Pearson Education Limited.

Bühler, Karl. 1990/1934. *Theory of Language*. Translated by Donald Fraser Goodwin. Amsterdam & Philadelphia: John Benjamins.

Cherryh, C. J. 1995. *Invader*. Legend Books.

Einstein, Albert. 1920. *Relativity: The Special and General Theory*. Translated by Robert W. Lawson. New York: Henry Holt. (Published in 2000 by Bartleby.com at www.bartleby.com/173)

Epstein, Richard. 2001. The definite article, accessibility, and the construction of discourse referents. *Cognitive Linguistics* 12 (4): 333–78.

Fabiszak, Małgorzata. 2010. An application of MacLaury's Vantage Theory to abstract categories: Identity and the process of categorisation. *Language Sciences* 32 (2): 276–90.

Głaz, Adam. 2010. On analogy: The architecture of Vantage Theory. In Danuta Stanulewicz, Tadeusz Z. Wolański and Joanna Redzimska (eds), *Lingua Terra Cognita II: A Festschrift for Professor Roman Kalisz*. Gdańsk: Wydawnictwo Uniwersytetu Gdańskiego, 259–79.

Głaz, Adam. 2012. *Extended Vantage Theory in Linguistic Application: The Case of the English Articles*. Lublin: Wydawnictwo UMCS.

Greenbaum, Sidney. 1996. *The Oxford English Grammar*. Oxford and New York: Oxford University Press.

Halliday, M. A. K., and Ruqaiya Hasan. 1976. *Cohesion in English*. London and New York: Longman.

Huddleston, Rodney and Geoffrey K. Pullum. 2002. *The Cambridge Grammar of the English Language*. Cambridge: Cambridge University Press.

Langacker, Ronald W. 1991. *Foundations of Cognitive Grammar. Vol. II: Descriptive Application*. Stanford: Stanford University Press.

Low, Ring Mei Han. 2005. The Phenomenon of the Word *The* in English – Discourse Functions and Distribution Patterns. Unpublished PhD thesis, State University of New York.

Löbner, Sebastian. 2011. Concept types and determination. *Journal of Semantics* 28 (3): 279–333.

MacLaury, Robert E. 1995. Vantage Theory. In John R. Taylor and Robert E. MacLaury (eds), *Language and the Cognitive Construal of the World*. Berlin & New York: Mouton de Gruyter, 231–76.

MacLaury, Robert E. 1997/2011. *Color and Cognition in Mesoamerica: Constructing Categories as Vantages*. Austin: University of Texas Press.

MacLaury, Robert E. 2002. Introducing Vantage Theory. *Language Sciences* 24 (5–6): 493–536.

MacLaury, Robert E. 2013a. Categorization as space–time analogy. In Adam Głaz, Marnie L. Moist and Elena Tribushinina (eds), *Vantage Theory: A View on Language, Cognition and Categorization*. Newcastle upon Tyne: Cambridge Scholars Publishing, 137–81.

MacLaury, Robert E. 2013b. Vantage Theory in outline. In Adam Głaz, Marnie L. Moist and Elena Tribushinina (eds), *Vantage Theory: A View on Language, Cognition and Categorization*. Newcastle upon Tyne: Cambridge Scholars Publishing, 66–136.

Porzig, Walter. 1924. Aufgaben der indogermanischen Syntax. In Johannes Friedrich, Johannes Baptista Hofmann, and Wilhelm Horn (eds), *Stand und Aufgaben der Sprachwissenschaft. Festschrift für Wilhelm Streitberg*. Heildelberg: Carl Winter, 126–51.

Preston, Dennis R. 1993. The uses of folk linguistics. *International Journal of Applied Linguistics* 3 (2): 159–259.

Quirk, Randolph, Sidney Greenbaum, Geoffrey Leech and Jan Svartvik. 1985. *A Comprehensive Grammar of the English Language*. London & New York: Longman.

Rosch, Eleanor H. 1975. Cognitive reference points. *Cognitive Psychology* 7 (4): 532–47.

Rosch, Eleanor H. 1978. Principles of categorization. In Eleanor H. Rosch and Barbara B. Lloyd (eds), *Cognition and Categorization*. Hillsdale, NJ: Lawrence Erlbaum Associates, 27–48.

Sullivan, William J. 2013. The myth of the zero article: A Relational Network disproof. In Marcin Kleban and Ewa Willim (eds), *PASE Papers in Linguistics*. Kraków: Wydawnictwo Uniwersytetu Jagiellońskiego, 115–27.

Taylor, John R. 1993. Some pedagogical implications of Cognitive Linguistics. In Richard A. Geiger and Brygida Rudzka-Ostyn (eds), *Conceptualizations and Mental Processing in Language*. Berlin and New York: Mouton de Gruyter, 201–23.

Zadeh, Lofti. 1965. Fuzzy sets. *Information and Control* 8 (3): 338–53

Chapter 17

DELIMITING LEXICAL SEMANTICS

A RADICAL CONTEXTUALIST VIEW

Kasia M. Jaszczolt

University of Cambridge

In the domain of lexical semantics, contextualism is a view according to which meanings of words can only be legitimately defined in the context of an utterance. This view can assume two forms: that of a free, contextually triggered meaning endowment or that of all-pervasive indexicalism. The opposing view, semantic minimalism, opts for relatively stable, abstract, context-free meanings. According to semantic minimalism, pragmatics does not enter in the domain of semantics save for a limited and clearly delineated class of indexical expressions. Minimalists claim that to divorce semantics from syntactic rules and from abstract lexical content is to reject literal meaning altogether and opt for variable speech-act meaning, which would have catastrophic results for theoretical rigour. This paper adds new arguments in favour of the abolition of such a divide. I argue for a pragmatics-rich account of word meaning in which meanings with different degrees of salience, cancellability (entrenchment), and proximity to what is standardly considered to be the abstract conceptual core are included. At the same time, I argue for a principled account that would search for precise constraints and algorithms for the composition of meaning.

1. Introduction: Contextualism, minimalism, and the role of the lexicon

The appropriate treatment of the lexicon is probably still the most under-researched aspect of the current post-Gricean debates concerning the scope of semantics and pragmatics. I begin by giving a brief description of the playing field before presenting my contribution to the inquiry. In the domain of lexical semantics, contextualism refers to a group of approaches according to which meanings of words can only be legitimately defined in the context of an utterance. These approaches can be broadly divided into two groups: those that favour a free, contextually triggered meaning endowment and those that opt for all-pervasive indexicalism. Late Wittgenstein's (1953) emphasis on language use and the lack of core, lexical meanings in preference to 'language games', as well as Travis's 'occasion-sensitivity' according to which '[w]ords [...] vary their semantics from one speaking of them to another' (1997: 123) instantiate the first camp in this sub-division, while Stanley's (e.g., 2000) logical forms that closely guide context-dependent information such as the contextually appropriate restriction of the quantifier domain exemplify the latter. On this view, a lexical item such as 'man' in the phrase 'every man' shares a node with semantic information pertaining to the appropriately restricted extension. The opposing (or at least allegedly opposing) view, semantic minimalism, opts for stable, abstract, context-free meanings, defined in relation to the external world. According to semantic minimalism, pragmatics does not enter in the domain of semantics save for a very limited and clearly delineated class of indexical expressions, or 'essentially context-sensitive expressions', known as the Basic Set as worked out by Kaplan (1989) and subsequently revised by Cappelen and Lepore (2005) and Borg (2012).[1] Minimalists claim that the semantic content cannot be dissociated from the externalist perspective in that the externalist perspective is essential for saving semantics from fuzziness, and also for being true to the modular account of language processing. Semantics relies on abstract word meanings and on abstract syntax. To divorce semantics from syntactic rules and from abstract lexical content would mean to reject literal meaning altogether and opt for variable speech-act meaning, which would, as the followers of minimalism claim, have catastrophic results for theoretical rigour. In Borg's (2010: 57) terms, '[i]f we dissolve the syntactic walls on what counts as semantic content we will be left with no way to reconstruct any walls at all'.

In the most recent debates concerning the semantics/pragmatics interface, however, the alleged polar opposition between minimalism and contextualism has consistently been blurred and it is so largely due to deeper considerations afforded to the lexicon. If semantics is to be minimal, then words that seem to justify the intrusion of context into the semantic representation (understood here as minimal but truth-conditional, *pace* Bach

---

[1] On Cappelen and Lepore's (2005: 144) version the set contains personal and demonstrative pronouns; adverbs 'here', 'there', 'now', 'today', 'yesterday', 'tomorrow', 'ago', 'hence(forth)'; adjectives 'actual' and 'present'; indicators of temporal reference, and possibly some other expressions. It should not come as a surprise that the class is vaguely defined and unclear as to its membership, allowing also for, as they say, 'unclear (potential borderline) cases' (ibid.).

2004, 2006) will only truly justify it when their status in lexical semantics testifies to this need for a pragmatic component. This requirement for an independent justification on the level of lexical semantics has been taken up in the recent literature by e.g., Vicente (2012), Asher (2011) and Borg (2012). In this paper I briefly assess some of these arguments, concluding that they do not tip the balance in the direction of minimalism and away from contextualism. I move on to proposing some new arguments in favour of the abolition of the semantics/pragmatics divide, adding them to the already rife collection in the contextualist tradition, concluding that a radical form of contextualism is the way forward. I point out that the clear-cut division between semantics and pragmatics adhered to by minimalists, and indeed also the indexical/nonindexical division, seem untenable in various domains such as for example first-person reference or temporal reference. Neither is it justified to tease apart various meanings of sentential connectives along the minimal content/*modulated* content (cf. Recanati, e.g., 2005, 2010, 2012) divide. Next, I suggest that the minimal/contextually enriched content divide is not the way forward for lexical semantics at large: either one keeps the lexical content artificially 'thin' and ends up with an artificially rich overlay of pragmatic adjustments, or one models lexical content as appropriately 'thick' and thereby pragmatic adjustment is already included on the level of words. Be that as it may, contextually relevant senses have to be let in through a window, door, or mouse hole, as long as they are let in sufficiently generously to reflect the speaker's intended content. And these choices all amount to radical contextualism about meaning *tout court*, *qua* radical contextualism about the truth-conditional content. In short, when we take the role of the lexicon into account, there is no minimalist stance that holds water; contextual semantics is the only option.

Keith Allan's contribution to this debate is considerable. For him the lexicon is rich: all quantity implicatures belong there, and so do various other probable, defeasible meanings, displaying various degrees of salience. Meanings are flexible in two ways: they are stored in 'a rational model of the mental lexicon or dictionary' (Allan 2012: 227) and also adaptable via semantic adjustment that can proceed towards literal as well as figurative senses (p. 228). In what follows I am applying some of his ideas for such richly construed lexicon to demonstrate that, following this line of argument, the distinction between minimalism and contextualism, so fashionable and celebrated in the last two decades or so, proves to be merely terminological and uninteresting. Keith, this is for you, with thanks for your inspiration and friendship, for the updates on Australian snakes and frogs, and with very best wishes.

2. The minimalist's way out?

Keeping semantics minimal can be justified in a variety of ways. One of them is to emphasise that there are many different things we 'do with words' anyway, so enriching what properly belongs in linguistic semantics conflates two different kinds of content and does not fit the purpose. This is essentially Cappelen and Lepore's (2005) argument. Another way is to emphasise that semantics needs to be modular and thereby the construal of the boundary between semantics and pragmatics has to reflect the nature of mental processes associated with utterance interpretation. This is Borg's (2004) argument. One can also dissociate semantics from propositions and from truth conditions and instead associate it strongly with the syntactic form of the sentence and with minimally construed lexical content. On this construal, put forward by Bach (2004, 2006), utterances can correspond to complete sentences that pertain to incomplete propositions and thereby can lack truth conditions. In what follows I will have little to say about the latter account as it seems to me that the problem addressed in it is orthogonal to the mainstream minimalism/contextualism debate. When one takes propositions out of the equation, the issue becomes merely terminological: do we want the label 'semantics' to be attached to the syntactic structure of the sentence or do we want it to be associated with some kind of thought, be it abstract or intended? If the first, we are outside the domain of truth-conditional semantics. If the latter, we debate the content of this truth-conditional representation and thereby the degree and types of pragmatic contribution. In what follows, it is the latter that I will understand as the proper debate between minimalism and contextualism.[2]

Next, keeping semantics minimal encounters the problem of the Basic Set.[3] As has been well acknowledged since Grice (1978) and Kaplan (1989), one cannot exclude pragmatic contribution completely from the truth-conditional content. Instead, one has to allow some degree of pragmatic intrusion, be it to disambiguate lexically and structurally ambiguous expressions (either pre-semantically or in the semantics) or to assign some contextually relevant reference to such slot-holders as 'I', 'he', 'yesterday' or 'there'. Both groups of pragmatic processes, that of disambiguation and

---

[2] For a more extensive discussion see Jaszczolt (in preparation).
[3] See fn 1.

that of reference assignment, allow for various interpretations though. First, polysemy and ambiguity are not clearly separable. Next, semantic ambiguity such as that pertaining to the scope of negation, the scope of quantifiers, the referential/attributive distinction, the *de re/de dicto* distinction can be either explained away as underspecification (we owe this largely to the Kempson-Atlas thesis dating back to the 1970s) or, for not faint-hearted survivors of the sense-generality alias radical pragmatics, alias semantic underspecification trend, it can be classified with ambiguity proper. This poses the problem of what to include and what to exclude from minimally construed semantics. Likewise, the set of context-sensitive expressions can be construed more, or less, narrowly. It appears that 'ready' in (1) or 'enough' in (2) have to be included in virtue of their openness to different truth-conditional interpretations: 'ready for what?' and 'enough for what?'.

(1) Lidia is ready.

(2) Lidia is not old enough.

The question arises as to what principles we ought to use for delimiting such a set. Emma Borg (2012) argues that belonging to this set has to be justified on independent grounds. For Borg (2012: 216), minimalism is a *'predominantly* context-insensitive semantics'[4] but any departure from reading the meaning off the lexicon and the structure has to be externally motivated; the use of context has to be systematic and it has to be made on the level of *types*, not *tokens*. 'I', 'he', 'now', 'then' exemplify such a type but the list inevitably has to grow to include items such as 'ready', 'enough', 'actual', and others. Here, she argues, systematicity can be derived from the presence of a syntactic construction where 'ready' enters into a logical form that requires an argument-like completion of the proposition, necessary for the truth-conditional evaluation. So, (1) corresponds to the logical form in (3).

(3) $\exists x$ Ready (l, x)

(adapted from Borg 2012: 202). However, the methodological problem with the qualification 'predominantly' cannot be explained away so easily. If word meanings are complex and structured, if they contain information about the constructions into which they enter, then these structures themselves are open to discussion in that they can conceal pragmatic aspects of meaning.

---

[4] Emphasis added.

Borg finds here a solution that allows her to, so to speak, have a cake and eat it: lexical items have semantic features but at the same time lexical meanings are atomistic; the features do not play a role in language processing. She calls it 'organizational lexical semantics': meanings are atomistic, there is no polysemy, but at the same time there is information in the lexicon that pertains to potential argument structures the lexical item may enter into. The logical form in (3) exemplifies such 'lexical' information associated with the item 'ready'.

Naturally, the view that mental lexicon contains information about syntactic structures is hardly new as far as lexical semantic accounts go but what seems to be novel is the juxtaposition of the various tenets that form this minimalist account, allowing her precisely to 'have the cake and eat it': there is no lexical decomposition, there is no structure to the words themselves, there is just esoteric association between one kind of information – (i) Fodor-like, atomistic 'locking onto reality' in using a word (cf. his *nomological locking*, Fodor 1998) and making it stand for a concept and (ii) a rich and useful array of structural information.

It is not clear how far this helping oneself to the richly construed set of semantic features can extend. If we consider Jackendoff's (2002) or Pustejovsky's (1995) rich lexical semantics, then we can help ourselves to a lot of different kinds of features indeed. If we consider Allan's (e.g., 2000, 2011, 2012) probabilistic meanings present in the lexicon, then we can also help ourselves to information pertaining to the degree of salience of the available senses. The consequences for the minimalism/contextualism debate are significant: a lot of pragmatics becomes shifted to the lexicon, and thereby it is shifted to what is supposed to be a minimalist kind of semantics, relying on 'independently motivated' senses. It is a great blow to minimalists though that this 'independent motivation' cannot possibly respect the semantics/pragmatics divide. Some remarks on such selected 'rich and pragmaticky' construals of lexical meaning are what I turn to next.

3. Contextualist lexicon

Attempts to account for an array of interrelated senses in the domain of lexical semantics are ample, albeit going in and out of fashion. Cohen (1971) argued for a rich meaning of sentential connectives, where the temporal and causal senses of 'and' are allocated a place, while Grice and post-Griceans swiftly allocated any such senses over and above those pertaining to the propositional logic equivalents to the domain of pragmatic inference – be it implicit, or, later, explicit. For Allan (2012: 227), lexicon is 'a bin for storing listemes', where 'listemes' are defined as 'language expressions whose meaning is (normally) not determinable from the meanings (if any) of their constituent forms and which, therefore, a language user must memorize as a combination of form, certain morphosyntactic properties, and meaning'. Lexicon is also a rightful place for pragmatic information such as that pertaining to the probability with which we use 'lamb' meaning meat and the probability with which we use it to mean pelt. Analogously, 'and' has the semantics of its propositional logic equivalent (conjunction) supplemented by an array of non-monotonically inferred senses. These senses, however, can arguably be algorithmically captured, which makes the lexical entry quite formal, neat and tidy rather than subjected to free pragmatic alterations.

Pragmatic contribution to the lexicon can be construed in a variety of ways. It can be captured as fairly formally presented available options as in Jackendoff's (e.g., 2002) conceptual semantics or Pustejovsky's (e.g., 1995) generative lexicon (incorporating encyclopaedic knowledge), or it can be left more open to contextual preferences, probabilities and motivated choices as in Asher's (2011) type-composition logic (TCL) or Allan's probabilistic meanings. In Asher's TCL, words are allocated *types* (such as e, t, or physical object). The types can be simple or complex, they can also be ambiguous, allowing for type accommodation (understood as in van der Sandt's 1992 account of presupposition as anaphora) and sensitive to presupposition satisfaction. TCL is a dynamic lexical semantics, an account of word meaning that had been conspicuously missing from earlier dynamic semantic accounts of sentences, discourses, and dialogues.[5] This account also caters for metaphorical meanings in that for metaphorical senses coercion is triggered by the failure of presupposition associated with the type. What we obtain there is a dynamic picture of lexical meaning where the contextually relevant sense springs out of the contextually adjusted semantic properties – but not as a choice from a list of possible senses but rather as a result of a principled, incremental processing of discourse. In Allan, the dynamism is accounted for in a very different way in that 'semantic specification in the lexicon should incorporate defeasible default (probable) meaning of a lexicon item together with the logically necessary components of lexical meaning' (Allan 2000: 212). In other words, we have here a 'bin' filled with necessary as well as more, or less, probable components of sense, some of which are

---

[5] See, e.g., Segmented Discourse Representation Theory (SDRT), Asher and Lascarides (2003).

there in virtue of some principles of rational communication akin to Grice's Quantity maxim, Horn's (1984) Q and R principles, Levinson's (2000) Q and I heuristics, relevance-theoretic cognitive effect balanced by processing effort, and so forth.

Now, probabilistic meanings have to come with degrees of probability. This aspect of the theory is still underdeveloped and Allan suggests affinities between credibility metrics and Giora's (2003) graded salience. Like salient meanings, they need not necessarily have to be literal; like salient meanings, probabilistic meanings can be inaccurate, they don't have to match the features of the relevant referent; they just have to be readily available in one's memory. For example, 'bull' is readily associated with the feature 'bovine' although it need not be so restricted, and 'lamb' is readily associated with lamb's meat, although it could also refer to pelt.

Returning to the minimalism/contextualism debate, the question arises what exactly is the impact on the debate of construing the lexicon as more, or less, pragmatics-rich. It appears that the debate has reached the point at which broadly and dynamically construed pragmatic aspects of meaning are pretty much unanimously admitted in the truth-conditional content. Where they are not (and this seems to apply only to Borg; see Cappelen and Hawthorne 2009, where Cappelen has progressed to a defence of a contextualist stance), the criterion for delimiting semantic content fails, as was argued in Section 2. In a nutshell, to qualify as an inherently context-sensitive expression, the expression has to be associated with an independent motivation for this context-sensitivity, while this independent motivation is itself merely a list of available syntactic constructions into which the item can enter to produce a more plausible truth-conditionally evaluable representation than the one that could be proposed without availing oneself of such syntactic information but instead making do with the structure that can be seen and heard. This produces the following quandary: While truth conditions are assumed to be an appropriate tool for semantic analysis, we resort to intuitions and apparently unsystematic, unaccountable preferences concerning what is to count as a complete or appropriate and what as an incomplete or inappropriate representation. If 'ready' is incomplete, producing an incomplete representation, and in need of consulting the constructions that contain it, then, arguably, 'happy', 'tall', 'bird', 'fish', 'smallpox', 'chair' or the infamous 'doorknob' (Fodor 1998) face a similar challenge of appropriateness. Indeed, so does the totality of the lexicon in view of the fact that nonliteral meanings are so pervasive and not clearly theoretically distinguishable from literal, as Recanati's (2004) elaborate classification of the senses of 'literal' demonstrates.

Attempts to bring together radical contextualism and rich lexical semantics are therefore not surprising. Vicente (2012) takes on board Travis's occasion-sensitivity and the relevance-theoretic form of contextualism on the one hand, and 'thick' lexical semantics of Pustejovsky and Jackendoff on the other, in order to argue that there is no need to be defeatist about lexical meaning and claim that word meaning does not determine truth conditions. In his view, both Travis and Gricean-style contextualists are wrong in construing word meaning 'thinly'. The exact argument is not clearly discernible in his paper but it seems to rely on the methodological preference for a thick construal of lexical semantics in that one would need special reasons for postulating incomplete meanings in need of completion in preference to complete meanings that yield to the slogan that 'meaning determines truth conditions'. For Vicente, the onus of proof lies with those who claim that it does not. Theoretical rigour of the postulates of thick lexical entries further strengthens the point.

All in all, it appears that contextualism is comfortably entrenched either on the level of propositions that are subjected to a truth-conditional analysis or on the level of lexical meanings (and *a fortiori* propositions as well). The next question to consider is that of the consequences of this state of affairs for the boundary construal between semantics and pragmatics and the practical consequences of this construal for some well acknowledged distinctions in the semantics of natural language expressions.

4. Radical Lexical Contextualism: Justification and evidence

4.1. Why pragmatics-rich lexical semantics?

There are many reasons for which pragmatics-rich lexical semantics is to be preferred. First, it accounts for a greater scope of possible meanings that words can convey. Second, and in the same vein, the conflation of semantic and pragmatic aspects of meaning reflects the fact that there is no clear boundary between defeasible and non-defeasible content, especially when metaphorical and other figurative language use is included. For example, in metaphorical use, the essential features of the object that would appear non-defeasible are the most common ones to be cancelled – to mention the use of 'star' or 'sun' where the features of a celestial body and gaseous substance are deleted, while accidental features such as appearing gold, shining or sparkling are preserved.⁶ At the same time, as has been amply demonstrated and extensively argued in the literature, there is no discernible cognitively plausible boundary between literal and nonliteral uses: a concept can be narrowed, broadened, or altered in a more substantial way, resulting sometimes in an altogether different extension corresponding to the new use, but it is more appropriate to look at these cases of concept adjustment in terms of degrees, a cline, rather than a binary metaphorical/literal distinction.⁷

Next, 'thick lexicon' reflects the fact of natural language that there does not seem to be a biunique mapping from semantic concepts to lexemes. For example, first-person reference can be rendered by personal pronouns, but it can also be achieved in some cases by using common nouns. Likewise, expressions used for first-person reference need not have their function limited to that indexical use and can be used for other purposes as well.⁸ In addition, self-referring does not seem to be an all-or-nothing affair: there are degrees with which we express self-reference, as exemplified by the use of generic 'one' in English. Similarly, when we consider temporal reference, time-tense mismatches are ample: a form that is specialised for present-time reference can be used for future or past eventualities. Equally, the use of an expression can vary between temporal or modal meaning, or temporal reference may in some languages (like Thai) be left largely to pragmatic inference.⁹

Finally, pragmatics-rich lexical semantics renders psychologically real content in that meanings that are intended by the speaker and are often relegated to pragmatic enrichment obtain a uniform treatment with abstract senses. Here we can account for the salience of the conditional perfection sense of 'if' (rendering 'just in case', 'only if') or the causal sense of 'and' ('and as a result', 'and therefore'), without employing the explanatory tools of speaker's intentions and unsystematic context-dependence. Instead, the senses are either listed in the lexicon or are derived, also in the lexicon, according to clear principles or rules, like in Allan's algorithmic treatment. Arguably, this pragmatic treatment of connectives within the lexicon can be extended even further to account for situations where, say, 'and', 'or' or

---

6   For a vintage account see Cohen (1971).
7   See, e.g., Carston (2002, Chapter 5).
8   I discuss this issue at length in Jaszczolt (2013a, 2013b).
9   I discuss this issue at length in Jaszczolt (2012a).

'if' are used to convey other senses than those of conjunction, disjunction or implication respectively. I expand on this point in Section 4.2 below.

4.2. An example: Sentential connectives

Sentential connectives pose two kinds of problems for a truth-conditional semanticist who avails herself of the metalanguage of propositional calculus.

Firstly, their meanings tend to go beyond those of their logical equivalents. The literature on this topic is ample: there are various proposals on the market of how to account for the temporal and causal meaning of 'and', for the exclusive meaning of 'or', for the meaning of 'if' that more resembles equivalence than material implication, and for the non-truth-functional negation, also known as metalinguistic negation (Horn 1985). Most of the solutions fall into the post-Gricean paradigm of, broadly speaking, intention-and-implicature based explanations, others follow rich, 'thick' lexical content with varying views on the admixture of pragmatics (see, e.g., Cohen 1971; Allan 2011) or derive at least some of the explanations from discourse rules, allowing for a computationally implementable explanation (Asher and Lascarides 2003).

Secondly, there are utterances expressing conditional meaning where the obvious equivalent in propositional calculus does not reflect the intended sense. For example, 'and' in (4) clearly conveys the sense of a conditional link in (4'), while 'or' in (5) reflects a more complex logical form pertaining to (5').

(4) Let him be late once and he will never turn up on time.
(4') If you let him be late once, he will never turn up on time.
(5) He doesn't know about the meeting or he would be here.
(5') He doesn't know about the meeting. If he did know, he would be here.

Klinedinst and Rothschild (2012) claim that such uses signal that 'and' and 'or' are lexically ambiguous but not just because their sense can be richer than that of the corresponding logical connective but rather because the conjunctive and the disjunctive meaning respectively is not present in such uses. Instead, they claim that in sentences such as these the function of the connective is to signal the change of the parameter for the evaluation of what follows. They call it an 'information-parameter change' use. While we could possibly try to accommodate such uses within one of the extant ambiguity accounts, they are so remote from the basic sense of the connective that it seems more appropriate to account for them pragmatically. And here is where the problem starts: enrichment will not suffice, what we need is a process that significantly alters the logical form of the proposition that is then subjected to the truth-conditional analysis. A minimalist would have to subject a 'wrong' kind of meaning to the truth-conditional analysis, an indexicalist-contextualist does not have a solution to offer in that the structure itself is substantially altered, while a radical contextualist has to forgo the restriction imposed by sentence structure and claim that the meaning of 'and' interacts here with the meanings of the propositions in what are effectively the antecedent and the consequent, yielding as a result an essentially context-sensitive relation.

Similarly far-reaching departures from the meaning of the logical connective can be observed in the case of the conditional in English. For example, arguably, indicative conditional can be analysed as having close semantic affinities with the interrogative 'if'. To do that, Starr (2011) construes the semantics by using the concept of transitions from one informational content to another – sentence meaning becomes 'information change potential' (modelled on Heim's 'context change potential'), where a semantic value of an expression is a mapping between two sets of possibilities. Construed in this way, the semantic task of 'if' is simply to select a set of contextual possibilities. The possibility of such a unary treatment of 'if' adds yet another argument in favour of a rich lexical semantics: 'if' is neither specialised for conditional use on the one hand, nor is it the only means to express the conditional sense on the other.

Next, speech-act conditionals such as (6) do not conform to the truth-functional analysis, not even with a conditional perfection to equivalence, but instead tend to function as hedges, hedging the illocutionary force in their role as politeness markers in (6) or the propositional content in their role as disclaimers as in (7).

(6) If you don't mind me saying, you look pale in this colour.

(7) If I remember well, *The Catcher in the Rye* was written by J.D. Salinger.

In addition, hedging allows for degrees of formulaicity, as the construction 'if you like' in (8) exemplifies.

(8) So I went in with a bone of complaint, if you like.

(from Elder 2012, source: ICE-GB). They can also have a more substantial function of conveying a speech act such as an offer or invitation as in (9).

(9) If you are thirsty, there are soft drinks in the fridge.

A related problem pertains to the fact that there are languages where a certain connective is not lexicalised. Wari', a Chapacura-Wanham language of the Amazon, and Tzeltal, a Mayan language spoken in Mexico, don't have words for 'or'. Maricopa, a Yuman language spoken in Arizona, does not have a word for 'and', and Guugu Yimithirr, an Australian Aboriginal language does not have a word for 'if'.[10] In Wari', disjunction is expressed by using modality markers and plain juxtaposition of propositions as in (10).

(10) **'am** 'e'   ca   **'am**   mi'   pin   ca
     Perhaps live 3SG.M. perhaps give complete 3SG.M.
     'Either he will live or he will die.'

(from Mauri and van der Auwera 2012: 391). Analogously, in Guugu Yimithirr, the conditional sense is rendered by modality and juxtaposition (see Evans and Levinson 2009: 443).

The question arises, to take the example of 'or', as to how to reconcile the intuitive plausibility of relying on logical disjunction as the core of the meaning of natural language disjunction with the observation that the natural language equivalent either has other salient uses as well, some of them only remotely related as in (5), or does not exist at all. I propose that the remote similarity of meaning as in (4) and (5) be subsumed under the pragmatics-rich lexicon, while the case represented in (6) be explained by appealing to the simple fact of the trade-offs between different levels of language in expressing semantic content. In other words, the semantic content of (6) makes use of the pragmatic, speech-act interpretation of the *if*-construction attained either via pragmatic inference or through default interpretation.[11] This interaction of various processes with a simple recovery of word meaning and sentence structure testifies to the fact that what is expressed in the lexicon in one language can be expressed by grammar or left to pragmatic inference or defaults in another. All in all, what looks like an overwhelming disorder is in fact quite an orderly and predictable situation once we allow for a radical, late-Wittgensteinian, contextualist perspective

---

[10] See Mauri and van der Auwera (2012) and Evans and Levinson (2009).
[11] These processes are further discussed in Section 4.3.

on the lexicon on the one hand, and recognise the interplay between levels of language in conveying sense on the other. Logical connectives can still be considered to be a semantic universal in the sense of a universal conceptual tool.[12]

4.3. Dénouement

All evidence considered, and by 'evidence' I mean both theoretical arguments and empirical findings, it would seem that there is no good reason to separate core, abstract meanings in lexical semantics from the array of adjustments, enrichments and shifts in the pragmatic overlay. Instead, there are plenty of good reasons, and some of them have been discussed above, for putting semantic and pragmatic aspects of meaning in one basket. To repeat, one of the primary reasons is that of the indiscernibility of the boundary between what is necessary and what is defeasible in word meaning. *A fortiori*, when we do not know the alleged 'core meaning', it is difficult to envisage what a 'shift' from the core to a different, context-relative sense would amount to. In other words, what Carston (e.g., 2002) calls concept broadening, concept narrowing, and in general '*ad hoc*' concept construction necessitates postulating a clear and uncontroversial starting point from which such processes can begin. No such core contents have, however, been uniformly agreed on in the literature.

On the other hand, the extent of context-dependent and at the same time cognitively salient meanings is overwhelming, which indicates that perhaps talking about such meanings in terms of shifts, adjustments, enrichments and the like is on the wrong track. Instead, an adequate theory of lexical semantics should subsume this variation in a principled, systematic way. Lists of senses clearly will not do, neither will 'thick' semantics that leaves out default and cancellable senses, or inferential but strongly salient (cancellable) senses. Let us call an orientation that caters for all these possible meanings Radical Lexical Contextualism (RLC). To repeat, to be implementable in broader accounts of discourse semantics, RLC has to be both psychologically plausible and formalized. That is, the senses have to be derivable along constrained and precisely defined procedures, which will in effect yield an algorithmic and yet pragmatics-rich account of meaning. The

---

[12] Cf. von Fintel and Matthewson (2008: 170) on the status of logical connectives as semantic universals: '…while perhaps none of the logical connectives are universally lexically expressed, there is no evidence that languages differ in whether or not logical connectives are present in their logical forms'.

extant 'thickly construed' lexical semantic theories are on the right track here but what requires elaboration is the construal of defeasible senses – à la Allan's probabilistic meanings with different degrees of salience, or, indeed, their source in Giora's (2003) lexical semantics with graded salience.

One aspect is conspicuously missing here though, and that is the listing of the *sources* from which defeasible information comes, and the *processes* which allow them to be incorporated in what we can call word meaning. Such sources and processes have been proposed in my Default Semantics (DS, Jaszczolt, e.g., 2005, 2009, 2010) and its sequel Interactive Semantics (IS, 2012b, in preparation) where they are used to analyse the main, primary meaning that is intended by a speaker and recovered by an addressee in a model situation of discourse.[13] The identified sources are as follows:

- world knowledge (WK);
- word meaning and sentence structure (WS);
- situation of discourse (SD);
- properties of the human inferential system (IS);
- stereotypes and presumptions about society and culture (SC).

The identified processes are as follows:

- processing of word meaning and sentence structure (PWS);
- social, cultural and world-knowledge defaults (SCWD);
- cognitive defaults (CD);
- conscious pragmatic inference (from situation of discourse, social and cultural assumptions, and world knowledge) (CPI).

Information coming from the identified sources is arrived at through the relevant types of interacting processes. Moreover, the mapping between the sources and the processes allows for fairly strict generalizations. Default Semantics is a radically contextualist account and the main idea is that the primary meaning that is subjected to the truth-conditional analysis is the main intended meaning, irrespective of its relation to the logical form of the uttered sentence. Semantic composition takes place *not* on the level of

---

[13] In Jaszczolt (2005, 2009, 2010) and elsewhere I call it the primary meaning intended by the Model Speaker and recovered by the Model Addressee, making use of a scenario on which the recovery of the intended content proceeds unhindered. Inferential meanings and default meanings then refer to senses that are arrived at, respectively, through conscious processing or automatically, below the level of conscious awareness, in the given situation of discourse.

logical form, be it a form that is (i) enriched through (i.a) indexing or (i.b) freely, or (ii) minimal, but rather on the level of the *merger of information* that comes from these identified sources. The merger is accomplished through the interaction of some of the identified processes listed above.[14] But at the same time, in spite of falling under the label of radical contextualism, such sources and processes allow in principle for the formalization of senses. They allow for representations where different aspects of the propositional content can be systematically ascribed to different processes. As such, this is a radical contextualist account that allows for the construction of algorithms. The pragmatics-rich lexicon affords algorithms such as for example Asher's (2011) or Allan's (2011), while sentences and discourses afford algorithms such as those proposed in SDRT (Asher and Lascarides 2003) or, with a lesser adherence to sentence grammar and with more emphasis on the interaction of extralinguistic sources, those developed in DS and IS.

Next, when we compare this group of proposals with free, 'top-down' modulation of Recanati's (e.g., 2004, 2007, 2010) truth-conditional pragmatics,[15] the advantages of the construal I depicted here are diaphanous. Recanati's modulation draws freely on contextual information and hence is totally unprincipled and intractable. A whiff of systematicity is preserved in that modulation is said to operate locally, intra-propositionally, and only on the constituents of the actual sentence (see, e.g., Recanati 2010: 23). In other words, modulation is local and interacts with semantic composition, but at the same time is 'top-down' and therefore, so to speak, unpredictable. An algorithmic account, even in spite of Recanati's declared adherence to sentence structure and thereby his affinities with indexicalists (Recanati 2012: 148), seems to be precluded. I return to this topic briefly in the conclusions.

With respect to lexical semantics, the question arises as to how this mechanism proposed in DS and IS can be employed for the purpose of representing the lexicon. If we make use of, for example, social, cultural and world-knowledge defaults on the level of the composition of the proposition, can we use them on the level of the WS source (word meaning and sentence structure) as well? If so, isn't the proposal in danger of massive redundancies and free choices as to where we want to place the defaults, in the lexicon or in the structure? The same question applies to the domain

---

[14] For a more detailed presentation, see the sources listed in fn 13.
[15] Examples of modulation are free enrichment, predicate transfer, and sense-extension. See, e.g., Recanati (2012).

of the process of conscious pragmatic inference (CPI): do we find it in the lexicon or rather in the proposition at large? It is evident then that the main question concerning the thick or thin construal of lexical meanings directly translates into the question concerning the level at which we want to place the 'pragmaticky' sources of meaning and the 'pragmaticky' processes adding to meaning composition. But if pragmatics is free to intrude either though the lexicon or through the structure, one may ask, where is the progress?

The progress lies precisely in the availability of the pragmatically triggered senses *both* to lexical composition and to the inter-constituent composition, and in the availability of an algorithmic explanation on both levels. Just as a lexical unit may afford default and inferential defeasible interpretations, so can a complex unit such as a quantifier noun phrase or a verb phrase with temporal reference. In addition, both types of interpretation are based on systematic principles. This is what I proposed elsewhere (Jaszczolt 2012b) as 'fluid characters' and 'flexible inferential bases': pragmatic processes pertain to units of different length, specified dynamically as the discourse progresses. Therefore, talking about the enrichment of 'and' or 'some' without talking about some particular context is not very helpful: Levinson-type presumed meanings (Levinson 2000), based on words or other predetermined, fixed units, just do not work, they create the need for postulating overwhelming and unrealistic cancellation. Flexible, pragmatics-rich lexicon and flexible, pragmatics-rich propositions are precisely what we need, and it is precisely what we find evidence for in observing how natural language discourse works.

It is worth pointing out that in order to justify this flexibility of the unit on which such processes operate there does not even seem to be any need for experimentation. Experimental method has recently been grossly overused in the analysis of meaning, producing as a result a false impression of scientific rigour where facts stare one in the face in everyday observation and everyday engagement in language use.[16]

5. Concluding remarks: Algorithms or 'holistic guesswork'?

In the preceding sections, I addressed the question as to what account of the lexicon appears to emerge from the current state of the minimalism/contextualism dispute. In this context, I argued for a pragmatics-rich

---

[16] See also Devitt (2006, 2010) and Ludlow (2011, Chapter 3) on the nature of evidence in linguistics.

account of word meaning in which meanings with different degrees of salience, cancellability (entrenchment), and proximity to what is standardly considered to be the abstract conceptual core are included. At the same time I argued for a principled account that would depart from the contextualist idea of 'free', 'top-down' enrichment but instead search for precise constraints or algorithms. To elaborate on the advantage of algorithmic accounts professed above, I conclude with a short comment on the following claim by Recanati (2012: 148):

> Is semantic interpretation a matter of holistic guesswork (like the interpretation of kicks under the table), rather than an algorithmic, grammar-driven process as formal semanticists have claimed? Contextualism: Yes. Literalism: No. [...] Like Stanley and the formal semanticists, I maintain that the semantic interpretation is grammar-driven.

Recanati clearly dissociates algorithmic accounts from the construal of meaning based on the interaction of various linguistic and non-linguistic processes whenever such a construal does not happen to be driven by the grammar of the sentence. Departing from the frame of sentence structure results for him in 'holistic guesswork', and thereby in the departure from systematicity and from any hope of an algorithmic account. Unless the interpretation can rely on the linguistic form, it becomes like 'interpreting kicks under the table' (ibid., after Stanley 2000).

It is unclear why this should be so. There seems to be no reason in principle why our conversational behaviour, and discourse meaning in general, should fall prey to an unsystematic account as soon as it affords due attention to indirectness by giving indirect meanings their due status of primary content. So, while Recanati's contextualism is 'radical' in the sense that for him word meanings are potentially always context-sensitive (Recanati 2012: 139),[17] it is not radical enough in that analogous flexibility in interpreting the main content of the utterance that can be quite independent from the structure of the sentence is denied. I have argued here that following the intended meaning on the level of both words and structures need not be restricted to what the logical form of the sentence dictates. There is no evidence in linguistic

---

[17] But note that for Recanati (2012: 141) the sense of an expression is 'a function of the lexical meaning of that expression and some factor x, where 'x' is whatever, in addition to lexical meaning, is needed to determine sense'. He endorses precisely the idea of a shift from some mysterious core lexical meaning that we have questioned above.

communication that such meanings afford greater psychological reality than indirect meanings – indeed, there is ample cross-linguistic evidence to the contrary. Semantic theory ought to follow this fact and open up to senses that are not grammar-driven. It also ought to search for algorithmic accounts of such senses, allowing for defeasible aspects of meanings to penetrate both the lexicon and sub-propositional units of different length. Just as there are regularities in lexical meaning and sentence meaning, so there are regularities in discourse meaning. Algorithmic accounts do work for lexical semantics, they also work for sentence meaning. There is no reason to doubt that they work for discourse meaning at large.

References

Allan, Keith. 2000. Quantity implicatures and the lexicon. In: Bert Peeters (ed.), *The Lexicon-Encyclopedia Interface*. Oxford: Elsevier, 169–217.

Allan, Keith. 2011. Graded salience: Probabilistic meanings in the lexicon. In: Kasia M. Jaszczolt and Keith Allan (eds), *Salience and Defaults in Utterance Processing*. Berlin: De Gruyter Mouton, 165–87.

Allan, Keith. 2012. Pragmatics in the (English) lexicon. In: Keith Allan and Kasia M. Jaszczolt (eds), *The Cambridge Handbook of Pragmatics*. Cambridge: Cambridge University Press, 227–50.

Asher, Nicholas. 2011. *Lexical Meaning in Context: A Web of Words*. Cambridge: Cambridge University Press.

Asher, Nicholas and Alex Lascarides. 2003. *Logics of Conversation*. Cambridge: Cambridge University Press.

Bach, Kent. 2004. Minding the gap. In: Claudia Bianchi (ed.), *The Semantics/Pragmatics Distinction*. Stanford, CA: CSLI Publications, 27–43.

Bach, Kent. 2006. The excluded middle: Semantic minimalism without minimal propositions. *Philosophy and Phenomenological Research* 73: 435–42.

Borg, Emma. 2004. *Minimal Semantics*. Oxford: Clarendon Press.

Borg, Emma. 2010. Minimalism and the content of the lexicon. In: Luca Baptista and Enrich H. Rast (eds), *Meaning and Context*. Berlin: Peter Lang, 51–77.

Borg, Emma. 2012. *Pursuing Meaning*. Oxford: Oxford University Press.

Cappelen, Herman and Ernie Lepore. 2005. *Insensitive Semantics: A Defense of Semantic Minimalism and Speech Act Pluralism*. Oxford: Blackwell.

Cappelen, Herman and John Hawthorne. 2009. *Relativism and Monadic Truth*. Oxford: Oxford University Press.

Carston, Robyn. 2002. *Thoughts and Utterances: The Pragmatics of Explicit Communication*. Oxford: Blackwell.

Cohen, L. Jonathan. 1971. Some remarks on Grice's views about the logical particles of natural language. In Y. Bar-Hillel (ed.), *Pragmatics of Natural Languages*. Dordrecht: D. Reidel, 50–68.

Devitt, Michael. 2006. *Ignorance of Language*. Oxford: Clarendon Press.

Devitt, Michael. 2010. What 'intuitions' are linguistic evidence? *Erkenntnis* 73: 251–64.

Elder, Chi-Hé. 2012. Conditional expressions: The case of metalinguistic *if you like*. Paper presented at AMPRA 1 (*First International Conference of the American Pragmatics Association*), Charlotte, N.C.

Evans, Nicholas and Stephen C. Levinson. 2009. The myth of language universals: Language diversity and its importance for cognitive science. *Behavioral and Brain Sciences* 32: 429–92.

von Fintel, Kai and Lisa Matthewson. 2008. Universals in semantics. *The Linguistic Review* 25: 139–201.

Fodor, Jerry A. 1998. *Concepts: Where Cognitive Science Went Wrong*. Oxford: Clarendon Press.

Giora, Rachel. 2003. *On Our Mind: Salience, Context, and Figurative Language*. Oxford: Oxford University Press.

Grice, H. Paul. 1978. Further notes on logic and conversation. In: Peter Cole (ed.), *Syntax and Semantics, Vol. 9*. New York: Academic Press. Reprinted in: H. Paul Grice. 1989. *Studies in the Way of Words*. Cambridge, MA: Harvard University Press, 41–57.

Horn, Lawrence R. 1984. Toward a new taxonomy for pragmatic inference: Q-based and R-based implicature. In Deborah Schiffrin (ed.), *Georgetown University Round Table on Languages and Linguistics 1984*. Washington, DC: Georgetown University Press, 11–42.

Horn, Lawrence R. 1985. Metalinguistic negation and pragmatic ambiguity. *Language* 61: 121–74.

Jackendoff, Ray. 2002. *Foundations of Language*. Oxford: Oxford University Press.

Jaszczolt, Kasia M. 2005. *Default Semantics: Foundations of a Compositional Theory of Acts of Communication*. Oxford: Oxford University Press.

Jaszczolt, Kasia M. 2009. *Representing Time: An Essay on Temporality as Modality*. Oxford: Oxford University Press.

Jaszczolt, Kasia M. 2010. Default Semantics. In Bernd Heine and Heiko Narrog (eds), *The Oxford Handbook of Linguistic Analysis*. Oxford: Oxford University Press, 215–46.

Jaszczolt, Kasia M. 2012a. Cross-linguistic differences in expressing time and universal principles of utterance interpretation. In: Luna Filipović and Kasia. M. Jaszczolt (eds), *Space and Time in Languages and Cultures: Linguistic Diversity*. Amsterdam: John Benjamins, 95–121.

Jaszczolt, Kasia M. 2012b. 'Pragmaticising' Kaplan: Flexible inferential bases and fluid characters. *Australian Journal of Linguistics* 32: 209–37.

Jaszczolt, Kasia M. 2013a. First-person reference in discourse: Aims and strategies. *Journal of Pragmatics* 48: 57–70.

Jaszczolt, Kasia M. 2013b. Contextualism and minimalism on *de se* belief ascription. In: Alessandro Capone and Neil Feit (eds), *Attitudes De Se: Linguistics, Epistemology, Metaphysics*. Stanford: CSLI Publications, 69–103.

Jaszczolt, Kasia M. in preparation. *Interactive Semantics*. Oxford: Oxford University Press.

Kaplan, David. 1989. Demonstratives: An essay on the semantics, logic, metaphysics, and epistemology of demonstratives and other indexicals. In: Joseph Almog, John Perry and Howard Wettstein (eds), *Themes from Kaplan*. New York: Oxford University Press, 481–563.

Klinedinst, Nathan and Daniel Rothschild. 2012. Connectives without truth tables. *Natural Language Semantics* 20: 137–75.

Levinson, Stephen C. 2000. *Presumptive Meanings: The Theory of Generalized Conversational Implicature*. Cambridge, MA: MIT Press.

Ludlow, Peter 2011. *The Philosophy of Generative Linguistics*. Oxford: Oxford University Press.

Mauri, Caterina and Johan van der Auwera. 2012. Connectives. In: Keith Allan and Kasia M. Jaszczolt (eds), *The Cambridge Handbook of Pragmatics*. Cambridge: Cambridge University Press, 377–401.

Pustejovsky, James. 1995. *The Generative Lexicon*. Cambridge, MA: MIT Press.

Recanati, François. 2004. *Literal Meaning*. Cambridge: Cambridge University Press.

Recanati, François. 2005. Literalism and contextualism: some varieties. In: Gerhard Preyer and Georg Peter (eds), *Contextualism in Philosophy: Knowledge, Meaning, and Truth*. Oxford: Clarendon Press, 171–96.

Recanati, François. 2007. *Perspectival Thought: A Plea for (Moderate) Relativism*. Oxford: Oxford University Press.

Recanati, François. 2010. *Truth-Conditional Pragmatics*. Oxford: Clarendon Press.

Recanati, François. 2012. Contextualism: Some varieties. In: Keith Allan and Kasia M. Jaszczolt (eds), *The Cambridge Handbook of Pragmatics*. Cambridge: Cambridge University Press, 135–49.

van der Sandt, Rob. 1992. Presupposition projection as anaphora resolution. *Journal of Semantics* 9: 333–77.

Stanley, Jason. 2000. Context and logical form. *Linguistics and Philosophy* 23: 391–34.

Starr, William B. 2011. Conditionals and questions. Unpublished ms, New York University.

Travis, Charles. 1997. Pragmatics. In: B. Hale and C. Wright (eds), *A Companion to the Philosophy of Language*. Oxford: B. Blackwell, 87–107. Reprinted in Charles Travis. 2008. *Occasion-Sensitivity: Selected Essays*. Oxford: Oxford University Press, 109–29.

Vicente, Agustin. 2012. On Travis cases. *Linguistics and Philosophy* 35: 3–19.

Wittgenstein, Ludwig. 1953. *Philosophische Untersuchungen / Philosophical Investigations*. Oxford: Blackwell. Reprinted in 1958 (second edition).

Chapter 18

WHERE DID PROTO NUCLEAR MICRONESIANS COME FROM?

A LINGUISTIC-TYPOLOGICAL PERSPECTIVE

Jae Jung Song
University of Otago

Historical linguists have proposed four hypotheses concerning Proto Nuclear Micronesians' migration route: Proto Nuclear Micronesians may have reached Micronesia from the Admiralty Islands, the Cristobal-Malaitan region, northern Vanuatu, or somewhere in the vast southeast Solomons-Vanuatu region. Unfortunately, there is no conclusive linguistic evidence, historical-comparative or otherwise, for any of the hypotheses. This article makes use of Johanna Nichols's population-typology model in an attempt to understand Proto Nuclear Micronesians' migration route better. This model has been developed to investigate geographical distributions of structural properties with a view to making inferences about human migration. In particular, the structural property of possessive classifiers, a defining characteristic of Micronesian languages, is selected in order to ascertain how this property is distributed in the wider areas surrounding Micronesia. Proto Nuclear Micronesians must have carried the propensity for possessive classifiers in their language(s) when travelling from somewhere into Micronesia. There is a distinct possibility that whomever Proto Nuclear Micronesians interacted (linguistically) with must have shared the same propensity. By interpreting the geographical cline of possessive classifiers from the lower to higher end, one may be able to trace the migration route of Proto Nuclear Micronesians back to their immediate homeland. This points to the Santa Cruz Islands as the place from which Proto Nuclear Micronesians entered Micronesia via northern Vanuatu.

1. Introduction

There are four different hypotheses concerning the genealogical position of Nuclear Micronesian languages within a wider context of the Oceanic subgrouping. First, Grace (1955) claims that languages of Micronesia – with the exception of Palauan and Chamorro – have their closest linguistic affiliations with those of the New Hebrides (now Vanuatu; cf. Map 1). Support for Grace's claim comes from Shutler and Marck (1975). Second, Smythe

(1970) points to a possible connection between languages of Micronesia and those of the Admiralty Islands (i.e., Manus Island), based largely on their lexical similarities.¹ Third, based on his lexical comparisons of Nuclear Micronesian languages and Cristobal-Malaitan languages in the Solomon Islands chain, Blust (1984) proposes a subgrouping hypothesis, bringing these two groups of languages together. Fourth, Pawley (1972) proposes what he calls 'North Hebridean-Central Pacific', a linguistic grouping that includes Fijian, Polynesian, and languages of the Banks, Torres and northern New Hebrides Islands. He believes that there is some evidence for including Kiribati, a Nuclear Micronesian language, in North Hebridean-Central Pacific. By extension, other Nuclear Micronesian languages should also belong to this grouping (Pawley 1972: 134). The position of Nuclear Micronesian within North Hebridean-Central Pacific remains unchanged in Pawley (1977), although the term 'Eastern Oceanic' is redefined to refer strictly to his earlier North Hebridean-Central Pacific (Jackson 1986: 215).

Based on these four different hypotheses, it is possible to propose at least four migration routes of Proto Nuclear Micronesians. First, Shutler and Marck's research suggests that Proto Nuclear Micronesians may have travelled from the Vanuatu region into Micronesia for settlement. More precisely, Shutler and Marck (1975: 101) identify northern Vanuatu as the area from which Micronesia was colonised. This migration route also seems to be favoured by Lynch, Ross and Crowley (2002: 119). The second possibility, deriving from Blust's (1984) work, is that Proto Nuclear Micronesians entered Micronesia from the Cristobal-Malaitan region of the main Solomon Islands chain. Third, regardless of the validity of his 'Eastern Oceanic' subgroup,² Pawley (1972: 140–1) indicates that the location of the Eastern Oceanic homeland may be somewhere in the southeast Solomons-New Hebrides region, because that is where the centre of diversity in Eastern Oceanic lies. From this, it follows that Proto Nuclear Micronesians may have migrated from somewhere in the vast southeast Solomons-New Hebrides region.³ Note that the vastness of this area is not surprising because Pawley's (1972, 1977)

---

[1] In what follows, Micronesia only refers to central and eastern Micronesia excluding western Micronesia (i.e., Yap, Palau and the Mariana Islands).

[2] Pawley (1981: 277, 301; also Pawley and Ross 1993: 440) now believes that evidence for this subgroup is unconvincing.

[3] Although Pawley (1972) identifies the larger southeast Solomons-New Hebrides region as the homeland of Proto Eastern Oceanic speakers, he recognises a closer linguistic affinity between Nuclear Micronesian and North Hebridean. Thus, Pawley (1972) may not be very different from Shutler and Marck (1975) insofar as the location of Proto Nuclear Micronesian homeland is concerned.

inclusion of Nuclear Micronesian languages in such a large subgroup does not make it possible to pinpoint any specific area as the homeland of Proto Nuclear Micronesians. Fourth, Smythe (1970: 1221) speaks of 'Micronesian infiltration' into the Admiralty Islands, leaving the question of Proto Nuclear Micronesians' homeland open. Smythe's scenario, however, does not fit in with archaeological evidence. Pottery evidence from these two areas (e.g., Athens 1990; Spriggs 1984) suggests that, if there was human migration between Micronesia and the Admiralty Islands, it is more likely to have been from the latter to the former than the converse. Furthermore, Ross (1988: 326) makes the suggestion that Micronesia and the Admiralty Islands may each have been settled by migrants from Mussau Island (i.e., the St Matthias Islands).[4] To wit, the Admiralty Islands or the St Matthias Islands may be a possible candidate for the homeland of Proto Nuclear Micronesians.

The four or five proposed migration routes for Proto Nuclear Micronesians are all well within the realms of possibility, probably the strongest being from northern Vanuatu (i.e., Shutler and Marck 1975) and the weakest from Micronesia to the Admiralty Islands (i.e., Smythe 1970). The problem, however, is that the linguistic evidence supporting them is far from conclusive (Lynch, Ross and Crowley 2002: 119). In fact, there is no consensus as to the genealogical position of Nuclear Micronesian within the Oceanic subgroup. Moreover, there has been no historical-comparative work on the external relationships of Nuclear Micronesian since Jackson (1986). It is almost as if the genealogical discussion of Nuclear Micronesian and the related question of Proto Nuclear Micronesians' migration route had come to a halt with the appearance of Jackson's work. It remains to be seen whether or not the absence of new Micronesian historical-comparative research may be an indication that historical-comparative linguistics has said all that it can possibly say about the external relationships of Nuclear Micronesian languages and about Proto Nuclear Micronesians' migration route(s). (Hopefully not!) This lack of new historical-comparative evidence, however,

---

[4] The present writer is not aware of any archaeological evidence in support of Ross's (1986) suggestion. As a matter of fact, there seems to be some evidence for material cultural artefacts imported into Mussau Island from other places including the Admiralty Islands (Kirch 1997: 145, 242–6; Spriggs 1997: 113). Between Mussau Island and Micronesia, on the other hand, the former was settled much earlier than the latter, as evidenced by the 'obsidians [...] from excavations of a Lapita pottery complex [on Eloaue in the St Matthias Islands], which elsewhere have been radiocarbon dated to around 3000 years ago' (Ambrose et al. 1981: 14). This date certainly is prior to the onset of Micronesian colonisation (i.e., 2000 BP, e.g., Intoh 1997: 20; but cf. Rehg 1995). This may at least preclude migration from Micronesia to Mussau Island.

calls for the need to ascertain whether or not there may be linguistic data, other than historical-comparative or lexicostatistical, that can be utilised to investigate the migration route(s) of Proto Nuclear Micronesians. Indeed the main objective of this paper is to argue for the existence of such linguistic evidence, based on the distribution of possessive classifiers, and to expatiate upon it, albeit in an exploratory manner. The paper makes use of Nichols's (1992) population-typology model in an attempt to understand Proto Nuclear Micronesians' migration route. This model has been developed to investigate geographical distributions of structural properties with a view to making inferences about human migration. In particular, the structural property of possessive classifiers, a defining characteristic of Micronesian languages, is selected in order to ascertain how this property is distributed in the wider areas surrounding Micronesia. Proto Nuclear Micronesians must have carried the propensity for possessive classifiers in their language(s) when travelling from somewhere into Micronesia. There is a distinct possibility that whomever Proto Nuclear Micronesians interacted (linguistically) with must have shared the same propensity. By interpreting the geographical cline of possessive classifiers from the lower to higher end, one may be able to trace the migration route of Proto Nuclear Micronesians back to their immediate homeland. This points to the Reefs-Santa Cruz Islands as the place from which Proto Nuclear Micronesians entered Micronesia via northern Vanuatu.

The remainder of the paper proceeds as follows. In section 2, the linguistic data used to propose the different migration routes for Proto Nuclear Micronesians will be surveyed with a view to demonstrating why it does not constitute conclusive evidence for any of the proposed migration routes. In section 3, Nichols's (1992) model will be outlined with very minor interpretative amendments. Section 4 examines the geographical distribution of possessive classifiers through the various areas surrounding Micronesia, proposing the Reefs-Santa Cruz Islands as the place from which Proto Nuclear Micronesians entered Micronesia. The paper concludes in section 5 with a summary and a brief comment on archaeological and genetic evidence in support of the proposal made in section 4.

2. The position of Nuclear Micronesian within Oceanic: An appraisal

In the present section, the linguistic evidence that the migration scenarios, as discussed in section 1, draw on will be discussed in order to explain why it is inconclusive. This will be based largely on Jackson's (1986) review of Smythe

(1970), Pawley (1972, 1977) and Blust (1984). The order of presentation here is from the strongest to the weakest migration scenario.

2.1. Shutler and Marck (1975)

The linguistic evidence in support of Grace's (1955) claim about Proto Nuclear Micronesians's homeland comes from Shutler and Marck's (1975) work, which in turn is based on Marck's (n.d.) 100-word lexicostatistical comparison of seven Nuclear Micronesian languages and three 'Eastern Oceanic' languages (cf. Marck 1975, 1986). Although Shutler and Marck (1975) make a laudable attempt to bring linguistics and archaeology together, their evidence is not historical-comparative one built on regular sound correspondences but lexicostatistically based. Moreover, the number of the 'Eastern Oceanic' languages included in Shutler and Marck's comparison is so small that it may be injudicious to draw firm conclusions or inferences from their work.

2.2. Pawley (1972, 1977)

Pawley (1972, 1977) proposes that Nuclear Micronesian languages may form a large subgroup not only with languages of the Banks, Torres and northern New Hebrides Islands (= Vanuatu), but also with Fijian and Polynesian. This subgroup is referred to by Pawley as Eastern Oceanic or North Hebridean-Central Pacific. He (1977) offers as many as ten properties in support of Eastern Oceanic. Jackson (1986: 220–1), however, has demonstrated that most of these are (i) merely retentions also reflected in non-Eastern Oceanic or non-Oceanic Austronesian languages, (ii) unattested in Nuclear Micronesian languages; or (iii) encumbered with 'too many irregularities to be considered as subgrouping evidence.'

There is, however, one piece of evidence put forth by Pawley (1977) that Jackson (1986: 215–220) dwells on at great length: loss of Proto Oceanic (POc) *R or its merger with POc *d. Four of the twelve lexical items examined by Jackson – POc *RuNma 'house', POc *qapaRa 'shoulder', POc *maRaqan 'light in weight' and POc *wakaR(i) 'root' – do exhibit an exact parallel between Proto Nuclear Micronesian and New Hebridean in terms of loss of *R or its merger with *d, thereby providing support for the subgrouping of these two groups. (Note that Jackson only deals with New Hebridean, because Pawley finds little evidence for linking Nuclear Micronesian with the Central Pacific branch of Eastern Oceanic.) This parallelism also suggests that *R was either lost or merged with *d in individual lexical items in New

Hebridean and Proto Nuclear Micronesian, although these lexical items themselves do not allow one to identify any specific dialect group in the New Hebrides from which Proto Nuclear Micronesian separated (Jackson 1986: 218).

However, when some of the other lexical items are scrutinised, there is 'extremely contradictory' evidence to the effect that the Banks Islands emerge not only as a New Hebridean area from which Proto Nuclear Micronesian may have derived, but also as an area from which Proto Nuclear Micronesian could not have derived! Moreover, there is counterevidence based on the reflexes of POc *meRa 'red' in Proto Nuclear Micronesian and New Hebridean, whereby it is indicated that *R must have been a distinct phoneme in Proto Nuclear Micronesian at the time of its separation from New Hebridean (and later merged with *d), and that *R must have been lost in New Hebridean subsequently to that separation.

This conundrum notwithstanding, Jackson (1986: 220) accepts the possibility that loss of *R and its merger with *d may have occurred in the 'ancestral' language of both Proto Nuclear Micronesian and New Hebridean, although he is quick to qualify this by saying that the whole thing can be 'entirely coincidental'. Nonetheless, the parallelism in the four lexical items is strong enough for him (1986: 220) to conclude that the Micronesian and New Hebridean reflexes of *R do not contradict the possibility that the two language groups subgroup together.

2.3. Blust (1984)

Blust (1984) puts forward a subgrouping hypothesis that links Nuclear Micronesian directly with languages of the Cristobal-Malaitan region. This subgroup is referred to by Blust (1984) as Malaita-Micronesian. 'The absence of clear phonological or syntactic innovations shared exclusively by the Nuclear Micronesian and Cristobal-Malaitan languages' leads him to draw heavily on lexical data, which comprise putative lexical, morphological and semantic innovations (Blust 1984: 101–2). There are twenty-eight such innovations discussed in Blust's (1984) work. As Blust himself acknowledges, however, the evidence arising from these innovations 'is limited' (p. 132). Nonetheless, he is firmly of the view that at least four of these innovations present a very strong case for his Malaita-Micronesian subgrouping hypothesis.

Jackson (1986: 221–5), however, does not share Blust's optimism. For instance, Blust's 'Proto Malaita-Micronesian' *pwaRusu 'nose' is attested outside the putative subgrouping, e.g., in Yapese. Jackson (p. 222) also makes reference to New Hebridean languages that seem to suggest that *pwaRusu was actually a compound made of two elements *pwa- and *Ru(n)su (both with meanings related to 'nose'), which may perhaps have been present as far back as in POc. Thus, there is every likelihood of *pwaRusu being a mere retention in Micronesian and Cristobal-Malaitan or having developed independently in the two groups, based on the two separate POc elements, *pwa- and *Ru(n)su. Similarly, the lexical innovation *masawa 'sea' is thought to have been 'a continuation of an earlier form' (p. 223). The problem with the other lexical innovation *maŋo 'breath, to breathe, fontanelle' is, as Jackson (pp. 223–4) explains, that there is too much inconsistency in meaning between Micronesian and Cristobal-Malaitan. This leads him to the view that the innovation in question is a very tenuous one. The semantic innovation that Blust (1984: 117) thinks provides 'a particularly compelling piece of evidence' for his Malaita-Micronesian subgroup comes from 'Proto Malaita-Micronesian' *lama 'lake, lagoon' (<POc *laman 'sea beyond the reef, deep blue sea'). Jackson (p. 224), however, points out that Arosi, Marshallese and Saipan Carolinian reflexes 'appear to continue the POc reference to *deep water* (albeit water which is relatively close to shore)'. Thus, he is of the opinion that *lama may independently have undergone the same semantic change in both Micronesian and Cristobal-Malaitan.

Jackson (1986: 225) concludes that Blust's (1984) Malaita-Micronesian subgroup is in need of conclusive evidence, because 'the innovative status of these forms [i.e., 'Proto Malaita-Micronesian' *pwaRusu, *masawa, *maŋo, and *lama] is not as certain as Blust believes'. With Blust's strongest evidence for his proposed subgrouping called into question, Jackson's circumspection seems to be well placed (also see Lichtenberk 2010 for indirect evidence against Blust's Malaita-Micronesian subgroup).

2.4. Smythe (1970)

Smythe (1970) develops the idea of linking Nuclear Micronesian with languages of the Admiralty Islands, based on lexical and grammatical similarities between the two. Blust (1984: 129), however, dismisses Smythe's view because it 'rests on virtually no solid evidence of exclusively shared lexical innovation.' Blust goes on to claim that, being of a general typological character, the few grammatical features that Smythe adduces in support also fail to uphold the Nuclear Micronesian-Admiralties hypothesis. Contrary to Blust's negative view, Jackson (1986: 225–6) argues that some of Smythe's lexical comparisons may collectively present a case for further investigation, although they may individually be problematic. Jackson (p. 226) also points to 'non-linguistic evidence for a connection between' Nuclear Micronesian and Admiralties languages, namely the geographical proximity and technological similarities (e.g., gardening techniques, and the appearance of canoes). In view of the nature of Smythe's linguistic evidence, however, it comes as no surprise that Jackson only speaks of a *connection* between the two language groups. The connection is not strong enough to warrant discussion of a *genealogical relationship* between them. It may well be due to sustained contact only.

2.5. Summary

Each of the subgrouping hypotheses involving Nuclear Micronesian is fraught with problems, empirical or methodological or even both. Thus, Proto Nuclear Micronesians' migration routes proposed on the basis of the subgrouping hypotheses cannot be taken to be conclusive, either (cf. Lynch, Ross and Crowley 2002: 119).

3. Geographical distribution of typological markers

Nichols (1992) has demonstrated in a most ingenious way the usefulness of linguistic typology in population migration research.[5] This kind of linguistic typology is referred to by Nichols as 'population typology'. The main objective of population typology is to discover 'principles governing the [geographical] distribution of structural features among the world's languages' with a view to making inferences about human migration and spread of languages, and thus to contributing to our understanding of linguistic prehistory (p. 2). Population typology diverges from the comparative method in that it deals with neither individual languages nor individual etyma, but rather populations of languages and geographical distributions of structural features and types (p. 280).

The interpretive model which Nichols (1992: 213–5) favours in an attempt to take account of her data is based on population genetics, wherein it is understood that one of the factors driving evolution is the tendency of genes to reach equilibrium in populations. How this happens is dependent crucially on two variables: (i) population size; and (ii) initial frequencies. The smaller

---

[5] As the reader recalls, Blust (1984: 129) takes a dim view of use of typological properties in subgrouping, to which typological evidence is 'of little relevance'. This may indeed also be the not uncommon perception of linguistic typology within historical linguistics. Thus, it may not be incorrect to say that some historical linguists will endorse Blust's pessimistic view without reservation, notwithstanding other linguists' efforts in demonstrating otherwise (see Shields 2011 for an overview).

the population, the sooner frequencies stabilise at 100% or 0%; and 100% for high initial frequencies or 0% for low initial frequencies. The skewing of a typological feature in the initial population of languages is postulated, for example, with less than half of the western languages with the feature, and more than half of the eastern languages with the feature. Then, just like biological genes, the skewing of frequencies has over time played out on an increasingly larger and larger scale, while stabilising at 0% or 100% at the extreme periphery.

Inclusive/exclusive oppositions in first-person pronouns have been identified as one such typological feature. The geographical distribution of these pronouns 'increases from area to area on a cline from west to east, and [also] with a clear distinction between Old World and colonized areas', with the extreme peripheral areas of Europe and (northern) Australia ending up with a zero frequency and a 100% frequency, respectively (Nichols 1992: 185, 196–8, 278). This global west-to-east cline, with a substantial difference between the Old World and the colonised areas in particular, is manifested by the respective percentages of languages having the distinction in question in the three macroareas, i.e., Old World, New World and Pacific. Exactly the same cline is observed also within each and every one of the three macroareas. What is so remarkable about this global west-to-east cline is that it mirrors the directionality or the vector of human migration itself, as is currently understood. The present paper draws its inspiration from this particular aspect of Nichols's work by making an attempt to interpret the geographical cline of the intensity – instead of frequency as in Nichols (1992) – of one typological property as reflecting the vector of Proto Nuclear Micronesian migration.

Determining the geographical distribution of properties is nothing new to genetics-based research on population migration. Genetic markers linked with specific human populations have been utilised in an attempt to reconstruct their migration routes, and also to locate their homelands, (e.g., O'Shaughnessy et al. 1990; Melton et al. 1998). This is possible because human populations, while interbreeding, contribute their genes to each other's gene pools. Different populations may have different unique genetic markers. By plotting genetic trails through populations, geneticists are able to make inferences about population migration.

Typological properties (or structural features) can likewise be plotted or traced over geographical areas, because they leave trails through populations of languages just as genetic markers leave trails through human populations. To give a simple hypothetical situation, suppose some of the languages indigenous to an area migrate into an uninhabited area, with other languages remaining in the old area. From this new area some languages continue to move into another uninhabited area, with other languages staying behind, and so on. Typological properties of the initial population of languages will then also be carried around by migrant languages. In other words, migrant languages will leave a trail of typological properties behind them. Far more frequently than not, languages migrate into already inhabited areas. Suppose some of the languages indigenous to an area move into an inhabited area while others, as in the case of the first situation, remain in the old area, and so on. Furthermore, migrant languages come in contact with pre-existing languages of the new area. The latter may then acquire typological properties from the former. (The converse is equally possible.) From this new area, some languages continue to move into another inhabited area, thereby yet again coming in contact with pre-existing languages. The latter's acquisition of typological properties from the former takes place again. The whole process may repeat itself over and over again. In this less simple hypothetical situation as well, migrant languages will leave a trail of typological properties behind them by opting to stay behind and/or by donating typological properties to pre-existing languages. By tracing such linguistic trails, it may be possible to draw inferences about population migration. Note that linguistic trails may inevitably cut across linguistic affiliations (i.e., linguistic subgroupings). This, however, is not unexpected because typological properties can be borrowed from one language group into another. Inferences to be drawn from linguistic trails do not concern linguistic subgrouping, but population migration.

It is quite possible, of course, that (nearby) areas where migrant languages have missed may also contain languages with the same typological properties by chance. In this case, there is much likelihood that these areas may incorrectly be included in the linguistic trail. Needless to say, inferences or conclusions drawn from such a 'false' linguistic trail are unlikely to provide an accurate reconstruction of population migration. However, linguistic trails are not merely geographically continuous lines of areas. Areas located on a 'genuine' linguistic trail may also vary from one another, with a given typological property increasing or decreasing in intensity (e.g., more or less complexity of the property) or in frequency (e.g., more or fewer languages with the property) from one end of the trail to the other. In other words, linguistic trails may constitute geographical clines of typological properties. This may need explanation. Suppose languages spoken in one area initially all have one and the same typological property, but some of them have additionally developed a propensity for expanding the property (i.e., high intensity), whereas others lack that propensity (i.e., low intensity). In other words, there is a disparity in intensity in the initial population of languages. When some of the languages migrate into a new area, the original disparity in intensity may also be carried from the old area to the new. The disparity, however, will now be displayed on a larger scale, that is, over the combined old and new areas. (The geographical scale will increase in proportion to the number of newly colonised areas.) The original disparity will thus play out on an increasingly larger scale as languages spread over time, although it will remain to be evident in each of the areas involved, albeit to varying degrees. The direct consequence of this is that the range of intensity will be different between the old and new areas to the effect that, for instance, the maximum level of intensity found in the new area may be higher than that found in the old area.[6] Thus, the initial disparity in the old area is manifested or 'replicated' by the disparity in the range of intensity between the old and the new area themselves, i.e., the old and the new area occupying the lower and the higher end of the intensity scale, respectively, as it were. This is schematised in Figure 1. The old area (or the left oval in Figure 1) exhibits a range of intensity from 1 to 3. (The higher the number, the greater the intensity.) The range of intensity in the first new area (or the middle oval) is from 2 to 5, and that in the second or last new area (or the right oval) from 4 to 8. The initial disparity in intensity in the old area is defined by the range of intensity in that area, i.e., from 1 to 3. This initial range of intensity then contrasts with the range of intensity in the first new area, i.e., from 2 to 5. In other words, the disparity in intensity in the combined old and first new area is between the range of intensity in the old area (i.e., 1 to 3) and that in the first new area (i.e., 2 to 5). Also note that the maximum level of intensity of the middle oval (i.e., 5) is greater than that of the left oval (i.e., 3); the maximum level of intensity of the right oval (i.e., 8) is greater than that of the middle oval. This is not unexpected, because, in order to play out the initial disparity on an increasingly larger scale, the maximum level of intensity in new areas will become higher than that in old areas (cf. Nichols 1992). In fact, one consequence of this may well be the maximal stabilisation of intensity at one extreme periphery of the geographical cline. Thus, by moving from the higher end of the geographical cline to the lower end (as in Figure 1), it may be possible to make inferences about population migration itself.

---

[6] It can work the other way around, the old area being the higher end of the intensity scale and the new area being the lower end of the scale. In this case, the property is 'dying out' as one moves further from the origin of dispersal.

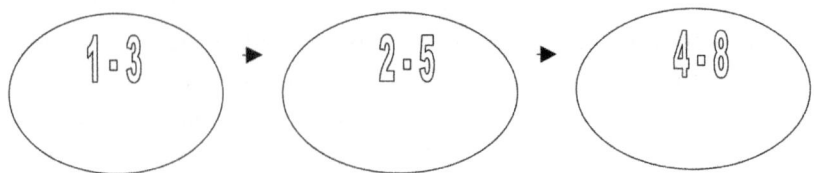

Figure 1. Geographical cline of intensity.
Note: The higher the number the greater the intensity of the typological marker. Each of the ovals represents a geographical area. ▶ = direction of migration

The preceding discussion suggests that an area that fails to fit in with a gradual geographical cline of intensity (e.g., by displaying a markedly different range of intensity) may not belong properly to the linguistic trail, even though it contains languages with the typological property in question. Such an area may have to be excluded from the linguistic trail, because languages in the area may always have had the property without having borrowed it from migrant languages. At best, the area may need to be regarded as suspect, insofar as the linguistics trail is concerned. By the same token, languages spoken in that area may also not form part of the linguistic trail.

This also implies that language groups that exhibit a comparable range of intensity may have migrated from, or stayed together in, one and the same area. For instance, it is difficult to expect language groups with a range of intensity to have travelled or spent time together with language groups without a similar range of intensity. It makes more sense to put together language groups with a comparable range of intensity, and to regard them as having dispersed from, or having spent time together in, the same area.

How does the preceding discussion apply to the topic of this paper? Proto Nuclear Micronesians did not originate from within Micronesia, but colonised the area from somewhere else. That much is uncontroversial. As discussed in section 2, geographically adjacent areas such as the Admiralty Islands, the St Matthias Islands, the Cristobal-Malaitan region, and the northern Vanuatu have all been put forth as the homeland for Proto Nuclear Micronesians. On the basis of geographical proximity alone, other adjacent areas, i.e., the Marianas, New Ireland, the western Solomon Islands (i.e., Bougainville, Choiseul and Santa Isabel) and Polynesia, should also be included in the list. On present evidence, however, three areas have emerged as strong candidates for the homeland of Proto Nuclear Micronesians: (i) the northern Vanuatu (or the greater southeast Solomons-Vanuatu region); (ii) the Cristobal-Malaitan region; and (iii) the Admiralty Islands. All located to the south of the Micronesian chain, these areas are more or less spread from east to west in that order. Thus, in terms of geographical propinquity Micronesia could have been settled from any one of the three, albeit with varying degrees of difficulty, or even from all of the three. If, however, there is a linguistic trail of the kind alluded to above, and if Micronesia is located on that trail, then it becomes crucial to ascertain whether or not any of the three areas is also found on the same trail. If, for example, one of the three areas is part of the linguistic trail whereas the other two are not, this will constitute evidence for the former being the homeland of Proto Nuclear Micronesians. Moreover, the other adjacent Oceanic-speaking areas, e.g., New Ireland, the western Solomon Islands and Polynesia, can also be assessed in order to determine whether or not they are located on the same trail, although there is currently no evidence, linguistic or otherwise, for them being Proto Nuclear Micronesians' homeland.[7] In other words, such a linguistic trail will also offer an opportunity to evaluate other available evidence or even the lack of evidence.

4. The linguistic trail of possessive classifiers

One of the typological properties that make Nuclear Micronesian languages stand out from the rest of the Oceanic group is that the former, with the sole exception of Kiribati, have an extremely large number of so-called possessive classifiers, ranging between fifteen and over twenty (Harrison 1988 and Song 1997; cf. Bender 1971: 457; see Allan 1977 for the classic overview of classifiers, and Aikhenvald 2003 for a recent treatment). As a matter of fact, Ulithian is reported to have as many as thirty-one possessive classifiers (Sohn and Bender 1973: 268–70). This indeed is a truly striking typological property of Nuclear Micronesian languages. The following examples come from Kusaiean (Lee 1975: 103–5, 242, 262).

(1a)   nu   na-k
       coconut   CL-1SG:POSS
       'my eating coconut'[8]

---

[7] The Mariana Islands are excluded because non-Oceanic, Austronesian languages are spoken there. There is ample evidence that this region was colonised from Southeast Asia (e.g., Craib 1983; Bellwood 1989; Intoh 1997).

[8] Abbreviations used in the examples: CL = possessive classifier; POSS = possessive; SG = singular.

(1b) mos   suhno-m
     breadfruit.tree CL-2SG:POSS
     'your breadfruit tree'

(1c) ik   osrwac-l
     fish   CL-3SG:POSS
     'his (or her) raw fish'

Note that in (1) the possessor marking (i.e., first, second or third person) is attached directly to the possessive classifier (i.e., *na-*, *suhno-* or *osrwac-*), whereby the semantic or culturally significant relation between the possessor and the possessed (i.e., *nu*, *mos*, *ik*) is explicitly indicated (cf. Lichtenberk 1983a, 1983b, 2009). Moreover, given possessor X and possessed Y, the 'edible' possessive classifier expresses that Y is food to X; the 'drinkable' possessive classifier indicates that Y is a drink to X, and so forth. It is thus possible that possessed Y, e.g., coconut, can enter into multiple relationships, e.g., food, drink and plant, with possessor X. This phenomenon is referred to as 'overlap' by Lynch (1973: 76). This is also why Lichtenberk (1983a: 148) chooses to refer to possessive classifiers as relational classifiers as opposed to 'sortal' or 'mensural' classifiers (cf. Allan 1977). The overlap is demonstrated by Ulithian (Sohn and Bender 1973: 270).

(2a) lawu-yi   ixi
     CL-my   fish
     'my fish, that I am keeping' [i.e., intimate property possession]

(2b) xala-yi   yixi
     CL-my   fish
     'my cooked-fish food' [i.e., cooked-food possession]

(2c) xocaa-yi   yixi
     CL-my   fish
     'my raw-fish food' [i.e., raw-food possession]

(2d) xolo-y   yixi
     CL-my   fish
     'my fish that I caught' [i.e., prey possession]

In comparison, non-Micronesian Oceanic languages have a much smaller number of possessive classifiers. In point of fact, Pawley (1973) and Lichtenberk (1985) have reconstructed only two or three possessive classifiers for POc, respectively.[9] The size of the possessive classifier system found in Nuclear Micronesian languages is truly something of a marvel.

What this suggests is that Proto Nuclear Micronesian must have had a very strong propensity for enlarging the possessive classifier system to an extent never witnessed anywhere else in the Pacific. Moreover, it is very difficult to imagine that such a strong propensity is something that came into being only after Proto Nuclear Micronesians had entered Micronesia (that is, Proto Nuclear Micronesian had only two or three possessive classifiers when its speakers first arrived in Micronesia). The dramatic increase from two or three possessive classifiers in POc to over twenty in present-day Nuclear Micronesian is something that could not possibly have been achieved in Micronesia alone. To put it differently, Proto Nuclear Micronesians must have carried the propensity for a large number of possessive classifiers in their languages from somewhere else into Micronesia. This in turn points to the distinct possibility that whomever they may have interacted linguistically – and also culturally and genetically – with must have shared the same typological propensity, if not equally strong. Moreover, the area where Proto Nuclear Micronesians intermingled with these people(s) must then have been the former's immediate or last inferable homeland. It is also within the realms of possibility that Proto Nuclear Micronesians and the latter people(s) may have derived from a third common area. It is expected that Nuclear Micronesian will be located at the higher end of the geographical cline or the linguistic trail of possessive classifiers. The largest size of the possessive classifier system in Oceanic is witnessed in Nuclear Micronesian, after all. By going from this higher end of the geographical cline towards the lower end, will it be possible to trace the migration route of Proto Nuclear Micronesians back to their immediate homeland (cf. Figure 1).

---

[9] Unlike Lichtenberk (1985), Pawley (1973: 163–4) only tentatively reconstructs *ma- 'drinkable' for POc. Ross (1988: 185), in contrast, believes 'that POc in fact had a somewhat larger collection of … [possessive] classifiers [than has so far been reconstructed], and that it is the most frequently used which have survived' (also see Ross and Naess 2007: 484). Lynch (1998: 122–30) seems to share Ross's position but also suggests that some languages (e.g., Micronesian) may further have expanded the possessive classifier system. However, no hard evidence has yet been published in support of these views. In the absence of such evidence, it is assumed in common with Pawley (1973) and Lichtenberk (1985) that POc had two or three possessive classifiers.

4.1. The data

In order to substantiate the claim that the linguistic trail of possessive classifiers exists in the Oceanic-speaking world, a survey of all the primary subgroups of Oceanic will be carried out here. Strictly speaking, geographical areas, not linguistic subgroupings, must be adopted for this purpose. There, however, is a reasonably good degree of correlation between geographical division and linguistic affiliation in the Oceanic-speaking world. Thus, use of linguistic subgroupings will have little bearing on the nature and quality of the data to be collected for the survey. This also seems to be a much more convenient option than to develop a set of criteria for dividing the Oceanic-speaking world into a number of geographical areas. Pawley and Ross's (1995: 51–7) nine primary subgroupings of Oceanic, as reproduced in Figure 2, will be utilised for the purposes of the present investigation.

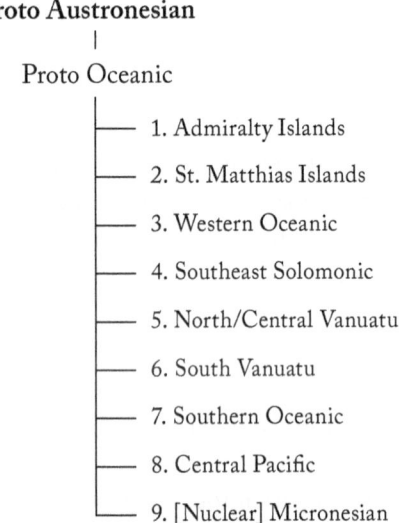

Figure 2. High-order and primary subgroups of Oceanic.

The Oceanic languages referred to or discussed in Lichtenberk (1985, 1986) and Ross (1988) were looked upon as a kind of 'convenience' database, from which languages could freely be selected for purposes of the survey. Not all of the languages listed in Lichtenberk (1985, 1986) and Ross (1988) were surveyed, however, because of either unavailability or lack of relevant or reliable information. Also included in the survey were three uncontroversially Austronesian (precisely, Oceanic) languages of the Eastern Outer Islands, i.e., Äiwoo, Asumboa and Tanimbili (Tryon 1994; Ross and Naess 2007). In addition to these three Eastern Outer languages, four Reefs-Santa Cruz languages from the Eastern Outer Islands, i.e., Natügu (a.k.a. Löndäi), Nanggu, Nea and Reefs, were included in the survey. There are three reasons for this. First, although there is a long-standing debate on whether the Reefs-Santa Cruz languages are Austronesian or Papuan (Wurm 1978; Lincoln 1978), there is an increasing amount of evidence for them to be Austronesian or precisely, Oceanic. In fact, Ross and Naess (2007: 459) go so far as to propose a primary subgroup for these languages under the name of Temotu (although they (p. 460) also acknowledge that the Austronesian status of the Santa Cruz languages 'remains to be demonstrated'). Second, as will later be argued, there is a strong possibility that it was these languages (or more accurately their progenitor(s)), not other Oceanic languages, that may have been the ones to expand the possessive classifier system, together with Proto Nuclear Micronesian, on a large scale. Third and most importantly, the main objective of the survey is to reconstruct population migration, not to establish linguistic subgroupings. Thus, in order to complete the whole picture of the linguistic trail, it is vital to include all (documented) languages of the area in the survey irrespective of their genealogical relationships.

Thus, data on as many as seventy seven non-Nuclear Micronesian Oceanic languages and nine Nuclear Micronesian languages were collected from the available sources (i.e., eighty six in total). It must be admitted, though, that a significant portion of the sample (i.e., 26.7%) came directly from Smythe's (1970) summary of grammatical properties of twenty-three Admiralties languages. Nonetheless, all the primary Oceanic subgroups were reasonably well represented in the sample. The names of the subgroups, followed by the number of surveyed languages in parentheses, are: the Admiralty Islands (23), St. Matthias Islands (1), Western Oceanic (14), Southeast Solomonic (10), North/Central Vanuatu (8), South Vanuatu (3), Southern Oceanic (5), Central Pacific (6), Eastern Outer Islands (7), and Nuclear Micronesian (9). The relevant data are summarized in tabular form in Appendix 1.

4.1.1. The Admiralty Islands

Smythe (1970: 1212) provides a brief summary of grammatical properties of twenty-three languages from this subgroup. These languages have one or two possessive classifiers, with the sole exception of Ninigo, which has as many as five. There are no languages in this subgroup that completely lack possessive classifiers, however. Thus, the number of possessive classifiers in almost all the Admiralties languages ranges from one to two.

4.1.2. St Matthias Islands

There is not much information on languages of the St Matthias Islands. Fortunately, there are data available on one of them, namely Mussau. Brownie and Brownie (2007: 77) list as many as fourteen possessive classifiers for Mussau.

4.1.3. Western Oceanic

The majority of the Western Oceanic languages may be said to have two possessive classifiers, although two of these, i.e., Mangap-Mbula and Banoni, seem to have a very dilapidated possessive classifier system. Five or six of these languages lack possessive classifiers completely. One or two have only one possessive classifier. The maximum number of possessive classifiers in Western Oceanic never exceeds the number of POc possessive classifiers, as has been reconstructed by Pawley (1973) and Lichtenberk (1985).

4.1.4. Southeast Solomonic

This subgroup is not very different from the Western Oceanic subgroup in terms of the number of possessive classifiers. The majority of these languages range from one to two in size. There are three languages that completely lack possessive classifiers, although one of them, Kwaio, may be said to have remnants of two possessive classifiers (Keesing 1985: 23–4, 115). Thus, the Southeast Solomonic languages can be said to deviate very little from the reconstructed POc (Pawley 1973; Lichtenberk 1985) or from Western Oceanic, insofar as the size of the possessive classifier system is concerned.

4.1.5. North/Central Vanuatu

The majority of the North/Central Vanuatu languages have four or more possessive classifiers. In fact, Sakao (Guy 1974) has as many as seven possessive classifiers, whereas Ambrym (Paton 1971) has six. There are two or three languages which lack possessive classifiers. The number of possessive classifiers in most of the North/Central Vanuatu languages exceeds that in Western Oceanic or Southeast Solomonic.

4.1.6. South Vanuatu

Two of the three South Vanuatu languages in the sample, i.e., Lenakel (Lynch 1978) and Anejom (Lynch 1982), exhibit as many as five possessive classifiers. The other language, Sye (Crowley 1998), lacks possessive classifiers. This subgroup is thus more akin to North/Central Vanuatu in terms of the number of possessive classifiers than either to Western Oceanic or to Southeast Solomonic.

4.1.7. Southern Oceanic

The number of possessive classifiers in this subgroup also ranges from none to possibly more than seven possessive classifiers. Tinrin has seven (Osumi 1995), whereas Iaai is said to have six (Tryon 1968b) or ten (Lynch 1998: 127). There are also two languages with no possessive classifiers (i.e., Dehu and Nengone) and one language with only one possessive classifier (i.e., Ajië).

4.1.8. Central Pacific

Fijian stands out from the rest of the Central Pacific subgroup in that it has three possessive classifiers (Milner 1972). The other Central Pacific languages, with the exception of Niuean and Rotuman, have the so-called *o/a* (i.e., inalienable vs. alienable, or uncontrolled vs. controlled) distinction. Niuean completely lost this Polynesian *o/a* distinction (Biggs 1971: 470), whereas Rotuman seems to have only a relic of POc possessive classifier *ka- 'edible/subordinate' in one of its so-called possessive prepositions (Churchward 1940: 31, Pawley 1972: 86, 1979: 21–2). The generalised *o/a* distinction cannot be strictly said to constitute the same type of possessive classifier system exhibited by other Oceanic languages, but it may well have been derived from the POc possessive classifier system (see Wilson 1982 for this view). At any rate, the maximum number of possessive classifiers found in Central Pacific does not deviate from what has been reconstructed for POc, notwithstanding its alteration of the original POc possessive classifier system.

4.1.9. Eastern Outer Islands

Two of the three uncontroversially Austronesian languages sampled from the Eastern Outer Islands, i.e., Asumboa and Tanimbili (both spoken on Utupua Island), have five possessive classifiers each, while the third, i.e., Äiwoo (the Reef Islands), has six. The four Reefs-Santa Cruz languages, which have not yet been conclusively demonstrated either as Austronesian or as Papuan, have far more possessive classifiers than Äiwoo, Asumboa or Tanimbili. Natügu has fourteen possessive classifiers, Nanggu eleven, Reefs ten, and Nea eight (Wurm 1969, 1972, 1978). These languages are the ones in the sample that approximate more closely to Nuclear Micronesian in terms of the size of the possessive classifier system than do any other subgroups.

4.1.10. Nuclear Micronesian

Not much will be said about this subgroup, except that it exceeds all the others in terms of the number of possessive classifiers by a decisive margin, and that only one Nuclear Micronesian language, Kiribati, lacks possessive classifiers (cf. Harrison 1988 and Song 1997). There is reason to suspect that Kiribati lost its possessive classifier system due to Polynesian influence (Song 1997: 44). Thus, apart from Kiribati, the size of the possessive classifier system in Nuclear Micronesian ranges from eight to thirty one. It is quite possible that Sonsorolese/Tobian may have more than eight possessive classifiers that they are reported to have (Capell 1969: 28).

4.2. *The geographical cline of possessive classifiers: An interpretation*

The preceding survey points to one significant fact. There are two 'sets' of language subgroups in Oceanic in terms of the quantitative range of possessive classifiers. In Oceanic subgroups such as Western Oceanic, Southeast Solomonic and Central Pacific, the maximum number of possessive classifiers never exceeds that of POc, i.e., two or three. The North/Central Vanuatu, South Vanuatu, Southern Oceanic and Eastern Outer Islands subgroups, on the other hand, contain languages the maximum number of possessive classifiers of which exceeds that of POc by a decisive margin. When, in fact, the areas where the language subgroups of the second 'set' are spoken are all connected (cf. the darkened areas in Map 1), an unbroken or uninterrupted line can literally be drawn from New Caledonia (i.e., Southern Oceanic) all the way to Micronesia (i.e., Nuclear Micronesian). In North/Central Vanuatu, South Vanuatu and Southern Oceanic, languages tend to have four to seven possessive classifiers. This trend continues well into the Eastern Outer Islands, with Asumboa and Tanimbili each having five possessive classifiers. (This area also contains Polynesian Outlier languages, i.e., Pileni and Tikopian-Anutan (Tryon 1994: 613).)[10] This geographical line is linked ultimately to Micronesia, where the size of possessive classifiers has 'exploded' into the range of eight or fourteen to thirty one. Moreover, Reefs-Santa Cruz languages are also located in the Eastern Outer Islands. For instance, one of these languages, Natügu, is reported to have as many as fourteen possessive classifiers. Thus, right on the doorstep of Micronesia are languages with a nearly comparable size of the possessive classifier system located. With the first 'set' of language subgroups ignored (i.e., lacking the propensity for enlarging the possessive classifier system beyond the size of POc; the undarkened areas in Map 1), the geographical line from New Caledonia to Micronesia may embody two separate clines with Vanuatu as the centre of dispersal: (i) a south-to-north cline from the lower end of

---

[10] The arrival of these Polynesian Outlier languages is understood to post-date that of Lapita colonisers and that of western Melanesians (Green 1976a: 50–1).

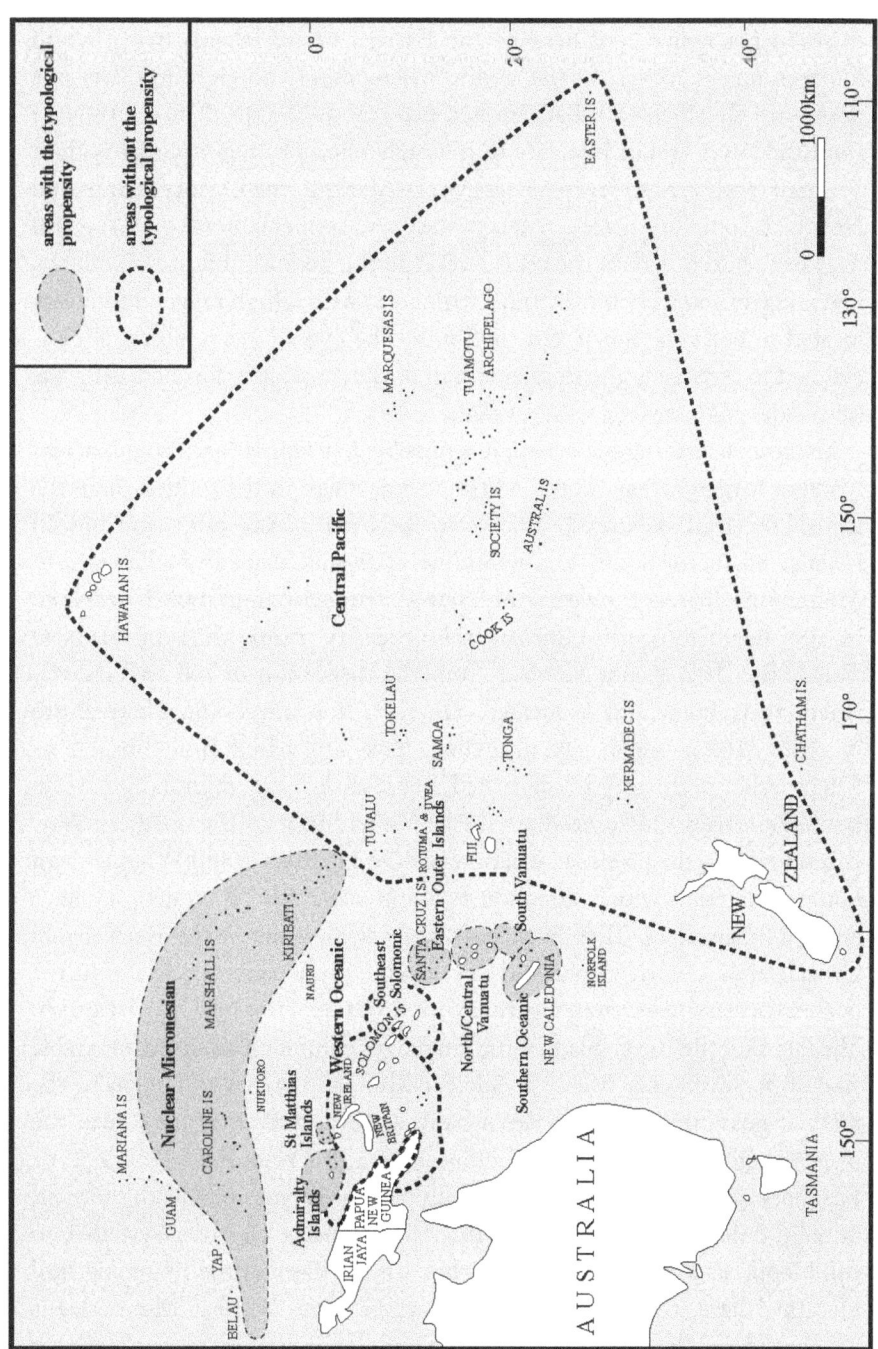

Map 1. Primary subgroups of Oceanic languages based on Pawley and Ross. (1953: 53)

intensity to the higher end of intensity, that is from Vanuatu (with zero to seven possessive classifiers) to the Eastern Outer Islands (with five to fourteen possessive classifiers), and to Micronesia (with eight to thirty one possessive classifiers; Kiribati ignored here), and (ii) a north-to-south cline from the lower end of intensity to the higher end of intensity, that is from Vanuatu (with zero to seven possessive classifiers) to the Loyalty Islands and New Caledonia (with zero to ten possessive classifiers). Note that Vanuatu has been chosen here as the centre of dispersal, because this area exhibits a low range of intensity on the trail, with areas with a high range of intensity located to both the north and the south. The overall geographical cline is claimed to constitute the linguistic trail of the propensity for increasing the size of the possessive classifier system.

In view of this linguistic trail, it is possible to propose that Proto Nuclear Micronesians may have travelled from somewhere in the south, where the rest of the trail is plotted. This vector of Micronesian migration indeed is reflected in the south-to-north cline of the intensity from Vanuatu to Micronesia (just as the vector of 'New Caledonian' migration is reflected in the north-to-south cline of the intensity from Vanuatu to New Caledonia). It may not be clear from the discussion of the trail exactly where their homeland is located. (In fact, it is irrelevant where Proto Nuclear Micronesians may ultimately have originated from, insofar as Micronesian prehistory is concerned, because one may eventually have to trace their origin to somewhere in the Vitiaz Strait or the northern New Britain region, the proposed location of POc à la Ross 1988.) What is clear, however, is from which direction Proto Nuclear Micronesians may have entered Micronesia. They must have spent some time in the Reefs-Santa Cruz Islands so that they could develop the propensity for enlarging the possessive classifier system together with Proto Reefs-Santa Cruz Islanders. The fact that the Reefs-Santa Cruz languages exhibit an almost comparable size of possessive classifiers to Nuclear Micronesian is a testament to the distinct possibility that the Reefs-Santa Cruz Islands may have been the place where Proto Nuclear Micronesians and Proto Reefs-Santa Cruz Islanders developed the typological propensity further before the former, once in Micronesia, finally brought the possessive classifier system into full bloom, as it were. This means that, on the basis of the linguistic trail identified here, the immediate homeland of Proto Nuclear Micronesians may have been the Reefs-Santa Cruz Islands, or at least that is the area that Proto Nuclear Micronesians left in the direction of Micronesia.

It is also quite possible that Proto Nuclear Micronesians and Proto Reefs-Santa Cruz Islanders may have travelled together from further down south in the trail, e.g., Vanuatu. In this scenario, Proto Nuclear Micronesians alone may then have continued to move further north from the Reefs-Santa Cruz Islands, leaving Proto Reefs-Santa Cruz Islanders behind. Alternatively, Proto Reefs-Santa Cruz Islanders may have migrated from Vanuatu to the Reefs-Santa Cruz Islands where they met pre-existing Proto Nuclear Micronesians. Whichever scenario is correct, the crucial point is that the two proto languages must have expanded the possessive classifier system together beyond the level witnessed nowhere else in the Pacific before parting company with each other *in* the Reefs-Santa Cruz Islands.[11] Thus, the entry point into Micronesia of Proto Nuclear Micronesians is none other than the Reefs-Santa Cruz Islands.

Three major areas have so far been proposed in Oceanic linguistics as the homeland of Proto Nuclear Micronesians: the Admiralty Islands, the Cristobal-Malaitan region, and the northern Vanuatu. The Admiralty Islands may possibly be a potential, albeit not very strong, candidate, because at least one language, i.e., Ninigo, is known to have as many as five possessive classifiers. As a matter of fact, not only the Admiralty Islands but also the St Matthias Islands (i.e., Mussau with fourteen possessive classifiers) form part of the linguistic trail. These two areas, however, could not have been the departure point for Proto Nuclear Micronesians. The 'transition' from the Admiralty Islands or the St Matthias Islands to Micronesia is less gradual in terms of intensity than that from the areas on the other side of the trail to Micronesia. From Vanuatu to the Reefs-Santa Cruz Islands and to Micronesia, the maximum number of possessive classifiers increases gradually from seven to fourteen to thirty one. By contrast, Ninigo and Mussau have five and fourteen possessive classifiers, respectively. The difference between five/fourteen possessive classifiers in the Admiralty/St Matthias Islands and thirty one in Micronesia, with no intervening groups of languages, is much too great to suggest that Proto Nuclear Micronesians may have spent time together with Proto Admiralty or St Matthias Islanders in the Admiralty Islands or the St Matthias Islands, respectively. It is more likely that both Ninigo and Mussau may have borrowed the propensity for

---

[11] The latter scenario may be in agreement with Green (1976a, 1976b), who argues on the basis of Lapita data that the arrival in the Santa Cruz Islands of non-Austronesian speakers occurred only in the post-Lapita period, because there is no evidence for a pre-Lapita occupation in the Santa Cruz Islands (McCoy and Cleghorn 1988: 112; cf. Spriggs 1984: 207, 1997: 7).

enlarging the possessive classifier system from Nuclear Micronesian some time after the colonisation of Micronesia. Also noteworthy in this context is that the maximum level of intensity in the Admiralty Islands has barely reached the minimum level of intensity in Micronesia. This suggests that the existence of a relatively high number of possessive classifiers in Ninigo or Mussau, in comparison with Western Oceanic or Southeast Solomonic, may well be due to comparatively recent contact between the two languages and Nuclear Micronesian (e.g., Spriggs 1997: 195), in fact, so recent that the level of intensity in the Admiralty Islands has not yet stabilised. As evidence in support of this view, attention is drawn to the fact that the size of the possessive classifier system in all other languages of the Admiralty Islands subgroup ranges only from one to two possessive classifiers, much smaller than that of North/Central Vanuatu, South Vanuatu and Southern Oceanic languages.

In the light of the linguistic trail, the second candidate, the Cristobal-Malaitan region (Blust 1984), turns out to be an extremely poor candidate for the Micronesian homeland. Languages spoken in that region (i.e., the Southeast Solomonic subgroup) do not even form part of the linguistic trail.

The picture emerging from the preceding discussion does also not match exactly the migration scenario built on Shutler and Marck's (1975) subgrouping hypothesis i.e., the northern Vanuatu, or more broadly, Pawley's (1972, 1977). However, at least this area is connected directly with the Reefs-Santa Cruz Islands not only in geographical terms, but also, more importantly, in terms of the linguistic trail. Proto Nuclear Micronesians may very well have reached the Reefs-Santa Cruz Islands from northern Vanuatu. (They must have come from somewhere else to the Reefs-Santa Cruz Islands.) If this is correct, it may also be possible to argue that Proto Nuclear Micronesians may have travelled from somewhere in northern Vanuatu or at least from that direction to the Reefs-Santa Cruz Islands. In this context, it is also worth taking note of the relatively long distance between northern Vanuatu and Micronesia, as opposed to that between either the Admiralty Islands or the St Matthias Islands and Micronesia. The distance between northern Vanuatu and Micronesia is matched by the gradually increasing intensity between them. The short distance between the Admiralty Islands or the St Matthias Islands and Micronesia, on the other hand, is matched by the abruptly increasing intensity between them. This may suggest that the 'transition' from northern Vanuatu to Micronesia may be of greater antiquity than that from either the Admiralty Islands or the St Matthias Islands to Micronesia. This in turn implies that the large size of the possessive classifier system witnessed in Micronesia may have derived from northern Vanuatu rather than from either the Admiralty Islands or the St Matthias Islands.

To wit, of the three potential homelands for Proto Nuclear Micronesians only the one derived from Shutler and Marck's (1975) hypothesis – or more broadly, Pawley's (1972, 1977) – fits in with what the linguistic trail of the typological propensity suggests: the Reefs-Santa Cruz Islands and, prior to that, northern Vanuatu.

5. Concluding remarks

The linguistic trail of the typological propensity points to the Reefs-Santa Cruz Islands and possibly also to northern Vanuatu as the immediate homeland of Proto Nuclear Micronesians. Insofar as lexicostatistical/historical-comparative linguistics is concerned, the main conclusion of the present paper is not incompatible with Shutler and Marck's (1975) or Pawley's (1972, 1977) subgrouping hypotheses. This conclusion also accords very well with both archaeological and genetic evidence. Based on the evidence from recovered pottery and cultural material artefacts, the southeast Solomons (i.e., the Reefs-Santa Cruz Islands) and northern Vanuatu have indeed been identified by archaeologists as the homeland of Proto Nuclear Micronesians (e.g., Athens 1990). Geneticists (e.g., O'Shaughnessy *et al.* 1990: 153), on the other hand, have proposed a broader area of (northern) Melanesia, that is, Vanuatu or the north Solomon Islands, as the Proto Nuclear Micronesian homeland.[12]

The migration route of Proto Nuclear Micronesians as proposed here on the basis of the linguistic trail is deemed plausible in physical terms also. That is, there are no reasons to regard the settlement of Micronesia by direct voyage from the Reefs-Santa Cruz Islands as improbable, as Irwin (1992) demonstrates by means of computer simulation. He (p. 122) explains that in one of his computer simulations, consisting of ten canoes sailing from the Reefs Islands by using realistic navigational skills, '[o]ne canoe reaches Banaba [a Kiribati-speaking island located in between the Kiribati Islands and Nauru], two reach Kiribati … [and t]he rest find seven separate landfalls in the Marshall Islands, three on the return leg of the journey after turning to sail home [see Map 1].' This particular test was carried out on

---

[12] Needless to say, this is not due to lack of precision in genetics-based population migration research but rather due to the relatively small number of sampled populations (Kirch 1997: 106). As the scope of their research is widened, geneticists will no doubt be able to locate the homeland of Proto Nuclear Micronesians in a more precise fashion.

the assumption that the canoes sailed off in January, 'a more difficult time', when they had to 'sail into the trade wind season of the northern hemisphere winter' (p. 122). Thus, direct voyage from the Reefs-Santa Cruz Islands to Micronesia is navigationally possible and feasible.

Finally, it goes without saying that the evidence from the linguistic trail is very limited. More languages have to be surveyed in order to strengthen the validity of the linguistic trail. Moreover, future research will need to look into the possibility of discovering other linguistic trails that may add weight to (or, as the case may be, detract from) the migration route of Proto Nuclear Micronesians that has been proposed here.[13] For these reasons alone, the nature of the present paper is highly exploratory. Nonetheless, it is hoped that it has achieved the objective of demonstrating the possibility of utilising linguistic-typological data in population migration research.

---

[13] Bender (1971: 457) mentions other typical Micronesian linguistic properties including elaborate demonstrative systems correlating with person categories and classification of nouns by numerals. The present writer's preliminary investigation has revealed, however, that the elaborate demonstrative systems seem to be confined to Nuclear Micronesian languages. They are not attested in any other Oceanic subgroups.

Appendix 1: Data

PRIMARY SUBGROUPS; Individual languages; (Sources); [Total number of possessive classifiers]

Note: ?? = possibly; ? = maybe; [X » Y], where X and Y represent the quantitative range of possessive classifiers

THE ADMIRALTY ISLANDS: [1 ≈ 5]	
Andra	(Smythe 1970) [2]
Aua	(Smythe 1970) [1]
Baluan	(Smythe 1970) [1]
Buyang	(Smythe 1970) [2]
Hus	(Smythe 1970) [2]
Levei	(Smythe 1970) [2]
Luf	(Smythe 1970) [2]
M'bunai	(Smythe 1970) [1]
Mokareng	(Smythe 1970) [2]
Mundrau	(Smythe 1970) [1]
Ninigo	(Smythe 1970) [5]
Nyada	(Smythe 1970) [1]
Pak	(Smythe 1970) [1]
Pityilu	(Smythe 1970) [1]
Ponam	(Smythe 1970) [1]
Rambutyo	(Smythe 1970) [1]
Sabon	(Smythe 1970) [1]
Sisi	(Smythe 1970) [2]
Sori	(Smythe 1970) [2]
Taui	(Smythe 1970) [2]
Tulu	(Smythe 1970) [2]
Warembu	(Smythe 1970) [1]
Yiru	(Smythe 1970) [1]

ST MATTHIAS ISLANDS:	
Mussau	(Brownie and Brownie 2007) [14]
WESTERN OCEANIC: [0 ≈ 2]	
Adzera	(Holzknecht 1986) [0]
Balawaia	(Kolia 1975) [1]
Banoni	(Lincoln 1976) [2?]
Kairiru	(Wivel 1981) [0]
Koliai-Kove	(Counts 1969) [2]
Labu	(Siegel 1984) [0]
Lara	(Lanyon-Orgill 1945) [1??]
Manam	(Lichtenberk 1983b) [2]
Mangap-Mbula	(Bugenhagen 1995) [2]
Mono-Alu	(Fagan 1986) [2]
Nakanai	(Johnston 1980) [0]
Nissan	(Todd 1978) [2]
Tigak	(Beaumont 1979) [0]
Tolai	(Mosel 1984) [2]
SOUTHEAST SOLOMONIC: [0 ≈ 2]	
Arosi	(Capell 1971) [1 or 2?]
Bugotu	(Ivens 1933) [2]
Inakona	(Capell 1930) [2??]
Kwara'ae	(Deck 1933–1934) [0]
Kwaio	(Keesing 1985) [0?]
Longgu	(Ivens 1934a) [1]
Oroha	(Ivens 1926–1928) [1 or 2??]
To'aba'ita	(Lichtenberk 1984) [0]
Ulawa	(Ivens 1913–1914) [1? or 2??]
Vaturanga	(Ivens 1934b) [2]

NORTH-CENTRAL VANUATU: [0 ≈ 7]	
Ambrym	(Paton 1971) [6]
Atchin	(Capell and Layard 1980) [4]
Big Nambas	(Fox 1979) [1?]
Namakir	(Sperlich 1991) [0]
Nguna	(Schütz 1969) [0]
Paamese	(Crowley 1982) [4]
Raxa	(Walsh 1966) [4]
Sakao	(Guy 1974) [7]
SOUTH VANUATU: [0 ≈ 5]	
Anejom	(Lynch 1982) [5]
Lenakel	(Lynch 1978) [5]
Sye	(Crowley 1998) [0]
SOUTHERN OCEANIC: [0 ≈ 10]	
Ajië	(Lichtenberk 1978) [1]
Dehu	(Tryon 1968a) [0]
Iaai	(Tryon 1968b, Lynch 1998) [6 or 10]
Nengone	(Tryon 1967) [0]
Tinrin	(Osumi 1995) [7]
CENTRAL PACIFIC: [0 ≈ 3]	
Fijian	(Milner 1972) [3]
Māori	(Bauer 1993) [2?]
Niuean	(Seiter 1980) [0]
Rapanui	(De Feu 1996) [2?]
Rotuman	(Churchward 1940) [1? or 2??]
Samoan	(Mosel and Hovdhaugen 1992) [2?]

EASTERN OUTER ISLANDS: [5 ≈ 14]	
Äiwoo	(Naess 2006) [6]
Asumboa	(Tryon 1994, per. comm.) [5]
Natügu (a.k.a Löndäi)	(Wurm 1972) [14]
Nanggu	(Wurm 1972) [11]
Nea	(Wurm 1972) [8]
Reefs	(Wurm 1972) [10]
Tanimbili	(Tryon 1994, pers. comm.) [5]
NUCLEAR MICRONESIAN: [0 ≈ 31] or [8 ≈31] if Kiribati is ignored	
Kiribati	(Groves, Groves and Jacobs 1985) [0]
Kusaiean	(Lee 1975) [19]
Marshallese	(Bender 1969, Zewen 1977) [14 or 15]
Mokilese	(Harrison 1976) [14 or more]
Ponapean	(Rehg 1981) [21 or more]
Sonsorolese/Tobian	(Capell 1969) [8 or more?]
Trukese	(Dyen 1965) [24 or more?]
Ulithian	(Sohn and Bender 1973) [31]
Woleaian	(Sohn 1975) [18]

References

Aikhenvald, Alexandra Y. 2003. *Classifiers: A Typology of Noun Categorization Devices*. Oxford: Oxford University Press.

Allan, Keith. 1977. Classifiers. *Language* 53: 285–311.

Ambrose, W. R., J. R. Bird and P. Duerden. 1981. The impermanence of obsidian sources in Melanesia. In F. Leach and J. Davidson (eds), *Archaeological Studies of Pacific Stone Resources*. Oxford: British Archaeological Reports, 1–19.

Athens, J. Stephen. 1990. Nan Madol pottery, Pohnpei. *Micronesica Supplement* 2: 17–32.

Bauer, Winifred. 1993. *Maori*. London: Routledge.

Beaumont, Clive H. 1979. *The Tigak Language of New Ireland*. Pacific Linguistics B-58. Canberra: Australian National University.

Bellwood, Peter S. 1989. The colonization of the Pacific: Some current hypotheses. In Adrian V.S. Hill and Susan W. Serjeantson (eds), *The Colonization of the Pacific: A Genetic Trail*. Oxford: Clarendon Press, 1–59.

Bender, Byron W. 1969. *Spoken Marshallese*. Honolulu: University of Hawaii Press.

Bender, Byron W. 1971. Micronesian languages. In Thomas A. Sebeok (ed.), *Current Trends in Linguistics. Vol. 8: Linguistics in Oceania*. The Hague: Mouton, 426–65.

Biggs, Bruce. 1971. The languages of Polynesia In Thomas A. Sebeok (ed.), *Current Trends in Linguistics. Vol. 8: Linguistics in Oceania*. The Hague: Mouton, 466–505.

Blust, Robert. 1984. Malaita-Micronesian: An Eastern Oceanic subgroup? *Journal of the Polynesian Society* 93 (2): 99–140.

Brownie, John and Marjo Brownie. 2007. *Mussau Grammar Essentials*. Ukarumpa: SIL-PNG Academic Publications.

Bugenhagen, Robert D. 1995. *A Grammar of Mangap-Mbula : An Austronesian Language of Papua New Guinea*. Pacific Linguistics C-101. Canberra: Australian National University.

Capell, Arthur. 1930. The language of Inakona, Guadalcanal, Solomon Islands. *Journal of the Polynesian Society* 39: 113–36.

Capell, Arthur. 1969. *Grammar and Vocabulary of the Language of Sonsorol-Tobi*. Sydney: University of Sydney.

Capell, Arthur. 1971. *Arosi Grammar*. Pacific Linguistics B-20. Canberra: Australian National University.

Capell, Arthur and John Layard. 1980. *Materials in Atchin, Malekula: Grammar, Vocabulary and Texts*. Pacific Linguistics D-20. Canberra: Australian National University.

Churchward, C. Maxwell. 1940. *Rotuman Grammar and Dictionary*. Sydney: Methodist Church of Australasia.

Counts, David R. 1969. *A Grammar of Kaliai-Kove*. Honolulu: University of Hawaii Press.

Craib, John L. 1983. Micronesian prehistory: An archaeological overview. *Science* 219: 922–7.

Crowley, Terry. 1982. *The Paamese Language of Vanuatu*. Pacific Linguistics B-87. Canberra: Australian National University.

Crowley, Terry. 1998. *An Erromangan (Sye) Grammar*. Honolulu: University of Hawaii Press.

Deck, Norman C. 1933–4. A grammar of the language spoken by the Kwara'ae people of Mala, British Solomon Islands. *Journal of the Polynesian Society* 42: 33–48, 133–44, 241–56; 43: 1–16, 85–100, 163–70, 246–57.

Du Feu, Veronica. 1996. *Rapanui*. London: Routledge.

Dyen, Isidore. 1965. *A sketch of Trukese Grammar*. New Haven: American Oriental Society.

Fagan, Joel L. 1986. *A grammatical Analysis of Mono-Alu (Bougainville Straits, Solomon Islands)*. Pacific Linguistics B-96. Canberra: Australian National University.

Fox, G. J. 1979. *Big Nambas Grammar*. Pacific Linguistics B-60. Canberra: Australian National University.

Grace, George W. 1955. Subgrouping of Malayo-Polynesian: A report of tentative findings. *American Anthropologist* 57 (2): 337–9.

Green, Roger C. 1976a. Languages of the Southeast Solomons and their historical relationships. In R. C. Green and M. M. Cresswell (eds), *Southeast Solomon Islands Culture History*. Royal Society of New Zealand Bulletin No. 11, 47–60.

Green, Roger C. 1976b. Lapita sites in the Santa Cruz Group. In R. C. Green and M. M. Cresswell (eds), *Southeast Solomon Islands Culture History*. Royal Society of New Zealand Bulletin No. 11, 245–65.

Groves, Terab'ata R., Gordon W. Groves and Roderick Jacobs. 1985. *Kiribatese: An Outline Description*. Pacific Linguistics D-64. Canberra: Australian National University.

Guy, Jaques B. M. 1974. *A Grammar of the Northern Dialect of Sakao*. Pacific Linguistics B-33. Canberra: Australian National University.

Harrison, Sheldon P. 1976. *Mokilese Reference Grammar*. Hawaii: University Press of Hawaii.

Harrison, Sheldon P. 1988. A plausible history for Micronesian possessive classifiers. *Oceanic Linguistics* 27: 63–78.

Holzknecht, Susanne. 1986. A morphology and grammar of Adzera (Amari dialect), Morobe Province, Papua New Guinea. *Papers in New Guinea Linguistics* 24: 77–166. Pacific Linguistics A-70.

Intoh, Michiko. 1997. Human dispersals into Micronesia. *Anthropological Science* 105 (1):15–28.

Irwin, Geoffrey. 1992. *The Prehistoric Exploration and Colonisation of the Pacific*. Cambridge: Cambridge University Press.

Ivens, Walter G. 1913–4. Grammar of the language of Ulawa, Solomon Islands. *Journal of the Polynesian Society* 22: 28–35, 96–103, 134–40, 219–24; 23: 21–7.

Ivens, Walter G. 1926–8. A study of the Oroha language, Mala, Solomon Islands. *Bulletin of the School of Oriental and African Studies* 4: 587–610.

Ivens, Walter G. 1933. A grammar of the language of Bugotu, Ysabel Island, Solomon Islands. *Bulletin of the School of Oriental and African Studies* 7: 141–77.

Ivens, Walter G. 1934a. A grammar of the language of Longgu, Guadalcanal, British Solomon Islands. *Bulletin of the School of Oriental and African Studies* 7: 601–21.

Ivens, Walter G. 1934b. A grammar of the language of Vaturanga, Guadalcanal, British Solomon Islands. *Bulletin of the School of Oriental and African Studies* 7: 349–75.

Jackson, Frederick H. 1986. On determining the external relationships of the Micronesian languages. In Paul Geraghty, Lois Carrington and S. A. Wurm (eds), *FOCAL II: Papers from the Fourth International Conference on Austronesian Linguistics*. Pacific Linguistics C-94. Canberra: Australian National University, 201–38.

Johnston, Raymond L. 1980. *Nakanai of New Britain: The Grammar of an Oceanic Language*. Pacific Linguistics B-70. Canberra: Australian National University.

Keesing, Roger M. 1985. *Kwaio Grammar*. Pacific Linguistics B-88. Canberra: Australian National University.

Kirch, Patrick V. 1997. *The Lapita Peoples: Ancestors of the Oceanic World*. Oxford: Blackwell.

Kolia, J. A. 1975. A Balawaia grammar sketch and vocabulary. In T. E. Dutton (ed.), *Studies in Languages of Central and South-East Papua*. Pacific Linguistics C-29. Canberra: Australian National University, 107–226.

Lanyon-Orgill, P. A. 1945. Grammar of the Pokau language, Central Division of Papua New Guinea. *Bulletin of the School of Oriental and African Studies* 11: 641–55.

Lee, Kee-dong. 1975. *Kusaiean Reference Grammar*. Honolulu: University Press of Hawaii.

Lichtenberk, Frantisek. 1978. A sketch of Houailou grammar. *University of Hawai'i Working Papers in Linguistics* 10 (2): 74–116.

Lichtenberk, Frantisek. 1983a. Relational classifiers. *Lingua* 60: 147–76.

Lichtenberk, Frantisek. 1983b. *A Grammar of Manam*. Honolulu: University of Hawaii Press.

Lichtenberk, Frantisek. 1984. To'aba'ita language of Malaita, Solomon Islands. *Working Papers in Anthropology, Archaeology, Linguistics, and Maori Studies*, No. 65. Department of Anthropology, University of Auckland.

Lichtenberk, Frantisek. 1985. Possessive constructions in Oceanic languages and in Proto-Oceanic. In Andrew Pawley and Lois Carrington (eds), *Austronesian Linguistics at the 15th Pacific Science Congress*. Pacific Linguistics C-88. Canberra: Australian National University, 93–140.

Lichtenberk, Frantisek. 1986. Syntactic-category change in Oceanic languages. *Oceanic Linguistics* 24: 1–84.

Lichtenberk, Frantisek. 2009. Oceania possessive classifiers. *Oceanic Linguistics* 48: 379–402.

Lichtenberk, Frantisek. 2010. Southeast Solomonic: A view from possessive constructions. *Oceanic Linguistics* 49: 259–77.

Lincoln, Peter C. 1976. *Describing Banoni, an Austronesian Language of Southwest Bougainville*. Unpublished PhD thesis, University of Hawaii.

Lincoln, Peter C. 1978. Reefs-Santa Cruz as Austronesian. In Stephen A. Wurm and Lois Carrington (eds), *Second InternationalConference on Austronesian Linguistics: Proceedings*. Pacific Linguistics C-61. Canberra: Australian National University, 929–67.

Lynch, John. 1973. Verbal aspects of possession in Melanesian languages. *Oceanic Linguistics* 12: 69–102.

Lynch, John. 1978. *A Grammar of Lenakel*. Pacific Linguistics B-55. Canberra: Australian National University.

Lynch, John. 1982. Anejom grammar sketch. *Papers in Linguistics of Melanesia* 4: 93–154. Pacific Linguistics A-64.

Lynch, John. 1998. *Pacific Languages: An Introduction*. Honolulu: University of Hawaii Press.

Lynch, John, Malcolm Ross and Terry Crowley (eds). 2002. *The Oceanic Languages*. London: Routledge.

Marck, Jeffrey C. 1975. *The Origin and Dispersal of the Proto Nuclear Micronesians*. Unpublished MA thesis, University of Iowa.

Marck, Jeffrey C. 1986. Micronesian dialects and the overnight voyage. *Journal of the Polynesian Society* 95: 253–8.

Marck, Jeffrey C. n.d. Towards a multiple working hypothesis approach to problems in nuclear Micronesian settlement. Unpublished ms.

McCoy, Patrick C. and Paul L. Cleghorn. 1988. Archaeological excavations on Santa Cruz (Nendö), southeast Solomon Islands: Summary report. *Archaeology in Oceania* 23: 104–15.

Melton, Terry, Stephanie Clifford, Jeremy Martinson, Mark Batzer and Mark Stoneking. 1998. Genetic evidence for the Proto-Austronesian homeland in Asia: mtDNA and nuclear DNA variation in Taiwanese aboriginal tribes. *American Journal of Human Genetics* 63: 1807–23.

Milner, G. B. 1972. *Fijian Grammar*. Suva: Government Press.

Mosel, Ulrike. 1984. *Tolai Syntax and Its Historical Development*. Pacific Linguistics B-92. Canberra: Australian National University.

Mosel, Ulrike and Even Hovdhaugen. 1992. *Samoan Reference Grammar*. Oslo: Scandinavian University Press.

Naess, Åshild. 2006. Bound nominal elements in Äiwoo (Reefs): A reappraisal of the 'multiple noun class systems'. *Oceanic Linguistics* 45: 269–96.

Nichols, Johanna. 1992. *Linguistic Diversity in Space and Time*. Chicago: University of Chicago Press.

O'Shaughnessy, D. F., A. V. S. Hill, D. K. Bowden, D. J. Weatherall and J. B. Clegg. 1990. Globin genes in Micronesia: Origins and affinities of Pacific Island peoples. *American Journal of Human Genetics* 46: 144–55.

Osumi, Midori. 1995. *Tinrin Grammar*. Honolulu: University of Hawaii Press.

Paton, W. F. 1971. *Ambrym (Lonwolwol) Grammar*. Pacific Linguistics B-19. Canberra: Australian National University.

Pawley, Andrew. 1972. On the internal relationships of Eastern Oceanic languages. In R. C. Green and M. Kelly (ed.), *Studies in Oceanic Culture History, vol. 3*. Honolulu: Bernice P. Bishop Museum, 1–142.

Pawley, Andrew. 1973. Some problems in Proto-Oceanic grammar. *Oceanic Linguistics* 12: 103–88.

Pawley, Andrew. 1977. On redefining 'Eastern Oceanic'. Unpublished ms.

Pawley, Andrew. 1979. New evidence on the position of Rotuman. *Working Papers in Anthropology, Archaeology, Linguistics, and Maori Studies*, No. 56. Department of Anthropology, University of Auckland.

Pawley, Andrew. 1981. Melanesian diversity and Polynesian homogeneity: A unified explanation for language. In J. Hollyman and A. Pawley (eds), *Studies in Pacific Languages and Cultures in Honour of Bruce Biggs*. Auckland: Linguistic Society of New Zealand, 269–309.

Pawley, Andrew and Malcolm Ross. 1993. Austronesian historical linguistics and culture history. *Annual Review of Anthropology* 22: 425–59.

Pawley, Andrew and Malcolm Ross. 1995. The prehistory of the Oceanic languages: A current view. In Peter Bellwood, James J. Fox and Darrell Tryon (eds), *The Austronesians*. Canberra: Department of Anthropology, Australian National University, 39–74.

Rehg, Kenneth L. 1981. *Ponapean reference grammar*. Honolulu: University Press of Hawaii.

Rehg, Kenneth L. 1995. The significance of linguistic interaction spheres in reconstructing Micronesian prehistory. *Oceanic Linguistics* 34: 305–25.

Ross, M. D. 1988. *Proto Oceanic and the Austronesian Languages of Western Melanesia*. Pacific Linguistics C-98. Canberra: Australian National University.

Ross, Malcolm and Åshild Naess. 2007. An Oceanic origin for Äiwoo, the language of the Reef Islands. *Oceanic Linguistics* 46: 456–98.

Schütz, Albert J. 1969. *Nguna Grammar*. Honolulu: University of Hawaii Press.

Seiter, William. 1980. *Studies in Niuean Syntax*. New York: Garland.

Shields, Kenneth. 2011. Linguistic typology and historical linguistics. In J. J. Song (ed.), *Oxford Handbook of Linguistic Typology*. Oxford: Oxford University Press, 551–67.

Shutler, Richard and Jeffrey C. Marck. 1975. On the dispersal of the Austronesian horticulturalists. *Archaeology and Physical Anthropology in Oceania* 10 (2): 81–113.

Siegel, Jeff. 1984. Introduction to the Labu language. *Papers in New Guinea Linguistics* 23: 83–157. Pacific Linguistics A-69. Canberra: Australian National University.

Smythe, W. E. 1970. Melanesian, Micronesian, and Indonesian features in languages of the Admiralty Islands. In S. A. Wurm and D. C. Laycock (eds), *Pacific Linguistic Studies in Honour of Arthur Capell*. Pacific Linguistics C-13. Canberra: Australian National University, 1209–34.

Sohn, Ho-Min. 1975. *Woleaian Reference Grammar*. Honolulu: University Press of Hawaii.

Sohn, Ho-Min and Byron W. Bender. 1973. *A Ulithian Grammar*. Pacific Linguistics C-27. Canberra: Australian National University.

Song, Jae Jung. 1997. The history of Micronesian possessive classifiers and benefactive marking in Oceanic languages. *Oceanic Linguistics* 36 (1): 29–64.

Sperlich, Wolfgang B. 1991. *Namakir: A Description of a Central Vanuatu Language*. Unpublished PhD thesis, University of Auckland.

Spriggs, Matthew. 1984. The Lapita cultural complex: Origins, distribution, contemporaries and successors. *The Journal of Pacific History* 19 (3–4): 202–23.

Spriggs, Matthew. 1997. *Island Melanesians*. Oxford: Blackwell.

Todd, Evelyn M. 1978. A sketch of Nissan (Nehan grammar). In S. A. Wurm and Lois Carrington (eds), *Second International Conference on Austronesian Linguistics: Proceedings*. Pacific Linguistics C-61. Canberra: Australian National University, 1181–239.

Tryon, D. T. 1967. *Nengone Grammar*. Pacific Linguistics B-6. Canberra: Australian National University.

Tryon, D. T. 1968a. *Dehu Grammar*. Pacific Linguistics B-7. Canberra: Australian National University.

Tryon, D. T. 1968b. *Iai Grammar*. Pacific Linguistics B-8. Canberra: Australian National University.

Tryon, D. T. 1994. Language contact and contact-induced language change in the Eastern Outer Islands, Solomon Islands. In Tom Dutton and Darrell T. Tryon (eds), *Language Contact and Change in the Austronesian World*. Berlin: Mouton de Gruyter, 611–48.

Walsh, David S. 1966. *The Phonology and Phrase Structure of Raxa*. Unpublished MA thesis, University of Auckland.

Wilson, William H. 1982. *Proto-Polynesian Possessive Marking*. Pacific Linguistics B-85. Canberra: Australian National University.

Wivel, Richard. 1981. *Kairiru Grammar*. Unpublished MA thesis, University of Auckland.

Wurm, Stephen A. 1969. The linguistic situation in the Reef and Santa Cruz Islands. *Pacific Linguistics* A 21: 47–105.

Wurm, Stephen A. 1972. Notes on the indication of possession with nouns in Reefs and Santa Cruz Islands languages. *Papers in Linguistics of Melanesia* 3: 85–113. Pacific Linguistics A-35.

Wurm, Stephen A. 1978. Reefs-Santa Cruz: Austronesian, but ..! In Stephen A. Wurm and Lois Carrington (eds), *Second International Conference on Austronesian Linguistics: Proceedings*. Pacific Linguistics C-61. Canberra: Australian National University. 969–1010.

Zewen, François X. N. 1977. *The Marshallese Language: A Study of Its Phonology, Morphology and Syntax*. Berlin: Dietrich Reimer.

NOTES ON CONTRIBUTORS

József Andor is Honorary Professor at the Department of English Linguistics of the University of Pécs in Hungary. 'My research interests include frame semantics, lexicalist approaches to the study of pragmatics, syntax and textology, as well as the corpus-based linguistic description of English and Hungarian. I have published widely in these fields in various journals, edited books and volumes of conference proceedings. I have followed publications by Keith Allan on a regular basis for several decades. I met him at various international conferences of cognitively based linguistics. Beyond this, let me add that life, interestingly, drifted us into a closer personal and intellectual relationship by way of his getting to know two of my children who visited Melbourne a couple of decades ago.'

Mike Balint pursued on and off courses of study in linguistics and literature at Tel Aviv University from 1968 to 1975, then transferred to undertake a research PhD on mental representations in language usage at La Trobe University in Melbourne, but left academia soon after to go into business. He resumed his PhD at Monash University upon retirement (with Keith as main supervisor), completing it in 2011. Currently Mike is an Adjunct Research Fellow in the Linguistics Program at Monash University.

Margaret à Beckett turned her years of experience and interest in cross-cultural communication in private industry and Australian Government service in Australia and overseas to advantage when she extended her education by becoming a member of the Monash University MA program in Applied Linguistics. This led to her initial introduction to Keith Allan as one of his students. She later entered academia as a lecturer in communication studies at Victoria University, continuing her research focus on cross-cultural and sociolinguistic aspects of language use. When she was admitted to the Monash PhD program, Margaret was able to further her connection with Keith, particularly during the sabbatical period of her primary supervisor, Dr Heather Bowe, when Keith was appointed her supervisor. His advice and guidance during this period had a direct bearing on the outcome of her studies and the material presented here, although '…he would possibly be as surprised as I am to find that it led to the inclusion of my research in this Festschrift dedicated to him'.

Réka Benczes (PhD 2005) is Senior Lecturer at the Department of American Studies, Eötvös Loránd University, Budapest, and Visiting Research Fellow at the Department of Central Eurasian Studies, Indiana University, Bloomington. Her main fields of interest centre around linguistic creativity, word formation and cognitive linguistics. She has been a great fan and follower of Keith's work – especially those on lexical semantics – from the very start of her doctoral studies. In 2009, she applied for a Group of Eight Postdoctoral Visiting Fellowship, and wrote to Keith out of the blue, asking for his recommendation. Keith immediately responded and gave his full support to the application. Thanks to Keith, Réka spent a wonderful five months at Monash, during which her interest increasingly turned to non-prototypical cases of word formation processes. While at Monash, Réka also had the chance to meet Kate Burridge, with whom the present volume is – hopefully – only the start of a long series of future collaborations.

Barry Blake is currently Emeritus Professor at La Trobe University. 'I began my academic career at Monash in 1966 as a postgraduate working on Australian languages. After a brief period in Sydney I returned to Monash in 1970 as a lecturer, later senior lecturer and associate professor before taking up the Foundation Chair of Linguistics at La Trobe in 1988. Keith Allan joined the department at Monash in 1978 and we were in almost daily contact for over a decade, though Keith worked in semantics and I on morpho-syntax, particularly the grammar of Australian languages. In retirement I have taken an interest in language and the supernatural culminating in *Secret Language* (OUP 2010), an interest inspired by the two books Keith and Kate Burridge wrote.'

Kate Burridge is Professor of Linguistics in the School of Languages, Cultures and Linguistics (Monash University). 'After completing a BA Honours degree at the University of Western Australia, I proceeded to the University of London where I did a PhD on syntactic change in medieval Dutch. My collaboration with Keith began in 1988 while I was still a fledgling academic at La Trobe University. Our many years of collaboration have led to numerous publications on the topics of euphemism, dysphemism, jargon, insult, slang, politeness, taboo, censorship, the use of figurative language, and language and the brain. These have been the most rewarding and the most enjoyable years of my academic life, and they have been the most illuminating. It was Keith who taught me how to write – it was also Keith who taught me how to swear.'

Pedro J. Chamizo Domínguez (Malaga, Spain, 1952) is a tenured professor at the Department of Philosophy of the University of Malaga and currently teaches Philosophy of Language and History of Science. In addition to several Spanish universities, he has taught in universities of Germany, Italy, Slovakia, and the United States. He has published books, collaboration books, and papers in the five continents, in Spanish, English, Slovak, and French. His research topics deal with: (1) translation studies; (2) figures of language (mainly metaphor and euphemism); and 3) the language of political correctness. His most recent and publications in English are: (1) *Semantics and Pragmatics of False Friends* (2008, London & New York); (2) 'Linguistic Interdiction: Its status quaestionis and possible future research lines' (in *Language Sciences* 31, 2009); and (3) (With Brigitte Nerlich) 'Metaphor and Truth in Rationalism and Romanticism' (in Armin Burkhardt and Brigitte Nerlich (eds), *Tropical Truth(s): The Epistemology of Metaphor and other Tropes*. Berlin: De Gruyter, 2010). He is honoured by Keith Allan's friendship since 1998, in spite of the fact that, unfortunately, 'we met only two times all through our lives'.

Thorstein Fretheim is Emeritus Professor at NTNU (Norwegian University of Science and Technology) in Trondheim, Norway, where he has been doing pragmatic research since the seventies, for the past two decades with a relevance-theoretic bias. His main concern has been with studies of reference, information structure, pragmatic particles, the semantics – pragmatics interface, the distinction between procedural and conceptual meaning, and the relationship between intonational phonology and pragmatics. He knows Keith mainly from conferences (including, of course, the IPrA conference in Melbourne in 2009) and from email correspondence on matters of mutual interest.

Adam Głaz (b. 1970) is Associate Professor at the Department of English, Marie Curie-Skłodowska University in Lublin, Poland, from which he also received his PhD in 2001. His research interests include cognitive semantics, the application of Vantage Theory (VT) to linguistic problems, point of view in language and linguistics, ethnolinguistics, and language/linguistics in science fiction. He is the author of two monographs: *The Dynamics of Meaning: Explorations in the Conceptual Domain of EARTH* (2002) and *Extended Vantage Theory: The Case of the English Articles* (2012), both published by Marie Curie-Skłodowska University Press. Adam Głaz and Keith Allan have guest edited a special issue of the journal *Language Sciences* (vol. 32, issue 2): 'Vantage Theory: Developments and Extensions'. It is to a large extent thanks to this project, which involved an extensive and intensive exchange of views, that Głaz has developed his model of Extended Vantage Theory (EVT), largely inspired by Allan's VT2.

Zofia Golebiowski completed her PhD in 2002 at Monash University under the supervision of Professor Keith Allan. She works at Deakin University in the Faculty of Arts and Education, where she is a discipline leader in TESOL and LOTE, and teaches postgraduate courses in discourse analysis, linguistics and intercultural communication for language classrooms. Zofia has published on intercultural variation in academic English, relational analyses of texts and tertiary.

Kasia M. Jaszczolt is Professor of Linguistics and Philosophy of Language at the University of Cambridge. She published extensively on various topics in semantics and pragmatics, including propositional attitude ascription, representation of time, semantics/pragmatics interface, her theory of Default Semantics, and ambiguity and underspecification. One of her current project concerns attitudes *de se* and first-person reference, the other is a theory of *Interactive Semantics* (in progress, OUP). Her authored books include *Representing Time* (2009, OUP), *Default Semantics* (2005, OUP), *Semantics and Pragmatics* (2002, Longman) and *Discourse, Beliefs and*

Intentions (1999, Elsevier). Among her editorial commitments are editing a book series, membership of various editorial boards, and editing several volumes, including *The Cambridge Handbook of Pragmatics* (2012, CUP, with Keith Allan). In 2012 she was elected member of Academia Europaea. See also http://people.pwf.cam.ac.uk/kmj21.

Zoltán Kövecses is Professor of Linguistics in the Department of American Studies at Eötvös Loránd University, Budapest, Hungary. His main research interests include the theory of metaphor and metonymy, the conceptualization of emotions, the relationship between cognition and culture, and the issue of cultural variation in metaphor. He has taught widely at several American and European universities, including the University of Nevada at Las Vegas (1994 and 1996), Rutgers University (1987, 1989, 1990), University of Massachusetts at Amherst (1987), Hamburg University (1992–1993), Odense University (2000), the University of California at Berkeley (2003), University of Granada (2005), and Heidelberg University (2012/13). He also serves on the advisory board of several scholarly journals, including *Cognitive Linguistics*, the *Annual Review of Cognitive Linguistics*, and he is one of the four editors of *Metaphor and Symbol*. His most important books include *Language, Mind, and Culture: A Practical Introduction* (OUP, 2006); *Metaphor in Culture: Universality and Variation* (CUP, 2005); *Metaphor: A Practical Introduction* (OUP, 2002/2010); *Metaphor and Emotion* (CUP, 2000); *Emotion Concepts* (New York & Berlin: Springer-Verlag, 1990); and *The Language of Love* (Bucknell UP, 1988). He received the prestigious Charles Simonyi Award in 2008 and he was a distinguished fellow in the Institute of Advanced Study at Durham University, United Kingdom. Zoltán has been a long-time admirer of Keith's work, especially on lexical semantics, greatly influencing his own.

Olav Kuhn is currently assistant lecturer in the School of Languages, Cultures and Linguistics (Monash University) with a research interest in everything from historical linguistics and bilingual education to the creation of planned or artificial human languages. Keith was Olav's PhD supervisor and he recalls the speed of Keith's highly informative feedback: 'No matter how slow or fast I was with drafts, Keith was faster.'

Adrienne Lehrer was a pre-doctoral Fulbright scholar when she first met Keith Allan in Edinburgh, studying semantic theory with John Lyons. They later became friends during her first trip to Australia, where she was a visiting professor at La Trobe in 1983 and he was teaching at Melbourne. Keith spent time in Tucson, Arizona on an exchange in 1989, during which Keith was an invited speaker at an NSF conference on semantic fields and frames. Adrienne has written mostly on lexical semantics, and her early works focused on semantic fields. More recently she studied word formation, especially lexical blends and other creative neologisms. Her books include *Semantic*

Fields and Lexical Structure (1974), *Frames, Fields, and Contrasts*, edited with Eva Kittay (1992), and *Wine and Conversation* (1983), which was completely revised as *Wine and Conversation, Second Edition* (2009). She taught linguistics at the University Rochester, where she received her PhD, then moved to the University of Arizona in 1974 to start the linguistics department there. During her trips to Australia, in addition to La Trobe, she was a visiting scholar at the Research School of Social Science, Australian National University. With her husband Keith Lehrer she co-authored articles on wine language, antonymy, and a sketch of a semantic theory.

Simon Musgrave is a lecturer in the School of Languages, Cultures and Linguistics at Monash University. 'I completed my doctorate at the University of Melbourne in 2002, and was then a post-doctoral researcher at Leiden University and an Australian Research Council post-doctoral fellow at Monash. My research interests include Austronesian languages, language documentation and language endangerment, African languages in Australia, communication in medical interactions, and the use of technology in linguistic research. Major publications include the edited volumes *Voice and Grammatical Relations in Austronesian* (2008) and *The Use of Databases in Cross-linguistic Research* (2009). I have also been closely involved in the Australian National Corpus project from an early stage. I met Keith Allan at the 2000 Australian Linguistic Institute, where I attended his course on The Semantics of Number and experienced total bewilderment – this was entirely due to my shortcomings. Fortunately, I managed to conceal this sorry state from Keith and he welcomed me as a colleague when I came to Monash in 2003, although this welcome perhaps owed something to the fact that my arrival represented a 100% increase in the male staff of the program. Over the ensuing years I valued Keith's willingness to discuss linguistic matters at any time and in any place, I admired his efficiency (and impatience) in dealing with administrative chores, and I enjoyed the post-seminar lunch and wine tradition which he had established.'

Finex Ndlovou is currently senior lecturer in the School of Behavioural, Cognitive and Social Sciences at the University of New England. 'I got to know Keith Allan as supervisor of my PhD research in 2005, which I completed in a record time of 21 months. From the very start of my PhD candidature Keith proved to be an easy-going, laid back but outstanding and generous HDR supervisor with extraordinary ability to let the research student dream and drive the research process. During my tenure as his PhD student Keith's role was always that of facilitating and guiding the research process with me doing all the work. Since then, Keith has become my academic mentor and colleague who has consistently supported me during my postdoctoral career development. One specific attribute of Keith that has stuck with me is his almost contagious sense of humour coupled with his depth of knowledge across the fields of theoretical linguistics and pragmatics. His ability to supervise my PhD thesis on the politics of language and nation building in postcolonial Africa demonstrated beyond any reasonable doubt that Keith is a dynamic and versatile academic capable of traversing, with relative ease, the various sub-disciplinary fields of linguistics. With the following motto "A neat desk is a sign of an idle mind", Keith's desk was never the neatest one because his mind was always busy. I don't regret that this rubbed off onto me.'

Deborah Perrott is currently Consultant Psychologist in Auckland. She writes: 'Professor Keith Allan was my primary supervisor as a PhD student between 2004–2011. I will always be grateful for his excellent supervision and support over such a critical period. As a mature age part-time student, working and raising children, Keith worked considerately and compassionately around my commitments and showed genuine hospitality and care to my family. Keith always kept a big picture approach to supervision. His turn-around time for a draft chapter was often within a 24-hour period and in most cases drafts were returned via email BEFORE 6am! This was not only motivating as a student but helped maintain the momentum to continue writing. His comments were encouraging, even when a re-write chapter was suggested! Keith has continued to encourage me to write and I will always be thankful that he provided me with such a positive experience as a PhD student. Many thanks for all your time and expertise. Your contribution to the field of linguistics and pragmatics in particular, is remarkable.'

Farzad Sharifian is Professor and Director of the Language and Society Centre at Monash University. He is the author of *Cultural Conceptualisations and Language* (John Benjamins, 2011) and the Founding Editor of the *International Journal of Language and Culture* (John Benjamins). Keith Allan was Farzad's mentor at Monash University for five years prior to his retirement.

Jae Jung Song was a former student of Keith Allan at Monash University, where he completed his BA (Honours) and PhD, the latter under Keith's co-supervision. Jae was very fortunate to have the privilege of being taught by Keith, who was not only a world-class linguist – and continues to be, even after his retirement! – but also never failed to provide him with academic and moral support. Jae's chapter in this volume is a small tribute to Keith's generosity, thoughtfulness and kindness. Jae is currently Professor of Linguistics at the University of Otago (New Zealand). He has previously taught at Monash University and the National University of Singapore. He has also held visiting appointments with Max Planck Institute for Evolutionary Anthropology (Leipzig) and La Trobe University (Melbourne). He is the author of *Causatives and Causation: A Universal-Typological Perspective* (Addison Wesley Longman, 1996), *Linguistic Typology: Morphology and Syntax* (Pearson, 2001), *The Korean Language: Structure, Use and Context* (Routledge, 2005) and *Word Order* (CUP, 2012), the editor of *The Oxford Handbook of Linguistic Typology* (OUP, 2011) and the co-editor, with Anna Siewierska, of *Case, Typology and Grammar* (John Benjamins, 1998).

INDEX

abusive swearing, 8
academic writing, 236–259
ACE, *see* Australian Corpus of English
Admiralty Islands, languages of 387–388, 397, 407
adolescents, assimilation 267
    communication problems, 273
aggression, and language disorders, 267
algorithms 374, 376, 377
Allan, Keith, vii–ix, 126, 219–220, 288–289, 361–362, 365–366
    VT2, 343–344
ambiguity, 363
    and translation, 286–289
American English
    binomial expressions, 65
    speakers of, 136–138
anaphors, 198–217
ancestral spirit, personal pronoun for, 189–190
Andean languages, 47
anger concepts, basis of, 152–153
animal names, for wines and wineries, 115–118, 120
antecedents, 200, 207–211, 216
antonymy, 103–104
applied linguistics, 262
appositional compounds, 57, 58, 59–60
archaisms, and translation, 286, 289–291
aroma, of wines, 109–111
ART, *see* Australian Radio Talkback Corpus
article usage, analysis of, 344–352, 356
    conceptualisations 342
Ash, John 16–17
ASJP, *see* automated similarity judgment program
assessment of communication capacities, 262–263, 269, 271
association, 104
audience, of academic texts, 236
AusNC, *see* Australian National Corpus
AustLit, 5
Australian Corpus of English, 5, 19
Australian English, history, 3–5
Australian languages, 47, 78, 94–95, 96
Australian National Corpus, 5, 18
Australian Radio Talkback Corpus, 5
Austronesian languages, retention rates, 35
automated similarity judgment program, 36, 47, 50, 51
Bailey, Nathan, 16
Balto-Slavic languages, lexical stability, 36–39
Barsalou, Lawrence, 143, 146
Basic Set, 360 fn1, 362
basic vocabulary, 38–39, 50–51
bastard, change in usage, 6–7
    difference from bugger, 27–29
    history, 13–14
    in dictionaries, 14–17
    public acceptability, 17–18
Bauer, Laurie, 58, 59
beer terminology, 120–121
Bercow Report, 264, 273
binomials, 65, 68 fn31
biological semantic distinctions, 74, 81–83
birds, gender in French, 81–83
blasphemy, 6
blends, 67
Blust, Robert, 382, 386–387
BNC, *see* British National Corpus
Borg, Emma, 363–364
Borges, J.L., 283
British English, speakers of, 136–138
British National Corpus, 126, 133–134
bugger, change in usage, 6–7
    difference from bastard, 27–29
    history, 11–13
    in Australian English, 13
    in dictionaries, 14–17
    public acceptability, 17–18
bureaucratic language, 63
butterflies, gender, 83

Caballero, Rosario, 112–113
Cano Mora, Laura, 126
Carter, Ronald, 126
categorisation, 60–62, 356
    of wine terminology, 104–109
Celtic languages, lexical stability, 36–39
censorship, of swearing, 10, 11
Central Pacific languages, 399, 409
Chesterton, G.K., translation of, 293
childhood–adolescence transition, 265
Chomskyan models, 309, 312 fn12, 324, 330, 331, 332

church members, personal pronoun for, 188–189
Claridge, Claudia, 126–127, 128
clarification, synonymous compounds for, 67–68
class inclusion, 103
clauses, as analytical unit, 240
coders, 317–318
coffee terminology, 121
cognate finding, 39–43
cognates
    Germanic languages, 43–47
    Indo-European languages, 51
cognition motivation, 355, 356
cognitive database, 305, 308, 327
cognitive distance, 340–342
Cognitive Grammar, 324
cognitive linguistics, 143
cognitive operations, 143–145, 147–148
cognitive plausibility, 308–313, 324, 325, 329
cognitive processes, 355, 356
coherence relations, 240, 247, 253, 256
coherence, pressure of, *see* pressure of coherence
collocations, and translation, 286, 295–296
colloquialisation, of English language, 5
colonial parlance, 3–4
common ground, 219–220
    and cultural schemas, 225–226
    lack of, 232
    presumptions, 314
communication disorders, 262–275
    consequences of, 268–269
    management of, 263
    prevention, 273–274
    research, 270
communication profiles, 271
communication screening, 271, 272
communicative tools, of *târof*, 228
communicatively impaired populations, 264–268
competing properties, and gender determination, 86–88
concept-dependent meanings, 372
conceptual replication, 355
Conceptual Semantics, 324
conceptual systems, 143–158, 144, 145
conceptual transfer, 202
Connectionism, 324
connectives, *see* sentential connectives
construal operations, *see* cognitive operations
context, 143–158
    and conceptual systems, 146
    database, 305, 310, 316
    in knowledge, 146–148
    role of, 312
    types, 157–158
contexts, changeability, 145, 148
contextualism, 359–377
contextualist lexicon, 364–367
conversation, and *târof*, 226–227
COOEE, *see* Corpus of Oz Early English
coordinate strength, 340–342
coordinated compounds, 58
Copernicus, N., translation of, 284
Corbett, Greville G., 80
core meanings, 372
Cornish, Francis, 200
corpus data, 18–27
Corpus of Oz Early English, 5, 18
counter-charms, 169
creation stories, 165
cultural categories, 221
cultural cognition, 220–221, 224
cultural conceptualisations, 221–222
cultural context, 157–158
cultural metaphors, 221–222
cultural schemas, 222–226
curses, 166–171

Default Semantics, 373–374
deference, and personal pronoun usage, 193
definite plurals, 352–354
defixiones, *see* curses
delexicalisation, of adverbs, 134
    of hyperbolic expressions, 127, 128, 138
depressed adolescents, communication skills, 266
depression, assessment of adolescents, 271
Descartes, R., translation of, 289–291
dialect formation, 3–4
differential concerns, 150–151
differential experiential focus, 153
digression frequency, 255, 256 fn3
discourse communities, 258
discourse flow, and elaborations, 256
discourse participation entities, 155–156
discursive overstatement, 125
distant language relationships, 47–50
diversity distribution, 37
    rankings, 41–42
    values, 52
domain knowledge, 151
dual semantic systems, 93–95, 97
dvandva compounds, 58
Dyen, Isidore, 35

Index | 427

early intervention, in communication disorders, 272–273
early language skills, as predictor, 266
Eastern Outer Islands languages, 399, 410
eating of texts, 172–173
editorial policies, 258–259
elaboration, 236–237
  addition, 246–247, 255, 256
  amplification, 243–244, 247, 253
  explanation, 244–245, 248
  extension, 242–243, 247–248
  instantiation ,246, 248, 255, 256
  reformulation, 245–246, 248, 255
elaborative pervasiveness, 247–248, 254
elaborative relations, 238, 241–242, 253, 254, 255
elaborative rhetoric, 236–259
embodied experience, and conceptual systems, 146
embodiment, 151–152
emphatic device, synonymous compounds as, 65–66
employment, communication assessment, 273
encoding, result of, 306
encyclopedia database, 308, 310, 317, 327
endearment, 9, 10
English language
  and Ndebele address system, 195
  as global lingua franca, 5
  lack of gender, 293
erroneous translation, 286
euphemistic register, *see* hlonipha register
evaluative expressions, for wine, 111–112
exemplification categories, 246
experimental method, 375
expletives, use of, 7–8
explicatures, 211, 216, 217
Extended Vantage Theory, 344–352, 356
external influences, on writing style, 257–258

false friends, and translation, 291–293
family functioning, and communication skills, 267
family relationship, and personal pronouns, 182–185
FARS, *see* Framework for the Analysis of the Rhetorical Structure of Texts
final phoneme, determination of, 79–80
final sounds, semantic features, 92–93
Finno-Ugrian, lexical stability, 36–39
first-person pronouns, 389
flexibility, of meanings, 361, 372–373, 375
form–referent relationship, 161–162

formal domains, and personal pronoun usage, 187–191
Framework for the Analysis of the Rhetorical Structure of Texts, 239–240
Frege, Gottlob, 310
French language, gender in, 73–100
friends, personal pronoun for, 191–192
functional communication, 264
functional integrity, 241
functors, 325–326

Galilei, Galileo, translation of, 285
GCSAusE, *see* Griffith Corpus of Spoken English
gender
  and personal pronoun usage, 194
  and translation, 286, 293–294
  disagreements, 77–78
  in French language, 73–100
  neutralisation, 80
  variation in French, 77–78, 88, 94, 95
generic terms, for species, 82–83
genetic markers, and migration, 389
German language
  gender in, 76
  gender variation, 95
  response words, 204–205
Germanic languages
  lexical stability, 36–39
  subgrouping, 43–47
Gervais, Marie-Marthe, 77
Gevaert, Caroline, 153
given names, and gender, 162
global context, 153–154
global stability rankings, 41, 42
glottochronology, 34
God, personal pronoun for, 187–188
golems, 169
Grace, George W., 381
Grahm, Randall 114, 119
grammar, modelling of, 303–332
grammatical coding, 316, 317
grammatical flexibility, of bugger, 14, 29 fn17
grammatical form, lexical licensing of, 321–324
grammaticalisation, of hyperbolic expressions, 127, 128, 138
graphemes, 306, 308
Greek rhetorics, 124
greetings, and common ground, 225
Griffith Corpus of Spoken English, 5
Grimes, Joseph, 237, 242
Grose, Francis, 17

Halliday, M.A.K., 236–237, 242
Härmä, Juharni, 80
harmfulness, and gender determination, 83–84
Hatcher, Anna Granville, 59–60
head movements, 205–207
Hebrew names, 165–166
Hegel, G.W.H., translation of, 286
hierarchy, of elaboration placement, 248–249
historical-comparative linguistics, 383–384
hlonipha register, 179, 190
Hobbs, Jerry, 237
holistic approach, to language use, 311–312
humans, gender of terms for, 91
hyperbole, 124–127
    and misrepresentation of truth, 125
hyperbolic adverbial collocations, 124–138
hyperbolic expression
    studies of, 125–126
    and vagueness, 126
hyponym-superordinate compounds, 58–64
hyponymy, 103
hypotactic elaboration, 242, 244, 245, 250, 256
Hyppolite, Jean, 286

ICE-AUS, *see* International Corpus of English
idioms, and translation, 286, 294–295
image schemas, 151–152
imprecatives, 6
in-group solidarity, and swearing, 9, 10
in-patient psychiatric samples, 267
inconceivably
    British National Corpus analysis, 133
    dictionary definitions, 129, 131–132
    syntactic functions, 128
    variance in collocates, 136–138
incredibly
    British National Corpus analysis, 133
    dictionary definitions, 129–132
    syntactic functions, 128
    variance in collocates, 136–138
Indo-Euralic relationship, 48, 49
Indo-European languages, 34
    lexical stability, 36–39
informal domains, and personal pronoun usage, 191–192
insults, 8–9
intensity, disparity in, 391
intensity cline, 391–392
Interactive Semantics, 373
intergenerational transfer of disorders, 270

interlocutory language usage, 308–309, 310, 311, 314, 316
internalised language knowledge, 304, 308, 310, 311, 313–314, 317
International Corpus of English, 5, 19
intrasentential elaborations, 257
Iranian diaspora, 228–229
Irish English, speakers of, 136–138
-ist language, 6–7

Jackendoff, Ray, 324, 330, 331
Jackson, Frederick H., 385–388
Jespersen, Otto, 57
Johnson, Samuel, 15–16

katadesmoi, *see* curses
Kempson-Atlas thesis, 363
kinship relations, and language use, 177, 193–194
knowledge representation theory, 309
Köpcke, K.M., 76
Koyré, A., 284–285
Krige, Eileen Jensen, 177, 194

languaculture, influence on writing, 254
language
    and cultural cognition, 221
    and cultural schemas, 224–225
    function of, 303–304
language magic, 166–171
Language of Thought Hypothesis, 324, 330
language process, 314
language relationships, analysis, 33–34
language system, 314
    database, 310, 327
Latin, noun classification, 96
Leech, Geoffrey, 126
legal language, 68
lemmas, 306, 307–308, 316
lexemes, 305, 306, 316, 317–318, 327
lexical database, 305, 308, 310, 314, 317, 322, 327
lexical licensing, 321–324
lexical persistence estimation, 34
lexical semantics, 359–377
lexical stability, of European languages, 36–39
lexicographers, 15–17
lexicon, role of, 359–361, 375–376
lexicostatistical methods, 33–39
licensing rules, 315
linguistic context, 154–155

linguistic evidence, of migration routes, 383–384, 393
linguistic pragmatics, origins, 125
linguistic trails, 390, 392, 393–405
listemes, 304, 314, 318, 319, 322, 365
local context, 153–154
logical form, encoding of, 217
logographs, 308
Longacre, Robert, 242
Lynch, Jack, 17

MacLaury, Robert E., 336–337
magic formulae, 167–168, 169
magic words, 167–168, 170
Malaita-Micronesian, 386–387
Marchand, Hans, 59
Marck, Jeffrey C., 381, 385, 405
marriage negotiations, personal pronouns in, 190–191
masculine and feminine oppositions, 89–90
mass, homogenous concept, 345–346
mass nouns, 345, 354
maternal health practitioners, 272–273
mateship, 9
Mayali language, noun classification, 96
McCarthy, Michael, 126
MCE, *see* Monash Corpus of Australian English
meaning, emergence of, 151, 152
meaning-content, 304, 305, 320, 321, 329 fn25
Mel'čuk, Igor A., 76, 80
memory capacity, 308
memory function, 314
mental health, 262–275
    assessment of, 264
    clinicians, education of, 270–271
mental representations, in language usage, 303–304
mentally represented lexicon, 313–321
merger of information, 374
merger representation, 304–308
Mesoamerican Color Survey, 336
message-content, 304, 312
metacoders, 319–320, 321–323, 327
metaphor use, 148, 154–158
metaphorical concepts, 143–158
    contextual grounding, 148–158
metaphors
    and context, 149–150
    and translation, 286, 296–298
migration, of languages, 389–391
migration routes, of Proto Nuclear Micronesians, 382–383, 388, 402–403

Minangkabau language, noun classification, 95
minimalism/contextualism debate, 361, 362, 364, 366, 375
Minimalist Program, 331
modelling, 304–308
Mon-Khmer languages, 34
Monash Corpus of Australian English, 5
monolingualism, 310, 313
Morente, Manuel García, 289–291
moths, gender, 83
multilingualism, 310, 313
Munsell chips, 336
Murrinh-Patha language, 78, 94–95

names, destruction of, 171
native speakers' judgment, 135–138
Ndebele language, 176–196
Nemesi, Attila L., 125–126
neurological processing, of bad language, 6
neuronal activities, of cognitive operations, 144
New Hebridean, 385–386
Ngan'gityemerri language, noun classification, 96
Nichols, Johanna, 384, 388, 389
Noble, Ann C., 110
nominal uses, of bastard and bugger, 19–23
non-Micronesian Oceanic languages, 395, 397
Norrick, Neal, 126
North/Central Vanuatu languages, 398, 409
Norwegian, response words, 205–217
noun classification systems, 73, 75
    semantic features, 95–96
Nuclear Micronesian languages, 393, 397, 399–400, 410
    as Oceanic subgroup, 384–388
number, in English, 343
numbers, in magic formulae, 168

Oceanic languages, subgroupings, 396–397, 401
officialese, *see* bureaucratic language
olfaction, and wine terminology, 109–111
organisational lexical semantics, 364
Ortega y Gasset, José, 293–294
    translation of, 297–298
orthography, and pronunciation, 79
Oswalt, Robert L., 35

palindromes, countering reversal, 170, 171
paratactic configurations, 255
paratactic elaboration, 242, 244, 245, 250

Parker, Robert M., 109
partners, personal pronoun for, 191
Pawley, Andrew, 382, 385–386, 405
Persian language, 226–227
personal names, as referent, 163, 173
personal pronoun usage
　age variable, 180–185
　　gender variable, 185–186, 194
　　social context, 187–192
personal pronouns, as address terms, 176–196
philosophers' writings, 283–300
physemes, 306, 307
physical environment, 156–158
plant names, for wines and wineries, 118
pleonastic compounds, *see* tautological compounds
plural usage, 346, 352–354
point of view, 340 fn2, 356
points of view, 326
polarity shift, of adverbs, 128, 135
polarity, of adverbs, 135–138
Polish academic writing, 254–255, 256
politeness, 178–179
politic behaviour, 178–179
polysemy, 363
　and translation, 286, 298–294
population-typology model, 384, 388–389
possessive classifiers, 393–405, 407–410
power of language, 165–166
pragmatic meanings, and cultural schemas, 225, 232
pragmatic processes, 362–363
pragmatics-rich lexical semantics, 367–368, 374, 375
pressure of coherence, 148–151
probablistic meanings, 365–366
procedural meaning, of response words, 202, 211, 216
processes of meaning, 373
pronunciation, and orthography, 79
proper names, 114, 161–174
propitious directions, 170
propositional attitude, 203–204, 216, 217
propositional content, 255, 257
propositionally expressed rules, 319
protectiveness, and gender determination, 84–86
Proto Nuclear Micronesians, origins, 381–410
psychiatric disorders, and communication disorders, 263–268
psychological benefit, of breaking taboos, 10
public education, and communication disorders, 273–274

Quine, Willard Van Orman, translated titles, 284 fn2
Quintilian, 125

radical contextualism, 361
radical lexical contextualism, 367–375
radical lexicalism, 303–332
Rawls, John, 291–293, 295–296
Recanati, François, 200, 374, 376
recursiveness, 250–253
redundancy, 56
Reefs-Santa Cruz Islands, and Proto Nuclear Micronesians, 402–406
reference points, 355
regional variance, 136
relational functioning, 240
relative stability indices, 35–36
relevance theory, 202 fn2, 217
religious profanity, *see* blasphemy
remote communities, and disorder risk, 274
Renner, Vincent, 64
repression, of swearing, 10, 11
respect, and personal pronoun usage, 193
respectful register, *see* hlonipha register
response words, 198–217
　and concepts, 201
　and context, 200, 216
　and encoded meaning, 201, 216, 217
　and head movements, 205–207
　and pragmatic processes, 202–204, 216
　inference, 199
　pitch profile, 199
retrieval capacity, 314
reversal, of actions, 169
　of names and texts, 169
rhetorical structure theory, 237, 242
Right-Hand Head Rule, 56, 62
Roman oratory, 125
Romance languages, lexical stability, 36–39
RSIs, *see* relative stability indices
RST, *see* rhetorical structure theory
runes, 170

saturation processes, 200, 216
schema theory, 222–223
schemas, functions of, 222–223
second-language development, 258–259
segmentation, of texts, 241
self-esteem, 265
semantic determination of noun classification, 78
semantic features
　and gender of French nouns, 99

Index | 431

final sounds/segments, 92–93
identifying in gender distinction, 90
semantic fields, 103–104, 122
semantic frames, 103–104
semantic minimalism, 360, 362–364
semantic oppositions, and word-final pronunciation, 100
semantic principles, and gender of nouns, 74
semantic prosody, 127, 137, 138
semantics/pragmatics divide, 359–361, 364, 367
sentential connectives, 369–372
sex, and gender of nouns, 74
shrinking words, 168, 170–171
Shutler, Richard, 381, 385, 405
Sibanda, Galen, 178
siblings, and personal pronoun usage, 193–194
signemes, 306, 307, 308, 320–321
skeuomorphs, 67 fn29
Skinner, Stephen, 16
smell, words for, 110
Smythe, W.E., 382, 387–388, 397
social context, of linguistic behaviour, 192–193, 194–195
social function, of swearing, 9
social functioning, of children and adolescents, 265
social interactions, schemas for, 223–224
social relations, Iranian, 228
social setting, 157–158
social space, and *târof*, 228
social taboos, 6, 27
sociocultural benefit, of breaking taboos, 10
socioeconomic disadvantage, and language skills, 274
socioeconomic factors, and mental health, 269
sociological writing, 238–239, 254, 257, 258
'soft' science texts, 238
solidarity, and personal pronoun usage, 193
sources of meaning, 373
South Vanuatu languages, 398, 409
Southeast Solomonic languages, 398, 408
Southern Oceanic languages, 399, 409
species–genus relationship, 59–60
speech pathologists
  and educationalists, 272
  in mental health, 272
  role 274, 275
Speech Pathology Association of Australia 263, 264
Spencer, Andrew, 57
spoken language, correspondence with written, 307–308
St Matthias Islands, languages, 398, 408
stability distribution, 37–38, 41, 48

Steiman, Harvey, 109
stress, and swearing, 10 fn6
student–teacher communication, 192
stylistic function, of swearing, 9–11
subgrouping, 43–47
supporting predicates, 237, 244
Surridge, Marie E., 76
Swadesh, Morris, 33, 34
Swadesh word lists, 36, 38, 40, 41, 47, 48, 49, 51, 52
Swahili, gender agreement, 96
swearing
  changes in patterns. 6–7
  functions of, 7–11
  history, 4–5
synonymous compounds, 64–68
synonymy, 103–104
syntactic functions, of adverbs, 128

taboos, relating to names, 163–165, 174
târof, 226–232
  as cultural schema, 230–232
tautological compound
  definition, 55–56, 57–58
  in English language, 55–69
taxonomy, of wine terminology, 110
tea terminology, 121
terroir
  in coffee descriptions, 121
  in wine descriptions, 114
tertiary education institutions, and communication assessment, 273
text segmentation, 241
Thomas, David, 34
titles, translations of, 284, 298–299
transemes, 306, 320–321
translation, 283–300
  and language theory, 311
  and misinterpretation, 286
  improving clarity, 285–286
  purpose of, 283–284
translator bias, 284
truth-conditional pragmatics, 201, 374
truth-conditional semantics, 362, 366, 369–370
Tucker, G. Richard, 76
type-composition logic, 365
typological markers, geographical distribution, 388–393

unbelievably
  British National Corpus analysis, 134
  dictionary definitions, 130–132

syntactic functions of, 128
variance in collocates, 136–138
universality, in knowledge, 145–146
unthinkably
British National Corpus analysis, 134
dictionary definitions, 130–132
syntactic functions of, 128
variance in collocates, 136–138
Uralic–Yukaghir relationship, 49
urbanisation, effect on Ndebele address system, 195

vagueness, and hyperbole usage, 126
Vantage Theory 336–342, 356
see also VT2
vantages, 338–339
Vanuatu, and Proto Nuclear Micronesians, 403–405
verbs of motion, in wine terminology, 112–113
Vicente, Agustin, 367
Vietnamese language, gender variation, 95
viewing modes, 345–352
Viollet-le-Duc, E.E., 284
VT2, 343–344

Wälchli, Bernhard, 64
Watts, Richard, 178–179
Western Oceanic languages, 398, 408
wine descriptors, 104–114
wine terminology, 103–122
wine writing, 110–111
wineries, names of, 114–120
wines, names of, 114–120
Wittgenstein, L., translation of, 286–288, 298–299
Word Grammar, 324
word-final phonemes, and gender, 76, 79–80, 96–97
word-final pronunciation, and semantic oppositions, 100
word-final sounds, and gender of nouns, 74
workplaces, personal pronoun usage, 190
World Color Survey, 336 fn1
written curses, destruction, 171

xenophobia, in language, 11
!Xóõ language, noun classification, 96

young offenders, language problems, 266

Zimbabwe, 176–177
Zubin, David A., 76
Zulu people, 177, 193–194